Film Stars and Their Awards

Film Stars and Their Awards

Who Won What for Movies, Theater and Television

ROGER LESLIE

McFarland & Company, Inc., Publishers

Jefferson, North Carolina, and London

LIBRARY OF CONGRESS CATALOGUING-IN-PUBLICATION DATA

Leslie, Roger.
Film stars and their awards : who won what for movies,
theater and television / Roger Leslie.
p.   cm.
Includes bibliographical references and index.

ISBN 978-0-7864-4017-7
softcover : 50# alkaline paper ∞

1. Motion pictures—Awards—Dictionaries.   2. Theater—
Awards—Dictionaries.   3. Television broadcasting—Awards—
Dictionaries.   4. Motion picture actors and actresses—
Credits—Dictionaries.   I. Title.
PN1993.9.L47   2008   791.43079—dc22   2008022984

British Library cataloguing data are available

On the cover: *background* ©2008 Comstock Images; *top* Meryl Streep
(Best Actress for *Sophie's Choice*), 1983 (Photofest);
bottom Ingrid Bergman and Albert Finney (Photofest);
Gene Hackman, George Clooney, Dame Helen Mirren,
Cate Blanchett ©2008 Shutterstock

Manufactured in the United States of America

McFarland & Company, Inc., Publishers
Box 611, Jefferson, North Carolina 28640
www.mcfarlandpub.com

Table of Contents

v

To my favorite actors,
who help make moviegoing
the greatest escape adventure ever

Special thanks to Jerry and Helen
for their patience and encouragement,
and to Brandon and Lauren
for their assistance

Preface

As an avid fan of motion pictures and a collector of movie reference books for more than thirty years, I was recently surprised to discover that some of my favorite stars received awards of which I'd previously been unaware. When I searched through both my personal collection and the performing arts reference section of the library I run, it was easy to find books about movie awards organized chronologically by year or alphabetically by film, but a gap existed for readers wanting a resource where all major award information for individual actors appeared in one convenient list. That realization inspired me to write *Film Stars and Their Awards*.

Two criteria determined the scope of this book: who has received awards and honors, and who has given the awards and honors. Though my goal seemed a bit ambitious for a single volume, I set out to recognize anyone who has earned recognition for acting in motion pictures with a nomination or competitive award win, either for an individual performance or as part of an ensemble, and anyone who received a special honor or tribute for movie acting.

Imagining that fans wanted a comprehensive list of accolades for their favorite stars, I also chose to include awards that male and female actors received in any area of filmmaking, such as directing, producing, writing, and composing. After all, sharing only the acting achievements of filmmakers such as Warren Beatty, Clint Eastwood, or Barbra Streisand would certainly seem incomplete. I noted the same gap concerning the actors' work in other media, and so included their major theater and television awards as well. That addition more appropriately acknowledges the tremendous, record-setting contributions of people like Alan Alda, Julie Harris, and Cloris Leachman.

After collecting data for individual competitive awards, it seemed only fitting that I also mention special tributes given to some actors for single performances or for their life-long contributions to the industry. Beyond the awards and tributes, I describe unique records that some actors set and highlight information about actors whose career or award recognition were particularly noteworthy.

As I compiled lists of actor recognitions from local and national groups, I realized how many organizations, film festivals, and critics groups emerge and disappear without impacting the industry. On the other hand, some organizations and film festivals rise far above others for credibility and longevity. As a result, my second criterion, determining which award-presenting organizations to include, narrowed to encompass the most influential and prestigious groups to honor movie actors with annual awards or tributes.

The organizations represented in this book still strive to secure a standard of excellence in filmmaking by recognizing influential films and encouraging technological innovation and artistic excellence. The impact that awards have on box office further shapes the film industry. Although detractors may bemoan the pomp and pageantry that have escalated among some awards presentations, the relevance of movie awards remains intact and continues to warrant study and to provide entertaining reading.

My research required revisiting some favorite books from my personal collection. While each has invaluable elements that contributed to my research, they are all arranged chronologically, they include acting awards as only one of many categories, and they all lack some information I included in this book. I love Robert Osborne's beautifully formatted *75 Years of Oscar,* which of course only covers the Academy Awards. Tom O'Neil has done fine work with *Movie Awards: The Ultimate, Unofficial Guide to the Oscars, the Golden Globes, Critics, Guild, & Indie Honors,* but it was last revised in 2002 and covers only some of the organizations in this book. Back in 1992 O'Neil also published a great television resource, *The Emmys,* which unfortunately has not been updated and which contains a very incomplete index. Michael Gebert's *The Encyclopedia of Movie Awards* from 1996 is helpful and comprehensive for a small paperback, but his text contains frequent, subjective, and often disparaging commentary about movies and stars.

My online research surprised me. I was disappointed to discover that many movie award websites are poorly organized and filled with gaps and gaffes. Even some organizations included in this book have official websites with no archives, cumbersome search capabilities, or missing and inconsistent data.

With this work, I hope I have filled a gap in performing arts collections. Even more, I hope I have provided for fans of so many wonderful actors a clearer picture of their contributions to the entertainment industry and the acknowledgments they have received for their work on stage, on television, and especially in motion pictures.

How to Use This Book

The entries are presented as follows:

Actor's Name

Type [of award or recognition] year ***Title*** (Nomination Category) Nominating organization [roman type = nominated but did not win; *italics* = won]

TYPE OF AWARD OR RECOGNITION

Movie: Competitive nominations and wins for work in motion pictures.
Theater: Competitive nominations and wins for stage work.
Television: Competitive nominations and wins for work on TV.
Tributes: Special awards for individual accomplishment or honors for career achievement.
Records: Records the actor set in regard to acting or other awards.
Highlights: Interesting background or information regarding an actor's award history.

YEAR

This is the year in which the film was released in the United States and was consequently eligible for most awards, or when it premiered in the U.K. if it was only up for British awards.

TITLE

Titles of movies, plays, and television productions are in ***bold italics***. Foreign films that are generally recognized by both their original language and their English version or translation cite the original language title followed by the English version in parentheses. English-language films released under different titles in the U.S. and the U.K. list their original, usually more familiar title, first, followed by the alternate title in parentheses.

NOMINATION CATEGORY

In most cases, an effort has been made to be as specific about category names as possible. For example, in movie awards, American actors nominated for British awards until 1968 competed as (Best Foreign Actor) or (Best Foreign Actress). Those nominations are distinguished from the (Best Actor) or (Best Actress) nominations they may have received from other organizations for the same film. Inexplicably, as the case of Leslie Caron illustrates, an actress might be nominated for (Best Foreign Actress) one year and (Best British Actress) another. Unless an error was discovered in a text or a mistake in a website, this reference work has remained true to the categories as they were published, even if they seemed illogical.

With theater awards, the slight variations in category names as the awards evolved have been honored. Thus, some nominations may be for (Best Supporting or Featured Actor, Dramatic) while later nominations for that same actor may be (Best Actor in a Featured Role, Play). Although both categories essentially honor the same kind of performance, the categories as they were written the year that award was presented are recorded.

Television awards have proven to be particularly cumbersome, especially during the early years of Emmys. For the same series, a star might be nominated for (Best Actress in a Comedy) one year, (Best Continued Performance by an Actress in a Comedy Series) the following year, and then (Best Actress in a Series, Dramatic or Comedy) the next. An attempt was made to be as faithful to each category as possible, honoring distinctions that some might consider minute. For example, for a single performance in a miniseries, an actor might get a SAG nomination for (Best Male Actor in a Television Movie or Miniseries), an Emmy nomination for (Best Supporting Actor in a Miniseries or Special), and a Golden Globe nomination for (Best Supporting Actor in a Series, Miniseries, or TV Movie). Though such fine differences might not matter to some, many readers would probably genuinely like those differences to be noted. The one distinction not made with Emmy was between the words Best and Outstanding. Early in Emmy's history, the television academy replaced the word Best with Outstanding. However, it seemed redundant to distinguish between (Best Actor in a Drama Series) for Globe and (Outstanding Actor in a Drama Series) for Emmy. For consistency, all television awards, like most of the movie and theater awards, are identified as Best.

Nominating Organization

Following the nomination category are the abbreviated names of the organizations which nominated the actor for that category in that movie. The organizations in regular roman font are nominations; organizations in *italics* denote award wins. The abbreviations and the organizations' full names are as follows:

Movie Awards

Academy	The Academy of Motion Picture Arts and Sciences (Oscar)
Berlin	Berlin International Film Festival
Board	National Board of Review
British	British Academy of Film and Television Arts (BAFTA)
Broadcast	Broadcast Film Critics Association
Cannes	Cannes Film Festival
Globe	The Hollywood Foreign Press Association (Golden Globe)
LA	Los Angeles Film Critics Association
New York	New York Film Critics Circle
SAG	Screen Actors Guild
Society	National Society of Film Critics
Spirit	Film Independent (Independent Spirit Awards)
Venice	Venice International Film Festival

Theater Awards

Tony   American Theater Wing (Antoinette Perry "Tony" Award)

Television Awards

Emmy   American Television Arts & Sciences (Emmy)
Globe   The Hollywood Foreign Press Association (Golden Globe)
SAG   Screen Actors Guild

Tributes

Organizations that appear only in the Tributes section, and are not abbreviated, are:

American Film Institute
Kennedy Center for the Performing Arts
Film Society of Lincoln Center
Emmy Hall of Fame

SOME SAMPLE ENTRIES WITH EXPLANATIONS

Freeman, Morgan

Movie: 2004: ***Million Dollar Baby*** (Best Supporting Actor) *Academy*, Globe, *SAG*, Broadcast (Best Ensemble) SAG.

In 2004, Freeman starred in ***Million Dollar Baby***. He was nominated for Best Supporting Actor from four organizations, listed in order of when the organizations were first formed and began giving awards. He won the Academy Award (wins are italicized), lost the Golden Globe, won the Screen Actors Guild award, and lost the Broadcast Film Critics Association prize. For that same film he was also recognized with his fellow cast members for Best Ensemble. He and his costars lost their Screen Actors Guild Award competition.

If an actor has been nominated for more than one movie in a single year, I divide those movie citations with a semicolon. For example, Phillip Seymour Hoffman was nominated for three movies in 2007. Each film, arranged alphabetically, is separated from the others by a semicolon:

Hoffman, Phillip Seymour

Movie: 2007: ***Before the Devil Knows You're Dead*** (Best Ensemble) Broadcast; ***Charlie Wilson's War*** (Best Supporting Actor) Academy, Globe, British, Broadcast; ***The Savages*** (Best Actor) *Spirit* (Best Actor, Musical or Comedy) Globe.

• AWARDS OTHER THAN ACTING—Each star's acting award categories are arranged alphabetically, and acting awards appear before non-acting award categories. Therefore, even though Orson Welles was best known for his directing, his categories appear in this order:

Welles, Orson

Movie: 1941: ***Citizen Kane*** (Best Acting) *Board* (Best Actor) Academy (Best Director) Academy (Best Picture, Producer) Academy, *New York, Board* (Best Original Screenplay) *Academy.*

Note also the extra explanatory term in the parentheses with Best Picture. Whenever there is a category that does not make clear what professional role the star had in that nomination category, it is clarified. Other examples include:

(Best Picture, Drama; Executive Producer)
(Best Variety Show, Star)
(Best Achievement in Children's Programming, Host)
(Best Information Special, Narrator)
(Best Comedy, Variety or Music Special; Producer and Star)

• SPECIAL AWARDS—Sometimes actors receive special awards for performances beyond the regular competitions where they are nominated and then win, or beyond the traditional choice of one Best Actor and one Best Actress at a film festival. Those wins are designated with a (special award) notation. For example, that notation appears for every star of the 1954 film ***Executive Suite,*** which received a special Best Ensemble award at the Venice Film Festival decades before Best Ensemble became a competitive category at any awards ceremony. Thus, part of Shelley Winters' citation appears as:

Winters, Shelley

Movie: 1954: ***Executive Suite*** (Best Ensemble) *Venice* (special award).

On the subject of Ensemble Awards, there are some organizations, especially in their early years, that presented Best Ensemble or Best Cast (for consistency, they are always listed as Best Ensemble) awards, but never recorded exactly how encompassing their cast list was to be. Whenever the exact cast information was not available from the organization that nominated them, the cast list was extended as far as possible, preferring to honor more stars than the organization might have intended rather than slight any who were meant to be part of that nominated or winning ensemble.

• MULTIPLE NOMINATION OR MULTIPLE WIN—When an actor receives a single award or nomination for two or more performances in a single year, those recognitions are followed by the parenthetical note "(multiple nomination)" or "(multiple win)." In 1981, for example, Isabelle Adjani won the Best Actress prize at the Cannes Film Festival for her performances in both ***Possession*** and ***Quartet***:

Adjani, Isabelle

Movie: 1981: ***Possession*** (Best Actress) *Cannes* (multiple win); ***Quartet*** (Best Actress) *Cannes* (multiple win).

Occasionally the "(multiple nomination)" or "(multiple win)" notations refer to movies with different years, as when Gene Hackman won a single British award for his Best Actor performances in both ***The French Connection*** (1971) and ***The Poseidon Adventure*** (1972).

Such disparities occur because films are not eligible for British award recognition until they premiere in the U.K., and often American films will open in the U.S. near the end of one year, and not reach European theaters until weeks or months later. Such multiple wins or nominations are never separated by more than one year, so it is still easy to determine which films shared the nomination or win.

Hackman, Gene

Movie: 1971: ***The French Connection*** (Best Actor) *Academy, New York, Board, British* (multiple win), (Best Actor, Drama) *Globe.* 1972: ***The Poseidon Adventure*** (Best Actor) *British* (multiple win).

• A Unique Challenge with Years— As explained under "Year" (page 3 above), all awards for a single performance are placed in the citation beginning with the year the film premiered in the United States. For this reason, Hackman's British Best Actor prize for ***The French Connection*** appears with all the other organizations that honored him for that performance.

In this case and in others like it, the date for the British award (and very rarely for a few other organizations) is inconsistent with the year an actor actually competed for awards for that performance. For example, Meryl Streep swept nearly every American film award for ***Sophie's Choice*** in competitions honoring movies released in 1982, but was nominated for that film at the British awards with the movies of 1983, after ***Sophie's Choice*** reached the U.K. and became eligible for their award competitions. This information has been streamlined so that each film is connected with only one year in order to avoid confusion and repetition:

Streep, Meryl

Movie: 1982: ***Sophie's Choice*** (Best Actress) *Academy, New York, Board,* British, *Society, LA* (Best Actress, Drama) *Globe.*

• Dated Order of Information— Actors who are nominated for a single performance on television will have a citation organized just like the movie and theater citations. Both of Hugh Jackman's television awards fit this description:

Jackman, Hugh

Television: 2005: ***The 58th Annual Tony Awards*** (Best Individual Performance in a Variety or Music Program, Host) *Emmy.* 2006: ***The 59th Annual Tony Awards*** (Best Individual Performance in a Variety or Music Program, Host) Emmy.

A variation on the dated order of information occurs for actors who starred in a television series and thus were nominated over several years for the same program. For actors who appeared regularly on a series, the citation begins with the span of years that the actor was a regular on the show and therefore eligible for award consideration. From 1974 to 1978, for instance, Jack Albertson starred in the series, ***Chico and the Man***. That is, he was on the show for four seasons: 1974–1975, 1975–1976, 1976–1977, and 1977–1978. During that time, he was nominated for an Emmy as Best Actor in a Comedy Series three times. He lost in the first season (indicated by 1975), won in the second season (1976), lost in the third season (1977), and was not nominated in the show's final season. That information appears like this:

Albertson, Jack

Television: 1974–1978 series ***Chico and the Man*** (Best Actor in a Comedy Series) 1975: Emmy. 1976: *Emmy.* 1977: Emmy.

For some actors this span of years is not necessarily the entire run of the series, especially if they earned nominations for guest performances. One example would be Carol Burnett, who made several guest appearances on the TV comedy ***Mad About You*** between 1996 and 1999. Even though she was only nominated for two of the three seasons she guest starred on the show, the entire span of time is included before the word "series" and the show's title to convey what years she was eligible for award consideration:

Burnett, Carol

Television: 1996–1999 series ***Mad About You*** (Best Guest Actress in a Comedy Series) 1997: *Emmy.* 1998: Emmy.

As indicated by the span of years, Burnett appeared on the show during the 1996–1997 season, the 1997–1998 season, and the 1998–1999 season. She won for the 1996–1997 season (indicated by 1997 after the category and the accompanying, italicized *Emmy*), lost for the 1997–1998 season, and was not nominated during the 1998–1999 season.

If guest appearances occur intermittently, that fact is indicated with a comma rather than a hyphen between dates:

Knight, Shirley

1987, 1990 series ***thirtysomething*** (Best Guest Actress in a Drama Series) 1987: *Emmy.* 1990: Emmy.

Shirley Knight guest starred on ***thirtysomething*** during the 1986–1987 season. She returned for a guest appearance during the 1989–1990 season. As the comma suggests, she was not on the show in the years between those seasons.

Some stars were nominated in different categories for the same television series, such as Shirley Jones in ***The Partridge Family***. In her case, as in some others', it made more sense to put her categories chronologically rather than alphabetically.

Jones, Shirley

Television: 1970–1974 series ***The Partridge Family*** (Best Actress in a Series, Musical or Comedy) 1971: Globe. (Best Actress in a Musical or Comedy Series or TV Movie) 1972: Globe.

For most stars nominated in numerous categories from different organizations, it was usually more helpful to arrange the categories for individual acting achievement alphabetically, and, if applicable, put Best Ensemble nominations last. During the run of ***Friends***, for example, Jennifer Aniston was nominated for

> Best Actress in a Comedy Series
> Best Actress in a Series, Musical or Comedy
> Best Female Actor in a Comedy Series
> Best Supporting Actress in a Comedy Series

Best Supporting Actress in a Series, Miniseries, or TV Movie
Best Ensemble

Her television award information looks like this:

Aniston, Jennifer

Television: 1994–2004 series *Friends* (Best Actress in a Comedy Series) 2002: *Emmy*. 2003: Emmy. 2004: Emmy. (Best Actress in a Series, Musical or Comedy) 2002: *Globe*. (Best Female Actor in a Comedy Series) 2001: SAG. 2002: SAG. (Best Supporting Actress in a Comedy Series) 2000: Emmy. 2001: Emmy. (Best Supporting Actress in a Series, Miniseries, or TV Movie) 2001: Globe. (Best Ensemble in a Comedy Series) 1995: *SAG*. 1998: SAG. 1999: SAG. 2000: SAG. 2001: SAG. 2002: SAG. 2003: SAG.

From 1994 to 2004, Aniston starred in *Friends*. In the category (Best Actress in a Comedy Series) she won the Emmy in 2002, and was nominated but did not win Emmys in 2003 and 2004. Under another category name (Best Actress in a Series, Musical or Comedy), she won the Golden Globe in 2002. For the SAG Awards, she was nominated in the category (Best Female Actor in a Comedy Series) in both 2001 and 2002, losing both years. Yet during the run of the show, she was sometimes up for Best Supporting Actress. In 2000 and 2001 she was nominated for Emmys as (Best Supporting Actress in a Comedy Series) and in 2001 she was up for a Golden Globe as (Best Supporting Actress in a Series, Miniseries, or TV Movie). As part of the cast of *Friends*, she was also nominated for (Best Ensemble in a Comedy Series) in 1995 and then every year from 1998 to 2003 by the Screen Actors Guild. She and her costars won in 1995.

• "---"—Three hyphens for Emmy nominations indicate a category where an actor was nominated for an award for no named series or special. In the first few years of the Emmy, actors might generally be nominated for Best Comedienne or Best Actor or Best Singer. Rather than put nothing between the date and the category, three hyphens were inserted so that readers know no data are missing. In 1956, for instance, Harry Belafonte was nominated for two Emmys, as Best Male Singer and for Best Specialty Act by a Singer or Group. Because the TV Academy did not nominate him in these categories for any particular program or special, his citation looks like this:

Belafonte, Harry

Television: 1956: --- (Best Male Singer) Emmy; --- (Best Specialty Act by a Singer or Group) Emmy.

• SHARED WINS OR NOMINATIONS—If an actor shared a win or nomination with a costar, that fact is indicated parenthetically immediately after the name of the organization that gave the nomination or award. For example, in 1962, Katharine Hepburn, Ralph Richardson, Jason Robards, and Dean Stockwell all shared a single Best Acting award from Cannes for their work in *Long Day's Journey into Night*. Shared wins differ from ties, where actors win separately in the same category, as when the National Board of Review gave Geena Davis and Susan Sarandon each a Best Actress prize for her work in *Thelma & Louise*. No special references appear for ties, and information about shared awards refers only to acting awards. No such notations follow wins for co-producing movies or television programs, co-authoring scripts, or collaborating on musical compositions.

- "*"—Any award information that requires elaboration is followed by an asterisk *
and then explained at the end of that actor's awards section.

While these notes offer quite a bit to comprehend, understanding the makeup of the
entries is made easier by the fact that the format is consistent for each of the thousands of
actors throughout the text.

Film Stars and Their Awards

Abdoo, Rose
Movie: 2005: *Good Night, and Good Luck* (Best Ensemble) SAG, Broadcast.

Abraham, F. Murray
Movie: 1984: *Amadeus* (Best Actor) *Academy,* British, *LA* (Best Actor, Drama) *Globe.*

Abril, Victoria
Movie: 1991: *Amantes (Lovers)* (Best Actress) *Berlin.*

Accorsi, Stefano
Movie: 2002: *Un viaggio chiamato amore* (Best Actor) *Venice.*

Ackland, Joss
Movie: 1988: *White Mischief* (Best Supporting Actor) British.

Adams, Amy
Movie: 2005: *Junebug* (Best Female Actor in a Supporting Role) SAG (Best Supporting Actress) Academy, *Society, Broadcast* (Best Supporting Female) *Spirit.* 2007: *Enchanted* (Best Actress) Broadcast (Best Actress, Musical or Comedy) Globe.

Adams, Brooke
Movie: 1992: *Gas Food Lodging* (Best Supporting Female) Spirit.

Adams, Evan
Movie: 1998: *Smoke Signals* (Best Debut Performance) *Spirit.* Highlights: Adams directed, co-produced, and starred in *Smoke Signals,* which he developed at the Sundance lab in 1995 and which won both the Filmmakers' Trophy and Audience Award at the 1998 Sundance Film Festival.

Adams, Jane
Movie: 1998: *Happiness* (Best Ensemble) *Board.*

Theater: 1994: *An Inspector Calls* (Best Featured Actress, Play) *Tony.*

Adams, Joe
Movie: 1954: *Carmen Jones* (New Star of the Year — Actor) *Globe.*

Adams, Joey Lauren
Movie: 1997: *Chasing Amy* (Best Actress, Musical or Comedy) Globe.

Adams, Mary
Movie: 1954: *Executive Suite* (Best Ensemble) *Venice* (special award).

Adams, Nick
Movie: 1963: *Twilight of Honor* (Best Supporting Actor) Academy.

Addy, Mark
Movie: 1997: *The Full Monty* (Best Supporting Actor) British (Best Ensemble) *SAG.*

Adjani, Isabelle
Movie: 1975: *L'Histoire d'Adèle H. (The Story of Adele H.)* (Best Actress) Academy, *New York, Board, Society.* 1981: *Possession* (Best Actress) *Cannes* (multiple win); *Quartet* (Best Actress) *Cannes* (multiple win). 1989: *Camille Claudel* (Best Actress) Academy, *Berlin.* Records: Adjani made it into the *2003 Guinness World Records* book as the actress who's won the most César Awards, France's highest film award presented by members of the Académie des Arts et Techniques du Cinema. Adjani began her winning streak in 1982 for *Possession* and earned her record-setting fourth Best Actress award in 1995 for *La Reine Margot.* Katharine Hepburn holds the record for the most acting Oscar wins with the same number of victories as Adjani. However, what took Hepburn 48 years to

11

accomplish for the American award, Adjani achieved in 13 for the French.

Adrian, Max

Movie: 1971: *The Boy Friend* (Best Supporting Actor) British.

Affleck, Ben

Movie: 1997: *Good Will Hunting* (Best Original Screenplay) *Academy, Broadcast* (Best Screenplay) *Globe* (Best Ensemble) SAG. 1998: *Shakespeare in Love* (Best Ensemble) SAG. 2006: *Hollywoodland* (Best Actor) *Venice* (Best Supporting Actor) Globe, Broadcast. 2007: *Gone Baby Gone* (Best Directorial Debut) *Board.* **Television:** 2001–2005 series *Project Greenlight* (Best Non-Fiction Program, Reality; Executive Producer) 2002: Emmy. (Best Reality Program, Executive Producer) 2004: Emmy. 2005: Emmy. **Tributes:** 1997: Special Filmmaking Achievement award for *Good Will Hunting* from Board (honor shared with coauthor and costar, Matt Damon).

Affleck, Casey

Movie: 2001: *Ocean's 11* (Best Ensemble) Broadcast. 2004: *Ocean's Twelve* (Best Ensemble) Broadcast. 2007: *The Assassination of Jesse James by the Coward Robert Ford* (Best Male Actor in a Supporting Role) SAG (Best Supporting Actor) Academy, *Board,* Globe, Broadcast; *Gone Baby Gone* (Best Ensemble) Broadcast.

Aghdashloo, Shohreh

Movie: 2003: *House of Sand and Fog* (Best Supporting Actress) Academy, *New York, LA* (Best Supporting Female) *Spirit.*

Agutter, Jenny

Movie: 1977: *Equus* (Best Supporting Actress) British. **Television:** 1972: *"The Snow Goose," Hallmark Hall of Fame* (Best Supporting Actress in a Drama) *Emmy.*

Aherne, Brian

Movie: 1939: *Juarez* (Best Supporting Actor) Academy.

Aiello, Danny

Movie: 1989: *Do the Right Thing* (Best Supporting Actor) Academy, Globe, *LA.* 1994: *Prêt-à-Porter (Ready-to-Wear)* (Best Ensemble) *Board.* **Television:** 1981: *"Family of Strangers," ABC Afterschool Special* (Outstanding Individual Achievement in Children's Programming, Performer) *Emmy.*

Aiken, Liam

Movie: 2004: *Lemony Snicket's A Series of Unfortunate Events* (Best Young Actor) Broadcast.

Aimée, Anouk

Movie: 1962: *Lois* (Best Foreign Actress) British. 1966: *Un Homme et une femme (A Man and a Woman)* (Best Actress) Academy (Best Actress, Drama) *Globe* (Best Foreign Actress) *British.* 1980: *Le Saut dans le vide (A Leap into the Void)* (Best Actress) *Cannes.* 1994: *Prêt-à-Porter (Ready-to-Wear)* (Best Ensemble) *Board.* **Tributes:** 2003: Honorary Golden Bear from Berlin.

Aitken, Maria

Movie: 1988: *A Fish Called Wanda* (Best Supporting Actress) British.

Alba, Jessica

Movie: 2005: *Sin City* (Best Ensemble) Broadcast. **Television:** 2000–2002 series *Dark Angel* (Best Actress in a Series, Drama) 2001: Globe.

Albert, Eddie

Movie: 1953: *Roman Holiday* (Best Foreign Actor) British (Best Supporting Actor) Academy. 1956: *The Teahouse of the August Moon* (Best Supporting Actor) Globe. 1972: *The Heartbreak Kid* (Best Supporting Actor) Academy, *Society.* 1974: *The Longest Yard* (Best Supporting Actor) Globe. **Highlights:** A spur-of-the-moment rule change suggested by one of its members cost Albert the New York Film Critics award for Best Supporting Actor in 1972 for *The Heartbreak Kid.* In that year's race, Albert earned the most points in the first round of voting, but not enough for a majority and a win. In previous years, subsequent balloting only required the most overall votes from the critics, but that year the critics changed the rules and required at least 50 percent of the total votes to win. After a few more ballots, Albert lost ground and the New York critics gave the award instead to Robert Duvall for *The Godfather.*

Albert, Edward

Movie: 1972: *Butterflies Are Free* (New Star of the Year — Actor) *Globe* (Best Actor, Musical or Comedy) Globe.

Albertson, Jack

Movie: 1968: *The Subject Was Roses* (Best Supporting Actor) *Academy.* **Theater:** 1965: *The Subject Was Roses* (Best Supporting or Featured Actor, Dramatic) *Tony.* 1973: *The Sunshine Boys* (Best Actor,

Dramatic) Tony. **Television:** 1974–1978 series *Chico and the Man* (Best Actor in a Comedy Series) 1975: Emmy. 1976: *Emmy*. 1977: Emmy. 1975: *Cher* (Best Continuing or Single Performance by a Supporting Actor in Variety or Music) *Emmy*. 1982: *My Body, My Child* (Best Supporting Actor in a Limited Series or a Special) Emmy. **Highlights:** Playwright Frank Gilroy was so moved by Albertson's performance as embittered father John Cleary in his Pulitzer Prize honored play *The Subject Was Roses* that Gilroy would allow a screen adaptation only if Albertson could reprise his Tony-winning role in the film. He did and became an Oscar winner as well.

Albright, Lola

Movie: 1966: *Lord Love a Duck* (Best Actress) *Berlin*. **Television:** 1958–1961 series *Peter Gunn* (Best Supporting Actress in a Dramatic Series) 1959: Emmy.

Alda, Alan

Movie: 1968: *Paper Lion* (New Star of the Year — Actor) Globe. 1978: *Same Time, Next Year* (Best Actor, Musical or Comedy) Globe. 1981: *The Four Seasons* (Best Actor, Musical or Comedy) Globe (Best Screenplay) Globe. 1989: *Crimes and Misdemeanors* (Best Supporting Actor) *New York, Board,* British. 2004: *The Aviator* (Best Supporting Actor) Academy, British (Best Ensemble) SAG. **Theater:** 1967: *The Apple Tree* (Best Actor, Musical) Tony. 1992: *Jake's Women* (Best Actor, Play) Tony. 2005: *Glengarry Glen Ross* (Best Actor in a Featured Role, Play) Tony. **Television:** 1972–1983 series *M*A*S*H* (Best Actor in a Series, Musical or Comedy) 1973: Globe. 1974: Globe. 1975: *Globe*. 1976: *Globe*. 1977: Globe. 1978: Globe. 1979: Globe. 1980: *Globe*. 1981: *Globe*. 1982: *Globe*. 1983: *Globe*. (Actor of the Year) 1974: *Emmy*. (Best Continued Performance by an Actor in a Leading Role in a Comedy Series) 1973: Emmy. (Best Actor in a Comedy Series) 1974: *Emmy*. 1975: Emmy. 1976: Emmy. 1977: Emmy. 1978: Emmy. 1979: Emmy. 1980: Emmy. 1981: Emmy. 1982: *Emmy*. 1983: Emmy. (Best Directing in a Comedy Series) 1975: Emmy. 1976: Emmy. 1977: *Emmy*. 1978: Emmy. 1979: Emmy. 1980: Emmy. 1981: Emmy. 1982: Emmy. 1983: Emmy. (Best Writing for a Comedy Series) 1977: Emmy. 1978: Emmy. 1979: *Emmy*. 1982: Emmy. 1974: *6 Rms Riv Vu* (Best Actor in a Drama) Emmy. 1978: *Kill Me If You Can* (Best Actor in a Drama or Comedy Special) Emmy. 1994: *And the Band Played On* (Best Supporting Actor in a Miniseries or Special) Emmy; *White Mile* (Best Actor in a Miniseries or TV Movie) Globe. 2000: *ER* (Best Guest Actor in a Drama Series) Emmy. 2001: *Club Land* (Best Male Actor in a Television Movie or Miniseries) SAG (Best Supporting Actor in a Mini-series or TV Movie) Emmy. 2004–2006 series *The West Wing* (Best Male Actor in a Drama Series) 2005: SAG. (Best Supporting Actor in a Drama Series) 2005: Emmy. 2006: *Emmy*. (Best Ensemble in a Drama Series) 2005: SAG. **Tributes:** 1994: Television Hall of Fame Inductee from Emmy. **Records:** Alda, who has 32 Emmy nominations and six Emmy wins to date, is the first person to win Emmys for acting, directing, and writing.

Alden, Jane

Movie: 1993: *Short Cuts* (Best Ensemble) *Venice* (special award).

Aleandro, Norma

Movie: 1985: *La historia official (The Official Story)* (Best Actress) *New York, Cannes.* 1987: *Gaby—A True Story* (Best Supporting Actress) Academy, Globe.

Alexander, Jane

Movie: 1970: *The Great White Hope* (New Star of the Year — Actress) Globe (Best Actress) Academy. 1976: *All the President's Men* (Best Supporting Actress) Academy. 1979: *Kramer vs. Kramer* (Best Supporting Actress) Academy, Globe. 1983: *Testament* (Best Actress) Academy, Globe. 1999: *The Cider House Rules* (Best Ensemble) SAG. **Theater:** 1969: *The Great White Hope* (Best Supporting or Featured Actress, Dramatic) *Tony*. 1973: *6 Rms Riv Vu* (Best Actress, Dramatic) Tony. 1974: *Find Your Way Home* (Best Actress, Dramatic) Tony. 1979: *First Monday in October* (Best Actress, Play) Tony. 1992: *The Visit* (Best Actress, Play) Tony. 1993: *The Sisters Rosensweig* (Best Actress, Play) Tony. 1998: *Honour* (Best Actress, Play) Tony. **Television:** 1976: *"Eleanor and Franklin," ABC Theatre* (Best Actress in a Comedy or Drama Special) Emmy. 1977: *"Eleanor and Franklin: The White House Years," ABC Theatre* (Best Actress in a Comedy or Drama Special) Emmy. 1981: *Playing for Time* (Best Supporting Actress in a Limited Series or Special) *Emmy*. 1984: *Calamity Jane* (Best Actress in a Limited Series or Special) Emmy. 1985: *Malice in Wonderland* (Best Actress in a Limited Series or Special) Emmy. 2000: *Law & Order: Special Victims Unit* (Best Guest Actress in a Drama Series) Emmy. 2005: *Warm Springs* (Best Supporting Actress in a Miniseries or TV Movie) *Emmy*.

Alice, Mary

Movie: 1990: *To Sleep with Anger* (Best Female Lead) Spirit. **Theater:** 1987: *Fences* (Best Actress in a Featured Role, Play) Tony. 1995: *Having Our Say*

(Best Actress, Play) Tony. **Television:** 1991–1993 series *I'll Fly Away* (Best Supporting Actress in a Drama Series) 1992: Emmy. 1993: *Emmy.*

Alison, Dorothy

Movie: 1952: *Mandy* (Most Promising Newcomer) British. 1956: *Reach for the Sky* (Best British Actress) British.

Allen, Joan

Movie: 1995: *Nixon* (Best Female Actor in a Leading Role) SAG (Best Supporting Actress) Academy, British, *Society, LA* (Best Ensemble) SAG. 1996: *The Crucible* (Best Supporting Actress) Academy, Globe, *Broadcast.* 1998: *Pleasantville* (Best Supporting Actress) *LA, Broadcast.* 2000: *The Contender* (Best Actress) Academy, Globe, Broadcast (Best Female Actor in a Leading Role) SAG (Best Female Lead) Spirit. 2005: *The Upside of Anger* (Best Actress) Broadcast. **Theater:** 1988: *Burn This* (Best Actress, Play) *Tony.* 1989: *The Heidi Chronicles* (Best Actress, Play) Tony. **Television:** 2002: *The Mists of Avalon* (Best Supporting Actress in a Miniseries or TV Movie) Emmy. **Records:** Allen's role as Pat Nixon earned her more awards for portraying a First Lady than any actress.

Allen, Karen

Movie: 1987: *The Glass Menagerie* (Best Supporting Female) Spirit.

Allen, Nancy

Movie: 1980: *Dressed to Kill* (New Star of the Year — Actress) Globe.

Allen, Sian Barbara

Movie: 1972: *You'll Like My Mother* (New Star of the Year — Actress) Globe.

Allen, Woody

Movie: 1975: *Love and Death* (Best Director) *Berlin* (special award). 1977: *Annie Hall* (Best Actor) Academy, British (Best Actor, Musical or Comedy) Globe (Best Director) *Academy, New York, Globe, British* (Best Screenplay) *Academy, New York, Globe, British, Society, LA.* 1978: *Interiors* (Best Director) Academy, Globe (Best Screenplay) Academy, Globe. 1979: *Manhattan* (Best Actor) British (Best Director) *New York,* British, *Society* (Best Screenplay) Academy, British. 1983: *Zelig* (Best Actor, Musical or Comedy) Globe (Best Screenplay) British. 1984: *Broadway Danny Rose* (Best Director) Academy (Best Screenplay) Academy, *British.* 1985: *The Purple Rose of Cairo* (Best Screenplay) Academy, *New York, Globe,*

British. 1986: *Hannah and Her Sisters* (Best Actor) British (Best Director) Academy, *New York, Board,* Globe, *British* (Best Screenplay) *Academy,* Globe, *British, LA.* 1987: *Radio Days* (Best Screenplay) Academy, British. 1989: *Crimes and Misdemeanors* (Best Director) Academy, British (Best Screenplay) Academy, British. 1990: *Alice* (Best Screenplay) Academy. 1992: *Husbands and Wives* (Best Screenplay) Academy, *British.* 1994: *Bullets Over Broadway* (Best Director) Academy (Best Screenplay) Academy, British, Spirit. 1995: *Mighty Aphrodite* (Best Screenplay) Academy. 1997: *Deconstructing Harry* (Best Screenplay) Academy. 2005: *Match Point* (Best Director) Globe (Best Screenplay) Academy, Globe. **Television:** 1959: *Sid Caesar's Chevy Hour* (Best Writing for a Single Musical or Variety Program) Emmy. **Tributes:** 1973: Special award for *Sleeper* from Board. 1975: Special Silver Bear Award for his complete works from Berlin. 1995: Career Golden Lion for directing from Venice. **Records:** With *Annie Hall*, Allen became the first person to win a Best Director Academy Award for a film he also starred in. Allen's Best Director and Best Screenplay wins for *Annie Hall* also made him the third person to earn both awards in the same year. Before him, Joseph L. Mankiewicz and Billy Wilder each did it twice. **Highlights:** All the years the Oscars were presented on Monday night, Allen used his long-standing gig playing jazz clarinet at Michael's Pub in New York City as his excuse for not being able to attend the Academy Awards ceremony. But according to Oscar legend, Allen's disinterest in attending the Academy Awards began when, at age 16, Allen discounted the Academy's credibility after he saw Marlon Brando lose the 1951 Best Actor race for his performance in *A Streetcar Named Desire.* Like Katharine Hepburn, Allen has attended the Oscars only once, and not in a year that he was even nominated. In 2002, the first Academy Awards telecast after the 9/11 disasters, Allen came on stage dressed impeccably in a tuxedo (another rarity) to offer a brief stand-up routine before introducing a Nora Ephron film tribute to his beloved New York.

Allgood, Sara

Movie: 1941: *How Green Was My Valley* (Best Acting) *Board* (Best Supporting Actress) Academy.

Allyson, June

Movie: 1951: *Too Young to Kiss* (Best Actress, Musical or Comedy) *Globe.* 1954: *Executive Suite* (Best Ensemble) *Venice* (special award). **Tributes:** 1954: Henrietta Award for World Film Favorite from Globe.

Alonso, Maria Conchita

Movie: 1996: *Caught* (Best Female Lead) Spirit.

Amalric, Mathieu

Movie: 2005: *Munich* (Best Supporting Actor) Society.

Ameche, Don

Movie: 1985: *Cocoon* (Best Supporting Actor) *Academy*. 1988: *Things Change* (Best Actor) *Venice* (win shared with costar).

Ames, Leon

Tributes: 1980: Life Achievement Award from the Screen Actors Guild. **Highlights:** Ames has the rare distinction of winning a lifetime achievement award despite never being nominated for any major acting award in any medium. His award, in recognition of his work in more than 100 motion pictures and four television series, came from the Screen Actors Guild, which he helped found in 1933.

Amis, Suzy

Movie: 1993: *The Ballad of Little Jo* (Best Female Lead) Spirit. 1995: *The Usual Suspects* (Best Ensemble) *Board*. 1997: *Titanic* (Best Ensemble) SAG.

Anderson, Anthony

Movie: 2005: *Hustle & Flow* (Best Ensemble) SAG. 2006: *The Departed* (Best Ensemble) *Board,* SAG, Broadcast.

Anderson, Carl

Movie: 1973: *Jesus Christ Superstar* (New Star of the Year — Actor) Globe (Best Actor, Musical or Comedy) Globe.

Anderson, Ernest

Movie: 1942: *In This Our Life* (Best Acting) *Board.*

Anderson, Gilbert M. "Bronco Billy"

Tributes: 1957: Honorary Oscar statuette for being a motion picture pioneer and for his contributions to the development of motion pictures as entertainment from Academy.

Anderson, Jeff

Movie: 1994: *Clerks* (Best Debut Performance) Spirit.

Anderson, Judith

Movie: 1940: *Rebecca* (Best Supporting Actress) Academy. Theater: 1948: *Medea* (Best Actress, Dramatic) Tony. 1982: *Medea* (Best Actress in a Featured Role, Play) Tony. **Television: 1951:** --- (Best Actress) Emmy. 1955: *"Macbeth," Hallmark Hall of Fame* (Best Actress in a Single Performance) *Emmy.* 1959: *"The Bridge of San Luis Rey," DuPont Show of the Month* (Best Single Performance by an Actress) Emmy. 1961: *"Macbeth," Hallmark Hall of Fame* (Best Single Performance by an Actress) *Emmy.* 1968: *"Elizabeth the Queen," Hallmark Hall of Fame* (Best Single Performance by an Actress in a Drama) Emmy. 1974: *"The Borrowers," Hallmark Hall of Fame* (Best Individual Achievement in Acting) Emmy. 1983: *"Medea," Kennedy Center Tonight* (Best Supporting Actress in a Limited Series or Special) Emmy. 1984–1987 series *Santa Barbara* (Best Supporting Actress in a Daytime Drama) 1986: Emmy. **Records:** Anderson is the first actor to win two Emmys for playing the same part in different productions. In 1953 Hallmark Hall of Fame produced a live telecast of *Macbeth* for NBC, and Anderson, as Lady Macbeth, won its only Emmy. Eight years later Hallmark assembled the same cast for a more elaborate production of Shakespeare's tragedy. This time the show swept its categories, bringing in five awards, including another for Anderson.

Andersson, Bibi

Movie: 1958: *Nara livet (Brink of Life)* (Best Actress) *Cannes* (win shared with costars). 1963: *Älskarinnan* (Best Actress) *Berlin.* 1967: *My Sister, My Love* (Best Foreign Actress) British (multiple nomination); *Persona* (Best Actress) *Society* (Best Foreign Actress) British (multiple nomination). 1974: *Scenes from a Marriage* (Best Supporting Actress) *Society.* **Records:** In 1967 Andersson became the first Best Actress winner from the newly formed National Society of Film Critics. In 1974, she set another record with them by becoming the first actor to win awards from that organization in two different categories.

Andersson, Harriet

Movie: 1962: *Through a Glass Darkly* (Best Foreign Actress) British. 1964: *Att älask* (Best Actress) *Venice.*

Andress, Ursula

Movie: 1963: *Dr. No* (New Star of the Year — Actress) *Globe.* **Tributes:** 1965: Henrietta Award for World Film Favorite from Globe.

Andrews, Harry

Movie: 1965: *The Agony and the Ecstasy* (Best Supporting Actor) *Board* (multiple win); *The Hill* (Best Supporting Actor) *Board* (multiple win), (Best British Actor) British.

Andrews, Jason

Movie: 1995: *Rhythm Thief* (Best Debut Performance) Spirit.

Andrews, Julie

Movie: 1964: *Mary Poppins* (Most Promising Newcomer) *British* (Best Actress) *Academy* (Best Actress, Musical or Comedy) *Globe*. 1965: *The Americanization of Emily* (Best British Actress) British (multiple nomination); *The Sound of Music* (Best Actress) Academy (Best Actress, Musical or Comedy) *Globe* (Best British Actress) British (multiple nomination). 1967: *Thoroughly Modern Millie* (Best Actress, Musical or Comedy) Globe. 1968: *Star!* (Best Actress, Musical or Comedy) Globe. 1970: *Darling Lili* (Best Actress, Musical or Comedy) Globe. 1979: *10* (Best Actress, Musical or Comedy) Globe. 1982: *Victor/Victoria* (Best Actress) Academy (Best Actress, Musical or Comedy) *Globe*. 1986: *Duet for One* (Best Actress, Drama) Globe; *That's Life!* (Best Actress, Musical or Comedy) Globe. Theater: 1957: *My Fair Lady* (Best Actress, Musical) Tony. 1961: *Camelot* (Best Actress, Musical) Tony. 1996: *Victor/Victoria* (Best Actress, Musical) Tony. Television: 1958: *Cinderella* (Best Single Performance by an Actress in a Leading or Supporting Role) Emmy. 1965: *The Andy Williams Show* (Best Individual Achievement in Entertainment, Performer) Emmy. 1972: *Julie and Carol at Lincoln Center* (Best Single Program in a Variety or Musical, Star) Emmy. 1973: *The Julie Andrews Hour* (Best Actress in a TV Series, Musical or Comedy) Globe (Best New Series, Star) Emmy (Best Variety Musical Series, Star) *Emmy*. 1995: *The Sound of Julie Andrews* (Best Individual Performance in a Variety or Music Program) Emmy. 2004: *Eloise at Christmastime* (Best Supporting Actress in a Miniseries or TV Movie) Emmy. 2005: *Broadway: The American Musical* (Best Nonfiction Series, Host) *Emmy*. Tributes: 1966, 1967, 1968, 1969: Henrietta Award for World Film Favorite from Globe. 2001: Honor from Kennedy Center for the Performing Arts. 2006: Life Achievement Award from SAG. Highlights: Despite Andrews' rise to Broadway fame as Eliza Doolittle in *My Fair Lady*, Warner Bros. didn't consider Andrews a worthy financial risk to cast her in the movie adaptation. Instead of *My Fair Lady*, Andrews filmed *Mary Poppins*, the first of a string of box office hits so huge that Andrews became one of the most bankable stars of the 1960s, earning four consecutive Golden Globes as World Film Favorite.

Andrews, Naveen

Movie: 1996: *The English Patient* (Best Ensemble) SAG. Television: 2004–present series *Lost* (Best Supporting Actor in a Drama Series) 2005: Emmy. (Best Supporting Actor in a Series, Miniseries, or TV Movie) 2005: Globe. (Best Ensemble in a Drama Series) 2005: *SAG*.

Andreyev, Boris

Movie: 1954: *Bolshaya semya (The Big Family)* *Cannes* (special ensemble award).

Angeli, Pier

Movie: 1951: *Teresa* (New Star of the Year — Actress) *Globe*. 1960: *The Angry Silence* (Best Foreign Actress) British. Tributes: 1954: Henrietta Award for World Film Favorite from Globe.

Aniston, Jennifer

Movie: 2002: *The Good Girl* (Best Female Lead) Spirit. Television: 1994–2004 series *Friends* (Best Actress in a Comedy Series) 2002: *Emmy*. 2003: Emmy. 2004: Emmy. (Best Actress in a Series, Musical or Comedy) 2002: *Globe*. (Best Female Actor in a Comedy Series) 2001: SAG. 2002: SAG. (Best Supporting Actress in a Comedy Series) 2000: Emmy. 2001: Emmy. (Best Supporting Actress in a Series, Miniseries, or TV Movie) 2001: Globe. (Best Ensemble in a Comedy Series) 1995: *SAG*. 1998: SAG. 1999: SAG. 2000: SAG. 2001: SAG. 2002: SAG. 2003: SAG.

Annabella

Movie: 1936: *Veille D'armes* (Best Actress) *Venice*.

Ann-Margret

Movie: 1961: *Pocketful of Miracles* (New Star of the Year — Actress) *Globe*. 1963: *Bye Bye Birdie* (Best Actress, Musical or Comedy) Globe. 1971: *Carnal Knowledge* (Best Supporting Actress) Academy, *Globe*. 1975: *Tommy* (Best Actress) Academy (Best Actress, Musical or Comedy) *Globe*. 1977: *Joseph Andrews* (Best Supporting Actress) Globe. Television: 1983: *Who Will Love My Children?* (Best Actress in a Limited Series or Special) Emmy (Best Actress in a Miniseries or TV Movie) *Globe*. 1984: *A Streetcar Named Desire* (Best Actress in a Limited Series or Special) Emmy (Best Actress in a Miniseries or TV Movie) *Globe*. 1987: *The Two Mrs. Grenvilles* (Best Actress in a Miniseries or Special) Emmy (Best Actress in a Miniseries, or TV Movie) Globe. 1993: *Alex Haley's Queen* (Best Supporting Actress in a Miniseries or Special) Emmy (Best Supporting Actress in a Series, Miniseries, or TV Movie) Globe. 1999: *Life of the Party: The Pamela Harriman Story* (Best Actress in a Miniseries or TV Movie) Emmy, Globe (Best Female Actor in a Television Movie or Miniseries) SAG. Highlights: Ann-Margret lost in two of the biggest upsets in Emmy history. In 1983, the press all but guaranteed that she would win for **Who Will Love My Children?** Instead, 76-year-old film great Barbara Stanwyck took the prize for **The Thorn Birds** and in her acceptance speech acknowledged Ann-Margret's great performance. The next year, Ann-Margret wowed critics playing Blanche DuBois in **A Streetcar Named Desire**, a role Tennessee Williams himself once said he wanted her to play. She lost again, to first-time Emmy nominee Jane Fonda for **The Dollmaker**. Although Ann-Margret has yet to win an Emmy, she's a Golden Globe favorite. She won for both the TV movies that she lost in Emmy upsets as well as for both films that brought her unsuccessful bids for Oscar.

Anton, Susan

Movie: 1979: **Goldengirl** (New Star of the Year — Actress) Globe.

Aoki, Devon

Movie: 2005: **Sin City** (Best Ensemble) Broadcast.

Archer, Anne

Movie: 1987: **Fatal Attraction** (Best Supporting Actress) Academy, Globe, British. 1993: **Short Cuts** (Best Ensemble) Venice (special award). **Records:** In 1971, Archer, daughter of movie actor John Archer and television actress Marjorie Lord, was selected as Miss Golden Globe to hand out awards. Sixteen years later, she became the first Miss Golden Globe to be nominated for a Globe for a motion picture performance.

Ardant, Fanny

Tributes: 2002: Silver Bear for outstanding artistic contribution in **8 Femmes (8 Women)** from Berlin (special ensemble award shared with costars).

Arden, Eve

Movie: 1945: **Mildred Pierce** (Best Supporting Actress) Academy. **Television:** 1953: --- (Best Comedienne) Emmy. 1952–1955 series **Our Miss Brooks** (Best Female Star, Regular Series) 1954: Emmy. (Best Actress Starring in a Regular Series) 1955: Emmy. (Best Actress—Continuing Performance) 1956: Emmy. 1956: --- (Best Comedienne) Emmy. 1957–1958 series **The Eve Arden Show** (Best Continuing Performance by an Actress in a Leading Role in a Dramatic or Comedy Series) 1958: Emmy. 1974: **"Mother of the Bride," ABC Afternoon Playbreak** (Best Actress in a Daytime Drama, Special Program) Emmy. **Highlights:** In 1952, Arden brought her popular radio character, Our Miss Brooks to television

and won an Emmy in its first season. When she took the character to the big screen in 1956, her show became one of the first in television history to be adapted into a full-length motion picture.

Arepina, Iya

Movie: 1954: **Bolshaya semya (The Big Family)** Cannes (special ensemble award).

Arinbasarova, Natalya

Movie: 1966: **Pervvy uchitel** (Best Actress) Venice.

Arkin, Alan

Movie: 1966: **The Russians Are Coming, the Russians Are Coming** (New Star of the Year — Actor) Globe (Most Promising Newcomer) British (Best Actor) Academy (Best Actor, Musical or Comedy) Globe. 1968: **The Heart Is a Lonely Hunter** (Best Actor) Academy, New York (Best Actor, Drama) Globe. 1969: **Popi** (Best Actor, Drama) Globe. 1975: **Hearts of the West** (Best Supporting Actor) New York. 2002: **Thirteen Conversations About One Thing** (Best Supporting Male) Spirit. 2006: **Little Miss Sunshine** (Best Male Actor in a Supporting Role) SAG (Best Supporting Actor) Academy, British, Broadcast (Best Supporting Male) Spirit (Best Ensemble) SAG, Broadcast. **Theater:** 1963: **Enter Laughing** (Best Supporting or Featured Actor, Dramatic) Tony. 1973: **The Sunshine Boys** (Best Director, Dramatic) Tony. **Television:** 1967: **"The Love Song of Barney Kempinski," ABC Stage 67** (Best Single Performance by an Actor in a Leading Role, Drama) Emmy. 1987: **Escape from Sobibor** (Best Actor in a Miniseries or Special) Emmy (Best Actor in a Miniseries or TV Movie) Globe. 1997: **Chicago Hope** (Best Guest Actor in a Drama Series) Emmy. 2003: **The Pentagon Papers** (Best Supporting Actor in a Miniseries or TV Movie) Emmy.

Arliss, George

Movie: 1929: **Disraeli** (Best Actor) Academy (multiple nomination). 1930: **The Green Goddess** (Best Actor) Academy (multiple nomination). **Records:** Arliss's Oscar win for **Disraeli** marked the first time an actor received an Academy Award for reprising a role he'd previously performed on stage. With **Disraeli**, Arliss went one step further, winning for a sound performance after having also starred in an earlier silent film version of the play. **Highlights:** In the first two years of the Academy Awards, winners were announced months ahead of the awards ceremony. To build suspense in the third year, the Academy theoretically planned to wait until the actual banquet to announce the winners. For the films of

1929/1930, it didn't work, as *Daily Variety* printed the voting results in that morning's edition of the paper. Even if they hadn't, the winners wouldn't have been a complete surprise. That year's Best Actor, Arliss and Best Actress, Norma Shearer had posed for photos with their statuettes two days before the awards ceremony. It wasn't until 1940 that the Academy secured their secret winners by putting the results in sealed envelopes to be opened on awards night.

 *For the 1929/1930 Academy Awards season, Arliss was nominated for both *The Green Goddess* as well as *Disraeli*. When the award was announced, he won only for *Disraeli*, but the Academy gave no reason why his multiple nomination resulted in only that single win.

Arnaz, Desi, Jr.

Movie: 1971: *Red Sky at Morning* (New Star of the Year — Actor) *Globe*. Television: 2002: *I Love Lucy 50th Anniversary Special* (Best Special Class Program, Executive Producer) Emmy.

Arnaz, Lucie

Movie: 1980: *The Jazz Singer* (Best Supporting Actress) Globe. Television: 1993: *Lucy and Desi: A Home Movie* (Best Informational Special, Executive Producer) *Emmy*. 2002: *I Love Lucy 50th Anniversary Special* (Best Special Class Program, Executive Producer) Emmy.

Arnold, Tracy

Movie: 1990: *Henry, Portrait of a Serial Killer* (Best Supporting Female) Spirit.

Arquette, Rosanna

Movie: 1985: *After Hours* (Best Female Lead) Spirit (Best Supporting Actress) British; *Desperately Seeking Susan* (Best Actress, Musical or Comedy) Globe (Best Supporting Actress) *British*. Television: 1983: *The Executioner's Song* (Best Actress in a Limited Series or Special) Emmy.

Arthur, Beatrice

Movie: 1974: *Mame* (Best Supporting Actress) Globe. Theater: 1966: *Mame* (Best Supporting or Featured Actress, Musical) *Tony*. Television: 1972–1978 series *Maude* (Best Actress in a Comedy Series) 1973: Emmy. 1974: Emmy. 1976: Emmy. 1977: *Emmy*. 1978: Emmy. (Best Actress in a Series, Musical or Comedy) 1973: Globe. 1974: Globe. 1976: Globe. 1978: Globe. 1978: *Laugh-In* (Best Continuing or Single Performance by a Supporting Actress in Variety or Music) Emmy. 1985–1992 series *The Golden Girls* (Best Actress in a Comedy Series) 1986: Emmy, Globe. 1987: Emmy, Globe. 1988: *Emmy*, Globe. 1989: Emmy, Globe. 2000: *Malcolm in the*

Middle (Best Guest Actress in a Comedy Series) Emmy.

Arthur, Jean

Movie: 1943: *The More the Merrier* (Best Actress) Academy.

Asano, Tadanobu

Movie: 2003: *Ruang rak noi nid mahasan* (Best Actor) *Venice*.

Ashcroft, Peggy

Movie: 1959: *The Nun's Story* (Best British Actress) British. 1969: *Three into Two Won't Go* (Best Supporting Actress) British. 1984: *A Passage to India* (Best Actress) *New York, Board, British* (Best Supporting Actress) *Academy, Globe, LA*. 1989: *Madame Sousatzka* (Best Supporting Actress) British; *She's Been Away* (Best Actress) *Venice* (win shared with costar). Television: 1985: *"The Jewel in the Crown," Masterpiece Theatre* (Best Actress in a Limited Series or Special) Emmy (Best Actress in a Miniseries or TV Movie) Globe. 1989: *"A Perfect Spy," Masterpiece Theatre* (Best Supporting Actress in a Miniseries or Special) Emmy. **Tributes:** 1989: A second Best Actress award for *She's Been Away* from Venice. **Records:** 28 years after earning the status of Dame Commander of the British Empire, Ashcroft became the first Dame of British Theater to also win an Academy Award. Winning the Best Supporting Actress Oscar at age 77 also made her the oldest star to win in that category.

Asher, Jane

Movie: 1971: *Deep End* (Best Supporting Actress) British.

Ashley, Elizabeth

Movie: 1964: *The Carpetbaggers* (Most Promising Newcomer) British (Best Supporting Actress) Globe. Theater: 1962: *Take Her, She's Mine* (Best Supporting or Featured Actress, Dramatic) *Tony*. 1964: *Barefoot in the Park* (Best Actress, Dramatic) Tony. 1975: *Cat on a Hot Tin Roof* (Best Actress, Dramatic) Tony. Television: 1990–1994 series *Evening Shade* (Best Supporting Actress in a Comedy Series) 1991: Emmy.

Ashton, John

Movie: 2007: *Gone Baby Gone* (Best Ensemble) Broadcast.

Assante, Armand

Movie: 1990: *Q & A* (Best Supporting Actor) Globe. 2007: *American Gangster* (Best Ensemble) SAG.

Television: 1988: *Jack the Ripper* (Best Supporting Actor in a Miniseries or Special) Emmy (Best Supporting Actor in a Miniseries or TV Movie) Globe. 1997: *Gotti* (Best Actor in a Miniseries or Special) *Emmy* (Best Actor in a Miniseries or TV Movie) Globe (Best Male Actor in a Television Movie or Miniseries) SAG. 1998: *The Odyssey* (Best Actor in a Miniseries or TV Movie) Globe.

Astaire, Fred

Movie: 1950: *Three Little Words* (Best Actor, Musical or Comedy) *Globe*. 1959: *On the Beach* (Best Supporting Actor) Globe. 1961: *The Pleasure of His Company* (Best Actor, Musical or Comedy) Globe. 1968: *Finian's Rainbow* (Best Actor, Musical or Comedy) Globe. 1974: *The Towering Inferno* (Best Supporting Actor) Academy, *Globe, British*. Television: 1959: *An Evening with Fred Astaire* (Best Single Performance by an Actor) *Emmy*. 1960: *Another Evening with Fred Astaire* (Best Performance in a Variety or Musical Program or Series) Emmy. 1961: *Astaire Time* (Best Performance in a Variety or Musical Program or Series) *Emmy*. 1968: *The Fred Astaire Show* (Best Music or Variety Program, Producer) Emmy. 1978: *A Family Upside Down* (Best Actor in a Drama or Comedy Special) *Emmy*. Tributes: 1949: Honorary Oscar statuette for his unique artistry and his contributions to the technique of musical pictures from Academy. 1960: Cecil B. DeMille award from Globe. 1973: Gala Tribute from the Film Society of Lincoln Center. 1978: Honor from Kennedy Center for the Performing Arts. 1981: Life Achievement Award from American Film Institute. 1990: Television Hall of Fame Inductee from Emmy. 1999: Ranked Number 5 on List of 25 Greatest Male Screen Legends of the 20th Century from American Film Institute. **Records:** Astaire was the first actor to be a Kennedy Center Honoree and the second, after actor/director/writer/composer Charlie Chaplin, to be honored by the Film Society of Lincoln Center.

Astin, Sean

Movie: 1994: *Kangaroo Court* (Best Live Action Short Film, Producer) Academy. 2001: *The Lord of the Rings: The Fellowship of the Ring* (Best Ensemble) SAG. 2002: *The Lord of the Rings: The Two Towers* (Best Ensemble) SAG. 2003: *The Lord of the Rings: The Return of the King* (Best Ensemble) *Board, SAG, Broadcast.*

Astor, Mary

Movie: 1941: *The Great Lie* (Best Acting) *Board* (multiple win), (Best Supporting Actress) *Academy*; *The Maltese Falcon* (Best Acting) *Board* (multiple win).

Atkins, Christopher

Movie: 1980: *The Blue Lagoon* (New Star of the Year — Actor) Globe.

Atkins, Eileen

Movie: 1983: *The Dresser* (Best Supporting Actress) British. 2001: *Gosford Park* (Best Ensemble) *SAG, Broadcast*. Theater: 1967: *The Killing of Sister George* (Best Actress, Dramatic) Tony. 1972: *Vivat! Vivat! Regina!* (Best Actress, Dramatic) Tony. 1995: *Indiscretions* (Best Actress, Play) Tony. 2004: *The Retreat from Moscow* (Best Actress, Play) Tony.

Atkinson, Rowan

Movie: 2003: *Love Actually* (Best Ensemble) Broadcast.

Attenborough, Richard

Movie: 1960: *The Angry Silence* (Best British Actor) British. 1962: *Dock Brief* (Best British Actor) British. 1964: *Guns at Batasi* (Best British Actor) *British* (multiple win); *Séance on a Wet Afternoon* (Best British Actor) *British* (multiple win). 1966: *The Sand Pebbles* (Best Supporting Actor) *Globe*. 1967: *Doctor Doolittle* (Best Supporting Actor) *Globe*. 1969: *Oh! What a Lovely War* (Best Director) British. 1977: *A Bridge Too Far* (Best Director) British. 1982: *Gandhi* (Best Director) *Academy, Globe, British* (Best Picture, Producer) *Academy, New York, Board, British* (Best Foreign Film, Producer) *Globe*. 1985: *A Chorus Line: The Movie* (Best Director) Globe. 1987: *Cry Freedom* (Best Director) Globe (Best Picture, Drama; Producer) Globe. 1993: *Shadowlands* (Best Director) British (Best Picture, Producer) British. **Tributes:** 1988: Honorary Award from Berlin. 1993: Special Alexander Korda Award for outstanding British Film of the Year for *Shadowlands* from British.

Audran, Stéphane

Movie: 1968: *Les Biches* (Best Actress) *Berlin*. 1972: *The Butchers* (Best Actress) British. 1973: *The Discreet Charm of the Bourgeoisie* (Best Actress) *British* (multiple win); *Just Before Nightfall* (Best Actress) *British* (multiple win). 1988: *Babette's Feast* (Best Actress) British.

Auer, Mischa

Movie: 1936: *My Man Godfrey* (Best Supporting Actor) Academy.

August, Pernilla

Movie: 1992: *The Best Intentions* (Best Actress)

Cannes. 2003: *Om jag vänder mig om* (Best Ensemble) *Berlin* (special award).

Aulin, Ewa

Movie: 1968: *Candy* (New Star of the Year — Actress) Globe.

Auteuil, Daniel

Movie: 1987: *Jean de Florette* (Best Supporting Actor) *British.* 1996: *Le Huitième jour (The Eighth Day)* (Best Actor) *Cannes* (win shared with costar).

Avery, Margaret

Movie: 1985: *The Color Purple* (Best Supporting Actress) Academy.

Aykroyd, Dan

Movie: 1989: *Driving Miss Daisy* (Best Supporting Actor) Academy. Television: 1975–1979 series *Saturday Night Live (NBC's Saturday Night)* (Best Continuing or Single Performance by a Supporting Actor in a Comedy-Variety or Music Series) 1978: Emmy. (Best Writing for a Comedy-Variety or Music Series) 1977: *Emmy.* 1978: Emmy. 1979: Emmy. (Best Comedy-Variety or Music Series, Star) 1979: Emmy.

Ayler, Ethel

Movie: 1990: *To Sleep with Anger* (Best Supporting Female) Spirit.

Ayres, Lew

Movie: 1938: *Holiday* (Best Acting) *Board* (multiple win); *Young Dr. Kildare* (Best Acting) *Board* (multiple win). 1948: *Johnny Belinda* (Best Actor) Academy. Television: 1975: *Kung Fu* (Best Single Performance by a Supporting Actor) Emmy.

Azaria, Hank

Movie: 1996: *The Birdcage* (Best Male Actor in a Supporting Role) SAG (Best Ensemble) *SAG.* Theater: 2004: *Monty Python's Spamalot* (Best Actor, Musical) Tony. Television: 1998: *Mad About You* (Best Guest Actor in a Comedy Series) Emmy. 1989–present series *The Simpsons* (Best Voice-Over Performance) 1998: *Emmy.* 2001: *Emmy.* 2003: *Emmy.* 1999: *"Tuesdays with Morrie," Oprah Winfrey Presents* (Best Male Actor in a Television Movie or Miniseries) SAG (Best Supporting Actor in a Miniseries or TV Movie) *Emmy.* 2003: *Friends* (Best Guest Actor in a Comedy Series) Emmy. 2004–2006 series *Huff* (Best Actor in a Drama Series) 2005: Emmy. (Best Male Actor in a Drama Series) 2004: SAG.

Azéma, Sabine

Movie: 1984: *A Sunday in the Country* (Best Supporting Actress) *Board.*

Bacall, Lauren

Movie: 1976: *The Shootist* (Best Actress) British. 1994: *Prêt-à-Porter (Ready-to-Wear)* (Best Ensemble) *Board.* 1996: *The Mirror Has Two Faces* (Best Female Actor in a Supporting Role) SAG (Best Supporting Actress) Academy, *Globe,* British. Theater: 1970: *Applause* (Best Actress, Musical) *Tony.* 1981: *Woman of the Year* (Best Actress, Musical) *Tony.* Television: 1973: *Applause* (Best Actress, Single Performance) Emmy. 1980: *The Rockford Files* (Best Actress, Drama Series) Emmy. 1988: *"Bacall on Bogart," Great Performances* (Best Information Special, Host) Emmy. Tributes: 1991: Career Achievement Award from Board. 1992: Cecil B. DeMille Award from Globe. 1996: Lifetime Achievement Award from Broadcast. 1997: Honorary Award from Berlin; Honor from Kennedy Center for the Performing Arts. 1999: Ranked Number 20 on List of 25 Greatest Female Screen Legends of the 20th Century from American Film Institute. **Records:** Bacall received the first Lifetime Achievement Award ever given by the Broadcast Film Critics Association.

Bacon, Kevin

Movie: 1994: *The River Wild* (Best Supporting Actor) Globe. 1995: *Apollo 13* (Best Ensemble) *SAG; Murder in the First* (Best Actor) *Broadcast* (Best Male Actor in a Supporting Role) SAG. 2003: *Mystic River* (Best Ensemble) SAG, Broadcast. 2004: *The Woodsman* (Best Male Lead) Spirit. **Highlights:** In a year when Nicholas Cage was sweeping every critical award for his performance as a depressed writer drinking himself to death in *Leaving Las Vegas,* Bacon pulled off the only critics' award upset when the Broadcast Film Critics named him their first Best Actor winner for playing real life convict Henri Young, an Alcatraz inmate driven to madness and murder after years of torturous solitary confinement in *Murder in the First.*

Baddeley, Hermione

Movie: 1959: *Room at the Top* (Best British Actress) British (Best Supporting Actress) Academy. Theater: 1963: *The Milk Train Doesn't Stop Here Anymore* (Best Actress, Dramatic) Tony. Television: 1974–1977 series *Maude* (Best Supporting Actress in a Series, Miniseries, or TV Movie) 1975: *Globe.*

Badham, Mary

Movie: 1962: *To Kill a Mockingbird* (Best Supporting Actress) Academy.

Badland, Annette

Movie: 1998: *Little Voice* (Best Ensemble) SAG.

Badu, Erykah

Movie: 1999: *The Cider House Rules* (Best Ensemble) SAG.

Baer, Robert

Movie: 2005: *Syriana* (Best Ensemble) Broadcast.

Bailey, Pearl

Television: 1986: *"Cindy Eller: A Modern Fairy Tale," ABC Afterschool Special* (Best Individual Achievement in Children's Programming, Performer) *Emmy.* Tributes: 1968: Special Tony Award for *Hello, Dolly!* 1976: Life Achievement Award from SAG.

Bainter, Fay

Movie: 1938: *Jezebel* (Best Supporting Actress) *Academy*; *White Banners* (Best Actress) Academy. 1961: *The Children's Hour* (Best Supporting Actress) Academy, Globe. **Records:** Bainter is the first performer to be nominated for both a lead and supporting acting Oscar in the same year. Her supporting actress win for *Jezebel* in 1938 started a trend that continued for fifty years: stars nominated for both awards lost the lead actor award and won supporting.

Baker, Carroll

Movie: 1956: *Giant* (New Star of the Year — Female) *Globe* (multiple win); *Baby Doll* (New Star of the Year — Female) *Globe* (multiple win), (Best Actress) Academy (Best Actress, Drama) Globe (Best Foreign Actress) British.

Baker, Diane

Movie: 1959: *The Diary of Anne Frank* (New Star of the Year — Female) Globe. 1963: *The Prize* (Best Supporting Actress) Globe. Television: 1966: *"Inherit the Wind," Hallmark Hall of Fame* (Best Performance by a Supporting Actress, Drama) Emmy. 1974: *"Can I Save My Children?" ABC Afternoon Playbreak* (Best Actress in a Daytime Drama Special) Emmy. 1985: *Barbara Taylor Bradford's A Woman of Substance* (Best Limited Series, Producer) Emmy.

Baker, Dylan

Movie: 1998: *Happiness* (Best Male Lead) Spirit (Best Ensemble) *Board.* Theater: 1991: *La Bête* (Best Actor in a Featured Role, Play) Tony.

Baker, Kathy

Movie: 1987: *Street Smart* (Best Supporting Actress) *Society* (Best Supporting Female) Spirit. 1999: *The Cider House Rules* (Best Ensemble) SAG. Television: 1992–1996 series *Picket Fences* (Best Actress in a Drama Series) 1993: *Emmy.* 1994: Emmy, *Globe.* 1995: *Emmy*, Globe. 1996: *Emmy*, Globe. (Best Female Actor in a Drama Series) 1994: *SAG.* 2000: *Touched by an Angel* (Best Guest Actress in a Drama Series) Emmy. 2001: *Boston Public* (Best Guest Actress in a Drama Series) Emmy. 2003: *Door to Door* (Best Supporting Actress in a Miniseries or TV Movie) Emmy.

Baker, Lenny

Movie: 1976: *Next Stop, Greenwich Village* (New Star of the Year — Male) Globe. Theater: 1977: *I Love My Wife* (Best Actor in a Featured Role, Musical) *Tony.*

Baker, Stanley

Movie: 1959: *Yesterday's Enemy* (Best British Actor) British. Television: 1977: *"How Green Was My Valley," Masterpiece Theatre* (Best Actor, Limited Series) Emmy.

Baker, Tom

Movie: 1971: *Nicholas and Alexandra* (New Star of the Year — Male) Globe (Best Supporting Actor) Globe.

Baker Hall, Philip

Movie: 1997: *Hard Eight* (Best Male Lead) Spirit; *Boogie Nights* (Best Ensemble) SAG. 1999: *Magnolia* (Best Ensemble) *Board*, SAG.

Balaban, Bob

Movie: 2001: *Gosford Park* (Best Ensemble) *SAG, Broadcast* (Best Picture, Producer) Academy (Best Picture, Musical or Comedy; Producer) Globe. 2003: *A Mighty Wind* (Best Screenplay) Spirit (Best Ensemble) Broadcast. 2005: *Capote* (Best Ensemble) SAG. Theater: 1979: *The Inspector General* (Best Actor in a Featured Role, Play) Tony.

Baldwin, Alec

Movie: 2000: *State and Main* (Best Ensemble) *Board.* 2003: *The Cooler* (Best Male Actor in a Supporting Role) SAG (Best Supporting Actor) Academy, *Board*, Globe, Broadcast. 2004: *The Aviator* (Best Ensemble) SAG. 2006: *The Departed* (Best Ensemble) *Board*, SAG, Broadcast. **Theater:** 1992: *A Streetcar Named Desire* (Best Actor, Play) Tony. **Television:** 1995: *Tennessee Williams' A Streetcar Named Desire* (Best Actor in a Miniseries or Special) Emmy (Best Actor in a Miniseries or TV Movie) Globe (Best Male Actor in a Television Movie or Miniseries) SAG. 2000: *Nuremberg* (Best Actor in a Miniseries or TV Movie) Globe (Best Male Actor in a Television Movie or Miniseries) SAG (Best Miniseries, Producer) Emmy. 2002: *Path to War* (Best Supporting Actor in a Miniseries or TV Movie) Emmy (Best Supporting Actor in a Series, Miniseries, or TV Movie) Globe. 2005–2006 series *Will & Grace* (Best Guest Actor in a Comedy Series) 2005: Emmy. 2006: Emmy. 2006–present series *30 Rock* (Best Actor in a Comedy Series) 2007: Emmy. (Best Actor in a Series, Musical or Comedy) 2006: *Globe*. 2007: Globe. (Best Male Actor in a Comedy Series) 2006: *SAG*. 2007: *SAG*. (Best Ensemble in a Comedy Series) 2007: SAG.

Baldwin, Greta

Movie: 1967: *Rogues' Gallery* (New Star of the Year — Female) Globe.

Baldwin, Stephen

Movie: 1995: *The Usual Suspects* (Best Ensemble) *Board*.

Bale, Christian

Movie: 1987: *Empire of the Sun* (Best Juvenile Performance) *Board*. 2007: *3:10 to Yuma* (Best Ensemble) SAG; *I'm Not There* (Best Ensemble) *Spirit* (special award).

Balin, Ina

Movie: 1960: *From the Terrace* (New Star of the Year — Female) *Globe* (Best Supporting Actress) Globe.

Balint, Eszter

Movie: 1990: *Bail Jumper* (Best Female Lead) Spirit.

Balk, Fairuza

Movie: 1992: *Gas Food Lodging* (Best Female Lead) *Spirit*. 2000: *Almost Famous* (Best Ensemble) SAG.

Ball, Lucille

Movie: 1960: *The Facts of Life* (Best Actress, Comedy or Musical) Globe. 1968: *Yours, Mine and Ours* (Best Actress, Comedy or Musical) Globe. 1974: *Mame* (Best Actress, Comedy or Musical) Globe. **Television:** 1952: --- (Best Comedian or Comedienne) Emmy. 1953: --- (Most Outstanding Personality) Emmy (Best Comedienne) *Emmy*. 1956: --- (Best Comedienne) Emmy. 1951–1957 series *I Love Lucy* (Best Female Star on a Regular Series) 1954: Emmy. (Best Actress Starring in a Regular Series) 1955: Emmy. (Best Actress in a Continuing Performance) 1956: *Emmy*. (Best Continuing Performance by a Comedienne in a Series) 1957: Emmy. (Best Continuing Performance — Female — in a Series by an Actress) 1958: Emmy. (Best Comedy Show, Producer) 1951: Emmy. (Best Situation Comedy, Producer) 1952: *Emmy*. 1953: *Emmy*. 1954: Emmy. 1962–1968 series *The Lucy Show (The Lucille Ball Show)* (Best Continued Performance by an Actress in a Comedy Series) 1963: Emmy. 1966: Emmy. 1967: *Emmy*. 1968: *Emmy*, Globe. 1968–1974 series *Here's Lucy* (Best Actress, Musical or Comedy Series) 1969: Globe. 1970: Globe. (Best Actress, Musical or Comedy Series or TV Movie) 1971: Globe. **Tributes:** 1978: Cecil B. DeMille Award from Globe. 1984: Television Hall of Fame Inductee from Emmy. 1986: Honor from Kennedy Center for the Performing Arts. **Records:** In 1984, Ball was honored with the first group of inductees to the Academy of Television Arts and Sciences Hall of Fame. Of the seven inductees that year, she was the only female.

Balsam, Martin

Movie: 1964: *The Carpetbaggers* (Best Supporting Actor) *Board*. 1965: *A Thousand Clowns* (Best Supporting Actor) *Academy*. 1973: *Summer Wishes, Winter Dreams* (Best Supporting Actor) Globe. 1974: *The Taking of Pelham 1-2-3* (Best Supporting Actor) British. 1976: *All the President's Men* (Best Supporting Actor) British. **Theater:** 1968: *You Know I Can't Hear You When the Water's Running* (Best Actor, Dramatic) *Tony*. **Television:** 1977: *"Raid on Entebee," The Big Event* (Best Supporting Actor in a Comedy or Drama Special) Emmy.

Bamji, Firdous

Movie: 2005: *The War Within* (Best Supporting Male) Spirit.

Bancroft, Anne

Movie: 1962: *The Miracle Worker* (Best Actress) *Academy, Board* (Best Actress, Drama) Globe (Best

Foreign Actress) *British*. 1964: ***The Pumpkin Eater*** (Best Actress) Academy, *Cannes* (Best Actress, Drama) *Globe* (Best Foreign Actress) *British*. 1967: ***The Graduate*** (Best Actress) Academy, British (Best Actress, Comedy or Musical) *Globe*. 1972: ***Young Winston*** (Best Actress) British. 1975: ***The Prisoner of Second Avenue*** (Best Actress) British. 1977: ***The Turning Point*** (Best Actress) Academy, *Board*, British (Best Actress, Drama) Globe. 1983: ***To Be or Not to Be*** (Best Actress, Comedy or Musical) Globe. 1984: ***Garbo Talks*** (Best Actress, Comedy or Musical) Globe. 1985: ***Agnes of God*** (Best Actress) Academy (Best Actress, Drama) Globe. 1986: ***'night, Mother*** (Best Actress, Drama) Globe. 1987: ***84 Charing Cross Road*** (Best Actress) *British*. 1995: ***How to Make an American Quilt*** (Best Ensemble) SAG. Theater: 1958: ***Two for the Seesaw*** (Best Supporting or Featured Actress, Dramatic) *Tony*. 1960: ***The Miracle Worker*** (Best Actress, Dramatic) *Tony*. 1978: ***Golda*** (Best Actress, Play) Tony. **Television:** 1970: ***Annie, the Women in the Life of a Man*** (Outstanding Variety or Musical Program, Star) *Emmy*. 1992: ***"Mrs. Cage," American Playhouse*** (Best Actress in a Miniseries or Special) Emmy; ***Neil Simon's Broadway Bound*** (Best Supporting Actress in a Miniseries or Special) Emmy. 1994: ***Oldest Living Confederate Widow Tells All*** (Best Supporting Actress in a Miniseries or Special) Emmy. 1996: ***The Homecoming*** (Best Female Actor in a Television Movie or Miniseries) SAG. 1999: ***Deep in My Heart*** (Best Supporting Actress in a Miniseries or TV Movie) *Emmy*. 2001: ***Haven*** (Best Supporting Actress in a Miniseries or TV Movie) Emmy. 2003: ***Tennessee Williams' The Roman Spring of Mrs. Stone*** (Best Female Actor in a Television Movie or Miniseries) SAG (Best Supporting Actress in a Miniseries or TV Movie) Emmy.

Bancroft, George

Movie: 1929: ***Thunderbolt*** (Best Actor) Academy.

Banderas, Antonio

Movie: 1996: ***Evita*** (Best Actor, Comedy or Musical) Globe. 1998: ***The Mask of Zorro*** (Best Actor, Comedy or Musical) Globe. **Theater:** 2003: ***Nine, the Musical*** (Best Actor, Musical) Tony. **Television:** 2004: ***And Starring Pancho Villa as Himself*** (Best Actor in a Miniseries or TV Movie) Emmy, Globe.

Banerjee, Karuna

Movie: 1958: ***The Unvanquished*** (Best British Actress) British.

Banerjee, Victor

Movie: 1984: ***A Passage to India*** (Best Actor) *Board*, British.

Bankhead, Tallulah

Movie: 1944: ***Lifeboat*** (Best Actress) *New York*. Theater: 1961: ***Midgie Purvis*** (Best Actress, Dramatic) Tony.

Banks, Caerthan

Movie: 1997: ***The Sweet Hereafter*** (Best Ensemble) *Board*.

Banks, Elizabeth

Movie: 2003: ***Seabiscuit*** (Best Ensemble) SAG.

Bannen, Ian

Movie: 1965: ***The Flight of the Phoenix*** (New Star of the Year — Male) Globe (Best Supporting Actor) Academy. 1973: ***The Offence*** (Best Supporting Actor) British. 1987: ***Hope and Glory*** (Best Supporting Actor) British. 1998: ***Waking Ned Devine*** (Best Ensemble) SAG.

Baquero, Ivana

Movie: 2006: ***Pan's Labyrinth*** (Best Young Actress) Broadcast.

Baranska, Jadwiga

Movie: 1976: ***Noce i dnie*** (Best Actress) *Berlin*.

Baranski, Christine

Movie: 1996: ***The Birdcage*** (Best Ensemble) *SAG*. 2002: ***Chicago*** (Best Ensemble) *SAG, Broadcast*. **Theater:** 1984: ***The Real Thing*** (Best Actress in a Featured Role, Play) *Tony*. 1989: ***Rumors*** (Best Actress in a Featured Role, Play) *Tony*. **Television:** 1995–1998 series ***Cybill*** (Best Female Actor in a Comedy Series) 1995: *SAG*. 1996: SAG. (Best Supporting Actress in a Comedy Series) 1995: *Emmy*. 1996: Emmy. 1997: Emmy. 1998: Emmy. (Best Supporting Actress in a Series, Miniseries, or TV Movie) 1995: Globe. 1996: Globe. 1999: ***Frasier*** (Best Guest Actress in a Comedy Series) Emmy.

Barber, Paul

Movie: 1997: ***The Full Monty*** (Best Ensemble) *SAG*.

Bardem, Javier

Movie: 2000: ***Before Night Falls*** (Best Actor) Academy, *Venice, Board, Society,* Broadcast (Best Actor, Drama) Globe (Best Male Lead) *Spirit*. 2004: ***Mar adentro (The Sea Inside)*** (Best Actor) *Venice,*

Broadcast (Best Actor, Drama) Globe. 2007: *No Country for Old Men* (Best Male Actor in a Supporting Role) SAG (Best Supporting Actor) *Academy, New York, Globe, British, Society, Broadcast* (Best Ensemble) *Board, SAG,* Broadcast.

Bardot, Brigitte

Movie: 1966: *Viva Maria* (Best Foreign Actress) British. **Highlights:** Bardot made arguably the biggest splash in Cannes Film Festival history when, at only age 18, she attended the April 1953 festival and instantly rose to international fame. An uninvited entrance to an elegant luncheon where she twirled in her skirt revealing how little she wore underneath and the admission that she had never seen a bikini, let alone wore one before that festival made her the media darling. A posed photo of her with 3,500 U.S. Navy sailors on the aircraft carrier *Midway* and some candid shots of Bardot with Kirk Douglas on the beach hit newsstands worldwide. Within days, one of the highest and brightest stars had vaulted into the celebrity stratosphere.

Barker, Eric

Movie: 1957: *Brothers in Law* (Most Promising Newcomer) *British.*

Barkin, Ellen

Movie: 1991: *Switch* (Best Actress, Musical or Comedy) Globe. **Television:** 1998: *"Before Women Had Wings," Oprah Winfrey Presents* (Best Actress in a Miniseries or TV Movie) *Emmy,* Globe.

Barlow, Thelma

Movie: 2005: *Mrs. Henderson Presents* (Best Ensemble) *Board.*

Barnes, Joanna

Movie: 1958: *Auntie Mame* (New Star of the Year — Actress) Globe.

Baron Cohen, Sacha

Movie: 2006: *Borat: Cultural Learning of America for Make Benefit Glorious Nation of Kazakhstan* (Best Actor) *LA* (Best Actor, Musical or Comedy) *Globe* (Best Adapted Screenplay) Academy (Best Comedy Movie, Executive Producer) *Broadcast* (Best Picture, Musical or Comedy; Executive Producer) Globe. 2007: *Sweeney Todd: The Demon Barber of Fleet Street* (Best Ensemble) Broadcast. **Television:** 2003–2004 series *Da Ali G Show* (Best Nonfiction Program, Alternative; Executive Producer) 2003: Emmy. (Best Variety, Music or Comedy

Series; Producer) 2005: Emmy. (Best Writing for Nonfiction Programming) 2003: Emmy. (Best Writing for a Variety, Music, or Comedy Series) 2005: Emmy.

Barrault, Marie-Christine

Movie: 1976: *Cousin, Cousine* (Best Actress) Academy.

Barraza, Adriana

Movie: 2006: *Babel* (Best Female Actor in a Supporting Role) SAG (Best Supporting Actress) Academy, Globe, Broadcast (Best Ensemble) SAG, Broadcast.

Barrie, Barbara

Movie: 1964: *One Potato, Two Potato* (Best Actress) *Cannes.* 1979: *Breaking Away* (Best Supporting Actress) Academy. 1999: *Judy Berlin* (Best Supporting Female) Spirit. **Theater:** 1971: *Company* (Best Supporting or Featured Actress, Musical) Tony. **Television:** 1980–1981 series *Breaking Away* (Best Supporting Actress, Drama Series) 1981: Emmy. 1991–1992 series *Law & Order* (Best Supporting Actress in a Drama Series) 1992: Emmy. 2003: *Law & Order: Special Victims Unit* (Best Guest Actress in a Drama Series) Emmy.

Barry, Raymond J.

Movie: 2006: *Steel City* (Best Supporting Male) Spirit.

Barrymore, Drew

Movie: 1982: *E.T. The Extra-Terrestrial* (Most Promising Newcomer) British. 1984: *Irreconcilable Differences* (Best Supporting Actress) Globe. **Television:** 1992: *Guncrazy* (Best Actress in a Miniseries or TV Movie) Globe. 2000: *Olive, the Other Reindeer* (Best Animated Program, Executive Producer) Emmy.

Barrymore, Ethel

Movie: 1944: *None but the Lonely Heart* (Best Acting) *Board* (Best Supporting Actress) *Academy.* 1946: *The Spiral Staircase* (Best Supporting Actress) Academy. 1947: *The Paradine Case* (Best Supporting Actress) Academy. 1949: *Pinky* (Best Supporting Actress) Academy. **Television:** 1955: *"The 13th Chair," Climax* (Best Actress in a Single Performance) Emmy. **Records:** Barrymore's 1944 Best Supporting Actress win, following brother Lionel's Best Actor win in 1930/1931 for *A Free Soul*, made them the first siblings to both win acting Oscars. Their brother John, also a talented and popular actor, was never even nominated. To date, Lionel and Ethel remain the only brother and sister to both win Academy Awards for acting.

Barrymore, Lionel

Movie: 1929: *Madame X* (Best Director) Academy. 1931: *A Free Soul* (Best Actor) *Academy*. Records: Up for Best Director in 1928/29 and Best Actor in 1930/31, Barrymore became the first person to receive Oscar nominations in two different categories. Although he lost the Best Director competition, he won Best Actor for *A Free Soul*, a film that set a Guinness world record. In the climactic courtroom scene, Barrymore, as alcoholic lawyer Stephen Ashe delivers a 14-minute soliloquy that remains the longest uninterrupted monologue in film history. Because film reels of the day lasted only ten minutes, director Clarence Brown achieved the feat by using more than one camera. Barrymore always considered the part of Ashe in *A Free Soul* his favorite screen role.

Barthelmess, Richard

Movie: 1927: *The Patent Leather Kid* (Best Actor) Academy. 1928: *The Noose* (Best Actor) Academy. Records: A founding member of the Academy of Motion Picture Arts and Sciences, Barthelmess was one of the first three actors to earn an Academy Award nomination. For the 1927/1928 season, he was recognized for both *The Patent Leather Kid* and *The Noose*. He lost to Emil Jannings, who won for *The Last Command* and *The Way of All Flesh*. Also in contention for Best Actor that year was Charlie Chaplin, up for one film, *The Circus*. During his career, Chaplin won both competitive and honorary Oscars, leaving Barthelmess the only one of the first three Best Actor nominees never to win an Academy Award.

Baryshnikov, Mikhail

Movie: 1977: *The Turning Point* (Best Supporting Actor) Academy, Globe. Theater: 1989: *Metamorphosis* (Best Actor, Play) Tony. Television: 1978: *The Nutcracker* (Best Individual Achievement in Children's Programming) Emmy. 1979: *Baryshnikov at the White House* (Best Individual Achievement in a Special Event) *Emmy*. 1980: *IBM Presents Baryshnikov on Broadway* (Best Variety or Music Program, Star) *Emmy*. 1982: *Baryshnikov in Hollywood* (Best Variety, Music, or Comedy Program, Star) Emmy. 1985: *Dance in America: Baryshnikov by Tharp with American Ballet Theatre* (Best Classical Performance in the Performing Arts, Host) Emmy. 1988: "*Celebrating Gershwin,*" *Great Performances* (Best Individual Performance in a Variety or Music Pro-

gram) Emmy; "*Dance in America: David Gordon's Made in U.S.A.,*" *Great Performances* (Best Individual Achievement, Classical) Emmy. 1989: "*Baryshnikov Dances Balanchine,*" *Great Performances* (Best Individual Performance in a Classical Music or Dance Program) *Emmy*. Tributes: 2000: Honor from Kennedy Center for the Performing Arts.

Basehart, Richard

Movie: 1951: *Fourteen Hours* (Best Actor) *Board*. 1956: *Moby Dick* (Best Supporting Actor) *Board*. 1957: *Time Limit* (Best Foreign Actor) British. Television: 1965: *Let My People Go* (Individual Achievement Award, Narrator) *Emmy*.

Basinger, Kim

Movie: 1984: *The Natural* (Best Supporting Actress) Globe. 1994: *Prêt-à-Porter (Ready-to-Wear)* (Best Ensemble) *Board*. 1997: *L.A. Confidential* (Best Actress) British (Best Female Actor in a Supporting Role) *SAG* (Best Supporting Actress) *Academy*, *Globe* (Best Ensemble) SAG. Records: In the Screen Actors Guild Awards' fourth year, Basinger and *Titanic*'s Gloria Stuart both won Best Supporting Actress, making their wins the first tie in SAG history. That award season Basinger won the major prizes for *L.A. Confidential* playing a Hollywood call girl who got clients by making herself look like Veronica Lake, a film siren whose only award recognition was a star on the Hollywood Walk of Fame.

Baskett, James

Tributes: 1947: Honorary Oscar statuette for his able and heart-warming characterization of Uncle Remus, friend and storyteller to the children of the world in Walt Disney's *Song of the South* from Academy. Records: When the Academy of Motion Picture Arts and Sciences gave Baskett an honorary Academy Award for playing Uncle Remus, he became the first African-American male to receive an acting Oscar. Before him, Hattie McDaniel set the first Oscar record for African-Americans when she was voted Best Supporting Actress for *Gone with the Wind* in 1939. The first male Black actor to win an Oscar in a competitive category was Sidney Poitier, who was voted Best Actor for *Lilies of the Field* in 1963.

Bass, Alfie

Movie: 1955: *The Bespoke Overcoat* (Best British Actor) British.

Basserman, Albert

Movie: 1940: *Foreign Correspondent* (Best Supporting Actor) Academy.

Bassett, Angela

Movie: 1993: *What's Love Got to Do with It* (Best Actress) Academy (Best Actress, Musical or Comedy) *Globe.* Television: 2001: *Ruby's Bucket of Blood* (Best Female Actor in a Television Movie or Miniseries) SAG. 2002: *The Rosa Parks Story* (Best Actress in a Miniseries or TV Movie) Emmy.

Bassett, Linda

Movie: 1999: *East Is East* (Best Actress) British.

Batalov, Aleksey

Movie: 1954: *Bolshaya semya (The Big Family)* Cannes (special ensemble award).

Bateman, Jason

Movie: 2007: *Juno* (Best Ensemble) Broadcast. Television: 2003–2006 series *Arrested Development* (Best Actor in a Comedy Series) 2005: Emmy. (Best Actor in a Series, Musical or Comedy) 2005: *Globe.* (Best Male Actor in a Comedy Series) 2004: SAG.

Bates, Alan

Movie: 1962: *A Kind of Loving* (Best British Actor) British. 1966: *Georgy Girl* (New Star of the Year — Actor) Globe (Best Actor, Musical or Comedy) Globe. 1967: *Far from the Madding Crowd* (Best Actor, Drama) Globe. 1968: *The Fixer* (Best Actor) Academy (Best Actor, Drama) Globe. 1969: *Women in Love* (Best Actor) British. 1990: *Hamlet* (Best Supporting Actor) British. 2001: *Gosford Park* (Best Ensemble) *SAG, Broadcast.* Theater: 1973: *Butley* (Best Actor, Dramatic) *Tony.* 2002: *Fortune's Fool* (Best Actor, Play) *Tony.*

Bates, Florence

Movie: 1942: *The Moon and Sixpence* (Best Acting) Board.

Bates, Kathy

Movie: 1990: *Misery* (Best Actress) *Academy* (Best Actress, Drama) *Globe.* 1991: *Fried Green Tomatoes (Fried Green Tomatoes at the Whistle Stop Café)* (Best Actress, Musical or Comedy) Globe (Best Supporting Actress) British. 1997: *Titanic* (Best Ensemble) SAG. 1998: *Primary Colors* (Best Female Actor in a Supporting Role) *SAG* (Best Supporting Actress) Academy, Globe, British, *Broadcast.* 2002: *About Schmidt* (Best Female Actor in a Supporting Role) SAG (Best Supporting Actress) Academy, *Board,* Globe, Broadcast. Theater: 1983: *'night, Mother* (Best Actress, Play) Tony. Television: 1996: *The Late Shift* (Best Female Actor in a Television Movie or Miniseries) *SAG* (Best Supporting Actress in a Miniseries or Special) Emmy (Best Supporting Actress in a Series, Miniseries, or TV Movie) *Globe.* 1999: *3rd Rock from the Sun* (Best Guest Actress in a Comedy Series) Emmy; *Dash and Lilly* (Best Director in a Miniseries or TV Movie) Emmy. 2000: *"Annie," The Wonderful World of Disney* (Best Female Actor in a Television Movie or Miniseries) SAG (Best Supporting Actress in a Miniseries or TV Movie) Emmy (Best Supporting Actress in a Series, Miniseries, or TV Movie) Globe. 2002: *My Sister's Keeper* (Best Female Actor in a Television Movie or Miniseries) SAG. 2003: *Six Feet Under* (Best Guest Actress in a Drama Series) Emmy. 2005: *Warm Springs* (Best Supporting Actress in a Miniseries or TV Movie) Emmy. 2006: *Ambulance Girl* (Best Actress in a Miniseries or TV Movie) Emmy.

Battle, Hinton

Movie: 2006: *Dreamgirls* (Best Ensemble) SAG, Broadcast. Theater: 1981: *Sophisticated Ladies* (Best Actor in a Featured Role, Musical) *Tony.* 1984: *The Tap Dance Kid* (Best Actor in a Featured Role, Musical) *Tony.* 1991: *Miss Saigon* (Best Actor in a Featured Role, Musical) *Tony.*

Bauer, Steven

Movie: 1983: *Scarface* (Best Supporting Actor) Globe. 2000: *Traffic* (Best Ensemble) *SAG.* Television: 1990: *Drug Wars: The Camarena Story* (Best Actor in a Miniseries or TV Movie) Globe.

Baur, Harry

Movie: 1937: *The Golem* (Best Acting) Board. 1938: *Un Carnet de bal* (Best Acting) Board.

Baxter, Anne

Movie: 1946: *The Razor's Edge* (Best Supporting Actress) *Academy, Globe.* 1950: *All About Eve* (Best Actress) Academy. Television: 1969: *The Name of the Game* (Best Single Performance by an Actress in a Leading Role) Emmy. **Records:** Because she'd already won a supporting Academy Award, Baxter insisted on being considered only for a lead actress nomination for *All About Eve*, even though many deemed costar Bette Davis's the starring role. When both women received nominations as Best Actress, Baxter and Davis became the first female stars from the same film to compete for a lead acting Academy Award.

On Oscar night, both actresses lost that competition to Judy Holliday in **Born Yesterday**.

Baxter, Warner

Movie: 1929: **In Old Arizona** (Best Actor) *Academy*. **Records:** Baxter was the first star to win a Best Actor Academy Award for a single performance and for a film with sound. At the first Oscar ceremony the previous year, Emil Jannings won Best Actor for his work in two movies (**The Last Command** and **The Way of All Flesh**), both silent pictures. Baxter won his Oscar for **In Old Arizona**, billed by 20th Century–Fox as the first 100 percent all-talking drama filmed outdoors. Baxter's win also made it the first western to earn an Academy Award.

Baye, Nathalie

Movie: 1999: **Une Liaison pornographique** (Best Actress) *Venice*.

Bazaka, Themis

Movie: 1985: **Petrina chronia** (Best Actress) *Venice*.

Beach, Adam

Movie: 2006: **Flags of Our Fathers** (Best Supporting Actor) Broadcast. **Television:** 2007: **Bury My Heart at Wounded Knee** (Best Actor in a Miniseries or TV Movie) Globe.

Beach, Michael

Movie: 1993: **Short Cuts** (Best Ensemble) *Venice* (special award).

Beals, Jennifer

Movie: 1983: **Flashdance** (Best Actress, Musical or Comedy) Globe.

Bean, Orson

Movie: 1999: **Being John Malkovich** (Best Ensemble) SAG. **Theater:** 1962: **Subways Are for Sleeping** (Best Supporting or Featured Actor, Musical) Tony.

Bean, Sean

Movie: 2001: **The Lord of the Rings: The Fellowship of the Ring** (Best Ensemble) SAG. 2003: **The Lord of the Rings: The Return of the King** (Best Ensemble) *Board, SAG, Broadcast*.

Béart, Emmanuelle

Tributes: 2002: Silver Bear for outstanding artistic contribution in **8 Femmes (8 Women)** from Berlin (special ensemble award shared with costars).

The Beatles

Movie: 1964: **A Hard Day's Night** (Most Promising Newcomers) British. 1970: **Let It Be** (Best Original Song Score) *Academy*.

Beatty, Ned

Movie: 1977: **Network** (Best Supporting Actor) Academy. 1991: **Hear My Song** (Best Supporting Actor) Globe. **Television:** 1979: **Friendly Fire** (Best Actor in a Limited Series or Special) Emmy. 1990: **Last Train Home** (Best Supporting Actor in a Miniseries or Special) Emmy.

Beatty, Warren

Movie: 1961: **Splendor in the Grass** (New Star of the Year — Actor) *Globe* (Best Actor, Drama) Globe. 1967: **Bonnie and Clyde** (Best Actor) Academy (Best Actor, Drama) Globe (Best Foreign Actor) British (Best Picture, Producer) Academy, British (Best Picture, Drama; Producer) Globe. 1975: **Shampoo** (Best Actor, Musical or Comedy) Globe (Best Picture, Musical or Comedy) Globe (Best Original Screenplay) Academy. 1978: **Heaven Can Wait** (Best Actor) Academy (Best Actor, Musical or Comedy) *Globe* (Best Director) Academy (Best Picture, Producer) Academy (Best Picture, Musical or Comedy; Producer) *Globe* (Best Adapted Screenplay) Academy. 1981: **Reds** (Best Actor) Academy, British (Best Actor, Drama) Globe (Best Director) *Academy, Board, Globe, LA* (Best Picture, Producer) Academy, *New York, Board* (Best Picture, Drama; Producer) Globe (Best Original Screenplay) Academy, Globe. 1990: **Dick Tracy** (Best Picture, Musical or Comedy; Producer) Globe. 1991: **Bugsy** (Best Actor) Academy, *Board* (Best Actor, Drama) Globe (Best Picture, Producer) Academy (Best Picture, Drama; Producer) *Globe*. 1998: **Bulworth** (Best Actor, Comedy or Musical) Globe (Best Original Screenplay) Academy, Globe, *LA* (Best Picture, Musical or Comedy; Producer) Globe. **Theater:** 1960: **A Loss of Roses** (Best Supporting or Featured Actor, Dramatic) Tony. **Tributes:** 1998: Career Golden Lion from Venice. 1999: Irving G. Thalberg Memorial Award from Academy. 2004: Honor from Kennedy Center for the Performing Arts. 2006: Cecil B. DeMille Award from Globe. 2008: Life Achievement Award from American Film Institute. **Records:** With his 1978 hit, **Heaven Can Wait**, Beatty tied the record that Orson Welles set with 1941's **Citizen Kane** by becoming the only star to receive four separate Academy Award nominations for a single film. Both men were up for Best Actor, Director, Picture (as producer) and Screenplay. In 1981, Beatty surpassed Welles by becoming the only person to achieve the feat twice, when he was up in the same four categories for *Reds*. Beatty didn't win any Oscars for *Heaven Can Wait*, but he again outranked Welles as an Oscar winner by being the sole recipient of the Best Director award for *Reds*. Welles also won one award for *Kane*, but he shared his Best Screenplay win with co-author Herman J. Mankiewicz.

Becker, Gerry

Movie: 1998: *Happiness* (Best Ensemble) *Board*.

Beckinsale, Kate

Movie: 2004: *The Aviator* (Best Ensemble) SAG.

Bedelia, Bonnie

Movie: 1983: *Heart Like a Wheel* (Best Actress, Drama) Globe. 1988: *Prince of Pennsylvania* (Best Supporting Female) Spirit. **Television:** 1994: *Fallen Angels* (Best Guest Actress in a Drama Series) Emmy.

Beery, Wallace

Movie: 1930: *The Big House* (Best Actor) Academy. 1931: *The Champ* (Best Actor) *Academy*. 1934: *Viva Villa!* (Best Actor) *Venice*. **Records:** When he received his surprise Best Actor Oscar for *The Champ*, Beery set three Oscar records: he suffered an Oscar loss for the shortest time period of anyone in films— namely a few minutes; he's the only actor in history to receive an Oscar although he didn't garner the most votes among the nominees; and he won an Oscar that, according to Academy rules, technically shouldn't have been given to him. Norma Shearer presented the Best Actor award for the films of 1931/32, and correctly read the winner, Fredric March for *Dr. Jekyll and Mr. Hyde*. As the ceremony continued to the next award, the judges scrambled through ballots and then abruptly summoned Academy president Conrad Nagel. After a brief, suspenseful conference, Nagel called Beery up to the podium and announced that Beery had tied Fredric March for Best Actor of the year. Re-tallies revealed that March had beat Beery by only one vote. Until the previous year, the Academy rules stated that any two nominees who earned within three votes of one another should both be given an award. But the year of the Beery/March race, the Academy changed that rule, rewritten to state that only an exact tie should net a double win. After considering the debate between the members who said Beery shouldn't have won and those who didn't feel it was right to take it from him after his victory had been announced, the Academy decided to let Beery keep his award.

Beglau, Bibiana

Movie: 2000: *Die Stille nach de Schuß (The Legends of Rita)* (Best Actress) *Berlin* (win shared with costar).

Begley, Ed

Movie: 1962: *Sweet Bird of Youth* (Best Supporting Actor) *Academy*, Globe. **Theater:** 1956: *Inherit the Wind* (Best Supporting or Featured Actor, Dramatic) *Tony*. **Television:** 1956: *"Patterns," Kraft Theatre* (Best Supporting Actor) Emmy. 1966: *"Inherit the Wind," Hallmark Hall of Fame* (Best Single Performance by an Actor in a Leading Role) Emmy.

Belafonte, Harry

Movie: 1996: *Kansas City* (Best Supporting Actor) *New York*. 2006: *Bobby* (Best Ensemble) SAG, Broadcast. **Theater:** 1954: *John Murray Anderson's Almanac* (Best Supporting or Featured Actor, Musical) *Tony*. **Television:** 1956: --- (Best Male Singer) Emmy; --- (Best Specialty Act by a Singer or Group) Emmy. 1960: *"Tonight with Belafonte," Revlon Revue* (Best Performance in a Variety or Musical Program) *Emmy*. 1961: *Belafonte, N.Y.* (Best Performance in a Variety or Musical Program) Emmy. 1971: *Harry and Lena* (Best Variety or Musical Program, Star) Emmy. **Tributes:** 1989: Honor from Kennedy Center for the Performing Arts. **Records:** Although Bill Cosby is often given credit for breaking the color barrier in television by getting a starring role and winning a 1966 Emmy for his acting in *I Spy*, it was actually Belafonte who first penetrated the wall that excluded African-Americans from television accolades. In 1960, Belafonte became the first Black performer to win an Emmy Award. Five years earlier he'd been nominated twice for an NBC special and lost the awards to Perry Como and Marcel Marceau, but in 1960 he beat out two Emmy favorites, Fred Astaire and Dinah Shore, and took home an Emmy for his critically acclaimed musical variety program, *Tonight with Belafonte*.

Bell, Jamie

Movie: 2000: *Billy Elliot* (Breakthrough Performance — Male) Broadcast (Best Actor) *British* (Best Male Actor in a Leading Role) SAG (Best Child Performer) *Broadcast* (Best Young Actor) *Board* (Best Ensemble) SAG. 2002: *Nicholas Nickleby* (Best Ensemble) *Board*.

Bell, Marshall

Movie: 2005: *Capote* (Best Ensemble) SAG.

Bellamy, Ralph

Movie: 1937: *The Awful Truth* (Best Supporting Actor) Academy. Theater: 1958: *Sunrise at Campobello* (Best Actor, Dramatic) *Tony*. Television: 1956: *"Fearful Decision," The U.S. Steel Hour* (Best Actor — Single Performance) Emmy. 1975: *"The Missiles of October," ABC Theatre* (Best Single Performance by a Supporting Actor) Emmy. 1983: *The Winds of War* (Best Supporting Actor, Limited Series or Special) Emmy. Tributes: 1983: Life Achievement Award from SAG. 1986: Special award for his unique artistry and his distinguished service to the profession of acting from Academy.

Beller, Kathleen

Movie: 1979: *Promises in the Dark* (Best Supporting Actress) Globe.

Bello, Maria

Movie: 2003: *The Cooler* (Best Female Actor in a Supporting Role) SAG (Best Supporting Actress) Globe. 2005: *A History of Violence* (Best Actress, Drama) Globe (Best Supporting Actress) *New York*, Broadcast. Television: 1997–1998 series *ER* (Best Ensemble) 1997: *SAG*.

Belmondo, Jean-Paul

Movie: 1962: *Leon Martin, Priest* (Best Foreign Actor) British. 1966: *Pierrot Le Fou* (Best Foreign Actor) British.

Bendix, William

Movie: 1942: *Wake Island* (Best Supporting Actor) Academy.

Benigni, Roberto

Movie: 1986: *Down by Law* (Best Male Lead) Spirit. 1998: *La Vita è Bella (Life Is Beautiful)* (Best Actor) *Academy, British* (Best Male Actor in a Leading Role) *SAG* (Best Ensemble) SAG (Best Director) Academy (Best Original Screenplay) Academy. Tributes: 1998: Grand Prix for *Life Is Beautiful* from Cannes; Special Filmmaking Achievement Award for *Life Is Beautiful* from Board. Records: With *Life Is Beautiful*, Italian actor/director/screenwriter Benigni set several movie firsts and seconds. After *Life Is Beautiful* became the highest grossing foreign film in history, it received seven Oscar nominations, a record-setting total for a foreign language movie. Three of those went to Benigni, for Best Actor, Best Director, and Best Screenplay, making him the first foreign filmmaker to be recognized in that many categories. When Benigni took home the Best Actor prize on Oscar night, he followed Laurence Olivier (*Hamlet*, 1948) as only the second person to direct himself to an Oscar-winning performance. That award also made Benigni the second person to win an Academy Award for a performance in a foreign language film. Fellow Italian Sophia Loren achieved the feat first when she won Best Actress for *Two Women* in 1961. Loren was on hand at the 1999 Oscar ceremony to present the award for Best Foreign Language Film. Her exuberant announcement that *Life Is Beautiful* won brought Benigni to the stage to accept the award on behalf of the film's producers, Elda Ferri and Gianluigi Braschi. Though he was overjoyed about this win, his response to picking up this award paled compared to his unforgettable reaction to hearing his name announced as Best Actor of the year when he rushed to the stage by literally leaping on the back of another attendee's seat, wrapping his arms around presenter Helen Hunt's legs and lifting her high in the air before setting her down and stepping to the podium to share a humorous, heartfelt, and heavy-accented thank you.

Bening, Annette

Movie: 1990: *The Grifters* (Best Supporting Actress) Academy, British, *Society*. 1991: *Bugsy* (Best Actress, Drama) Globe. 1995: *The American President* (Best Actress, Musical or Comedy) Globe. 1999: *American Beauty* (Best Actress) Academy, *British* (Best Actress, Drama) Globe (Best Female Actor in a Leading Role) *SAG* (Best Ensemble) *SAG*. 2004: *Being Julia* (Best Actress) Academy, *Board*, Broadcast (Best Actress, Musical or Comedy) *Globe* (Best Female Actor in a Leading Role) SAG. 2006: *Running with Scissors* (Best Actress, Musical or Comedy) Globe. Theater: 1987: *Coastal Disturbances* (Best Actress in a Featured Role, Play) Tony. Television: 2006: *Mrs. Harris* (Best Actress in a Miniseries or TV Movie) Emmy, Globe (Best Female Actor in a Television Movie or Miniseries) SAG.

Benjamin, Paul

Movie: 2003: *The Station Agent* (Best Ensemble) SAG.

Benjamin, Richard

Movie: 1970: *Diary of a Mad Housewife* (Best Actor, Musical or Comedy) Globe. 1975: *The Sunshine Boys* (Best Supporting Actor) *Globe*. Television: 1967–1968 series *He & She* (Best Continued Performance by an Actor in a Comedy) 1968: Emmy.

Benson, Robby

Movie: 1973: *Jeremy* (New Star of the Year — Actor) Globe. Television: 1982: *Two of a Kind* (Best Actor in a Miniseries or TV Movie) Globe.

Bentivoglio, Fabrizio

Movie: 1993: *Un' Anima divisa in due* (Best Actor) *Venice*.

Bentley, Wes

Movie: 1999: *American Beauty* (Breakthrough Performance — Male) *Board* (Best Supporting Actor) British (Best Ensemble) *SAG*.

Berenger, Tom

Movie: 1986: *Platoon* (Best Supporting Actor) Academy, *Globe*. Television: 1993: *Cheers* (Best Guest Actor in a Comedy Series) Emmy.

Berenson, Marisa

Movie: 1972: *Cabaret* (New Star of the Year — Actress) Globe (Best Supporting Actress) *Board*, Globe, British.

Bergen, Candice

Movie: 1966: *The Group* (New Star of the Year — Actress) Globe (multiple nomination), *The Sand Pebbles* (New Star of the Year — Actress) Globe (multiple nomination). 1979: *Starting Over* (Best Supporting Actress) Academy, Globe. 1982: *Gandhi* (Best Supporting Actress) British. **Television:** 1988–1998 series *Murphy Brown* (Best Actress in a Comedy Series) 1989: *Emmy*. 1990: *Emmy*. 1991: Emmy. 1992: *Emmy*. 1993: Emmy. 1994: *Emmy*. 1995: *Emmy*. (Best Actress in a Series, Musical or Comedy) 1989: *Globe*. 1990: Globe. 1991: Globe. 1992: *Globe*. 1993: Globe. 1994: Globe. 1995: Globe. 1996: Globe. (Best Female Actor in a Comedy Series) 1994: SAG. 1995: SAG. 2005–present series *Boston Legal* (Best Female Actor in a Comedy Series) 2005: SAG. (Best Supporting Actress in a Drama Series) 2006: Emmy. (Best Supporting Actress in a Series, Miniseries, or TV Movie) 2005: Globe. (Best Ensemble in a Comedy Series) 2005: SAG. (Best Ensemble in a Drama Series) 2006: SAG. 2007: SAG. **Highlights:** When Bergen won her first Emmy for *Murphy Brown*, she ended her acceptance speech by dedicating her win to her father, Edgar Bergen, the Television Academy's first president who never won an Emmy himself. After seven nominations and four wins for *Murphy Brown*, Bergen withdrew her name from Emmy eligibility to let other actresses win. Helen Hunt, who'd lost three times while Bergen was still in competition, won four consecutive Emmys for *Mad About You* after Bergen's withdrawal.

Bergen, Edgar

Tributes: 1937: Honorary Oscar wooden statuette for his outstanding comedy creation, Charlie McCarthy from Academy. 1978: Life Achievement Award from SAG.

Bergen, Polly

Movie: 1963: *The Caretakers* (Best Actress, Drama) Globe. Theater: 2001: *Follies* (Best Actress in a Featured Role, Musical) Tony. Television: 1958: *"The Helen Morgan Story," Playhouse 90* (Best Actress in a Single Performance for a Lead or Supporting Role) *Emmy*. 1983: *The Winds of War* (Best Supporting Actress in a Limited Series or Special) Emmy. 1989: *War and Remembrance* (Best Supporting Actress in a Miniseries or Special) Emmy. **Highlights:** In 1957 when women had much less power in the entertainment industry and female stars rarely had the freedom or clout to helm projects independently, Bergen purchased the television rights to Helen Morgan's story and convinced CBS to air it. Her efforts paid off handily when she took home the Emmy that year for her performance of the troubled torch singer.

Berger, Helmut

Movie: 1969: *The Damned* (New Star of the Year — Actor) Globe.

Bergerac, Jacques

Movie: 1956: *Marie-Antoinette reine de France (Shadow of the Guillotine)* (New Foreign Star of the Year — Actor) *Globe* (multiple win)*; *Strange Intruder* (New Foreign Star of the Year — Actor) *Globe* (multiple win)*.

   *The Hollywood Foreign Press did not designate a particular film for which they honored Bergerac as their new male foreign star of the year. These two titles denote the two movies he starred in in the year he received the Golden Globe.

Bergman, Ingrid

Movie: 1941: *Rage in Heaven* (Best Acting) *Board*. 1943: *For Whom the Bell Tolls* (Best Actress) Academy. 1944: *Gaslight* (Best Acting) *Board* (Best Actress) *Academy*, Globe. 1945: *The Bells of St. Mary's* (Best Actress) Academy, *New York* (multiple win), *Globe*; *Spellbound* (Best Actress) *New York* (multiple win). 1948: *Joan of Arc* (Best Actress) Academy.

1956: *Anastasia* (Best Actress) *Academy*, *New York* (Best Actress, Drama) *Globe*. 1958: *The Inn of the Sixth Happiness* (Best Actress) *Board* (Best Actress, Drama) Globe (Best Foreign Actress) British; *Indiscreet* (Best Actress, Musical or Comedy) Globe. 1969: *Cactus Flower* (Best Actress, Musical or Comedy) Globe. 1974: *Murder on the Orient Express* (Best Supporting Actress) *Academy*, *British*. 1978: *Autumn Sonata* (Best Actress) Academy, *New York*, *Board*, *Society* (Best Actress, Drama) Globe. Theater: 1947: *Joan of Lorraine* (Best Actress, Dramatic) *Tony*. Television: 1960: *"The Turn of the Screw," Ford Startime* (Best Single Performance by a Lead or Supporting Actress) *Emmy*. 1961: *24 Hours in a Woman's Life* (Best Single Performance by an Actress in a Leading Role) Emmy. 1982: *A Woman Called Golda* (Best Actress in a Limited Series or Special) *Emmy* (Best Actress in a Miniseries or TV Movie) *Globe*. Tributes: 1999: Ranked Number 4 on List of 25 Greatest Female Screen Legends of the 20th Century from American Film Institute. Records: Bergman is the first to win three acting Oscars that include both lead and supporting awards. She won Best Actress for *Gaslight* and *Anastasia* then Supporting Actress for *Murder on the Orient Express*. Before her, only two stars won three acting Academy Awards: Walter Brennan (all for Best Supporting Actor) and Katharine Hepburn (all for Best Actress). Since Bergman's win, only Jack Nicholson has matched her achievement by winning twice for lead actor and once for supporting. Bergman's history with the Academy was punctuated with apologies. Favored to win Best Actress in 1943 for *For Whom the Bell Tolls*, Bergman lost to Jennifer Jones in *The Song of Bernadette*. Later than evening Jones found Bergman backstage and apologized for beating her. Bergman's 1956 Best Actress award for *Anastasia* is generally considered the Academy's way of apologizing to Bergman and welcoming her back to Hollywood after the film community shunned her and boycotted her films because of her marriage-breaking relationship with director Robert Rossellini. While accepting her third Oscar for 1974's *Murder on the Orient Express*, Bergman complimented the performance of fellow nominee, Valentina Cortese of *Day for Night* and asked her forgiveness for taking the Oscar away from her. Highlights: Bergman won Emmys for her first and last small-screen performances. She picked up the first award for her debut performance on American television for her harrowing portrayal of the haunted governess in the TV adaptation of Henry James's *The Turn of the Screw*. Bergman ended her career with a memorable portrayal of Israel's Prime Minister Golda Meir. Just weeks after Emmy's blue ribbon panel secretly picked her as Best Actress of the year for her performance in *A Woman Called Golda*, Bergman died of breast cancer on her 67th birthday. At that year's Emmys, Bergman's daughter, art critic Pia Lindstrom accepted on her mother's behalf.

Bergman, Sandahl

Movie: 1982: *Conan the Barbarian* (New Star of the Year — Actress) *Globe*. Records: Bergman won the very last New Female Star of the Year Golden Globe ever given. The year before, Pia Zadora caused a swirl of controversy by winning New Star of the Year for the critically scalded *Butterfly* over the likes of Kathleen Turner in *Body Heat* and Elizabeth McGovern in *Ragtime*. With complaints still coming in a year later, the Hollywood Foreign Press decided to drop the New Star categories for good.

Bergner, Elisabeth

Movie: 1935: *Escape Me Never* (Best Actress) Academy.

Berkley, Elizabeth

Movie: 1996: *The First Wives Club* (Best Ensemble) *Board*.

Berlin, Jeannie

Movie: 1972: *The Heartbreak Kid* (Best Supporting Actress) Academy, *New York*, Globe, *Society*.

Bernal, Gael Garcìa

Movie: 2001: *Y tu mamá también* (Best First Time Actor) *Venice* (win shared with costar). 2004: *Diarios de motocicleta (The Motorcycle Diaries)* (Best Actor) British. 2006: *Babel* (Best Ensemble) SAG, Broadcast.

Bernhard, Sandra

Movie: 1983: *The King of Comedy* (Best Supporting Actress) *Society*.

Berry, Halle

Movie: 2001: *Monster's Ball* (Best Actress) *Academy*, *Board*, *Berlin*, British (Best Actress, Drama) Globe (Best Female Actor in a Leading Role) *SAG*. 2005: *Lackawanna Blues* (Best First Feature, Producer) Spirit. Television: 1999: *Introducing Dorothy Dandridge* (Best Actress in a Miniseries or TV Movie) *Emmy*, *Globe* (Best Female Actor in a Television Movie or Miniseries) *SAG* (Best TV Movie, Executive Producer) Emmy. 2005: *Lackawanna Blues* (Best TV Movie, Executive Producer) Emmy; *Their Eyes Were Watching God* (Best Actress in a Miniseries or TV Movie) Emmy, Globe. Records: For the first 73 years of Oscar, Best Actress remained the only acting category that no African-American had ever won. In 2001, Berry became the first Black actress to take home a Best Actress Oscar, beating out such formidable and popular competitors as Sissy Spacek for *In the Bedroom* and Nicole Kidman for *Moulin Rouge!* In her tearful acceptance speech, Berry acknowledged some of the African-American actresses who in the past had been nominated for but didn't win the honor, most notably Dorothy Dandridge, whom Berry had portrayed in a television movie two years earlier that earned Berry an Emmy, Golden Globe, and Screen Actors Guild award.

Bettany, Paul

Movie: 2001: *A Beautiful Mind* (Best Ensemble) SAG. 2003: *Master and Commander: The Far Side of the World* (Best Supporting Actor) British, Broadcast.

Betti, Laura

Movie: 1968: *Teorema* (Best Actress) *Venice.*

Beymer, Richard

Movie: 1961: *West Side Story* (New Star of the Year — Actor) *Globe* (Best Actor, Musical or Comedy) Globe.

Bickford, Charles

Movie: 1943: *The Song of Bernadette* (Best Supporting Actor) Academy. 1947: *The Farmer's Daughter* (Best Supporting Actor) Academy. 1948: *Johnny Belinda* (Best Supporting Actor) Academy. 1955: *Not as a Stranger* (Best Supporting Actor) *Board.*

Bikel, Theodore

Movie: 1958: *The Defiant Ones* (Best Supporting Actor) Academy. Theater: 1958: *The Rope Dancers* (Best Supporting or Featured Actor, Dramatic) Tony. 1960: *The Sound of Music* (Best Supporting or Featured Actor, Musical) Tony.

Bin, Li

Movie: 2001: *Beijing Bicycle* (Best Young Actor) *Berlin* (win shared with costar).

Binoche, Juliette

Movie: 1993: *Trois Couleurs: Bleu (Blue)* (Best Actress) *Venice* (Best Actress, Drama) Globe. 1996: *The English Patient* (Best Actress) *Berlin* (Best Female Actor in a Supporting Role) SAG (Best Supporting Actress) *Academy, Board,* Globe, *British* (Best Ensemble) SAG. 2000: *Chocolat* (Best Actress) Academy, British (Best Actress, Musical or Comedy) Globe (Best Female Actor in a Leading Role) SAG (Best Ensemble) SAG. Theater: 2001: *Betrayal* (Best Actress, Play) Tony. Tributes: 1993: Honorary Award from Berlin. Highlights: Although Paris-born Binoche made an impressive impact in Anthony Minghella's *The English Patient* in 1996, that year never-before–nominated screen legend Lauren Bacall had a lock on the Best Supporting Actress Oscar for her performance in *The Mirror Has Two Faces.* An audible gasp swept across the Shrine Auditorium when Kevin Spacey announced Binoche as the winner. At the podium, Binoche confessed that she didn't prepare an acceptance speech because she too thought Bacall would win.

Birch, Thora

Movie: 1999: *American Beauty* (Best Supporting Actress) British (Best Ensemble) *SAG.* 2001: *Ghost World* (Best Actress, Musical or Comedy) Globe. Television: 2003: *Homeless to Harvard: The Liz Murray Story* (Best Actress in a Miniseries or TV Movie) Emmy.

Bisset, Jacqueline

Movie: 1968: *The Sweet Ride* (New Star of the Year — Actress) Globe. 1978: *Who Is Killing the Great Chefs of Europe?* (Best Actress, Musical or Comedy) Globe. 1984: *Under the Volcano* (Best Supporting Actress) Globe. Television: 1999: *Joan of Arc* (Best Supporting Actress in a Series, Miniseries, or TV Movie) Globe (Best Supporting Actress in a Miniseries or TV Movie) Emmy.

Bityukov, Boris

Movie: 1954: *Bolshaya semya (The Big Family)* *Cannes* (special ensemble award).

Björk

Movie: 2000: *Dancer in the Dark* (Best Musical Performance by a Film Actress) *Board* (Best Actress) *Cannes,* Broadcast (Best Actress, Drama) Globe (Best Song, "I've Seen It All") Academy, Globe.

Björnstrand, Gunnar

Movie: 1956: *Smiles of a Summer Night* (Best Foreign Actor) British.

Black, Jack

Movie: 2003: *School of Rock* (Best Actor, Musical or Comedy) Globe.

Black, Karen

Movie: 1970: *Five Easy Pieces* (Best Supporting Actress) Academy, *New York, Board, Globe.* 1974: *The Great Gatsby* (Best Supporting Actress) *Globe.* 1975: *The Day of the Locust* (Best Actress, Drama) Globe. **Records:** Black dazzled as Jack Nicholson's dense, sexually voracious girlfriend in *Five Easy Pieces,* but she ended up sharing the spotlight at awards that year. Black earned the Supporting Actress prize from the New York Film Critics and the National Board of Review, but then lost the National Society of Film Critics award to *Pieces* co-star, Lois Smith. At the Golden Globes, it was Black, not Smith, who earned the nomination. Black's name was announced as the winner at the Globes—along with fellow nominee Maureen Stapleton for *Airport,* making Black and Stapleton the first to tie for a Golden Globe acting award.

Black, Lucas

Movie: 1996: *Sling Blade* (Best Ensemble) SAG.

Blackman, Jeremy

Movie: 1999: *Magnolia* (Best Ensemble) *Board,* SAG.

Blades, Ruben

Movie: 1985: *Crossover Dreams* (Best Male Lead) Spirit. **Television:** 1991: *The Josephine Baker Story* (Best Supporting Actor in a Miniseries or Special) Emmy. 1992: *Crazy from the Heart* (Best Actor in a Miniseries or Special) Emmy.

Blair, Betsy

Movie: 1955: *Marty* (Best Supporting Actress) Academy (Best Foreign Actress) *British.*

Blair, Linda

Movie: 1973: *The Exorcist* (New Star of the Year — Actress) Globe (Best Supporting Actress) Academy, *Globe.*

Blake, Robert

Movie: 1973: *Electra Glide in Blue* (Best Actor, Drama) Globe. **Television:** 1975–1978 series *Baretta* (Best Actor in a Drama) 1975: *Emmy.* 1976: *Globe.* 1977: Emmy. 1983: *Blood Feud* (Best Actor in a Limited Series or Special) Emmy (Best Actor in a Miniseries or TV Movie) Globe. 1993: *Judgment Day: The John List Story* (Best Actor in a Miniseries or Special) Emmy.

Blake Nelson, Tim

Movie: 2005: *Syriana* (Best Ensemble) Broadcast.

Blakely, Colin

Movie: 1977: *Equus* (Best Supporting Actor) British.

Blakley, Ronee

Movie: 1975: *Nashville* (New Star of the Year — Female) Globe (Best Supporting Actress) Academy, *Board,* Globe, British.

Blanc, Michel

Movie: 1986: *Ménage* (Best Actor) *Cannes.* 1994: *Prêt-à-Porter (Ready-to-Wear)* (Best Ensemble) *Board.*

Blancan, Bernard

Movie: 2006: *Days of Glory* (Best Actor) *Cannes* (win shared with costars).

Blanchard, Pierre

Movie: 1935: *Crime et châtiment* (Best Actor) *Venice.* 1938: *Un Carnet de Bal* (Best Acting) *Board.*

Blanchett, Cate

Movie: 1998: *Elizabeth* (Best Actress) Academy, *British, Broadcast* (Best Actress, Drama) *Globe* (Best Female Actor in a Leading Role) SAG. 1999: *The Talented Mr. Ripley* (Best Supporting Actress) British. 2001: *Bandits* (Best Actress, Musical or Comedy) Globe (Best Female Actor in a Supporting Role) SAG; *The Lord of the Rings: The Fellowship of the Ring* (Best Supporting Actress) *Board* (multiple win), (Best Ensemble) SAG; *The Man Who Cried* (Best Supporting Actress) *Board* (multiple win); *The Shipping News* (Best Supporting Actress) *Board* (multiple win). 2002: *The Lord of the Rings: The Two Towers* (Best Ensemble) SAG. 2003: *The Lord of the Rings: The Return of the King* (Best Ensemble) *Board, SAG, Broadcast; Veronica Guerin* (Best Actress, Drama) Globe. 2004: *The Aviator* (Best Female Actor in a Supporting Role) *SAG* (Best Supporting Actress) *Academy,* Globe, *British,* Society (multiple nomination), Broadcast (Best Ensemble) SAG; *Coffee and Cigarettes* (Best Supporting Actress) Society (multiple nomination), (Best Supporting Female) Spirit; *The Life Aquatic with Steve Zissou* (Best Ensemble) Broadcast. 2006: *Babel* (Best Ensemble) SAG, Broadcast; *Notes on a Scandal* (Best Female Actor in a Supporting Role) SAG (Best Supporting Actress) Academy, Globe, Broadcast. 2007: *Elizabeth: The Golden Age* (Best Actress) Academy, British, Broadcast (Best Actress, Drama) Globe (Best Female Actor in a Leading Role) SAG; *I'm Not There* (Best Actress) *Venice* (Best Female Actor in a Supporting Role) SAG (Best Supporting Actress) Academy, *Globe,* British, *Society,* Broadcast

(Best Supporting Female) *Spirit* (Best Ensemble) *Spirit* (special award).

Bledel, Alexis

Movie: 2005: *Sin City* (Best Ensemble) Broadcast.

Bleibtreu, Moritz

Movie: 2006: *Elementarteilchen (The Elementary Particles)* (Best Actor) *Berlin*.

Blethyn, Brenda

Movie: 1996: *Secrets and Lies* (Best Actress) Academy, *Cannes, British, LA* (Best Actress, Drama) *Globe* (Best Female Actor in a Leading Role) SAG. 1998: *Little Voice* (Best Female Actor in a Supporting Role) SAG (Best Supporting Actress) Academy, Globe, British (Best Ensemble) SAG. 2000: *Saving Grace* (Best Actress, Musical or Comedy) Globe. 2005: *Pride and Prejudice* (Best Supporting Actress) British. Television: 2001: *Anne Frank* (Best Supporting Actress in a Miniseries or TV Movie) Emmy.

Blondell, Joan

Movie: 1951: *The Blue Veil* (Best Supporting Actress) Academy. 1965: *The Cincinnati Kid* (Best Supporting Actress) *Board*, Globe. 1977: *Opening Night* (Best Supporting Actress) Globe. Theater: 1958: *The Rope Dancers* (Best Supporting or Featured Actress, Dramatic) Tony. Television: 1968–1970 series *Here Come the Brides* (Best Continuing Performance by an Actress in a Dramatic Series) 1969: Emmy. 1970: Emmy.

Blonsky, Nikki

Movie: 2007: *Hairspray* (Best Actress, Musical or Comedy) Globe (Best Young Actress) *Broadcast* (Best Ensemble) SAG, *Broadcast*.

Bloom, Claire

Movie: 1952: *Limelight* (Most Promising Newcomer) *British*. Theater: 1999: *Electra* (Best Actress in a Featured Role, Play) Tony. Television: 1982: *"Brideshead Revisited," Great Performances* (Best Supporting Actress in a Limited Series or Special) Emmy.

Bloom, Orlando

Movie: 2001: *The Lord of the Rings: The Fellowship of the Ring* (Best Ensemble) SAG. 2002: *The Lord of the Rings: The Two Towers* (Best Ensemble) SAG. 2003: *The Lord of the Rings: The Return of the King* (Best Ensemble) *Board, SAG, Broadcast*.

Blount, Lisa

Movie: 1982: *An Officer and a Gentleman* (New Star of the Year — Actress) Globe. 2001: *The Accountant* (Best Live Action Short Film, Producer) *Academy*.

Blunt, Emily

Movie: 2006: *The Devil Wears Prada* (Best Supporting Actress) Globe, British. Television: 2006: *Gideon's Daughter* (Best Supporting Actress in a Series, Miniseries, or TV Movie) *Globe*.

Blyth, Ann

Movie: 1945: *Mildred Pierce* (Best Supporting Actress) Academy.

Bogarde, Dirk

Movie: 1960: *Song Without End* (Best Actor, Musical or Comedy) Globe. 1961: *Victim* (Best British Actor) British. 1963: *The Servant* (Best British Actor) *British*. 1965: *Darling* (Best British Actor) *British*. 1967: *Accident* (Best British Actor) British. 1971: *Death in Venice* (Best Actor) British. Television: 1982: *The Patricia Neal Story* (Best Actor in a Miniseries or TV Movie) Globe.

Bogart, Humphrey

Movie: 1937: *Black Legion* (Best Acting) *Board*. 1941: *High Sierra* (Best Acting) *Board* (multiple win); *The Maltese Falcon* (Best Acting) *Board* (multiple win). 1943: *Casablanca* (Best Actor) Academy. 1944: *To Have and Have Not* (Best Acting) *Board*. 1951: *The African Queen* (Best Actor) *Academy* (Best Foreign Actor) British. 1954: *The Caine Mutiny* (Best Actor) Academy. Tributes: 1999: Ranked Number 1 on List of 25 Greatest Male Screen Legends of the 20th Century from American Film Institute. Highlights: Although Bogart's fine performance in *The African Queen* made him a worthy contender for Best Actor against Marlon Brando in *A Streetcar Named Desire*, some enthusiastic marketing certainly helped put Bogart in the winner's circle. When he read that Brando refused to campaign to win the Oscar that year, Bogart had his publicist barrage *Daily Variety* with ads excerpting his best reviews and more than once treated his colleagues and fellow Oscar-voters to rounds of drinks at Romanoff's. After he won, claimed *Daily Variety* reporter and Academy Award staple Army Archerd, Bogart was back at Romanoff's for a celebration that lasted a week.

Bogosian, Eric

Movie: 1988: *Talk Radio* (Best Male Lead) Spirit. Tributes: 1988: Honorary Silver Bear for outstanding individual achievement as actor and screenwriter for *Talk Radio* from Berlin.

Bolger, Emma

Movie: 2003: *In America* (Best Young Actor/Actress) Broadcast (Best Ensemble) SAG.

Bolger, Sarah

Movie: 2003: *In America* (Best Supporting Female) Spirit (Best Young Actor/Actress) Broadcast (Best Ensemble) SAG.

Bolkan, Florinda

Movie: 1975: *A Brief Vacation* (Best Actress) *LA*.

Bonaiuto, Anna

Movie: 1993: *Dove siete? Io sono qui (Where Are You? I'm Here)* (Best Supporting Actress) *Venice*.

Bond, Margery

Movie: 1993: *Short Cuts* (Best Ensemble) *Venice* (special award).

Bondi, Beulah

Movie: 1936: *The Gorgeous Hussy* (Best Supporting Actress) Academy. 1938: *Of Human Hearts* (Best Supporting Actress) Academy. **Television:** 1977: *The Waltons* (Best Single Performance by an Actress in a Comedy or Drama) *Emmy*.

Bonham Carter, Helena

Movie: 1992: *Howards End* (Best Supporting Actress) British. 1997: *The Wings of the Dove* (Best Actress) Academy, *Board*, British, *LA*, *Broadcast* (Best Actress, Drama) Globe (Best Female Actor in a Leading Role) SAG. 2007: *Sweeney Todd: The Demon Barber of Fleet Street* (Best Actress, Musical or Comedy) Globe (Best Ensemble) Broadcast. **Television:** 1993: *Fatal Deception: Mrs. Lee Harvey Oswald* (Best Actress in a Miniseries or TV Movie) Globe. 1998: *Merlin* (Best Supporting Actress in a Miniseries or TV Movie) Emmy (Best Supporting Actress in a Series, Miniseries, or TV Movie) Globe. 2002: *Live from Baghdad* (Best Actress in a Miniseries or TV Movie) Emmy, Globe.

Bonnaire, Sandrine

Movie: 1986: *Vagabond* (Best Actress) *LA*. 1995: *La Cérémonie (The Ceremony)* (Best Actress) *Venice* (win shared with costar).

Bonneville, Hugh

Movie: 2001: *Iris* (Best Supporting Actor) British (Best Young Actor) *Berlin*.

Booth, Shirley

Movie: 1952: *Come Back, Little Sheba* (Best Actress) *Academy, New York, Board, Cannes* (Best Actress, Drama) *Globe* (Best Foreign Actress) British. 1954: *About Mrs. Leslie* (Best Foreign Actress) British. **Theater:** 1949: *Goodbye, My Fancy* (Best Supporting or Featured Actress, Dramatic) *Tony*. 1950: *Come Back, Little Sheba* (Best Actress, Dramatic) *Tony*. 1953: *Time of the Cuckoo* (Best Actress, Dramatic) *Tony*. **Television:** 1961–1966 series *Hazel* (Best Actress in a Series) 1962: *Emmy*. 1963: *Emmy*, Globe. 1964: Emmy. 1967: *"The Glass Menagerie," CBS Playhouse* (Best Single Performance by an Actress in a Drama) Emmy. **Records:** Booth is the first star to win the Best Actress Oscar for her film debut, and the first to win Best Actress from both the National Board of Review and the New York Film Critics. Though *Come Back, Little Sheba* was her initial film experience, it was nowhere near the first time she'd given that performance. After winning the Academy Award, she acknowledged her other nominees by admitting that she'd had plenty of time to hone her interpretation of well-meaning but frumpy and disillusioned Lola Delaney, as she'd played the role on stage hundreds of times before reprising the part for the movie. Only fellow nominee Julie Harris (also in her film debut) shared Booth's long-standing connection to her nominated role, as Harris was also recreating her Broadway role (for *The Member of the Wedding*). The other nominees, Joan Crawford (*Sudden Fear*), Bette Davis (*The Star*), and Susan Hayward (*With a Song in My Heart*), were playing their parts for the first time. In all, Booth won four awards for *Sheba*, a sweep for that time period, and only lost one award for which she was nominated: at the British Academy's awards, Leslie Caron won for *Lili*. **Highlights:** Booth followed Fredric March as only the second person to win an Oscar and a Tony in the same year. She won her *Come Back, Little Sheba* Academy Award in 1953 then that year won the third Tony of her career for *Time of the Cuckoo*.

Boothe, Powers

Movie: 2005: *Sin City* (Best Ensemble) Broadcast. **Television:** 1980: *Guyana Tragedy: The Story of Jim Jones* (Best Actor in a Limited Series or Special) *Emmy*. 2004–2006 series *Deadwood* (Best Ensemble in a Drama Series) 2006: SAG. **Records:** By crossing the picket line during an industry boycott of the 1980 Emmys, Boothe became the first star to be the lone actor at an entire awards ceremony. When he won his competition, he accepted his Emmy and explained that he honored his fellow actors but felt he had to do what he believed for himself. His comments earned him a standing ovation.

Borchers, Cornell

Movie: 1954: *The Divided Heart* (Best Foreign Actress) *British.*

Borgnine, Ernest

Movie: 1955: *Marty* (Best Actor) *Academy, New York, Board* (Best Actor, Drama) *Globe* (Best Foreign Actor) *British.* 1988: *Spike of Bensonhurst* (Best Supporting Male) Spirit. **Television:** 1962–1966 series *McHale's Navy* (Best Continued Performance by an Actor in a Series) 1963: Emmy. 1980: *"All Quiet on the Western Front," Hallmark Hall of Fame* (Best Supporting Actor in a Limited Series or Special) Emmy. 2007: *A Grandpa for Christmas* (Best Actor in a Miniseries or TV Movie) Globe.

Borisov, Oleg

Movie: 1990: *Edinstvenijat suidetel* (Best Actor) *Venice.*

Borstein, Alex

Movie: 2005: *Good Night, and Good Luck* (Best Ensemble) SAG, Broadcast.

Bosco, Philip

Movie: 1996: *The First Wives Club* (Best Ensemble) *Board.* **Theater:** 1961: *The Rape of the Belt* (Best Supporting or Featured Actor, Dramatic) Tony. 1984: *Heartbreak House* (Best Featured Actor, Play) Tony. 1987: *You Never Can Tell* (Best Actor, Play) Tony. 1989: *Lend Me a Tenor* (Best Actor, Play) *Tony.* 1996: *Moon Over Buffalo* (Best Actor, Play) Tony. 2005: *12 Angry Men* (Best Actor, Play) Tony.

Bottoms, Joseph

Movie: 1974: *The Dove* (New Star of the Year — Actor) *Globe.*

Bottoms, Timothy

Movie: 1971: *Johnny Got His Gun* (New Star of the Year — Actor) Globe.

Bouajila, Sami

Movie: 2006: *Days of Glory* (Best Actor) *Cannes* (win shared with costars).

Bouchez, Élodie

Movie: 1998: *The Dreamlife of Angels* (Best Actress) *Cannes* (win shared with costar).

Bourvil

Movie: 1956: *La Traversée de Paris* (Best Actor) *Venice.*

Bower, Tom

Movie: 1985: *Wildrose* (Best Male Lead) Spirit.

Bowman, Lisa

Movie: 1995: *River of Grass* (Best Debut Performance) Spirit.

Boyd, Billy

Movie: 2001: *The Lord of the Rings: The Fellowship of the Ring* (Best Ensemble) SAG. 2002: *The Lord of the Rings: The Two Towers* (Best Ensemble) SAG. 2003: *The Lord of the Rings: The Return of the King* (Best Ensemble) *Board, SAG, Broadcast.*

Boyd, Guy

Movie: 1983: *Streamers* (Best Actor) *Venice* (win shared with costars).

Boyd, Stephen

Movie: 1956: *The Man Who Never Was* (Most Promising Newcomer) British. 1959: *Ben-Hur* (Best Supporting Actor) *Globe.* 1962: *Billy Rose's Jumbo* (Best Actor, Musical or Comedy) Globe.

Boyer, Charles

Movie: 1937: *Conquest* (Best Acting) *Board* (Best Actor) Academy. 1938: *Algiers* (Best Actor) Academy. 1944: *Gaslight* (Best Actor) Academy. 1952: *The Happy Time* (Best Actor, Drama) Globe. 1961: *Fanny* (Best Actor) Academy. 1974: *Stravinsky* (Best Supporting Actor) *New York.* **Theater:** 1963: *Lord Pengo* (Best Actor, Dramatic) Tony. **Television:** 1957: *Four Star Playhouse* (Best Continuing Performance by an Actor in a Dramatic Series) Emmy. 1965: *The Louvre* (Individual Achievement Award, Narrator) *Emmy.* **Tributes:** 1942: Honorary Oscar statuette for his progressive cultural achievement in establishing the French Research Foundation in Los Angeles as a source for the Hollywood Motion Picture industry from Academy. 1952: Special award for his distinguished stage performance in *Don Juan in Hell*, thereby assisting in a new theatre trend from Tony.

Boyle, Lara Flynn

Movie: 1993: *Equinox* (Best Supporting Female) Spirit. 1998: *Happiness* (Best Ensemble) *Board.* **Television:** 1997–2003 series *The Practice* (Best

Supporting Actress in a Drama Series) 1999: Emmy. (Best Ensemble in a Drama Series) 1998: SAG. 1999: *SAG.* 2000: SAG.

Bracco, Lorraine

Movie: 1990: *GoodFellas* (Best Supporting Actress) Academy, Globe, *LA.* Television: 1999–2007 series *The Sopranos* (Best Actress in a Drama Series) 1999: Emmy. 2000: Emmy, Globe. 2001: Emmy, Globe. 2002: Globe. (Best Female Actor in a Drama Series) 1999: SAG. 2001: SAG. 2002: SAG. (Best Supporting Actress in a Drama Series) 2007: Emmy. (Best Ensemble in a Drama Series) 1999: *SAG.* 2000: SAG. 2001: SAG. 2002: SAG. 2004: SAG. 2006: SAG. 2007: *SAG.*

Bracken, Eddie

Movie: 1944: *Hail the Conquering Hero* (Best Acting) *Board.* Theater: 1978: *Hello, Dolly!* (Best Actor, Musical) Tony.

Bradley, David

Movie: 1969: *Kes* (Most Promising Newcomer) *British.*

Brady, Alice

Movie: 1936: *My Man Godfrey* (Best Supporting Actress) Academy. 1937: *In Old Chicago* (Best Supporting Actress) *Academy.* **Records:** Brady was the first star to have her Oscar stolen, and even before she got it. Laid up at home with a broken ankle, Brady didn't attend the Academy Award ceremony the year she was up for *In Old Chicago.* When her name was announced as the winner, a man came to the podium, accepted on her behalf and left. Only later was it discovered that she hadn't sent the man in her place, no one knew who he was, and he absconded with the award. The Academy presented Brady with a replacement less than two weeks later. Her original has never materialized.

Braff, Zach

Movie: 2004: *Garden State* (Best Directorial Debut) *Board* (Best First Feature, Director) *Spirit* (Best First Screenplay) Spirit. Television: 2001–2008 series *Scrubs* (Best Actor in a Comedy Series) 2005: Emmy. (Best Actor in a Series, Musical or Comedy) 2004: Globe. 2005: Globe. 2006: Globe.

Braga, Sonia

Movie: 1980: *Dona Flor and Her Two Husbands* (Most Promising Newcomer) British. 1985: *Kiss of the Spider Woman* (Best Supporting Actress) Globe.

1988: *Moon Over Parador* (Best Supporting Actress) Globe. Television: 1995: *The Burning Season* (Best Supporting Actress in a Miniseries or Special) Emmy (Best Supporting Actress in a Series, Miniseries, or TV Movie) Globe.

Branagh, Kenneth

Movie: 1989: *Henry V* (Best Actor) Academy, British (Best New Director) *New York* (Best Director) Academy, *Board, British.* 1992: *Swan Song* (Best Live Action Short Film, Producer) Academy. 1993: *Much Ado About Nothing* (Best Feature, Producer) Spirit (Best Picture, Musical or Comedy; Producer) Globe. 1995: *Othello* (Best Male Actor in a Supporting Role) SAG. 1996: *Hamlet* (Best Adapted Screenplay) Academy. 2007: *Sleuth* (Best Director) *Venice* (special award). Television: 2001: *Conspiracy* (Best Actor in a Miniseries or TV Movie) *Emmy*, Globe. 2002: *Shackleton* (Best Actor in a Miniseries or TV Movie) Emmy. 2005: *Warm Springs* (Best Actor in a Miniseries or TV Movie) Emmy, Globe (Best Male Actor in a Television Movie or Miniseries) SAG.

Brand, Neville

Movie: 1954: *Riot in Cell Block 11* (Best Foreign Actor) British.

Brandauer, Klaus Maria

Movie: 1981: *Mephisto* (Most Promising Newcomer) British. 1985: *Out of Africa* (Best Supporting Actor) Academy, *New York, Board, Globe,* British. Television: 2000: *Introducing Dorothy Dandridge* (Best Supporting Actor in a Miniseries or TV Movie) Emmy (Best Supporting Actor in a Series, Miniseries, or TV Movie) Globe. **Tributes:** 1987: Honorary Award from Berlin.

Brando, Marlon

Movie: 1951: *A Streetcar Named Desire* (Best Actor) Academy. 1952: *Viva Zapata!* (Best Actor) Academy, *Cannes* (Best Foreign Actor) *British.* 1953: *Julius Caesar* (Best Actor) Academy (Best Foreign Actor) *British.* 1954: *On the Waterfront* (Best Actor) *Academy, New York* (Best Actor, Drama) Globe (Best Foreign Actor) *British.* 1956: *The Teahouse of the August Moon* (Best Actor, Musical or Comedy) Globe. 1957: *Sayonara* (Best Actor) Academy (Best Actor, Drama) Globe. 1958: *The Young Lions* (Best Foreign Actor) British. 1963: *The Ugly American* (Best Actor, Drama) Globe. 1972: *The Godfather* (Best Actor) *Academy,* British (multiple nomination), (Best Actor, Drama) *Globe; The Nightcomers* (Best Actor) British (multiple nomination). 1973: *Last Tango in Paris* (Best Actor) Academy, *New York,*

British, *Society*. 1989: *A Dry White Season* (Best Supporting Actor) Academy, Globe, British. **Television:** 1979: *Roots: The Next Generation* (Best Supporting Actor in a Limited Series or Special) *Emmy*. **Tributes:** 1954, 1955, 1972, 1973: Henrietta Award for World Film Favorite from Globe. 1999: Ranked Number 4 on List of 25 Greatest Male Screen Legends of the 20th Century from American Film Institute. **Records:** Brando won the first three Best Foreign Actor awards ever given by British. **Highlights:** Brando's vacillating interest in awards remained newsworthy for decades. For his first three Oscar nominations, Brando refused to campaign to win and avoided the awards ceremonies. With *On the Waterfront*, Brando reconsidered his stance, supported efforts to campaign on behalf of the movie and ended up winning four Best Actor prizes. Finally attending award ceremonies, Brando was a fan favorite and his Oscar acceptance speech was especially warm and gracious. Several nominations followed over the next twenty years without much fanfare. But the emotional climate surrounding Brando's reactions to his nominations for 1972's *The Godfather* demonstrated a clear swing back to the more obstinate pre–*Waterfront* Brando. When nominated for the Golden Globe, Brando sent a note to the Foreign Press informing them that he wouldn't attend their ceremony and wanted no one else to accept on his behalf, citing the United States' lack of honor, imperialism, military intrusions upon other countries, and disrespect for Native and African-Americans as some of his reasons for not wanting to accept the award. When he did win the Golden Globe, presenter Carol Burnett so tactfully glossed over his absence that his refusal caused barely a ripple. That all changed on Oscar night. Brando gave no response to his Academy Award nomination, sending no note to the Academy suggesting another refusal. When Roger Moore and Liv Ullmann announced Brando as the winner, unknown actress Maria Cruz stepped up to the podium dressed in Native American garb, introduced herself to the audience as Sacheen Littlefeather, and refused the award for Brando because of Hollywood's demeaning depiction of Native Americans. Cruz continued Brando's stunning refusal backstage by reading a 15-page letter he'd written further expounding on his reasons for protesting. Despite mixed reactions from Academy members, they nevertheless stayed true to their desire to honor great acting by nominating Brando again the next year for *Last Tango in Paris* and once more in 1989 for *A Dry White Season*. His *Godfather* snub proved the pinnacle of Brando's seismographic award reactions, as he remained neutral about award acknowledgments thereafter by simply ignoring them.

Braschi, Nicoletta

Movie: 1998: *La Vita è Bella (Life Is Beautiful)* (Best Ensemble) SAG.

Brasseur, Pierre

Movie: 1957: *Porte des lilas* (Best Foreign Actor) British.

Bratt, Benjamin

Movie: 2000: *Traffic* (Best Ensemble) *SAG*. **Television:** 1995–1999 series *Law & Order* (Best Supporting Actor in a Drama Series) 1999: Emmy. (Best Ensemble) 1996: SAG. 1997: SAG. 1998: SAG. 1999: SAG.

Brennan, Eileen

Movie: 1971: *The Last Picture Show* (Best Supporting Actress) British. 1980: *Private Benjamin* (Best Supporting Actress) Academy. **Television:** 1980–1981 series *Taxi* (Best Actress in a Comedy Series) 1981: Emmy. 1981–1983 series *Private Benjamin* (Best Actress in a Series, Musical or Comedy) 1981: *Globe*. 1982: Globe. (Best Supporting Actress in a Comedy, Variety, or Music Series) 1981: *Emmy*. 1982: Emmy. 1983: Emmy. 1989: *Newhart* (Best Guest Actress in a Comedy Series) Emmy. 1991: *thirtysomething* (Best Guest Actress in a Drama Series) Emmy. 2004: *Will & Grace* (Best Guest Actress in a Comedy Series) Emmy.

Brennan, Walter

Movie: 1936: *Come and Get It* (Best Supporting Actor) *Academy*. 1938: *Kentucky* (Best Supporting Actor) *Academy*. 1940: *The Westerner* (Best Supporting Actor) *Academy*. 1941: *Sergeant York* (Best Supporting Actor) Academy. **Television:** 1957–1963 series *The Real McCoys* (Best Actor — Continuing Character — in a Comedy Series) 1959: Emmy. **Records:** Not only did Brennan win the first Best Supporting Actor Oscar ever presented, but he also became the first person to win three acting Oscars. Even more impressive, he won all three awards within only five years, taking home the first, third, and fifth Supporting Actor Academy Awards ever presented. Brennan's early work as a Hollywood extra contributed markedly to his record-setting Oscar wins. From 1937 through 1944, the Academy allowed the 15,000 acting extras to vote in the annual Academy Awards competition. Brennan had worked as a $5 extra in films for many years before Samuel Goldwyn gave him his break as an actor. According to *Daily Variety*, Brennan's ties to extras impacted the voting every time he was nominated during that period, tipping the scale for his wins and enabling him to become the first triple acting Oscar winner in history.

Breslin, Abigail

Movie: 2006: *Little Miss Sunshine* (Best Female Actor in a Supporting Role) SAG (Best Supporting Actress) Academy, British (Best Young Actress) *Broadcast* (Best Ensemble) *SAG, Broadcast.*

Brian, David

Movie: 1949: *Intruder in the Dust* (Best Supporting Actor) Globe.

Bridges, Beau

Movie: 1968: *For Love of Ivy* (Best Supporting Actor) Globe. 1989: *The Fabulous Baker Boys* (Best Supporting Actor) *Society.* **Television:** 1992: *Without Warning: The James Brady Story* (Best Actor in a Miniseries or TV Movie) *Emmy, Globe.* 1993: *The Positively True Adventures of the Alleged Texas Cheerleader-Murdering Mom* (Best Supporting Actor in a Miniseries or TV Movie) *Emmy* (Best Supporting Actor in a Series, Miniseries, or TV Movie) *Globe.* 1995: *5 American Kids—5 American Hangouts* (Best Information Special, Narrator) Emmy; *The Outer Limits* (Best Guest Actor in a Drama Series) Emmy. 1996: *Kissinger and Nixon* (Best Actor in a Miniseries or Special) Emmy; *Losing Chase* (Best Actor in a Miniseries or TV Movie) Globe. 1997: *Hidden in America* (Best Actor in a Miniseries or Special) Emmy (Best Male Actor in a Television Movie or Miniseries) SAG; *The Second Civil War* (Best Supporting Actor in a Miniseries or Special) *Emmy.* 1999: *Inherit the Wind* (Best Supporting Actor in a Miniseries or TV Movie) Emmy. 2000: *P.T. Barnum* (Best Actor in a Miniseries or TV Movie) Emmy. 2002: *We Were the Mulvaneys* (Best Actor in a Miniseries or TV Movie) Emmy. 2007: *My Name Is Earl* (Best Guest Actor in a Comedy Series) Emmy.

Bridges, Chris "Ludacris"

Movie: 2005: *Crash* (Best Ensemble) *SAG, Broadcast*; *Hustle & Flow* (Best Ensemble) SAG.

Bridges, Jeff

Movie: 1971: *The Last Picture Show* (Best Supporting Actor) Academy. 1974: *Thunderbolt and Lightfoot* (Best Supporting Actor) Academy. 1984: *Starman (John Carpenter's Starman)* (Best Actor) Academy (Best Actor, Drama) Globe. 1991: *The Fisher King* (Best Actor, Musical or Comedy) Globe. 1993: *American Heart* (Best Male Lead) *Spirit.* 2000:

The Contender (Best Male Actor in a Supporting Role) SAG (Best Supporting Actor) Academy, Globe, Broadcast. 2003: *Seabiscuit* (Best Ensemble) SAG. 2004: *The Door in the Floor* (Best Male Lead) Spirit. **Tributes:** 2004: Career Achievement Award from Board.

Bright, Cameron

Movie: 2004: *Birth* (Best Young Actor) Broadcast. 2006: *Thank You for Smoking* (Best Young Actor) Broadcast.

Brissac, Virginia

Movie: 1954: *Executive Suite* (Best Ensemble) *Venice* (special award).

Broadbent, Jim

Movie: 1998: *Little Voice* (Best Ensemble) SAG. 1999: *Topsy-Turvy* (Best Actor) *Venice,* British. 2001: *Iris* (Best Actor) British (Best Male Actor in a Supporting Role) SAG (Best Supporting Actor) *Academy, Board* (multiple win), *Globe, LA* (multiple win), Broadcast; *Moulin Rouge!* (Best Supporting Actor) *Board* (multiple win), *British, LA* (multiple win), (Best Ensemble) SAG. 2002: *Nicholas Nickleby* (Best Ensemble) *Board.* **Television:** 2002: *The Gathering Storm* (Best Supporting Actor in a Miniseries or TV Movie) Emmy (Best Supporting Actor in a Series, Miniseries, or TV Movie) Globe. 2007: *Longford* (Best Actor in a Miniseries or TV Movie) Emmy, *Globe.* **Highlights:** Not since Thomas Mitchell starred in the three movies that took 11 of the 17 competitive Oscars in 1939 had a Best Supporting Actor winner been in so many films up for awards as Broadbent in 2001. In *Iris,* the film which brought him his award, Broadbent co-starred with Best Supporting Actress nominee Kate Winslet and Best Actress nominee Judi Dench. He also appeared in films that put two other actresses in contention for Best Actress: Nicole Kidman in *Moulin Rouge!* and Renée Zellweger in *Bridget Jones's Diary.* From the three films that year, only Broadbent went home an acting winner.

Broderick, Matthew

Movie: 1986: *Ferris Bueller's Day Off* (Best Actor, Musical or Comedy) Globe. **Theater:** 1983: *Brighton Beach Memoirs* (Best Actor in a Featured Role, Play) *Tony.* 1995: *How to Succeed in Business Without Really Trying!* (Best Actor, Musical) *Tony.* 2001: *The Producers* (Best Actor, Musical) Tony. **Television:** 1993: *A Life in the Theatre* (Best Supporting Actor in a Miniseries or Special) Emmy.

Brodie, V. S.

Movie: 1994: *Go Fish* (Best Supporting Female) Spirit.

Brodsky, Vlastimil

Movie: 1975: *Jakob der Lügner (Jacob the Liar)* (Best Actor) *Berlin.*

Brody, Adrien

Movie: 2000: *Restaurant* (Best Male Lead) Spirit. 2002: *The Pianist* (Best Actor) *Academy*, British, *Society* (Best Actor, Drama) Globe (Best Male Actor in a Leading Role) SAG. **Records:** Brody's Best Actor Oscar nomination for *The Pianist* in 2002 marked the first time an actor in his initial Oscar race competed against four previous Academy Award recipients: one-time winners Nicholas Cage and Daniel Day-Lewis, twice victorious Michael Caine and triple golden boy, Jack Nicholson. When 29-year-old Brody won, he became the youngest star to win the Best Actor Academy Award, taking the record from then-reigning champ of 25 years, Richard Dreyfuss, who was 30 when he picked up his Best Actor award for 1977's *The Goodbye Girl.*

Brolin, James

Movie: 2000: *Traffic* (Best Ensemble) SAG. **Television:** 1969–1976 series *Marcus Welby, M.D.* (Best Supporting Actor in a Drama Series) 1970: *Emmy.* 1971: Emmy. 1972: Emmy. 1973: Emmy. (Best Supporting Actor in a Television Series) 1970: *Globe.* (Best Supporting Actor in a Series or Television Movie) 1971: Globe. (Best Supporting Actor in a Series, Miniseries, or TV Movie) 1972: *Globe.* 1983–1988 series *Hotel* (Best Actor in a Drama Series) 1984: Globe. 1985: Globe. 2004: *The Reagans* (Best Actor in a Miniseries or TV Movie) Emmy, Globe.

Brolin, Josh

Movie: 2007: *American Gangster* (Best Ensemble) SAG; *No Country for Old Men* (Best Ensemble) *Board, SAG,* Broadcast.

Bronson, Charles

Television: 1961: *"Memory in White," GE Theatre* (Best Performance in a Supporting Role by an Actor or Actress in a Single Program) Emmy. **Tributes:** 1971: Henrietta Award for World Film Favorite from Globe.

Brooks, Albert

Movie: 1985: *Lost in America* (Best Screenplay) *Society.* 1987: *Broadcast News* (Best Supporting Actor) Academy. 1996: *Mother* (Best Screenplay) *New York, Society.*

Brooks, Mel

Movie: 1968: *The Producers* (Best Original Story and Screenplay) *Academy* (Best Screenplay) Globe. 1974: *Blazing Saddles* (Best Screenplay) British (Best Song, "Blazing Saddles") Academy; *Young Frankenstein* (Best Adapted Screenplay) Academy. 1976: *Silent Movie* (Best Actor, Musical or Comedy) Globe. 1977: *High Anxiety* (Best Actor, Musical or Comedy) Globe (Best Picture, Musical or Comedy; Producer) Globe. 2005: *The Producers* (Best Original Song, "There's Nothing Like a Show on Broadway") Globe. **Theater:** 2001: *The Producers* (Best Book of a Musical, Writer) *Tony* (Best Musical, Producer) *Tony* (Best Original Musical Score, Composer) *Tony.* **Television:** 1954–1957 series *Caesar's Hour* (Best Comedy Writing) 1956: Emmy. 1958: Emmy. (Best Comedy Writing — Variety or Situation Comedy) 1957: Emmy. 1965–1970 series *Get Smart* (Best Writing Achievement in Comedy) 1966: Emmy. 1967: *Sid Caesar, Imogene Coca, Carl Reiner, Howard Morris Special* (Best Writing Achievement in Variety) *Emmy.* 1996–1999 series *Mad About You* (Best Guest Actor in a Comedy Series) 1997: *Emmy.* 1998: *Emmy.* 1999: *Emmy.* 2003: *Jakers! The Adventures of Piggley Winks* (Best Performer in an Animated Program) Emmy. **Records:** With *The Producers*, Brooks became the first person to adapt his Academy Award–winning screenplay into a Tony Award–winning musical. That achievement also made him one of only nine icons to win an Emmy, Grammy, Oscar, and a Tony, and the only one to win three of those awards for adaptations of the same work. For *The Producers* he won one Oscar, two Grammys, and three Tonys.

Brosnan, Pierce

Movie: 2005: *The Matador* (Best Actor, Musical or Comedy) Globe. **Television:** 1984: *Nancy Astor* (Best Supporting Actor in a Series, Miniseries, or TV Movie) Globe.

Brown, Blair

Movie: 1981: *Continental Divide* (Best Actress, Musical or Comedy) Globe. **Theater:** 2000: *Copenhagen* (Best Actress in a Featured Role, Play) *Tony.* **Television:** 1983: *Kennedy* (Best Actress in a Miniseries or TV Movie) Globe. 1987–1991 series *The Days and Nights of Molly Dodd* (Best Actress in a

Comedy Series) 1987: Emmy. 1988: Emmy. 1989: Emmy. 1990: Emmy. 1991: Emmy.

Brown, Georgia

Movie: 1971: *The Raging Moon* (Best Supporting Actress) British. **Theater:** 1963: *Oliver!* (Best Actress, Musical) Tony. 1990: *Threepenny Opera* (Best Actress, Musical) Tony. **Television:** 1990: *Cheers* (Best Guest Actress in a Comedy Series) Emmy.

Brown, Kimberly J.

Movie: 1999: *Tumbleweeds* (Best Debut Performance) *Spirit.*

Brown, Rob

Movie: 2000: *Finding Forrester* (Best Child Performer) Broadcast.

Browne, Leslie

Movie: 1977: *The Turning Point* (Best Supporting Actress) Academy, Globe.

Browning, Emily

Movie: 2004: *Lemony Snicket's A Series of Unfortunate Events* (Best Young Actress) Broadcast.

Bruckner, Agnes

Movie: 2003: *Blue Car* (Best Female Lead) Spirit.

Bryan, Dora

Movie: 1961: *A Taste of Honey* (Best British Actress) *British.*

Bryan, Jane

Movie: 1939: *We Are Not Alone* (Best Acting) *Board.*

Bryant, Joy

Movie: 2006: *Bobby* (Best Ensemble) SAG, Broadcast.

Brynner, Yul

Movie: 1956: *Anastasia* (Best Actor) *Board* (multiple win); *The King and I* (Best Actor) *Academy, Board* (multiple win), (Best Actor, Musical or Comedy) Globe; *The Ten Commandments* (Best Actor) *Board* (multiple win). **Theater:** 1952: *The King and I* (Best Supporting or Featured Actor, Musical) *Tony.* **Tributes:** 1985: Special award honoring his 4,525 performances in *The King and I* from Tony.

Buchholz, Horst

Movie: 1998: *La Vita è Bella (Life Is Beautiful)* (Best Ensemble) SAG.

Bujold, Genevieve

Movie: 1969: *Anne of the Thousand Days* (Best Actress) Academy (Best Actress, Drama) *Globe.* 1988: *Dead Ringers* (Best Supporting Actress) *LA* (multiple win); *The Moderns* (Best Supporting Actress) *LA* (multiple win). **Television:** 1968: *"Saint Joan," Hallmark Hall of Fame* (Best Single Performance by an Actress in a Drama) Emmy.

Bullock, Sandra

Movie: 1995: *While You Were Sleeping* (Best Actress, Musical or Comedy) Globe. 2000: *Miss Congeniality* (Best Actress, Musical or Comedy) Globe. 2005: *Crash* (Best Ensemble) *SAG, Broadcast.*

Buono, Victor

Movie: 1962: *What Ever Happened to Baby Jane?* (Best Supporting Actor) Academy, Globe.

Burke, Billie

Movie: 1938: *Merrily We Live* (Best Supporting Actress) Academy.

Burke, Kathy

Movie: 1997: *Nil by Mouth* (Best Actress) *Cannes,* British.

Burke, Robert John

Movie: 2005: *Good Night, and Good Luck* (Best Ensemble) SAG, Broadcast.

Burnett, Carol

Movie: 1972: *Pete 'n' Tillie* (Best Actress, Musical or Comedy) Globe. 1978: *A Wedding* (Best Supporting Actress) Globe. 1981: *The Four Seasons* (Best Actress, Musical or Comedy) Globe. 1982: *Annie* (Best Actress, Musical or Comedy) Globe. **Theater:** 1960: *Once Upon a Mattress* (Best Actress, Musical) Tony. 1996: *Moon Over Buffalo* (Best Actress, Play) Tony. **Television:** 1959–1962 series *The Garry Moore Show* (Best Performance in a Variety or Musical Program or Series) 1962: *Emmy.* 1963: *Julie and Carol at Carnegie Hall* (Best Performance in a Variety or Musical Program or Series) *Emmy.* 1967–1978 series *The Carol Burnett Show* (Best Actress in a Comedy or Musical Series) 1969: *Globe.* 1972: Globe. 1973: Globe. 1974: Globe. 1975: Globe. 1976: *Globe.* 1977: *Globe.* 1978: Globe. (Best Actress in a Comedy or Musical Series or TV Movie) 1971: *Globe.* (Best Actress in a Television Series) 1967: *Globe.* (Best Variety or Musical Series, Star) 1969: Emmy. 1970: Emmy. 1971: Emmy. 1972: *Emmy.* 1973: Emmy. 1974: *Emmy.* 1975: *Emmy.* 1976: Emmy. 1977: Emmy. 1978:

Emmy. 1972: *Julie and Carol at Lincoln Center* (Best Single Program, Variety or Musical; Star) Emmy. 1974: *6 Rms Riv Vu* (Best Actress in a Drama) Emmy. 1977: *Sills and Burnett at the Met* (Best Comedy-Variety or Music Special, Star) Emmy. 1979: *Friendly Fire* (Best Actress in a Limited Series or Special) Emmy. 1982: *Life of the Party: The Story of Beatrice* (Best Actress in a Miniseries or TV Movie) Globe. 1983: *Texaco Star Theater: Opening Night* (Best Individual Performance in a Variety or Music Program) Emmy. 1990: *Carol & Company* (Best Actress in a Comedy or Musical Series) Globe. 1993: *The Larry Sanders Show* (Best Guest Actress in a Comedy Series) Emmy. 1995: *Men, Movies and Carol* (Best Individual Performance in a Variety or Music Program) Emmy. 1996–1999 series *Mad About You* (Best Guest Actress in a Comedy Series) 1997: *Emmy.* 1998: Emmy. 2002: *The Carol Burnett Show "Show Stoppers"* (Best Variety, Music or Comedy Special; Executive Producer) Emmy. **Tributes:** 1969: Special award from Tony. 1985: Television Hall of Fame Inductee from Emmy. 2003: Honor from Kennedy Center for the Performing Arts.

Burns, Catherine

Movie: 1969: *Last Summer* (Best Supporting Actress) Academy.

Burns, Edward

Movie: 1998: *Saving Private Ryan* (Best Ensemble) SAG.

Burns, George

Movie: 1975: *The Sunshine Boys* (Best Actor, Musical or Comedy) Globe (Best Supporting Actor) *Academy.* 1980: *Going in Style* (Best Actor) *Venice* (win shared with costars). **Television:** 1978: *The George Burns One-Man Show* (Best Comedy-Variety or Music Special, Star) Emmy. 1984: *George Burns Celebrates 80 Years in Show Business* (Best Individual Performance in a Variety or Music Program) Emmy. 1990: *A Conversation with...* (Best Performance in Informational Programming) *Emmy.* **Tributes:** 1988: Honor from Kennedy Center for the Performing Arts. 1989: Television Hall of Fame Inductee from Emmy (honor shared with spouse, Gracie Allen). 1994: Life Achievement Award from SAG. **Records:** 69 days after his 80th birthday, Burns picked up a Best Supporting Actor Oscar for *The Sunshine Boys*, making him the oldest person to win an Academy Award for acting. Fourteen years later, Jessica Tandy broke his age record: at 80 years and 293 days old, she was 124 days older than Burns when she won Best Actress for *Driving Miss Daisy*. Nevertheless, Burns still holds the record for oldest

actor to win a supporting Oscar. **Highlights:** Before *The Sunshine Boys* in 1975, Burns hadn't made a film since 1939's *Honolulu.* Upon winning the Oscar, the always quick-witted Burns quipped that he was so excited that he would keep making one movie every thirty-six years. He ended up making several more films over the next few years, including the successful *Oh, God* pictures and *Going in Style*, for which he and co-stars Art Carney and Lee Strasberg received an acting award at the Venice Film Festival.

Burns, Megan

Movie: 2000: *Liam* (Best First Time Actress) *Venice.*

Burrus, Bob

Movie: 2002: *Tully* (Best Debut Performance) Spirit.

Burstyn, Ellen

Movie: 1971: *The Last Picture Show* (Best Supporting Actress) Academy, *New York*, Globe, *Society.* 1973: *The Exorcist* (Best Actress) Academy (Best Actress, Drama) Globe. 1974: *Alice Doesn't Live Here Anymore* (Best Actress) *Academy*, *British* (Best Actress, Drama) Globe. 1978: *Same Time, Next Year* (Best Actress) Academy (Best Actress, Musical or Comedy) *Globe.* 1980: *Resurrection* (Best Actress) Academy (Best Actress, Drama) Globe. 1995: *How to Make an American Quilt* (Best Ensemble) SAG. 2000: *Requiem for a Dream* (Best Actress) Academy, Broadcast (Best Actress, Drama) Globe (Best Female Actor in a Leading Role) SAG (Best Female Lead) *Spirit.* **Theater:** 1975: *Same Time, Next Year* (Best Actress, Dramatic) *Tony.* **Television:** 1981: *The People vs. Jean Harris* (Best Actress in a Limited Series or Special) Emmy (Best Actress in a Miniseries or TV Movie) Globe. 1987: *"Pack of Lies," Hallmark Hall of Fame* (Best Actress in a Miniseries or Special) Emmy. 2006: *Mrs. Harris* (Best Supporting Actress in a Miniseries or TV Movie) Emmy. 2007: *Mitch Albom's For One More Day* (Best Female Actor in a Television Movie or Miniseries) SAG. **Tributes:** 1988: Honorary Award from Berlin. 2000: Career Achievement Award from Board. **Records:** Burstyn set two award records, one related to her work in movies and the other for a performance on television. In 2000, Burstyn won the first Career Achievement award ever presented by the Broadcast Film Critics. In 1996, they gave Lauren Bacall a similar honor, but hers was a Lifetime Achievement award. In 2006, Burstyn earned an Emmy nomination for the shortest performance ever to receive major award recognition in any medium. In the TV movie *Mrs. Harris*, Burstyn had a total of 14 or 9 seconds of screen time (depending on how you count the time her face appears on camera), spoke two lines consisting of 38 words, and was billed simply as "Ex-Lover #3" or "Steady." Critics such as *The Los Angeles Times*' Tom O'Neil suggested that her name recognition led many Emmy voters to select her without knowing the brevity of her appearance and railed for a change in the Emmy rule that would allow such an unexpected nomination. Not everyone felt so negatively about the nomination and some even shared their joy that the fine actress was getting more recognition. The good-natured Burstyn, who did not submit her name for Emmy consideration, took the media debate in stride, even joking that her next ambition would be to get nominated for seven seconds, and, eventually, to get nominated for a film in which she didn't even appear. Burstyn was not present when the award was given in that category to Cloris Leachman, who set an Emmy record with that victory by becoming the first person to win nine acting Emmys.

Burton, Richard

Movie: 1952: *My Cousin Rachel* (New Star of the Year — Actor) *Globe* (Best Supporting Actor) Academy. 1953: *The Robe* (Best Actor) Academy. 1959: *Look Back in Anger* (Best Actor, Drama) Globe (Best British Actor) British. 1964: *Becket* (Best Actor) Academy (Best Actor, Drama) Globe. 1965: *The Spy Who Came In from the Cold* (Best Actor) Academy (Best British Actor) *British*. 1966: *Who's Afraid of Virginia Woolf?* (Best Actor) Academy (Best Actor, Drama) Globe. 1967: *The Taming of the Shrew* (Best Actor, Musical or Comedy) Globe (Best British Actor) British (Best Picture, Musical or Comedy; Producer) Globe. 1969: *Anne of the Thousand Days* (Best Actor) Academy (Best Actor, Drama) Globe. 1977: *Equus* (Best Actor) Academy (Best Actor, Drama) *Globe*. **Theater:** 1958: *Time Remembered* (Best Actor, Dramatic) Tony. 1961: *Camelot* (Best Actor, Musical) *Tony*. 1964: *Hamlet* (Best Actor, Dramatic) Tony. **Television:** 1985: *Ellis Island* (Best Supporting Actor in a Limited Series or Special) Emmy. **Tributes:** 1968: Henrietta Award for World Film Favorite from Globe. 1976: Special award from Tony. **Highlights:** A top contender for the Oscar nearly every time he was nominated, Burton was expected to break his losing streak and finally take home the prize for his affecting turn as spiritually torn psychiatrist Martin Dysart in *Equus*, adapted from Peter Shaffer's Tony winning play. On Oscar night, Sylvester Stallone announced that the winner was Richard ... Dreyfuss for *The Goodbye Girl*. That seventh loss made Burton the most nominated actor in Academy history never to win the award.

Burton, Tyrone

Movie: 1997: *Squeeze* (Best Debut Performance) Spirit (nomination shared with costars).

Buscemi, Steve

Movie: 1989: *Mystery Train* (Best Supporting Male) Spirit. 1992: *Reservoir Dogs* (Best Supporting Male) *Spirit*. 1996: *Trees Lounge* (Best First Screenplay) Spirit. 2001: *Ghost World* (Best Supporting Actor) *New York*, Globe, *Society* (Best Supporting Male) *Spirit*. **Television:** 2002–2006 series *The Sopranos* (Best Supporting Actor in a Drama Series) 2004: Emmy. (Best Director of a Drama Series) 2001: Emmy. (Best Ensemble in a Drama Series) 2004: SAG. **Highlights:** A favorite actor of many indie filmmakers, especially the Coen Brothers, Buscemi is one of the most nominated Independent Spirit award actors and one of its first multiple winners. Although he is attracted to smaller films, Buscemi nevertheless enjoys big fame, even ranking #52 on the United Kingdom's *Empire Magazine* October 1997 list of The Top 100 Movie Stars of All Time.

Busey, Gary

Movie: 1978: *The Buddy Holly Story* (Most Promising Newcomer) British (New Generation) *LA* (Best Actor) Academy, *Society* (Best Actor, Musical or Comedy) Globe.

Bushman, Francis X.

Tributes: 1959: Special Achievement Award from Globe in honor of the performance of his career for playing Messala in the 1925 silent version of *Ben-Hur*, given the year the new sound remake was released.

Bustric, Sergio Bini

Movie: 1998: *La Vita è Bella (Life Is Beautiful)* (Best Ensemble) SAG.

Butler, Paul

Movie: 2007: *Before the Devil Knows You're Dead* (Best Ensemble) Broadcast.

Butterworth, Donna

Movie: 1965: *The Family Jewels* (New Star of the Year — Actor) Globe.

Buttons, Red

Movie: 1957: *Sayonara* (Most Promising Newcomer) British (Best Supporting Actor) *Academy, Globe*. 1965: *Harlow* (Best Supporting Actor) Globe. 1969: *They Shoot Horses, Don't They?* (Best Supporting Actor) Globe. **Television:** 2005: *ER* (Best Guest Actor in a Drama Series) Emmy.

Byington, Spring

Movie: 1938: *You Can't Take It with You* (Best Supporting Actress) Academy. 1950: *Louisa* (Best Actress, Musical or Comedy) Globe. **Television:** 1954–1959 series *December Bride* (Best Continuing Performance by an Actress in a Leading Role) 1958: Emmy. (Best Actress in a Leading Role — Continuing Character — Comedy Series) 1959: Emmy.

Bynes, Amanda

Movie: 2007: *Hairspray* (Best Ensemble) SAG, *Broadcast.*

Byrne, Gabriel

Movie: 1995: *The Usual Suspects* (Best Ensemble) *Board.* **Theater:** 2000: *A Moon for the Misbegotten* (Best Actor, Play) Tony.

Byrne, Rose

Movie: 2000: *The Goddess of 1967* (Best Actress) *Venice.* **Television:** 2007–present series *Damages* (Best Supporting Actress in a Series, Miniseries, or TV Movie) 2007: Globe.

Caan, James

Movie: 1965: *Lady in a Cage* (New Star of the Year — Actor) Globe. 1972: *The Godfather* (Best Supporting Actor) Academy, Globe. 1974: *The Gambler* (Best Actor, Drama) Globe. 1975: *Funny Lady* (Best Actor, Musical or Comedy) Globe. **Television:** 1972: *"Brian's Song," ABC Movie of the Week* (Best Single Performance by an Actor in a Leading Role) Emmy.

Caan, Scott

Movie: 2001: *Ocean's 11* (Best Ensemble) Broadcast. 2004: *Ocean's Twelve* (Best Ensemble) Broadcast.

Caesar, Adolph

Movie: 1984: *A Soldier's Story* (Best Supporting Actor) Academy, Globe, *LA.*

Cage, Nicolas

Movie: 1987: *Moonstruck* (Best Actor, Musical or Comedy) Globe. 1989: *Vampire's Kiss* (Best Male Lead) Spirit. 1992: *Honeymoon in Vegas* (Best Actor, Musical or Comedy) Globe. 1995: *Leaving Las Vegas* (Best Actor) *Academy, New York, Board,* British, *Society, LA* (Best Actor, Drama) *Globe* (Best Male Lead) Spirit (Best Male Actor in a Leading Role) *SAG.* 2002: *Adaptation* (Best Actor) Academy, British (Best Actor, Musical or Comedy) Globe (Best Male Actor in a Leading Role) SAG (Best Ensemble) SAG. **Highlights:** Few performances have swept the awards the way Cage's suicidal meltdown did in 1995's *Leaving Las Vegas.* His astounding ten nominations and record-setting seven wins meant that he won nearly every major award an actor could have received that year. Cage missed a perfect 10-for-10 record by losing the Independent Spirit Award to Sean Penn, who won for *Dead Man Walking,* the Broadcast Film Critics prize to Kevin Bacon in *Murder in the First,* and the BAFTA to British actor Nigel Hawthorne, who took that top prize for *The Madness of King George.*

Cagney, James

Movie: 1938: *Angels with Dirty Faces* (Best Acting) *Board* (Best Actor) Academy, *New York.* 1939: *Roaring Twenties* (Best Acting) *Board.* 1942: *Yankee Doodle Dandy* (Best Acting) *Board* (Best Actor) *Academy, New York.* 1955: *Love Me or Leave Me* (Best Actor) Academy. **Tributes:** 1974: Life Achievement Award from American Film Institute. 1977: Life Achievement Award from SAG. 1980: Honor from Kennedy Center for the Performing Arts. 1981: Special award from Board. 1999: Ranked Number 8 on List of 25 Greatest Male Screen Legends of the 20th Century from American Film Institute. **Records:** Cagney, whom George M. Cohan himself had chosen to play him in the movie version of *Yankee Doodle Dandy,* won his New York Film Critics Circle Award for that film by one of the highest vote ratios in the organization's history. On the very first ballot (itself an impressive feat), 13 of the 15 participating critics chose Cagney. The other two votes went to Humphrey Bogart in *Casablanca,* a 1943 film in most competitions that had been released in New York in '42. To illustrate just how impressive Cagney's second win was, when he won that same award two year's earlier for *Angels with Dirty Faces,* it had taken nine rounds of voting to make him a clear winner. When he later went on to win an Oscar for *Yankee Doodle Dandy,* Cagney became the first star to win an Academy Award for a song-and-dance role. **Highlights:** Because he won his Academy Award in the spring of 1943 when metal was in short supply due to World War II, Cagney, as well as that year's Best Actress Greer Garson, received plaster Oscar replicas at the ceremony instead of the usual bronze, gold plated statuettes. (Supporting winners were still being given plaques instead of statuettes as they had since 1936.) All acting winners for the films of 1943 and 1944 received the same plaster replicas. After the war, all those stars received regular statuettes like those given before and after the war.

Caine, Michael

Movie: 1965: ***The Ipcress File*** (Best British Actor) British. 1966: ***Alfie*** (Best Actor) Academy, *Society* (Best Actor, Drama) Globe (Best British Actor) British; ***Gambit*** (Best Actor, Musical or Comedy) Globe. 1972: ***Sleuth*** (Best Actor) Academy (Best Actor, Drama) Globe. 1983: ***Educating Rita*** (Best Actor) Academy, *British* (Best Actor, Musical or Comedy) *Globe;* ***The Honorary Consul*** (Best Actor) British. 1986: ***Hannah and Her Sisters*** (Best Actor) British (Best Supporting Actor) *Academy,* Globe. 1988: ***Dirty Rotten Scoundrels*** (Best Actor, Musical or Comedy) Globe. 1998: ***Little Voice*** (Best Actor) British (Best Actor, Musical or Comedy) *Globe* (Best Ensemble) SAG. 1999: ***The Cider House Rules*** (Best Male Actor in a Supporting Role) *SAG* (Best Supporting Actor) *Academy,* Globe, British (Best Ensemble) SAG. 2001: ***Last Orders*** (Best Ensemble) Board. 2002: ***The Quiet American*** (Best Actor) Academy, British (Best Actor, Drama) Globe. Television: 1988: ***Jack the Ripper*** (Best Actor in a Miniseries or TV Movie) *Globe.* 1990: ***Jekyll & Hyde*** (Best Actor in a Series or Special) Emmy (Best Actor in a Miniseries or TV Movie) Globe. 1994: ***World War II: When Lions Roared*** (Best Actor in a Miniseries or Special) Emmy. 1997: ***Mandela and de Klerk*** (Best Supporting Actor in a Miniseries or Special) Emmy (Best Supporting Actor in a Miniseries or TV Movie) Globe. 1988: **Tributes:** 1998: Career Achievement Award from Board. 2004: Gala Tribute from the Film Society of Lincoln Center. **Records:** In 1966, Caine won the first Best Actor prize ever presented by the National Society of Film Critics. It turned out to be his first major award and the only one he received for the seminal role of ***Alfie,*** which made him an international star.

Calder-Marshall, Anna

Movie: 1970: ***Pussycat, Pussycat, I Love You*** (New Star of the Year — Actress) Globe. Television: 1969: **"*Male of the Species,*" *Prudential's On Stage*** (Best Single Performance by an Actress in a Supporting Role) *Emmy.*

Calhern, Louis

Movie: 1950: ***The Magnificent Yankee*** (Best Actor) Academy (Best Actor, Drama) Globe. 1954: ***Executive Suite*** (Best Ensemble) *Venice* (special award).

Callan, Michael

Movie: 1959: ***The Flying Fontaines*** (New Star of the Year — Actor) Globe. 1960: ***Because They're Young*** (New Star of the Year — Actor) *Globe.*

Calleia, Joseph

Movie: 1938: ***Algiers*** (Best Acting) *Board.*

Callow, Simon

Movie: 1986: ***A Room with a View*** (Best Supporting Actor) British. 1994: ***Four Weddings and a Funeral*** (Best Supporting Actor) British. 1998: ***Shakespeare in Love*** (Best Ensemble) *SAG.*

Calloway, Kirk

Movie: 1973: ***Cinderella Liberty*** (New Star of the Year — Actor) Globe.

Calvert, Phyllis

Movie: 1952: ***Mandy*** (Best British Actress) British.

Campbell, Glen

Movie: 1969: ***True Grit*** (New Star of the Year — Male) Globe. Television: 1969–1972 series ***The Glen Campbell Goodtime Hour*** (Best Actor in a Musical or Comedy Series) 1970: Globe.

Campbell, Jessica

Movie: 1999: ***Election*** (Best Debut Performance) Spirit.

Campbell, Tisha

Movie: 1990: ***House Party*** (Best Supporting Female) Spirit.

Campbell Bower, Jamie

Movie: 2007: ***Sweeney Todd: The Demon Barber of Fleet Street*** (Best Ensemble) Broadcast.

Caneele, Severine

Movie: 1999: ***L'Humanité (Humanity)*** (Best Actress) *Cannes.*

Canerday, Natalie

Movie: 1996: ***Sling Blade*** (Best Ensemble) SAG.

Cannavale, Bobby

Movie: 2003: ***The Station Agent*** (Best Ensemble) SAG. Television: 2005: ***Will & Grace*** (Best Guest Actor in a Comedy Series) *Emmy.*

Cannon, Dyan

Movie: 1969: ***Bob & Carol & Ted & Alice*** (Best New Star of the Year — Actress) Globe (Best Actress, Musical or Comedy) Globe (Best Supporting Actress) Academy, *New York.* 1971: ***Such Good Friends*** (Best

Actress, Drama) Globe. 1976: **Number One** (Best Live Action Short Film, Producer) Academy. 1978: **Heaven Can Wait** (Best Supporting Actress) Academy, *Globe.*

Cannon, Nick

Movie: 2006: **Bobby** (Best Ensemble) SAG, Broadcast.

Canovas, Anne

Movie: 1994: **Prêt-à-Porter (Ready-to-Wear)** (Best Ensemble) *Board.*

Cantarini, Giorgio

Movie: 1998: **La Vita è Bella (Life Is Beautiful)** (Best Ensemble) SAG.

Cantinflas

Movie: 1956: **Around the World in 80 Days** (Best Actor, Musical or Comedy) *Globe.* 1960: **Pepe** (Best Actor, Musical or Comedy) Globe. Tributes: 1960: Special Achievement Award from Globe. **Records:** Cantinflas's Golden Globe for **Around the World in 80 Days** made him the first Mexican star to become an award-winning actor in American films. He appeared in Mexican films beginning in 1936 and reached international fame portraying Passepartout in Mike Todd's sweeping, all-star opus.

Cantor, Eddie

Tributes: 1956: Honorary Oscar statuette for distinguished service to the film industry from Academy. 1962: Life Achievement Award from SAG.

Capote, Truman

Movie: 1976: **Murder by Death** (New Star of the Year—Male) Globe. Tributes: 1967: Special award for adapting his story, "A Christmas Memory" to television for **ABC Stage 67** from Emmy.

Capshaw, Kate

Movie: 1995: **How to Make an American Quilt** (Best Ensemble) SAG.

Capucine

Movie: 1960: **Song Without End** (Best Actress, Musical or Comedy) Globe.

Cara, Irene

Movie: 1980: **Fame** (Best Actress, Musical or Comedy) Globe. 1983: **Flashdance** (Best Song, "Flashdance ... What a Feeling") *Academy, Globe.*

Cardellini, Linda

Movie: 2005: **Brokeback Mountain** (Best Ensemble) SAG.

Cardinale, Claudia

Movie: 1984: **Claretta** (Best Actress) *Venice.* Tributes: 1993: Career Golden Lion from Venice. 2002: Honorary Golden Bear from Berlin.

Carell, Steve

Movie: 2006: **Little Miss Sunshine** (Best Ensemble) *SAG, Broadcast.* Television: 2005–present series **The Office** (Best Actor in a Comedy Series) 2006: Emmy. 2007: Emmy. (Best Actor in a Series, Musical or Comedy) 2005: *Globe.* 2006: Globe. 2007: Globe. (Best Male Actor in a Comedy Series) 2006: SAG. 2007: SAG. (Best Ensemble in a Comedy Series) 2006: *SAG.* 2007: *SAG.*

Carey, Harry

Movie: 1939: **Mr. Smith Goes to Washington** (Best Supporting Actor) Academy.

Carides, Gia

Movie: 2002: **My Big Fat Greek Wedding** (Best Ensemble) SAG, Broadcast.

Carillo, Elpidia

Movie: 1986: **Salvador** (Best Female Lead) Spirit.

Carlin, Lynn

Movie: 1968: **Faces** (Best Supporting Actress) Academy. 1971: **Taking Off** (Best Actress) British.

Carlisi, Olimpia

Movie: 1977: **The Middle of the World** (Most Promising Newcomer) British.

Carlyle, Robert

Movie: 1997: **The Full Monty** (Best Actor) *British* (Best Ensemble) *SAG.* Television: 2006: **Human Trafficking** (Best Supporting Actor in a Miniseries or TV Movie) Emmy.

Carney, Art

Movie: 1974: **Harry and Tonto** (Best Actor) *Academy* (Best Actor, Musical or Comedy) *Globe.* 1977: **The Late Show** (Best Actor) *Society.* 1980: **Going in Style** (Best Actor) *Venice* (win shared with costars). Theater: 1969: **Lovers** (Best Actor, Dramatic) Tony. Television: 1952–1954; 1956; 1966–1970 series **The Jackie Gleason Show** (Best Series Supporting Actor)

1954: *Emmy*. (Best Supporting Actor in a Regular Series) 1955: *Emmy*. (Best Supporting Performance by an Actor) 1957: Emmy. (Best Special Individual Achievement, Performer) 1966: Emmy. 1967: *Emmy*. 1968: *Emmy*. 1956: --- (Best Comedian) Emmy. 1955–1956 series *The Honeymooners* (Best Actor in a Supporting Role) 1956: *Emmy*. 1960: *Art Carney V.I.P. Special* (Best Program Achievement in the Field of Humor, Star) *Emmy*. 1976: *"Katherine," The ABC Sunday Night Movie* (Best Single Performance by a Supporting Actor in a Comedy or Drama Special) Emmy. 1984: *"Terrible Joe Moran," An ITT Theatre Special* (Best Supporting Actor in a Limited Series or Special) *Emmy*. 1987: *The Cavanaughs* (Best Guest Performer in a Comedy Series) Emmy. 1990: *Where Pigeons Go to Die* (Best Actor in a Miniseries or Special) Emmy. **Tributes:** 2004: Television Hall of Fame Inductee from Emmy. **Records:** In the early years of television, Carney proved the importance of supporting players by winning the first Supporting Actor Emmy and then going on to win a then-record total of five Emmys for his portrayal as Ed Norton, sidekick to Jackie Gleason's Ralph Cramden in *The Jackie Gleason Show* and *The Honeymooners*. **Highlights:** Carney's heavy campaigning for the Oscar resulted in a win over some of the biggest names in a few of the biggest movies of the 1970s. *Harry and Tonto*, a small-budget film with moderate box office appeal starring a television actor who had not had much public exposure in several years, seemed to have all the markings of a film that could hope, at best, for a nomination in recognition for Carney's fine work. Before the Oscars, Carney hit the talk show circuit hard, appearing on nearly every national, and even many regional talk shows. His diligence paid off, and his performance won over screen heavyweights in now-classic roles, including Jack Nicholson in *Chinatown*, Dustin Hoffman in *Lenny*, and Al Pacino in *The Godfather Part II*. The fifth nominee for Best Actor that year was Albert Finney for *Murder on the Orient Express*, which earned the highest international grosses of any British film to that time.

Caron, Leslie

Movie: 1953: *Lili* (Best Actress) Academy (Best Foreign Actress) *British*. 1958: *Gigi* (Best Actress, Musical or Comedy) Globe. 1961: *Fanny* (Best Actress, Drama) Globe. 1963: *The L-Shaped Room* (Best Actress) Academy (Best Actress, Drama) *Globe* (Best British Actress) *British*. 2000: *Chocolat* (Best Ensemble) SAG. **Television:** 2007: *Law & Order: Special Victims Unit* (Best Guest Actress in a Drama Series) *Emmy*.

Carradine, David

Movie: 1976: *Bound for Glory* (Best Actor) *Board* (Best Actor, Drama) Globe. 2004: *Kill Bill: Vol. 2* (Best Supporting Actor) Globe. **Television:** 1972–1975 series *Kung Fu* (Best Continued Performance by an Actor in a Leading Role) 1973: Emmy (Best Actor in a Drama Series) 1973: Globe. 1985: *North and South* (Best Supporting Actor in a Series, Miniseries, or TV Movie) Globe.

Carrera, Barbara

Movie: 1975: *The Master Gunfighter* (New Star of the Year — Actress) Globe. 1983: *Never Say Never Again* (Best Supporting Actress) Globe.

Carrey, Jim

Movie: 1994: *The Mask* (Best Actor, Musical or Comedy) Globe. 1997: *Liar Liar* (Best Actor, Musical or Comedy) Globe. 1998: *The Truman Show* (Best Actor, Drama) *Globe*. 1999: *Man on the Moon* (Best Actor, Musical or Comedy) *Globe* (Best Male Actor in a Leading Role) SAG. 2000: *Dr. Seuss' How the Grinch Stole Christmas* (Best Actor, Musical or Comedy) Globe. 2004: *Eternal Sunshine of the Spotless Mind* (Best Actor) British (Best Actor, Drama) Globe.

Carroll, Diahann

Movie: 1974: *Claudine* (Best Actress) Academy (Best Actress, Musical or Comedy) Globe. **Theater:** 1962: *No Strings* (Best Actress, Musical) *Tony*. **Television:** 1963: *Naked City* (Best Single Performance by an Actress in a Leading Role) Emmy. 1968–1971 series *Julia* (Best Continuing Performance by an Actress in a Comedy Series) 1969: Emmy. (Best Actress in a Television Series) 1969: *Globe*. (Best Actress in a Series, Musical or Comedy) 1970: Globe. 1989: *A Different World* (Best Guest Actress in a Comedy Series) Emmy. **Records:** The ageless beauty first found acclaim on stage, but widened her appeal on television where she became the first African-American female to star in her own primetime television show as Julia, a widowed nurse raising a young son and dealing with politics and prejudice in the health field. She lost her one bid for a *Julia* Emmy to Hope Lange in *The Ghost and Mrs. Muir*, but won a Golden Globe for a fine performance that helped break barriers for women, for African-Americans, and for single working mothers.

Carroll, Nancy

Movie: 1930: *The Devil's Holiday* (Best Actress) Academy.

Carroll, Pat

Movie: 2000: *Songcatcher* (Best Supporting Female) Spirit. Theater: 1956: *Catch a Star* (Best Supporting or Featured Actress, Musical) Tony. Television: 1954, 1956–1957 series *Caesar's Hour* (Best Continuing Supporting Performance by an Actress in a Dramatic or Comedy Series) 1956: *Emmy*. 1957: Emmy.

Carson, Jack

Movie: 1942: *The Male Animal* (Best Acting) *Board*.

Cartaxo, Marcelia

Movie: 1986: *A Hora da estrela (The Hour of the Star)* (Best Actress) *Berlin*.

Carter, Jim

Movie: 1998: *Shakespeare in Love* (Best Ensemble) *SAG*.

Cartlidge, Katrin

Movie: 1998: *Claire Dolan* (Best Female Lead) Spirit.

Cascio, Salvatore

Movie: 1990: *Cinema Paradiso* (Best Supporting Actor) *British*.

Cass, Peggy

Movie: 1958: *Auntie Mame* (Best Supporting Actress) Academy, Globe. Theater: 1957: *Auntie Mame* (Best Supporting or Featured Actress, Dramatic) *Tony*.

Cassavetes, John

Movie: 1960: *Shadows* (Best Picture, Producer) *Venice*, British. 1967: *The Dirty Dozen* (Best Supporting Actor) Academy, Globe. 1968: *Faces* (Best Original Story and Screenplay) Academy. 1970: *Husbands* (Best Screenplay) Globe. 1974: *A Woman Under the Influence* (Best Director) Academy, Globe (Best Screenplay) Globe. 1980: *Gloria* (Best Picture, Director) *Venice*. Television: 1980: *Flesh and Blood* (Best Supporting Actor in a Limited Series or Special) Emmy. Tributes: 1960: Nominated for the United Nations Award for *Shadows* from British. 1986: Lifetime Achievement from LA. Highlights: Cassavetes set the standard for independent filmmakers by maintaining creative control of his projects and making masterpieces on a small budget. His efforts so inspired the industry that the Independent Spirit Awards have a category expressly named for him. The John Cassavetes Award is given to the best feature made under $500,000.

Cassel, Jean-Pierre

Movie: 1994: *Prêt-à-Porter (Ready-to-Wear)* (Best Ensemble) *Board*.

Cassel, Seymour

Movie: 1968: *Faces* (Best Supporting Actor) Academy, *Society*.

Cassel, Vincent

Movie: 2004: *Ocean's Twelve* (Best Ensemble) Broadcast.

Casseus, Gabriel

Movie: 1995: *New Jersey Drive* (Best Debut Performance) Spirit.

Cassidy, Lane

Movie: 1993: *Short Cuts* (Best Ensemble) *Venice* (special award).

Castaneda, Pedro

Movie: 2007: *August Evening* (Best Male Lead) Spirit.

Castellano, Richard

Movie: 1970: *Lovers and Other Strangers* (Best Supporting Actor) Academy. Theater: 1969: *Lovers and Other Strangers* (Best Supporting or Featured Actor, Dramatic) Tony.

Castle-Hughes, Keisha

Movie: 2003: *Whale Rider* (Best Actress) Academy (Best Female Actor in a Supporting Role) SAG (Best Young Actor or Actress) *Broadcast*. Records: At 13 years and 309 days old, Castle-Hughes became the youngest star in history to earn a Best Actress Academy Award nomination. The New Zealand actress played Paikea "Pai" Apirana in the 2003 New Zealand/German film, *Whale Rider*. Castle-Hughes found herself in prestigious company, as her fellow nominees were Diane Keaton for *Something's Gotta Give*, Samantha Morton for *In America*, Naomi Watts for *21 Grams*, and that year's winner, Charlize Theron for *Monster*.

Cazale, John

Movie: 1975: *Dog Day Afternoon* (Best Supporting Actor) Globe. Highlights: Before his untimely death in 1978, Cazale starred in five movies and set the record as the only actor to have every film in which he appeared earn a Best Picture Academy Award nomination. His record was extended in 1990 when footage of his earlier *Godfather* work was included in *The Godfather, Part III*, which also earned a Best Picture nod. Of those six motion pictures, half (*The Godfather, The Godfather Part II*, and *The Deer Hunter*) won. In 1974, one of his films (*The Conversation*) lost to another (*The Godfather Part II*).

Ceccarelli, Sandra

Movie: 2001: *Luce dei miei occhi (Light of My Eyes)* (Best Actress) *Venice.*

Cera, Michael

Movie: 2007: *Juno* (Best Young Actor) Broadcast (Best Ensemble) Broadcast; *Superbad* (Best Young Actor) Broadcast.

Chakiris, George

Movie: 1961: *West Side Story* (New Star of the Year — Actor) Globe (Best Supporting Actor) *Academy, Globe.* Highlights: Chakiris appeared as Jets' gang leader, Riff in the London stage version of *West Side Story*, but then won the part of Riff's rival gang leader, Bernardo for the film adaptation.

Chandler, Jeff

Movie: 1950: *Broken Arrow* (Best Supporting Actor) Academy.

Channing, Carol

Movie: 1967: *Thoroughly Modern Millie* (Best Supporting Actress) Academy, *Globe.* Theater: 1956: *The Vamp* (Best Actress, Musical) Tony. 1961: *Show Girl* (Best Actress, Musical) Tony. 1964: *Hello, Dolly!* (Best Actress, Musical) *Tony.* 1974: *Lorelei* (Best Actress, Musical) Tony. Tributes: 1968: Special award from Tony. 1995: Lifetime Achievement Award from Tony.

Channing, Stockard

Movie: 1975: *The Fortune* (New Star of the Year — Actress) Globe. 1993: *Six Degrees of Separation* (Best Actress) Academy (Best Actress, Drama) Globe. 1995: *Smoke* (Best Female Actor in a Supporting Role) SAG. 1996: *The First Wives Club* (Best Ensemble) *Board.* 1998: *The Baby Dance* (Best Supporting Female) Spirit. Theater: 1985: *Joe Egg* (Best Actress, Play) *Tony.* 1986: *The House of Blue Leaves* (Best Actress in a Featured Role, Play) Tony. 1991: *Six Degrees of Separation* (Best Actress, Play) Tony. 1992: *Four Baboons Adoring the Sun* (Best Actress, Play) Tony. 1999: *The Lion in Winter* (Best Actress, Play) Tony. Television: 1988: *Joseph Wambaugh's Echoes in the Darkness* (Best Supporting Actress in a Miniseries or Special) Emmy. 1990: *Perfect Witness* (Best Supporting Actress in a Miniseries or Special) Emmy. 1994: *Avonlea (Road to Avonlea or Tales of Avonlea)* (Best Guest Actress in a Drama Series) Emmy. 1996: *An Unexpected Family* (Best Actress in a Miniseries or Special) Emmy (Best Female Actor in a Television Movie or Miniseries) SAG. 1998: *The Baby Dance* (Best Actress in a Miniseries or TV Movie) Emmy, Globe (Best Female Actor in a Television Movie or Miniseries) SAG. 1999–2006 series *The West Wing* (Best Female Actor in a Drama Series) 2001: SAG. 2003: SAG. (Best Supporting Actress in a Drama Series) 2000: Emmy. 2001: Emmy. 2002: *Emmy.* 2003: Emmy. 2004: Emmy. 2005: Emmy. (Best Ensemble in a Drama Series) 2001: *SAG.* 2002: SAG. 2003: SAG. 2004: SAG. 2000: *The Truth About Jane* (Best Female Actor in a Television Movie or Miniseries) SAG. 2002: *The Matthew Shepard Story* (Best Female Actor in a Television Movie or Miniseries) *SAG* (Best Supporting Actress in a Miniseries or TV Movie) *Emmy.* 2005: *Jack* (Best Performer in a Children's, Youth, or Family Special) *Emmy.* 2005–2006 series *Out of Practice* (Best Actress in a Comedy Series) 2006: Emmy.

Chaplin, Charles

Movie: 1928: *The Circus* (Best Actor) Academy (Best Comedy Direction) Academy.* 1940: *The Great Dictator* (Best Acting) *Board* (Best Actor) Academy, *New York* (Best Picture, Producer) Academy (Best Original Screenplay) Academy. 1947: *Monsieur Verdoux* (Best Original Screenplay) Academy. 1972: *Limelight* (Best Dramatic Score) *Academy.* Tributes: 1928: Honorary Oscar for versatility and genius in writing, acting, directing, and producing *The Circus* from Academy. 1971: Special award for the incalculable effect he has had in making motion pictures the art form of the century from Academy. 1972: Career Golden Lion from Venice; Gala Tribute from the Film Society of Lincoln Center. 1999: Ranked Number 10 on List of 25 Greatest Male Screen Legends of the 20th Century from American Film Institute. Records: 1972 was a good year for Chaplin. Not only was he the first honoree ever to be given a gala tribute by The Film Society of Lincoln Center, but he also set an Academy Award record by winning an Oscar the longest time after completing a motion picture. In 1952, he filmed *Limelight*, which United Artist distributed to only a few cities because of the McCarthy-era political climate through which Chaplin did not fare very well. 20 years later, the film was re-released and premiered in Los Angeles for the first time, finally making it eligible for Oscar consideration. The year after he returned to Hollywood for an emotional tribute and special award from the Academy, Chaplin (along with Raymond Rasch and Larry Russell) received his first and only competitive Oscar, not for Best Director or Best Actor, but for Best Original Dramatic Score.

*After nominating Chaplin for *The Circus*, the Academy withdrew the nominations and instead gave him an honorary Oscar for writing, acting in, directing, and producing the film.

Chaplin, Geraldine

Movie: 1965: *Doctor Zhivago* (New Star of the Year — Actress) Globe. 1975: *Nashville* (Best Supporting Actress) Globe. 1977: *Welcome to L.A.* (Best Supporting Actress) *British*. 1992: *Chaplin* (Best Supporting Actress) Globe. **Highlights:** Chaplin received her third Golden Globe nomination for *Chaplin*, a 1992 biopic of her father in which she had the unique distinction of playing her own grandmother, Hannah Chaplin.

Chapman, Andi

Movie: 1993: *Short Cuts* (Best Ensemble) *Venice* (special award).

Charbonneau, Patti

Movie: 1986: *Desert Hearts* (Best Female Lead) Spirit.

Charisse, Cyd

Movie: 1957: *Silk Stockings* (Best Actress, Musical or Comedy) Globe.

Chase, Chevy

Movie: 1978: *Foul Play* (New Star of the Year — Actor) Globe (Best Actor, Musical or Comedy) Globe. **Television:** 1976–1977 series *NBC's Saturday Night (Saturday Night Live)* (Best Continuing or Single Performance by a Supporting Actor in a Variety or Music Program) 1976: *Emmy*. 1977: Emmy. (Best Writing in a Comedy-Variety or Music Series) 1976: *Emmy*. 1977: Emmy. 1978: *The Paul Simon Special* (Best Writing for a Comedy-Variety or Music Special) *Emmy*.

Chatterton, Ruth

Movie: 1929: *Madame X* (Best Actress) Academy. 1930: *Sarah and Son* (Best Actress) Academy. **Records:** Athough in the earliest years of the Academy the judging panel only considered rather than formally announced nominees, Chatterton became the first star to be in contention for acting Oscars in consecutive years. For the 1928/1929 season, the sec-

ond in the Academy's existence, she was up for *Madame X*, and lost to Mary Pickford in *Coquette*. The following season, she lost her bid for *Sarah and Son* to Norma Shearer in *The Divorcee*. The year of her second nomination, Chatterton tied Gloria Swanson in another Oscar record: the first stars to earn acting nominations in different years. Swanson had been up for Best Actress for *Sadie Thompson* the first year the Academy gave awards, and then was up against Chatterton the third year, this time for *The Trespasser*. Neither Chatterton nor Swanson ever won an Oscar.

Chávez, Julio

Movie: 2007: *El Otro (The Other)* (Best Actor) *Berlin*.

Chaykin, Maury

Movie: 1997: *The Sweet Hereafter* (Best Ensemble) *Board*.

Cheadle, Don

Movie: 1995: *Devil in a Blue Dress* (Best Male Actor in a Supporting Role) SAG (Best Supporting Actor) *Society, LA*. 1997: *Boogie Nights* (Best Ensemble) SAG. 2000: *Traffic* (Best Ensemble) *SAG*. 2001: *Ocean's 11* (Best Ensemble) Broadcast; *Things Behind the Sun* (Best Supporting Male) Spirit. 2004: *Hotel Rwanda* (Best Actor) Academy, Broadcast (Best Actor, Drama) Globe (Best Male Actor in a Leading Role) SAG (Best Ensemble) SAG; *Ocean's Twelve* (Best Ensemble) Broadcast. 2005: *Crash* (Best Male Actor in a Supporting Role) SAG (Best Supporting Actor) British (Best First Feature, Producer) *Spirit* (Best Ensemble) *SAG, Broadcast*. 2007: *Talk to Me* (Best Male Lead) Spirit. **Television:** 1998: *The Rat Pack* (Best Supporting Actor in a Miniseries or TV Movie) Emmy (Best Supporting Actor in a Series, Miniseries, or TV Movie) *Globe*. 1999: *A Lesson Before Dying* (Best Actor in a Miniseries or TV Movie) Emmy. 2002: *Things Behind the Sun* (Best Supporting Actor in a Miniseries or TV Movie) Emmy. 2003: *ER* (Best Guest Actor in a Drama Series) Emmy. **Tributes:** 2007: Joel Siegel Award from Broadcast.

Chekhov, Michael

Movie: 1945: *Spellbound* (Best Supporting Actor) Academy.

Chen, Tina

Movie: 1970: *The Hawaiians* (Best Supporting Actress) Globe. **Television:** 1967: *"The Final War of Olly Winter," CBS Playhouse* (Best Supporting Actress in a Drama) Emmy.

Cher

Movie: 1982: *Come Back to the 5 and Dime, Jimmy Dean, Jimmy Dean* (Best Supporting Actress) Globe. 1983: *Silkwood* (Best Supporting Actress) Academy, *Globe*, British. 1985: *Mask* (Best Actress) Cannes (Best Actress, Drama) Globe. 1987: *Moonstruck* (Best Actress) *Academy*, British (Best Actress, Musical or Comedy) *Globe*. **Television:** 1971–1974 series *The Sonny and Cher Comedy Hour* (Best Actress in a Musical or Comedy Series) 1973: *Globe*. (Best Single Program, Variety or Musical, Star) 1972: Emmy. (Best Variety Series — Musical, Star) 1972: Emmy. (Best Variety Musical Series, Star) 1973: Emmy. 1974: Emmy. 1975–1976 series *Cher* (Best Comedy-Variety or Music Series) 1975: Emmy. 1996: *If These Walls Could Talk* (Best Supporting Actress in a Series, Miniseries, or TV Movie) Globe. 2000: *Cher: Live in Concert from the MGM Grand in Las Vegas* (Best Individual Performance in a Variety or Music Program) Emmy. 2003: *Cher — The Farewell Tour* (Best Variety, Music or Comedy Special; Executive Producer) *Emmy*. **Records:** Cher, whose chart-topping single, "Half-Breed" focused on her part–Cherokee ancestry, is the first Oscar-winning actor identified with her Native American heritage. Playing Italian New Yorker Loretta Castorini in *Moonstruck* brought Cher the Academy Award.

Cherkassov, Nikolai

Movie: 1937: *Deputat Baltiki (Baltic Deputy)* (Best Acting) *Board*.

Chester, Craig

Movie: 1992: *Swoon* (Best Male Lead) Spirit.

Cheung, Maggie

Movie: 1992: *Ruan ling yu (Center Stage)* (Best Actress) *Berlin*. 2004: *Clean* (Best Actress) *Cannes*.

Chevalier, Maurice

Movie: 1929: *The Love Parade* (Best Actor) Academy. 1930: *The Big Pond* (Best Actor) Academy. 1957: *Love in the Afternoon* (Best Actor, Musical or Comedy) Globe. 1958: *Gigi* (Best Actor, Musical or Comedy) Globe. 1961: *Fanny* (Best Actor, Drama) Globe. **Tributes:** 1958: Honorary Oscar statuette for his contributions to the world of entertainment for more than half a century from Academy; Cecil B. DeMille Award from Globe. 1968: Special award from Tony.

Chico

Movie: 1938: *The Adventures of Chico* (Best Acting) *Board*.

Chin, May

Movie: 1993: *The Wedding Banquet* (Best Female Lead) Spirit.

Chiu-Wai, Tony Leung

Movie: 2000: *In the Mood for Love* (Best Actor) *Cannes*.

Christensen, Erika

Movie: 2000: *Traffic* (Best Ensemble) *SAG*.

Christensen, Hayden

Movie: 2001: *Life as a House* (Breakthrough Performance — Male) *Board* (Best Male Actor in a Supporting Role) SAG (Best Supporting Actor) Globe.

Christie, Julie

Movie: 1963: *Billy Liar* (Best British Actress) British. 1965: *Darling* (Best Actress) *Academy*, *New York*, *Board* (multiple win), (Best Actress, Drama) Globe (Best British Actress) *British*; *Doctor Zhivago* (Best Actress) *Board* (multiple win), (Best British Actress) British (multiple nomination); *Fahrenheit 451* (Best British Actress) British (multiple nomination). 1971: *The Go-Between* (Best Actress) British; *McCabe and Mrs. Miller* (Best Actress) Academy. 1973: *Don't Look Now* (Best Actress) British. 1975: *Shampoo* (Best Actress, Musical or Comedy) Globe. 1997: *Afterglow* (Best Actress) Academy, *New York*, *Society* (Best Female Lead) *Spirit*. 2004: *Finding Neverland* (Best Supporting Actress) British (Best Ensemble) SAG. 2007: *Away from Her* (Best Actress) Academy, *New York*, *Board*, British, *Society*, *Broadcast* (Best Actress, Drama) *Globe* (Best Female Actor in a Leading Role) *SAG*.

Christopher, Dennis

Movie: 1979: *Breaking Away* (New Star of the Year — Actor) Globe (Most Promising Newcomer) *British*.

Chtchelkanova, Ekaterina

Movie: 2002: *Chicago* (Best Ensemble) *SAG, Broadcast*.

Chung, David

Movie: 1993: *The Ballad of Little Jo* (Best Supporting Male) Spirit.

Church, Thomas Haden

Movie: 2004: *Sideways* (Best Male Actor in a Supporting Role) SAG (Best Supporting Actor) Academy, *Board*, Globe, *Society, LA, Broadcast* (Best Supporting Male) *Spirit* (Best Ensemble) *SAG, Broadcast*. **Television:** 2006: ***Broken Trail*** (Best Male Actor in a Television Movie or Miniseries) SAG (Best Supporting Actor in a Miniseries or TV Movie) *Emmy* (Best Supporting Actor in a Series, Miniseries, or TV Movie) Globe. **Highlights:** Church auditioned for a supporting role in Thomas Payne's ***About Schmidt***, but when Payne cast Dermot Mulroney instead, he promised Church a part in his next film, which turned out to be ***Sideways***. Church bulldozed through the part of self-indulgent has-been actor Jack with such relish, he instantly found himself the recipient of nearly every critical award presented that year. However, ***Sideways*** lost momentum toward the end of the awards season and was usurped by ***Million Dollar Baby***, which came from seemingly nowhere to be the odds on favorite come Oscar time. At the Golden Globes, Church lost to Clive Owen for ***Closer***. Although the ***Sideways*** cast ended up with the coveted Ensemble award at the SAGs, the Academy Award for Best Supporting Actor that year went to Morgan Freeman as part of ***Million Dollar Baby***'s triumphant night.

Churikova (Tschurikova), Inna

Movie: 1984: ***Woenno-polewoj roman (A Front Romance)*** (Best Actress) *Berlin*.

Cilento, Diane

Movie: 1963: ***Tom Jones*** (Best Supporting Actress) Academy. **Theater:** 1956: ***Tiger at the Gates*** (Best Supporting or Featured Actress, Dramatic) Tony.

Citi, Franco

Movie: 1962: ***Accattone*** (Best Foreign Actor) British.

Citran, Roberto

Movie: 1994: ***Il Toro*** (Best Supporting Actor) *Venice*.

Clark, Candy

Movie: 1973: ***American Graffiti*** (Best Supporting Actress) Academy.

Clark, Petula

Movie: 1968: ***Finian's Rainbow*** (Best Actress, Musical or Comedy) Globe.

Clarkson, Patricia

Movie: 1998: ***High Art*** (Best Supporting Female) Spirit. 1999: ***The Green Mile*** (Best Ensemble) SAG. 2002: ***Far from Heaven*** (Best Supporting Actress) *New York, Society*. 2003: ***Pieces of April*** (Best Female

Actor in a Supporting Role) SAG (Best Supporting Actress) Academy, *Board* (multiple win), Globe, *Society* (multiple win), Broadcast (Best Supporting Female) Spirit; ***The Station Agent*** (Best Female Actor in a Leading Role) SAG (Best Supporting Actress) *Board* (multiple win), *Society* (multiple win), (Best Ensemble) SAG. 2005: ***Good Night, and Good Luck*** (Best Ensemble) SAG, Broadcast. **Television:** 2002–2006: ***Six Feet Under*** (Best Guest Actress in a Drama Series) 2002: *Emmy*. 2006: *Emmy*.

Clayburgh, Jill

Movie: 1978: ***An Unmarried Woman*** (Best Actress) Academy, *Cannes*, British (Best Actress, Drama) Globe. 1979: ***Luna*** (Best Actress, Drama) Globe; ***Starting Over*** (Best Actress) Academy (Best Actress, Musical or Comedy) Globe. 1981: ***First Monday in October*** (Best Actress, Musical or Comedy) Globe. **Television:** 1975: *"Hustling," Special World Premiere ABC Saturday Night* (Best Actress in a Special Program) Emmy. 2005: ***Nip/Tuck*** (Best Guest Actress in a Drama Series) Emmy.

Cleese, John

Movie: 1988: ***A Fish Called Wanda*** (Best Actor) British (Best Actor, Musical or Comedy) Globe (Best Original Screenplay) Academy, British. **Television:** 1987: ***Cheers*** (Best Guest Actor in a Comedy Series) *Emmy*. 1998: ***3rd Rock from the Sun*** (Best Guest Actor in a Comedy Series) Emmy. 2002: ***The Human Face with John Cleese*** (Best Nonfiction Information Special, Writer and Host) Emmy. 2004: ***Will & Grace*** (Best Guest Actor in a Comedy Series) Emmy.

Clift (George), Jeanette

Movie: 1975: ***The Hiding Place*** (New Star of the Year — Actress) Globe (Most Promising Newcomer) British.

Clift, Montgomery

Movie: 1948: ***The Search*** (Best Actor) Academy. 1951: ***A Place in the Sun*** (Best Actor) Academy. 1953: ***From Here to Eternity*** (Best Actor) Academy. 1961: ***Judgment at Nuremberg*** (Best Supporting Actor) Academy, Globe (Best Foreign Actor) British.

Clooney, George

Movie: 2000: ***O Brother, Where Art Thou?*** (Best Actor, Musical or Comedy) *Globe*. 2001: ***Ocean's 11*** (Best Ensemble) Broadcast. 2004: ***Ocean's Twelve*** (Best Ensemble) Broadcast. 2005: ***Good Night, and Good Luck*** (Best Supporting Actor) British (Best Director) Academy, Globe, British, Spirit, Broadcast (Best Picture, Producer) *Venice* (special award),

Board, Broadcast (Best Original Screenplay) Oscar, Globe, British (Best Screenplay) *Venice* (Best Writer) Broadcast (Best Ensemble) SAG, Broadcast; *Syriana* (Best Male Actor in a Supporting Role) SAG (Best Supporting Actor) *Academy, Globe*, British, Broadcast (Best Ensemble) Broadcast. 2007: *Michael Clayton* (Best Actor) Academy, *Board*, British, Broadcast (Best Actor, Drama) Globe (Best Male Actor in a Leading Role) SAG. **Television:** 1995–1998 series *ER* (Best Actor in a Drama Series) 1995: Emmy, Globe. 1996: Emmy, Globe. 1997: Globe. (Best Male Actor in a Drama Series) 1995: SAG. 1996: SAG. (Best Ensemble in a Drama Series) 1995: *SAG*. 1996: *SAG*. 1997: *SAG*. 1998: *SAG*. **Tributes:** 2002: Special Filmmaking Achievement Award for *Confessions of a Dangerous Mind* from Board. **Records:** Thanks to his directing and screenwriting contributions to *Good Night, and Good Luck* and his acting in *Syriana*, Clooney became the first person to earn three Academy Award nominations between two films in the same year. He also became the first person to get a Best Director nomination for one film in the same year he received an acting nomination for another. He outdid even that record at the British Academy of Film and Television Awards in 2005 when he scored a record-setting four nominations in three different categories for his work in both films. The British Academy nominated him for Best Supporting Actor for *Syriana* and for Best Supporting Actor, Best Director, and Best Original Screenwriter for *Good Night, and Good Luck*. He went home empty-handed from the BAFTAs, but took home the Best Supporting Actor Academy Award for *Syriana*.

Close, Glenn

Movie: 1982: *The World According to Garp* (Best Supporting Actress) Academy, *Board*, LA. 1983: *The Big Chill* (Best Supporting Actress) Academy. 1984: *The Natural* (Best Supporting Actress) Academy. 1985: *Maxie* (Best Actress, Musical or Comedy) Globe. 1987: *Fatal Attraction* (Best Actress) Academy (Best Actress, Drama) Globe. 1988: *Dangerous Liaisons* (Best Actress) Academy, British. 1996: *101 Dalmatians* (Best Actress, Musical or Comedy) Globe. **Theater:** 1980: *Barnum* (Best Actress in a Featured Role, Musical) Tony. 1984: *The Real Thing* (Best Actress, Play) *Tony*. 1992: *Death and the Maiden* (Best Actress, Play) *Tony*. 1995: *Sunset Boulevard* (Best Actress, Musical) *Tony*. **Television:** 1984: *"Something About Amelia," An ABC Theatre Presentation* (Best Actress in a Limited Series or Special) Emmy (Best Actress in a Miniseries or TV Movie) Globe. 1991: *"Sarah, Plain and Tall," Hallmark Hall of Fame* (Best Actress in a Miniseries or

Special) Emmy, Globe (Best Comedy or Drama Special or Miniseries, Executive Producer) Emmy. 1993: *"Skylark," Hallmark Hall of Fame* (Best Actress in a Miniseries or Special) Emmy. 1995: *Serving in Silence: The Margarethe Cammermeyer Story* (Best Actress in a Miniseries or TV Movie) *Emmy*, Globe (Best Female Actor in a Television Movie or Miniseries) SAG (Best Made for TV Movie, Executive Producer) Emmy. 1997: *In the Gloaming* (Best Actress in a Miniseries or Special) Emmy (Best Female Actor in a Television Movie or Miniseries) SAG. 2002: *Will & Grace* (Best Guest Actress in a Comedy Series) Emmy. 2004: *The Lion in Winter* (Best Actress in a Miniseries or TV Movie) Emmy, *Globe* (Best Female Actor in a Television Movie or Miniseries) *SAG*. 2005–2006 series *The Shield* (Best Actress in a Drama Series) 2005: Emmy, Globe. 2007–present series *Damages* (Best Actress in a Drama Series) 2007: *Globe*. (Best Female Actor in a Drama Series) 2007: SAG.

Clunes, Martin

Movie: 1998: *Shakespeare in Love* (Best Ensemble) *SAG*.

Cobb, Lee J.

Movie: 1954: *On the Waterfront* (Best Supporting Actor) Academy. 1957: *12 Angry Men* (Best Supporting Actor) Globe. 1958: *The Brothers Karamazov* (Best Supporting Actor) Academy. 1963: *Come Blow Your Horn* (Best Supporting Actor) Globe. **Television:** 1958: *"No Deadly Medicine," Studio One* (Best Single Performance by a Leading or Supporting Actor) Emmy. 1960: *"Project Immortality," Playhouse 90* (Best Single Performance by a Leading or Supporting Actor) Emmy. 1967: *Death of a Salesman* (Best Single Performance by an Actor in a Leading Role in a Drama) Emmy.

Cobo, Yohana

Movie: 2006: *Volver* (Best Actress) *Cannes* (win shared with costars).

Coburn, Charles

Movie: 1941: *The Devil and Miss Jones* (Best Supporting Actor) Academy. 1942: *H. M. Pulham, Esq.* (Best Acting) *Board* (multiple win); *In This Our Life* (Best Acting) *Board* (multiple win); *Kings Row* (Best Acting) *Board* (multiple win). 1943: *The More the Merrier* (Best Supporting Actor) *Academy*. 1946: *The Green Years* (Best Supporting Actor) Academy. **Records:** Coburn became the first Best Supporting Actor Oscar winner to receive a full-sized Oscar statuette for his win. From 1936 to 1942, supporting actor and actress winners received a plaque with a miniature statuette attached.

Coburn, James

Movie: 1998: *Affliction* (Best Male Actor in a Supporting Role) SAG (Best Supporting Actor) *Academy* (Best Supporting Male) Spirit. Television: 2002: *The Mists of Avalon* (Best Miniseries, Executive Producer) Emmy.

Coco, James

Movie: 1972: *Man of La Mancha* (Best Supporting Actor) Globe. 1981: *Only When I Laugh* (Best Supporting Actor) Academy, Globe. Theater: 1970: *Last of the Red Hot Lovers* (Best Actor, Dramatic) Tony. Television: 1982–1983 series *St. Elsewhere* (Best Supporting Actor in a Drama Series) 1983: *Emmy.*

Coe, Barry

Movie: 1959: *A Private's Affair* (New Star of the Year — Actor) *Globe.*

Coffey, Scott

Movie: 1989: *Shag* (Best Supporting Male) Spirit.

Colbert, Claudette

Movie: 1934: *It Happened One Night* (Best Actress) *Academy.* 1935: *Private Worlds* (Best Actress) Academy. 1944: *Since You Went Away* (Best Actress) Academy. Theater: 1959: *The Marriage-Go-Round* (Best Actress, Dramatic) Tony. Television: 1987: *The Two Mrs. Grenvilles* (Best Supporting Actress in a Miniseries or Special) Emmy (Best Supporting Actress in a Series, Miniseries, or TV Movie) *Globe.* Tributes: 1984: Gala Tribute from Film Society of Lincoln Center. 1989: Honor from Kennedy Center for the Performing Arts. 1999: Ranked Number 12 on List of 25 Greatest Female Screen Legends of the 20th Century from American Film Institute. **Records:** Colbert was the first French-born actress to win an Academy Award. 62 years after her win, Juliette Binoche became the second when she was named Best Supporting Actress for *The English Patient.* Both women, as well as 2007 Best Actress winner Marion Cotillard, were born in Paris. The most notable French actress to win an Oscar, Simone Signoret (Best Actress for *Room at the Top* in 1959) was born in Wiesbaden, Germany. **Highlights:** It's hard to imagine, since she starred in three of the Best Picture nominated films of 1934 (*Cleopatra, Imitation of Life* and *It Happened One Night*) that Colbert could be unaware of the still relatively new Academy Awards, but according to Oscar lore, that's why, instead of attending the awards ceremony, Colbert was boarding a train when her name was announced as Best Actress for *It Happened One Night.* Friends rushed to the train station, yanked her off the Chief and hurried her to the awards ceremony with the help of a police escort. The teary and flustered Colbert had to ask what the award was on her way to the ceremony and then left before her film made the first sweep of all five major awards (Picture, Actor, Actress, Director and Screenplay) in Academy history. She had to race back to the station because the train she'd boarded earlier was being held for her. Originally, Colbert turned down the part of runaway heiress Ellie Andrews in *It Happened One Night*, then only took the job when Columbia promised her $50,000 for 30 days of filming. It became the defining role of her career.

Coleman, Charlotte

Movie: 1994: *Four Weddings and a Funeral* (Best Supporting Actress) British.

Collette, Toni

Movie: 1995: *Muriel's Wedding* (Best Actress, Musical or Comedy) Globe. 1999: *The Sixth Sense* (Best Supporting Actress) Academy. 2002: *About a Boy* (Best Supporting Actress) British; *The Hours* (Best Ensemble) SAG, Broadcast. 2006: *Little Miss Sunshine* (Best Actress, Musical or Comedy) Globe (Best Supporting Actress) British (Best Ensemble) *SAG, Broadcast.* Theater: 2000: *The Wild Party* (Best Actress, Musical) Tony. Television: 2006: *Tsunami, the Aftermath* (Best Supporting Actress in a Miniseries or TV Movie) Emmy (Best Supporting Actress in a Series, Miniseries, or TV Movie) Globe.

Collinge, Patricia

Movie: 1941: *The Little Foxes* (Best Acting) *Board* (Best Supporting Actress) Academy.

Collins, Clifton, Jr.

Movie: 2000: *Traffic* (Best Ensemble) *SAG.* 2005: *Capote* (Best Ensemble) SAG. Television: 2006: *Thief* (Best Supporting Actor in a Miniseries or TV Movie) Emmy.

Collins, Pauline

Movie: 1989: *Shirley Valentine* (Best Actress) Academy, *British* (Best Actress, Musical or Comedy) Globe. Theater: 1989: *Shirley Valentine* (Best Actress, Play) *Tony.*

Collins, Stephen

Movie: 1996: *The First Wives Club* (Best Ensemble) *Board.* Television: 1987: *The Two Mrs. Grenvilles* (Best Supporting Actor in a Miniseries or Special) Emmy.

Colman, Ronald

Movie: 1929: *Bulldog Drummond* (Best Actor) Academy; *Condemned* (Best Actor) Academy. 1942: *Random Harvest* (Best Actor) Academy. 1947: *A Double Life* (Best Actor) *Academy, Globe.*

Coltrane, Robbie

Movie: 2001: *Harry Potter and the Philosopher's Stone* (Best Supporting Actor) British. 2004: *Ocean's Twelve* (Best Ensemble) Broadcast.

Compson, Betty

Movie: 1928: *The Barker* (Best Actress) Academy.

Connelly, Jennifer

Movie: 2000: *Requiem for a Dream* (Best Supporting Female) Spirit. 2001: *A Beautiful Mind* (Best Female Actor in a Leading Role) SAG (Best Supporting Actress) *Academy, Globe, British, Broadcast* (Best Ensemble) SAG. 2003: *House of Sand and Fog* (Best Actress) Broadcast.

Connery, Sean

Movie: 1986: *The Name of the Rose* (Best Actor) *British.* 1987: *The Untouchables* (Best Supporting Actor) *Academy, Board, Globe,* British. 1989: *Indiana Jones and the Last Crusade* (Best Supporting Actor) Globe, British. 1990: *The Hunt for Red October* (Best Actor) British. Theater: 1998: *Art* (Best Play, Producer) *Tony.* Tributes: 1965, 1968, 1971: Henrietta Award for World Film Favorite from Globe. 1993: Honorary Award from Board. 1995: Cecil B. DeMille Award from Globe. 1997: Gala Tribute from Film Society of Lincoln Center. 1999: Honor from Kennedy Center for the Performing Arts. 2006: Life Achievement Award from American Film Institute. Records: With his Best Supporting Actor win for 1987's *The Untouchables*, Connery became the first actor to receive an Academy Award for a film based on a television series.

Connolly, Billy

Movie: 1997: *Mrs. Brown* (Best Actor) British (Best Male Actor in a Supporting Role) SAG. Tributes: 2003: Lifetime Achievement from British.

Considine, Paddy

Movie: 2003: *In America* (Best Ensemble) SAG.

Considine, Tim

Movie: 1954: *Executive Suite* (Best Ensemble) *Venice* (special award).

Constantine, Michael

Movie: 2002: *My Big Fat Greek Wedding* (Best Ensemble) SAG, Broadcast. Television: 1969–1974 series *Room 222* (Best Supporting Actor in a Musical or Comedy Program) 1970: *Emmy*, Globe. 1971: Emmy. 1976–1977 series *Sirota's Court* (Best Actor in a Musical or Comedy Program) 1976: Globe.

Conti, Tom

Movie: 1983: *Merry Christmas, Mr. Lawrence* (Best Actor) *Board* (multiple win); *Reuben, Reuben* (Best Actor) Academy, *Board* (multiple win), (Best Actor, Drama) Globe. Theater: 1979: *Whose Life Is It Anyway?* (Best Actor, Play) *Tony.* Television: 1986: *Nazi Hunter: The Beate Klarsfeld Story* (Best Supporting Actor in a Series, Miniseries, or TV Movie) Globe.

Cooper, Chris

Movie: 1996: *Lone Star* (Best Male Lead) Spirit. 1999: *American Beauty* (Best Male Actor in a Supporting Role) SAG (Best Ensemble) *SAG.* 2002: *Adaptation* (Best Male Actor in a Supporting Role) SAG (Best Supporting Actor) *Academy, Board, Globe,* British, *LA, Broadcast* (Best Ensemble) SAG. 2003: *Seabiscuit* (Best Male Actor in a Supporting Role) SAG (Best Ensemble) SAG. 2005: *Capote* (Best Ensemble) SAG; *Syriana* (Best Ensemble) Broadcast. Television: 2003: *My House in Umbria* (Best Supporting Actor in a Miniseries or TV Movie) Emmy.

Cooper, Gary

Movie: 1936: *Mr. Deeds Goes to Town* (Best Actor) Academy. 1941: *Sergeant York* (Best Acting) *Board* (Best Actor) *Academy, New York.* 1942: *The Pride of the Yankees* (Best Actor) Academy. 1943: *For Whom the Bell Tolls* (Best Actor) Academy. 1952: *High Noon* (Best Actor) *Academy* (Best Actor, Drama) *Globe.* 1956: *Friendly Persuasion* (Best Actor, Drama) Globe. Tributes: 1960: Honorary Oscar statuette for his many memorable screen performances and the international recognition he, as an individual, has gained for the motion picture industry from Academy. 1999: Ranked Number 11 on List of 25 Greatest Male Screen Legends of the 20th Century from American Film Institute. Highlights: Cooper's unassuming World War I hero, Sergeant York, earned him his first Oscar and proved a powerful icon for Allied soldiers and civilians during World War II. "Coop" brought that same low key heroism to aging marshal Will Kane in *High Noon*, making him only the third actor (after Spencer Tracy and Fredric March) to win two Best Actor Academy Awards. Just after learning that Cooper had been diagnosed with incurable cancer, his good friend

James Stewart tearfully accepted the 1960 honorary Oscar on his behalf. One month later, Cooper died.

Cooper, Gladys

Movie: 1942: *Now, Voyager* (Best Supporting Actress) Academy. 1943: *The Song of Bernadette* (Best Supporting Actress) Academy. 1964: *My Fair Lady* (Best Supporting Actress) Academy. **Theater:** 1956: *The Chalk Garden* (Best Actress, Dramatic) Tony. 1962: *A Passage to India* (Best Actress, Dramatic) Tony. **Television:** 1965: *The Rogues* (Best Individual Achievement in Entertainment, Actress) Emmy.

Cooper, Jackie

Movie: 1931: *Skippy* (Best Actor) Academy. **Television:** 1959–1962 series *Hennesey* (Best Actor in a Series) 1961: Emmy. 1962: Emmy. 1974: *M*A*S*H* (Best Director of a Comedy Series) *Emmy*. 1979: *The White Shadow* (Best Director of a Drama Series) *Emmy*. **Records:** At age ten Cooper became the first adolescent to receive an Oscar nomination. He lost Best Actor for *Skippy* to Lionel Barrymore in *A Free Soul*. Cooper's record as the youngest Best Actor nominee still stands. The youngest Best Actress nominee was 13-year-old Keisha Castle-Hughes for 2003's *Whale Rider*. **Highlights:** Though he lost his only Academy Award bid for Best Actor, Cooper made a memorable impression at that year's ceremony by falling asleep while leaning against Marie Dressler, who had to ease Cooper off her shoulder when her name was announced as Best Actress for her performance in *Min and Bill*. Cooper actually didn't fade too early that evening. At the November 10, 1931, ceremony, the acting awards weren't presented until after midnight.

Corbett, John

Movie: 2002: *My Big Fat Greek Wedding* (Best Ensemble) SAG, Broadcast. **Television:** 1990–1995 series *Northern Exposure* (Best Supporting Actor in a Drama Series) 1992: Emmy. (Best Supporting Actor in a Series, Miniseries, or TV Movie) 1992: Globe. 2001–2002 series *Sex and the City* (Best Supporting Actor in a Series, Miniseries, or TV Movie) 2001: Globe.

Corby, Ellen

Movie: 1948: *I Remember Mama* (Best Supporting Actress) Academy, *Globe*. **Television:** 1972–1979 series *The Waltons* (Best Actress in a Drama Series) 1972: Globe. (Best Supporting Actress in a Drama Series) 1973: *Emmy, Globe*. 1974: Emmy, Globe. 1975: *Emmy*. 1976: *Emmy*, Globe. 1977: Emmy. 1978: Emmy.

Corrigan, Kevin

Movie: 1996: *Walking and Talking* (Best Supporting Male) Spirit. 2007: *American Gangster* (Best Ensemble) SAG.

Cort, Bud

Movie: 1971: *Harold and Maude* (Most Promising Newcomer) British (Best Actor, Musical or Comedy) Globe. 2004: *The Life Aquatic with Steve Zissou* (Best Ensemble) Broadcast.

Cortese, Valentina

Movie: 1973: *Nuit américaine (Day for Night)* (Best Supporting Actress) Academy, *New York*, Globe, *British, Society*.

Costa, Mary

Movie: 1972: *The Great Waltz* (New Star of the Year — Actress) Globe.

Costanza, Anthony Roth

Movie: 1998: *A Soldier's Daughter Never Cries* (Best Debut Performance) Spirit.

Costello, Deirdre

Movie: 1997: *The Full Monty* (Best Ensemble) *SAG*.

Costner, Kevin

Movie: 1990: *Dances with Wolves* (Best Actor) Academy, British (Best Actor, Drama) Globe (Best Director) *Academy, Board, Globe,* British (Best Picture, Producer) *Academy, Board,* British (Best Picture, Drama; Producer) *Globe*. 1991: *JFK* (Best Actor, Drama) Globe. 1996: *Tin Cup* (Best Actor, Musical or Comedy) Globe. 2005: *The Upside of Anger* (Best Supporting Actor) Broadcast. **Tributes:** 1990: Outstanding Single Achievement for *Dances with Wolves* from Berlin.

Cotillard, Marion

Movie: 2007: *La Vie en Rose* (Best Actress) *Academy, Venice, British, LA,* Broadcast (Best Actress, Musical or Comedy) *Globe* (Best Female Actor in a Leading Role) SAG. **Records:** With her Best Actress Oscar win for *La Vie en Rose*, Cotillard became the first actor to win a competitive Academy Award for a performance entirely in French. Past acting winners from foreign language films were Italian — Sophia Loren in *Two Women* and Roberto Benigni for *Life Is Beautiful*. Robert De Niro and Benicio Del Toro won Best Supporting Actor Oscars for speaking foreign languages in American films — De Niro spoke Italian in *The Godfather Part II* and Del Toro spoke Spanish in *Traffic*.

Cotten, Joseph

Movie: 1949: *Portrait of Jenny* (Best Actor) *Venice.*

Cotton, Curtis, III

Movie: 2000: *George Washington* (Best Debut Performance) Spirit (nomination shared with costars).

Coulouris, George

Movie: 1941: *Citizen Kane* (Best Acting) *Board.*

Courtenay, Tom

Movie: 1962: *The Loneliness of the Long Distance Runner* (Most Promising Newcomer) *British.* 1963: *Billy Liar* (Best British Actor) British. 1964: *King and Country* (Best Actor) *Venice* (Best British Actor) British. 1965: *Doctor Zhivago* (Best Supporting Actor) Academy. 1983: *The Dresser* (Best Actor) Academy, British (Best Actor, Drama) *Globe.* 2001: *Last Orders* (Best Ensemble) *Board.* 2002: *Nicholas Nickleby* (Best Ensemble) *Board.* **Theater:** 1977: *Otherwise Engaged* (Best Actor, Play) Tony. 1982: *The Dresser* (Best Actor, Play) Tony.

Cox, Brian

Movie: 2001: *L.I.E.* (Best Male Lead) Spirit. 2002: *Adaptation* (Best Ensemble) SAG. **Television:** 2000: *Nuremberg* (Best Actor in a Miniseries or TV Movie) Globe (Best Male Actor in a Television Movie or Miniseries) SAG (Best Supporting Actor in a Miniseries or TV Movie) *Emmy.* 2002: *Frasier* (Best Guest Actor in a Comedy Series) Emmy. 2004–2006 series *Deadwood* (Best Ensemble in a Drama Series) 2006: SAG.

Craig, Daniel

Movie: 2006: *Casino Royale* (Best Actor) British; *Infamous* (Best Supporting Male) Spirit. **Records:** In 1969, George Lazenby was nominated for a New Star of the Year Golden Globe for playing James Bond in *On Her Majesty's Secret Service*, and in the 1970s both Sean Connery and Roger Moore earned the Golden Globe's Henrietta Awards for World Film Favorite for their Bond movies' box office successes. But when the 2006 British awards were announced, Craig became the first star to earn a Best Actor nomination for playing Bond. He, like nearly every other actor nominated for any Best Actor award that year, lost to Forest Whitaker in *The Last King of Scotland.*

Craig, Michael

Movie: 1958: *Sea of Sand* (Best British Actor) British. 1960: *The Angry Silence* (Best Original Story and Screenplay) Academy.

Craig, Wendy

Movie: 1963: *The Servant* (Most Promising Newcomer) British.

Crain, Jeanne

Movie: 1949: *Pinky* (Best Actress) Academy.

Craney, Heather

Movie: 2004: *Vera Drake* (Best Supporting Actress) British.

Crawford, Broderick

Movie: 1949: *All the King's Men* (Best Actor) *Academy, New York, Globe.*

Crawford, Joan

Movie: 1945: *Mildred Pierce* (Best Actress) *Academy, Board.* 1947: *Possessed* (Best Actress) Academy. 1952: *Sudden Fear* (Best Actress) Academy (Best Actress, Drama) Globe. 1962: *What Ever Happened to Baby Jane?* (Best Foreign Actress) British. **Tributes:** 1954: Cecil B. DeMille Award nomination from Globe. 1969: Cecil B. DeMille Award from Globe. 1999: Ranked Number 10 on List of 25 Greatest Female Screen Legends of the 20th Century from American Film Institute. **Records:** Crawford's career was going through a dry spell until she earned a surprise Best Actress win from the National Board of Review for *Mildred Pierce.* Seeing the potential to make it a comeback performance, Crawford became one of the first stars to use her own publicist to generate Oscar buzz and also to campaign vigorously herself to win more awards. The New York Film Critics didn't bite, picking Ingrid Bergman over Crawford for her back-to-back hits, *The Bells of St. Mary's* and *Spellbound.* But the Academy did, and going into Oscar night, Crawford was considered one of the front-runners to win. Overwrought by the stress of competing, Crawford stayed home, claiming to have the flu, and listened to the ceremony broadcast over the radio. *Pierce* director, Michael Curtiz came to Crawford's bedside to deliver her Oscar. Never one to bypass publicity, Crawford made sure photographers were present, and the moment became front page news the next day.

Crawford, Michael

Movie: 1965: *The Knack ... and How to Get It* (Most Promising Newcomer) British. **Theater:** 1988: *The Phantom of the Opera* (Best Actor, Musical) *Tony.* **Television:** 1998: *Michael Crawford in Concert* (Best Performance in a Variety or Music Program) Emmy.

Crenna, Richard

Movie: 1984: *The Flamingo Kid* (Best Supporting Actor) Globe. Television: 1957–1962 series *The Real McCoys* (Best Supporting Actor — Continuing Performance — in a Comedy Series) 1959: Emmy. 1964–1965 series *Slattery's People* (Best Actor in a Series) 1964: Globe. (Best Individual Achievement in Entertainment) 1965: Emmy. (Best Continued Performance by an Actor in a Leading Role in a Dramatic Series) 1966: Emmy. 1985: *"The Rape of Richard Beck,"* An ABC Theatre Presentation (Best Actor in a Limited Series or Special) *Emmy*, Globe.

Cribbins, Bernard

Movie: 1970: *The Railway Children* (Best Supporting Actor) British.

Crisp, Donald

Movie: 1941: *How Green Was My Valley* (Best Acting) *Board* (Best Supporting Actor) *Academy.*

Cristal, Linda

Movie: 1958: *The Perfect Furlough* (New Star of the Year — Actress) *Globe.* Television: 1967–1971 series *The High Chaparral* (Best Actress in a Drama Series) 1969: *Globe.* 1970: Globe. (Best Continued Performance by an Actress in a Leading Role in a Dramatic Series) 1971: Emmy. (Best Continued Performance by an Actress in a Supporting Role in a Dramatic Series) 1968: Emmy.

Cromwell, James

Movie: 1995: *Babe* (Best Supporting Actor) Academy. 1997: *L.A. Confidential* (Best Ensemble) SAG. 1999: *The Green Mile* (Best Ensemble) SAG. Television: 2000: *RKO 281* (Best Supporting Actor in a Miniseries or TV Movie) Emmy. 2001: *ER* (Best Guest Actor in a Drama Series) Emmy. 2003–2005 series *Six Feet Under* (Best Guest Actor in a Drama Series) 2003: Emmy. (Best Ensemble in a Drama Series) 2004: SAG. 2005: SAG.

Cronyn, Hume

Movie: 1944: *The Seventh Cross* (Best Supporting Actor) Academy. 1996: *Marvin's Room* (Best Ensemble) SAG. Theater: 1961: *Big Fish, Little Fish* (Best Actor, Dramatic) Tony. 1964: *Hamlet* (Best Supporting or Featured Actor, Dramatic) *Tony.* 1965: *Slow Dance on the Killing Ground* (Best Producer, Dramatic) Tony. 1967: *A Delicate Balance* (Best Actor, Dramatic) Tony. 1978: *The Gin Game* (Best Actor, Play) Tony (Best Play, Producer) Tony. 1986: *The Petition* (Best Actor, Play) Tony. Television: 1984:

"The Dollmaker," An ABC Theatre Presentation (Best Writing in a Limited Series or Special) Emmy. 1988: *Foxfire* (Best Actor in a Miniseries or Special) Emmy. 1990: *Age-Old Friends* (Best Actor in a Miniseries or Special) *Emmy.* 1992: *Christmas on Division Street* (Best Actor in a Miniseries or Special) Emmy; *Neil Simon's Broadway Bound* (Best Supporting Actor in a Miniseries or Special) *Emmy* (Best Supporting Actor in a Series, Miniseries, or TV Movie) Globe. 1994: *"To Dance with the White Dog,"* Hallmark Hall of Fame (Best Actor in a Miniseries or Special) *Emmy.* 1997: *12 Angry Men* (Best Supporting Actor in a Miniseries or TV Movie) Emmy. Tributes: 1986: Honor from Kennedy Center for the Performing Arts (honor shared with spouse, Jessica Tandy). 1994: Lifetime Achievement Award from Tony. Records: When Cronyn won his Emmy for *Age-Old Friends* in 1991, he and wife Jessica Tandy became the only married couple to each win acting Tonys and Emmys. Cronyn won his Tony in 1964, followed by Tandy and her first Tony in 1978 (for *The Gin Game*) and her Emmy in 1988 (for *Foxfire*).

Crosbie, Annette

Movie: 1976: *The Slipper and the Rose* (Best Supporting Actress) British.

Crosby, Bing

Movie: 1941: *Birth of the Blues* (Best Acting) *Board* (multiple win); *The Road to Zanzibar* (Best Acting) *Board* (multiple win). 1944: *Going My Way* (Best Acting) *Board* (Best Actor) *Academy.* 1945: *The Bells of St. Mary's* (Best Actor) Academy. 1951: *Here Comes the Groom* (Best Actor, Musical or Comedy) Globe. 1954: *The Country Girl* (Best Actor) Academy, *Board.* Tributes: 1959: Cecil B. DeMille Award from Globe. Records: Crosby was the first star to receive Oscar nominations for playing the same character in two different films. He was nominated and won for his portrayal of amiable Father O'Malley in *Going My Way* in 1944, and then received a nomination the following year when he reprised the character in the sequel, *The Bells of St. Mary's*. In 1945, he lost to Ray Milland, whose performance in *The Lost Weekend* won Milland every Best Actor award given that year.

Cross, David

Movie: 2007: *I'm Not There* (Best Ensemble) *Spirit* (special award).

Cross, Flora

Movie: 2005: *Bee Season* (Best Young Actress) Broadcast.

Cross, Joseph

Movie: 2006: **Running with Scissors** (Best Young Actress) Broadcast.

Crosse, Rupert

Movie: 1969: **The Reivers** (Best Supporting Actor) Academy.

Crouse, Lindsay

Movie: 1984: **Places in the Heart** (Best Supporting Actress) Academy.

Crowe, Russell

Movie: 1997: **L.A. Confidential** (Best Ensemble) SAG. 1999: **The Insider** (Best Actor) Academy, Board, British, Society, LA, Broadcast (Best Actor, Drama) Globe (Best Male Actor in a Leading Role) SAG. 2000: **Gladiator** (Best Actor) Academy, British, Broadcast (Best Actor, Drama) Globe (Best Male Actor in a Leading Role) SAG (Best Ensemble) SAG. 2001: **A Beautiful Mind** (Best Actor) Academy, British, Broadcast (Best Actor, Drama) Globe (Best Male Actor in a Leading Role) SAG (Best Ensemble) SAG. 2003: **Master and Commander: The Far Side of the World** (Best Actor) Broadcast (Best Actor, Drama) Globe. 2005: **Cinderella Man** (Best Actor) Broadcast (Best Actor, Drama) Globe (Best Male Actor in a Leading Role) SAG. 2007: **3:10 to Yuma** (Best Ensemble) SAG; **American Gangster** (Best Ensemble) SAG.

Crowley, Pat

Movie: 1953: **Forever Female** (New Star of the Year — Actress) Globe (multiple win); **Money from Home** (New Star of the Year — Actress) Globe (multiple win).

Crowley, Yvonne

Movie: 1970: **Ryan's Daughter** (Best Supporting Actress) British.

Croze, Maria-Josée

Movie: 2003: **Les Invasions barbares (The Barbarian Invasions)** (Best Actress) Cannes.

Crudup, Billy

Movie: 1998: **The Hi-Lo Country** (Breakthrough Performance — Male) Board. 2000: **Almost Famous** (Best Ensemble) SAG; **Jesus' Son** (Best Male Lead) Spirit. Theater: 2002: **The Elephant Man** (Best Actor, Play) Tony. 2005: **The Pillowman** (Best Actor, Play) Tony. 2007: **The Coast of Utopia** (Best Actor in a Featured Role, Play) Tony.

Cruise, Tom

Movie: 1983: **Risky Business** (Best Actor, Musical or Comedy) Globe. 1989: **Born on the Fourth of July** (Best Actor) Academy, British (Best Actor, Drama) Globe. 1992: **A Few Good Men** (Best Actor, Drama) Globe. 1996: **Jerry Maguire** (Best Actor) Academy, Board (Best Actor, Musical or Comedy) Globe (Best Male Actor in a Leading Role) SAG. 1999: **Magnolia** (Best Male Actor in a Supporting Role) SAG (Best Supporting Actor) Academy, Globe (Best Ensemble) Board, SAG. 2003: **The Last Samurai** (Best Actor, Drama) Globe.

Cruz, Penélope

Movie: 2006: **Volver** (Best Actress) Academy, Cannes (win shared with costars), British, Broadcast (Best Actress, Drama) Globe (Best Female Actor in a Leading Role) SAG.

Crystal, Billy

Movie: 1989: **When Harry Met Sally...** (Best Actor, Musical or Comedy) Globe. 1991: **City Slickers** (Best Actor, Musical or Comedy) Globe. 1992: **Mr. Saturday Night** (Best Actor, Musical or Comedy) Globe. Theater: 2005: **700 Sundays** (Special Theatrical Event) Tony. Television: 1985: **Saturday Night Live** (Best Individual Performance in a Variety or Music Program) Emmy. 1987: **The 29th Annual Grammy Awards** (Best Individual Performance in a Variety or Music Program, Host) Emmy. 1988: **All Star Toast to the Improv** (Best Individual Performance in a Variety or Music Program) Emmy; **The 30th Annual Grammy Awards** (Best Individual Achievement — Special Events) Emmy. 1989: **The 31st Annual Grammy Awards** (Best Performance in Special Events) Emmy. 1990: **Billy Crystal: Midnight Train to Moscow** (Best Individual Performance in a Variety or Music Program) Emmy (Best Variety, Music, or Comedy Special, Executive Producer) Emmy (Best Writing in a Variety or Music Program) Emmy. 1991: **The 63rd Annual Academy Awards** (Best Individual Performance in a Variety or Music Program, Host) Emmy (Best Writing in a Variety or Music Program) Emmy. 1992: **The 64th Annual Academy Awards** (Best Individual Performance in a Variety or Music Program, Host) Emmy (Best Writing in a Variety or Music Program) Emmy. 1993: **The 65th Annual Academy Awards** (Best Individual Performance in a Variety or Music Program, Host) Emmy. 1996: **Comic Relief VII** (Best Individual Performance in a Variety or Music Program, Host) Emmy. 1997: **The 69th Annual Academy Awards** (Best Individual Performance in a Variety or Music Program, Host) Emmy. 1998: **The 70th Annual Academy Awards** (Best Individual Performance in a

Variety or Music Program, Host) *Emmy*. 2000: *The 72nd Annual Academy Awards* (Best Individual Performance in a Variety or Music Program, Host) Emmy. 2001: *61** (Best Director of a Miniseries, TV Movie, or Special) Emmy (Best TV Movie, Executive Producer) Emmy. 2004: *The 76th Annual Academy Awards* (Best Individual Performance in a Variety or Music Program, Host) Emmy. **Highlights:** Like Bob Hope, one of his predecessors, Crystal has hosted the Academy Awards ceremony many times, has made some wonderful films, would love to get some Oscar recognition, yet never makes the final cut for a nomination. After Oscar nods eluded him for *When Harry Met Sally...* and *City Slickers*, Crystal was especially hopeful that *Mr. Saturday Night* would put him among the Best Actor nominees. Although his costar David Paymer was up for Best Supporting Actor, Crystal again missed out. His one consolation: he has at least won three of his Emmys for hosting the Academy Awards.

Cucciolla, Riccardo

Movie: 1971: *Sacco and Vanzetti* (Best Actor) *Cannes*.

Culkin, Kieran

Movie: 1999: *The Cider House Rules* (Best Ensemble) SAG. 2002: *Igby Goes Down* (Best Actor, Musical or Comedy) Globe (Best Young Actor/Actress) *Broadcast*.

Culkin, Macaulay

Movie: 1990: *Home Alone* (Best Actor, Musical or Comedy) Globe.

Culkin, Rory

Movie: 2000: *You Can Count on Me* (Best Debut Performance) Spirit (Best Child Performer) Broadcast.

Cumming, Alan

Movie: 2001: *The Anniversary Party* (Best First Feature) Spirit (Best First Screenplay) Spirit. 2002: *Nicholas Nickleby* (Best Ensemble) *Board*. **Theater:** 1998: *Cabaret* (Best Actor, Musical) *Tony*.

Cummings, Quinn

Movie: 1977: *The Goodbye Girl* (Best Supporting Actress) Academy, Globe.

Curtis, Jamie Lee

Movie: 1983: *Trading Places* (Best Supporting Actress) *British*. 1988: *A Fish Called Wanda* (Best Actress) British (Best Actress, Musical or Comedy) Globe. 1994: *True Lies* (Best Actress, Musical or Comedy) *Globe* (Best Female Actor in a Supporting Role) SAG. 2003: *Freaky Friday* (Best Actress, Musical or Comedy) Globe. **Television:** 1989–1992 series *Anything But Love* (Best Actress in a Musical or Comedy Series) 1989: *Globe*. 1991: Globe. 1995: *The Heidi Chronicles* (Best Actress in a Miniseries or TV Movie) Globe. 1998: *Nicholas' Gift* (Best Actress in a Miniseries or TV Movie) Emmy. **Records:** Winning the Best Actress Golden Globe in 1989 for *Anything but Love* made her immediate family a Globe-winning trio. In 1957, her father, Tony Curtis, won the Henrietta Award for World Film Favorite. In 1960, he won the award again, the same year her mother, Janet Leigh earned the Best Supporting Actress prize for her performance as ill-fated embezzler Marion Crane in *Psycho*. Jamie Lee's win made them the first parents and child to all win for acting. Previously, Judy Garland, Vincente Minnelli, and their daughter, Liza had earned Globes, but not all for acting. Vincente won his for directing *Gigi* in 1958.

Curtis, Tony

Movie: 1957: *Sweet Smell of Success* (Best Foreign Actor) British. 1958: *The Defiant Ones* (Best Actor) Academy (Best Actor, Drama) Globe (Best Foreign Actor) British. 1968: *The Boston Strangler* (Best Actor, Drama) Globe. **Television:** 1980: *Moviola: The Scarlett O'Hara War* (Best Actor in a Limited Series or Special) Emmy. **Tributes:** 1957, 1960: Henrietta Award for World Film Favorite from Globe.

Cusack, Joan

Movie: 1988: *Working Girl* (Best Supporting Actress) Academy. 1997: *In & Out* (Best Supporting Actress) Academy, *New York*, Globe, *Broadcast*.

Cusack, John

Movie: 1999: *Being John Malkovich* (Best Male Lead) Spirit (Best Ensemble) SAG. 2000: *High Fidelity* (Best Actor, Musical or Comedy) Globe.

Cusack, Susie

Movie: 1993: *Short Cuts* (Best Ensemble) *Venice* (special award).

Cutanda, Eddie

Movie: 1997: *Squeeze* (Best Debut Performance) Spirit (nomination shared with costars).

Cuthbert, Elisha

Movie: 2003: *Love Actually* (Best Ensemble) Broadcast. **Television:** 2001–2004 series *24* (Best Ensemble) 2002: SAG. 2004: SAG.

Cybulski, Zbigniew

Movie: 1959: *Ashes and Diamonds* (Best Foreign Actor) British.

Dabney, Augusta

Movie: 1957: *That Night* (Best Foreign Actress) British.

Dafoe, Willem

Movie: 1986: *Platoon* (Best Male Lead) Spirit (Best Supporting Actor) Academy. 1990: *Wild at Heart* (Best Supporting Male) Spirit. 1996: *The English Patient* (Best Ensemble) SAG. 2000: *Shadow of the Vampire* (Best Male Actor in a Supporting Role) SAG (Best Supporting Actor) Academy, Globe, *LA* (Best Supporting Male) *Spirit*. 2004: *The Life Aquatic with Steve Zissou* (Best Ensemble) Broadcast.

Dahlbeck, Eva

Movie: 1958: *Nara livet (Brink of Life)* (Best Actress) *Cannes* (win shared with co-stars). 1956: *Smiles of a Summer Night* (Best Foreign Actress) British.

Dailey, Dan

Movie: 1948: *When My Baby Smiles at Me* (Best Actor) Academy. 1950: *When Willie Comes Marching Home* (Best Actor, Musical or Comedy) Globe. Television: 1969–1970 series *The Governor and J.J.* (Best Actor in a Comedy or Musical Series) 1969: *Globe*.

Dale, James Badge

Movie: 2006: *The Departed* (Best Ensemble) *Board*, SAG, Broadcast.

Dale, Jim

Movie: 1966: *Georgy Girl* (Best Song, "Georgy Girl") Academy, Globe. 1973: *Adolf Hitler, My Part of His Downfall* (Most Promising Newcomer) British. Theater: 1975: *Scapino* (Best Actor, Dramatic) Tony. 1980: *Barnum* (Best Actor, Musical) *Tony*. 1985: *Joe Egg* (Best Actor, Play) Tony. 1997: *Candide* (Best Actor, Musical) Tony. 2006: *The Threepenny Opera* (Best Actor in a Featured Role, Musical) Tony.

Dall, John

Movie: 1945: *The Corn Is Green* (Best Supporting Actor) Academy.

Daltrey, Roger

Movie: 1975: *Tommy* (New Star of the Year — Actor) Globe.

Damon, Mark

Movie: 1960: *The Fall of the House of Usher* (New Star of the Year — Actor) *Globe.*

Damon, Matt

Movie: 1997: *Good Will Hunting* (Best Breakthrough Performer) *Broadcast* (Best Actor) Academy (Best Actor, Drama) Globe (Best Male Actor in a Leading Role) SAG (Best Original Screenplay) *Academy, Broadcast* (Best Screenplay) *Globe* (Best Ensemble) SAG. 1998: *Saving Private Ryan* (Best Ensemble) SAG. 1999: *The Talented Mr. Ripley* (Best Actor, Drama) Globe. 2001: *Ocean's 11* (Best Ensemble) Broadcast. 2004: *Ocean's Twelve* (Best Ensemble) Broadcast. 2005: *Syriana* (Best Ensemble) Broadcast. 2006: *The Departed* (Best Ensemble) *Board*, SAG, Broadcast. Television: 2001–2005 series *Project Greenlight* (Best Non-Fiction Program, Reality; Executive Producer) 2002: Emmy. (Best Reality Program, Executive Producer) 2004: Emmy. 2005: Emmy. Tributes: 1997: Silver Bear for Outstanding Single Achievement for *Good Will Hunting* from Berlin; Special Filmmaking Achievement award for *Good Will Hunting* from Board (honor shared with coauthor and costar, Ben Affleck). Records: Damon's and Ben Affleck's Best Original Screenplay Oscar win for *Good Will Hunting* marked the first time that actors won screenwriting Academy Awards in three consecutive years. The wonderboys of 1997, Damon and Affleck followed on the heels of Best Adapted Screenplay winners Emma Thompson, who adapted Jane Austen's *Sense and Sensibility* in 1995 and Billy Bob Thornton, who extended his short film, *Some Folks Call It a Sling Blade* into the feature-length *Sling Blade* in 1996.

Dance, Charles

Movie: 2001: *Gosford Park* (Best Ensemble) *SAG, Broadcast.* Television: 2006: *"Bleak House," Masterpiece Theatre* (Best Actor in a Miniseries or TV Movie) Emmy.

Dandridge, Dorothy

Movie: 1954: *Carmen Jones* (Best Actress) Academy (Best Foreign Actress) British. 1959: *Porgy and Bess* (Best Actress, Musical or Comedy) Globe. Records: In 1954, Dandridge's performance as *Carmen Jones* made her the first African-American to earn an Academy Award nomination in the lead acting category.

Danes, Claire

Movie: 2002: *The Hours* (Best Ensemble) SAG, Broadcast. Television: 1994–1995 series *My So-*

Called Life (Best Actress in a Drama Series) 1994: *Globe*. 1995: Emmy.

D'Angelo, Beverly

Movie: 1980: *Coal Miner's Daughter* (Best Supporting Actress) Globe. Television: 1984: *"A Streetcar Named Desire," An ABC Theatre Presentation* (Best Supporting Actress in a Limited Series or Special) Emmy.

Daniels, Jeff

Movie: 1985: *The Purple Rose of Cairo* (Best Actor, Musical or Comedy) Globe. 1986: *Something Wild* (Best Actor, Musical or Comedy) Globe. 2002: *The Hours* (Best Ensemble) SAG, Broadcast. 2005: *The Squid and the Whale* (Best Actor) Society (Best Actor, Musical or Comedy) Globe (Best Male Lead) Spirit; *Good Night, and Good Luck* (Best Ensemble) SAG, Broadcast.

Dano, Paul (Franklin)

Movie: 2001: *L.I.E.* (Best Debut Performance) *Spirit*. 2006: *Little Miss Sunshine* (Best Supporting Male) Spirit (Best Young Actor) *Broadcast* (Best Ensemble) *SAG, Broadcast*. 2007: *There Will Be Blood* (Best Supporting Actor) British.

Danton, Ray

Movie: 1955: *I'll Cry Tomorrow* (New Star of the Year — Actor) *Globe*.

Darby, Kim

Movie: 1969: *True Grit* (Most Promising Newcomer) British; *Generation* (Best Actress, Musical or Comedy) Globe. Television: 1976: *Rich Man, Poor Man* (Best Single Performance by a Supporting Actress in a Comedy or Drama Series) Emmy.

Darin, Bobby

Movie: 1961: *Come September* (New Star of the Year — Actor) *Globe*. 1962: *Pressure Point* (Best Actor, Drama) Globe. 1963: *Captain Newman, M.D.* (Best Supporting Actor) Academy, Globe. 1965: *That Funny Feeling* (Best Song, "That Funny Feeling") Globe.

Darrieux, Danielle

Movie: 1937: *Mayerling* (Best Acting) *Board*. Tributes: 2002: Silver Bear for outstanding artistic contribution in *8 Femmes (8 Women)* from Berlin (special ensemble award shared with costars). Records: With 65 years separating her two award recognitions, Darrieux appears to have the longest span be-

tween honors among the major awards. Throughout a career that has spanned eight decades, Darrieux continued working in the United States as well as in Europe, where she has won César Awards (including their lifetime achievement recognition) from her native France.

Darst, Danny

Movie: 1993: *Short Cuts* (Best Ensemble) *Venice* (special award).

Darvi, Bella

Movie: 1953: *The Egyptian* (New Star of the Year — Actress) *Globe* (multiple win); *Hell and High Water* (New Star of the Year — Actress) *Globe* (multiple win); *Money from Home* (New Star of the Year — Actress) Globe.

Darwell, Jane

Movie: 1940: *The Grapes of Wrath* (Best Acting) *Board* (Best Supporting Actress) *Academy*. Records: When 61-year-old Darwell won her Academy Award for 1940's *The Grapes of Wrath*, she became the first person over 60 to win a supporting Oscar.

Da Silva, Howard

Movie: 1963: *David and Lisa* (Best Foreign Actor) British. Theater: 1960: *Fiorello!* (Best Supporting or Featured Actor, Musical) Tony. Television: 1978: *"Verna: USO Girl," Great Performances* (Best Supporting Actor in a Comedy or Drama Special) *Emmy*.

Davidson, Jaye

Movie: 1992: *The Crying Game* (Most Auspicious Debut) *Board* (Best Supporting Actor) Academy, British.

Davies, Jeremy

Movie: 1994: *Spanking the Monkey* (Best Debut Performance) Spirit. 1998: *Saving Private Ryan* (Best Ensemble) SAG.

Davis, Bette

Movie: 1935: *Dangerous* (Best Actress) *Academy*. 1937: *Kid Galahad* (Best Actress) *Venice* (multiple win); *Marked Woman* (Best Actress) *Venice* (multiple win). 1938: *Jezebel* (Best Actress) *Academy*. 1939: *Dark Victory* (Best Acting) *Board* (multiple win), (Best Actress) Academy; *The Old Maid* (Best Acting) *Board* (multiple win). 1940: *The Letter* (Best Actress) Academy. 1941: *The Little Foxes* (Best Acting) *Board* (Best Actress) Academy. 1942: *Now, Voyager*

(Best Actress) Academy. 1944: *Mr. Skeffington* (Best Actress) Academy. 1950: *All About Eve* (Best Actress) Academy, *New York*, *Cannes* (Best Actress, Drama) Globe. 1952: *The Star* (Best Actress) Academy. 1961: *Pocketful of Miracles* (Best Actress, Musical or Comedy) Globe. 1962: *What Ever Happened to Baby Jane?* (Best Actress) Academy (Best Actress, Drama) Globe (Best Foreign Actress) British. **Television:** 1974: *Warner Bros. Movies: A Fifty Year Salute* (Best Special Classification of Outstanding Programming, Host) Emmy. 1979: *Strangers: The Story of a Mother and Daughter* (Best Actress in a Limited Series or Special) *Emmy*. 1980: *White Mama* (Best Actress in a Limited Series or Special) Emmy. 1983: *Little Gloria ... Happy at Last* (Best Supporting Actress in a Limited Series or Special) Emmy. **Tributes:** 1973: Cecil B. DeMille Award from Globe. 1977: Life Achievement Award from American Film Institute. 1987: Honor from Kennedy Center for the Performing Arts. 1989: Gala Tribute from Film Society of Lincoln Center. 1999: Ranked Number 2 on List of 25 Greatest Female Screen Legends of the 20th Century from American Film Institute. **Records:** Davis missed reaching her personal goal of being the most Oscared actor in history by one year. Luise Rainer became the first twice-honored actor in 1937. The following year Davis achieved the same feat with a Best Actress win for *Jezebel*, but so did Best Actor Spencer Tracy and Best Supporting Actor Walter Brennan. Within only two years, Brennan passed their record by winning his third supporting award, and in 1981 Katharine Hepburn became the first, and so far only, person to win four acting Oscars. Although Davis missed her goal for award wins, she did set the Academy record for most nominations when she received her tenth nod in 1962 for *What Ever Happened to Baby Jane?* Kate Hepburn beat that record with an eleventh nomination for *The Lion in Winter* in 1968. Meryl Streep now has the most nominations, 14. Davis set another award record in 1977 by being the first woman to receive a Life Achievement Award from the American Film Institute.

Davis, Brad

Movie: 1978: *Midnight Express* (New Star of the Year — Actor) *Globe* (Most Promising Newcomer) British (Best Actor) British (Best Actor, Drama) Globe.

Davis, Geena

Movie: 1988: *The Accidental Tourist* (Best Supporting Actress) *Academy*. 1991: *Thelma & Louise* (Best Actress) Academy, *Board*, British (Best Actress, Drama) Globe. 1992: *A League of Their Own* (Best Actress, Musical or Comedy) Globe. 1994: *Speechless* (Best Actress, Musical or Comedy) Globe. **Television:** 2005–2006 series *Commander in Chief* (Best Actress in a Drama Series) 2005: *Globe*. 2006: Emmy. (Best Female Actor in a Dramas Series) 2005: SAG.

Davis, Hope

Movie: 2003: *The Secret Lives of Dentists* (Best Actress) *New York* (multiple win), (Best Supporting Female) Spirit; *American Splendor* (Best Actress) *New York* (multiple win), (Best Supporting Actress) Globe.

Davis, Judy

Movie: 1980: *My Brilliant Career* (Most Promising Newcomer) *British* (Best Actress) *British*. 1984: *A Passage to India* (Best Actress) Academy. 1988: *High Tide* (Best Actress) *Society*. 1991: *Barton Fink* (Best Supporting Actress) *New York* (multiple win); *Impromptu* (Best Female Lead) *Spirit*; *Naked Lunch* (Best Supporting Actress) *New York* (multiple win). 1992: *Husbands and Wives* (Best Actress) British (Best Supporting Actress) Academy, *Board*, Globe, *Society*, LA. **Television:** 1982: *A Woman Called Golda* (Best Supporting Actress in a Limited Series or Special) Emmy. 1992: *"One Against the Wind,"* *Hallmark Hall of Fame* (Best Actress in a Miniseries or Special) Emmy (Best Actress in a Miniseries or TV Movie) *Globe*. 1995: *Serving in Silence: The Margarethe Cammermeyer Story* (Best Supporting Actress in a Miniseries or TV Movie) *Emmy* (Best Supporting Actress in a Series, Miniseries, or TV Movie) Globe. 1998: *"The Echo of Thunder,"* *Hallmark Hall of Fame* (Best Actress in a Miniseries or TV Movie) Emmy. 1999: *A Cooler Climate* (Best Actress in a Miniseries or TV Movie) Emmy (Best Female Actor in a Television Movie or Miniseries) SAG; *Dash and Lilly* (Best Actress in a Miniseries or TV Movie) Emmy, Globe. 2001: *Life with Judy Garland: Me and My Shadows* (Best Actress in a Miniseries or TV Movie) *Emmy, Globe* (Best Female Actor in a Television Movie or Miniseries) *SAG*. 2004: *The Reagans* (Best Actress in a Miniseries or TV Movie) Emmy, Globe. 2006: *A Little Thing Called Murder* (Best Actress in a Miniseries or TV Movie) Emmy. 2007: *The Starter Wife* (Best Supporting Actress in a Miniseries or TV Movie) *Emmy*. **Highlights:** Davis's uncanny ability to immerse herself so completely into a character that viewers forget it's Davis on screen acting has made her a favorite actress to portray real-life people, some of whom are familiar to her movie and television audiences. Famous people she has earned award recognition for playing include author George Sand in *Impromptu*, playwright Lillian Hellman in *Dash and Lilly*, first lady

Nancy Reagan in *The Reagans*, and, in the role that won every television acting award she could garner, actress/singer Judy Garland in *Life with Judy Garland: Me and My Shadows*.

Davis, Ossie

Movie: 1968: *The Scalphunters* (Best Supporting Actor) Globe. Theater: 1958: *Jamaica* (Best Supporting or Featured Actor, Musical) Tony. 1970: *Purlie* (Best Musical, Book Writer) Tony. Television: 1969: *"Teacher, Teacher" Hallmark Hall of Fame* (Best Single Performance by an Actor in a Leading Role) Emmy. 1978: *King* (Best Continuing Performance by a Supporting Actor in a Drama Series) Emmy. 1997: *Miss Evers' Boys* (Best Supporting Actor in a Miniseries or Special) Emmy. 2005: *The L Word* (Best Guest Actor in a Drama Series) Emmy. Tributes: 2000: Life Achievement Award from SAG. 2004: Honor from Kennedy Center for the Performing Arts (honor shared with spouse, Ruby Dee).

Davis, Phil

Movie: 2004: *Vera Drake* (Best Supporting Actor) British.

Davis, Viola

Movie: 2002: *Antwone Fisher* (Best Supporting Female) Spirit. Theater: 1996: *Seven Guitars* (Best Actress in a Featured Role, Play) Tony. 2001: *King Hedley II* (Best Actress in a Featured Role, Play) *Tony*.

Davison, Bruce

Movie: 1990: *Longtime Companion* (Best Supporting Actor) Academy, *New York, Globe, Society* (Best Supporting Male) *Spirit*. 1993: *Short Cuts* (Best Ensemble) *Venice* (special award). Television: 1998: *Touched by an Angel* (Best Guest Actor in a Drama Series) Emmy.

Dawson, Rosario

Movie: 2005: *Sin City* (Best Ensemble) Broadcast.

Day, Doris

Movie: 1958: *The Tunnel of Love* (Best Actress, Musical or Comedy) Globe. 1959: *Pillow Talk* (Best Actress) Academy (Best Actress, Musical or Comedy) Globe. 1960: *Midnight Lace* (Best Actress, Drama) Globe. 1962: *Billy Rose's Jumbo* (Best Actress, Musical or Comedy) Globe. 1963: *Move Over, Darling* (Best Actress, Musical or Comedy) Globe. Television: 1968–1973 series *The Doris Day Show* (Best Actress in a Series) 1968: Globe. Tributes: 1954, 1957, 1959, 1962, 1965: Henrietta Award for World Film Favorite from Globe. 1988: Cecil B. DeMille Award from Globe.

Day-Lewis, Daniel

Movie: 1985: *My Beautiful Laundrette* (Best Supporting Actor) *New York* (multiple win), *Board* (multiple win). 1986: *A Room with a View* (Best Supporting Actor) *New York* (multiple win), *Board* (multiple win). 1989: *My Left Foot* (Best Actor) *Academy, New York, British, Society, LA* (Best Actor, Drama) Globe. 1992: *The Last of the Mohicans* (Best Actor) British. 1993: *In the Name of the Father* (Best Actor) Academy, British (Best Actor, Drama) Globe. 1997: *The Boxer* (Best Actor, Drama) Globe. 2002: *Gangs of New York* (Best Actor) Academy, *New York, British, LA, Broadcast* (Best Actor, Drama) Globe (Best Male Actor in a Leading Role) *SAG*. 2007: *There Will Be Blood* (Best Actor) *Academy, New York, British, Society, LA, Broadcast* (Best Actor, Drama) *Globe* (Best Male Actor in a Leading Role) *SAG*. Tributes: 2005: Honorary Award from Berlin.

Dayan, Assaf

Movie: 1970: *Promise at Dawn* (New Star of the Year — Actor) Globe.

Dean, James

Movie: 1955: *East of Eden* (Best Actor) Academy (Best Foreign Actor) British; *Rebel Without a Cause* (Best Foreign Actor) British. 1956: *Giant* (Best Actor) Academy. Tributes: 1955: Special Posthumous Award for Best Dramatic Actor for *East of Eden* from Globe. 1956: Henrietta Award for World Film Favorite from Globe. 1999: Ranked Number 18 on List of 25 Greatest Male Screen Legends of the 20th Century from American Film Institute. Records: In 1955 at age 24, Dean was killed in a highway accident while driving his Porsche. When the Oscar nominations were announced later that year, Dean became the first male actor to receive a posthumous nomination. The following year, he became the only actor to be posthumously nominated twice. He lost in 1955 to Ernest Borgnine for *Marty* and in 1956 to Yul Brynner for *The King and I*. Hedda Hopper had campaigned for the Academy to give Dean a special posthumous award just as the Hollywood Foreign Press had, but Academy rules disqualified current nominees from receiving special tributes.

Dean, Quentin

Movie: 1967: *In the Heat of the Night* (Best Supporting Actress) Globe.

De Banzie, Brenda

Movie: 1954: *Hobson's Choice* (Best British Actress) British. Theater: 1958: *The Entertainer* (Best Supporting or Featured Actress, Dramatic) Tony.

Debbouze, Jamel

Movie: 2006: *Days of Glory* (Best Actor) *Cannes* (win shared with costars).

Dee, Ruby

Movie: 1961: *A Raisin in the Sun* (Best Supporting Actress) *Board*. 2007: *American Gangster* (Best Female Actor in a Supporting Role) *SAG* (Best Supporting Actress) Academy (Best Ensemble) SAG. Television: 1964: *The Nurses* (Best Single Performance by an Actress in a Leading Role) Emmy. 1979: *Roots: The Next Generation* (Best Supporting Actress in a Limited Series or Special) Emmy. 1988: *Gore Vidal's Lincoln* (Best Supporting Actress in a Miniseries or Special) Emmy. 1990: *China Beach* (Best Guest Actress in a Drama Series) Emmy. 1991: *"Decoration Day," Hallmark Hall of Fame* (Best Supporting Actress in a Miniseries or Special) *Emmy*. 1993: *Evening Shade* (Best Guest Actress in a Comedy Series) Emmy. 1999–2007 series *Little Bill* (Best Performer in an Animated Series) 2002: Emmy. Tributes: 2000: Life Achievement Award from SAG. 2004: Honor from Kennedy Center for the Performing Arts (honor shared with spouse, Ossie Davis).

Dee, Sandra

Movie: 1957: *Until They Sail* (New Star of the Year — Actress) *Globe*.

Degermark, Pia

Movie: 1967: *Elvira Madigan* (New Star of the Year — Actress) Globe (Most Promising Newcomer) British (Best Actress) *Cannes*.

de Havilland, Olivia

Movie: 1939: *Gone with the Wind* (Best Supporting Actress) Academy. 1941: *Hold Back the Dawn* (Best Actress) Academy. 1946: *To Each His Own* (Best Actress) *Academy*. 1948: *The Snake Pit* (Best Actress) Academy, *Venice, New York, Board*. 1949: *The Heiress* (Best Actress) *Academy, New York, Globe*. 1952: *My Cousin Rachel* (Best Actress, Drama) Globe. Television: 1986: *Anastasia: The Mystery of Anna* (Best Supporting Actress in a Miniseries or Special) Emmy (Best Supporting Actress in a Series, Miniseries, or TV Movie) *Globe*. Records: de Havilland is on record for having thanked the most people in a single Oscar acceptance speech. When she won her first

Academy Award for the 1946 tearjerker, *To Each His Own*, she thanked 27 people. That Best Actress win, combined with her sister Joan Fontaine's in the same category for 1941's *Suspicion*, made them the first sisters to both win Academy Awards and the first siblings to win acting Oscars for leading roles. In 1948 de Havilland set another award record when her performance in *The Snake Pit* became the only acting award that the New York Film Critics Circle selected unanimously on the first ballot.

De La Serna, Rodrigo

Movie: 2004: *Diarios de motocicleta (The Motorcycle Diaries)* (Best Debut Performance) *Spirit* (Best Supporting Actor) British.

De La Tour, Frances

Movie: 2006: *The History Boys* (Best Supporting Actress) British. Theater: 2006: *The History Boys* (Best Actress in a Featured Role, Play) *Tony*.

Delevanti, Cyril

Movie: 1964: *The Night of the Iguana* (Best Supporting Actor) Globe.

Delon, Alain

Movie: 1963: *The Leopard* (New Star of the Year — Actor) Globe. Tributes: 1995: Honorary Golden Bear from Berlin.

Delpy, Julie

Movie: 2004: *Before Sunset* (Best Actress) Society.

Del Toro, Benicio

Movie: 1995: *The Usual Suspects* (Best Supporting Male) *Spirit* (Best Ensemble) *Board*. 1996: *Basquiat* (Best Supporting Male) *Spirit*. 2000: *Traffic* (Best Actor) *Berlin* (Best Male Actor in a Leading Role) *SAG* (Best Supporting Actor) *Academy, New York, Globe, British, Society*, Broadcast (Best Ensemble) SAG. 2003: *21 Grams* (Best Actor) *Venice* (special audience award), British, *Spirit* (special award shared with costars), (Best Male Actor in a Supporting Role) SAG (Best Supporting Actor) Academy, Broadcast. 2005: *Sin City* (Best Ensemble) Broadcast. Records: Although *Traffic* was an English language film, Del Toro's nearly entire Spanish-language part made him the first actor to deliver an Oscar-winning performance in Spanish. Until then, all non–English speaking Oscar-winning performances were Italian. In all, Del Toro received eight major awards for his work in *Traffic*. He lost only one race, as the Broadcast Film Critics gave their award to Joaquin Phoenix for his work in three films: *Gladiator, Quills*, and *The Yards*.

Demarest, William

Movie: 1946: *The Jolson Story* (Best Supporting Actor) Academy. Television: 1965–1972 series *My Three Sons* (Best Supporting Actor in a Comedy Series) 1968: Emmy. Highlights: Demarest earned his only big screen award recognition for *The Jolson Story*, playing the fictional mentor of actor Al Jolson, star of the first feature length film with sound, *The Jazz Singer*. One of Jolson's costars in that groundbreaking talkie was Demarest.

de Medeiros, Maria

Movie: 1994: *Três Irmãos* (Best Actress) *Venice*.

Demongeot, Mylene

Movie: 1957: *The Witches of Salem* (Most Promising Newcomer) British.

DeMunn, Jeffrey

Movie: 1999: *The Green Mile* (Best Ensemble) SAG. Theater: 1983: *K2* (Best Actor, Play) Tony.

Dench, Judi

Movie: 1965: *Four in the Morning* (Most Promising Newcomer) *British*. 1985: *Wetherby* (Best Supporting Actress) British. 1986: *A Room with a View* (Best Supporting Actress) *British*. 1987: *84 Charing Cross Road* (Best Supporting Actress) British. 1988: *A Handful of Dust* (Best Supporting Actress) British. 1997: *Mrs. Brown* (Best Actress) Academy, *British* (Best Actress, Drama) *Globe* (Best Female Actor in a Leading Role) SAG. 1998: *Shakespeare in Love* (Best Female Actor in a Supporting Role) SAG (Best Supporting Actress) *Academy*, Globe, *British*, *Society* (Best Ensemble) *SAG*. 2000: *Chocolat* (Best Female Actor in a Supporting Role) *SAG* (Best Supporting Actress) Academy, Globe, British, Broadcast (Best Ensemble) SAG. 2001: *Iris* (Best Actress) Academy, *British* (Best Actress, Drama) Globe (Best Female Actor in a Leading Role) SAG; *The Shipping News* (Best Female Actor in a Supporting Role) SAG (Best Supporting Actress) British. 2005: *Mrs. Henderson Presents* (Best Actress) Academy, British, Broadcast (Best Actress, Musical or Comedy) Globe (Best Female Actor in a Leading Role) SAG (Best Ensemble) *Board*. 2006: *Notes on a Scandal* (Best Actress) Academy, British, Broadcast (Best Actress, Drama) Globe (Best Female Actor in a Leading Role) SAG. Theater: 1999: *Amy's View* (Best Actress, Play) *Tony*. Television: 2000: *The Last of the Blonde Bombshells* (Best Actress in a Miniseries or TV Movie) Emmy, *Globe* (Best Female Actor in a Television Movie or Miniseries) SAG.

Deneuve, Catherine

Movie: 1968: *Belle de jour* (Best Actress) British. 1992: *Indochine* (Best Actress) Academy. 1998: *Place vendôme* (Best Actress) *Venice*. Tributes: 1997: Honorary Golden Bear from Berlin. 2002: Silver Bear for outstanding artistic contribution in *8 Femmes (8 Women)* from Berlin (special ensemble award shared with costars).

Denham, Maurice

Movie: 1954: *The Purple Plain* (Best British Actor) British.

De Niro, Robert

Movie: 1973: *Bang the Drum Slowly* (Best Supporting Actor) *New York*; *Mean Streets* (Best Supporting Actor) *Society*. 1974: *The Godfather Part II* (Most Promising Newcomer) British (Best Supporting Actor) *Academy*. 1976: *Taxi Driver* (Best Actor) Academy, *New York*, British, *Society*, *LA* (Best Actor, Drama) Globe. 1977: *New York, New York* (Best Actor, Musical or Comedy) Globe. 1978: *The Deer Hunter* (Best Actor) Academy, British (Best Actor, Drama) Globe. 1980: *Raging Bull* (Best Actor) *Academy*, *New York*, *Board*, British, *LA* (Best Actor, Drama) *Globe*. 1983: *The King of Comedy* (Best Actor) British. 1988: *Midnight Run* (Best Actor, Musical or Comedy) Globe. 1990: *Awakenings* (Best Actor) Academy, *New York* (multiple win), *Board*; *GoodFellas* (Best Actor) *New York* (multiple win), British. 1991: *Cape Fear* (Best Actor) Academy (Best Actor, Drama) Globe. 1996: *Marvin's Room* (Best Ensemble) SAG. 1997: *Wag the Dog* (Best Picture, Musical or Comedy; Producer) Globe. 1999: *Analyze This* (Best Actor, Musical or Comedy) Globe. 2000: *Meet the Parents* (Best Actor, Musical or Comedy) Globe. Tributes: 1993: Career Golden Lion from Venice. 2003: Life Achievement Award from American Film Institute. Records: De Niro is the first actor to win an Oscar for a foreign language performance in an American film. In *The Godfather Part II*, he speaks only Italian in the flashback scenes as young Vito Corleone. Playing that character to an Oscar win makes that De Niro performance a double record-setter, as he also became the first actor to win an Oscar portraying a character that already brought someone else Oscar gold. Two years earlier, Marlon Brando won (and refused) his second Best Actor Oscar playing the aging Corleone while De Niro played him as the young man rising to power. Highlights: By gaining 60 pounds for the latter scenes of *Raging Bull,* De Niro joins others who put on considerable weight for what became the most award-honored role of their careers. Among them, Elizabeth Taylor risked her image as a stunning beauty by adding 30 pounds to play foulmouthed Martha in *Who's Afraid of Virginia Woolf?* and Shelley Winters gained 40 pounds to play the struggling but ultimately valiant shipwrecked passenger Belle Rosen in *The Poseidon Adventure*. While reports on exactly how many pounds the stars actually gained for their roles varies slightly, the *1999 Guinness Book of World Records* claims that De Niro put on 60 pounds, thus giving him the record for Most Weight Gained for a Film Appearance.

Dennis, Sandy

Movie: 1966: *Who's Afraid of Virginia Woolf?* (Best Supporting Actress) *Academy,* Globe. 1970: *The Out-of-Towners* (Best Actress, Musical or Comedy) Globe. Theater: 1963: *A Thousand Clowns* (Best Supporting or Featured Actress, Dramatic) *Tony.* 1964: *Any Wednesday* (Best Actress, Dramatic) *Tony.*

de Palma, Rossy

Movie: 1994: *Prêt-à-Porter (Ready-to-Wear)* (Best Ensemble) *Board.*

Depardieu, Gèrard

Movie: 1983: *Danton* (Best Actor) *Society* (multiple win); *The Return of Martin Guerre* (Best Actor) *Society* (multiple win). 1985: *Police* (Best Actor) *Venice.* 1987: *Jean De Florette* (Best Actor) British. 1990: *Cyrano de Bergerac* (Best Actor) Academy, *Cannes,* British; *Green Card* (Best Actor, Musical or Comedy) *Globe.* Television: 2002: *Napoleon* (Best Miniseries, Producer) Emmy. Tributes: 1997: Career Golden Lion from Venice. Records: Depardieu's prolific output made him a major leading man of French film in the 1980s and built such momentum that he became France's top male star of that decade. By the end of the 1990s, Depardieu had won ten Césars (French acting awards) and become France's highest-earning actor.

Depp, Johnny

Movie: 1990: *Edward Scissorhands* (Best Actor, Musical or Comedy) Globe. 1993: *Benny and Joon* (Best Actor, Musical or Comedy) Globe. 1994: *Ed Wood* (Best Actor, Musical or Comedy) Globe. 2000: *Chocolat* (Best Ensemble) SAG. 2003: *Pirates of the Caribbean: The Curse of the Black Pearl* (Best Actor) Academy, British, Broadcast (Best Actor, Musical or Comedy) Globe (Best Male Actor in a Leading Role) *SAG.* 2004: *Finding Neverland* (Best Actor) Academy, British, Broadcast (Best Actor, Drama) Globe (Best Male Actor in a Leading Role) SAG (Best Ensemble) SAG. 2005: *Charlie and the Chocolate Factory* (Best Actor, Musical or Comedy) Globe. 2006: *Pirates of the Caribbean: Dead Man's Chest* (Best Actor, Musical or Comedy) Globe. 2007: *Sweeney Todd: The Demon Barber of Fleet Street* (Best Actor) Academy, Broadcast (Best Actor, Musical or Comedy) *Globe* (Best Ensemble) Broadcast.

Dequenne, Emilie

Movie: 1999: *Rosetta* (Best Actress) *Cannes.*

Derek, Bo

Movie: 1979: *10* (New Star of the Year — Actress) Globe.

Dern, Bruce

Movie: 1971: *Drive, He Said* (Best Supporting Actor) *Society.* 1974: *The Great Gatsby* (Best Supporting Actor) Globe. 1978: *Coming Home* (Best Supporting Actor) Academy, Globe. 1982: *That Championship Season* (Best Actor) *Berlin.*

Dern, Laura

Movie: 1985: *Smooth Talk* (New Generation) *LA* (Best Female Lead) Spirit. 1986: *Blue Velvet* (Best Female Lead) Spirit. 1991: *Rambling Rose* (Best Actress) Academy (Best Actress, Drama) Globe. Television: 1992: *Afterburn* (Best Actress in a Miniseries or Special) Emmy (Best Actress in a Miniseries or TV Movie) *Globe.* 1994: *Fallen Angels* (Best Guest Actress in a Drama Series) Emmy. 1997: *Ellen* (Best Guest Actress in a Comedy Series) Emmy. 1998: *The Baby Dance* (Best Actress in a Miniseries or TV Movie) Globe. Tributes: 2006: Lifetime Achievement award from Spirit (award shared with director David Lynch). Records: With back-to-back Female Lead nominations during the first two years of the Independent Spirit awards, Dern set the record as the first actor to earn multiple nominations from the then fledgling group. Dern and her mother, actress Diane Ladd also made Oscar history when they became the first mother and daughter to be nominated for acting Oscars the same year (and for the same film) as Dern and Ladd were up for Best Actress and Best Supporting Actress, respectively, for *Rambling Rose.*

De Rossi, Barbara

Movie: 1985: *Mamma Ebe* (Best Actress) *Venice.*

Desailly, Jean

Movie: 1959: *Maigret Sets a Trap* (Best Foreign Actor) British.

Deschanel, Zooey

Movie: 2003: *All the Real Girls* (Best Female Lead) Spirit.

De Sica, Vittorio

Movie: 1949: *The Bicycle Thief* (Best Director) Board. 1957: *A Farewell to Arms* (Best Supporting Actor) Academy.

De Soto, Rosanna

Movie: 1988: *Stand and Deliver* (Best Supporting Female) *Spirit*.

Deutsch, Ernst

Movie: 1948: *Der Prozeß* (Best Actor) *Venice*.

Devine, Loretta

Movie: 2004: *Woman Thou Art Loosed* (Best Supporting Female) Spirit.

DeVito, Danny

Movie: 1986: *Ruthless People* (Best Actor, Musical or Comedy) Globe. 1987: *Throw Momma from the Train* (Best Actor, Musical or Comedy) Globe. 1995: *Get Shorty* (Best Ensemble) SAG (Best Picture, Drama; Producer) Globe. 1997: *L.A. Confidential* (Best Ensemble) SAG. 1999: *Man on the Moon* (Best Picture, Musical or Comedy; Producer) Globe. 2000: *Erin Brockovich* (Best Picture, Producer) Academy (Best Picture, Drama; Producer) Globe. Television: 1978–1983 series *Taxi* (Best Supporting Actor in a Comedy or Comedy-Variety or Music Series) 1979: Emmy. (Best Supporting Actor in a Comedy or Variety or Music Series) 1981: *Emmy*. 1982: Emmy. 1983: Emmy. (Best Supporting Actor in a Series, Miniseries, or TV Movie) 1978: Globe. 1979: *Globe*. 1980: Globe. 1981: Globe. 2004: *Friends* (Best Guest Actor in a Comedy Series) Emmy.

De Wilde, Brandon

Movie: 1953: *Shane* (Best Supporting Actor) Academy. Tributes: 1952: Special Achievement Award for Best Juvenile Performance for *The Member of the Wedding* from Globe. Records: De Wilde made a highly acclaimed stage debut at age seven in Carson McCullers' play, *The Member of the Wedding*. For his performance as John Henry West, De Wilde became the first child star to win the prestigious Donaldson Award.

Diamond, Neil

Movie: 1973: *Jonathan Livingston Seagull* (Best Original Score) *Globe* (Best Song, "Lonely Looking Sky") Globe. 1980: *The Jazz Singer* (Best Actor, Musical or Comedy) Globe (Best Song, "Love on the Rocks") Globe. Television: 1977: *The Neil Diamond Special* (Best Comedy-Variety or Music Special, Star) Emmy. 1978: *Neil Diamond: I'm Glad You're Here with Me Tonight* (Best Comedy-Variety or Music Special, Star) Emmy.

Diamond, Reed

Movie: 2005: *Good Night, and Good Luck* (Best Ensemble) SAG, Broadcast.

Diaz, Cameron

Movie: 1998: *There's Something About Mary* (Best Actress) *New York* (Best Actress, Musical or Comedy) Globe. 1999: *Being John Malkovich* (Best Female Actor in a Supporting Role) SAG (Best Supporting Actress) Globe, British (Best Ensemble) SAG. 2001: *Vanilla Sky* (Best Female Actor in a Supporting Role) SAG (Best Supporting Actress) Globe, Broadcast. 2002: *Gangs of New York* (Best Supporting Actress) Globe.

Diaz, Melonie

Movie: 2006: *A Guide to Recognizing Your Saints* (Best Supporting Female) Spirit.

DiCaprio, Leonardo

Movie: 1993: *What's Eating Gilbert Grape?* (New Generation) *LA* (Best Supporting Actor) Academy, *Board*, Globe. 1996: *Marvin's Room* (Best Ensemble) SAG. 1997: *Titanic* (Best Actor, Drama) Globe (Best Ensemble) SAG; *William Shakespeare's Romeo & Juliet* (Best Actor) *Berlin*. 2002: *Catch Me If You Can* (Best Actor, Drama) Globe. 2004: *The Aviator* (Best Actor) Academy, British, Broadcast (Best Actor, Drama) *Globe* (Best Male Actor in a Leading Role) SAG (Best Ensemble) SAG. 2006: *Blood Diamond* (Best Actor) Academy, Broadcast (Best Actor, Drama) Globe (Best Male Actor in a Leading Role) SAG; *The Departed* (Best Actor) British, Broadcast (Best Actor, Drama) Globe (Best Male Actor in a Supporting Role) SAG (Best Ensemble) *Board*, SAG, Broadcast.

Dickens, Kim

Movie: 2001: *Things Behind the Sun* (Best Female Lead) Spirit. Television: 2004–2006 series *Deadwood* (Best Ensemble in a Drama Series) 2006: SAG.

Dickinson, Angie

Movie: 1959: *Rio Bravo* (New Star of the Year — Actress) *Globe*. Television: 1974–1978 series *Police Woman* (Best Actress in a Drama Series) 1975:

Emmy, *Globe*. 1976: Emmy, Globe. 1977: Emmy, Globe. 1978: Globe.

Dierker, Brian

Movie: 2007: *Into the Wild* (Best Ensemble) SAG.

Diesel, Vin

Movie: 1998: *Saving Private Ryan* (Best Ensemble) SAG.

Dietrich, Marlene

Movie: 1930: *Morocco* (Best Actress) Academy. 1957: *Witness for the Prosecution* (Best Actress, Drama) Globe. Tributes: 1968: Special award from Tony. 1999: Ranked Number 9 on List of 25 Greatest Female Screen Legends of the 20th Century from American Film Institute.

Diggs, Taye

Movie: 2002: *Chicago* (Best Ensemble) *SAG, Broadcast*. 2005: *Rent* (Best Ensemble) Broadcast.

Dillahunt, Garret

Movie: 2007: *No Country for Old Men* (Best Ensemble) *Board, SAG*, Broadcast.

Dillane, Stephen

Movie: 2002: *The Hours* (Best Ensemble) SAG, Broadcast. Theater: 2000: *The Real Thing* (Best Actor, Play) *Tony*.

Dillman, Bradford

Movie: 1958: *In Love and War* (New Star of the Year — Actor) *Globe*. 1959: *Compulsion* (Best Actor) *Cannes* (win shared with costars). Television: 1963: *"The Voice of Charlie Pont," Premiere, Presented by Fred Astaire* (Best Single Performance by an Actor in a Leading Role) Emmy. 1975: *"The Last Bride of Salem," ABC Afternoon Playbreak* (Best Actor in a Daytime Drama Special) *Emmy*.

Dillon, Matt

Movie: 1989: *Drugstore Cowboy* (Best Male Lead) *Spirit*. 2005: *Crash* (Best Male Actor in a Supporting Role) SAG (Best Supporting Actor) Academy, Globe, British, Broadcast (Best Supporting Male) *Spirit* (Best Ensemble) *SAG, Broadcast*.

Dillon, Melinda

Movie: 1976: *Bound for Glory* (New Star of the Year — Actress) Globe. 1977: *Close Encounters of the Third Kind* (Best Supporting Actress) Academy.

1981: *Absence of Malice* (Best Supporting Actress) Academy. 1999: *Magnolia* (Best Ensemble) *Board*, SAG. Theater: 1963: *Who's Afraid of Virginia Woolf?* (Best Supporting or Featured Actress, Dramatic) Tony.

Dinklage, Peter

Movie: 2003: *The Station Agent* (Best Male Lead) Spirit (Best Male Actor in a Leading Role) SAG (Best Ensemble) SAG.

Ditchburn, Anne

Movie: 1978: *Slow Dancing in the Big City* (New Star of the Year — Actress) Globe.

Divine

Movie: 1988: *Hairspray* (Best Supporting Male) Spirit.

Dix, Richard

Movie: 1931: *Cimarron* (Best Actor) Academy.

Dobronravov, Ivan

Movie: 2003: *Vozvrashcheniye (The Return)* (Best Actor) *Venice* (win shared with costars).

Dobronravova, Yelena

Movie: 1954: *Bolshaya semya (The Big Family)* *Cannes* (special ensemble award).

Dollenmayer, Kate

Movie: 2005: *Funny Ha Ha* (Best Actress) Society.

Donahue, Troy

Movie: 1959: *A Summer Place* (New Star of the Year — Actor) *Globe*.

Donat, Robert

Movie: 1938: *The Citadel* (Best Acting) *Board* (Best Actor) Academy. 1939: *Goodbye, Mr. Chips* (Best Actor) *Academy*. 1954: *Lease of Life* (Best British Actor) British. 1958: *The Inn of the Sixth Happiness* (Best Actor, Drama) Globe.

Donlevy, Brian

Movie: 1939: *Beau Geste* (Best Supporting Actor) Academy.

D'Onofrio, Vincent

Movie: 1993: *Household Saints* (Best Male Lead) Spirit. Television: 1998: *Homicide: Life on the Street* (Best Guest Actor in a Drama Series) Emmy.

Donovan, Martin

Movie: 1996: *The Portrait of a Lady* (Best Supporting Actor) *Society*. Television: 2006–present series *Weeds* (Best Ensemble in a Comedy Series) 2006: SAG.

Donovan, Tate

Movie: 1993: *Inside Monkey Zetterland* (Best Supporting Male) Spirit. 2005: *Good Night, and Good Luck* (Best Ensemble) SAG, Broadcast.

Dooley, Paul

Movie: 1979: *Breaking Away* (Best Supporting Actor) *Board*. 2007: *Hairspray* (Best Ensemble) SAG, *Broadcast*. Television: 1994: *Dream On* (Best Guest Actor in a Comedy Series) Emmy. 2000: *The Practice* (Best Guest Actor in a Drama Series) Emmy.

DoQui, Robert

Movie: 1993: *Short Cuts* (Best Ensemble) *Venice* (special award).

Doug, Doug E.

Movie: 1991: *Hangin' with the Homeboys* (Best Male Lead) Spirit.

Douglas, Kirk

Movie: 1949: *Champion* (Best Actor) Academy. 1951: *Detective Story* (Best Actor, Drama) Globe. 1952: *The Bad and the Beautiful* (Best Actor) Academy. 1956: *Lust for Life* (Best Actor) Academy, *New York* (Best Actor, Drama) *Globe*. 1962: *Lonely Are the Brave* (Best Foreign Actor) British. Television: 1986: *Amos* (Best Actor in a Miniseries or Special) Emmy (Best Actor in a Miniseries or TV Movie) Globe. 1992: *Tales from the Crypt* (Best Actor in a Drama Special) Emmy. 2000: *Touched by an Angel* (Best Guest Actor in a Drama Series) Emmy. Tributes: 1967: Cecil B. DeMille Award from Globe. 1988: Career Achievement Award from Board. 1991: Life Achievement Award from American Film Institute. 1994: Honor from Kennedy Center for the Performing Arts. 1995: Honorary award for being a creative and moral force in the motion picture community from Academy. 1998: Life Achievement Award from SAG. 1999: Ranked Number 17 on List of 25 Greatest Male Screen Legends of the 20th Century from American Film Institute. 2001: Honorary Golden Bear from Berlin.

Douglas, Melvyn

Movie: 1963: *Hud* (Best Supporting Actor) *Academy, Board*, Globe. 1970: *I Never Sang for My Father* (Best Actor) Academy (Best Actor, Drama) Globe.

1979: *Being There* (Best Supporting Actor) *Academy, New York, Globe, LA* (multiple win); *The Seduction of Joe Tynan* (Best Supporting Actor) *LA* (multiple win). Theater: 1960: *The Best Man* (Best Actor, Dramatic) *Tony*. Television: 1966: *"Inherit the Wind," Hallmark Hall of Fame* (Best Single Performance by an Actor in a Leading Role in a Drama) Emmy. 1968: *"Do Not Go Gentle into That Good Night," CBS Playhouse* (Best Single Performance by an Actor in a Leading Role in a Drama) *Emmy*. Records: Douglas wasn't present at the award ceremony to accept his second Best Supporting Actor Oscar for *Being There* because, he told reporters, he resented being up against an 8-year-old. At 78, Douglas was in the running against young Justin Henry in *Kramer vs. Kramer*. Their age gap put Douglas in the record books for winning an Oscar over another nominee 70 years younger than he.

Douglas, Michael

Movie: 1969: *Hail, Hero!* (New Star of the Year — Actor) Globe. 1975: *One Flew Over the Cuckoo's Nest* (Best Picture, Producer) *Academy* (Best Picture, Drama; Producer) *Globe*. 1979: *The China Syndrome* (Best Picture, Drama; Producer) Globe. 1984: *Romancing the Stone* (Best Picture, Musical or Comedy; Producer) *Globe*. 1987: *Fatal Attraction* (Best Actor) British; *Wall Street* (Best Actor) *Academy, Board* (Best Actor, Drama) *Globe*. 1989: *The War of the Roses* (Best Actor, Musical or Comedy) Globe. 1995: *The American President* (Best Actor, Musical or Comedy) Globe. 2000: *Traffic* (Best Ensemble) *SAG*; *Wonder Boys* (Best Actor) British, *LA*, Broadcast (Best Actor, Drama) Globe. Television: 1972–1976 series *The Streets of San Francisco* (Best Actor in a Drama Series) 1974: Globe. (Best Supporting Actor in a Drama) 1974: Emmy. (Best Continuing Performance by a Supporting Actor in a Drama Series) 1975: Emmy. 1976: Emmy. 2002: *Will & Grace* (Best Guest Actor in a Comedy Series) Emmy. Tributes: 2003: Cecil B. DeMille Award from Globe. 2007: Career Achievement award from Board. Records: Douglas is the first actor to win a Best Picture award for a film he produced. In 1963, Michael's father, Kirk had starred in a stage production of Ken Kesey's anti-establishment novel, *One Flew Over the Cuckoo's Nest* and bought the movie rights. After a dozen years of trying to launch the film project, Kirk Douglas finally relinquished the reigns to Michael, who ended up producing a film version that won the Best Picture Golden Globe and became the second movie in Oscar history (after 1934's *It Happened One Night*) to sweep the top five awards (Best Picture, Actor, Actress, Director, and Screenplay). Douglas set another record when he won the Cecil B. DeMille award at the Golden Globes 36 years after his father Kirk received the same honor, making them the first father/son actors to both earn the prestigious recognition.

Douglas, Paul

Movie: 1954: *Executive Suite* (Best Ensemble) *Venice* (special award).

Dourif, Brad

Movie: 1975: *One Flew Over the Cuckoo's Nest* (New Star of the Year — Actor) *Globe* (Best Supporting Actor) Academy, *British*. 2002: *The Lord of the Rings: The Two Towers* (Best Ensemble) SAG. Television: 2004–2006 series *Deadwood* (Best Supporting Actor in a Drama Series) 2004: Emmy. (Best Ensemble in a Drama Series) 2006: SAG.

Downey, Robert, Jr.

Movie: 1992: *Chaplin* (Best Actor) Academy, *British* (Best Actor, Drama) Globe. 1993: *Short Cuts* (Best Ensemble) *Venice* (special award). 2005: *Good Night, and Good Luck* (Best Ensemble) SAG, Broadcast. Television: 2000–2001 series *Ally McBeal* (Best Male Actor in a Comedy Series) 2000: *SAG*. (Best Supporting Actor in a Comedy Series) 2001: Emmy. (Best Supporting Actor in a Series, Miniseries, or TV Movie) 2000: *Globe*. (Best Ensemble in a Comedy Series) 2000: SAG.

Do-yeon, Jeon

Movie: 2007: *Secret Sunshine* (Best Actress) *Cannes*.

Draven, Jamie

Movie: 2000: *Billy Elliot* (Best Ensemble) SAG.

Dresser, Louise

Movie: 1928: *A Ship Comes In* (Best Actress) Academy.

Dressler, Marie

Movie: 1930: *Min and Bill* (Best Actress) *Academy*. 1932: *Emma* (Best Actress) Academy. Records: Winning the Best Actress Oscar the day after her 62nd birthday, Dressler became the oldest Oscar winning actor. Dressler made an astounding eight motion pictures in 1930, most notably as the waterfront hag Marthy in *Anna Christie*, a rare departure of a dramatic role for the former vaudevillian turned comedic actress, and as Min Divot in the tragicomic *Min and Bill*, which earned her an Academy Award. Her other films of 1930: *Caught Short, Chasing Rainbows, Derelict, The Girl Said No, Let Us Be Gay*, and *One Romantic Night*. A hefty and unglamorous actress (she titled her autobiography *The Life Story of an Ugly Duckling*) Dressler was an unlikely movie star, but she was as popular as she was talented, and for four years reigned as the number one box office draw in the country. That achievement made her the oldest #1 Box Office Star, a world record that still stands today.

Dreyfuss, Richard

Movie: 1973: *American Graffiti* (Best Actor, Musical or Comedy) Globe. 1975: *Jaws* (Best Actor) British. 1977: *The Goodbye Girl* (Best Actor) *Academy, British, LA* (Best Actor, Musical or Comedy) *Globe*. 1987: *Nuts* (Best Supporting Actor) Globe. 1995: *Mr. Holland's Opus* (Best Actor) Academy (Best Actor, Drama) Globe. Television: 2001–2002 series *The Education of Max Bickford* (Best Male Actor in a Drama Series) 2001: SAG. 2001: *The Day Reagan Was Shot* (Best Male Actor in a Television Movie or Miniseries) SAG. Records: At age 30 Richard Dreyfuss became the youngest star to win a Best Actor Academy Award, for the 1977 Neil Simon comedy, *The Goodbye Girl*. He held the record for 25 years until 29-year-old Adrien Brody won in the same category for *The Pianist* in 2002. Dreyfuss's 1977 win was a surprise. Although he received Best Actor prizes from the L.A. Film Critics and the Hollywood Foreign Press, all eyes were on Richard Burton that year, who set the record for most nominations (eight) without a win. Burton had wanted to win, and his absorbing performance as a psychiatrist forced to look at his own shortcomings while treating a young man's sexual obsession with horses in *Equus* was a true tour-de-force. When Sylvester Stallone announced the winner that night, however, it was Richard Dreyfuss, not Burton he summoned to the podium. An ebullient Dreyfuss leapt to the stage and accepted his honor for playing egotistical but good hearted struggling actor Elliot Garfield in Neil Simon's *The Goodbye Girl*.

Driscoll, Bobby

Tributes: 1949: Honorary miniature Oscar statuette for outstanding juvenile actor from Academy. Records: A favorite actor in Disney films of the 1940s, Driscoll was the first "live" actor to sign a contract with Disney's animation studios.

Driver, Minnie

Movie: 1997: *Good Will Hunting* (Best Female Actor in a Supporting Role) SAG (Best Supporting Actress) Academy (Best Ensemble) SAG. Television: 2007–present series *The Riches* (Best Actress in a Drama Series) 2007: Emmy, Globe.

Dueñas, Lola

Movie: 2006: *Volver* (Best Actress) *Cannes* (win shared with costars).

Duggan, Gerry

Movie: 1959: *The Siege of Pinchgut* (Most Promising Newcomer) British.

Dukakis, Olympia

Movie: 1987: *Moonstruck* (Best Supporting Actress) *Academy, Board, Globe, British, LA*. **Television:** 1991: *Lucky Day* (Best Supporting Actress in a Miniseries or Special) Emmy. 1992: *Sinatra* (Best Supporting Actress in a Series, Miniseries, or TV Movie) Globe. 1998: *Armistead Maupin's More Tales of the City* (Best Actress in a Miniseries or Movie) Emmy (Best Female Actor in a Television Movie or Miniseries) SAG. 1999: *Joan of Arc* (Best Supporting Actress in a Miniseries or TV Movie) Emmy. **Highlights:** Dukakis went five-for-five at awards time in 1987 for playing Cher's wise and only slightly jaded mother in *Moonstruck*. Capitalizing on her naturally sharp wit, Dukakis delivered some unforgettable lines in Norman Jewison's romantic comedy. While the crackling script won screenwriter John Patrick Shanley the Best Screenplay Oscar, Dukakis is said to have adlibbed some of her humorous lines.

Duke (Astin), Patty

Movie: 1962: *The Miracle Worker* (New Star of the Year — Actress) *Globe* (Best Supporting Actress) *Academy, Globe*. 1969: *Me, Natalie* (Best Actress, Musical or Comedy) *Globe*. **Television:** 1963–1966 series *The Patty Duke Show* (Best Actress in a Series) 1965: Globe. (Best Continued Performance by an Actress in a Comedy Series) 1964: Emmy. 1970: *My Sweet Charlie* (Best Single Performance by an Actress in a Leading Role) *Emmy*. 1977: *"The Captains and the Kings," NBC's Best Seller* (Best Actress in a Limited Series) *Emmy*. 1978: *A Family Upside Down* (Best Supporting Actress in a Drama or Comedy Special) Emmy; *Having Babies* (Best Single Performance by an Actress in a Drama or Comedy Series) Emmy. 1980: *The Miracle Worker* (Best Actress in a Limited Series or Special) *Emmy*. 1981: *Family Specials* (Best Individual Achievement in Children's Programming, Star) Emmy; *The Women's Room* (Best Supporting Actress in a Limited Series or Special) Emmy. 1984: *George Washington* (Best Supporting Actress in a Limited Series or Special) Emmy. 1999: *Touched by an Angel* (Best Guest Actress in a Drama Series) Emmy. **Records:** At 14, Duke became the first juvenile star to win an Academy Award in a competitive category. Until she re-ceived her Best Supporting Actress Oscar portraying Helen Keller in the 1962 film, *The Miracle Worker*, the only juveniles to win Oscars (there were 12 in all, from Shirley Temple in 1934 to Hayley Mills in 1960) were honored as Special Award recipients and given miniature statuettes. In the year Duke won, she beat another child actress, Mary Badham of *To Kill a Mockingbird*. Two years later, Duke set her first television record when her sitcom, *The Patty Duke Show* made her the youngest actor to have a television series bearing her name. She set another TV record when she won the Emmy for the 1980 television adaptation of her big screen hit, *The Miracle Worker*, this time with Duke in the role of teacher, Annie Sullivan. It was the first time an actor won both an Academy Award and Emmy for the same film, but playing different roles.

Dullea, Keir

Movie: 1962: *David and Lisa* (New Star of the Year — Actor) *Globe* (Most Promising Newcomer) British.

Dunaway, Faye

Movie: 1967: *Hurry Sundown* (Best New Star of the Year — Actress) Globe (Most Promising Newcomer) *British* (multiple win); *Bonnie and Clyde* (Most Promising Newcomer) *British* (multiple win), (Best Actress) Academy (Best Actress, Drama) Globe. 1970: *Puzzle of a Downfall Child* (Best Actress, Drama) Globe. 1974: *Chinatown* (Best Actress) Academy, British (Best Actress, Drama) Globe. 1975: *Three Days of the Condor* (Best Actress, Drama) Globe. 1976: *Network* (Best Actress) *Academy*, British (Best Actress, Drama) *Globe*. 1987: *Barfly* (Best Actress, Drama) Globe. **Television:** 1984: *Ellis Island* (Best Supporting Actress in a Series, Miniseries, or TV Movie) *Globe*. 1994: *Columbo: It's All in the Game* (Best Guest Actress in a Drama Series) *Emmy* (Best Actress in a Series, Miniseries, or TV Movie) Globe. 1997: *The Twilight of the Gods* (Best Female Actor in a Television Movie or Miniseries) SAG. 1998: *Gia* (Best Supporting Actress in a Series, Miniseries, or TV Movie) *Globe*. 2000: *Running Mates* (Best Supporting Actress in a Series, Miniseries, or TV Movie) Globe.

Duncan, Michael Clarke

Movie: 1999: *The Green Mile* (Best Male Actor in a Supporting Role) SAG (Best Supporting Actor) Academy, Globe, *Broadcast* (Best Ensemble) SAG. 2005: *Sin City* (Best Ensemble) Broadcast.

Duncan, Sandy

Movie: 1971: *Million Dollar Duck* (New Star of the Year — Actress) Globe; *Star-Spangled Girl* (Best

Actress, Musical or Comedy) Globe. **Theater:** 1969: *Canterbury Tales* (Best Supporting or Featured Actress, Musical) Tony. 1971: *The Boy Friend* (Best Actress, Musical) Tony. 1980: *Peter Pan* (Best Actress, Musical) Tony. **Television:** 1971 series *Funny Face* (Best Actress in a Comedy Series) 1972: Emmy. 1977: *Roots* (Best Single Performance by a Supporting Actress in a Comedy or Drama Series) Emmy.

Dundas, Jennifer

Movie: 1996: *The First Wives Club* (Best Ensemble) *Board*.

Dunn, James

Movie: 1945: *A Tree Grows in Brooklyn* (Best Supporting Actor) *Academy*.

Dunn, Michael

Movie: 1965: *Ship of Fools* (Best Supporting Actor) Academy. **Theater:** 1964: *The Ballad of the Sad Café* (Best Supporting or Featured Actor, Dramatic) Tony.

Dunne, Griffin

Movie: 1985: *After Hours* (Best Actor, Musical or Comedy) Globe. 1995: *Duke of Groove* (Best Live Action Short Film) Academy. 1998: *Running on Empty* (Best Picture, Drama; Producer) Globe. **Television:** 1996: *Frasier* (Best Guest Actor in a Comedy Series) Emmy.

Dunne, Irene

Movie: 1931: *Cimarron* (Best Actress) Academy. 1936: *Theodora Goes Wild* (Best Actress) Academy. 1937: *The Awful Truth* (Best Actress) Academy. 1939: *Love Affair* (Best Actress) Academy. 1948: *I Remember Mama* (Best Actress) Academy. **Tributes:** 1985: Honor from Kennedy Center for the Performing Arts.

Dunnock, Mildred

Movie: 1951: *Death of a Salesman* (Best Supporting Actress) Academy. 1952: *Viva Zapata!* (Best Supporting Actress) Globe. 1956: *Baby Doll* (Best Supporting Actress) Academy, Globe. 1957: *Peyton Place* (Best Supporting Actress) Globe. **Television:** 1967: *Death of a Salesman* (Best Single Performance by an Actress in a Leading Role in a Drama) Emmy.

Dunst, Kirsten

Movie: 1994: *Interview with the Vampire* (Best Supporting Actress) Globe.

Duong, Phuong

Movie: 1997: *Squeeze* (Best Debut Performance) Spirit (nomination shared with costars).

Duprez, June

Movie: 1944: *None but the Lonely Heart* (Best Acting) *Board*.

Duquenne, Pascal

Movie: 1996: *Le huitième jour (The Eighth Day)* (Best Actor) *Cannes* (win shared with costar).

Durand, Kevin

Movie: 2007: *3:10 to Yuma* (Best Ensemble) SAG.

Durano, Giustino

Movie: 1998: *La Vita è Bella (Life Is Beautiful)* (Best Ensemble) SAG.

Durante, Jimmy

Movie: 1962: *Billy Rose's Jumbo* (Best Actor, Musical or Comedy) Globe. **Television:** 1952: --- (Best Comedian or Comedienne) Emmy. 1953: --- (Best Comedian) *Emmy* (Most Outstanding Personality) Emmy.

Durbin, Deanna

Tributes: 1938: Honorary miniature Oscar statuette for her significant contribution in bringing to the screen the spirit and personification of youth, and as a juvenile player setting a high standard of ability and achievement from Academy.

Durning, Charles

Movie: 1975: *Dog Day Afternoon* (Best Supporting Actor) *Board*, Globe. 1982: *The Best Little Whorehouse in Texas* (Best Supporting Actor) Academy. 1983: *To Be or Not to Be* (Best Supporting Actor) Academy, Globe. 2000: *State and Main* (Best Ensemble) *Board*. **Theater:** 1990: *Cat on a Hot Tin Roof* (Best Actor in a Featured Role, Play) *Tony*. **Television:** 1975: *Queen of the Stardust Ballroom* (Best Actor in a Special Program) Emmy. 1977: *"The Captains and the Kings," NBC's Best Seller* (Best Supporting Actor in a Comedy or Drama Series) Emmy (Best Supporting Actor in a Series, Miniseries, or TV Movie) Globe. 1980: *Attica* (Best Supporting Actor in a Limited Series or Special) Emmy. 1985: *Death of a Salesman* (Best Supporting Actor in a Miniseries or Special) Emmy. 1990: *The Kennedys of Massachusetts* (Best Supporting Actor in a Miniseries or Special) *Globe*. 1990–1994 series *Evening Shade* (Best Supporting Actor in a

Comedy Series) 1991: Emmy. 1992: Emmy. 1998: *Homicide: Life on the Street* (Best Guest Actor in a Drama Series) Emmy. 2005: *NCIS* (Best Guest Actor in a Drama Series) Emmy. **Tributes:** 2007: Life Achievement Award from SAG.

Dutton, Charles S.

Movie: 1998: *Blind Faith* (Best Supporting Male) Spirit. 1999: *Cookie's Fortune* (Best Supporting Male) Spirit. **Theater:** 1985: *Ma Rainey's Black Bottom* (Best Actor in a Featured Role, Play) Tony. 1990: *The Piano Lesson* (Best Actor, Play) Tony. **Television:** 1995: *"The Piano Lesson," Hallmark Hall of Fame* (Best Actor in a Miniseries or Special) Emmy (Best Actor in a Miniseries or TV Movie) Globe. 1998: *Blind Faith* (Best Male Actor in a Television Movie or Miniseries) SAG. 1999: *Oz* (Best Guest Actor in a Drama Series) Emmy. 2000: *The Corner* (Best Directing for a Miniseries, TV Movie, or Special) *Emmy*. 2002: *The Practice* (Best Guest Actor in a Drama Series) *Emmy*. 2003: *Without a Trace* (Best Guest Actor in a Drama Series) *Emmy*.

Duvall, Robert

Movie: 1972: *The Godfather* (Best Supporting Actor) Academy, *New York*, British. 1976: *Network* (Best Supporting Actor) British. 1979: *Apocalypse Now* (Best Supporting Actor) Academy, *Globe, British*. 1980: *The Great Santini* (Best Actor) Academy. 1981: *True Confessions* (Best Actor) *Venice*. 1983: *Tender Mercies* (Best Actor) *Academy, New York, LA* (Best Actor, Drama) *Globe*. 1985: *The Lightship* (Best Actor) *Venice*. 1991: *Rambling Rose* (Best Male Lead) Spirit. 1996: *Sling Blade* (Best Ensemble) SAG. 1997: *The Apostle* (Best Actor) Academy, *Society, LA* (Best Male Lead) *Spirit* (Best Male Actor in a Leading Role) SAG (Best Director) *Spirit* (Best Screenplay) Spirit. 1998: *A Civil Action* (Best Male Actor in a Supporting Role) *SAG* (Best Supporting Actor) Academy, Globe. **Television:** 1989: *Lonesome Dove* (Best Actor in a Miniseries or Special) Emmy (Best Actor in a Miniseries or TV Movie) *Globe*. 1993: *Stalin* (Best Actor in a Miniseries or Special) Emmy (Best Actor in a Miniseries or TV Movie) *Globe*. 1997: *The Man Who Captured Eichmann* (Best Actor in a Miniseries or Special) Emmy (Best Male Actor in a Television Movie or Miniseries) SAG. 2006: *Broken Trail* (Best Actor in a Miniseries or TV Movie) *Emmy*, Globe (Best Male Actor in a Television Movie or Miniseries) SAG (Best Miniseries or TV Movie, Executive Producer) *Emmy*. **Tributes:** 1997: Career Achievement Award from Board. **Records:** Duvall is the first actor in movie history to win two Golden Globes in a tie with another actor. In 1979, he picked up his first Globe

as Best Supporting Actor for *Apocalypse Now*, sharing the prize with Melvyn Douglas for *Being There*. Four years later, he was in the running for Best Actor, Drama for *Tender Mercies*, and won alongside Tom Courtenay for *The Dresser*. Since those wins, Duvall has been nominated for only one other Globe for acting in motion pictures, but lost for his supporting performance in *A Civil Action* to Ed Harris in *The Truman Show*. Although he was never an individual Globe winner for his work in motion pictures, he was the exclusive winner twice for his work in television: in 1989 for *Lonesome Dove* and in 1993 for *Stalin*.

Duvall, Shelley

Movie: 1977: *Three Women* (Best Actress) *Cannes, British, LA*. **Television:** 1988: *Shelley Duvall's Tall Tales and Legends* (Best Children's Program, Executive Producer) Emmy. 1992: *Shelley Duvall's Bedtime Stories* (Best Animated Program for Programming One Hour or Less, Executive Producer) Emmy.

Dzundza, George

Movie: 1983: *Streamers* (Best Actor) *Venice* (win shared with costars).

Eagels, Jeanne

Movie: 1929: *The Letter* (Best Actress) Academy. **Records:** At age 35, Eagels received an Oscar nod and died of a heroin overdose, making her, at only the second Academy Awards ceremony, the first posthumous nominee. She lost to Mary Pickford for *Coquette*. In 1940 Bette Davis received an Oscar nomination for playing the same role in a remake of *The Letter*, but lost to Ginger Rogers in *Kitty Foyle*. Eagels's life became the subject of a 1957 biopic, *Jeanne Eagels*, with Kim Novak portraying the stage and screen beauty.

Eastwood, Clint

Movie: 1988: *Bird* (Best Director) *Globe*. 1992: *Unforgiven* (Best Actor) Academy, *LA* (Best Director) *Academy, Globe*, British, *Society, LA* (Best Picture, Producer) *Academy*, British, *Society, LA* (Best Picture, Drama; Producer) Globe. 1995: *The Bridges of Madison County* (Best Picture, Drama; Producer) Globe. 2003: *Mystic River* (Best Director) Academy, Globe, *Society*, Broadcast (Best Picture, Producer) Academy, *Board*, Broadcast (Best Picture, Drama; Producer) Globe (Best Composer) Broadcast. 2004: *Million Dollar Baby* (Best Actor) Academy, Society (Best Director) *Academy, New York, Globe*, Society, Broadcast (Best Picture, Producer) *Academy, Society,* Broadcast (Best Picture, Drama; Producer)

Globe (Best Score) Globe (Best Ensemble) SAG. 2006: *Flags of Our Fathers* (Best Director) Globe; *Letters from Iwo Jima (Iwo Jima kara no tegami)* (Best Director) Academy, Globe, Broadcast (Best Picture, Producer) Academy, *Board, LA,* Broadcast (Best Foreign Language Film, Producer) *Globe.* 2007: *Grace Is Gone* (Best Score) Globe (Best Song, "Grace Is Gone") Globe. **Tributes:** 1970: Henrietta Award for World Film Favorite from Globe. 1987: Cecil B. DeMille Award from Globe. 1994: Irving G. Thalberg Memorial Award from Academy. 1996: Life Achievement Award from American Film Institute; Gala Tribute from the Film Society of Lincoln Center. 1999: Career Achievement Award from Board. 2000: Honor from Kennedy Center for the Performing Arts; Career Golden Lion from Venice. 2002: Future Film Festival Digital Award for *Blood Work* from Venice; Life Achievement Award from SAG. 2004: Special Filmmaking Achievement Award for producing, directing, acting, and composing the score of *Million Dollar Baby* from Board. **Records:** While everyone from Shirley Temple and John Wayne to Doris Day and Sophia Loren have been singled out as the most popular star in the world during more than one year, Eastwood is the only actor in history to have appeared on the list of Top 10 box office draws nineteen consecutive times. He topped the list every year from 1968 to 1986.

Eckhart, Aaron

Movie: 1997: *In the Company of Men* (Best Debut Performance) *Spirit.* 2006: *Thank You for Smoking* (Best Male Lead) Spirit (Best Actor, Musical or Comedy) Globe.

Edwards, Stacy

Movie: 1997: *In the Company of Men* (Best Female Lead) Spirit. **Television:** 1994–2000 series *Chicago Hope* (Best Ensemble in a Drama Series) 1994: SAG. 1995: SAG. 1996: SAG. 1997: SAG.

Efron, Zac

Movie: 2007: *Hairspray* (Best Ensemble) SAG, *Broadcast.*

Egan, Peter

Movie: 1973: *The Hireling* (Most Promising Newcomer) *British.*

Egan, Richard

Movie: 1953: *The Glory Brigade* (New Star of the Year — Actor) *Globe* (multiple win); *The Kid from Left Field* (New Star of the Year — Actor) *Globe* (multiple win).

Eggar, Samantha

Movie: 1965: *The Collector* (Best Actress) Academy, Cannes (Best Actress, Drama) *Globe.*

Ehle, Jennifer

Movie: 1997: *Wilde* (Best Supporting Actress) British. **Theater:** 2000: *The Real Thing* (Best Actress, Play) *Tony.* 2007: *The Coast of Utopia* (Best Actress in a Featured Role, Play) *Tony.*

Eichhorn, Lisa

Movie: 1979: *Yanks* (New Star of the Year — Actress) Globe (Best Actress, Drama) Globe; *The Europeans* (Best Supporting Actress) British.

Eisenberg, Jesse

Movie: 2005: *The Squid and the Whale* (Best Supporting Male) Spirit (Best Young Actor) Broadcast.

Ejiofor, Chiwetel

Movie: 2003: *Love Actually* (Best Ensemble) Broadcast. 2006: *Kinky Boots* (Best Actor, Musical or Comedy) Globe. 2007: *American Gangster* (Best Ensemble) SAG; *Talk to Me* (Best Supporting Male) *Spirit.* **Television:** 2006: *Tsunami, The Aftermath* (Best Actor in a Series, Miniseries, or TV Movie) Globe.

Ekberg, Anita

Movie: 1955: *Blood Alley* (New Star of the Year — Actress) *Globe.*

Eklund, Jakob

Movie: 2003: *Om jag vänder mig om* (Best Ensemble) *Berlin* (special award).

Elba, Idris

Movie: 2007: *American Gangster* (Best Ensemble) SAG.

Elg, Taina

Movie: 1956: --- (New Foreign Star of the Year — Actress) *Globe.* 1957: *Les Girls* (Best Actress, Musical or Comedy) *Globe.* **Theater:** 1975: *Where's Charley?* (Best Supporting or Featured Actress, Musical) Tony.

Elise, Kimberly

Movie: 2004: *Woman Thou Art Loosed* (Best Female Lead) Spirit.

Elizabeth, Shannon

Movie: 2003: *Love Actually* (Best Ensemble) Broadcast.

Elizondo, Hector

Movie: 1990: *Pretty Woman* (Best Supporting Actor) Globe. Television: 1992: *"Mrs. Cage," American Playhouse* (Best Supporting Actor in a Miniseries or Special) Emmy. 1994–2000 series *Chicago Hope* (Best Male Actor in a Drama Series) 1994: SAG. (Best Supporting Actor in a Drama Series) 1995: Emmy. 1996: Emmy. 1997: *Emmy*. 1998: Emmy. (Best Ensemble in a Drama Series) 1994: SAG. 1995: SAG. 1996: SAG. 1997: SAG.

Elliman, Yvonne

Movie: 1973: *Jesus Christ Superstar* (Best Actress, Musical or Comedy) Globe.

Elliott, Alison

Movie: 1997: *The Wings of the Dove* (Best Female Actor in a Supporting Role) SAG.

Elliott, Denholm

Movie: 1973: *A Doll's House* (Best Supporting Actor) British. 1979: *Saint Jack* (Best Supporting Actor) British. 1981: *Raiders of the Lost Ark* (Best Supporting Actor) British. 1983: *Trading Places* (Best Supporting Actor) *British*. 1984: *A Private Function* (Best Supporting Actor) *British*. 1985: *Defense of the Realm* (Best Supporting Actor) *British*. 1986: *A Room with a View* (Best Supporting Actor) Academy, British.

Ellis, Aunjanue

Movie: 2004: *Ray* (Best Ensemble) SAG.

Elphick, Michael

Movie: 1984: *Gorky Park* (Best Supporting Actor) British.

Elsom, Isobel

Movie: 1941: *Ladies in Retirement* (Best Acting) *Board*.

Elvin, Justin

Movie: 1998: *Happiness* (Best Ensemble) *Board*.

Emerson, Hope

Movie: 1950: *Caged* (Best Supporting Actress) Academy. Television: 1958–1959 series *Peter Gunn* (Best Supporting Actress — Continuing Character — in a Dramatic Series) 1959: Emmy.

Engel, Georgia

Movie: 1971: *Taking Off* (Best Supporting Actress) British. Television: 1972–1977 series *The Mary Tyler Moore Show* (Best Continuing Performance by a Supporting Actress in a Comedy Series) 1976: Emmy. 1977: Emmy. 2003–2005 series *Everybody Loves Raymond* (Best Guest Actress in a Comedy Series) 2003: Emmy. 2004: Emmy. 2005: Emmy.

Epps, Shareeka

Movie: 2006: *Half Nelson* (Best Female Lead) *Spirit* (Best Young Actress) Broadcast.

Ermey, R. Lee

Movie: 1987: *Full Metal Jacket* (Best Supporting Actor) Globe.

Erwin, Stuart

Movie: 1936: *Pigskin Parade* (Best Supporting Actor) Academy.

Esposito, Giancarlo

Movie: 1994: *Fresh* (Best Supporting Male) Spirit. 1995: *The Usual Suspects* (Best Ensemble) *Board*.

Esposito, Jennifer

Movie: 2005: *Crash* (Best Ensemble) *SAG, Broadcast*.

Essex, David

Movie: 1973: *That'll Be the Day* (Most Promising Newcomer) British.

Estevez, Emilio

Movie: 2006: *Bobby* (Best Ensemble) SAG, Broadcast.

Etel, Alex

Movie: 2005: *Millions* (Best Young Actor) Broadcast.

Evanofski, Candace

Movie: 2000: *George Washington* (Best Debut Performance) Spirit (nomination shared with costars).

Evans, Edith

Movie: 1959: *The Nun's Story* (Best Supporting Actress) *Board*, Globe. 1963: *Tom Jones* (Best British Actress) British (Best Supporting Actress) Academy. 1964: *The Chalk Garden* (Best British Actress) British (Best Supporting Actress) Academy, *Board*. 1967: *The Whisperers* (Best Actress) Academy, *New York, Board*, Berlin (Best Actress, Drama) *Globe* (Best British Actress) *British*. Television: 1970: *David Copperfield* (Best Single Performance by an Actress in a Leading Role) Emmy.

Everett, Rupert

Movie: 1984: *Another Country* (Best Newcomer to Film) British. 1994: *Prêt-à-Porter (Ready-to-Wear)* (Best Ensemble) *Board.* 1997: *My Best Friend's Wedding* (Best Supporting Actor) Globe, British. 1999: *An Ideal Husband* (Best Actor, Musical or Comedy) Globe.

Ewell, Tom

Movie: 1955: *The Seven Year Itch* (Best Actor, Musical or Comedy) *Globe.* Theater: 1953: *The Seven Year Itch* (Best Actor, Dramatic) *Tony.* Television: 1975–1978 series *Baretta* (Best Continued Performance by a Supporting Actor in a Drama Series) 1977: Emmy.

Eziashi, Maynard

Movie: 1991: *Mister Johnson* (Best Actor) *Berlin.*

Faber, Matthew

Movie: 1996: *Welcome to the Dollhouse* (Best Supporting Male) Spirit.

Fabray, Nanette

Theater: 1949: *Love Life* (Best Actress, Musical) *Tony.* 1963: *Mr. President* (Best Actress, Musical) Tony. Television: 1956: --- (Best Comedienne) *Emmy.* 1955–1956 series *Caesar's Hour* (Best Actress in a Supporting Role) 1956: *Emmy.* (Best Continuing Performance by a Comedienne in a Series) 1957: *Emmy.* Tributes: 1986: Life Achievement Award from SAG. Records: In 1955, Fabray (along with Phil Silvers, who won Best Actor and Best Comedian) became the first actor to win two Emmys in different acting categories for the same show. Fabray was a popular choice in 1955 when she accepted her awards as Best Supporting Actress and then as Best Comedienne in *Caesar's Hour*, thanking Sid Caesar tearfully because she had just retired from his show. However, when she won Best Comedienne in a Continuing Series the next year, her win grew criticism instead of praise. Somehow Fabray was nominated in 1956 even though she had quit *Caesar's Hour* the previous year and had not starred in a single episode. The Academy Board investigated the complaint and stuck by the win because the period of consideration was the calendar year of 1956, not the television season of fall 1956 through spring 1957. Fabray had still been filming *Caesar's Hour* in spring of 1956, which that year's awards covered. Of the actresses Fabray beat that year — Edie Adams, Gracie Allen, Lucille Ball, and Ann Sothern — Sothern was the most vocal about her objections.

Faith, Adam

Movie: 1974: *Stardust* (Best Supporting Actor) British.

Falana, Lola

Movie: 1970: *The Liberation of L. B. Jones* (New Star of the Year — Actress) Globe. Theater: 1975: *Doctor Jazz* (Best Actress, Musical) Tony.

Falco, Edie

Movie: 1992: *Laws of Gravity* (Best Female Lead) Spirit. 2002: *Sunshine State* (Best Supporting Actress) *LA.* Television: 1999–2007 series *The Sopranos* (Best Actress in a Drama Series) 1999: *Emmy, Globe.* 2000: Emmy, Globe. 2001: *Emmy*, Globe. 2002: *Globe.* 2003: *Emmy.* 2004: Emmy, Globe. 2006: Globe. 2007: Emmy, Globe. (Best Female Actor in a Drama Series) 1999: *SAG.* 2000: SAG. 2001: SAG. 2002: *SAG.* 2004: SAG. 2006: SAG. 2007: *SAG.* (Best Ensemble in a Drama Series) 1999: *SAG.* 2000: SAG. 2001: SAG. 2002: SAG. 2004: SAG. 2006: SAG. 2007: *SAG.*

Falconer, Deborah

Movie: 1993: *Short Cuts* (Best Ensemble) *Venice* (special award).

Falk, Peter

Movie: 1960: *Murder, Inc.* (New Star of the Year — Actor) Globe (Best Supporting Actor) Academy. 1961: *Pocketful of Miracles* (Best Supporting Actor) Academy. Television: 1961: *"Cold Turkey," The Law and Mr. Jones* (Best Single Performance by an Actor or Actress) Emmy. 1962: *"The Price of Tomatoes," Dick Powell Theater (The Dick Powell Show)* (Best Single Performance by an Actor) *Emmy.* 1971–1978, 1989–2003 series *"Columbo," NBC Mystery Movie* (*"Columbo," NBC Sunday Mystery Movie*) (Best Actor in a Drama Series or TV Movie) 1971: Globe. (Best Actor in a Drama Series) 1972: *Globe.* 1973: Globe. 1974: Globe. 1975: Globe. 1977: Globe. 1990: Globe. (Best Continued Performance by an Actor in a Leading Role) 1972: *Emmy.* 1973: Emmy. (Best Lead Actor in a Limited Series) 1974: Emmy. 1975: *Emmy.* 1976: *Emmy.* 1977: Emmy. 1978: Emmy. 1990: *Emmy.* 1991: Emmy. 1994: Emmy. 1991: *Columbo and the Murder of a Rock Star* (Best Actor in a Miniseries or TV Movie) Globe. 1993: *Columbo: It's All in the Game* (Best Actor in a Miniseries or TV Movie) Globe.

Fanning, Dakota

Movie: 2001: *I Am Sam* (Best Young Actor/Actress) *Broadcast* (Best Female Actor in a Supporting Role)

SAG. 2004: *Man on Fire* (Best Young Actress) Broadcast. 2005: *War of the Worlds* (Best Young Actress) *Broadcast.* 2006: *Charlotte's Web* (Best Young Actress) Broadcast.

Farentino, James

Movie: 1966: *The Pad ... and How to Use It* (New Star of the Year — Actor) *Globe.* Television: 1978: *Jesus of Nazareth* (Best Supporting Actor in a Comedy or Drama Special) Emmy.

Farina, Carolyn

Movie: 1990: *Metropolitan* (Best Female Lead) Spirit.

Faris, Anna

Movie: 2005: *Brokeback Mountain* (Best Ensemble) SAG.

Farmer, Gary

Movie: 1989: *Powwow Highway* (Best Supporting Male) Spirit. 1995: *Dead Man* (Best Supporting Male) Spirit. 1998: *Smoke Signals* (Best Supporting Male) Spirit.

Farmiga, Vera

Movie: 2005: *Down to the Bone* (Best Actress) Society, *LA* (Best Female Lead) Spirit. 2006: *The Departed* (Best Ensemble) *Board*, SAG, Broadcast.

Farnsworth, Richard

Movie: 1978: *Comes a Horseman* (Best Supporting Actor) Academy, *Board, Society.* 1983: *The Grey Fox* (Best Actor, Drama) Globe. 1999: *The Straight Story* (Best Actor) Academy, *New York* (Best Actor, Drama) Globe (Best Male Lead) *Spirit.* Television: 1985: *Chase* (Best Supporting Actor in a Series, Miniseries, or TV Movie) Globe. Records: Farnsworth holds the Academy Award record as the oldest performer to be nominated in the Best Actor category. Farnsworth was 78 when he earned his Oscar nod for *The Straight Story*, an understated film about a man who takes a 250-mile journey on his riding mower to visit his brother in another state and make amends before he dies. In truth, Fransworth was himself dying of cancer during the production. He lived through award season, but succumbed to his illness soon after.

Farrow, Mia

Movie: 1964: *Guns at Batasi* (New Star of the Year — Actress) *Globe.* 1968: *Rosemary's Baby* (Best Actress) British (multiple nomination), (Best Actress, Drama) Globe; *Secret Ceremony* (Best Actress) British (multiple nomination). 1969: *John and Mary* (Best Actress) British (multiple nomination), (Best Actress, Musical or Comedy) Globe. 1984: *Broadway Danny Rose* (Best Actress, Musical or Comedy) Globe. 1985: *The Purple Rose of Cairo* (Best Actress) British (Best Actress, Musical or Comedy) Globe. 1986: *Hannah and Her Sisters* (Best Actress) British. 1990: *Alice* (Best Actress) *Board* (Best Actress, Musical or Comedy) Globe. Television: 1964–1966 series *Peyton Place* (Best Actress in a Series) 1965: Globe. 1999: *Forget Me Never* (Best Actress in a Miniseries or TV Movie) Globe. Tributes: 1969: Henrietta Award for World Film Favorite from Globe.

Fatone, Joey

Movie: 2002: *My Big Fat Greek Wedding* (Best Ensemble) SAG, Broadcast.

Fawcett, Farrah

Movie: 1986: *Extremities* (Best Actress, Drama) Globe. 1997: *The Apostle* (Best Supporting Female) Spirit. Television: 1976–1977 series *Charlie's Angels* (Best Actress in a Drama Series) 1976: Globe. 1984: *The Burning Bed* (Best Actress in a Limited Series or Special) Emmy (Best Actress in a Miniseries or TV Movie) Globe. 1986: *Nazi Hunter: The Beate Klarsfeld Story* (Best Actress in a Miniseries or TV Movie) Globe. 1987: *Poor Little Rich Girl: The Barbara Hutton Story* (Best Actress in a Miniseries or TV Movie) Globe. 1989: *Small Sacrifices* (Best Actress in a Miniseries or Special) Emmy (Best Actress in a Miniseries or TV Movie) Globe. 2003: *The Guardian* (Best Guest Actress in a Drama Series) Emmy.

Faye, Denise

Movie: 2002: *Chicago* (Best Ensemble) SAG, Broadcast.

Feldman, Marty

Movie: 1976: *Silent Movie* (Best Supporting Actor) Globe.

Feore, Colm

Movie: 2002: *Chicago* (Best Ensemble) SAG, Broadcast.

Ferrari, Isabella

Movie: 1995: *Romanzo di un giovane povero* (Best Supporting Actress) *Venice.*

Ferrell, Will

Movie: 2005: *The Producers* (Best Supporting Actor) Globe. 2006: *Stranger Than Fiction* (Best Actor,

Musical or Comedy) Globe. **Television:** 2001: *Saturday Night Live* (Best Individual Performance in a Variety or Music Program) Emmy.

Ferrer, José

Movie: 1948: *Joan of Arc* (Best Supporting Actor) Academy. 1950: *Cyrano de Bergerac* (Best Actor) *Academy* (Best Actor, Drama) *Globe.* 1952: *Moulin Rouge* (Best Actor) Academy. 1954: *The Caine Mutiny* (Best Foreign Actor) British. **Theater:** 1947: *Cyrano de Bergerac* (Best Actor, Dramatic) *Tony.* 1952: *The Shrike* (Best Actor, Dramatic) *Tony* (Best Director) *Tony* (multiple win); *The Fourposter* (Best Director) *Tony* (multiple win); *Stalag 17* (Best Director) *Tony* (multiple win). 1958: *Oh, Captain!* (Best Musical, Book Writer) Tony. **Television:** 1951: --- (Best Actor) Emmy. 1956: *Cyrano de Bergerac* (Best Actor in a Single Performance) Emmy. **Records:** Ferrer is the first actor to win a Tony Award and then Academy Award for the same role after he reprised his 1947 stage performance as lovelorn Cyrano de Bergerac for the 1950 film adaptation. Ferrer is also the first actor to receive nominations for both an Oscar and Emmy. He earned each nomination in 1950.

Ferrer, Miguel

Movie: 2000: *Traffic* (Best Ensemble) *SAG.*

Ferrera, America

Movie: 2002: *Real Women Have Curves* (Best Debut Performance) Spirit. **Television:** 2006–present series *Ugly Betty* (Best Actress in a Comedy Series) 2006: *Globe.* 2007: *Emmy*, Globe. (Best Female Actor in a Comedy Series) 2006: *SAG.* 2007: SAG. (Best Ensemble in a Comedy Series) 2006: SAG. 2007: SAG.

Ferris, Barbara

Movie: 1965: *Catch Us If You Can* (Most Promising Newcomer) British.

Feuilliere, Edwige

Movie: 1952: *Olivia* (Best Foreign Actress) British.

Fichtner, William

Movie: 2005: *Crash* (Best Ensemble) *SAG, Broadcast.*

Field, Betty

Movie: 1940: *Of Mice and Men* (Best Acting) *Board.*

Field, Sally

Movie: 1977: *Smokey and the Bandit* (Best Actress, Musical or Comedy) Globe. 1979: *Norma Rae* (Best Actress) *Academy, New York, Board, Cannes, Society, LA* (Best Actress, Drama) *Globe.* 1981: *Absence of Malice* (Best Actress, Drama) Globe. 1982: *Kiss Me Goodbye* (Best Actress, Musical or Comedy) Globe. 1984: *Places in the Heart* (Best Actress) *Academy* (Best Actress, Drama) *Globe.* 1985: *Murphy's Romance* (Best Actress, Musical or Comedy) Globe. 1989: *Steel Magnolias* (Best Actress, Drama) Globe. 1994: *Forrest Gump* (Best Female Actor in a Supporting Role) SAG (Best Supporting Actress) British. **Television:** 1977: *"Sybil," The Big Event* (Best Actress in a Drama or Comedy Special) *Emmy.* 1995: *A Woman of Independent Means* (Best Actress in a Miniseries or Special) Emmy (Best Actress in a Miniseries or TV Movie) Globe (Best Female Actor in a Television Movie or Miniseries) SAG (Best Miniseries, Executive Producer) Emmy. 1999: *A Cooler Climate* (Best Actress in a Miniseries or TV Movie) Emmy (Best Female Actor in a Television Movie or Miniseries) SAG. 2000: *David Copperfield* (Best Female Actor in a Television Movie or Miniseries) SAG. 2000–2003, 2006 series *ER* (Best Female Actor in a Drama Series) 2000: SAG. (Best Guest Actress in a Drama Series) 2001: *Emmy.* 2003: Emmy. 2006–present series *Brothers and Sisters* (Best Actress in a Drama Series) 2007: *Emmy*, Globe. (Best Female Actor in a Drama Series) 2007: SAG. **Tributes:** 1996: Honorary Award from Berlin. **Records:** With new awards cropping up every decade and eventually exploding in the 1980s and '90s, the idea of an awards sweep continues to evolve. For her work in *Norma Rae*, Field is the first star to win the six awards that constituted a sweep in 1979: The Oscar, The Golden Globe, the National Board of Review, the National Society of Film Critics, and the New York and the L.A. Film Critics Awards. Her winning streak began with the Cannes Film Festival award for Best Actress, giving her seven victories for that performance. She won every competitive prize for which she was nominated that year. Since then, the well-regarded Screen Actors Guild and the Broadcast Film Critics prize are among the top ranking organizations whose selection for an acting award would now be included in a sweep.

Field, Todd

Movie: 1993: *Ruby in Paradise* (Best Supporting Male) Spirit. 2001: *In the Bedroom* (Best Picture, Producer) Academy, Board, Broadcast (Best Picture, Drama; Producer) Globe (Best Director) *Board* (Best First Feature) *Spirit* (Best First Picture) *New York* (Best Adapted Screenplay) Academy (Best Screenplay) *Board,* Spirit. 2006: *Little Children* (Best Adapted Screenplay) Academy (Best Screenplay) Globe (Best Writer) Broadcast.

Fields, Gracie

Movie: 1943: *Holy Matrimony* (Best Acting) *Board.* Television: 1957: *"Old Lady Shows Her Medals,"* *The U.S. Steel Hour* (Best Single Performance by an Actress) Emmy.

Fiennes, Joseph

Movie: 1998: *Elizabeth* (Best Breakthrough Performer) *Broadcast* (multiple win); *Shakespeare in Love* (Best Breakthrough Performer) *Broadcast* (multiple win), (Best Actor) British (Best Male Actor in a Leading Role) SAG (Best Ensemble) *SAG.*

Fiennes, Ralph

Movie: 1993: *Schindler's List* (Best Supporting Actor) Academy, *New York*, Globe, *British*, *Society*. 1996: *The English Patient* (Best Actor) Academy, British (Best Actor, Drama) Globe (Best Male Actor in a Leading Role) SAG (Best Ensemble) SAG. 1999: *The End of the Affair* (Best Actor) British. 2005: *The Constant Gardner* (Best Actor) British. **Theater:** 1995: *Hamlet* (Best Actor, Play) *Tony.* 2006: *Faith Healer* (Best Actor, Play) Tony. **Records:** Trained at the Royal Academy of Dramatic Art and once a member of the Royal Shakespeare Company, Fiennes is the only actor in the history of Broadway to win a Tony Award for a portrayal of Shakespeare's melancholy Dane, Hamlet.

Fierstein, Harvey

Movie: 1988: *Torch Song Trilogy* (Best Male Lead) Spirit. **Theater:** 1983: *Torch Song Trilogy* (Best Actor, Play) *Tony* (Best Play, Writer) *Tony.* 1984: *La Cage aux folles* (Best Book of a Musical, Writer) *Tony.* 2003: *Hairspray* (Best Actor, Musical) *Tony.* **Television:** 1992 series *Cheers* (Outstanding Supporting Actor in a Comedy Series) 1992: Emmy.

Figueroa, Efrain

Movie: 1997: *Star Maps* (Best Supporting Male) Spirit.

Finch, Peter

Movie Award: 1956: *A Town Like Alice* (Best British Actor) *British.* 1957: *Windom's Way* (Best British Actor) British. 1959: *The Nun's Story* (Best British Actor) British. 1960: *The Trials of Oscar Wilde* (Best British Actor) *British.* 1961: *No Love for Johnny* (Best Actor) *Berlin* (Best British Actor) *British.* 1967: *Far from the Madding Crowd* (Best Actor) *Board.* 1971: *Sunday, Bloody Sunday* (Best Actor) Academy, *British, Society* (Best Actor, Drama) Globe. 1976: *Network* (Best Actor) *Academy*, British (Best Actor, Drama) *Globe.* **Television:** 1977: *"Raid on Entebbe,"* *The Big Event* (Best Actor in a Drama or Comedy Special) Emmy. **Records:** Finch was the first (and still only) actor to receive a posthumous Academy Award. Excited by his likely nomination for *Network*, Finch campaigned enthusiastically, guest starring on many national talk shows. Soon after he appeared on *The Tonight Show with Johnny Carson*, Finch had a heart attack and died. A shaken Carson shared the news with his audience and paid a brief, compassionate tribute to the talented actor. **Highlights:** The Academy faced an awkward situation when Finch died two months before the Oscar ceremonies honoring the films of 1976. After Marlon Brando sent an actress pretending to be a Native American onstage to refuse his 1972 Oscar, the Academy strove to prevent such unpleasant surprises by establishing a rule that no one but the winner could accept an award. They hadn't factored in posthumous nominations or wins. Compounding the potential problem that year was the fact that many industry insiders admired Finch's widow and thought it most appropriate for her to accept on her husband's behalf. Despite some bad press, the Academy held to its rule and chose *Network*'s screenwriter, Paddy Chayevsky to accept the award for Best Actor and say a quick thank you if Finch won. When Liv Ullmann opened the envelope and announced Finch as the winner, Chayevsky did come forward, then took it upon himself to break the Academy rule and invited Finch's widow to the podium to say a few words on behalf of her late husband. The audience, the fans, and the Academy seemed pleased. Mrs. Finch gave a sweet and moving acceptance speech, reiterating how much Finch loved acting and the people with whom he worked over the years.

Finlay, Frank

Movie: 1965: *Othello* (Most Promising Newcomer) British (Best Supporting Actor) Academy, Globe. 1982: *The Return of the Soldier* (Best Supporting Actor) British.

Finney, Albert

Movie: 1961: *Saturday Night and Sunday Morning* (Most Promising Newcomer) *British* (Best Actor) *Board* (Best British Actor) British. 1963: *Tom Jones* (New Star of the Year — Actor) *Globe* (Best Actor) Academy, *Venice*, *New York* (Best Actor, Musical or Comedy) Globe (Best British Actor) British. 1970: *Scrooge* (Best Actor, Musical or Comedy) *Globe.* 1971: *Gumshoe* (Best Actor) British. 1974: *Murder on the Orient Express* (Best Actor) Academy, British. 1982: *Shoot the Moon* (Best Actor) British (Best Actor, Drama) Globe. 1983: *The Dresser* (Best

Actor) Academy, *Berlin*, British (Best Actor, Drama) Globe. 1984: *Under the Volcano* (Best Actor) Academy, *LA* (Best Actor, Drama) Globe. 2000: *Erin Brockovich* (Best Male Actor in a Supporting Role) *SAG* (Best Supporting Actor) Academy, Globe, British, Broadcast; *Traffic* (Best Ensemble) *SAG*. 2003: *Big Fish* (Best Supporting Actor) Globe, British. 2004: *Ocean's Twelve* (Best Ensemble) Broadcast. 2007: *Before the Devil Knows You're Dead* (Best Ensemble) Broadcast. **Theater:** 1964: *Luther* (Best Actor, Dramatic) Tony. 1968: *Joe Egg* (Best Actor, Dramatic) Tony. **Television:** 1990: *The Image* (Best Actor in a Miniseries or Special) Emmy. 2002: *The Gathering Storm* (Best Actor in a Miniseries or TV Movie) *Emmy*, *Globe* (Best Male Actor in a Television Movie or Miniseries) SAG. **Records:** Finney may be one of Oscar's most overlooked actors, but he has earned accolades from many critics' associations and developed tremendous box office appeal during his career. In 1974, Finney led what *Entertainment Weekly* critic, Lisa Schwarzbaum considers the greatest big-name ensemble cast of all time in the screen adaptation of Agatha Christie's *Murder on the Orient Express*. As fastidious Belgian sleuth, Hercule Poirot, Finney had the starring role amid a trainload of supporting actor suspects including Lauren Bacall, Ingrid Bergman, Sean Connery, Wendy Hiller, Anthony Perkins, and Vanessa Redgrave. He alone carried the climactic scene where Poirot solves the murder with an impressive 23-minute monologue, one of the longest in film history. Thanks in large part to the appeal of Finney and his ensemble, *Murder on the Orient Express* earned £35,733,867 ($27,634,716), making the 1974 film the most commercially successful British movie to date.

Fiorentino, Linda

Movie: 1994: *The Last Seduction* (Best Actress) *New York*, British (Best Female Lead) *Spirit*. **Highlights:** Fiorentino earned two awards and great buzz for her performance in *The Last Seduction*, but her road to Oscar consideration was eclipsed when the movie's producers, struggling to find an audience, premiered the film in the U.S. on HBO. Broadcasting the movie on television made the film, and Fiorentino's praiseworthy performance, ineligible for the Oscar.

Firth, Colin

Movie: 1996: *The English Patient* (Best Ensemble) SAG. 1998: *Shakespeare in Love* (Best Ensemble) *SAG*. 2001: *Bridget Jones's Dairy* (Best Supporting Actor) British. 2003: *Love Actually* (Best Ensemble) Broadcast. **Television:** 2001: *Conspiracy* (Best Supporting Actor in a Miniseries or TV Movie) Emmy.

Firth, Peter

Movie: 1977: *Equus* (Best Supporting Actor) Academy, *Globe*. **Theater:** 1975: *Equus* (Best Actor, Dramatic) Tony.

Fishburne, Laurence

Movie: 1992: *Deep Cover* (Best Male Lead) Spirit. 1993: *What's Love Got to Do with It* (Best Actor) Academy. 2003: *Mystic River* (Best Ensemble) SAG, Broadcast. 2006: *Bobby* (Best Ensemble) SAG, Broadcast. **Theater:** 1992: *Two Trains Running* (Best Actor in a Featured Role, Play) *Tony*. **Television:** 1993: *Tribeca* (Best Guest Actor in a Drama Series) *Emmy*. 1996: *The Tuskegee Airmen* (Best Actor in a Miniseries or Special) Emmy (Best Actor in a Miniseries or TV Movie) Globe (Best Male Actor in a Television Movie or Miniseries) SAG. 1997: *Miss Evers' Boys* (Best Actor in a Miniseries or Special) Emmy (Best Made for TV Movie, Executive Producer) *Emmy*.

Fisher, Frances

Movie: 1997: *Titanic* (Best Ensemble) SAG.

Fisher, Gregor

Movie: 2003: *Love Actually* (Best Ensemble) Broadcast.

Fitzgerald, Barry

Movie: 1944: *Going My Way* (Best Actor) Academy, *New York* (Best Supporting Actor) *Academy, Globe*. **Records:** Fitzgerald is the only actor to receive two Oscar nominations for the same performance. In 1944, he co-starred with Bing Crosby in *Going My Way*. Though Crosby got top billing, Fitzgerald and Crosby both had leading roles. Unclear about which category he belonged in, Academy voters ended up nominating him as both Best Actor and Best Supporting Actor. He won the supporting honor and lost Best Actor to Crosby.

Fitzgerald, Geraldine

Movie: 1939: *Dark Victory* (Best Acting) *Board* (multiple win); *Wuthering Heights* (Best Acting) *Board* (multiple win), (Best Supporting Actress) Academy. **Theater:** 1982: *Mass Appeal* (Best Director, Play) Tony. **Television:** 1979: *Special Treat* (Best Children's Programming, Performer) Emmy. 1988: *The Golden Girls* (Best Guest Performance in a Comedy Series) Emmy.

Flanagan, Fionnula

Movie: 1998: *Waking Ned Devine* (Best Ensemble) SAG. **Theater:** 1974: *Ulysses in Nighttown* (Best

Supporting or Featured Actress, Dramatic) Tony. Television: 1976: *Rich Man, Poor Man* (Best Single Performance by a Supporting Actress in a Comedy or Drama Series) *Emmy*. 1978–1979 series *How the West Was Won* (Best Actress in a Drama Series) 1978: Emmy.

Flanagan, Maile

Movie: 2004: *Ocean's Twelve* (Best Ensemble) Broadcast.

Flannagan, Mark

Movie: 1999: *Magnolia* (Best Ensemble) *Board*, SAG.

Flannery, Susan

Movie: 1974: *The Towering Inferno* (New Star of the Year — Actress) *Globe*. Television: 1966–1975 series *Days of Our Lives* (Best Actress in a Daytime Drama Series) 1975: *Emmy*. 1977: *"The Moneychangers," NBC World Premiere Movie, The Big Event* (Best Actress in a Limited Series) Emmy. 1987–present series *The Bold and the Beautiful* (Best Actress in a Daytime Drama Series) 2000: *Emmy*. 2001: Emmy. 2002: *Emmy*. 2003: *Emmy*. 2005: Emmy. 2006: Emmy.

Fletcher, Louise

Movie: 1975: *One Flew Over the Cuckoo's Nest* (Best Actress) *Academy, British* (Best Actress, Drama) *Globe*. Television: 1996: *Picket Fences* (Best Guest Actress in a Drama Series) Emmy. 2004: *Joan of Arcadia* (Best Guest Actress in a Drama Series) Emmy.

Flockhart, Calista

Movie: 1996: *The Birdcage* (Best Ensemble) *SAG*. Television: 1997–2002 series *Ally McBeal* (Best Actress in a Comedy Series) 1998: Emmy. 1999: Emmy. 2001: Emmy. (Best Actress in a Series, Musical or Comedy) 1997: *Globe*. 1998: Globe. 1999: Globe. 2000: Globe. 2001: Globe. (Best Female Actor in a Comedy Series) 1997: SAG. 1998: SAG. 1999: SAG. 2000: SAG. (Best Ensemble in a Comedy Series) 1997: SAG. 1998: *SAG*. 1999: SAG. 2000: SAG.

Flon, Suzanne

Movie: 1961: *Tu ne Tueras Point* (Best Actress) *Venice*.

Flores, Lysa

Movie: 1997: *Star Maps* (Best Debut Performance) Spirit.

Flynn, Neil

Movie: 1999: *Magnolia* (Best Ensemble) *Board*, SAG.

Foch, Nina

Movie: 1954: *Executive Suite* (Best Supporting Actress) Academy, *Board* (Best Ensemble) *Venice* (special award). Television: 1979–1980 series *Lou Grant* (Best Supporting Actress in a Drama Series) Emmy.

Folland, Alison

Movie: 1997: *All Over Me* (Best Female Lead) Spirit.

Fonda, Bridget

Movie: 1989: *Scandal* (Best Supporting Actress) Globe; *Shag* (Best Supporting Female) Spirit. Television: 1997: *In the Gloaming* (Best Supporting Actress in a Miniseries or Special) Emmy. 2001: *No Ordinary Baby* (Best Actress in a Miniseries or TV Movie) Globe.

Fonda, Henry

Movie: 1939: *Young Mr. Lincoln* (Best Acting) *Board*. 1940: *The Grapes of Wrath* (Best Acting) *Board* (multiple win), (Best Actor) Academy; *The Return of Frank James* (Best Acting) *Board* (multiple win). 1957: *12 Angry Men* (Best Actor, Drama) Globe (Best Foreign Actor) *British* (Best Picture, Producer) Academy, Globe. 1981: *On Golden Pond* (Best Actor) *Academy, Board*, British (Best Actor, Drama) *Globe*. Theater: 1948: *Mister Roberts* (Best Actor, Dramatic) *Tony*. 1975: *Clarence Darrow* (Best Actor, Dramatic) Tony. Television: 1973: *"The Red Pony," Bell System Family Theatre* (Best Single Performance by an Actor) Emmy. 1975: *IBM Presents Clarence Darrow* (Best Actor in a Drama or Comedy Special) Emmy. 1980: *"Gideon's Trumpet," Hallmark Hall of Fame* (Best Actor in a Limited Series or Special) Emmy. Tributes: 1978: Life Achievement Award from American Film Institute. 1979: Cecil B. DeMille Award from Globe; Special award from Tony; Honor from Kennedy Center for the Performing Arts. 1980: Special award in recognition of his brilliant accomplishments and enduring contribution to the art of motion pictures from Academy. 1999: Ranked Number 6 on List of 25 Greatest Male Screen Legends of the 20th Century from American Film Institute. **Records:** When, at 76 years and 317 days old, Fonda won the Academy Award for *On Golden Pond*, he became the oldest star to win Best Actor. The victory also made Henry and Jane Fonda the first father and daughter to both win Oscars in the competitive acting categories. Overall, they're the second father/daughter winners.

In 1970, John Mills was named Best Supporting Actor for *Ryan's Daughter*, ten years after daughter Hayley received a special juvenile award for *Pollyanna*. Henry and Jane Fonda are also the only father/daughter pair to receive nominations for the same movie (*On Golden Pond*).

Fonda, Jane

Movie: 1961: *Tall Story* (New Star of the Year — Actress) *Globe*. 1962: *Period of Adjustment* (Best Actress, Musical or Comedy) Globe. 1965: *Cat Ballou* (Best Actress, Musical or Comedy) Globe (Best Foreign Actress) British. 1966: *Any Wednesday* (Best Actress, Musical or Comedy) Globe. 1967: *Barefoot in the Park* (Best Foreign Actress) British. 1969: *They Shoot Horses, Don't They?* (Best Actress) Academy, *New York*, British (Best Actress, Drama) Globe. 1971: *Klute* (Best Actress) *Academy, New York,* British, *Society* (Best Actress, Drama) *Globe*. 1977: *Julia* (Best Actress) Academy, *British* (Best Actress, Drama) *Globe*. 1978: *California Suite* (Best Actress) *LA* (multiple win); *Comes a Horseman* (Best Actress) *LA* (multiple win); *Coming Home* (Best Actress) *Academy, LA* (multiple win), (Best Actress, Drama) *Globe*. 1979: *The China Syndrome* (Best Actress) Academy, *British* (Best Actress, Drama) Globe. 1981: *On Golden Pond* (Best Supporting Actress) Academy, Globe, British. 1986: *The Morning After* (Best Actress) Academy. **Theater:** 1960: *There Was a Little Girl* (Best Supporting or Featured Actress, Dramatic) Tony. **Television:** 1984: *"The Dollmaker," An ABC Theatre Presentation* (Best Actress in a Limited Series or Special) *Emmy* (Best Actress in a Miniseries or TV Movie) Globe. 1995: *A Century of Women* (Best Informational Series, Narrator) Emmy. **Tributes:** 1972, 1978, 1979: Henrietta Award for World Film Favorite from Globe. 2001: Gala Tribute from Film Society of Lincoln Center. 2006: Career Achievement Award from Board. 2007: Lifetime Achievement Award from Cannes. **Records:** Thanks to a hot streak of consecutive, hugely successful films that included *Coming Home, Comes a Horseman, California Suite, The Electric Horseman,* and *The China Syndrome*, Fonda ended the 1970s as one of the biggest box office stars of the decade and won the last two Henrietta Awards for World Film Favorite given by the Hollywood Foreign Press.

Fonda, Peter

Movie: 1963: *The Victors* (New Star of the Year — Actor) Globe. 1969: *Easy Rider* (Best Story and Screenplay) Academy. 1997: *Ulee's Gold* (Best Actor) Academy, *New York* (Best Actor, Drama) *Globe* (Best Male Lead) Spirit (Best Male Actor in a Leading Role) SAG. 2007: *3:10 to Yuma* (Best Ensemble) SAG. **Television:** 1998: *The Tempest* (Best Actor in a Series, Miniseries, or TV Movie) Globe. 1999: *The Passion of Ayn Rand* (Best Male Actor in a Television Movie or Miniseries) SAG (Best Supporting Actor in a Miniseries or TV Movie) Emmy (Best Supporting Actor in a Series, Miniseries, or TV Movie) *Globe*.

Fontaine, Joan

Movie: 1940: *Rebecca* (Best Acting) *Board* (Best Actress) Academy. 1941: *Suspicion* (Best Acting) *Board* (Best Actress) *Academy, New York*. 1943: *The Constant Nymph* (Best Actress) Academy. **Television:** 1979: *Ryan's Hope* (Best Cameo Appearance on a Daytime Drama Series) Emmy. **Records:** When Fontaine earned an Oscar nomination for Alfred Hitchcock's *Suspicion* the same year her sister, Olivia de Havilland was up for *Hold Back the Dawn*, they became the first siblings to compete for the same acting Academy Award. The media focused on their competition for Best Actress, playing up the rivalry while the sisters sat together at a table talking and laughing amiably. After Fontaine won, de Havilland congratulated her sister with a smile and a handshake. Fontaine's win set two records: she was the first to beat a sibling for an acting Oscar and ultimately gave the only Oscar-winning performance in a Hitchcock film.

Fontani, Amerigo

Movie: 1998: *La Vita è Bella (Life Is Beautiful)* (Best Ensemble) SAG.

Fontanne, Lynn

Movie: 1931: *The Guardsman* (Best Actress) Academy. **Theater:** 1959: *The Visit* (Best Actress, Dramatic) Tony. **Television:** 1965: *"The Magnificent Yankee," Hallmark Hall of Fame* (Best Individual Achievement in Entertainment, Actor or Performer) *Emmy*. 1967: *"Anastasia," Hallmark Hall of Fame* (Best Single Performance by an Actress in a Leading Role in a Drama) Emmy. **Tributes:** 1970: Special award from Tony. 1980: Honor from Kennedy Center for the Performing Arts. **Records:** In 1965 Fontanne and her husband, Alfred Lunt became the first married couple to both win acting Emmys when they each received an award for their work in *The Magnificent Yankee*, a TV adaptation of Emmet Lavery's Broadway play about Supreme Court Justice Oliver Wendell Holmes. Previously, husband and wife Desi Arnaz and Lucille Ball had shared Emmy wins for *I Love Lucy*, but as co-producers.

Ford, Glenn

Movie: 1956: *The Teahouse of the August Moon* (Best Actor, Musical or Comedy) Globe. 1957: *Don't Go Near the Water* (Best Actor, Musical or Comedy) Globe. 1958: *The Sheepman* (Best Foreign Actor) British. 1961: *Pocketful of Miracles* (Best Actor, Musical or Comedy) *Globe.*

Ford, Harrison

Movie: 1985: *Witness* (Best Actor) Academy, British (Best Actor, Drama) Globe. 1986: *The Mosquito Coast* (Best Actor, Drama) Globe. 1993: *The Fugitive* (Best Actor, Drama) Globe. 1995: *Sabrina* (Best Actor, Musical or Comedy) Globe. Tributes: 2000: Life Achievement Award from American Film Institute. 2001: Cecil B. DeMille Award from Globe.

Ford, Paul

Movie: 1967: *The Comedians* (Best Supporting Actor) *Board.* Theater: 1963: *Never Too Late* (Best Actor, Dramatic) Tony. Television: 1955–1959 series *The Phil Silvers Show* (also *Sergeant Bilko*, *Bilko*, or *You'll Never Get Rich*) (Best Supporting Performance by an Actor) 1957: Emmy. (Best Continuing Supporting Performance by an Actor in a Dramatic or Comedy Series) 1958: Emmy. 1963: *"The Teahouse of the August Moon," Hallmark Hall of Fame* (Best Performance in a Supporting Role by an Actor) Emmy.

Forrest, Frederic

Movie: 1972: *When the Legends Die* (New Star of the Year — Actor) Globe. 1979: *Apocalypse Now* (Best Supporting Actor) *Society* (multiple win); *The Rose* (Best Supporting Actor) Academy, Globe, *Society* (multiple win).

Forrest, Steve

Movie: 1953: *The Kid from Left Field* (New Star of the Year — Actor) Globe; *So Big* (New Star of the Year — Actor) *Globe.*

Forster, Robert

Movie: 1997: *Jackie Brown* (Best Supporting Actor) Academy.

Forsythe, Rosemary

Movie: 1965: *Shenandoah* (New Star of the Year — Actress) Globe.

Forsythe, William

Movie: 1992: *The Waterdance* (Best Supporting Male) Spirit.

Foster, Ben

Movie: 2007: *3:10 to Yuma* (Best Ensemble) SAG.

Foster, Jodie

Movie: 1976: *Taxi Driver* (New Generation) *LA* (Most Promising Newcomer) *British* (multiple win), (Best Supporting Actress) Academy, *British* (multiple win), *Society*; *Bugsy Malone* (Most Promising Newcomer) *British* (multiple win), (Best Supporting Actress) *British* (multiple win); *Freaky Friday* (Best Actress, Musical or Comedy) Globe. 1988: *The Accused* (Best Actress) *Academy, Board*, British (Best Actress, Drama) *Globe*; *Five Corners* (Best Female Lead) *Spirit*. 1991: *The Silence of the Lambs* (Best Actress) *Academy, New York, British* (Best Actress, Drama) *Globe*. 1994: *Nell* (Best Actress) Academy (Best Actress, Drama) Globe (Best Female Actor in a Leading Role) *SAG* (Best Picture, Drama; Producer) Globe. 1997: *Contact* (Best Actress, Drama) Globe. 2007: *The Brave One* (Best Actress, Drama) Globe. Television: 1998: *The Baby Dance* (Best TV Movie, Executive Prodcuer) Emmy. Tributes: 1996: Honorary Award from Berlin. Records: Foster's performance in *Nell* made her the first SAG Best Actress winner. It was a surprising though popular win, as Foster had won no major critics' awards for that performance and had even lost the Golden Globe to *Blue Sky*'s Jessica Lange, who ended up victorious over Foster for the Oscar later that awards season.

Fox, Bernard

Movie: 1997: *Titanic* (Best Ensemble) SAG.

Fox, Edward

Movie: 1971: *The Go-Between* (Best Supporting Actor) *British*. 1977: *A Bridge Too Far* (Best Supporting Actor) *British, Society*. 1982: *Gandhi* (Best Supporting Actor) British. 2002: *Nicholas Nickleby* (Best Ensemble) *Board*.

Fox, James

Movie: 1963: *The Servant* (Most Promising Newcomer) *British*. 1965: *Those Magnificent Men in Their Flying Machines* (New Star of the Year — Actor) Globe. 1984: *A Passage to India* (Best Supporting Actor) British.

Fox, Kerry

Movie: 2001: *Intimacy* (Best Actress) *Berlin*.

Fox, Michael J.

Movie: 1985: *Back to the Future* (Best Actor, Musical or Comedy) Globe. Television: 1982–1989 series

Family Ties (Best Actor in a Comedy Series) 1986: *Emmy*. 1987: *Emmy*. 1988: *Emmy*. 1989: Emmy. (Best Actor is a Series, Musical or Comedy) 1985: Globe. 1986: Globe. 1988: *Globe*. (Best Supporting Actor in a Comedy Series) 1985: Emmy. 1996–2000 series *Spin City* (Best Actor in a Comedy Series) 1997: Emmy. 1998: Emmy. 1999: Emmy. 2000: *Emmy*. (Best Actor is a Series, Musical or Comedy) 1996: Globe. 1997: *Globe*. 1998: *Globe*. 1999: *Globe*. (Best Male Actor in a Comedy Series) 1998: *SAG*. 1999: *SAG*. 2006: **Boston Legal** (Best Guest Actor in a Drama Series) Emmy. **Highlights:** Fox worked hard to win the role of young conservative Alex P. Keaton in *Family Ties*, but studio head Brandon Tartikoff didn't want to give him the role because he said he couldn't imagine Fox's face looking good on a lunch box. After he won the role and an Emmy, Fox had his image printed on a lunch box and sent it to Tartikoff, who good-naturedly displayed it in his office.

Foxx, Jamie

Movie: 2004: **Collateral** (Best Actor) *Society* (multiple win), (Best Male Actor in a Supporting Role) SAG (Best Supporting Actor) Academy, Globe, British, Broadcast; **Ray** (Best Actor) *Academy, Board, British, Society* (multiple win), *Broadcast* (Best Actor, Musical or Comedy) *Globe* (Best Male Actor in a Leading Role) *SAG* (Best Ensemble) SAG; **Redemption** (Best Male Lead) Spirit. 2006: **Dreamgirls** (Best Ensemble) SAG, Broadcast. **Television:** 2004: **Redemption** (Best Actor in a Miniseries or TV Movie) Globe (Best Male Actor in a Television Movie or Miniseries) SAG. **Records:** In 2004, Foxx became the first African-American to receive two acting Oscar nominations in the same year. He won Best Actor for **Ray** but lost Best Supporting Actor (for **Collateral**) to another Black actor, Morgan Freeman in that year's Best Picture, **Million Dollar Baby**.

Franciosa, Anthony

Movie: 1957: **A Hatful of Rain** (Best Actor) Academy, *Venice* (Best Actor, Drama) Globe. 1959: **Career** (Best Actor, Drama) *Globe*. 1964: **Rio Conchos** (Best Actor, Drama) Globe. **Theater:** 1956: **A Hatful of Rain** (Best Supporting or Featured Actor, Dramatic) Tony.

Frangione, Jim

Movie: 2000: **State and Main** (Best Ensemble) *Board*.

Franklin, Marcus Carl

Movie: 2007: **I'm Not There** (Best Supporting Male) Spirit (Best Ensemble) *Spirit* (special award).

Franklin, Pamela

Movie: 1969: **The Prime of Miss Jean Brodie** (Best Supporting Actress) *Board*, British. **Television:** 1966: **"Eagle in a Cage," Hallmark Hall of Fame** (Best Supporting Actress in a Drama) Emmy.

Fraser, Brendan

Movie: 2005: **Crash** (Best Ensemble) *SAG, Broadcast*.

Fraser, John

Movie: 1960: **The Trials of Oscar Wilde** (Best British Actor) British.

Fraser, Liz

Movie: 1959: **I'm All Right Jack** (Most Promising Newcomer) British.

Freeman, Martin

Movie: 2003: **Love Actually** (Best Ensemble) Broadcast.

Freeman, Morgan

Movie: 1987: **Street Smart** (Best Supporting Actor) Academy, *New York*, Globe, *Society, LA* (Best Supporting Male) *Spirit*. 1989: **Driving Miss Daisy** (Best Actor) Academy, *Board* (Best Actor, Musical or Comedy) *Globe*. 1994: **The Shawshank Redemption** (Best Actor) Academy (Best Actor, Drama) Globe (Best Male Actor in a Leading Role) SAG. 2004: **Million Dollar Baby** (Best Male Actor in a Supporting Role) *SAG* (Best Supporting Actor) *Academy*, Globe, Society, Broadcast (Best Ensemble) SAG. 2007: **Gone Baby Gone** (Best Ensemble) Broadcast. **Theater:** 1978: **The Mighty Gents** (Best Actor in a Featured Role, Play) Tony. **Tributes:** 1989: Special Performance Award for **Driving Miss Daisy** from Berlin (win shared with costar, Jessica Tandy). 2003: Career Achievement Award from Board. **Highlights:** Since Freeman won his first award for **Street Smart**, he has shared the spotlight with another African-American male in the other years he's had big award wins. In 1989, Freeman took home the Golden Globe for Best Actor, Musical or Comedy for **Driving Miss Daisy** while his **Glory** co-star, Denzel Washington was voted Best Supporting Actor. In 2004, Freeman was the odds-on favorite to win the Best Supporting Actor Oscar in the pivotal role of former boxer and story narrator, Scrappy in **Million Dollar Baby** while Jamie Foxx was a shoo-in to cap off his Best Actor sweep for **Ray** with an Academy Award. As expected, both men won, making it the second time Freeman shared a night of award success with another Black male winner.

Fresnay, Pierre

Movie: 1938: *Grand Illusion* (Best Acting) *Board*. 1947: *Monsieur Vincent* (Best Actor) *Venice*. 1952: *Dieu a Besoin des Hommes* (Best Foreign Actor) British. 1956: *La Defroque* (Best Foreign Actor) British.

Frey, Leonard

Movie: 1971: *Fiddler on the Roof* (Best Supporting Actor) Academy. Theater: 1975: *The National Health* (Best Supporting or Featured Actor, Dramatic) Tony.

Fricker, Brenda

Movie: 1989: *My Left Foot* (Best Supporting Actress) *Academy*, Globe, *LA*.

Friedlander, Judah

Movie: 2003: *American Splendor* (Best Supporting Male) Spirit.

Friel, Austin

Movie: 1993: *Short Cuts* (Best Ensemble) *Venice* (special award).

Friel, Cassie

Movie: 1993: *Short Cuts* (Best Ensemble) *Venice* (special award).

Friel, Dustin

Movie: 1993: *Short Cuts* (Best Ensemble) *Venice* (special award).

Fry, Stephen

Movie: 1997: *Wilde* (Best Actor, Drama) Globe. 2001: *Gosford Park* (Best Ensemble) *SAG, Broadcast*. Theater: 1987: *Me and My Gal* (Best Book of a Musical, Writer) Tony.

Fugit, Patrick

Movie: 2000: *Almost Famous* (Best Breakthrough Performer) Broadcast (Best Ensemble) SAG.

Furlong, Edward

Movie: 1993: *American Heart* (Best Supporting Male) Spirit.

Futterman, Dan

Movie: 1996: *The Birdcage* (Best Ensemble) *SAG*. 2005: *Capote* (Best Adapted Screenplay) Academy, British (Best Screenplay) Society, *LA, Spirit* (Best Writer) Broadcast.

Fyffe, Will

Movie: 1938: *To the Victor* (Best Acting) *Board*.

Gabbriellini, Edoardo

Movie: 1997: *Ovosodo* (Best Actor) *Venice*.

Gabin, Jean

Movie: 1938: *Grand Illusion* (Best Acting) *Board*. 1939: *Port of Shadows* (Best Acting) *Board*. 1951: *La Nuit est mon royaume* (Best Actor) *Venice*. 1954: *L'air de Paris* (Best Actor) *Venice* (multiple win); *Touchez Pas au Grisbi* (Best Actor) *Venice* (multiple win). 1957: *Pig Across Paris* (Best Foreign Actor) British. 1959: *Archimède, le Clochard* (Best Actor) *Berlin; Maigret Sets a Trap* (Best Foreign Actor) British. 1971: *Le Chat* (Best Actor) *Berlin*.

Gable, Clark

Movie: 1934: *It Happened One Night* (Best Actor) *Academy*. 1935: *Mutiny on the Bounty* (Best Actor) Academy. 1939: *Gone with the Wind* (Best Actor) Academy. 1958: *Teacher's Pet* (Best Actor, Musical or Comedy) Globe. 1959: *But Not for Me* (Best Actor, Musical or Comedy) Globe. **Tributes:** 1999: Ranked Number 7 on List of 25 Greatest Male Screen Legends of the 20th Century from American Film Institute. **Records:** Gable didn't need a music cue to remind him not to overstay his welcome at the podium when accepting his Best Actor Academy Award for 1934's *It Happened One Night* as he has one of the shortest acceptance speeches on record. He reached the podium, took award in hand, said a quick thank you and exited the stage. **Highlights:** Because Gable won his Best Actor award two decades before the Academy started requiring winners to sign an agreement not to sell their Oscars, Gable's estate put his Oscar up for auction through Christie's in 1996. An unidentified bidder paid $607,500 for Gable's statuette. To the Academy's great relief, the mystery bidder turned out to be director Steven Spielberg, who gave the award back to the Academy.

Gabor, Zsa Zsa

Tributes: 1957: Special Achievement Award as Most Glamorous Actress from Globe. **Records:** Gabor holds the distinction of being honored as an actress in a category created for her. During its early days, the Hollywood Foreign Press Association sometimes created special achievement categories to acknowledge an accomplishment or, in Gabor's case, to honor a celebrity's unique star quality. In 1957, they named her Most Glamour Actress, the only time they gave such an award.

Gainsbourg, Charlotte

Movie: 2007: *I'm Not There* (Best Ensemble) *Spirit* (special award).

Galifianakis, Zach

Movie: 2007: *Into the Wild* (Best Ensemble) SAG.

Gallagher, Peter

Movie: 1993: *Short Cuts* (Best Ensemble) *Venice* (special award). 1999: *American Beauty* (Best Ensemble) *SAG*. Theater: 1986: *Long Day's Journey into Night* (Best Actor in a Featured Role, Play) Tony.

Gallo, Carla

Movie: 1994: *Spanking the Monkey* (Best Supporting Female) *Spirit*.

Gam, Rita

Movie: 1952: *The Thief* (New Star of the Year — Actress) Globe. 1962: *No Exit* (Best Actress) *Berlin* (win shared with costar).

Gamblin, Jacques

Movie: 2002: *Laissez-passer (Safe Conduct)* (Best Actor) *Berlin*.

Gambon, Michael

Movie: 2001: *Gosford Park* (Best Ensemble) *SAG, Broadcast*. 2004: *The Life Aquatic with Steve Zissou* (Best Ensemble) Broadcast. Theater: 1997: *Skylight* (Best Actor, Play) Tony. Television: 2002: *Path to War* (Best Actor in a Miniseries or TV Movie) Emmy, Globe.

Gandolfini, James

Movie: 1995: *Get Shorty* (Best Ensemble) SAG. Television: 1999–2007 series *The Sopranos* (Best Actor in a Drama Series) 1999: Emmy, *Globe*. 2000: *Emmy*, Globe. 2001: *Emmy*, Globe. 2002: Globe. 2003: *Emmy*. 2004: Emmy. 2007: Emmy. (Best Male Actor in a Drama Series) 1999: *SAG*. 2000: SAG. 2001: SAG. 2002: *SAG*. 2004: SAG. 2006: SAG. 2007: *SAG*. (Best Ensemble in a Drama Series) 1999: *SAG*. 2000: SAG. 2001: SAG. 2002: SAG. 2004: SAG. 2006: SAG. 2007: *SAG*.

Garai, Romola

Movie: 2002: *Nicholas Nickleby* (Best Ensemble) *Board*.

Garber, Victor

Movie: 1996: *The First Wives Club* (Best Ensemble) *Board*. 1997: *Titanic* (Best Ensemble) SAG. Theater: 1978: *Deathtrap* (Best Actor in a Featured Role, Play) Tony. 1982: *Little Me* (Best Actor, Musical) Tony. 1989: *Lend Me a Tenor* (Best Actor, Play) Tony. 1994: *Damn Yankees* (Best Actor, Musical) Tony. Television: 2001: *Frasier* (Best Guest Actor in a Comedy Series) Emmy; *Life with Judy Garland: Me and My Shadows* (Best Supporting Actor in a Miniseries or TV Movie) Emmy. 2001–2006 series *Alias* (Best Supporting Actor in a Drama Series) 2002: Emmy. 2003: Emmy. 2004: Emmy. 2005: *Will & Grace* (Best Guest Actor in a Comedy Series) Emmy.

Garbo, Greta

Movie: 1930: *Anna Christie* (Best Actress) Academy; *Romance* (Best Actress) Academy. 1935: *Anna Karenina* (Best Actress) *New York*. 1937: *Camille* (Best Acting) *Board* (Best Actress) Academy, *New York*. 1939: *Ninotchka* (Best Acting) *Board* (Best Actress) Academy. 1941: *The Two-Faced Woman* (Best Acting) *Board*. Tributes: 1954: Honorary Oscar statuette for her unforgettable screen performances. 1999: Ranked Number 5 on List of 25 Greatest Female Screen Legends of the 20th Century from American Film Institute. Records: Garbo was the first to win a Best Actress award from the New York Film Critics when they honored her for *Anna Karenina* in 1935. She was an unlikely choice to win any award because by then she'd already established her reputation as a recluse, and the New York Critics knew their winning star wouldn't be on hand to accept their award. The first round of ballots put Garbo just one vote ahead of Katharine Hepburn for *Alice Adams*, who herself was becoming known for avoiding awards presentations. In the second round, Garbo won resoundingly. Two years later the New York Critics rewarded Garbo again, this time for *Camille*. She appreciated their recognition so much that she tried to attend their 1940 gala. However, when she was bombarded by fans outside the elevators of the Rainbow Room, Garbo rushed back to the Ritz Tower where the autograph seekers had hired a 24-hour sentry service to keep Garbo, registered as Clara Brown, from escaping without their notice. The traumatized Garbo never made the effort to attend an awards ceremony again.

Garcia, Andy

Movie: 1990: *The Godfather, Part III* (Best Supporting Actor) Academy, Globe. 2001: *Ocean's 11* (Best Ensemble) Broadcast. 2004: *Ocean's Twelve* (Best Ensemble) Broadcast. Television: 2001: *For Love or Country: The Arturo Sandoval Story* (Best Actor in a Miniseries or TV Movie) Emmy, Globe (Best TV Movie, Executive Producer) Emmy.

Gardenia, Vincent

Movie: 1973: *Bang the Drum Slowly* (Best Supporting Actor) Academy. 1987: *Moonstruck* (Best Supporting Actor) Academy. **Theater:** 1972: *The Prisoner of Second Avenue* (Best Supporting or Featured Actor, Dramatic) *Tony*. 1979: *Ballroom* (Best Actor, Musical) Tony. **Television:** 1990: *Age-Old Friends* (Best Supporting Actor in a Miniseries or Special) *Emmy*.

Gardner, Ava

Movie: 1953: *Mogambo* (Best Actress) Academy. 1956: *Bhowani Junction* (Best Foreign Actress) British. 1959: *On the Beach* (Best Foreign Actress) British. 1964: *The Night of the Iguana* (Best Actress, Drama) Globe (Best Foreign Actress) British. **Tributes:** 1999: Ranked Number 25 on List of 25 Greatest Female Screen Legends of the 20th Century from American Film Institute.

Garfield, John

Movie: 1938: *Four Daughters* (Best Acting) *Board* (Best Supporting Actor) Academy. 1947: *Body and Soul* (Best Actor) Academy.

Garfunkel, Art

Movie: 1971: *Carnal Knowledge* (Best Supporting Actor) Globe.

Gargan, William

Movie: 1940: *They Knew What They Wanted* (Best Supporting Actor) Academy. **Tributes:** 1967: Life Achievement Award from SAG.

Garin, Vladimir

Movie: 2003: *Vozvrashcheniye (The Return)* (Best Actor) *Venice* (win shared with costars).

Garity, Troy

Movie: 2003: *Soldier's Girl* (Best Supporting Male) Spirit. **Television:** 2003: *Soldier's Girl* (Best Actor in a Miniseries or TV Movie) Globe.

Garland, Judy

Movie: 1954: *A Star Is Born* (Best Actress) Academy (Best Actress, Musical or Comedy) *Globe* (Best Foreign Actress) British. 1961: *Judgment at Nuremberg* (Best Supporting Actress) Academy, Globe. **Television:** 1955: --- (Best Female Singer) Emmy. 1962: *The Judy Garland Show* (Best Performance in a Variety or Musical Program) Emmy. 1963–1964 series *The Judy Garland Show* (Best Performance in a Variety or Musical Program or Series) 1964: Emmy. **Tributes:** 1939: Honorary miniature Oscar statuette for her outstanding performance as a screen juvenile during the past year from Academy. 1952: Special award for an important contribution to the revival of vaudeville through her recent stint at the Palace Theatre from Tony. 1961: Cecil B. DeMille Award from Globe. 1999: Ranked Number 8 on List of 25 Greatest Female Screen Legends of the 20th Century from American Film Institute.

Garner, James

Movie: 1957: *Sayonara* (New Star of the Year — Actor) *Globe*. 1963: *Wheeler Dealers* (Best Actor, Musical or Comedy) Globe. 1985: *Murphy's Romance* (Best Actor) Academy (Best Actor, Musical or Comedy) Globe. 2004: *The Notebook* (Best Male Actor in a Supporting Role) SAG. **Television:** 1957–1960 series *Maverick* (Best Actor in a Drama Series) 1959: Emmy. 1974–1980 series *The Rockford Files* (Best Actor in a Drama Series) 1976: Emmy. 1977: *Emmy*, Globe. 1978: Emmy, Globe. 1979: Emmy, Globe. 1980: Emmy. 1981–1982 series *Bret Maverick* (Best Actor in a Drama Series) 1982: Emmy. (Best Actor in a Musical or Comedy Series) 1982: Globe. 1984: *"Heartsounds," An ABC Theatre Presentation* (Best Actor in a Limited Series or Special) Emmy, Globe. 1986: *"The Promise," Hallmark Hall of Fame* (Best Actor in a Miniseries or Special) Emmy, *Globe* (Best Drama or Comedy Special, Executive Producer) *Emmy*. 1989: *"My Name Is Bill W.," Hallmark Hall of Fame* (Best Supporting Actor in a Miniseries or Special) Emmy (Best Drama or Comedy Special, Executive Producer) Emmy. 1990: *"Decoration Day," Hallmark Hall of Fame* (Best Actor in a Miniseries or Special) Emmy, *Globe*. 1993: *Barbarians at the Gate* (Best Actor in a Miniseries or Special) Emmy (Best Actor in a Miniseries or TV Movie) *Globe*. 1994: *"Breathing Lessons," Hallmark Hall of Fame* (Best Actor in a Miniseries or Special) Emmy (Best Actor in a Miniseries or TV Movie) Globe; *The Rockford Files: I Still Love L.A.* (Best Male Actor in a Television Movie or Miniseries) SAG. 1995: *The Rockford Files* (Best Male Actor in a Television Movie or Miniseries) SAG. 1998: *Legalese* (Best Male Actor in a Television Movie or Miniseries) SAG. **Tributes:** 1991: Television Hall of Fame Inductee from Emmy. 2004: Life Achievement Award from SAG. **Highlights:** Garner had small parts in over forty motion pictures before being recognized by the Hollywood Foreign Press as New Star of the Year in the role of Marlon Brando's military pal, Captain Mike Bailey in *Sayonara*, the film adaptation of James Michener's sprawling Korean War novel.

Garner, Jennifer

Movie: 2007: *Juno* (Best Ensemble) Broadcast. **Television:** 2001–2006 series *Alias* (Best Actress in a Drama Series) 2002: Emmy, *Globe*. 2003: Emmy, Globe. 2004: Emmy, Globe. 2005: Emmy, Globe.

Garner, Peggy Ann

Tributes: 1945: Honorary miniature Oscar statuette for outstanding juvenile actress from Academy.

Garr, Teri

Movie: 1982: *Tootsie* (Best Supporting Actress) Academy, British. 1994: *Prêt-à-Porter (Ready-to-Wear)* (Best Ensemble) *Board*.

Garson, Greer

Movie: 1939: *Goodbye, Mr. Chips* (Best Actress) Academy. 1940: *Pride and Prejudice* (Best Acting) *Board*. 1941: *Blossoms in the Dust* (Best Actress) Academy. 1942: *Mrs. Miniver* (Best Acting) *Board* (multiple win), (Best Actress) *Academy*; *Random Harvest* (Best Acting) *Board* (multiple win). 1943: *Madame Curie* (Best Actress) Academy. 1944: *Mrs. Parkington* (Best Actress) Academy. 1945: *The Valley of Decision* (Best Actress) Academy. 1960: *Sunrise at Campobello* (Best Actress) Academy, *Board* (Best Actress, Drama) *Globe*. **Records:** Decades before movie sequels became commonplace, Garson was the first female actor to win an Oscar for a role and then reprise it in a sequel. Eight years after winning Best Actress as *Mrs. Miniver* she starred in *The Miniver Story*. For her *Mrs. Miniver* win, Garson is on record for having given the longest acceptance speech in Academy Award history. Though rumors have inflated the time up to an unbelievable 40+ minutes, more reliable sources registered the official time to be about 5½ minutes. Nonetheless, Garson's lengthy, though sincere and heartfelt acceptance, remained the subject of jokes for years, and contributed markedly to the Academy's subsequent request that winners keep acceptance speeches brief.

Gassman, Vittorio

Movie: 1975: *Profumo di donna (Scent of a Woman)* (Best Actor) *Cannes*. **Tributes:** 1996: Career Golden Lion from Venice.

Gavin, John

Movie: 1958: *A Time to Love and a Time to Die* (New Star of the Year — Actor) *Globe*.

Gaynor, Janet

Movie: 1927: *Seventh Heaven* (Best Actress) *Academy* (multiple win); *Street Angel* (Best Actress) *Academy* (multiple win). 1928: *Sunrise* (Best Actress) *Academy* (multiple win). 1937: *A Star Is Born* (Best Actress) Academy. **Records:** Not only is Gaynor the first to win a Best Actress Oscar, but she is also the only actor to win a single Oscar for three performances and the only actress to win her Academy Award for silent films.

Gaynor, Mitzi

Movie: 1958: *South Pacific* (Best Actress, Musical or Comedy) Globe.

Gazzara, Ben

Movie: 1998: *Happiness* (Best Ensemble) *Board*. **Theater:** 1956: *A Hatful of Rain* (Best Actor, Dramatic) Tony. 1975: *Hughie and Duet* (Best Actor, Dramatic) Tony. 1977: *Who's Afraid of Virginia Woolf?* (Best Actor, Play) Tony. **Television:** 1965–1968 series *Run for Your Life* (Best Continued Performance by an Actor in a Leading Role in a Dramatic Series) 1967: Emmy. 1968: Emmy. (Best Actor in a Series) 1966: Globe. 1967: Globe. 1968: Globe. 1986: *An Early Frost* (Best Actor in a Miniseries or TV Movie) Emmy. 2003: *Hysterical Blindness* (Best Supporting Actor in Miniseries or TV Movie) *Emmy*.

Gazzo, Michael V.

Movie: 1974: *The Godfather Part II* (Best Supporting Actor) Academy.

Geddes, Barbara Bel

Movie: 1948: *I Remember Mama* (Best Supporting Actress) Academy. **Theater:** 1956: *Cat on a Hot Tin Roof* (Best Actress, Dramatic) Tony. 1961: *Mary, Mary* (Best Actress, Dramatic) Tony. **Television:** 1978–1984, 1985–1990 series *Dallas* (Best Actress in a Drama Series) 1979: Emmy, Globe. 1980: *Emmy*, Globe. 1981: Emmy, Globe.

Genn, Leo

Movie: 1951: *Quo Vadis?* (Best Supporting Actor) Academy.

George, Chief Dan

Movie: 1970: *Little Big Man* (Best Supporting Actor) Academy, *New York*, Globe, *Society*.

George, Gladys

Movie: 1936: *Valiant Is the Word for Carrie* (Best Actress) Academy.

George, Götz

Movie: 1995: *Der Totmacher* (Best Actor) *Venice*.

Geraghty, Brian

Movie: 2006: *Bobby* (Best Ensemble) SAG, Broadcast.

Gere, Richard

Movie: 1982: *An Officer and a Gentleman* (Best Actor, Drama) Globe. 1990: *Pretty Woman* (Best Actor, Musical or Comedy) Globe. 2002: *Chicago* (Best Male Actor in a Leading Role) SAG (Best Actor, Musical or Comedy) *Globe* (Best Ensemble) *SAG, Broadcast*. 2007: *I'm Not There* (Best Ensemble) *Spirit* (special award). Television: 1994: *And the Band Played On* (Best Supporting Actor in a Miniseries or Special) Emmy. Tributes: 1997: Freedom of Expression Award for *Red Corner* from Board.

Gheorghiu, Luminita

Movie: 2006: *The Death of Mr. Lazarescu* (Best Supporting Actress) *LA*.

Gholson, Julie

Movie: 1974: *Where the Lilies Bloom* (New Star of the Year — Actress) Globe.

Giachetti, Fosco

Movie: 1942: *Bengasi* (Best Actor) *Venice*.

Giallelis, Stathis

Movie: 1963: *America, America* (New Star of the Year — Actor) *Globe* (Best Actor, Drama) Globe.

Giamatti, Paul

Movie: 2003: *American Splendor* (Breakthrough Performance — Male) *Board* (Best Male Lead) Spirit. 2004: *Sideways* (Best Actor) *New York*, Society, Broadcast (Best Actor, Musical or Comedy) Globe (Best Male Actor in a Leading Role) SAG (Best Male Lead) *Spirit* (Best Ensemble) *SAG, Broadcast*. 2005: *Cinderella Man* (Best Male Actor in a Supporting Role) *SAG* (Best Supporting Actor) Academy, Globe, *Broadcast*.

Giannini, Giancarlo

Movie: 1973: *Film d'amore e d'anarchia (Love and Anarchy)* (Best Actor) *Cannes*. 1976: *Seven Beauties* (Best Actor) Academy.

Gibson, Henry

Movie: 1975: *Nashville* (Best Supporting Actor) Globe, *Society*. Television: 1968–1971 series *Rowan and Martin's Laugh-In* (Best Supporting Actor in a Series) 1970: Globe.

Gibson, Mel

Movie: 1995: *Braveheart* (Best Director) *Academy, Globe*, British, *Broadcast* (Best Picture, Producer) *Academy*, Board (Best Picture, Drama; Producer) Globe. 1996: *Ransom* (Best Actor, Drama) Globe. 2000: *What Women Want* (Best Actor, Musical or Comedy) Globe. 2006: *Apocalypto* (Best Foreign Language Film, Producer) Globe (Best Film Not in English, Producer) British. Tributes: 1995: Special Filmmaking Achievement Award for *Braveheart* from Board. Records: In 1995 Gibson received the first Special Filmmaking Achievement Award introduced as an annual special honor by the National Board of Review, and also won the first Best Director prize ever given by the newly formed Broadcast Film Critics Association.

Gielgud, John

Movie: 1953: *Julius Caesar* (Best British Actor) *British*. 1964: *Becket* (Best Supporting Actor) Academy. 1974: *Murder on the Orient Express* (Best Supporting Actor) *British*. 1977: *Providence* (Best Actor) *New York*. 1981: *Arthur* (Best Supporting Actor) *Academy, New York, Globe*, British, *LA*. 1985: *Plenty* (Best Supporting Actor) British, *Society* (multiple win), *LA* (multiple win); *The Shooting Party* (Best Supporting Actor) *Society* (multiple win), *LA* (multiple win). 1996: *Shine* (Best Supporting Actor) British (Best Ensemble) SAG. Theater: 1961: *Big Fish, Little Fish* (Best Director, Dramatic) *Tony*. 1963: *The School for Scandal* (Best Director, Dramatic) Tony. 1965: *Tiny Alice* (Best Actor, Dramatic) Tony. 1971: *Home* (Best Actor, Dramatic) Tony. Television: 1982: *"Brideshead Revisited," Great Performances* (Best Supporting Actor in a Limited Series or Special) Emmy. 1984: *"The Master of Ballantrae," Hallmark Hall of Fame* (Best Supporting Actor in a Limited Series or Special) Emmy. 1985: *Romance on the Orient Express* (Best Supporting Actor in a Limited Series or Special) Emmy. 1988: *War and Remembrance* (Best Actor in a Limited Series or Special) Emmy; *War and Remembrance, Part I–VII* (Best Supporting Actor in a Miniseries or TV Movie) *Globe*. 1989: *War and Remembrance, Part VIII–XII* (Best Actor in a Miniseries or TV Movie) Globe. 1991: *"Summer's Lease," Masterpiece Theatre* (Best Actor in a Miniseries or Special) *Emmy*. Tributes: 1959: Special award for contribution to theater for his extraordinary insight in the writings of Shakespeare as demonstrated in his one-man play, *Ages of Man* from Tony.

Gilbert, Sara

Movie: 1992: *Poison Ivy* (Best Supporting Female) Spirit. Television: 1988–1997 series *Roseanne* (Best

Supporting Actress in a Comedy Series) 1993: Emmy. 1994: Emmy.

Gilford, Jack

Movie: 1973: *Save the Tiger* (Best Supporting Actor) Academy, Globe. **Theater:** 1963: *A Funny Thing Happened on the Way to the Forum* (Best Supporting or Featured Actor, Musical) Tony. 1967: *Cabaret* (Best Actor, Musical) Tony. **Television:** 1978: *Big Blue Marble* (Best Performer in Children's Programming) *Emmy.* 1989: *The Golden Girls* (Best Guest Actor in a Comedy Series) Emmy; *thirtysomething* (Best Guest Actor in a Drama Series) Emmy.

Gingold, Hermione

Movie: 1958: *Gigi* (Best Supporting Actress) *Globe.* 1962: *The Music Man (Meredith Willson's The Music Man)* (Best Supporting Actress) Globe. **Theater:** 1973: *A Little Night Music* (Best Supporting or Featured Actress, Musical) Tony.

Girardot, Annie

Movie: 1961: *Rocco and His Brothers* (Best Foreign Actress) British. 1965: *Trois Chambers à Manhattan* (Best Actress) *Venice.*

Gish, Lillian

Movie: 1946: *Duel in the Sun* (Best Supporting Actress) Academy. 1967: *The Comedians* (Best Supporting Actress) Globe. 1987: *The Whales of August* (Best Actress) *Board* (Best Female Lead) Spirit. **Tributes:** 1970: Special Oscar for superlative artistry and for distinguished contribution to the progress of motion pictures from Academy. 1982: Honor from Kennedy Center for the Performing Arts. 1984: Life Achievement Award from American Film Institute. 1987: Lifetime Achievement Award from Board. 1999: Ranked Number 17 on List of 25 Greatest Female Screen Legends of the 20th Century from American Film Institute. **Records:** Gish, widely considered The First Lady of the Silent Screen, holds the Guinness world record for having the longest career as a leading film actress and a record for having been a film actress the longest before earning a competitive acting award. She made her screen debut in *An Unseen Enemy* in 1912. 75 years and 86 films later, Gish made her last movie, *The Whales of August.* At awards time, the National Board of Review gave Gish a lifetime achievement award at the same ceremony where she tied for the Best Actress prize with Holly Hunter in *Broadcast News.* After that long wait to awards night accolades, Gish was forced by her doctor to stay home after she fell one month before the National Board's ceremony. Friend and First Lady of the American Theater Helen Hayes accepted the awards on Gish's behalf. Gish recuperated from injuries sustained in the fall and lived five more years but never made another film and won no more movie awards until AFI listed her as one of their 25 Screen Legends in an end-of-the-century poll six years after Gish died.

Glantzman-Leib, Lila

Movie: 1998: *Happiness* (Best Ensemble) *Board.*

Gleason, Jackie

Movie: 1961: *The Hustler* (Best Supporting Actor) Academy, *Board*, Globe. 1962: *Gigot* (Best Actor, Drama) Globe. **Theater:** 1960: *Take Me Along* (Best Actor, Musical) *Tony.* **Television:** 1952: --- (Best Comedian) Emmy. 1952–1970 series *The Jackie Gleason Show* (Best Male Star in a Regular Series) 1953: Emmy. (Best Actor Starring in a Regular Series) 1954: Emmy. (Best Written Comedy Material, Writer) 1954: Emmy. 1954–1955: *The Honeymooners* (Best Actor — Continuing Performace) 1955: Emmy. 1963: *Jackie Gleason and His American Scene Magazine* (Best Actor in a Series) Globe. **Tributes:** 1986: Television Hall of Fame Inductee from Emmy.

Gleason, James

Movie: 1941: *Here Comes Mr. Jordan* (Best Acting) *Board* (multiple win), (Best Supporting Actor) Academy; *Meet John Doe* (Best Acting) *Board* (multiple win).

Glen, Iain

Movie: 1990: *Silent Scream* (Best Actor) *Berlin.*

Glover, Danny

Movie: 1990: *To Sleep with Anger* (Best Male Lead) *Spirit.* 2001: *The Royal Tenenbaums* (Best Ensemble) Broadcast. 2006: *Dreamgirls* (Best Ensemble) SAG, Broadcast. **Television:** 1988: *Mandela* (Best Actor in a Miniseries or Special) Emmy. 1989: *Lonesome Dove* (Best Supporting Actor in a Miniseries or Special) Emmy. 1996: *Fallen Angels* (Best Guest Actor in a Drama Series) Emmy. 2000: *Freedom Song* (Best Male Actor in a Television Movie or Miniseries) SAG (Best Supporting Actor in a Miniseries or TV Movie) Emmy.

Gluschenko, Jewgenija

Movie: 1983: *Wljubljon po sobstvennomu zhelaniju (Love by Request)* (Best Actress) *Berlin.*

Goddard, Paulette

Movie: 1943: *So Proudly We Hail* (Best Supporting Actress) Academy.

Goldberg, Adam

Movie: 1998: *Saving Private Ryan* (Best Ensemble) SAG. 2001: *A Beautiful Mind* (Best Ensemble) SAG.

Goldberg, Whoopi

Movie: 1985: *The Color Purple* (Best Actress) Academy, *Board* (Best Actress, Drama) *Globe*. 1990: *Ghost* (Best Supporting Actress) *Academy, Globe, British*. 1992: *Sister Act* (Best Actress, Musical or Comedy) Globe. Theater: 2002: *Thoroughly Modern Millie* (Best Musical, Producer) *Tony*. Television: 1986: *Moonlighting* (Best Guest Actress in a Drama Series) Emmy. 1991: *A Different World* (Best Guest Actress in a Comedy Series) Emmy. 1994: *The 66th Annual Academy Awards* (Best Individual Performance in a Variety or Music Program) Emmy. 1996: *The 68th Annual Academy Awards* (Best Performance in a Variety or Music Program, Host) Emmy; *Comic Relief VII* (Best Performance in a Variety or Music Program, Host) Emmy. 2005: *Whoopi Back to Broadway, the 20th Anniversary* (Best Individual Performance in a Variety or Music Program) Emmy. Records: Oscar winner Goldberg set two Oscar records in 1994, not for acting but for emceeing. At the 66th Annual Academy Awards for the films of 1993, Goldberg became the first African-American and the first female ever to serve as solo host at the awards ceremony. She received favorable reviews for her work and hosted again for the films of 1995, 1998, and 2001, when African-Americans again made Oscar history as Denzel Washington and Halle Berry became the first Black actors to win Best Actor and Best Actress in the same year.

Goldblum, Jeff

Movie: 1992: *Deep Cover* (Best Supporting Male) Spirit. 1995: *Little Surprises* (Best Live Action Short Film) Academy. 2004: *The Life Aquatic with Steve Zissou* (Best Ensemble) Broadcast. Television: 2005: *Will & Grace* (Best Guest Actor in a Comedy Series) Emmy.

Goldoni, Lelia

Movie: 1960: *Shadows* (Most Promising Newcomer) British. 1974: *Alice Doesn't Live Here Anymore* (Best Supporting Actress) British.

Golino, Valerie

Movie: 1986: *Storia d'amore* (Best Actress) *Venice*.

Golisano, Francesco

Movie: 1952: *Miracolo a Milano* (Best Foreign Actor) British.

Gómez, Fernando Fernàn

Movie: 1977: *El Anacoreta* (Best Actor) *Berlin*. 1984: *Los Zancos* (Best Actor) *Venice*. 1985: *Stico* (Best Actor) *Berlin*.

Gomez, José Louis

Movie: 1976: *Pascual Duarte* (Best Actor) *Cannes*.

Gomez, Marie

Movie: 1966: *The Professionals* (New Star of the Year — Actress) Globe.

Gomez, Thomas

Movie: 1947: *Ride the Pink Horse* (Best Supporting Actor) Academy.

Gooding, Cuba, Jr.

Movie: 1996: *Jerry Maguire* (Best Male Actor in a Supporting Role) *SAG* (Best Supporting Actor) *Academy*, Globe, *Broadcast*. 2007: *American Gangster* (Best Ensemble) SAG. Records: With his Best Supporting Actor win for *Jerry Maguire*, Gooding became the first African-American to win an acting prize from the Broadcast Film Critics Association.

Goodman, John

Movie: 1991: *Barton Fink* (Best Supporting Actor) Globe. Television: 1988–1997 series *Roseanne* (Best Actor in a Comedy Series) 1989: Emmy. 1990: Emmy. 1991: Emmy. 1992: Emmy. 1993: Emmy. 1994: Emmy. 1995: Emmy. (Best Actor in a Series, Musical or Comedy) 1988: Globe. 1989: Globe. 1990: Globe. 1992: *Globe*. (Best Male Actor in a Comedy Series) 1994: SAG. 1995: *Kingfish: The Story of Huey P. Long* (Best Actor in a Miniseries or Special) Emmy. 1995: *Tennessee Williams' A Streetcar Named Desire* (Best Supporting Actor in a Miniseries or Special) Emmy. 2007: *Studio 60 on the Sunset Strip* (Best Guest Actor in a Drama Series) *Emmy*.

Goodwin, Deidre

Movie: 2002: *Chicago* (Best Ensemble) *SAG, Broadcast*.

Goodwin, Raven

Movie: 2002: *Lovely & Amazing* (Best Debut Performance) Spirit. 2003: *The Station Agent* (Best Ensemble) SAG.

Gordon, Dexter

Movie: 1986: *'Round Midnight* (Best Actor) Academy (Best Actor, Drama) Globe (Best Music Score) *LA*.

Gordon, Jade

Movie: 1999: *Sugar Town* (Best Debut Performance) Spirit.

Gordon, Ruth

Movie: 1947: *A Double Life* (Best Original Screenplay) Academy. 1950: *Adam's Rib* (Best Story and Screenplay) Academy. 1952: *Pat and Mike* (Best Story and Screenplay) Academy. 1965: *Inside Daisy Clover* (Best Supporting Actress) Academy, *Globe*. 1968: *Rosemary's Baby* (Best Supporting Actress) *Academy, Globe*. 1971: *Harold and Maude* (Best Actress, Musical or Comedy) Globe. **Theater:** 1956: *The Matchmaker* (Best Actress, Dramatic) Tony. **Television:** 1976: *Rhoda* (Best Single Performance by a Supporting Actress in a Comedy or Drama Series) Emmy. 1977: *"The Great Houdinis," The ABC Friday Night Movie* (Best Supporting Actress in a Comedy or Drama Special) Emmy. 1979: *Taxi* (Best Actress in a Comedy Series) *Emmy*. 1985: *The Secret World of the Very Young* (Best Individual Achievement in Information Programming, Performer) Emmy. **Records:** When she was voted Best Supporting Actress for *Rosemary's Baby* in 1968, 72-year-old Gordon became the first person over 70 to win a competitive acting Oscar. Accepting her Academy Award after 53 years as a stage and screen actress and a playwright and screenwriter, an elated Gordon chided that if she hadn't won this time, her husband refused to bring her to the awards again. Beaming, she then wondered aloud why it took the Academy so long, and confessed to feeling encouraged and groovy about winning.

Gosling, Ryan

Movie: 2001: *The Believer* (Best Male Lead) Spirit. 2006: *Half Nelson* (Breakthrough Performance — Male) *Board* (Best Actor) Academy, Broadcast (Best Male Lead) *Spirit* (Best Male Actor in a Leading Role) SAG. 2007: *Lars and the Real Girl* (Best Actor) Broadcast (Best Actor, Musical or Comedy) Globe (Best Male Actor in a Leading Role) SAG.

Gossett, Louis, Jr.

Movie: 1982: *An Officer and a Gentleman* (Best Supporting Actor) *Academy, Globe*. **Television:** 1977: *Roots* (Best Single Performance by an Actor in a Drama or Comedy Series) *Emmy*. 1978: *The Sentry Collection Presents Ben Vereen—His Roots* (Best Continuing or Single Performance by a Supporting Actor in Variety or Music) Emmy. 1979: *Backstairs at the White House* (Best Actor in a Limited Series or Special) Emmy. 1980–1981 series *Palmerstown, U.S.A.* (Best Actor in a Drama Series) 1981: Emmy. 1984: *Sadat* (Best Actor in a Limited Series or Special) Emmy (Best Actor in a Miniseries or TV Movie) Globe. 1987: *A Gathering of Old Men* (Best Actor in a Miniseries or Special) Emmy. 1991: *The Josephine Baker Story* (Best Supporting Actor in a Series, Miniseries, or TV Movie) *Globe*. 1997: *Touched by an Angel* (Best Guest Actor in a Drama Series) Emmy. **Records:** For his role as relentless but ultimately wise drill sergeant Emil Foley in *An Officer and a Gentleman*, Gossett became the first African-American to win the Best Supporting Actor Oscar. Prior to his winning, only two Black stars had won competitive Oscars: Hattie McDaniel (*Gone with the Wind*, 1939) and Sidney Poitier (*Lilies of the Field*, 1963). **Highlights:** When Gossett won the Emmy for Outstanding Lead Actor for a Single Performance in a Drama or Comedy Series, all the other nominees were his co-stars in *Roots*. His performance as Fiddler beat out John Amos as Toby (Kunta Kinte as an adult), LaVar Burton as Kunta Kinte/Toby Reynolds, and Ben Vereen as "Chicken" George Moore.

Gough, Michael

Movie: 1971: *The Go-Between* (Best Supporting Actor) British. **Theater:** 1979: *Bedroom Farce* (Best Actor in a Featured Role, Play) *Tony*. 1988: *Breaking the Code* (Best Actor in a Featured Role, Play) Tony.

Gould, Elliott

Movie: 1969: *Bob & Carol & Ted & Alice* (Best Actor) British (multiple nomination), (Best Supporting Actor) Academy. 1970: *M*A*S*H* (Best Actor) British (multiple nomination), (Best Actor, Musical or Comedy) Globe. 2001: *Ocean's 11* (Best Ensemble) Broadcast. 2004: *Ocean's Twelve* (Best Ensemble) Broadcast.

Gourmet, Olivier

Movie: 2002: *Le Fils (The Son)* (Best Actor) *Cannes*.

Grabowska, Barbara

Movie: 1981: *Goraczka* (Best Actress) *Berlin*.

Grace, April

Movie: 1999: *Magnolia* (Best Ensemble) *Board*, SAG.

Grace, Topher

Movie: 2000: *Traffic* (Best Ensemble) *SAG*. 2004: *In Good Company* (Breakthrough Performance — Male) *Board* (multiple win); *Ocean's Twelve* (Best Ensemble) Broadcast; *P.S.* (Breakthrough Performance — Male) *Board* (multiple win).

Graham, Heather

Movie: 1989: *Drugstore Cowboy* (Best Supporting Female) Spirit. 1997: *Boogie Nights* (Best Ensemble) SAG. 2006: *Bobby* (Best Ensemble) SAG, Broadcast.

Grahame, Gloria

Movie: 1947: *Crossfire* (Best Supporting Actress) Academy. 1952: *The Bad and the Beautiful* (Best Supporting Actress) *Academy*, Globe.

Grant, Cary

Movie: 1941: *Penny Serenade* (Best Actor) Academy. 1944: *None but the Lonely Heart* (Best Actor) Academy. 1958: *Indiscreet* (Best Actor, Musical or Comedy) Globe. 1959: *Operation Petticoat* (Best Actor, Musical or Comedy) Globe. 1960: *The Grass Is Greener* (Best Actor, Musical or Comedy) Globe. 1962: *That Touch of Mink* (Best Actor, Musical or Comedy) Globe. 1963: *Charade* (Best Foreign Actor) British (Best Actor, Musical or Comedy) Globe. Tributes: 1969: Honorary Oscar for his unique mastery of the art of screen acting with the respect and affection of his colleagues from Academy. 1981: Honor from Kennedy Center for the Performing Arts. 1999: Ranked Number 2 on List of 25 Greatest Male Screen Legends of the 20th Century from American Film Institute.

Grant, Hugh

Movie: 1987: *Maurice* (Best Actor) *Venice* (win shared with costar). 1994: *Four Weddings and a Funeral* (Best Actor) *British* (Best Actor, Musical or Comedy) *Globe*. 1995: *Sense and Sensibility* (Best Ensemble) SAG. 1999: *Notting Hill* (Best Actor, Musical or Comedy) Globe. 2002: *About a Boy* (Best Actor, Musical or Comedy) Globe. 2003: *Love Actually* (Best Ensemble) Broadcast.

Grant, Lee

Movie: 1951: *Detective Story* (Best Actress) *Cannes* (Best Supporting Actress) Academy, Globe. 1967: *In the Heat of the Night* (Best Supporting Actress) Globe. 1970: *The Landlord* (Best Supporting Actress) Academy, Globe. 1975: *Shampoo* (Best Supporting Actress) *Academy*, Globe. 1976: *Voyage of the Damned* (Best Supporting Actress) Academy, Globe. Television: 1965–1966 series *Peyton Place* (Best Supporting Actress in a Drama) 1966: Emmy. 1969: *Judd for the Defense* (Best Single Performance by an Actress) Emmy. 1971: *The Neon Ceiling* (Best Single Performance by an Actress) *Emmy*; *Ransom for a Dead Man* (Best Single Performance by an Actress) Emmy. 1974: *The Shape of Things* (Best Supporting Actress in a Comedy-Variety, Variety, or Music Program) Emmy. 1975–1976 series *Fay* (Best Actress in a Comedy Series) 1976: Emmy. 1993: *Citizen Cohn* (Best Supporting Actress in a Miniseries or Special) Emmy. Highlights: Due to an Emmy rule change in 1966, supporting players on regular dramas could compete against stars on big budget TV movies and specials. A snobbish editorial in *The Hollywood Reporter* grumbled about the prospect of a *Peyton Place* star actually beating a *Hallmark Hall of Fame* actor. When Grant's name was announced at the Emmys that year for *Peyton Place* over some *Hallmark Hall of Fame* nominees, the audience bounded to its feet amid thunderous applause. Grant responded to the ovation by telling her peers that the feeling was mutual and exiting the stage. Hers remains one of the shortest and best loved acceptance speeches in award history.

Grant, Richard E.

Movie: 1994: *Prêt-à-Porter (Ready-to-Wear)* (Best Ensemble) *Board*. 2001: *Gosford Park* (Best Ensemble) *SAG*, Broadcast.

Granville, Bonita

Movie: 1936: *These Three* (Best Supporting Actress) Academy. Records: In 1936, the first year the Academy added supporting categories for actors, Granville earned a nomination for Best Supporting Actress. Because she was only 13 at the time, she became the first female child star to compete for an Oscar. She lost to Gale Sondergaard in *Anthony Adverse*.

Gray, Spalding

Movie: 1987: *Swimming to Cambodia* (Best Male Lead) Spirit (Best Screenplay) Spirit.

Gray-Stanford, Jason

Movie: 2001: *A Beautiful Mind* (Best Ensemble) SAG.

Greenberg, Ari

Movie: 1996: *The First Wives Club* (Best Ensemble) *Board*.

Greene, Graham

Movie: 1990: *Dances with Wolves* (Best Supporting Actor) Academy. 1999: *The Green Mile* (Best Ensemble) SAG. 2002: *Skins* (Best Male Lead) Spirit.

Greene, Peter

Movie: 1992: *Laws of Gravity* (Best Male Lead) Spirit. 1995: *The Usual Suspects* (Best Ensemble) *Board.*

Greenstreet, Sydney

Movie: 1941: *The Maltese Falcon* (Best Supporting Actor) Academy. 1942: *Across the Pacific* (Best Acting) *Board.* **Highlights:** Robust (he weighed nearly 300 pounds) and dependable character actor Greenstreet received an Oscar nomination for his first screen role, playing ruthless Kasper Gutman in the film noir classic, *The Maltese Falcon.*

Greenwood, Bruce

Movie: 1997: *The Sweet Hereafter* (Best Ensemble) *Board.* 2005: *Capote* (Best Ensemble) SAG. 2007: *I'm Not There* (Best Ensemble) *Spirit* (special award).

Greenwood, Joan

Movie: 1963: *Tom Jones* (Best Supporting Actress) Globe.

Gregg, Clark

Movie: 1999: *The Adventures of Sebastian Cole* (Best Supporting Male) Spirit. 2000: *State and Main* (Best Ensemble) *Board.*

Grey, Jennifer

Movie: 1987: *Dirty Dancing* (Best Actress, Musical or Comedy) Globe.

Grey, Joel

Movie: 1972: *Cabaret* (Most Promising Newcomer) *British* (Best Supporting Actor) *Academy, Board, Globe, Society.* 1985: *Remo Williams: The Adventure Begins* (Best Supporting Actor) Globe. **Theater:** 1967: *Cabaret* (Best Supporting or Featured Actor, Musical) *Tony.* 1969: *George M!* (Best Actor, Musical) Tony. 1975: *Goodtime Charley* (Best Actor, Musical) Tony. 1979: *The Grand Tour* (Best Actor, Musical) Tony. **Television:** 1993: *Brooklyn Bridge* (Best Guest Actor in a Comedy Series) Emmy. **Records:** Grey is the first actor to win in a tie with another actor for two different critical awards. 1972 was a strong and varied year for supporting actors, as award-worthy performances came in dramas, comedies, and musicals. The three Corleone brothers in *The Godfather* saga (Al Pacino, James Caan, and Robert Duvall) were all in contention for different awards, as was Eddie Albert for his comic turn in *The Heartbreak Kid* and Grey for his androgynous emcee in Bob Fosse's musical, *Cabaret.* Both the National Board of Review and National Society of Film Critics spread the wealth by declaring ties: Grey shared his Board win with Al Pacino and his Society win with Eddie Albert. The only race Grey lost that year was from the New York Film Critics, who crowned Duvall their winner.

Grier, David Alan

Movie: 1983: *Streamers* (Best Actor) *Venice* (win shared with costars). **Theater:** 1982: *The First* (Best Actor in a Featured Role, Musical) Tony.

Grier, Pam

Movie: 1997: *Jackie Brown* (Best Female Actor in a Leading Role) SAG (Best Actress, Musical or Comedy) Globe.

Gries, Jon

Movie: 2004: *Napoleon Dynomite* (Best Supporting Male) Spirit.

Griffith, Corrine

Movie: 1929: *The Divine Lady* (Best Actress) Academy.

Griffith, Hugh

Movie: 1959: *Ben-Hur* (Best Supporting Actor) *Academy, Board.* 1963: *Tom Jones* (Best British Actor) British (Best Supporting Actor) Academy, Globe. 1968: *The Fixer* (Best Supporting Actor) Globe; *Oliver!* (Best Supporting Actor) Globe. **Theater:** 1958: *Look Homeward, Angel* (Best Actor, Dramatic) Tony.

Griffith, Melanie

Movie: 1984: *Body Double* (Best Supporting Actress) Globe, *Society.* 1986: *Something Wild* (Best Actress, Musical or Comedy) Globe. 1988: *Working Girl* (Best Actress) Academy, British (Best Actress, Musical or Comedy) *Globe.* **Television:** 1995: *Buffalo Girls* (Best Supporting Actress in a Series, Miniseries, or TV Movie) Globe. 2000: *RKO 281* (Best Supporting Actress in a Miniseries or TV Movie) Emmy (Best Supporting Actress in a Series, Miniseries, or TV Movie) Globe. **Records:** Griffith is the first Miss Golden Globe to win a Globe for her work in motion pictures. In 2006 Griffith set another record by becoming the first former Miss Golden Globe to have a daughter become a Miss Golden Globe as well when Dakota Johnson, her child with actor Don Johnson, was selected to pass out the awards.

Griffiths, Rachel

Movie: 1998: *Hilary and Jackie* (Best Female Actor in a Supporting Role) SAG (Best Supporting Actress) Academy. Television: 2001–2005 series *Six Feet Under* (Best Actress in a Drama Series) 2002: Emmy, Globe. (Best Supporting Actress in a Drama Series) 2003: Emmy. (Best Supporting Actress in a Series, Miniseries, or TV Movie) 2001: *Globe.* (Best Ensemble in a Drama Series) 2001: SAG. 2002: *SAG.* 2003: *SAG.* 2004: SAG. 2005: SAG. 2006–present series *Brothers and Sisters* (Best Supporting Actress in a Drama Series) 2007: Emmy. (Best Supporting Actress in a Series, Miniseries, or TV Movie) 2007: Globe.

Griffiths, Richard

Movie: 2006: *The History Boys* (Best Actor) British. Theater: 2006: *The History Boys* (Best Actor, Play) *Tony.*

Grimes, Gary

Movie: 1971: *Summer of '42* (New Star of the Year — Actor) Globe (Most Promising Newcomer) British.

Grinberg, Anouk

Movie: 1996: *Mon homme* (Best Actress) *Berlin.*

Gritsenko, Nikolai

Movie: 1954: *Bolshaya semya (The Big Family)* *Cannes* (special ensemble award).

Grodin, Charles

Movie: 1972: *The Heartbreak Kid* (Best Actor, Musical or Comedy) Globe. Television: 1978: *The Paul Simon Special* (Best Writing in a Comedy-Variety or Music Special) *Emmy.*

Gua, Ah-Leh

Movie: 1993: *The Wedding Banquet* (Best Supporting Female) Spirit.

Guard, Dominic

Movie: 1971: *The Go-Between* (Most Promising Newcomer) *British.*

Guardino, Harry

Movie: 1958: *Houseboat* (Best Supporting Actor) Globe. 1962: *The Pigeon That Took Rome* (Best Supporting Actor) Globe. Theater: 1960: *One More River* (Best Supporting or Featured Actor, Dramatic) Tony.

Guastaferro, Vincent

Movie: 2000: *State and Main* (Best Ensemble) *Board.*

Guest, Christopher

Movie: 1997: *Waiting for Guffman* (Best Male Lead) Spirit (Best Screenplay) Spirit. 2000: *Best in Show* (Best Director) Spirit. 2003: *A Mighty Wind* (Best Screenplay) Spirit (Best Song, "A Mighty Wind") *Broadcast* (Best Ensemble) Broadcast. 2005: *Mrs. Henderson Presents* (Best Ensemble) *Board.* Television: 1976: *Lily Tomlin* (Best Writing in a Comedy-Variety or Music Special) *Emmy.*

Gugino, Carla

Movie: 2005: *Sin City* (Best Ensemble) Broadcast. 2007: *American Gangster* (Best Ensemble) SAG.

Guinness, Alec

Movie: 1950: *Kind Hearts and Coronets* (Best Actor) *Board.* 1952: *The Lavender Hill Mob* (Best Actor) Academy. 1955: *The Prisoner* (Best British Actor) British. 1957: *The Bridge on the River Kwai* (Best Actor) *Academy, New York, Board* (Best Actor, Drama) *Globe* (Best British Actor) *British.* 1958: *The Horse's Mouth* (Best Actor) *Venice* (Best Screenplay) Academy, British. 1960: *Tunes of Glory* (Best British Actor) British. 1977: *Star Wars* (Best Supporting Actor) Academy, Globe. 1988: *Little Dorrit* (Best Supporting Actor) Academy, Globe, *LA.* Theater: 1964: *Dylan* (Best Actor, Dramatic) *Tony.* Television: 1960: *"The Wicked Scheme of Jebal Deeks," Ford Startime* (Best Single Performance by a Lead or Supporting Actor) Emmy. 1983: *Smiley's People* (Best Actor in a Limited Series or Special) Emmy. Tributes: 1979: Honorary Oscar for advancing the art of screen acting through a host of memorable and distinguished performances from Academy. 1987: Gala Tribute from the Film Society of Lincoln Center. 1988: Honorary Golden Bear from Berlin.

Guzmán, Luis

Movie: 1997: *Boogie Nights* (Best Ensemble) SAG. 1999: *The Limey* (Best Supporting Male) Spirit; *Magnolia* (Best Ensemble) *Board*, SAG. 2000: *Traffic* (Best Ensemble) *SAG.*

Gwenn, Edmund

Movie: 1947: *Miracle on 34th Street* (Best Supporting Actor) *Academy, Globe.* 1950: *Mister 880* (Best Supporting Actor) Academy, *Globe.*

Gwisdek, Michael

Movie: 1999: *Nachtgestalten (Nightshapes)* (Best Actor) *Berlin*.

Gyllenhaal, Jake

Movie: 2001: *Donnie Darko* (Best Male Lead) Spirit. 2005: *Brokeback Mountain* (Best Male Actor in a Supporting Role) SAG (Best Supporting Actor) Academy, *Board*, *British*, Broadcast (Best Ensemble) SAG.

Gyllenhaal, Maggie

Movie: 2002: *Secretary* (Breakthrough Performance — Female) *Board* (Best Actress, Musical or Comedy) Globe (Best Female Lead) Spirit. 2005: *Happy Endings* (Best Supporting Female) Spirit. 2006: *Sherrybaby* (Best Actress, Drama) Globe.

Hackett, Joan

Movie: 1966: *The Group* (Best Foreign Actress) British. 1981: *Only When I Laugh* (Best Supporting Actress) Academy, *Globe*. **Television:** 1962: *Ben Casey* (Best Performance in a Supporting Role by an Actress) Emmy.

Hackman, Gene

Movie: 1967: *Bonnie and Clyde* (Best Supporting Actor) Academy, *Society*. 1970: *I Never Sang for My Father* (Best Supporting Actor) Academy. 1971: *The French Connection* (Best Actor) *Academy, New York, Board, British* (multiple win), (Best Actor, Drama) Globe. 1972: *The Poseidon Adventure* (Best Actor) *British* (multiple win). 1974: *The Conversation* (Best Actor) *Board*, British (Best Actor, Drama) Globe. 1975: *The French Connection II* (Best Actor) British (multiple nomination), (Best Actor, Drama) Globe; *Night Moves* (Best Actor) British (multiple nomination). 1978: *Superman* (Best Supporting Actor) British. 1983: *Under Fire* (Best Supporting Actor) Globe. 1985: *Twice in a Lifetime* (Best Actor, Drama) Globe. 1988: *Mississippi Burning* (Best Actor) Academy, *Board*, Berlin (Best Actor, Drama) Globe. 1992: *Unforgiven* (Best Supporting Actor) *Academy, New York, Globe, British, Society, LA*. 1995: *Get Shorty* (Best Ensemble) SAG. 1996: *The Birdcage* (Best Ensemble) SAG. 2001: *The Royal Tenenbaums* (Best Actor) *Society* (Best Actor, Musical or Comedy) *Globe* (Best Ensemble) Broadcast. **Tributes:** 2002: Cecil B. De-Mille Award from Globe. **Records:** Hackman's small role in Warren Beatty's *Lilith* led Beatty to remember him when casting *Bonnie and Clyde* in 1967. Hackman's performance as Buck Barrow, Clyde's good-natured and easily led astray brother earned him the first National Society of Film Critics award in the new category of Best Supporting Actor. Since that first win,

Hackman has gone on to share the record with Jack Nicholson for winning an award from more major organizations than any other actor or actress. Except for the Venice and Cannes film festivals and the Independent Spirit awards, Hackman has won at least one prize from every other major film group or festival. **Highlights:** Hackman's Best Actor Oscar win is sandwiched between the only two actors to date who've refused their awards. The year before Hackman won for *The French Connection*, George C. Scott ignored his Oscar win for *Patton*. The year after, Marlon Brando rejected his award for *The Godfather*.

Hagen, Jean

Movie: 1952: *Singin' in the Rain* (Best Supporting Actress) Academy. **Television:** 1953–1956 series *Make Room for Daddy* (Best Actress — Continuing Performance) 1955: Emmy. (Best Supporting Actress in a Regular Series) 1955: Emmy. (Best Actress in a Supporting Role) 1956: Emmy.

Hale, Elvi

Movie: 1957: *True as a Turtle* (Most Promising Newcomer) British.

Hale, Georgina

Movie: 1974: *Mahler* (Most Promising Newcomer) *British*.

Haley, Jackie Earle

Movie: 2006: *Little Children* (Best Male Actor in a Supporting Role) SAG (Best Supporting Actor) Academy, *New York*.

Hall, Danielle

Movie: 2002: *Beneath Clouds* (Best Young Actress) *Berlin*.

Hall, Grayson

Movie: 1964: *The Night of the Iguana* (Best Supporting Actress) Academy, Globe.

Hall, Irma P.

Movie: 2004: *The Lady Killers* (Best Actress) *Cannes* (special award).

Halsey, Brett

Movie: 1960: *Desire in the Dust* (New Star of the Year — Actor) *Globe*.

Hamilton, George

Movie: 1959: *Crime and Punishment, USA* (New Star of the Year) *Globe* (Best Foreign Actor) British.

1961: *Light in the Piazza* (Best Foreign Actor) British. 1979: *Love at First Bite* (Best Actor, Musical or Comedy) Globe. 1981: *Zorro, the Gay Blade* (Best Actor, Musical or Comedy) Globe.

Hamlin, Harry

Movie: 1978: *Movie, Movie* (New Star of the Year — Actor) Globe. Television: 1986–1991 series *L.A. Law* (Best Actor in a Drama Series) 1987: Globe. 1988: Globe. 1989: Globe.

Hampton, Jim

Movie: 1974: *The Longest Yard* (New Star of the Year — Actor) Globe.

Hancock, Anthony

Movie: 1961: *The Rebel* (Most Promising Newcomer) British.

Hancock, Barbara

Movie: 1968: *Finian's Rainbow* (New Star of the Year — Actress) Globe (Best Supporting Actress) Globe.

Handy, Rachael

Movie: 2000: *George Washington* (Best Debut Performance) Spirit (nomination shared with costars).

Hanks, Tom

Movie: 1988: *Big* (Best Actor) Academy, *LA* (multiple win), (Best Actor, Musical or Comedy) *Globe*; *Punchline* (Best Actor) *LA* (multiple win). 1993: *Philadelphia* (Best Actor) *Academy*, Berlin (Best Actor, Drama) *Globe*; *Sleepless in Seattle* (Best Actor, Musical or Comedy) Globe. 1994: *Forrest Gump* (Best Actor) *Academy, Board*, British (Best Actor, Drama) *Globe* (Best Male Actor in a Leading Role) *SAG*. 1995: *Apollo 13* (Best Ensemble) *SAG*. 1998: *Saving Private Ryan* (Best Actor) Academy, British (Best Actor, Drama) Globe (Best Male Actor in a Leading Role) SAG (Best Ensemble) SAG. 1999: *The Green Mile* (Best Ensemble) SAG. 2000: *Cast Away* (Best Actor) Academy, *New York*, British, Broadcast (Best Actor, Drama) *Globe* (Best Male Actor in a Leading Role) SAG. 2007: *Charlie Wilson's War* (Best Actor, Musical or Comedy) Globe. Television: 1998: *From the Earth to the Moon* (Best Directing for a Miniseries or Movie) Emmy (Best Miniseries, Executive Producer) *Emmy*. 2002: *Band of Brothers* (Best Directing for a Miniseries, TV Movie, or Drama Special) *Emmy* (Best Miniseries, Executive Producer) *Emmy* (Best Writing for a Miniseries, TV Movie, or Dramatic Special) Emmy; *We Stand Alone Together: The Men of Easy Company* (Best Non-Fiction Informational Special, Executive Producer) Emmy. **Tributes:** 2002: Life Achievement Award from American Film Institute. **Records:** While many life achievement awards mark the closing years of a person's career or even recall the body of work that has ended, Hanks' win turned that idea upside down when, at age 46, Hanks became the youngest recipient of AFI's Life Achievement Award. **Highlights:** The immensely likeable Hanks makes an indelible impression nearly any time he accepts an award. When Emma Thompson announced Hanks the Best Actor of 1993 for his role of a gay lawyer fighting job discrimination while dying of AIDS in *Philadelphia*, the audience rose to its feet for a long and generous standing ovation. As he concluded his eloquent speech, which acknowledged two gay role models who had impacted him in his youth and concluded with a teary remembrance of the many victims who had succumbed to AIDS to that time, the audience bookmarked the moment with a second standing ovation. The following year, when Hanks won the first Best Actor SAG award ever given for his endearing interpretation of the simple yet stellar title character in *Forrest Gump*, he punctuated his acceptance speech by pulling out his Screen Actor's Guild card. That gesture became the first history-making moment at the SAG awards and inspired a future taped segment of guild members showing their cards and explaining the history of how they got it.

Hannah, John

Movie: 1994: *Four Weddings and a Funeral* (Best Supporting Actor) British.

Harada, Ann

Movie: 1998: *Happiness* (Best Ensemble) *Board*.

Harden, Marcia Gay

Movie: 1996: *The First Wives Club* (Best Ensemble) *Board*. 2000: *Pollock* (Best Supporting Actress) *Academy, New York* (Best Supporting Female) Spirit. 2003: *Mystic River* (Best Supporting Actress) Academy, Broadcast (Best Ensemble) SAG, Broadcast. 2006: *American Gun* (Best Supporting Female) Spirit. 2007: *Into the Wild* (Best Ensemble) SAG. Theater: 1993: *Angels in America: Millennium Approaches* (Best Actress in a Featured Role, Play) Tony. Television: 2007: *Law & Order: Special Victims Unit* (Best Guest Actress in a Drama Series) Emmy.

Harding, Ann

Movie: 1930: *Holiday* (Best Actress) Academy. **Records:** Harding was the first female to have a lead position in the Screen Actors Guild when it formed. In October 1933 several actors met at Frank Morgan's home where they started SAG, elected Eddie Cantor their first president, and gave the vice-president position to three people: Fredric March, Adolphe Menjou, and Harding.

Hardwicke, Cedric

Movie: 1943: *The Cross of Lorraine* (Best Acting) Board (multiple win); *The Moon Is Down* (Best Acting) Board (multiple win). Theater: 1959: *A Majority of One* (Best Actor, Dramatic) Tony.

Harlow, Jean

Tributes: 1999: Ranked Number 22 on List of 25 Greatest Female Screen Legends of the 20th Century from American Film Insitute.

Harper, Hill

Movie: 2000: *The Visit* (Best Male Lead) Spirit.

Harper, Tess

Movie: 1983: *Tender Mercies* (Best Supporting Actress) Globe. 1986: *Crimes of the Heart* (Best Supporting Actress) Academy. 2007: *No Country for Old Men* (Best Ensemble) Board, SAG, Broadcast.

Harper, Valerie

Movie: 1974: *Freebie and the Bean* (New Star of the Year — Actress) Globe. 1979: *Chapter Two* (Best Supporting Actress) Globe. Television: 1970–1974 series *The Mary Tyler Moore Show* (Best Supporting Actress in a Comedy Series) 1971: *Emmy*. 1972: *Emmy*. 1973: *Emmy*. 1974: Emmy. (Best Supporting Actress in a Series, Miniseries, or TV Movie) 1971: Globe. 1972: Globe. 1974–1978 series *Rhoda* (Best Actress in a Comedy Series) 1975: *Emmy*. 1976: Emmy. 1977: Emmy. 1978: Emmy. (Best Actress in a Series, Musical or Comedy) 1975: *Globe*. 1976: Globe.

Harrelson, Woody

Movie: 1996: *The People vs. Larry Flynt* (Best Actor) Academy (Best Actor, Drama) Globe (Best Male Actor in a Leading Role) SAG. 2006: *A Prairie Home Companion* (Best Ensemble) Broadcast. 2007: *No Country for Old Men* (Best Ensemble) Board, SAG, Broadcast. Television: 1985–1993 series *Cheers* (Best Supporting Actor in a Comedy) 1987: Emmy. 1988: Emmy. 1989: *Emmy*. 1990: Emmy. 1991: Emmy. 1999: *Frasier* (Best Guest Actor in a Comedy Series) Emmy.

Harris, Barbara

Movie: 1965: *A Thousand Clowns* (Best Actress, Musical or Comedy) Globe. 1971: *Who Is Harry Kellerman and Why Is He Saying Those Terrible Things About Me?* (Best Supporting Actress) Academy. 1975: *Nashville* (Best Supporting Actress) Globe. 1976: *Family Plot* (Best Actress, Musical or Comedy) Globe; *Freaky Friday* (Best Actress, Musical or Comedy) Globe. Theater: 1962: *From the Second City* (Best Supporting or Featured Actress, Musical) Tony. 1966: *On a Clear Day You Can See Forever* (Best Actress, Musical) Tony. 1967: *The Apple Tree* (Best Actress, Musical) *Tony*.

Harris, Ed

Movie: 1989: *Jacknife* (Best Supporting Actor) Globe. 1995: *Apollo 13* (Best Male Actor in a Supporting Role) SAG (Best Supporting Actor) Academy, Globe, Broadcast (multiple win), (Best Ensemble) SAG; *Just Cause* (Best Supporting Actor) Broadcast (multiple win); *Nixon* (Best Supporting Actor) Broadcast (multiple win), (Best Ensemble) SAG. 1998: *Stepmom* (Best Supporting Actor) Board (multiple win); *The Truman Show* (Best Supporting Actor) Academy, Board (multiple win), *Globe*, British. 2000: *Pollock* (Best Actor) Academy. 2001: *A Beautiful Mind* (Best Ensemble) SAG. 2002: *The Hours* (Best Male Actor in a Supporting Role) SAG (Best Supporting Actor) Academy, Globe, British (Best Ensemble) SAG, Broadcast. 2005: *A History of Violence* (Best Supporting Actor) *Society*. 2007: *Gone Baby Gone* (Best Ensemble) Broadcast. Theater: 1986: *Precious Sons* (Best Actor, Play) Tony. Television: 1996: *Riders of the Purple Sage* (Best Male Actor in a Television Movie or Miniseries) SAG. 2005: *Empire Falls* (Best Actor in a Miniseries or TV Movie) Emmy, Globe (Best Male Actor in a Television Movie or Miniseries) SAG. Records: Ed Harris tied with Kevin Spacey to become the first actors to win the Best Supporting Actor prize from the newly formed Broadcast Film Critics Association in 1995. With Harris winning for three performances (*Apollo 13, Just Cause*, and *Nixon*) and Spacey winning for four (*Outbreak, Seven, Swimming with Sharks*, and *The Usual Suspects*) they also became the first actors to share a single award for so many performances. That same year Harris's performance in *Apollo 13* made him the first actor to win two SAG awards, and the first actor to win two SAGs for a single performance. He was named Best Supporting Actor and was also part of the cast that won Best Ensemble that year as well.

Harris, Julie

Movie: 1952: *The Member of the Wedding* (Best Actress) Academy. 1955: *I Am a Camera* (Best Foreign Actress) British. Theater: 1952: *I Am a Camera* (Best Actress, Dramatic) Tony. 1956: *The Lark* (Best Actress, Dramatic) *Tony*. 1964: *Marathon '33* (Best

Actress, Dramatic) Tony. 1966: *Skyscraper* (Best Actress, Musical) Tony. 1969: *Forty Carats* (Best Actress, Dramatic) *Tony*. 1973: *The Last of Mrs. Lincoln* (Best Actress, Dramatic) *Tony*. 1974: *The Au Pair Man* (Best Actress, Dramatic) Tony. 1977: *The Belle of Amherst* (Best Actress, Play) *Tony*. 1991: *Lucifer's Child* (Best Actress, Play) Tony. 1997: *The Gin Game* (Best Actress, Play) Tony. **Television:** 1956: *"A Wind from the South," The U.S. Steel Hour* (Best Actress—Single Performance) Emmy. 1959: *"Little Moon of Alban," Hallmark Hall of Fame* (Best Single Performance by an Actress) *Emmy*. 1960: *"Ethan Frome," DuPont Show of the Month* (Best Single Performance by an Actress, Lead or Supporting) Emmy. 1962: *"Victoria Regina," Hallmark Hall of Fame* (Best Single Performance by an Actress in a Leading Role) *Emmy*. 1965: *"The Holy Terror," Hallmark Hall of Fame* (Best Individual Achievement in Entertainment) Emmy. 1967: *"Anastasia," Hallmark Hall of Fame* (Best Single Performance by an Actress in a Leading Role in a Drama) Emmy. 1977: *"The Last of Mrs. Lincoln," Hollywood Television Theatre* (Best Actress in a Drama or Comedy Special) Emmy. 1981–1987 series *Knots Landing* (Best Supporting Actress in a Drama Series) 1982: Emmy. 1988: *The Woman He Loved* (Best Supporting Actress in a Miniseries or Special) Emmy. 1998: *"Ellen Foster," Hallmark Hall of Fame* (Best Supporting Actress in a Miniseries or TV Movie) Emmy. 2000: *Not for Ourselves Alone: The Story of Elizabeth Cady Stanton* (Best Voice-Over Performance) Emmy. **Tributes:** 2002: Special Lifetime Achievement Award from Tony. 2005: Honor from Kennedy Center for the Performing Arts.

Harris, Neil Patrick

Movie: 1988: *Clara's Heart* (Best Supporting Actor) Globe. **Television:** 1989–1993 series *Doogie Howser, M.D.* (Best Actor in a Comedy or Musical Series) 1991: Globe. 2005–present series *How I Met Your Mother* (Best Supporting Actor in a Comedy Series) 2007: Emmy.

Harris, Richard

Movie: 1963: *This Sporting Life* (Best Actor) Academy, *Cannes* (Best British Actor) British. 1967: *Camelot* (Best Actor, Musical or Comedy) *Globe*. 1990: *The Field* (Best Actor, Drama) Globe. 2000: *Gladiator* (Best Ensemble) SAG. **Television:** 1972: *"The Snow Goose," Hallmark Hall of Fame* (Best Single Performance by an Actor in a Leading Role) Emmy.

Harris, Robin

Movie: 1990: *House Party* (Best Supporting Male) Spirit.

Harris, Rosemary

Movie: 1983: *The Ploughman's Lunch* (Best Supporting Actress) British. 1994: *Tom & Viv* (Best Supporting Actress) Academy, *Board*. 2007: *Before the Devil Knows You're Dead* (Best Ensemble) Broadcast. **Theater:** 1966: *The Lion in Winter* (Best Actress, Dramatic) *Tony*. 1972: *Old Times* (Best Actress, Dramatic) Tony. 1976: *The Royal Family* (Best Actress, Play) Tony. 1984: *Heartbreak House* (Best Actress, Play) Tony. 1985: *Pack of Lies* (Best Actress, Play) Tony. 1986: *Hay Fever* (Best Actress, Play) Tony. 1996: *A Delicate Balance* (Best Actress, Play) Tony. 2000: *Waiting in the Wings* (Best Actress, Play) Tony. **Television:** 1976: *"Notorious Woman," Masterpiece Theatre* (Best Actress in a Limited Series) Emmy (Best Actress in a Drama) Globe. 1978: *"Holocaust," The Big Event* (Best Actress in a Limited Series) Emmy (Best Actress in a Drama) *Globe*.

Harrison, Mýa (Mýa)

Movie: 2002: *Chicago* (Best Ensemble) SAG, Broadcast.

Harrison, Rex

Movie: 1963: *Cleopatra* (Best Actor) Academy, *Board* (Best Actor, Drama) Globe. 1964: *My Fair Lady* (Best Actor) *Academy, New York* (Best Actor, Musical or Comedy) *Globe* (Best British Actor) British. 1965: *The Agony and the Ecstasy* (Best Actor, Drama) Globe. 1967: *Doctor Doolittle* (Best Actor, Musical or Comedy) Globe. **Theater:** 1949: *Anne of the Thousand Days* (Best Actor, Dramatic) *Tony*. 1957: *My Fair Lady* (Best Actor, Musical) *Tony*. 1984: *Heartbreak House* (Best Actor, Play) Tony. **Tributes:** 1965: Henrietta Award for World Film Favorite from Globe. 1969: Special award from Tony. **Highlights:** Harrison had played the part of snobbish linguistic professor Henry Higgins 1,006 times on stage before reprising the role for the motion picture version of *My Fair Lady* and winning the Oscar, Golden Globe, and New York Film Critics Circle award.

Harrow, Lisa

Movie: 1997: *Sunday* (Best Female Lead) Spirit.

Harry, Deborah (Debbie)

Movie: 1980: *American Gigolo* (Best Song, "Call Me") Globe. 1988: *Hairspray* (Best Supporting Female) Spirit.

Hart, Andrea

Movie: 1998: *Miss Monday* (Best Debut Performance) Spirit.

Hart, Ian

Movie: 1995: *Nothing Personal* (Best Supporting Actor) *Venice*.

Hartley, Mariette

Movie: 1962: *Guns in the Afternoon* (Most Promising Newcomer) British. **Television:** 1978: *"The Last Hurrah," Hallmark Hall of Fame* (Best Supporting Actress in a Drama or Comedy Special) Emmy. 1978–1979 series *The Incredible Hulk* (Best Actress in a Drama Series) 1979: *Emmy*. 1979–1980 series *The Rockford Files* (Best Actress in a Drama Series) 1980: Emmy. 1980: *The Halloween That Almost Wasn't* (Best Individual Achievement in Children's Programming, Star) Emmy. 1983: *M.A.D.D.: Mothers Against Drunk Drivers* (Best Actress in a Limited Series or Special) Emmy. 1983–1984 series *Goodnight, Beantown* (Best Actress in a Comedy Series) 1983: Emmy.

Hartman, Elizabeth

Movie: 1965: *A Patch of Blue* (New Star of the Year — Actress) *Globe* (Best Actress) Academy (Best Actress, Drama) Globe. 1966: *You're a Big Boy Now* (Best Actress, Musical or Comedy) Globe.

Hartnett, Josh

Movie: 2005: *Sin City* (Best Ensemble) Broadcast.

Harvey, Laurence

Movie: 1959: *Expresso Bongo* (Best British Actor) British; *Room at the Top* (Best Actor) Academy (Best British Actor) British. 1962: *The Wonderful World of the Brothers Grimm* (Best Actor, Drama) Globe. **Tributes:** 1967: Henrietta Award for World Film Favorite from Globe.

Hassett, Marilyn

Movie: 1975: *The Other Side of the Mountain* (New Star of the Year — Actress) *Globe* (Best Actress, Drama) Globe.

Hathaway, Anne

Movie: 2002: *Nicholas Nickleby* (Best Ensemble) Board. 2005: *Brokeback Mountain* (Best Ensemble) SAG.

Hattangady, Rohini

Movie: 1982: *Gandhi* (Best Supporting Actress) *British*.

Hauer, Rutger

Movie: 2005: *Sin City* (Best Ensemble) Broadcast. **Television:** 1987: *Escape from Sobibor* (Best Supporting Actor in a Series, Miniseries, or TV Movie) *Globe*. 1994: *Fatherland* (Best Actor in a Miniseries or TV Movie) Globe.

Hauser, Cole

Movie: 2000: *Tigerland* (Best Supporting Male) Spirit.

Hauser, Wings

Movie: 1987: *Tough Guys Don't Dance* (Best Supporting Male) Spirit.

Havers, Nigel

Movie: 1981: *Chariots of Fire* (Best Supporting Actor) British.

Hawke, Ethan

Movie: 2001: *Training Day* (Best Male Actor in a Supporting Role) SAG (Best Supporting Actor) Academy. 2004: *Before Sunset* (Best Adapted Screenplay) Academy (Best Screenplay) Society, Spirit. 2007: *Before the Devil Knows You're Dead* (Best Ensemble) Broadcast. **Theater:** 2007: *The Coast of Utopia* (Best Actor in a Featured Role, Play) Tony.

Hawkes, John

Movie: 2007: *American Gangster* (Best Ensemble) SAG.

Hawkins, Jack

Movie: 1952: *Mandy* (Best British Actor) British. 1953: *The Cruel Sea* (Best British Actor) British. 1955: *The Prisoner* (Best British Actor) British. 1956: *The Long Arm* (Best British Actor) British. **Television:** 1975: *"QB VII," ABC Movie Special* (Best Single Performance by a Supporting Actor in a Comedy or Drama Special) Emmy.

Hawkins, Sally

Movie: 2008: *Happy-Go-Lucky* (Best Actress) *Berlin*.

Hawkins, Screamin' Jay

Movie: 1989: *Mystery Train* (Best Supporting Male) Spirit.

Hawn, Goldie

Movie: 1969: *Cactus Flower* (New Star of the Year — Actress) Globe (Best Actress) British (multiple nomination), (Best Supporting Actress) *Academy, Globe*. 1970: *There's a Girl in My Soup* (Best Actress) British (multiple nomination). 1972: *Butterflies Are*

Free (Best Actress, Musical or Comedy) Globe. 1975: *Shampoo* (Best Actress, Musical or Comedy) Globe. 1976: *The Duchess and the Dirtwater Fox* (Best Actress, Musical or Comedy) Globe. 1978: *Foul Play* (Best Actress, Musical or Comedy) Globe. 1980: *Private Benjamin* (Best Actress) Academy (Best Actress, Musical or Comedy) Globe. 1982: *Best Friends* (Best Actress, Musical or Comedy) Globe. 1996: *The First Wives Club* (Best Ensemble) *Board*. 2002: *The Banger Sisters* (Best Actress, Musical or Comedy) Globe. **Television:** 1968–1970 series *Rowan and Martin's Laugh-In* (Special Classification Achievement, Star) 1969: Emmy. (Special Classification of Outstanding Program, Star) 1970: Emmy. 1980: *Goldie and Liza Together* (Best Variety or Music Program, Star) Emmy.

Hawthorne, Nigel

Movie: 1994: *The Madness of King George* (Best Actor) Academy, *British*. **Theater:** 1991: *Shadowlands* (Best Actor, Play) *Tony*.

Hayakawa, Sessue

Movie: 1957: *The Bridge on the River Kwai* (Best Supporting Actor) Academy, *Board*, Globe.

Hayden, Sterling

Movie: 1964: *Dr. Strangelove: Or How I Learned to Stop Worrying and Love the Bomb* (Best Foreign Actor) British.

Hayek, Salma

Movie: 2002: *Frida* (Best Actress) Academy, British, Broadcast (Best Actress, Drama) Globe (Best Female Actor in a Leading Role) SAG. **Television:** 2006–present series *Ugly Betty* (Best Guest Actress in a Comedy Series) 2007: Emmy. (Best Comedy Series, Executive Producer) 2007: Emmy.

Hayes, Helen

Movie: 1931: *The Sin of Madelon Claudet* (Best Actress) *Academy, Venice*. 1956: *Anastasia* (Best Actress, Drama) Globe. 1970: *Airport* (Best Supporting Actress) *Academy*. 1974: *Herbie Rides Again* (Best Actress, Musical or Comedy) Globe. **Theater:** 1947: *Happy Birthday* (Best Actress, Dramatic) *Tony*. 1958: *Time Remembered* (Best Actress, Dramatic) *Tony*. 1970: *Harvey* (Best Actress, Dramatic) Tony. **Television:** 1951: --- (Best Actress) Emmy. 1952: --- (Best Actress) Emmy. 1953: --- (Best Actress) *Emmy*. 1957: *"Mrs. Gilling and the Skyscraper," Alcoa Hour* (Best Single Performance by a Lead or Supporting Actress) Emmy. 1959: *"One Red Rose for Christmas," U.S. Steel Hour* (Best Single Perfor-

mance by an Actress) Emmy. 1972: *"Do Not Fold, Spindle, or Mutilate," Movie of the Week* (Best Single Performance by an Actress) Emmy. 1974: *"The Snoop Sisters," NBC Tuesday Mystery Movie* (Best Actress in a Limited Series) Emmy. 1976: *Hawaii Five-0* (Best Single Appearance by an Actress in a Drama or Comedy Series) Emmy. 1978: *A Family Upside Down* (Best Actress in a Drama or Comedy Special) Emmy. **Tributes:** 1980: Lawrence Langner Memorial Award for distinguished lifetime achievement in the American theatre from Tony. 1981: Honor from Kennedy Center for the Performing Arts. **Records:** Hayes set acting records during two very different eras of American film. Early in the history of talkies, Hayes won Best Actress at the first Venice International Film Festival in 1932 for her performance as a self-sacrificing mother in *The Sin of Madelon Claudet*, a role that also earned her her first Oscar. Then in 1970, with film innovation and risk cresting, Hayes earned a second Oscar as resilient old stowaway Ada Quonsett in *Airport* and set two Academy Award records. By winning the award 38 years after receiving her first Oscar, she set the record for longest time span between wins. At the same time, she also became the first performer to win Oscars for both a leading and supporting role. **Highlights:** Although her illustrious career earned her the title of First Lady of the American Theater and even resulted in a Broadway theater being named after her (Helen Hayes Theater is at 240 West 44th Street in New York), she was nominated for only three Tony Awards and won three (two competitive and one special) despite spending nearly an entire century as a stage actress. Earning an Emmy award in 1952 made Hayes the first actor to win an Oscar, a Tony, and an Emmy.

Hayes, Isaac

Movie: 1971: *Shaft* (Best Original Dramatic Score) Academy, *Globe* (Best Song, "The Theme from Shaft") *Academy*, Globe. 2005: *Hustle & Flow* (Best Ensemble) SAG.

Hayter, James

Movie: 1952: *The Pickwick Papers* (Best British Actor) British.

Hayward, Susan

Movie: 1947: *Smash-Up, the Story of a Woman* (Best Actress) Academy. 1949: *My Foolish Heart* (Best Actress) Academy. 1952: *With a Song in My Heart* (Best Actress) Academy (Best Actress, Musical or Comedy) *Globe*. 1955: *I'll Cry Tomorrow* (Best Actress) Academy, *Cannes* (Best Foreign Actress) British. 1958: *I Want to Live* (Best Actress) *Academy*,

New York (Best Actress, Drama) *Globe* (Best Foreign Actress) British. **Tributes:** 1952: Henrietta Award for World Film Favorite from Globe.

Hayworth, Jill

Movie: 1960: *Exodus* (New Star of the Year — Actress) Globe.

Hayworth, Rita

Movie: 1964: *Circus World* (Best Actress, Drama) Globe. **Tributes:** 1999: Ranked Number 19 on List of 25 Greatest Female Screen Legends of the 20th Century from American Film Institute.

Healy, Katherine

Movie: 1982: *Six Weeks* (New Star of the Year — Actress) Globe.

Healy, Pat

Movie: 1999: *Magnolia* (Best Ensemble) *Board*, SAG.

Heatherton, Joey

Movie: 1963: *Twilight of Honor* (New Star of the Year — Actress) Globe.

Heche, Anne

Movie: 1997: *Donnie Brasco* (Best Supporting Actress) *Board* (multiple win); *Wag the Dog* (Best Supporting Actress) *Board* (multiple win). **Theater:** 2004: *Twentieth Century* (Best Actress, Play) Tony. **Television:** 1987–1991 series *Another World* (Best Younger Actress in a Daytime Drama Series) 1988: Emmy. 1990: *Emmy*. 2004: *Gracie's Choice* (Best Supporting Actress in a Miniseries or TV Movie) Emmy.

Heckart, Eileen

Movie: 1956: *The Bad Seed* (Best Supporting Actress) Academy, *Globe*. 1972: *Butterflies Are Free* (Best Supporting Actress) *Academy*. 1996: *The First Wives Club* (Best Ensemble) *Board*. **Theater:** 1958: *The Dark at the Top of the Stairs* (Best Supporting or Featured Actress, Dramatic) Tony. 1961: *Invitation to a March* (Best Supporting or Featured Actress, Dramatic) Tony. 1970: *Butterflies Are Free* (Best Supporting or Featured Actress, Dramatic) Tony. **Television:** 1975: *"Wedding Band," ABC Theatre* (Best Single Performance by a Supporting Actress in a Comedy or Drama Special) Emmy. 1976–1977 series *The Mary Tyler Moore Show* (Best Single Performance by a Supporting Actress in a Comedy or Drama Series) 1976: Emmy. 1977: Emmy. 1979: *Backstairs at the White House* (Best Supporting

Actress in a Limited Series or Special) Emmy. 1980: *F.D.R.: The Last Year* (Best Supporting Actress in a Limited Series or Special) Emmy. 1988: *The Cosby Show* (Best Guest Performer in a Comedy Series) Emmy. 1994: *Love & War* (Best Guest Actress in a Comedy Series) *Emmy*. **Tributes:** 2000: Tony honor for excellence in theatre from Tony.

Hedaya, Dan

Movie: 1995: *The Usual Suspects* (Best Ensemble) *Board*. 1996: *The First Wives Club* (Best Ensemble) *Board*; *Marvin's Room* (Best Ensemble) SAG. **Television:** 1994: *NYPD Blue* (Best Guest Actor in a Drama Series) Emmy.

Hedren, Tippi

Movie: 1963: *The Birds* (New Star of the Year — Actress) *Globe*. **Records:** Hedren is the first actress to have both a daughter and granddaughter selected as Miss Golden Globe. In 1975 her daughter, Melanie Griffith had the honor, and then in 2006 granddaughter Dakota Johnson handed out awards.

Heflin, Van

Movie: 1942: *Johnny Eager* (Best Supporting Actor) *Academy*. 1953: *Shane* (Best Foreign Actor) British. **Television:** 1968: *A Case of Libel* (Best Single Performance by an Actor in a Leading Role) Emmy. **Records:** When 32-year-old Heflin picked up a Best Supporting Actor Oscar in 1942, he became the youngest Academy Award winning male actor.

Hemingway, Mariel

Movie: 1976: *Lipstick* (New Star of the Year — Actress) Globe. 1979: *Manhattan* (Best Supporting Actress) Academy, British. **Television:** 1992: *Civil Wars* (Best Actress in a Drama Series) Globe.

Hemmings, David

Movie: 2001: *Last Orders* (Best Ensemble) *Board*.

Hemsley, Estelle

Movie: 1959: *Take a Giant Step* (Best Supporting Actress) Globe.

Hendler, Daniel

Movie: 2004: *El Abrazo partido (Lost Embrace)* (Best Actor) *Berlin*.

Hendry, Ian

Movie: 1962: *Live Now, Pay Later* (Most Promising Newcomer) British. 1971: *Get Carter* (Best Supporting Actor) British.

Henley, Georgie

Movie: 2005: *The Chronicles of Narnia: The Lion, the Witch, and the Wardrobe* (Best Young Actress) Broadcast.

Henry, Buck

Movie: 1967: *The Graduate* (Best Adapted Screenplay) Academy (Best Screenplay) Globe, *British*. 1978: *Heaven Can Wait* (Best Director) Academy. 1993: *Short Cuts* (Best Ensemble) *Venice* (special award). Television: 1964–1965 series *That Was the Week That Was* (Best Individual Achievement in Entertainment, Writer) 1965: Emmy. 1965–1970 series *Get Smart* (Best Writing Achievement in Comedy) 1966: Emmy. 1967: *Emmy*.

Henry, Justin

Movie: 1971: *Kramer vs. Kramer* (New Star of the Year — Actor) Globe (Best Supporting Actor) Academy, Globe. Records: As the child caught in the emotional crossfire of his parents' divorce in *Kramer vs. Kramer*, 8-year-old Henry became the youngest actor nominated for a competitive Oscar. He lost to an actor 70 years older than he — Melvyn Douglas, for *Being There*.

Henson, Taraji P.

Movie: 2005: *Hustle & Flow* (Best Ensemble) SAG. Television: 2007–present series *Boston Legal* (Best Ensemble in a Drama Series) 2007: SAG.

Hepburn, Audrey

Movie: 1953: *Roman Holiday* (Best Actress) *Academy, New York* (Best Actress, Drama) *Globe* (Best British Actress) *British*. 1954: *Sabrina (Sabrina Fair)* (Best Actress) Academy (Best British Actress) British. 1956: *War and Peace* (Best Actress, Drama) Globe (Best British Actress) British. 1957: *Love in the Afternoon* (Best Actress, Musical or Comedy) Globe. 1959: *The Nun's Story* (Best Actress) Academy, *New York* (Best Actress, Drama) Globe (Best British Actress) *British*. 1961: *Breakfast at Tiffany's* (Best Actress) Academy (Best Actress, Musical or Comedy) Globe. 1963: *Charade* (Best Actress, Musical or Comedy) Globe (Best British Actress) *British*. 1964: *My Fair Lady* (Best Actress, Musical or Comedy) Globe. 1967: *Two for the Road* (Best Actress, Musical or Comedy) Globe; *Wait Until Dark* (Best Actress) Academy (Best Actress, Drama) Globe. Theater: 1954: *Ondine* (Best Actress, Dramatic) *Tony*. Television: 1993: *Gardens of the World* (Best Individual Achievement in Informational Programming, Host) *Emmy*. Tributes: 1954: Henrietta Award for World Film Favorite from Globe. 1968: Special award from Tony. 1989: Cecil B. DeMille Award from Globe. 1991: Gala Tribute from Film Society of Lincoln Center. 1992: Jean Hersholt Humanitarian Award from Academy; Life Achievement Award from SAG. 1999: Ranked Number 3 on List of 25 Greatest Female Screen Legends of the 20th Century from American Film Institute. **Highlights:** In many movie trivia books, Hepburn is listed among the actresses to win an Oscar for her first performance. But *Roman Holiday*, the film in which Hepburn captured American hearts and a Best Actress Academy Award for her dazzling performance of a runaway princess desperately yearning for a normal life, was only her first American film. Before it she had parts in several French and British movies, including the classic comedy, *The Lavender Hill Mob* starring Alec Guinness. Hepburn's elegance kept her an Academy favorite her entire life. She received five Oscar nominations in all, and the most buzz-worthy time she didn't get the nomination, she sailed through the controversy with her trademark regal charm. After Julie Andrews had made such a splash as Eliza Doolittle on Broadway in *My Fair Lady*, it seemed unfathomable to many that producers, leery of casting a star unknown to movie audiences in their multi-million dollar production, instead gave the role to Hepburn, whose singing voice would be dubbed by Marni Nixon. The film opened to rave reviews, with most critics saying that their initial reticence about Hepburn continued through her shaky start as the cockney flower girl, but disappeared completely as she made her transformation into a lady. That same year, Walt Disney cast Julie Andrews in *Mary Poppins*. At Oscar time, both films dominated the nominations list, with *My Fair Lady* netting a near record-setting twelve. None of those nominations went to Hepburn. Scandal sheets stirred the gossip pot vigorously, trying hard to create a controversy between the two stars, but Andrews and Hepburn, with unflinching elegance, would have none of it. Hepburn presented at that year's award show, and she and Andrews got along famously. Years later, the Academy again chose to honor Hepburn with the Jean Hersholt Humanitarian Award for her tireless efforts as a UNICEF ambassador. Hepburn died of colon cancer one week after learning she was to be honored. Sean Ferrer, her son by first husband, actor Mel Ferrer, accepted the award on her behalf.

Hepburn, Katharine

Movie: 1933: *Little Women* (Best Actress) *Venice*; *Morning Glory* (Best Actress) *Academy*. 1935: *Alice Adams* (Best Actress) Academy. 1940: *The Philadelphia Story* (Best Actress) Academy, *New York*. 1942:

Woman of the Year (Best Actress) Academy. 1951: *The African Queen* (Best Actress) Academy (Best Foreign Actress) British. 1952: *Pat and Mike* (Best Actress, Musical or Comedy) Globe. 1955: *Summertime (Summer Madness)* (Best Actress) Academy (Best Foreign Actress) British. 1956: *The Rainmaker* (Best Actress) Academy (Best Actress, Drama) Globe (Best Foreign Actress) British. 1959: *Suddenly, Last Summer* (Best Actress) Academy (Best Actress, Drama) Globe. 1962: *Long Day's Journey into Night* (Best Acting) *Cannes* (win shared with costars), (Best Actress) Academy (Best Actress, Drama) Globe. 1967: *Guess Who's Coming to Dinner* (Best Actress) *Academy, British* (multiple win), (Best Actress, Drama) Globe. 1968: *The Lion in the Winter* (Best Actress) *Academy, British* (multiple win), (Best Actress, Drama) Globe. 1981: *On Golden Pond* (Best Actress) *Academy, British* (Best Actress, Drama) Globe. **Theater:** 1970: *Coco* (Best Actress, Musical) Tony. 1982: *The West Side Waltz* (Best Actress, Play) Tony. **Television:** 1974: *The Glass Menagerie* (Best Actress in a Drama) Emmy. 1975: *"Love Among the Ruins," ABC Theatre* (Best Actress in a Special Drama or Comedy Program) *Emmy.* 1979: *The Corn Is Green* (Best Actress in a Limited Series or Special) Emmy. 1986: *Mrs. Delafield Wants to Marry* (Best Actress in a Miniseries or Special) Emmy; *The Spencer Tracy Legacy: A Tribute by Katharine Hepburn* (Best Information Special, Host) Emmy. 1992: *The Man Upstairs* (Best Actress in a Miniseries or TV Movie) Globe. 1993: *Katharine Hepburn: All About Me* (Best Information Special, Host) Emmy. 1994: *One Christmas* (Best Female Actor in a Television Movie or Miniseries) SAG. **Tributes:** 1979: Life Achievement Award from SAG. 1990: Honor from Kennedy Center for the Performing Arts. 1999: Ranked Number 1 on List of 25 Greatest Female Screen Legends of the 20th Century from American Film Institute. **Records:** With *The Lion in Winter* in 1968, Hepburn set several Academy Award records. Her nomination for the film was her eleventh, making her the most nominated actor to date. When she won, Hepburn also became the first performer to win three leading actor Academy Awards (Walter Brennan had previously won three supporting awards). She shared the award that year with fellow Best Actress winner Barbra Streisand, who won for *Funny Girl*. Their mutual win was the result of the first exact tie in Academy history. (In 1931/32, the vote results were so close between Wallace Beery in *The Champ* and Fredric March in *Dr. Jeckyll and Mr. Hyde* that the Academy gave both stars a Best Actor award.) Finally, Hepburn's win came on the heels of her winning Best Actress the year before for *Guess Who's Coming to Dinner*, making her the third actor (after Luise Rainer and,

interestingly, her lifelong love, Spencer Tracy) to win acting Oscars in consecutive years. In 1981, Hepburn broke her own three–Oscar win record by winning a fourth for *On Golden Pond*. Over the years, Hepburn has still maintained her greatest Oscar record: to date, she is the only person to win four acting Oscars. Ironically, the most Oscared actress in history remained among the least interested in the award. Hepburn participated in only two Oscar ceremonies, and only once in person. Hepburn helped celebrate Oscar's 40th birthday by taping a brief explanation about the history of the Academy Awards that introduced a montage of past winners at the 1967 ceremony. She taped her segment dressed as Eleanor of Aquitaine from the set of *The Lion in Winter*, the film for which Hepburn would win her third Oscar the following year. The only time Hepburn attended an Oscar telecast was in 1973, a year she wasn't even nominated, to present the Irving G. Thalberg Memorial Award to producer and friend, Lawrence Weingarten.

Heredia, Wilson Jermaine

Movie: 2005: *Rent* (Best Ensemble) Broadcast. **Theater:** 1996: *Rent* (Best Actor in a Featured Role, Musical) *Tony.*

Hernandez, Juano

Movie: 1949: *Intruder in the Dust* (New Star of the Year — Actor) Globe. **Records:** Hernandez's performance in *Intruder in the Dust* not only earned him the first Golden Globe nomination of any Black actor but also made him the first Black actor in the race for Best Actor from The New York Film Critics. He stayed in the running for that award until the critics cast their sixth ballot and picked Broderick Crawford for *All the King's Men*, with nine votes, over Ralph Richardson (*The Fallen Idol* and *The Heiress*) with five, and Hernandez with three.

Hershey, Barbara

Movie: 1986: *Hannah and Her Sisters* (Best Supporting Actress) British. 1987: *Shy People* (Best Actress) *Cannes*. 1988: *The Last Temptation of Christ* (Best Supporting Actress) Globe; *A World Apart* (Best Actress) *Cannes* (win shared with costars). 1996: *The Portrait of a Lady* (Best Supporting Actress) Academy, Globe, *Society, LA*. **Television:** 1990: *A Killing in a Small Town* (Best Actress in a Miniseries or Special) *Emmy* (Best Actress in a Miniseries or TV Movie) *Globe*. 1991: *Paris Trout* (Best Actress in a Miniseries or Special) Emmy. **Records:** American actors seldom fare as well at Cannes as they do in American and British film competitions, which makes Hershey's record even more impressive: she is the first actress ever to be named Best Actress in two consecutive years at the Cannes Film Festival. In 1987, she won for *Shy People* in the role of Ruth, an overbearing and manipulative mother of her adult sons. The following year, Hershey shared the Cannes Film Festival Best Actress prize with her *A World Apart* costars, Jodhi May and Linda Mvusi. In the drama, Hershey shone as anti–Apartheid crusader Diana Roth.

Hersholt, Jean

Tributes: 1939: Special plaque to The Motion Picture Relief Fund with Hersholt as its acting president acknowledging its services to the industry during the past year and its progressive leadership from Academy. 1948: Special award statuette on square wood base in recognition of his service to the Motion Picture Academy during four terms as president from Academy. 1949: Special Oscar statuette for distinguished service to the motion picture industry from Academy. 1954: Cecil B. DeMille Award from Globe. **Records:** Hersholt's greatest commemoration came soon after his death in 1956 when the Academy of Motion Pictures Arts and Sciences established the Jean Hersholt Humanitarian Award to honor individuals whose altruistic efforts bring credit to the motion picture industry. Hersholt was an original member and one-time president of the Academy, as well as president and co-founder of the Motion Picture Relief Fund.

Heslov, Grant

Movie: 2005: *Good Night, and Good Luck* (Best Ensemble) SAG, Broadcast (Best Picture, Producer) Academy (Best Original Screenplay) Academy, Globe.

Heston, Charlton

Movie: 1956: *The Ten Commandments* (Best Actor, Drama) Globe. 1959: *Ben-Hur* (Best Actor) *Academy* (Best Actor, Drama) Globe. 1962: *The Pigeon That Took Rome* (Best Actor, Musical or Comedy) Globe. **Television:** 1952: --- (Best Actor) Emmy. 1953: --- (Best Actor) Emmy. 1996: *Andersonville Diaries* (Best Information Special, Narrator) Emmy. **Tributes:** 1961: Henrietta Award for World Film Favorite from Globe. 1966: Cecil B. DeMille Award from Globe. 1971: Life Achievement Award from SAG. 1977: Jean Hersholt Humanitarian Award from Academy. 1997: Honor from Kennedy Center for the Performing Arts.

Heywood, Anne

Movie: 1967: *The Fox* (Best Actress, Drama) Globe.

Heywood, Pat

Movie: 1968: *Romeo and Juliet* (Best Supporting Actress) British.

Hickey, William

Movie: 1985: *Prizzi's Honor* (Best Supporting Actor) Academy. **Television:** 1990: *Tales from the Crypt* (Best Guest Actor in a Drama Series) Emmy.

Hidari, Sachiko

Movie: 1964: *Kanajo to kare* (Best Actress) *Berlin* (multiple win); *Nippon Konchuki* (Best Actress) *Berlin* (multiple win).

Higgins, John Michael

Movie: 2003: *A Mighty Wind* (Best Screenplay) Spirit (Best Ensemble) Broadcast.

Higgins, Michael

Movie: 2000: *State and Main* (Best Ensemble) *Board*.

Highmore, Freddie

Movie: 2004: *Finding Neverland* (Best Male Actor in a Supporting Role) SAG (Best Young Actor) *Broadcast* (Best Ensemble) SAG. 2005: *Charlie and the Chocolate Factory* (Best Young Actor) *Broadcast*. 2006: *A Good Year* (Best Young Actor) Broadcast. 2007: *August Rush* (Best Young Actor) Broadcast. **Records:** Highmore's four consecutive nominations for Best Young Actor, as well as his back-to-back victories, make him the most honored young nominee and winner from Broadcast.

Hill, Bernard

Movie: 1997: *Titanic* (Best Ensemble) SAG. 2002: *The Lord of the Rings: The Two Towers* (Best Ensemble) SAG. 2003: *The Lord of the Rings: The Return of the King* (Best Ensemble) *Board, SAG, Broadcast*.

Hiller, Wendy

Movie: 1938: *Pygmalion* (Best Acting) *Board* (Best Actress) Academy. 1958: *Separate Tables* (Best British Actress) British (Best Supporting Actress) *Academy*, Globe. 1960: *Sons and Lovers* (Best British Actress) British. 1963: *Toys in the Attic* (Best Supporting Actress) Globe. 1966: *A Man for All Seasons* (Best Supporting Actress) Academy. **Theater:** 1958: *A Moon for the Misbegotten* (Best Actress, Dramatic) Tony.

Hiortaf-Ornäs, Barbro

Movie: 1958: *Nara Livet (Brink of Life)* (Best Actress) *Cannes* (win shared with costars).

Hirsch, Emile

Movie: 2007: *Into the Wild* (Breakthrough Performance by an Actor) *Board* (Best Actor) Broadcast (Best Male Actor in a Leading Role) SAG (Best Ensemble) SAG.

Hirsch, Judd

Movie: 1980: *Ordinary People* (Best Supporting Actor) Academy, Globe. 2001: *A Beautiful Mind* (Best Ensemble) SAG. **Theater:** 1980: *Talley's Folly* (Best Actor, Play) Tony. 1986: *I'm Not Rappaport* (Best Actor, Play) *Tony.* 1992: *Conversations with My Father* (Best Actor, Play) *Tony.* **Television:** 1978: *Rhoda* (Best Single Appearance by an Actor in a Drama or Comedy Series) Emmy. 1978–1983 series *Taxi* (Best Actor in a Comedy Series) 1979: Emmy. 1980: Emmy. 1981: *Emmy.* 1982: Emmy. 1983: *Emmy.* (Best Actor in a Series, Musical or Comedy) 1979: Globe. 1980: Globe. 1981: Globe. 1982: Globe. 1983: Globe. 1988–1992 series *Dear John* (Best Actor in a Series, Musical or Comedy) 1989: *Globe.* 1990: Globe.

Hoechlin, Tyler

Movie: 2002: *Road to Perdition* (Best Young Actor/Actress) Broadcast.

Hoffman, Dustin

Movie: 1967: *The Graduate* (New Star of the Year — Actor) *Globe* (Most Promising Newcomer) *British* (Best Actor) Academy (Best Actor, Musical or Comedy) Globe. 1969: *John and Mary* (Best Actor) *British* (multiple win), (Best Actor, Musical or Comedy) Globe; *Midnight Cowboy* (Best Actor) Academy, *British* (multiple win), (Best Actor, Drama) Globe. 1970: *Little Big Man* (Best Actor) British. 1974: *Lenny* (Best Actor) Academy, British (Best Actor, Drama) Globe. 1976: *All the President's Men* (Best Actor) British (multiple nomination); *Marathon Man* (Best Actor) British (multiple nomination), (Best Actor, Drama) Globe. 1979: *Agatha* (Best Actor) *Society* (multiple win); *Kramer vs. Kramer* (Best Actor) *Academy, New York*, British, *Society* (multiple win), *LA* (Best Actor, Drama) *Globe.* 1982: *Tootsie* (Best Actor) Academy, *British, Society* (Best Actor, Musical or Comedy) *Globe.* 1988: *Rain Man* (Best Actor) *Academy,* British (Best Actor, Drama) *Globe.* 1991: *Hook* (Best Actor, Musical or Comedy) Globe. 1997: *Wag the Dog* (Best Actor) Academy (Best Actor, Musical or Comedy) Globe (Best Male Actor in a Leading Role) SAG. 2004: *Finding Neverland* (Best Ensemble) SAG. **Theater:** 1990: *The Merchant of Venice* (Best Actor, Play) Tony. **Television:** 1985: *Death of a Salesman* (Best Actor in a Miniseries or Special) *Emmy* (Best Actor in a Miniseries or TV Movie) *Globe* (Best Drama or Comedy Special, Executive Producer) Emmy. **Tributes:** 1989: Honorary Golden Bear from Berlin. 1996: Career Golden Lion from Venice; Cecil B. DeMille Award from Globe. 1999: Life Achievement Award from American Film Institute. 2005: Gala Tribute from Film Society of Lincoln Center. **Highlights:** In 1975, after losing three Oscar races, Hoffman called the Academy Awards dirty and obscene. But at each of his Best Actor wins, he set aside his criticism to be genuinely appealing when accepting his awards. At the podium after winning for *Kramer vs. Kramer*, Hoffman inspired chuckles by observing that Oscar has no genetalia and is holding a sword. When he won again for *Rain Man* nine years later, he acknowledged his fellow nominees even though, he said, he knew they didn't vote for him, sparking more laughter and embarking on a second well-received acceptance speech.

Hoffman, Philip Seymour

Movie: 1997: *Boogie Nights* (Best Ensemble) SAG. 1998: *Happiness* (Best Supporting Male) Spirit (Best Ensemble) *Board.* 1999: *Magnolia* (Best Supporting Actor) *Board* (multiple win), (Best Ensemble) *Board*, SAG; *The Talented Mr. Ripley* (Best Supporting Actor) *Board* (multiple win); *Flawless* (Best Male Actor in a Leading Role) SAG. 2000: *Almost Famous* (Best Ensemble) SAG; *State and Main* (Best Ensemble) *Board.* 2005: *Capote* (Best Actor) *Academy, Board, British, Society, LA, Broadcast* (Best Actor, Drama) *Globe* (Best Male Lead) *Spirit* (Best Male Actor in a Leading Role) *SAG* (Best Ensemble) SAG. 2007: *Before the Devil Knows You're Dead* (Best Ensemble) Broadcast; *Charlie Wilson's War* (Best Supporting Actor) Academy, Globe, British, Broadcast; *The Savages* (Best Actor, Musical or Comedy) Globe (Best Male Lead) *Spirit.* **Theater:** 2000: *True West* (Best Actor, Play) Tony. 2003: *Long Day's Journey into Night* (Best Actor in a Featured Role, Play) Tony. **Television:** 2005: *Empire Falls* (Best Supporting Actor in a Miniseries or TV Movie) Emmy. **Records:** In *Capote* Hoffman's interpretation of the author with effete charm yet a fierce determination that borders on the sinister earned him an astounding 18 Best Actor awards. His perfect sweep of all the major awards was interrupted by a single performance. Instead of Hoffman, the New York Film Critics preferred Heath Ledger, whose work as Ennis del Mar in *Brokeback Mountain* earned Ledger the Gotham Critics' Best Actor prize.

Hogan, Paul

Movie: 1986: *"Crocodile" Dundee* (Best Actor) British (Best Actor, Musical or Comedy) *Globe* (Best

Original Screenplay) Academy, British. **Records:** Hogan became an international celebrity thanks to his star turn as the irresistibly likeable title character of *"Crocodile" Dundee*, the $328 million box office smash that became the highest grossing Australian movie in cinema history.

Holbrook, Hal

Movie: 2007: *Into the Wild* (Best Male Actor in a Supporting Role) SAG (Best Supporting Actor) Academy, Broadcast (Best Ensemble) SAG. **Theater:** 1966: *Mark Twain Tonight* (Best Actor, Dramatic) *Tony*. **Television:** 1967: *Mark Twain Tonight!* (Best Single Performance by an Actor in a Leading Role in a Drama) Emmy. 1969: *The Whole World Is Watching* (Best Single Performance by an Actor in a Supporting Role) Emmy. 1970–1971 series *The Senator—The Bold Ones* (Best Continued Performance by an Actor in a Leading Role in a Dramatic Series) 1971: *Emmy*. 1971: *"A Clear and Present Danger," World Premiere NBC Saturday Night at the Movies* (Best Single Performance by an Actor in a Leading Role) Emmy. 1973: *"That Certain Summer," Wednesday Movie of the Week* (Best Single Performance by an Actor in a Leading Role) Emmy. 1974: *"Pueblo," ABC Theatre* (Best Actor in a Drama) *Emmy* (Actor of the Year— Special) *Emmy*. 1976: *Sandburg's Lincoln* (Best Actor in a Limited Series) *Emmy*. 1978: *The Awakening Land* (Best Actor in a Limited Series) Emmy; *"Our Town," The Bell System Special* (Best Actor in a Drama or Comedy Special) Emmy. 1988: *Portrait of America: New York City* (Best Performance in Informational Programming, Host) Emmy. 1989: *Portrait of America: Alaska* (Best Performance in Informational Programming, Host) *Emmy*.

Holden, Donald

Movie: 2000: *George Washington* (Best Debut Performance) Spirit (nomination shared with costars).

Holden, William

Movie: 1940: *Our Town* (Best Acting) *Board*. 1942: *The Remarkable Andrew* (Best Acting) *Board*. 1950: *Sunset Boulevard* (Best Actor) Academy. 1953: *Stalag 17* (Best Actor) *Academy*. 1954: *Executive Suite* (Best Ensemble) *Venice* (special award). 1955: *Picnic* (Best Foreign Actor) British. 1976: *Network* (Best Actor) Academy, British. **Television:** 1973: *The Blue Knight* (Best Actor in a Limited Series) *Emmy*. **Tributes:** 1999: Ranked Number 25 on List of 25 Greatest Male Screen Legends of the 20th Century from American Film Institute. **Highlights:** One of the most moving moments in Oscar history occurred when William Holden presented a special lifetime

achievement award to mentor and friend Barbara Stanwyck in 1981. That night he reiterated an often shared story about owing his entire career to Stanwyck after she fought for him to keep his first starring role in 1939's *Golden Boy* after he was almost fired from the production. A visibly moved Stanwyck acknowledged her "Golden Boy" in her acceptance speech.

Hollander, Tom

Movie: 2001: *Gosford Park* (Best Ensemble) *SAG, Broadcast.*

Holliday, Judy

Movie: 1950: *Born Yesterday* (Best Actress) *Academy* (Best Actress, Drama) Globe (Best Actress, Musical or Comedy) *Globe*; *Adam's Rib* (Best Supporting Actress) Globe. 1952: *The Marrying Kind* (Best Foreign Actress) British. 1954: *Phffft!* (Best Foreign Actress) British. 1956: *The Solid Gold Cadillac* (Best Actress, Musical or Comedy) Globe. 1960: *Bells Are Ringing* (Best Actress, Musical or Comedy) Globe. **Theater:** 1957: *Bells Are Ringing* (Best Actress, Musical) *Tony*. **Records:** Thanks to unforgettable work in *Adam's Rib* and *Born Yesterday*, Holliday is the only star to be nominated for Best Actress, Drama; Best Actress, Comedy or Musical; and Best Supporting Actress Golden Globes in a single year. Holliday's work in *Born Yesterday*, a comedy that had some dramatic scenes, is also the only single performance to earn anyone Golden Globe nominations in both the Drama and the Musical or Comedy categories.

Holliday, Kene

Movie: 2007: *Great World of Sound* (Best Supporting Male) Spirit.

Holliman, Earl

Movie: 1956: *The Rainmaker* (Best Supporting Actor) *Globe*. **Television:** 1992: *Delta* (Best Supporting Actor in a Series, Miniseries, or TV Movie) Globe.

Holloway, Stanley

Movie: 1964: *My Fair Lady* (Best Supporting Actor) Academy, Globe. **Theater:** 1957: *My Fair Lady* (Best Supporting or Featured Actor, Musical) Tony.

Holm, Celeste

Movie: 1947: *Gentleman's Agreement* (Best Supporting Actress) *Academy, Globe*. 1949: *Come to the Stable* (Best Supporting Actress) Academy. 1950: *All About Eve* (Best Supporting Actress) Academy.

Television: 1968: *Insight* (Best Achievement in Daytime Programming, Performer) Emmy. 1979: *Backstairs at the White House* (Best Supporting Actress in a Limited Series or Special) Emmy. 1987: *Loving* (Best Guest Actress in a Daytime Drama Series) Emmy.

Holm, Ian

Movie: 1958: *The Bofors Gun* (Best Supporting Actor) *British*. 1981: *Chariots of Fire* (Best Supporting Actor) Academy, *British*. 1984: *Greystoke—The Legend of Tarzan, Lord of the Apes* (Best Supporting Actor) British. 1994: *The Madness of King George* (Best Supporting Actor) British. 1997: *The Sweet Hereafter* (Best Ensemble) *Board*. 2001: *The Lord of the Rings: The Fellowship of the Ring* (Best Ensemble) SAG. 2003: *The Lord of the Rings: The Return of the King* (Best Ensemble) *Board, SAG, Broadcast*. 2004: *The Aviator* (Best Ensemble) SAG. **Theater:** 1967: *The Homecoming* (Best Supporting or Featured Actor, Dramatic) *Tony*. **Television:** 1999: *"King Lear," Mobil Masterpiece Theatre* (Best Actor in a Miniseries or TV Movie) Emmy. 2001: *The Last of the Blonde Bombshells* (Best Supporting Actor in a Miniseries or TV Movie) Emmy.

Holt, Tim

Movie: 1942: *The Magnificent Ambersons* (Best Acting) *Board*.

Homolka, Oscar

Movie: 1948: *I Remember Mama* (Best Supporting Actor) Academy. 1956: *War and Peace* (Best Supporting Actor) Globe.

Hooks, Kevin

Movie: 1972: *Sounder* (New Star of the Year—Actor) Globe. **Television:** 2000: *The Color of Friendship* (Best Children's Program, Producer) *Emmy*.

Hope, Bob

Movie: 1960: *The Facts of Life* (Best Actor, Musical or Comedy) Globe. 1961: *Bachelor in Paradise* (Best Actor, Musical or Comedy) Globe. **Television:** 1961: *The Bob Hope Buick Show* (Best Program Achievement in the Field of Humor, Producer) Emmy. 1965: *The Bob Hope Special* (Best Individual Achievement by an Actor or Performer) Emmy. 1966: *Chrysler Presents The Bob Hope Christmas Special* (Best Variety Special, Executive Producer) *Emmy*. 1967: *Chrysler Presents The Bob Hope Christmas Special* (Best Variety Special, Executive Producer) Emmy. 1968: *Chrysler Presents The Bob Hope Christmas Special* (Best Musical or Variety Program, Execu-

tive Producer) Emmy. **Tributes:** 1940: Honorary special silver plaque award in recognition of his unselfish services to the motion picture industry from Academy. 1944: Honorary Life Membership in the Academy of Motion Picture Arts and Sciences for his many services to the academy from Academy. 1952: Honorary Oscar statuette for his contributions to the laughter of the world, his service to the motion picture industry, and his devotion to the American premise from Academy. 1957: Special Achievement Golden Globe Award for being an Ambassador of Good Will from Globe. 1959: Jean Hersholt Humanitarian Award from Academy. 1962: Cecil B. DeMille Award from Globe. 1965: Honorary gold medal for unique and distinguished service to our industry and the academy from Academy; Life Achievement Award from SAG. 1979: Gala Tribute from the Film Society of Lincoln Center. 1985: Honor from Kennedy Center for the Performing Arts. 1987: Television Hall of Fame Inductee from Emmy. **Records:** Despite never winning a single award in regular competition (with the exception of his television show winning an Emmy in 1965), Hope holds the record of receiving more honorary awards and tributes than any other movie actor. According to the ***Guinness Book of World Records***, he is the most honored entertainer in history, and his accolades beyond his movie and television tributes include the USA's highest civilian honors—the Congressional Gold Medal (1963); Medal of Merit (1966); the Medal of Freedom (1969); Distinguished Service Gold Medal (1971), and Distinguished Public Service Medal (1973). He was also appointed Honorary Brigadier of the U.S. Marine Corps and has 44 honorary degrees. **Highlights:** Hope hosted the Oscars 18 times, 11 years as solo host and seven times as co-host. While presiding over the ceremony, Hope often quipped about always being overlooked by the Academy at nomination time. Though Hope never did receive a single nomination for any of his films, he was the first to receive some unique Academy tributes, including a silver plaque in 1940 and a gold medal in 1965.

Hopkins, Anthony

Movie: 1968: *The Lion in Winter* (Best Supporting Actor) British. 1978: *Magic* (Best Actor) British (Best Actor, Drama) Globe. 1991: *The Silence of the Lambs* (Best Actor) *Academy, New York, British* (Best Actor, Drama) Globe (Best Supporting Actor) *Board*. 1993: *The Remains of the Day* (Best Actor) Academy, *Board* (multiple win), *British, LA* (multiple win), (Best Actor, Drama) Globe; *Shadowlands* (Best Actor) *Board* (multiple win), British, *LA* (multiple win). 1995: *Nixon* (Best Actor) Academy (Best

Actor, Drama) Globe (Best Male Actor in a Leading Role) SAG (Best Ensemble) SAG. 1997: *Amistad* (Best Male Actor in a Supporting Role) SAG (Best Supporting Actor) Academy, Globe, *Broadcast*. 2006: *Bobby* (Best Ensemble) SAG, Broadcast. **Television:** 1976: *The Lindbergh Kidnapping Case* (Best Actor in a Drama or Comedy Special) *Emmy*. 1981: *The Bunker* (Best Actor in a Limited Series or Special) *Emmy*. 1982: *"The Hunchback of Notre Dame,"* *Hallmark Hall of Fame* (Best Actor in a Limited Series or Special) Emmy. 1988: *The Tenth Man* (Best Actor in a Miniseries or TV Movie) Globe. 1990: *Great Expectations* (Best Supporting Actor in a Miniseries or Special) Emmy. **Tributes:** 2005: Cecil B. DeMille Award from Globe. **Records:** Only on screen a little over 16 minutes, Hopkins's Oscar-winning turn as Hannibal Lechter in *The Silence of the Lambs* is the shortest Oscar-winning performance for a leading role in Academy history. **Highlights:** Both of Hopkins's Emmy wins were upsets. In 1976, the much-praised miniseries, *Eleanor and Franklin* was predicted to take the lion's share of awards. Although it won eleven, its Best Actor hopeful, Edward Herrmann, lost to Hopkins as Bruno Hauptmann, the immigrant perhaps unjustly executed for *The Lindbergh Kidnapping Case*. In 1981, odds-makers were betting either on Richard Chamberlain to win Best Actor for *Shogun* or Peter O'Toole to sneak in with a win for *Masada*. Instead, Hopkins pulled past both of them and won as Adolph Hitler in *The Bunker*.

Hopkins, Joseph C.

Movie: 1993: *Short Cuts* (Best Ensemble) *Venice* (special award).

Hopkins, Miriam

Movie: 1935: *Becky Sharp* (Best Actress) Academy. 1949: *The Heiress* (Best Supporting Actress) Globe. **Records:** Hopkins earned the first Golden Globe nomination for Best Supporting Actress when the Hollywood Foreign Press decided to acknowledge the runners-up in each of their award categories. Previously, the Golden Globes cited only winners.

Hopper, Dennis

Movie: 1969: *Easy Rider* (Best Original Story and Screenplay) Academy. 1986: *Blue Velvet* (Best Male Lead) Spirit (Best Supporting Actor) Globe, *Society, LA* (multiple win); *Hoosiers* (Best Supporting Actor) Academy, Globe, *LA* (multiple win). **Television:** 1991: *Paris Trout* (Best Actor in a Miniseries or Special) Emmy. **Tributes:** 1969: Special Best First Work award for *Easy Rider* from Cannes.

Hordern, Michael

Movie: 1976: *The Slipper and the Rose* (Best Supporting Actor) British.

Horrocks, Jane

Movie: 1991: *Life Is Sweet* (Best Supporting Actress) *Society, LA*. 1998: *Little Voice* (Best Actress) British (Best Actress, Musical or Comedy) Globe (Best Female Actor in a Leading Role) SAG (Best Ensemble) SAG.

Hoskins, Bob

Movie: 1980: *The Long Good Friday* (Best Actor) British. 1983: *The Honorary Consul* (Best Supporting Actor) British. 1986: *Mona Lisa* (Best Actor) Academy, *New York, Cannes, British, Society, LA* (Best Actor, Drama) *Globe*. 1988: *Who Framed Roger Rabbit* (Best Actor, Musical or Comedy) Globe. 1995: *Nixon* (Best Ensemble) SAG. 2001: *Last Orders* (Best Ensemble) *Board*. 2005: *Mrs. Henderson Presents* (Best Supporting Actor) Globe (Best Ensemble) *Board*.

Hoss, Nina

Movie: 2007: *Yella* (Best Actress) *Berlin*.

Houghton, Katharine

Movie: 1967: *Guess Who's Coming to Dinner* (New Star of the Year — Actress) Globe.

Hoult, Nicholas

Movie: 2002: *About a Boy* (Best Young Actor/Actress) Broadcast.

Hounsou, Djimon

Movie: 1997: *Amistad* (Best Actor, Drama) Globe. 2000: *Gladiator* (Best Ensemble) SAG. 2003: *In America* (Best Supporting Actor) Academy (Best Supporting Male) *Spirit* (Best Ensemble) SAG. 2006: *Blood Diamond* (Best Male Actor in a Supporting Role) SAG (Best Supporting Actor) Academy, *Board, Broadcast*.

Houseman, John

Movie: 1953: *Julius Caesar* (Best Picture, Producer) Academy. 1956: *Lust for Life* (Best Picture, Drama; Producer) Globe. 1973: *The Paper Chase* (Best Supporting Actor) *Academy, Board, Globe*. **Television:** 1978–1979 series *The Paper Chase* (Best Actor in a Drama Series) 1978: Globe. 1979: Globe. 1980: *"Gideon's Trumpet," Hallmark Hall of Fame* (Best Drama or Comedy Special, Executive Producer) Emmy. 1983: *The Winds of War* (Best Supporting Actor in a Series, Miniseries, or TV Movie) Globe.

Howard, Hilary

Movie: 2001: *Kaaterskill Falls* (Best Debut Performance) Spirit (nomination shared with costars).

Howard, Leslie

Movie: 1933: *Berkeley Square* (Best Actor) Academy. 1938: *Pygmalion* (Best Actor) Academy, *Venice*.

Howard, Ron

Movie: 1976: *The Shootist* (Best Supporting Actor) Globe. 1995: *Apollo 13* (Best Director) Globe. 2001: *A Beautiful Mind* (Best Director) *Academy*, Globe, British, *Broadcast* (Best Picture, Producer) *Academy*, British, *Broadcast* (Best Picture, Drama; Producer) *Globe*. 2005: *Cinderella Man* (Best Director) Broadcast. Television: 1974–1984 series *Happy Days* (Best Actor in a Comedy Series) 1977: *Globe*. 1982: *Through the Magic Pyramid* (Best Children's Program, Executive Producer) Emmy. 1998: *From the Earth to the Moon* (Best Miniseries, Producer) *Emmy*. 1999–2001 series *The PJs* (Best Animated Program of One Hour or Less, Executive Producer) 1999: Emmy. 2003–2006 series *Arrested Development* (Best Comedy Series, Executive Producer) 2004: *Emmy*, Globe. 2005: Emmy, Globe. 2006: Emmy. Records: Howard (*A Beautiful Mind*) and Baz Lurhmann (*Moulin Rouge!*) shared the Best Director honors from the Broadcast Film Critics in 2001, becoming the first directors to win in a tie from that organization.

Howard, Terrence (Dashon)

Movie: 1999: *The Best Man* (Best Supporting Male) Spirit. 2004: *Ray* (Best Ensemble) SAG. 2005: *Crash* (Breakthrough Performance — Male) *Board* (multiple win), (New Generation) *LA* (multiple win), (Best Supporting Actor) Broadcast (Best Ensemble) *SAG, Broadcast*; *Get Rich or Die Tryin'* (Breakthrough Performance — Male) *Board* (multiple win), (New Generation) *LA* (multiple win); *Hustle & Flow* (Breakthrough Performance — Male) *Board* (multiple win), (New Generation) *LA* (multiple win), (Best Actor) Academy, Broadcast (Best Male Lead) Spirit (Best Actor, Drama) Globe (Best Ensemble) SAG (Best Song, "Hustle and Flow") *Broadcast*.

Howard, Trevor

Movie: 1953: *The Heart of the Matter* (Best British Actor) British. 1957: *Manuela* (Best British Actor) British. 1958: *The Key* (Best British Actor) *British*. 1960: *Sons and Lovers* (Best Actor) Academy (Best Actor, Drama) Globe. 1968: *The Charge of the Light Brigade* (Best Actor) British. 1970: *Ryan's Daughter* (Best Supporting Actor) Globe. Television: 1963:

"The Invincible Mr. Disraeli," Hallmark Hall of Fame (Best Single Performance by an Actor in a Leading Role) *Emmy*. 1966: *"Eagle in a Cage,"* Hallmark Hall of Fame (Best Single Performance by an Actor in a Leading Role in a Drama) Emmy. 1975: *"The Count of Monte Cristo," Bell System Family Theatre* (Best Single Performance by a Supporting Actor in a Comedy or Drama Special) Emmy. 1986: *Christmas Eve* (Best Supporting Actor in a Series, Miniseries, or TV Movie) Globe.

Hudson, Jennifer

Movie: 2006: *Dreamgirls* (Breakthrough Performance — Female) *Board* (Best Female Actor in a Supporting Role) *SAG* (Best Supporting Actress) *Academy, New York, Globe, British, Broadcast* (Best Ensemble) SAG, Broadcast.

Hudson, Kate

Movie: 2000: *Almost Famous* (Best Breakthrough Performer) *Broadcast* (Best Female Actor in a Supporting Role) SAG (Best Supporting Actress) Academy, *Globe*, British, Broadcast (Best Ensemble) SAG.

Hudson, Rock

Movie: 1956: *Giant* (Best Actor) Academy. Tributes: 1958, 1959, 1960, 1962, 1965: Henrietta Award for World Film Favorite from Globe.

Huffman, Felicity

Movie: 2005: *Transamerica* (Best Actress) Academy, *Board*, Broadcast (Best Actress, Drama) *Globe* (Best Female Actor in a Leading Role) SAG (Best Female Lead) *Spirit*. Television: 1998–2000 series *Sports Night* (Best Ensemble in a Comedy Series) 1999: SAG. 2004–present series *Desperate Housewives* (Best Actress in a Comedy Series) 2005: *Emmy*. 2007: Emmy. (Best Actress in a Series, Musical or Comedy) 2005: Globe. 2006: Globe. 2007: Globe. (Best Female Actor in a Comedy Series) 2005: *SAG*. 2006: SAG. (Best Ensemble in a Comedy Series) 2005: *SAG*. 2006: SAG. 2007: SAG.

Huison, Steve

Movie: 1997: *The Full Monty* (Best Ensemble) *SAG*.

Hulce, Tom

Movie: 1984: *Amadeus* (Best Actor) Academy (Best Actor, Drama) Globe. 1988: *Dominick and Eugene* (Best Actor, Drama) Globe. Theater: 1990: *A Few Good Men* (Best Actor, Play) Tony. 2007: *Spring Awakening* (Best Musical, Producer) *Tony*. Television: 1990: *Murder in Mississippi* (Best Actor in a Miniseries or Special) Emmy (Best Actor in a

Miniseries or TV Movie) Globe. 1995: *The Heidi Chronicles* (Best Supporting Actor in a Miniseries or Special) *Emmy* (Best Supporting Actor in a Series, Miniseries, or TV Movie) Globe.

Hull, Josephine

Movie: 1950: *Harvey* (Best Supporting Actress) *Academy, Globe.* Highlights: Universal Studios claimed that Hull received her Oscar for *Harvey* on the day that also marked her fiftieth anniversary as an actress. Universal honored her with a special photo session the day after the Academy Awards with Hull surrounded by her award, a huge anniversary cake, several of the studio's contract players, and someone dressed in a rabbit suit as Harvey.

Hüller, Sandra

Movie: 2006: *Requiem* (Best Actress) *Berlin.*

Humphries, Barry

Movie: 2002: *Nicholas Nickleby* (Best Ensemble) *Board.*

Hunnam, Charlie

Movie: 2002: *Nicholas Nickleby* (Best Ensemble) *Board.*

Hunnicutt, Arthur

Movie: 1952: *The Big Sky* (Best Supporting Actor) Academy.

Hunt, Bonnie

Movie: 1999: *The Green Mile* (Best Ensemble) SAG. Television: 2002–2004 series *Life with Bonnie* (Best Actress in a Comedy Series) 2003: Globe. 2004: Emmy, Globe.

Hunt, Helen

Movie: 1997: *As Good as It Gets* (Best Actress) *Academy* (Best Actress, Musical or Comedy) *Globe* (Best Female Actor in a Leading Role) *SAG.* 2006: *Bobby* (Best Ensemble) SAG, Broadcast. Television: 1992–1999 series *Mad About You* (Best Actress in a Comedy Series) 1993: Emmy. 1994: Emmy. 1995: Emmy. 1996: *Emmy.* 1997: *Emmy.* 1998: *Emmy.* 1999: *Emmy.* (Best Actress in a Series, Musical or Comedy) 1992: Globe. 1993: *Globe.* 1994: *Globe.* 1995: Globe. 1996: *Globe.* 1997: Globe. (Best Female Actor in a Comedy Series) 1994: *SAG.* 1996: SAG. 1997: SAG. (Best Ensemble in a Comedy Series) 1994: SAG. 1995: SAG. 1996: SAG. 1997: SAG. (Best Comedy Series, Producer) 1997: Emmy. Records: When chosen Best Actress for the film *As Good as It Gets*, Hunt be-

came the first actress to win an Oscar for a leading role while currently starring in a television program (*Mad About You*). Goldie Hawn, Cloris Leachman, and Lee Grant each were starring on television shows when they won their Oscars, but all as Best Supporting Actress.

Hunt, Linda

Movie: 1983: *The Year of Living Dangerously* (Best Supporting Actress) *Academy, New York, Board, Globe, LA.* 1994: *Prêt-à-Porter (Ready-to-Wear)* (Best Ensemble) *Board.* Theater: 1984: *End of the World* (Best Actress, Play) Tony. Records: Thanks to her performance as male photojournalist Billy Kwan in *The Year of Living Dangerously*, Hunt is the first actor to win an Oscar playing a character of another gender.

Hunter, Holly

Movie: 1987: *Broadcast News* (Best Actress) Academy, *New York, Board, Berlin, LA* (Best Actress, Musical or Comedy) Globe. 1993: *The Firm* (Best Supporting Actress) Academy, British; *The Piano* (Best Actress) *Academy, New York, Board, Cannes, British, Society, LA* (Best Actress, Drama) *Globe.* 2003: *Thirteen* (Best Female Actor in a Supporting Role) SAG (Best Supporting Actress) Academy, Globe, British, Broadcast. Television: 1989: *Roe vs. Wade* (Best Actress in a Miniseries or Special) *Emmy* (Best Actress in a Miniseries or TV Movie) Globe. 1993: *The Positively True Adventures of the Alleged Texas Cheerleader-Murdering Mom* (Best Actress in a Miniseries or Special) *Emmy* (Best Actress in a Miniseries or TV Movie) Globe. 2000: *Harlan County War* (Best Actress in a Miniseries or TV Movie) Emmy, Globe. 2001: *Things You Can Tell Just by Looking at Her* (Best Supporting Actress in a Miniseries or TV Movie) Emmy; *When Billie Beat Bobby* (Best Actress in a Miniseries or TV Movie) Emmy. 2007–present series *Saving Grace* (Best Actress in a Drama Series) 2007: Globe. (Best Female Actor in a Drama Series) 2007: SAG. Records: It took 66 years before the Oscars nominated two actors in different categories at a single ceremony. In 1993, Hunter and Emma Thompson both vied for Best Supporting Actress (for *The Firm* and *In the Name of the Father*, respectively) and Best Actress (*The Piano* and *The Remains of the Day*, respectively.) Going into the Oscars Hunter was on one of the strongest runs of Best Actress wins in award history for her role in Jane Campion's atmospheric *The Piano*, and she capped her Best Actress sweep with another victory. In 1993 Hunter set another record by becoming the first star to win an acting Oscar and Emmy in a single year. In addition to her Academy

Award for **The Piano**, Hunter took home an Emmy for **The Positively True Adventures of the Alleged Texas Cheerleader-Murdering Mom.**

Hunter, Kim

Movie: 1951: **A Streetcar Named Desire** (Best Supporting Actress) *Academy, Globe.* Television: 1979–1980 series **The Edge of Night** (Best Actress in a Daytime Drama) 1980: Emmy.

Huppert, Isabelle

Movie: 1977: **The Lace Maker** (Most Promising Newcomer) *British.* 1978: **Violette Nozière** (Best Actress) *Cannes.* 1988: **Une affaire de femmes** (Best Actress) *Venice.* 1995: **La Cérémonie (The Ceremony)** (Best Actress) *Venice* (win shared with costar). 2001: **La Pianiste (The Piano Teacher)** (Best Actress) *Cannes.* Tributes: 2002: Silver Bear for outstanding artistic contribution in **8 Femmes (8 Women)** from Berlin (special ensemble award shared with costars). 2005: Career Golden Lion from Venice.

Hurt, John

Movie: 1971: **10 Rillington Place** (Best Supporting Actor) *British.* 1978: **Midnight Express** (Best Supporting Actor) *Academy, Globe, British.* 1979: **Alien** (Best Supporting Actor) *British.* 1980: **The Elephant Man** (Best Actor) *Academy, British* (Best Actor, Drama) *Globe.* 1990: **The Field** (Best Supporting Actor) *British.*

Hurt, Mary Beth

Movie: 1978: **Interiors** (Most Promising Newcomer) *British.* 2006: **The Dead Girl** (Best Supporting Female) *Spirit.* Theater: 1976: **Trelawny of the "Wells"** (Best Actress in a Featured Role, Play) *Tony.* 1982: **Crimes of the Heart** (Best Actress in a Featured Role, Play) *Tony.* 1986: **Benefactors** (Best Actress, Play) *Tony.*

Hurt, William

Movie: 1980: **Altered States** (New Star of the Year — Actor) *Globe.* 1985: **Kiss of the Spider Woman** (Best Actor) *Academy, Board* (win shared with costar), *Cannes, British, LA* (Best Actor, Drama) *Globe.* 1986: **Children of a Lesser God** (Best Actor) *Academy* (Best Actor, Drama) *Globe.* 1987: **Broadcast News** (Best Actor) *Academy* (Best Actor, Musical or Comedy) *Globe.* 2005: **A History of Violence** (Best Supporting Actor) *Academy, New York, LA*; **Syriana** (Best Ensemble) *Broadcast.* 2007: **Into the Wild** (Best Ensemble) *SAG.* Theater: 1985: **Hurlyburly** (Best Actor in a Featured Role, Play) *Tony.* Records: Hurt's critically acclaimed portrait of Molina, a pris-

oner who survives his incarceration thanks to elaborate, fantastical stories in **Kiss of the Spider Woman**, is the first actor to win major awards, including the Oscar, for playing an openly gay character.

Hussey, Olivia

Movie: 1968: **Romeo and Juliet** (New Star of the Year — Actress) *Globe.*

Hussey, Ruth

Movie: 1940: **The Philadelphia Story** (Best Supporting Actress) *Academy.* Television: 1954: **"Craig's Wife," Lux Video Theatre** (Best Actress in a Single Performance) *Emmy.*

Huston, Anjelica

Movie: 1985: **Prizzi's Honor** (Best Supporting Actress) *Academy, New York, Board, Globe, British, Society, LA.* 1987: **The Dead** (Best Supporting Female) *Spirit.* 1989: **Crimes and Misdemeanors** (Best Supporting Actress) *British*; **Enemies: A Love Story** (Best Supporting Actress) *Academy, Society.* 1990: **The Grifters** (Best Actress) *Academy, Society* (multiple win), *LA* (multiple win), (Best Actress, Drama) *Globe* (Best Female Lead) *Spirit*; **The Witches** (Best Actress) *Society* (multiple win), *LA* (multiple win). 1991: **The Addams Family** (Best Actress, Musical or Comedy) *Globe.* 1993: **Addams Family Values** (Best Actress, Musical or Comedy) *Globe*; **Manhattan Murder Mystery** (Best Supporting Actress) *British.* 1995: **The Crossing Guard** (Best Female Actor in a Supporting Role) *SAG* (Best Supporting Actress) *Globe.* 2001: **The Royal Tenenbaums** (Best Ensemble) *Broadcast.* 2004: **The Life Aquatic with Steve Zissou** (Best Ensemble) *Broadcast.* Television: 1989: **Lonesome Dove** (Best Actress in a Miniseries or Special) *Emmy* (Best Supporting Actress in a Series, Miniseries, or TV Movie) *Globe.* 1993: **Family Pictures** (Best Actress in a Miniseries or TV Movie) *Globe.* 1995: **Buffalo Girls** (Best Actress in a Miniseries or Special) *Emmy* (Best Female Actor in a Television Movie or Miniseries) *SAG.* 1997: **Bastard Out of Carolina** (Best Directing for a Miniseries or Special) *Emmy.* 2002: **The Mists of Avalon** (Best Female Actor in a Television Movie or Miniseries) *SAG* (Best Supporting Actress in a Miniseries or TV Movie) *Emmy.* 2004: **Iron Jawed Angels** (Best Supporting Actress in a Miniseries or TV Movie) *Emmy* (Best Supporting Actress in a Series, Miniseries, or TV Movie) *Globe.* Records: Following her grandfather Walter Huston's Best Supporting Actor win and her father's Best Director win (both for **The Treasure of the Sierra Madre** in 1948), Anjelica's Best Supporting Actress Academy Award victory for **Prizzi's**

Honor made the Hustons the first family to have three generations of Oscar winners. Their achievement earned them a place in the *2005 Guinness Book of World Records* as the family with Most Oscar–winning Generations.

Huston, Danny

Movie: 2002: *ivans xtc.* (Best Male Lead) Spirit. 2004: *The Aviator* (Best Ensemble) SAG.

Huston, John

Movie: 1940: *Dr. Ehrlich's Magic Bullet* (Best Original Screenplay) Academy. 1941: *The Maltese Falcon* (Best Screenplay) Academy; *Sergeant York* (Best Original Screenplay) Academy. 1948: *The Treasure of the Sierra Madre* (Best Director) *Academy, New York, Globe* (Best Screenplay) *Academy, Board.* 1950: *The Asphalt Jungle* (Best Director) Academy, *Board*, Globe (Best Screenplay) Academy, Globe. 1951: *The African Queen* (Best Director) Academy (Best Screenplay) Academy. 1952: *Moulin Rouge* (Best Director) Academy. 1956: *Moby Dick* (Best Director) *New York, Board.* 1957: *Heaven Knows, Mr. Allison* (Best Adapted Screenplay) Academy. 1962: *Freud* (Best Director) Globe. 1963: *The Cardinal* (Best Supporting Actor) Academy, *Globe.* 1964: *The Night of the Iguana* (Best Director) Globe. 1974: *Chinatown* (Best Supporting Actor) Globe, British. 1975: *The Man Who Would Be King* (Best Adapted Screenplay) Academy. 1985: *Prizzi's Honor* (Best Director) Academy, *New York, Globe, Society.* 1987: *The Dead* (Best Director) Spirit. **Tributes:** 1979: Career Achievement from LA. 1980: Gala Tribute from Film Society of Lincoln Center. 1983: Life Achievement Award from American Film Institute. 1984: Career Achievement from Board. 1985: Career Golden Lion from Venice. **Records:** Huston set two records at the twenty-first Academy Awards by becoming part of the first father-son pair to win Oscars and by directing two stars to Oscar victories for different films in the same year. In 1948, he directed *The Treasure of the Sierra Madre*, picking up Best Director and Best Screenplay Oscars for himself and seeing his father, Walter, win Best Supporting Actor as *Treasure*'s crusty prospector. That same night, Claire Trevor was named Best Supporting Actress as gun moll Gaye Dawn in Huston's *Key Largo*. In 1985, when Huston's daughter Anjelica won Best Supporting Actress for his film, *Prizzi's Honor*, Huston became the first person to direct a parent and an offspring to Oscar victory.

Huston, Walter

Movie: 1936: *Dodsworth* (Best Actor) Academy, *New York.* 1941: *All That Money Can Buy* (Best Acting) *Board* (Best Actor) Academy. 1942: *Yankee Doodle Dandy* (Best Supporting Actor) Academy. 1948: *The Treasure of the Sierra Madre* (Best Actor) *Board* (Best Supporting Actor) *Academy, Globe.* **Records:** Walter and John Huston became the first father/son Oscar winners when they picked up awards for *The Treasure of the Sierra Madre*. The Hustons took home three Academy Awards that night: John for his direction and screenplay, and Walter as Best Supporting Actor.

Hutchison, Doug

Movie: 1999: *The Green Mile* (Best Ensemble) SAG.

Hutton, Betty

Movie: 1944: *The Miracle of Morgan's Creek* (Best Acting) *Board.* 1950: *Annie Get Your Gun* (Best Actress, Musical or Comedy) Globe.

Hutton, Timothy

Movie: 1980: *Ordinary People* (New Star of the Year — Actor) *Globe* (Most Promising Newcomer) British (Best Supporting Actor) *Academy, Globe, LA.* 1981: *Taps* (Best Actor, Drama) Globe. **Television:** 1981: *A Long Way Home* (Best Actor in a Miniseries or TV Movie) Globe. **Records:** When 20-year-old Hutton won an Oscar for *Ordinary People* in 1980, he became the youngest Best Supporting Actor winner in Academy history. Hutton also holds the record as youngest male actor to win an Oscar in a competitive category.

Hyde, Jonathan

Movie: 1997: *Titanic* (Best Ensemble) SAG.

Hyer, Martha

Movie: 1958: *Some Came Running* (Best Supporting Actress) Academy.

Ifans, Rhys

Movie: 1999: *Notting Hill* (Best Supporting Actor) British.

Infante, Pedro

Movie: 1957: *Tizoc* (Best Actor) Berlin.

Ireland, John

Movie: 1949: *All the King's Men* (Best Supporting Actor) Academy.

Irons, Jeremy

Movie: 1981: *The French Lieutenant's Woman* (Best Actor) British. 1986: *The Mission* (Best Actor, Drama)

Globe. 1988: *Dead Ringers* (Best Actor) *New York*. 1990: *Reversal of Fortune* (Best Actor) *Academy, Society, LA* (Best Actor, Drama) *Globe*. **Theater:** 1984: *The Real Thing* (Best Actor, Play) *Tony*. **Television:** 1982: *"Brideshead Revisited," Great Performances* (Best Actor in a Limited Series or Special) Emmy (Best Actor in a Miniseries or TV Movie) Globe. 1997: *The Great War and the Shaping of the 20th Century* (Best Voice-Over Performance) *Emmy*. 2006: *Elizabeth I* (Best Male Actor in a Television Movie or Miniseries) *SAG* (Best Supporting Actor in a Miniseries or TV Movie) *Emmy* (Best Supporting Actor in a Series, Miniseries, or TV Movie) *Globe*.

Irving, Amy

Movie: 1983: *Yentl* (Best Supporting Actress) Academy. 1988: *Crossing Delancey* (Best Actress, Musical or Comedy) Globe. 2000: *Traffic* (Best Ensemble) *SAG*. **Television:** 1986: *Anastasia: The Mystery of Anna* (Best Actress in a Miniseries or TV Movie) Globe.

Ivanov, Vlad

Movie: 2007: *4 luni, 3 saptamani si 2 zile (4 Months, 3 Weeks, and 2 Days)* (Best Supporting Actor) *LA*.

Ivashov, Vladimir

Movie: 1961: *Ballad of a Soldier* (Best Foreign Actor) British.

Ives, Burl

Movie: 1958: *The Big Country* (Best Supporting Actor) *Academy, Globe*.

Izewska, Teresa

Movie: 1958: *Kanal* (Most Promising Newcomer) British.

Izzard, Eddie

Movie: 2004: *Ocean's Twelve* (Best Ensemble) Broadcast. **Theater:** 2003: *A Day in the Death of Joe Egg* (Best Actor, Play) Tony. **Television:** 2000: *Eddie Izzard: Dress to Kill* (Best Individual Performance in a Variety or Music Program) *Emmy* (Best Variety, Music, or Comedy Special; Executive Producer) Emmy (Best Writing for a Variety, Music, or Comedy Program) *Emmy*.

Jackman, Hugh

Movie: 2001: *Kate and Leopold* (Best Actor, Musical or Comedy) Globe. **Theater:** 2004: *The Boy from Oz* (Best Actor, Musical) *Tony*. **Television:** 2005:

The 58th Annual Tony Awards (Best Individual Performance in a Variety or Music Program, Host) *Emmy*. 2006: *The 59th Annual Tony Awards* (Best Individual Performance in a Variety or Music Program, Host) Emmy.

Jackson, Glenda

Movie: 1970: *Women in Love* (Best Actress) *Academy, New York, Board*, British, *Society* (Best Actress, Drama) Globe. 1971: *Mary, Queen of Scots* (Best Actress, Drama) Globe; *Sunday, Bloody Sunday* (Best Actress) Academy, *British*. 1973: *A Touch of Class* (Best Actress) *Academy*, British (Best Actress, Musical or Comedy) *Globe*. 1975: *Hedda* (Best Actress) Academy (Best Actress, Drama) Globe. 1976: *The Incredible Sarah* (Best Actress, Drama) Globe. 1978: *Stevie** (Best Actress) *New York, Board* (Best Actress, Drama) Globe. **Theater:** 1966: *Marat/Sade* (Best Supporting or Featured Actress, Dramatic) Tony. 1981: *Rose* (Best Actress, Play) Tony. 1985: *Strange Interlude* (Best Actress, Play) Tony. 1988: *Macbeth* (Best Actress, Play) Tony. **Television:** 1972: *Elizabeth R* (Best Continued Performance by an Actress in a Leading Role in a Dramatic Series) *Emmy*; *"Shadow in the Sun," Elizabeth R* (Best Single Performance by an Actress in a Leading Role) *Emmy*; *"The Lion's Club," Elizabeth R* (Best Single Performance by an Actress in a Leading Role) Emmy. 1982: *The Patricia Neal Story* (Best Actress in a Limited Series or Special) Emmy (Best Actress in a Miniseries or TV Movie) Globe. 1984: *Sakharov* (Best Actress in a Miniseries or TV Movie) Globe. **Records:** Jackson is the first person to win two regular competition Emmy Awards for one performance. In 1972, Jackson starred in the multiple-episode one-season series *Elizabeth R*. She won not only for her performance in the entire series, but also for her individual performance in one of the episodes. For that second award, she beat out three other actresses as well as herself for another episode of *Elizabeth R*.

*Because of distribution problems for *Stevie*, Jackson won these awards and nominations for the film in 1981, three years after it was originally shot and had its initial limited release.

Jackson, Gordon

Movie: 1959: *Yesterday's Enemy* (Best British Actor) British. **Television:** 1976: *"Upstairs, Downstairs," Masterpiece Theatre* (Best Single Performance by a Supporting Actor in a Comedy or Drama Series) *Emmy*.

Jackson, Joshua

Movie: 2006: *Bobby* (Best Ensemble) SAG, Broadcast.

116

Jackson, Philip

Movie: 1998: *Little Voice* (Best Ensemble) SAG.

Jackson, Samuel L.

Movie: 1991: *Jungle Fever* (Best Supporting Actor) *New York*. 1994: *Pulp Fiction* (Best Male Lead) *Spirit* (Best Male Actor in a Supporting Role) SAG (Best Supporting Actor) Academy, Globe, *British*. 1996: *A Time to Kill* (Best Supporting Actor) Globe. 1997: *Hard Eight* (Best Supporting Male) Spirit; *Jackie Brown* (Best Actor) *Berlin* (Best Actor, Musical or Comedy) Globe. Television: 1994: *Against the Wall* (Best Actor in a Miniseries or TV Movie) Globe.

Jacob, Irène

Movie: 1991: *The Double Life of Véronique* (Best Actress) *Cannes*. 1994: *Trois couleurs: Rouge (Three Colours Red)* (Best Actress) British.

Jacobi, Derek

Movie: 1991: *Dead Again* (Best Supporting Actor) British. 2000: *Gladiator* (Best Ensemble) SAG. 2001: *Gosford Park* (Best Ensemble) *SAG, Broadcast*. Theater: 1985: *Much Ado About Nothing* (Best Actor, Play) *Tony*. 1988: *Breaking the Code* (Best Actor, Play) Tony. Television: 1982: *Inside the Third Reich* (Best Supporting Actor in a Limited Series or Special) Emmy. 1988: *"The Tenth Man," Hallmark Hall of Fame* (Best Supporting Actor in a Miniseries or Special) *Emmy* (Best Supporting Actor in a Series, Miniseries, or TV Movie) Globe. 2001: *Frasier* (Best Guest Actor in a Comedy Series) *Emmy*.

Jacobson, Peter

Movie: 2005: *Good Night, and Good Luck* (Best Ensemble) SAG, Broadcast.

Jaeckel, Richard

Movie: 1971: *Sometimes a Great Notion* (Best Supporting Actor) Academy.

Jaffe, Sam

Movie: 1950: *The Asphalt Jungle* (Best Actor) *Venice* (Best Supporting Actor) Academy. Television: 1961–1965 series *Ben Casey* (Best Supporting Actor) 1962: Emmy.

Jaffrey, Madhur

Movie: 1965: *Shakespeare–Wallah* (Best Actress) *Berlin*.

Jaffrey, Saeed

Movie: 1985: *My Beautiful Laundrette* (Best Supporting Actor) British.

Jagger, Dean

Movie: 1949: *Twelve o'Clock High* (Best Supporting Actor) *Academy*. 1954: *Executive Suite* (Best Ensemble) *Venice* (special award). Television: 1963–1965 series **Mr. Novak** (Best Continued Performance by an Actor in a Series) 1964: Emmy. (Best Individual Achievement in Entertainment, Performer) 1965: Emmy. 1980: *This Is the Life* (Best Performance in a Daytime Religious Program) *Emmy*.

James, Geraldine

Movie: 1989: *She's Been Away* (Best Actress) *Venice* (win shared with costar). Theater: 1990: *The Merchant of Venice* (Best Actress, Play) Tony.

Janda, Krystyna

Movie: 1990: *Interrogation* (Best Actress) *Cannes*.

Jandl, Ivan

Tributes: 1948: Honorary miniature Oscar statuette for outstanding juvenile performance in *The Search* from Academy; Special Achievement award for best juvenile performance for *The Search* from Globe. Records: Jandl is the first child star to receive the special juvenile Academy Award for a specifically named motion picture. In previous years, when the likes of Shirley Temple, Deanna Durbin, and Margaret O'Brien won the award, the Academy honored child stars for their work that year whether they starred in one or, in Temple's case, as many as nine features.

Jane, Thomas

Movie: 1997: *Boogie Nights* (Best Ensemble) SAG.

Jankowska-Cieslak, Jadwiga

Movie: 1982: *Another Way* (Best Actress) *Cannes*.

Janney, Allison

Movie: 1999: *American Beauty* (Best Ensemble) SAG. 2002: *The Hours* (Best Ensemble) SAG, Broadcast. 2005: *Our Very Own* (Best Supporting Female) Spirit. 2007: *Hairspray* (Best Ensemble) SAG, *Broadcast*; *Juno* (Best Ensemble) Broadcast. Theater: 1998: *A View from the Bridge* (Best Actress, Play) Tony. Television: 1999–2006 series **The West Wing** (Best Actress in a Drama Series) 2002: *Emmy*, Globe. 2003: Emmy, Globe. 2004: *Emmy*. 2006: Emmy. (Best Female Actor in a Drama Series) 2000: *SAG*. 2001: *SAG*. 2002: SAG. 2003: SAG. 2004: SAG. (Best Supporting Actress in a Drama Series) 2000: *Emmy*. 2001: *Emmy*. (Best Supporting Actress in a Series, Miniseries, or TV Movie) 2000: Globe. 2001:

Globe. (Best Ensemble in a Drama Series) 2000: *SAG*. 2001: *SAG*. 2002: SAG. 2003: SAG. 2004: SAG. 2005: SAG.

Jannings, Emil

Movie: 1927: *The Way of All Flesh* (Best Actor) *Academy* (multiple win). 1928: *The Last Command* (Best Actor) *Academy* (multiple win). 1937: *Der Herrscher* (Best Actor) *Venice*. Records: Officially, Jannings is the first person to receive an Oscar. Because he was returning to his home in Germany and could not attend the first Academy Awards ceremony on May 16, 1929, the Academy presented him with his Best Actor statuette before he left for Europe. Arriving in Berlin on Oscar night, Jannings sent a telegram assuring the Academy that he would cherish the recognition of his artistic endeavors during his stay in the United States.

Janssen, David

Movie: 1960: *Hell to Eternity* (New Star of the Year — Actor) Globe. Television: 1963–1967 series *The Fugitive* (Best Actor in a Series) 1964: Globe. 1965: *Globe*. (Best Continued Performance by an Actor in a Series) 1964: Emmy. (Best Continued Performance by an Actor in a Dramatic Series) 1966: Emmy. 1967: Emmy.

Jarman, Claude, Jr.

Tributes: 1946: Honorary miniature Oscar statuette for outstanding juvenile actor from Academy.

Jay, Ricky

Movie: 1997: *Boogie Nights* (Best Ensemble) SAG. 1999: *Magnolia* (Best Ensemble) *Board*, SAG. 2000: *State and Main* (Best Ensemble) *Board*.

Jean-Baptiste, Marianne

Movie: 1996: *Secrets and Lies* (Best Supporting Actress) Academy, Globe, British. Television: 2002–present series *Without a Trace* (Best Ensemble in a Drama Series) 2003: SAG.

Jefford, Barbara

Movie: 1967: *Ulysses* (Best British Actress) British.

Jeffries, Lionel

Movie: 1966: *The Spy with a Cold Nose* (Best Actor, Musical or Comedy) Globe.

Jemison, Eddie

Movie: 2001: *Ocean's 11* (Best Ensemble) Broadcast. 2004: *Ocean's Twelve* (Best Ensemble) Broadcast.

Jenkins, Richard

Movie: 1996: *Flirting with Disaster* (Best Supporting Male) Spirit. Television: 2002 series *Six Feet Under* (Best Ensemble) 2002: *SAG*.

Jenney, Lucinda

Movie: 1993: *American Heart* (Best Supporting Female) Spirit.

Jentsch, Julia

Movie: 2005: *Sophie Scholl—Die letzten Tage (Sophie Scholl—The Final Days)* (Best Actress) *Berlin*.

Jessel, George

Tributes: 1949: Jean Hersholt Humanitarian Award from Academy.

Jeter, Michael

Movie: 1999: *The Green Mile* (Best Ensemble) SAG. Theater: 1990: *Grand Hotel, the Musical* (Best Actor in a Featured Role, Musical) *Tony*. Television: 1990–1994 series *Evening Shade* (Best Supporting Actor in a Comedy Series) 1991: Emmy. 1992: *Emmy*. 1993: Emmy. (Best Supporting Actor in a Series, Miniseries, or TV Movie) 1991: Globe. 1993: *Picket Fences* (Best Guest Actor in a Drama Series) Emmy. 1996: *Chicago Hope* (Best Guest Actor in a Drama Series) Emmy.

Johansson, Scarlett

Movie: 1996: *Manny & Lo* (Best Female Lead) Spirit. 2003: *Lost in Translation* (New Generation) *LA* (multiple win), (Best Actress) *Venice*, British (Best Supporting Actress) Broadcast (Best Actress, Musical or Comedy) Globe; *Girl with the Pearl Earring* (New Generation) *LA* (multiple win), (Best Actress) British (Best Actress, Drama) Globe. 2004: *A Love Song for Bobby Long* (Best Actress, Drama) Globe. 2005: *Match Point* (Best Supporting Actress) Globe.

Johar, I. S.

Movie: 1958: *Harry Black* (Best British Actor) British.

Johns, Glynis

Movie: 1942: *The Invaders* (Best Acting) *Board*. 1960: *The Sundowners* (Best Supporting Actress) Academy. 1962: *The Chapman Report* (Best Actress, Drama) Globe. Theater: 1973: *A Little Night Music* (Best Actress, Musical) *Tony*.

Johns, Tracy Camila

Movie: 1986: *She's Gotta Have It* (Best Female Lead) Spirit.

Johnson, A. J.

Movie: 1990: *House Party* (Best Supporting Female) Spirit.

Johnson, Ariyan

Movie: 1993: *Just Another Girl on the I.R.T.* (Best Female Lead) Spirit.

Johnson, Ben

Movie: 1971: *The Last Picture Show* (Best Supporting Actor) *Academy, New York, Board, Globe, British.*

Johnson, Celia

Movie: 1946: *Brief Encounter* (Best Actress) *Academy, New York.* 1947: *This Happy Breed* (Best Actress) *Board.* 1952: *I Believe in You* (Best British Actress) British. 1953: *The Captain's Paradise* (Best British Actress) British. 1969: *The Prime of Miss Jean Brodie* (Best Supporting Actress) *British.*

Johnson, Katie

Movie: 1955: *The Ladykillers* (Best British Actress) *British.*

Johnson, Lynn-Holly

Movie: 1979: *Ice Castles* (New Star of the Year — Actress) Globe.

Johnson, Margaret

Movie: 1955: *Touch and Go* (Best British Actress) British.

Jolie, Angelina

Movie: 1999: *Girl, Interrupted* (Best Female Actor in a Supporting Role) SAG (Best Supporting Actress) *Academy, Globe, Broadcast.* 2007: *A Mighty Heart* (Best Actress) Broadcast (Best Actress, Drama) Globe (Best Female Actor in a Leading Role) SAG (Best Female Lead) Spirit. Television: 1998: *George Wallace* (Best Supporting Actress in a Miniseries or TV Movie) Emmy (Best Supporting Actress in a Series, Miniseries, or TV Movie) *Globe; Gia* (Best Actress in a Miniseries or TV Movie) Emmy, *Globe* (Best Female Actor in a Television Movie or Miniseries) *SAG.*

Jones, Bruce

Movie: 1997: *The Full Monty* (Best Ensemble) *SAG.*

Jones, Carolyn

Movie: 1957: *Marjorie Morningstar* (New Star of the Year — Actress) *Globe; The Bachelor Party* (Best Supporting Actress) Academy. Television: 1963–1964 series *Burke's Law* (Best Actress in a Series) 1963: Globe.

Jones, Cherry

Movie: 2004: *Ocean's Twelve* (Best Ensemble) Broadcast. Theater: 1991: *Our Country's Good* (Best Actress, Play) Tony. 1995: *The Heiress* (Best Actress, Play) *Tony.* 2000: *A Moon for the Misbegotten* (Best Actress, Play) Tony. 2005: *Doubt* (Best Actress, Play) *Tony.*

Jones, Dean

Movie: 1971: *Million Dollar Duck* (Best Actor, Musical or Comedy) Globe.

Jones, James Earl

Movie: 1970: *The Great White Hope* (New Star of the Year — Actor) *Globe* (Best Actor) Academy (Best Actor, Drama) Globe. 1974: *Claudine* (Best Actor, Musical or Comedy) Globe. 1987: *Matewan* (Best Supporting Male) Spirit. 1995: *Cry the Beloved Country* (Best Male Actor in a Leading Role) SAG. Theater: 1969: *The Great White Hope* (Best Actor, Dramatic) *Tony.* 1987: *Fences* (Best Actor, Play) *Tony.* 2005: *On Golden Pond* (Best Actor, Play) Tony. Television: 1964: *East Side, West Side* (Best Single Performance by an Actor) Emmy. 1990: *By Dawn's Early Light* (Best Supporting Actor in a Miniseries or Special) Emmy. 1990–1991 series *Gabriel's Fire* (Best Actor in a Drama Series) 1990: *Emmy,* Globe. 1991: *Heat Wave* (Best Supporting Actor in a Miniseries or Special) *Emmy.* 1991–1992 series *Pros and Cons* (Best Actor in a Drama Series) 1991: Globe. 1994: *Picket Fences* (Best Guest Actor in a Drama Series) Emmy. 1995 series *Under One Roof* (Best Supporting Actor in a Drama Series) 1995: Emmy. 1997: *Frasier* (Best Guest Actor in a Comedy Series) Emmy. 2004: *Everwood* (Best Guest Actor in a Drama Series) Emmy. Tributes: 1995: Career Achievement Award from Board. 2002: Honor from Kennedy Center for the Performing Arts.

Jones, January

Movie: 2003: *Love Actually* (Best Ensemble) Broadcast. Television: 2007–present series *Mad Men* (Best Ensemble in a Drama Series) 2007: SAG.

Jones, Jeffrey

Movie: 1984: *Amadeus* (Best Supporting Actor) Globe. Television: 2004–2006 series *Deadwood* (Best Ensemble in a Drama Series) 2006: SAG.

Jones, Jennifer

Movie: 1943: *The Song of Bernadette* (Best Actress) *Academy, Globe.* 1944: *Since You Went Away* (Best Supporting Actress) Academy. 1945: *Love Letters* (Best Actress) Academy. 1946: *Duel in the Sun* (Best Actress) Academy. 1955: *Love Is a Many-Splendored Thing* (Best Actress) Academy. 1974: *The Towering Inferno* (Best Supporting Actress) Globe. **Records:** With *The Song of Bernadette*, 24-year-old Jones became the first star to win the Golden Globe's Best Actress Award. Jones won both the Academy Award and Golden Globe for what is generally considered her debut performance on the silver screen. Actually, it was only her first performance as Jennifer Jones. In 1939 she had roles in two films (*New Frontier* and the serial, *Dick Tracy's G-Men*) under her given name, Phyllis Isley.

Jones, Shirley

Movie: 1960: *Elmer Gantry* (Best Supporting Actress) *Academy, Board, Globe.* 1962: *The Music Man (Meredith Willson's The Music Man)* (Best Actress, Musical or Comedy) Globe. **Television:** 1970: *"Silent Night, Lonely Night," World Premiere Movie* (Best Single Performance by an Actress in a Leading Role) Emmy. 1970–1974 series *The Partridge Family* (Best Actress in a Series, Musical or Comedy) 1971: Globe. (Best Actress in a Musical or Comedy Series or TV Movie) 1972: Globe. 2006: *Hidden Places* (Best Female Actor in a Television Movie or Miniseries) SAG (Best Supporting Actress in a Miniseries or TV Movie) Emmy.

Jones, Tommy Lee

Movie: 1980: *Coal Miner's Daughter* (Best Actor, Musical or Comedy) Globe. 1991: *JFK* (Best Supporting Actor) Academy, British. 1993: *The Fugitive* (Best Supporting Actor) *Academy, Globe,* British, *LA.* 2005: *The Three Burials of Melquiades Estrada* (Best Actor) *Cannes* (Best Feature, Producer) Spirit. 2006: *A Prairie Home Companion* (Best Ensemble) Broadcast. 2007: *In the Valley of Elah* (Best Actor) Academy; *No Country for Old Men* (Best Male Actor in a Supporting Role) SAG (Best Supporting Actor) British (Best Ensemble) *Board, SAG,* Broadcast. **Television:** 1983: *The Executioner's Song* (Best Actor in a Limited Series or Special) *Emmy.* 1989: *Lonesome Dove* (Best Actor in a Miniseries or Special) Emmy (Best Supporting Actor in a Series, Miniseries, or TV Movie) Globe. 1995: *The Good Old Boys* (Best Male Actor in a Television Movie or Miniseries) SAG. **Records:** When he won Best Supporting Actor for *The Fugitive*, Jones became the first actor to win an Academy Award playing a character originally created for a television series. (Sean Connery, an Oscar winner for the 1987 movie version of *The Untouchables*, played a character created for the film). Jones's character, Deputy Samuel Gerard was an updated version of Lieutenant Philip Gerard, played by Barry Morse in the 1963–1967 series. Jones played Sam Gerard again in the movie, *U.S. Marshalls*, a sequel to the film, *The Fugitive*. In a short-lived TV update of the television show that aired during the 2000–2001 season, Lieutenant Philip Gerard and was played by Mykelti Williamson.

Jonze, Spike

Movie: 1999: *Being John Malkovich* (Best Breakthrough Performer) *Broadcast* (multiple win), (Best Director) Academy; *Three Kings* (Best Breakthrough Performer) *Broadcast* (multiple win). 2002: *Adaptation* (Best Director) Globe.

Jordan, Clint

Movie: 2001: *Virgil Bliss* (Best Debut Performance) Spirit.

Jourdan, Louis

Movie: 1958: *Gigi* (Best Actor, Musical or Comedy) Globe.

Jouvet, Louis

Movie: 1938: *Un Carnet de Bal* (Best Acting) *Board.*

Judd, Ashley

Movie: 1993: *Ruby in Paradise* (Best Female Lead) *Spirit.* 2004: *De-Lovely* (Best Actress, Musical or Comedy) Globe. **Television:** 1996: *Norma Jean and Marilyn* (Best Actress in a Miniseries or Special) Emmy (Best Actress in a Miniseries or TV Movie) Globe.

Julia, Raul

Movie: 1982: *Tempest* (Best Supporting Actor) Globe. 1985: *Kiss of the Spider Woman* (Best Actor) *Board* (win shared with costar), (Best Actor, Drama) Globe. 1988: *Moon Over Parador* (Best Supporting Actor) Globe. **Theater:** 1972: *Two Gentlemen of Verona* (Best Actor, Musical) Tony. 1975: *Where's Charley?* (Best Actor, Musical) Tony. 1977: *The Threepenny Opera* (Best Actor, Musical) Tony. 1982: *Nine* (Best Actor, Musical) Tony. **Television:** 1995: *The Burning Season* (Best Actor in a Miniseries or Special) *Emmy* (Best Actor in a Miniseries or TV Movie) *Globe* (Best Male Actor in a Television Movie or Miniseries) *SAG.*

Jurado, Katy

Movie: 1952: *High Noon* (New Star of the Year — Actress) Globe (Best Supporting Actress) *Globe.*

1954: *Broken Lance* (Best Supporting Actress) Academy.

Jürgens, Curd

Movie: 1955: *Les Héros sont fatigués* (Best Actor) *Venice.* 1958: *The Enemy Below* (Best Foreign Actor) British (multiple nomination); *The Inn of the Sixth Happiness* (Best Foreign Actor) British (multiple nomination).

Kadochnikov, Pavel

Movie: 1954: *Bolshaya semya (The Big Family) Cannes* (special ensemble award).

Kahn, Jonathan

Movie: 1976: *The Sailor Who Fell from Grace with the Sea* (New Star of the Year — Actor) Globe.

Kahn, Madeline

Movie: 1973: *What's Up, Doc?* (New Star of the Year — Actress) Globe; *Paper Moon* (Best Supporting Actress) Academy, Globe. 1974: *Blazing Saddles* (Best Supporting Actress) Academy; *Young Frankenstein* (Best Supporting Actress) Globe. Theater: 1974: *Boom Boom Room* (Best Actress, Dramatic) Tony. 1978: *On the Twentieth Century* (Best Actress, Musical) Tony. 1989: *Born Yesterday* (Best Actress, Play) Tony. 1993: *The Sisters Rosensweig* (Best Actress, Play) *Tony.* Television: 1983–1984 series *Oh, Madeline* (Best Actress in a Series, Musical or Comedy) 1983: Globe. 1987: *"Wanted: The Perfect Guy," ABC Afterschool Special* (Best Performer in Children's Programming) *Emmy.*

Kallianiotes, Helena

Movie: 1972: *Kansas City Bomber* (Best Supporting Actress) Globe.

Kaminska, Ida

Movie: 1966: *The Shop on Main Street* (Best Actress) Academy (Best Actress, Drama) Globe.

Kane, Carol

Movie: 1975: *Hester Street* (Best Actress) Academy. Television: 1981–1983 series *Taxi* (Best Actress in a Comedy Series) 1982: *Emmy.* (Best Supporting Actress in a Comedy Series) 1983: *Emmy.* (Best Supporting Actress in a Series, Miniseries, or TV Movie) 1982: Globe. 1996: *Chicago Hope* (Best Guest Actress in a Drama Series) Emmy.

Karina, Anna

Movie: 1961: *Une femme est une femme (A Woman Is a Woman)* (Best Actress) *Berlin.*

Kastner, Peter

Movie: 1966: *You're a Big Boy Now* (Most Promising Newcomer) British.

Kasznar, Kurt

Movie: 1952: *The Happy Time* (Best Supporting Actor) Globe. Theater: 1960: *The Sound of Music* (Best Supporting or Featured Actor, Musical) Tony.

Katz, Jonathan

Movie: 2000: *State and Main* (Best Ensemble) *Board.* Television: 1995–1999 series, *Dr. Katz, Professional Therapist* (Best Voice-Over Performance) 1995: *Emmy.*

Kaufman, Christine

Movie: 1961: *Town Without Pity* (New Star of the Year — Actress) *Globe.*

Kay, Billy

Movie: 2001: *L.I.E.* (Best Supporting Male) Spirit.

Kayaru, Artel

Movie: 2002: *Dahmer* (Best Debut Performance) Spirit.

Kaye, Celia

Movie: 1964: *Island of the Blue Dolphin* (New Star of the Year — Actress) *Globe.*

Kaye, Danny

Movie: 1951: *On the Riviera* (Best Actor, Musical or Comedy) *Globe.* 1952: *Hans Christian Andersen* (Best Actor, Musical or Comedy) Globe. 1956: *The Court Jester* (Best Actor, Musical or Comedy) Globe. 1958: *Me and the Colonel* (Best Actor, Musical or Comedy) *Globe.* Television: 1963: *The Danny Kaye Show with Lucille Ball* (Best Performance in a Variety or Musical Program or Series) Emmy. 1963–1967 series *The Danny Kaye Show* (Best Performance in a Variety or Musical Program or Series) 1964: *Emmy.* (Best Individual Achievement in Entertainment, Performer) 1965: Emmy. 1981: *Skokie* (Best Actor in a Miniseries or TV Movie) Globe. 1982: *Live from Lincoln Center: An Evening with Danny Kaye* (Best Classical Program in the Performing Arts, Star) Emmy. 1986: *The Cosby Show* (Best Guest Performer in a Comedy Series) Emmy. Tributes: 1953: Special award for heading a variety bill at the Palace Theatre from Tony. 1954: Honorary Oscar statuette for his unique talents, his service to the Academy, the motion picture industry, and the American people from Academy. 1981: Jean Hersholt

Humanitarian Award from Academy. 1982: Life Achievement Award from SAG. 1984: Honor from Kennedy Center for the Performing Arts.

Kazan, Lainie

Movie: 1982: *My Favorite Year* (Best Supporting Actress) Globe. 2002: *My Big Fat Greek Wedding* (Best Ensemble) SAG, Broadcast. Theater: 1993: *My Favorite Year* (Best Actress in a Featured Role, Musical) Tony. Television: 1988: *St. Elsewhere* (Best Guest Performer in a Drama Series) Emmy.

Keaton, Buster

Tributes: 1959: Honorary Oscar statuette for his unique talents which brought immortal comedies to the screen from Academy. 1999: Ranked Number 21 on List of 25 Greatest Male Screen Legends of the 20th Century from American Film Institute.

Keaton, Diane

Movie: 1977: *Annie Hall* (Best Actress) *Academy*, *New York*, *British*, *Society* (Best Actress, Musical or Comedy) *Globe* (Best Supporting Actress) *Board*; *Looking for Mr. Goodbar* (Best Actress, Drama) Globe. 1979: *Manhattan* (Best Actress) British. 1981: *Reds* (Best Actress) Academy, British (Best Actress, Drama) Globe. 1982: *Shoot the Moon* (Best Actress, Drama) Globe. 1984: *Mrs. Soffel* (Best Actress, Drama) Globe. 1987: *Baby Boom* (Best Actress, Musical or Comedy) Globe. 1993: *Manhattan Murder Mystery* (Best Actress, Musical or Comedy) Globe. 1996: *Marvin's Room* (Best Actress) Academy (Best Female Actor in a Leading Role) SAG (Best Ensemble) SAG; *The First Wives Club* (Best Ensemble) *Board*. 2003: *Something's Gotta Give* (Best Actress) Academy, *Board*, Broadcast (Best Actress, Musical or Comedy) *Globe* (Best Female Actor in a Leading Role) SAG. Theater: 1969: *Play It Again, Sam* (Best Supporting or Featured Actress, Dramatic) Tony. Television: 1995: *Amelia Earhart: The Final Flight* (Best Actress in a Miniseries or Special) Emmy (Best Actress in a Miniseries or TV Movie) Globe (Best Female Actor in a Television Movie or Miniseries) SAG. Tributes: 2007: Gala Tribute from Film Society of Lincoln Center. Highlights: Keaton is one of the few people in film history to earn awards playing a character based on herself. She picked up five Best Actress prizes as Annie Hall, from a screenplay written by ex-lover Woody Allen about the rise and bittersweet fall of their relationship. While many actresses have earned award recognition for biographies, Keaton holds the unique status of sweeping most of the awards in 1977 for an autobiographical work.

Keaton, Michael

Movie: 1988: *Beetlejuice* (Best Actor) *Society* (multiple win); *Clean and Sober* (Best Actor) *Society* (multiple win). Television: 2002: *Live from Baghdad* (Best Actor in a Miniseries or TV Movie) Globe. 2007: *The Company* (Best Male Actor in a Television Movie or Miniseries) SAG.

Kedrova, Lila

Movie: 1964: *Zorba the Greek* (Best Foreign Actress) British (Best Supporting Actress) *Academy*, Globe. Theater: 1984: *Zorba* (Best Actress in a Featured Role, Musical) *Tony*. Highlights: While several actors have translated their Tony Award–winning stage roles into Oscar-winning film performances, Kedrova is one of the few who did it the other way around. She got the part of dying French courtesan Madame Hortense in the 1964 film *Zorba the Greek* after actress Simone Signoret withdrew from the movie during production. The following spring, the Academy voted her Best Supporting Actress. When she and co-star Anthony Quinn reprised their roles for the stage musical *Zorba* twenty years later, she won the Tony.

Keener, Catherine

Movie: 1992: *Johnny Suede* (Best Female Lead) Spirit. 1996: *Walking and Talking* (Best Female Lead) Spirit. 1999: *Being John Malkovich* (Best Female Actor in a Supporting Role) SAG (Best Supporting Actress) Academy, *New York*, Globe (Best Ensemble) SAG. 2002: *Lovely & Amazing* (Best Female Lead) Spirit. 2005: *The 40-Year-Old Virgin* (Best Supporting Actress) Society (multiple nomination), *LA* (multiple win); *The Ballad of Jack and Rose* (Best Supporting Actress) Society (multiple nomination), *LA* (multiple win); *Capote* (Best Female Actor in a Supporting Role) SAG (Best Supporting Actress) Academy, British, Society (multiple nomination), *LA* (multiple win), Broadcast (Best Ensemble) SAG; *The Interpreter* (Best Supporting Actress) Society (multiple nomination), *LA* (multiple win). 2007: *Into the Wild* (Best Female Actor in a Supporting Role) SAG (Best Supporting Actress) Broadcast (Best Ensemble) SAG. Records: Keener is the first actor to win a single Los Angeles Film Critics Award for four performances. Before her, several stars won for two performances, but only two actors, Meryl Streep and Edward Norton, won for three. But Keener topped them all in 2005 by being acknowledged for a stunning four performances. Her win seems even more impressive when considering the range of films for which she won. *Capote* was a literary biography, *The Ballad of Jack and Rose* was a tragic drama, *The 40-Year-Old Virgin* was a comedy, and *The Interpreter* was a political thriller.

Keillor, Garrison

Movie: 2006: *A Prairie Home Companion* (Best Ensemble) Broadcast.

Keitel, Harvey

Movie: 1991: *Bugsy* (Best Supporting Actor) Academy, Globe, *Society* (multiple win); *Mortal Thoughts* (Best Supporting Actor) *Society* (multiple win); *Thelma & Louise* (Best Supporting Actor) *Society* (multiple win). 1992: *Bad Lieutenant* (Best Male Lead) *Spirit*; *Reservoir Dogs* (Best First Feature, Producer) Spirit. Tributes: 1995: Silver Bear Special Jury Prize for *Smoke* from Berlin.

Keith, David

Movie: 1982: *An Officer and a Gentleman* (New Star of the Year — Actor) Globe (Best Supporting Actor) Globe.

Kellaway, Cecil

Movie: 1948: *The Luck of the Irish* (Best Supporting Actor) Academy. 1967: *Guess Who's Coming to Dinner* (Best Supporting Actor) Academy.

Keller, Marthe

Movie: 1976: *Marathon Man* (Best Supporting Actress) Globe. Theater: 2001: *Judgment at Nuremberg* (Best Actress in a Featured Role, Play) Tony.

Kellerman, Sally

Movie: 1970: *M*A*S*H* (Best Supporting Actress) Academy, Globe. 1994: *Prêt-à-Porter (Ready-to-Wear)* (Best Ensemble) *Board*.

Kelley, Elijah

Movie: 2007: *Hairspray* (Best Ensemble) SAG, *Broadcast*.

Kelly, David

Movie: 1998: *Waking Ned Devine* (Best Male Actor in a Supporting Role) SAG (Best Ensemble) SAG.

Kelly, Gene

Movie: 1942: *For Me and My Gal* (Best Acting) *Board*. 1945: *Anchors Aweigh* (Best Actor) Academy. 1951: *An American in Paris* (Best Actor, Musical or Comedy) Globe. 1969: *Hello, Dolly!* (Best Director) Globe. Television: 1959: *Omnibus* (Best Choreography for Television) Emmy. 1966: *The Julie Andrews Show* (Best Special Classification of Individual Achievement, Performer) Emmy. 1967: *Jack and the Beanstalk* (Best Children's Program, Producer) *Emmy*. Tributes: 1951: Honorary Oscar statuette in appreciation of his versatility as an actor, singer, director, and dancer, and specifically for his brilliant achievements in the art of choreography on film from Academy. 1957: Special award for promoting international understanding through the film *The Happy Road* from Globe. 1980: Cecil B. DeMille Award from Globe. 1982: Honor from Kennedy Center for the Performing Arts. 1985: Life Achievement Award from American Film Institute. 1988: Life Achievement Award from SAG. 1999: Ranked Number 15 on AFI's List of 25 Male Screen Legends from American Film Institute.

Kelly, Grace

Movie: 1953: *Mogambo* (Best Supporting Actress) Academy, *Globe*. 1954: *The Country Girl* (Best Actress) *Academy, New York* (multiple win), *Board* (multiple win), (Best Actress, Drama) *Globe* (Best Foreign Actress) British; *Dial M for Murder* (Best Actress) *New York* (multiple win), *Board* (multiple win), (Best Foreign Actress) British; *Rear Window* (Best Actress) *New York* (multiple win), *Board* (multiple win). Tributes: 1955: Henrietta Award for World Film Favorite from Globe. 1999: Ranked Number 13 on List of 25 Greatest Female Screen Legends of the 20th Century from American Film Institute. Records: Kelly holds the record for the most award recognition for the shortest film career. Even though her five-year screen career included only 11 films, she won major awards for four of them, received two honors for fan popularity and even ranked among AFI's Screen Legends.

Kelly, Laura Michelle

Movie: 2007: *Sweeney Todd: The Demon Barber of Fleet Street* (Best Ensemble) Broadcast.

Kelly, Nancy

Movie: 1956: *The Bad Seed* (Best Actress) Academy. Theater: 1955: *The Bad Seed* (Best Actress, Dramatic) *Tony*. Television: 1957: *"The Pilot," Studio One* (Best Single Performance by an Actress) Emmy.

Kemp, Jeremy

Movie: 1966: *The Blue Max* (Most Promising Newcomer) British.

Kendal, Jennifer

Movie: 1981: *36 Chowringhee Lane* (Best Actress) British.

Kendall, Kay

Movie: 1957: *Les Girls* (Best Actress, Musical or Comedy) *Globe*.

Kendrick, Anna

Movie: 2003: *Camp* (Best Debut Performance) Spirit. 2007: *Rocket Science* (Best Supporting Female) Spirit. **Theater:** 1998: *High Society* (Best Featured Actress, Musical) Tony.

Kennedy, Arthur

Movie: 1949: *Champion* (Best Supporting Actor) Academy. 1951: *Bright Victory* (Best Actor) Academy, *New York* (Best Actor, Drama) Globe. 1955: *Trial* (Best Supporting Actor) Academy, *Globe*. 1957: *Peyton Place* (Best Supporting Actor) Academy. 1958: *Some Came Running* (Best Supporting Actor) Academy. **Theater:** 1949: *Death of a Salesman* (Best Supporting or Featured Actor, Dramatic) *Tony*.

Kennedy, George

Movie: 1967: *Cool Hand Luke* (Best Supporting Actor) *Academy*, Globe. 1970: *Airport* (Best Supporting Actor) Globe.

Kennedy, Jo

Movie: 1985: *Wrong World* (Best Actress) *Berlin*.

Kensit, Patsy

Movie: 1991: *Twenty-One* (Best Female Lead) Spirit.

Kerr, Deborah

Movie: 1947: *The Adventuress* (Best Actress) *New York* (multiple win); *Black Narcissus* (Best Actress) *New York* (multiple win). 1949: *Edward, My Son* (Best Actress) Academy, Globe. 1953: *From Here to Eternity* (Best Actress) Academy. 1955: *The End of the Affair* (Best British Actress) British. 1956: *The King and I* (Best Actress) Academy (Best Actress, Musical or Comedy) *Globe*; *Tea and Sympathy* (Best British Actress) British; 1957: *Heaven Knows, Mr. Allison* (Best Actress) Academy, *New York* (Best Actress, Drama) Globe. 1958: *Separate Tables* (Best Actress) Academy (Best Actress, Drama) Globe. 1960: *The Sundowners* (Best Actress) Academy, *New York* (Best British Actress) British. 1964: *The Chalk Garden* (Best British Actress) British. **Television:** 1985: *Barbara Taylor Bradford's A Woman of Substance* (Best Supporting Actress in a Limited Series or Special) Emmy. **Tributes:** 1958: Henrietta Award for World Film Favorite from Globe. 1993: Special award statuette in appreciation for a full career's worth of elegant and beautifully crafted performances from Academy. **Records:** Though notoriously overlooked by Oscar, Kerr was a darling of the New York Film Critics, setting their record by becoming the first thespian to earn three acting awards from them. In 1947, lead critic Bosley Crowther championed her sweep of twelve votes in only the second round of polling for her work in *The Adventuress* and *Black Narcissus*. Twelve votes earned Kerr a second New York Film Critics Circle award in 1957, and in 1960 a majority of votes, rather than the ⅔ vote required in the past, gave Kerr a third Gotham prize. Except for the special Oscar Kerr received in 1993, it was the last major award of her career.

Kerr, John

Movie: 1956: *Tea and Sympathy* (New Star of the Year — Actor) *Globe*. **Theater:** 1954: *Tea and Sympathy* (Best Supporting or Featured Actor, Dramatic) *Tony*.

Khan, Irfan

Movie: 2007: *The Namesake* (Best Supporting Male) Spirit.

Kidman, Nicole

Movie: 1991: *Billy Bathgate* (Best Supporting Actress) Globe. 1995: *To Die For* (Best Actress) British, *Broadcast* (Best Actress, Musical or Comedy) *Globe*. 2001: *Moulin Rouge!* (Best Actress) Academy, Broadcast (Best Actress, Musical or Comedy) *Globe* (Best Ensemble) SAG; *The Others* (Best Actress) British (Best Actress, Drama) Globe. 2002: *The Hours* (Best Actress) *Academy, Berlin* (win shared with costars), *British*, Broadcast (Best Actress, Drama) *Globe* (Best Female Actor in a Leading Role) SAG (Best Ensemble) SAG, Broadcast. 2003: *Cold Mountain* (Best Actress) Broadcast (Best Actress, Drama) Globe. 2004: *Birth* (Best Actress, Drama) Globe. **Records:** Kidman won the first Best Actress prize ever given by the Broadcast Film Critics Association for her satiric performance in *To Die For*.

Kikuchi, Rinko

Movie: 2006: *Babel* (Breakthrough Performance — Female) *Board* (Best Female Actor in a Supporting Role) SAG (Best Supporting Actress) Academy, Globe, Broadcast (Best Ensemble) SAG, Broadcast.

Kilcher, Q'Orianka

Movie: 2005: *The New World* (Breakthrough Performance — Female) *Board* (Best Young Actress) Broadcast.

Kim, Jacqueline

Movie: 2002: *Charlotte Sometimes* (Best Supporting Female) Spirit.

Kimbrough, Linda

Movie: 2000: *State and Main* (Best Ensemble) *Board.*

King, Jaime

Movie: 2005: *Sin City* (Best Ensemble) Broadcast.

King, Regina

Movie: 2004: *Ray* (Best Ensemble) SAG.

Kingsley, Ben

Movie: 1982: *Gandhi* (New Star of the Year — Actor) *Globe* (Most Promising Newcomer) *British* (Best Actor) *Academy, New York, Board, British, LA* (Best Actor, Drama) *Globe.* 1991: *Bugsy* (Best Supporting Actor) Academy, Globe. 1993: *Schindler's List* (Best Supporting Actor) British. 2001: *Sexy Beast* (Best Male Actor in a Supporting Role) SAG (Best Supporting Actor) Academy, Globe, *Broadcast.* 2003: *House of Sand and Fog* (Best Actor) Academy, Broadcast (Best Actor, Drama) Globe (Best Male Lead) Spirit (Best Male Actor in a Leading Role) SAG. **Television:** 1989: *Murderers Among Us: The Simon Wiesenthal Story* (Best Actor in a Miniseries or Special) Emmy (Best Actor in a Miniseries or TV Movie) Globe. 1995: *Joseph* (Best Supporting Actor in a Miniseries or Special) Emmy. 1998: *The Tale of Sweeney Todd* (Best Male Actor in a Television Movie or Miniseries) SAG. 2001: *Anne Frank* (Best Actor in a Miniseries or TV Movie) Emmy, Globe (Best Male Actor in a Television Movie or Miniseries) *SAG.* 2006: *Mrs. Harris* (Best Actor in a Miniseries or TV Movie) Emmy, Globe. **Records:** After 36 years of handing out Golden Globe awards for Best New Star of the Year, the Hollywood Foreign Press gave Kingsley the last one as New Star of the Year — Actor for his title role in 1982's *Gandhi.* The New Female Star that year was Sandahl Bergman for *Conan the Barbarian.* Controversy over Israeli tycoon Meshulam Riklis allegedly buying the award the previous year for young wife Pia Zadora in the panned *Butterfly* led the Foreign Press to do away with the New Star categories altogether. **Highlights:** Kingsley achieved the rare feat of winning two Golden Globes for the same performance, as he snagged the Best Actor, Drama and New Star of the Year — Actor for his pitch-perfect portrayal of India's peace leading Mahatma Gandhi.

Kinnear, Greg

Movie: 1997: *As Good as It Gets* (Best Male Actor in a Supporting Role) SAG (Best Supporting Actor) Academy, *Board,* Globe. 2006: *Little Miss Sunshine* (Best Ensemble) *SAG, Broadcast.*

Kinski, Nastassja

Movie: 1980: *Tess* (New Star of the Year — Actress) *Globe* (Best Actress, Drama) Globe.

Kinsolving, Lee

Movie: 1960: *The Dark at the Top of the Stairs* (Best Supporting Actor) Globe.

Kirkland, Sally

Movie: 1987: *Anna* (Best Actress) Academy, *LA* (Best Actress, Drama) *Globe* (Best Female Lead) *Spirit.* **Television:** 1991: *The Haunted* (Best Actress in a Miniseries or TV Movie) Globe. **Highlights:** Movie scholar Tom O'Neil called Kirkland's efforts to woo movie award voters after the release of *Anna* the most aggressive one-person campaign in film history. On her own, she bought a rash of ads in *Daily Variety,* guest starred on the major talk shows and even sent letters to every member of the Academy of Motion Picture Arts and Sciences. Her tactics paid off. In a strong year for Best Actress contenders, Kirkland triumphed over such stellar Independent Spirit nominees as Joanne Woodward in *The Glass Menagerie* and screen legend Lillian Gish in her last film, *The Whales of August.* At the Golden Globes, Kirkland outranked Faye Dunaway in her big screen comeback in *Barfly* and dynamic Glenn Close in the most talked about role of her career as crazed, jilted lover Alex Forrest in *Fatal Attraction.*

Kitzmiller, John

Movie: 1957: *Dolina miru (Valley of Peace)* (Best Actor) *Cannes.*

Kline, Kevin

Movie: 1982: *Sophie's Choice* (Best New Star of the Year — Actor) Globe (Most Outstanding Newcomer to Film) British. 1988: *A Fish Called Wanda* (Best Actor) British (Best Supporting Actor) *Academy.* 1991: *Soapdish* (Best Actor, Musical or Comedy) Globe. 1993: *Dave* (Best Actor, Musical or Comedy) Globe. 1997: *In & Out* (Best Actor, Musical or Comedy) Globe. 2001: *Life as a House* (Best Male Actor in a Leading Role) SAG. 2004: *De-Lovely* (Best Actor, Musical or Comedy) Globe. 2006: *A Prairie Home Companion* (Best Ensemble) Broadcast. **Theater:** 1978: *On the Twentieth Century* (Best Actor in a Featured Role, Musical) *Tony.* 1981: *The Pirates of Penzance* (Best Actor, Musical) *Tony.* 2004: *Henry IV* (Best Actor, Play) Tony. **Television:** 2007: *As You Like It* (Best Male Actor in a Television Movie or Miniseries) *SAG.* **Highlights:** Rarely does an actor reach Oscar victory from total award obscurity, but Kline managed to do just that in 1988 in his uproarious interpretation of crazed and conniving wannabe stud Otto West in Charles Crichton's zany British comedy, **A Fish Called Wanda**. Throughout the awards season, Kline's name never came up when winners or even nominees were announced. Never until Oscar, that is. Still, even going into Academy Awards night, little attention was given to Kline to win Best Supporting Actor, as focus remained on fellow nominees Alec Guinness (**Little Dorrit**), Martin Landau (**Tucker: The Man and His Dream**), River Phoenix (**Running on Empty**), and Dean Stockwell (**Married to the Mob**), all of whom had won critics' or industry awards for their work. But when Michael Caine (presenting with Sean Connery and Roger Moore) announced Kline the winner, Kline's frenetic performance became the rarest of Oscar winners: a comic role with no prior accolades. After his Oscar win, Kline found himself among the British Best Actor nominees, but lost that competition to his **A Fish Called Wanda** co-star, John Cleese.

Kline, Owen

Movie: 2005: **The Squid and the Whale** (Best Young Actor) Broadcast.

Klugman, Jack

Movie: 1969: **Goodbye, Columbus** (Best Supporting Actor) British. **Theater:** 1960: **Gypsy** (Best Supporting or Featured Actor, Musical) Tony. **Television:** 1964: **The Defenders** (Best Single Performance by an Actor) *Emmy.* 1970–1975 series **The Odd Couple** (Best Continued Performance by an Actor in a Leading Role in a Comedy Series) 1971: *Emmy.* 1972: Emmy. 1973: *Emmy.* (Best Actor in a Comedy Series) 1974: Emmy. 1975: Emmy. (Best Actor in a Series, Musical or Comedy) 1971: Globe. 1973: *Globe.* 1976–1983 series **Quincy** (Best Actor in a Drama Series) 1977: Emmy. 1978: Emmy. 1979: Emmy. 1980: Emmy.

Knight, Gladys

Movie: 1976: **Pipe Dreams** (New Star of the Year — Actress) Globe.

Knight, Shirley

Movie: 1960: **The Dark at the Top of the Stairs** (New Star of the Year — Actress) Globe (Best Supporting Actress) Academy, Globe. 1962: **Sweet Bird of Youth** (Best Supporting Actress) Academy, Globe. 1967: **Dutchman** (Best Actress) *Venice.* **Theater:** 1976: **Kennedy's Children** (Best Actress in a Featured Role, Play) *Tony.* 1997: **The Young Man from Atlanta** (Best Actress, Play) Tony. **Television:** 1981: **Playing for Time** (Best Supporting Actress in a Limited Series or Special) Emmy. 1987, 1990 series **thirtysomething** (Best Guest Actress in a Drama Series) 1987: *Emmy.* 1990: Emmy. 1989: **The Equalizer** (Best Guest Actress in a Drama Series) Emmy. 1991–1992 series **Law & Order** (Best Actress in a Drama Series) 1992: Emmy. 1995: **Indictment: The McMartin Trial** (Best Supporting Actress in a Miniseries or Special) *Emmy* (Best Supporting Actress in a Series, Miniseries, or TV Movie) Globe; **NYPD Blue** (Best Guest Actress in a Drama Series) *Emmy.* 2006: **Desperate Housewives** (Best Guest Actress in a Comedy Series) Emmy.

Knightley, Keira

Movie: 2003: **Love Actually** (Best Ensemble) Broadcast. 2005: **Pride and Prejudice** (Best Actress) Academy, Society, Broadcast (Best Actress, Musical or Comedy) Globe. 2007: **Atonement** (Best Actress) British (Best Actress, Drama) Globe.

Knoch, Lucy

Movie: 1954: **Executive Suite** (Best Ensemble) *Venice* (special award).

Knowles, Beyoncé

Movie: 2006: **Dreamgirls** (Best Actress, Musical or Comedy) Globe (Best Ensemble) SAG, Broadcast (Best Original Song, "Listen") Globe, *Broadcast.**

*Although Knowles is generally credited as one of the writers of the song, "Listen," the Academy nominated the song but only considered the primary songwriters for its Best Song nomination, thereby excluding Knowles.

Knox, Alexander

Movie: 1944: **Wilson** (Best Actor) Academy, *Globe.*

Köhler, Juliane

Movie: 1999: **Aimée & Jaguar** (Best Actress) *Berlin* (win shared with costar).

Kohner, Susan

Movie: 1958: **The Gene Krupa Story** (New Star of the Year — Actress) *Globe.* 1959: **Imitation of Life** (Best Supporting Actress) Academy, *Globe.* 1962: **Freud** (Best Supporting Actress) Globe.

Korjus, Miliza

Movie: 1938: **The Great Waltz** (Best Supporting Actress) Academy.

Korzun, Dina

Movie: 2005: **Forty Shades of Blue** (Best Female Lead) Spirit.

Kossoff, David

Movie: 1954: *The Young Lovers* (Most Promising Newcomer) *British*. 1955: *A Kid for Two Farthings* (Best British Actor) British.

Kotler, Oded

Movie: 1967: *Three Days and a Child* (New Star of the Year — Actor) Globe (Best Actor) *Cannes*.

Kozlowski, Linda

Movie: 1986: *"Crocodile" Dundee* (Best Supporting Actress) Globe.

Krabbé, Jeroen

Movie: 2004: *Ocean's Twelve* (Best Ensemble) Broadcast.

Kristofferson, Kris

Movie: 1973: *Pat Garrett & Billy the Kid* (Most Promising Newcomer) British. 1976: *A Star Is Born* (Best Actor, Musical or Comedy) *Globe*. 1984: *Songwriter* (Best Original Song Score) Academy. 2007: *I'm Not There* (Best Ensemble) *Spirit* (special award).

Krössner, Renate

Movie: 1980: *Solo Sunny* (Best Actress) *Berlin*.

Kruger, Hardy

Movie: 1965: *The Flight of the Phoenix* (Best Supporting Actor) Globe.

Krumholtz, David

Movie: 2006: *Bobby* (Best Ensemble) SAG, Broadcast.

Kruschen, Jack

Movie: 1960: *The Apartment* (Best Supporting Actor) Academy.

Kudoh, Youki

Movie: 1989: *Mystery Train* (Best Female Lead) Spirit.

Kudrow, Lisa

Movie: 1998: *The Opposite of Sex* (Best Supporting Actress) *New York* (Best Supporting Female) Spirit. Television: 1994–2004 series *Friends* (Best Female Actor in a Comedy Series) 1995: SAG. 1998: SAG. 1999: *SAG*. 2003: SAG. (Best Supporting Actress in a Comedy Series) 1995: Emmy. 1997: Emmy. 1998: *Emmy*. 1999: Emmy. 2000: Emmy 2001: Emmy. (Best

Supporting Actress in a Series, Miniseries, or TV Movie) 1995: Globe. (Best Ensemble in a Comedy Series) 1995: *SAG*. 1998: SAG. 1999: SAG. 2000: SAG. 2001: SAG. 2002: SAG. 2003: SAG. 2005–2006 series *The Comeback* (Best Actress in a Comedy Series) 2006: Emmy.

Kurilov, Sergei

Movie: 1954: *Bolshaya semya (The Big Family)* *Cannes* (special ensemble award).

Kurtiz, Tuncel

Movie: 1986: *Hiuch Ha'Gdu (The Smile of the Lamb)* (Best Actor) *Berlin*.

Kutcher, Ashton

Movie: 2006: *Bobby* (Best Ensemble) SAG, Broadcast.

Kuznetsova, Vera

Movie: 1954: *Bolshaya semya (The Big Family)* *Cannes* (special ensemble award).

Kwan, Nancy

Movie: 1960: *The World of Suzie Wong* (New Star of the Year — Actress) *Globe* (Best Actress, Drama) Globe.

Kyo, Machiko

Movie: 1956: *The Teahouse of the August Moon* (Best Actress, Musical or Comedy) Globe.

LaBeouf, Shia

Movie: 2006: *Bobby* (Best Ensemble) SAG, Broadcast.

Ladd, Alan

Tributes: 1953, 1954: Henrietta Award for World Film Favorite from Globe.

Ladd, David

Movie: 1958: *The Proud Rebel* (New Star of the Year — Actor) Globe (Best Supporting Actor) Globe. Tributes: 1958: Special Achievement Award as Best Juvenile for *The Proud Rebel* from Globe.

Ladd, Diane

Movie: 1974: *Alice Doesn't Live Here Anymore* (Best Supporting Actress) Academy, Globe, *British*. 1990: *Wild at Heart* (Best Supporting Actress) Academy, Globe. 1991: *Rambling Rose* (Best Supporting Actress) Academy, Globe (Best Supporting Female)

Spirit. **Television:** 1980–1981 series *Alice* (Best Supporting Actress in a Series, Miniseries, or TV Movie) 1980: *Globe.* 1993: *Dr. Quinn, Medicine Woman* (Best Guest Actress in a Drama Series) Emmy. 1994: *Grace Under Fire* (Best Guest Actress in a Comedy Series) Emmy. 1997: *Touched by an Angel* (Best Guest Actress in a Drama Series) Emmy. **Records:** When both Diane Ladd and daughter, Laura Dern earned Oscar nods in their respective categories for *Rambling Rose*, they made Academy Award history by becoming the first mother and daughter nominated for acting Oscars for the same movie and even the first mother/daughter to be up for their awards in the same year. That year Ladd and Dern also became the first mother/daughter team to present an Oscar, as they announced the Best Visual Effects award, which went in *Terminator 2: Judgment Day.*

LaGarde, Jocelyne

Movie: 1966: *Hawaii* (Best Supporting Actress) Academy, *Globe.*

Lage, Jordan

Movie: 2000: *State and Main* (Best Ensemble) Board.

Lahti, Christine

Movie: 1984: *Swing Shift* (Best Supporting Actress) Academy, *New York,* Globe. 1988: *Running on Empty* (Best Actress) *LA* (Best Actress, Drama) Globe. 1995: *Lieberman in Love* (Best Live Action Short Film, Co-producer) *Academy.* **Television:** 1987: *Amerika* (Best Supporting Actress in a Miniseries or Special) Emmy (Best Supporting Actress in a Series, Miniseries, or TV Movie) Globe. 1990: *No Place Like Home* (Best Actress in a Miniseries or Special) Emmy (Best Actress in a Miniseries or TV Movie) *Globe.* 1995–1999 series *Chicago Hope* (Best Actress in a Drama Series) 1996: Emmy, Globe. 1997: Emmy, *Globe.* 1998: *Emmy.* 1999: Emmy. (Best Female Actor in a Drama Series) 1995: SAG. 1996: SAG. 1997: SAG. 1998: SAG. (Best Ensemble in a Drama Series) 1994: SAG. 1995: SAG. 1996: SAG. 1997: SAG. 2001: *An American Daughter* (Best Actress in a Miniseries or TV Movie) Globe. 2004–2005 series *Jack and Bobby* (Best Actress in a Drama Series) 2004: Globe. (Best Female Actor in a Drama Series) 2004: SAG.

Lake, Ricki

Movie: 1988: *Hairspray* (Best Female Lead) Spirit.

Lambetti, Ella

Movie: 1959: *A Matter of Dignity* (Best Foreign Actress) British.

Lamore, Morris

Movie: 2000: *State and Main* (Best Ensemble) Board.

Lampe, Jutta

Movie: 1981: *Die Bleierne Ziet* (Best Actress) *Venice* (win shared with costar).

Lampreave, Chus

Movie: 2006: *Volver* (Best Actress) *Cannes* (win shared with costars).

Lamure, Dominique

Tributes: 2002: Silver Bear for outstanding artistic contribution in *8 Femmes (8 Women)* from Berlin (special ensemble award shared with costars).

Lancaster, Burt

Movie: 1953: *From Here to Eternity* (Best Actor) Academy, *New York.* 1956: *The Rainmaker* (Best Actor, Drama) Globe; *Trapeze* (Best Actor) *Berlin.* 1960: *Elmer Gantry* (Best Actor) *Academy, New York* (Best Actor, Drama) *Globe* (Best Foreign Actor) British. 1962: *Bird Man of Alcatraz* (Best Actor) Academy, *Venice* (Best Actor, Drama) Globe (Best Foreign Actor) *British.* 1981: *Atlantic City* (Best Actor) Academy, *New York, British, Society, LA* (Best Actor, Drama) Globe. 1983: *Local Hero* (Best Supporting Actor) British. **Theater:** 1957: *Separate Tables* (Best Play, Producer) Tony. **Television:** 1990: *The Phantom of the Opera* (Best Actor in a Miniseries or TV Movie) Globe. **Tributes:** 1991: Life Achievement Award from SAG. 1999: Ranked Number 19 on List of 25 Greatest Male Screen Legends of the 20th Century from American Film Institute.

Lanchester, Elsa

Movie: 1938: *The Beachcomber* (Best Acting) Board. 1949: *Come to the Stable* (Best Supporting Actress) Academy. 1957: *Witness for the Prosecution* (Best Supporting Actress) Academy, *Globe.* **Records:** When Lanchester and husband Charles Laughton both received Best Acting awards from the National Board of Review in 1938 for their work in *The Beachcomber*, they became the first married couple to win awards for performances in the same motion picture. **Highlights:** Lanchester's character, Miss Plimsoll in *Witness for the Prosecution* was not in the original Agatha Christie story or stage play. When adapting the play for cinema, Christie added the role of the pestering nurse devoted to Laughton's Sir Wilfred Robards expressly for Lanchester so she could look after her ailing husband on the set.

Landa, Alfredo

Movie: 1984: *Los Santos innocentes (The Holy Innocents)* (Best Actor) *Cannes* (win shared with co-star).

Landau, Martin

Movie: 1988: *Tucker: The Man and His Dream* (Best Supporting Actor) Academy, *Globe.* 1989: *Crimes and Misdemeanors* (Best Supporting Actor) Academy. 1994: *Ed Wood* (Best Male Actor in a Supporting Role) *SAG* (Best Supporting Actor) *Academy, New York, Globe*, British, *Society, LA.* **Television:** 1966–1969 series *Mission: Impossible* (Best Actor in a Television Series) 1967: *Globe.* (Best Continued Performance by an Actor in a Leading Role in a Dramatic Series) 1967: Emmy. 1968: Emmy. 1969: Emmy. 2004–2005 series *Without a Trace* (Best Guest Actor in a Drama Series) 2004: Emmy. 2005: Emmy. 2007: *Entourage* (Best Guest Actor in a Comedy Series) Emmy. **Tributes:** 1990: Honorary Award from Berlin. **Records:** Landau is the first Hollywood actor to win an Oscar playing another Hollywood actor. In *Ed Wood*, he portrayed horror film legend Bela Lugosi. He won six awards for the performance and was nominated for the British, which he lost in 1995 to Tim Roth in *Rob Roy.*

Lane, Charles

Movie: 1989: *Sidewalk Stories* (Best Male Lead) Spirit (Best Director) Spirit (Best First Feature, Director) Spirit.

Lane, Diane

Movie: 1999: *A Walk on the Moon* (Best Female Lead) Spirit. 2002: *Unfaithful* (Best Actress) Academy, *New York, Society*, Broadcast (Best Actress, Drama) Globe (Best Female Actor in a Leading Role) SAG. 2003: *Under the Tuscan Sun* (Best Actress, Musical or Comedy) Globe. **Television:** 1989: *Lonesome Dove* (Best Actress in a Miniseries or Special) Emmy.

Lane, Nathan

Movie: 1996: *The Birdcage* (Best Actor, Musical or Comedy) Globe (Best Male Actor in a Supporting Role) SAG (Best Ensemble) *SAG.* 2002: *Nicholas Nickleby* (Best Ensemble) *Board.* 2005: *The Producers* (Best Actor, Musical or Comedy) Globe. **Theater:** 1992: *Guys and Dolls* (Best Actor, Musical) Tony. 1996: *A Funny Thing Happened on the Way to the Forum* (Best Actor, Musical) *Tony.* 2001: *The Producers* (Best Actor, Musical) *Tony.* **Television:** 1995: *Frasier* (Best Guest Actor in a Comedy Series) Emmy. 1998: *Mad About You* (Best Guest Actor in a Comedy Series) Emmy.

Lang, Ben

Movie: 1990: *The Plot Against Harry* (Best Supporting Male) Spirit.

Lange, Hope

Movie: 1957: *Peyton Place* (Best Supporting Actress) Academy, Globe. **Television:** 1968–1970 series *The Ghost and Mrs. Muir* (Best Actress in a Comedy Series) 1968: Globe. 1969: *Emmy.* 1970: *Emmy.* 1973: *"That Certain Summer," Wednesday Movie of the Week* (Best Single Performance by an Actress) Emmy.

Lange, Jessica

Movie: 1976: *King Kong* (Best New Star of the Year — Actress) *Globe.* 1982: *Frances* (Best Actress) Academy (Best Actress, Drama) Globe; *Tootsie* (Best Actress) British (Best Supporting Actress) *Academy, New York, Globe, Society.* 1984: *Country* (Best Actress) Academy (Best Actress, Drama) Globe. 1985: *Sweet Dreams* (Best Actress) Academy. 1989: *Music Box* (Best Actress) Academy (Best Actress, Drama) Globe. 1994: *Blue Sky* (Best Actress) *Academy, LA* (Best Actress, Drama) *Globe* (Best Female Actor in a Leading Role) SAG. 1997: *A Thousand Acres* (Best Actress, Drama) Globe. **Television:** 1992: *O, Pioneers!* (Best Actress in a Miniseries or TV Movie) Globe. 1995: *Tennessee Williams' A Streetcar Named Desire* (Best Actress in a Miniseries or Special) Emmy (Best Actress in a Miniseries or TV Movie) *Globe.* 2003: *Normal* (Best Actress in a Miniseries or TV Movie) Emmy, Globe. **Tributes:** 2006: Gala Tribute from Film Society of Lincoln Center. **Records:** Lange holds the record for longest period between filming a role and winning an Oscar for it. Film production of *Blue Sky* wrapped in 1991, but soon after director Tony Richardson died and the film's distributing studio went bankrupt. Three years later, the movie found a new distributor and opened to rave reviews for Lange as a sexually charged, bi-polar housewife. On Oscar night, she took home her second Academy Award, her first for a leading role.

Langella, Frank

Movie: 1970: *Diary of a Mad Housewife* (New Star of the Year — Actor) Globe (Best Supporting Actor) *Board.* 2005: *Good Night, and Good Luck* (Best Supporting Actor) Society (Best Ensemble) SAG, Broadcast. 2007: *Starting Out in the Evening* (Best Male Lead) Spirit. **Theater:** 1975: *Seascape* (Best Supporting or Featured Actor, Dramatic) *Tony.* 1978: *Dracula* (Best Actor, Play) Tony. 2002: *Fortune's Fool* (Best Actor in a Featured Role, Play) *Tony.* 2004:

Match (Best Actor, Play) Tony. 2007: *Frost/Nixon* (Best Actor, Play) *Tony*. **Television:** 1983: *"I, Leonard: A Journey of the Mind," IBM Presents* (Best Individual Achievement in Informational Programming, Star) Emmy.

Lansbury, Angela

Movie: 1944: *Gaslight* (Best Supporting Actress) Academy. 1945: *The Picture of Dorian Gray* (Best Supporting Actress) Academy, *Globe*. 1962: *All Fall Down* (Best Supporting Actress) *Board* (multiple win); *The Manchurian Candidate* (Best Supporting Actress) Academy, *Board* (multiple win), *Globe*. 1970: *Something for Everyone* (Best Actress, Musical or Comedy) Globe. 1971: *Bedknobs and Broomsticks* (Best Actress, Musical or Comedy) Globe. 1978: *Death on the Nile* (Supporting Actress) *Board*, British. **Theater:** 1966: *Mame* (Best Actress, Musical) *Tony*. 1969: *Dear World* (Best Actress, Musical) *Tony*. 1975: *Gypsy* (Best Actress, Musical) *Tony*. 1979: *Sweeney Todd* (Best Actress, Musical) *Tony*. 2007: *Deuce* (Best Actress, Play) Tony. **Television:** 1983: *The Gift of Love: A Christmas Story* (Best Supporting Actress in a Series, Miniseries, or TV Move) Globe. 1983: *Little Gloria ... Happy at Last* (Best Actress in a Limited Series or Special) Emmy. 1984–1996 series *Murder, She Wrote* (Best Actress in a Drama Series) 1984: *Globe*. 1985: Emmy, Globe. 1986: Emmy, *Globe*. 1987: Emmy, Globe. 1988: Emmy, Globe. 1989: Emmy, *Globe*. 1990: Emmy, Globe. 1991: Emmy, *Globe*. 1992: Emmy, Globe. 1993: Emmy. 1994: Emmy, Globe. 1995: Emmy. 1996: Emmy. (Best Female Actor in a Drama Series) 1994: SAG. 1985: *"Sweeney Todd," Great Performances* (Best Individual Performance in a Variety or Music Program) Emmy. 1987: *The 1987 Tony Awards* (Best Individual Performance in a Variety or Music Program) Emmy. 1990: *The 43rd Annual Tony Awards* (Best Individual Performance in a Variety or Music Program) Emmy. 2004: *"The Blackwater Lightship," Hallmark Hall of Fame* (Best Supporting Actress in a Miniseries or Special) Emmy. 2005: *Law & Order: Special Victims Unit/Trial by Jury* (Best Guest Actress in a Drama Series) Emmy. **Tributes:** 1996: Life Achievement Award from SAG; Television Hall of Fame Inductee from Emmy. 2000: Honor from Kennedy Center for the Performing Arts. **Records:** With 18 nominations and not a single win, Lansbury holds the record as the nominated actor most overlooked by Emmy. For years, soap star Susan Lucci held the record until in 1999, on her nineteenth nomination for *All My Children*, she finally won Best Actress in a Daytime Drama. Although Lansbury has yet to win, she keeps racking up nominations, guaranteeing either a longer non-

win record or the chance at an eventual new record for most nominations before a win. But her television records are not all marred by defeats. Thanks to her work in *Murder, She Wrote*, which earned Lansbury a dozen Emmy nominations, one for each year she starred as mystery writer and amateur sleuth Jessica "J.B." Fletcher, Lansbury holds the record for starring in the longest running mystery drama in TV history.

Laslo, Hanna

Movie: 2005: *Free Zone* (Best Actress) *Cannes*.

Lasser, Louise

Movie: 1998: *Happiness* (Best Ensemble) *Board*.

Lathan, Sanaa

Movie: 2000: *Love & Basketball* (Best Female Lead) Spirit. **Theater:** 2004: *A Raisin in the Sun* (Best Actress in a Featured Role, Play) Tony.

Latifah, Queen

Movie: 1996: *Set It Off* (Best Supporting Female) Spirit. 2002: *Chicago* (Best Female Actor in a Supporting Role) SAG (Best Supporting Actress) Academy, Globe, British (Best Ensemble) *SAG, Broadcast*. 2007: *Hairspray* (Best Ensemble) SAG, *Broadcast*. **Television:** 2007: *Life Support* (Best Actress in a Miniseries or TV Movie) Emmy, *Globe* (Best Female Actor in a Television Movie or Miniseries) *SAG*.

Laughton, Charles

Movie: 1933: *The Private Life of Henry VIII* (Best Actor) *Academy*. 1935: *Mutiny on the Bounty* (Best Actor) Academy, *New York* (multiple win); *Ruggles of Red Gap* (Best Actor) *New York* (multiple win). 1938: *The Beachcomber* (Best Acting) *Board*. 1957: *Witness for the Prosecution* (Best Actor) Academy (Best Actor, Drama) Globe (Best Foreign Actor) British. 1962: *Advise and Consent* (Best Foreign Actor) British. **Records:** When Laughton picked up the Best Actor Academy Award for his comically robust portrayal of Henry VIII, he became the first star to win an Oscar for a movie not made in Hollywood. Alexander Korda directed the United Artist biopic in England. Two years later, Laughton set another record when he picked up the first Best Actor award ever given by the New York Film Critics Circle for his work in *Mutiny on the Bounty* and *Ruggles of Red Gap*.

Laurel, Stan

Tributes: 1960: Honorary Oscar statuette for his creative pioneering in the field of cinema comedy from Academy. 1963: Life Achievement Award from SAG.

Laurie, Hugh

Movie: 1995: *Sense and Sensibility* (Best Ensemble) SAG. Television: 2004–present series *House* (Best Actor in a Drama Series) 2005: Emmy, *Globe*. 2006: *Globe*. 2007: Emmy, Globe. (Best Male Actor in a Drama Series) 2005: SAG. 2006: *SAG*. 2007: SAG.

Laurie, Piper

Movie: 1961: *The Hustler* (Best Actress) Academy (Best Foreign Actress) British. 1976: *Carrie* (Best Supporting Actress) Academy, Globe. 1986: *Children of a Lesser God* (Best Supporting Actress) Academy. Television: 1958: *"The Deaf Heart," Studio One* (Best Single Performance — Lead or Supporting — by an Actress) Emmy. 1958: *"The Days of Wine and Roses," Playhouse 90* (Best Single Performance by an Actress) Emmy. 1981: *The Bunker* (Best Supporting Actress in a Limited Series or Special) Emmy. 1983: *The Thorn Birds* (Best Supporting Actress in a Limited Series or Special) Emmy (Best Supporting Actress in a Series, Miniseries, or TV Movie) Globe. 1983–1984 series *St. Elsewhere* (Best Supporting Actress in a Drama Series) 1984: Emmy. 1986: *"The Promise," Hallmark Hall of Fame* (Best Supporting Actress in a Miniseries or Special) *Emmy* (Best Supporting Actress in a Series, Miniseries, or TV Movie) Globe. 1990–1991 series *Twin Peaks* (Best Actress in a Drama Series) 1990: Emmy. 1991: Emmy. (Best Supporting Actress in a Series, Miniseries, or TV Movie) 1990: *Globe*. 1999: *Frasier* (Best Guest Actress in a Comedy Series) Emmy.

Lavi, Dahlia

Movie: 1962: *Two Weeks in Another Town* (New Star of the Year — Actress) Globe.

Lavronenko, Konstantin

Movie: 2003: *Vozvrashcheniye (The Return)* (Best Actor) *Venice* (win shared with costars). 2007: *The Banishment* (Best Actor) *Cannes*.

Law, John Philip

Movie: 1966: *The Russians Are Coming, the Russians Are Coming* (New Star of the Year — Actor) Globe.

Law, Jude

Movie: 1999: *The Talented Mr. Ripley* (Best Supporting Actor) Academy, Globe, *British*. 2001: *A.I.: Artificial Intelligence* (Best Supporting Actor) Globe. 2003: *Cold Mountain* (Best Actor) Academy, British (Best Actor, Drama) Globe. 2004: *The Aviator* (Best Ensemble) SAG; *Closer* (Best Ensemble)

Board, Broadcast. Theater: 1995: *Indiscretions* (Best Actor in a Featured Role, Play) Tony.

Laydu, Claude

Movie: 1953: *Jounal d'un cure de campagne* (Best Actor) British.

Lazenby, George

Movie: 1969: *On Her Majesty's Secret Service* (New Star of the Year — Actor) Globe.

Leach, Rosemary

Movie: 1973: *That'll Be the Day* (Best Supporting Actress) British. 1986: *A Room with a View* (Best Supporting Actress) British.

Leachman, Cloris

Movie: 1971: *The Last Picture Show* (Best Supporting Actress) *Academy, Board*, Globe, *British*. 1973: *Charley and the Angel* (Best Actress, Musical or Comedy) Globe. 1974: *Young Frankenstein* (Best Actress, Musical or Comedy) Globe. 2004: *Spanglish* (Best Female Actor in a Supporting Role) SAG. Television: 1970–1975 series *The Mary Tyler Moore Show* (Best Supporting Actress in a Comedy Series) 1972: Emmy. 1973: Emmy. 1974: *Emmy*. (Best Single Performance by a Supporting Actress in a Comedy or Drama Series) 1975: *Emmy*. 1973: *"A Brand New Life," Tuesday Movie of the Week* (Best Single Performance by an Actress in a Leading Role) *Emmy*. 1974: *"The Migrants," CBS Playhouse 90* (Best Actress in a Drama) Emmy. 1975: *Cher* (Best Continuing or Single Performance by a Supporting Actress in a Variety or Music Program) *Emmy*. 1976: *Telly ... Who Loves Ya, Baby?* (Best Continuing or Single Performance by a Supporting Actress in a Variety or Music Program) Emmy. 1975–1977 series *Phyllis* (Best Actress in a Comedy Series) 1976: Emmy. (Best Actress in a Series, Musical or Comedy) 1976: *Globe*. 1977: *It Happened One Christmas* (Best Supporting Actress in a Drama or Comedy Special) Emmy. 1983: *"The Woman Who Willed a Miracle," ABC Afterschool Special* (Best Performer in Children's Programming) *Emmy*. 1984: *Ernie Kovacs: Between the Laughter* (Best Supporting Actress in a Limited Series or Special) Emmy; *Screen Actors Guild 50th Anniversary Special* (Best Individual Performance in a Variety or Music Program) *Emmy*. 1998: *Promised Land* (Best Guest Actress in a Drama Series) *Emmy*. 2001–2006 series *Malcolm in the Middle* (Best Guest Actress in a Comedy Series) 2001: Emmy. 2002: *Emmy*. 2003: Emmy. 2004: Emmy. 2005: Emmy. 2006: *Emmy*. 2005: *Joan of Arcadia* (Best Guest Actress in a Drama Series) Emmy. 2006:

Mrs. Harris (Best Female Actor in a Television Movie or Miniseries) SAG (Best Supporting Actress in a Miniseries or TV Movie) Emmy. **Records:** After *The Mary Tyler Moore Show* costars Mary Tyler Moore and Ed Asner kept swapping first place as the stars with the most Emmy wins, Leachman quietly outdid them both, earning her record-setting ninth Emmy award in 2006 for another guest appearance as the coarse, self-centered grandmother on *Malcolm in the Middle*. A versatile and tireless performer, Leachman has won her Emmys for the most varied of categories. Her first two Emmys came in the Supporting Actress in a Comedy category in the role of neurotic landlady Phyllis Lindstrom on *The Mary Tyler Moore Show*. Later Emmys came for television movies (*A Brand New Life*), variety shows (*Cher*), variety specials (*Screen Actors Guild 50th Anniversary Special*), guest appearances on series dramas (*Promised Land*) and comedies (*Malcolm in the Middle*), and even a Daytime Emmy for children's programming (*The Woman Who Willed a Miracle*). **Highlights:** During the run of groundbreaking sitcom, *The Mary Tyler Moore Show* Leachman was still making films and played what she later called the most difficult role of her life. In Peter Bogdanovich's eloquent black-and-white film adaptation of Larry McMurtry's novel, *The Last Picture Show* she played Ruth Popper, the too-easily dismissed wife of a gym teacher who engages in a clandestine affair with sullen teenager Sonny Crawford (Timothy Bottoms). Her final scene, a mesmerizing tour-de-force that many believe clinched her multiple award wins for Best Supporting Actress, was almost cut from the film. But left in, it closes the arc to her storyline with starkness and then an elegant sadness that quite aptly punctuated the tone of the entire film. In a tight race for the Oscar with her *The Last Picture Show* co-star, Ellen Burstyn and Ann-Margret in *Carnal Knowledge*, Leachman came out victorious, becoming only the second actor (after Goldie Hawn two years earlier) to win an Academy Award in acting while currently starring as a regular on a television series.

Leal, Sharon

Movie: 2006: *Dreamgirls* (Best Ensemble) SAG, Broadcast.

Léaud, Jean-Pierre

Movie: 1960: *Les Quatre cents coups (The 400 Blows)*, (Most Promising Newcomer) British. 1966: *Masculin-Féminin* (Best Actor) *Berlin*.

Lederer, Francis

Movie: 1939: *Confessions of a Nazi Spy* (Best Acting) *Board*.

Ledger, Heath

Movie: 2005: *Brokeback Mountain* (Best Actor) Academy, *New York*, British, Society, Broadcast (Best Actor, Drama) Globe (Best Male Lead) Spirit (Best Male Actor in a Leading Role) SAG (Best Ensemble) SAG. 2007: *I'm Not There* (Best Ensemble) *Spirit* (special award).

Ledoyen, Virginie

Tributes: 2002: Silver Bear for outstanding artistic contribution in *8 Femmes (8 Women)* from Berlin (special ensemble award shared with costars).

Lee, Christopher

Movie: 2001: *The Lord of the Rings: The Fellowship of the Ring* (Best Ensemble) SAG. 2002: *The Lord of the Rings: The Two Towers* (Best Ensemble) SAG.

Lee, Damian Jewan

Movie: 2000: *George Washington* (Best Debut Performance) Spirit (nomination shared with costars).

Lee, Jason

Movie: 1997: *Chasing Amy* (Best Supporting Male) *Spirit*. 2000: *Almost Famous* (Best Ensemble) SAG. **Television:** 2005–present *My Name Is Earl* (Best Actor in a Series, Musical or Comedy) 2005: Globe. 2006: Globe. (Best Male Actor in a Comedy Series) 2005: SAG. 2006: SAG. (Best Ensemble in a Comedy Series) 2005: SAG.

Lee, Peggy

Movie: 1955: *Pete Kelly's Blues* (Best Supporting Actress) Academy. **Televison:** 1956: --- (Best Female Singer) Emmy.

Lee, Sheryl

Movie: 1992: *Twin Peaks: Fire Walk with Me* (Best Female Lead) Spirit.

Leeds, Andrea

Movie: 1937: *Stage Door* (Best Supporting Actress) Academy.

Le Gallienne, Eva

Movie: 1980: *Resurrection* (Best Supporting Actress) Academy, *Board*. **Theater:** 1981: *To Grandmother's House We Go* (Best Actress, Play) Tony. **Television:** 1978: *The Royal Family* (Best Supporting Actress in a Drama or Comedy Special) *Emmy*. **Tributes:** 1964: Special award celebrating her 50th year as an actress, honored for her work with the National Repertory

Company from Tony. **Records:** In competition for the Best Supporting Actress Academy Award for *Resurrection* at age 82, Le Gallienne became the oldest actor to be nominated for an Oscar. She held the record for 17 years until 87-year-old Gloria Stuart competed in the same category for *Titanic*. Both actresses lost, Le Gallienne to Mary Steenburgen for *Melvin and Howard* and Stuart to Kim Basinger for *L.A. Confidential*. **Highlights:** Like Helen Hayes, The First Lady of the American Theater, Le Gallienne contributed more to theater than perhaps any other actor. Inspired by Sarah Bernhardt and tutored by Constance Collier, London-born Le Gallienne broadened America's view of and accessibility to live theater by expanding the repertory system which gave stage actors a permanent place to perform and grow, the results of which still thrive in regional theaters across the United States. She drove down ticket prices (at her Civic Repertory Theatre, she charged only $1.50 per ticket, five times less than tickets of the time) so that theater was accessible to more of society.

Légitimus, Darling

Movie: 1983: *Rue cases nègres* (Best Actress) *Venice*.

Le Gros, James

Movie: 1995: *Living in Oblivion* (Best Supporting Male) Spirit. **Television:** 2000–2001 series *Ally McBeal* (Best Ensemble in a Comedy Series) 2000: SAG.

Leguizamo, John

Movie: 1995: *To Wong Foo, Thanks for Everything, Julie Newmar* (Best Supporting Actor) Globe. 2001: *Moulin Rouge!* (Best Ensemble) SAG. **Theater:** 1998: *Freak* (Best Actor, Play) Tony. **Television:** 1999: *John Leguizamo's Freak* (Best Performance in a Variety or Music Special) *Emmy* (Best Variety, Music, or Comedy Special; Executive Producer) Emmy.

Leigh, Janet

Movie: 1960: *Psycho* (Best Supporting Actress) Academy, *Globe*.

Leigh, Jennifer Jason

Movie: 1990: *Last Exit to Brooklyn* (Best Supporting Actress) *New York* (multiple win); *Miami Blues* (Best Supporting Actress) *New York* (multiple win). 1993: *Short Cuts* (Best Ensemble) *Venice* (special award). 1994: *Mrs. Parker and the Vicious Circle* (Best Actress) *Society* (Best Actress, Drama) Globe (Best Female Lead) Spirit. 1995: *Georgia* (Best Ac-

tress) *New York* (Best Female Lead) Spirit. 2001: *The Anniversary Party* (Best First Feature) Spirit (Best First Screenplay) Spirit. 2007: *Margot at the Wedding* (Best Supporting Female) Spirit.

Leigh, Vivien

Movie: 1939: *Gone with the Wind* (Best Acting) *Board* (multiple win), (Best Actress) *Academy, New York*. 1940: *Waterloo Bridge* (Best Acting) *Board* (multiple win). 1951: *A Streetcar Named Desire* (Best Actress) *Academy, Venice, New York* (Best Actress, Drama) Globe (Best British Actress) *British*. **Theater:** 1963: *Tovarich* (Best Actress, Musical) *Tony*. **Tributes:** 1999: Ranked Number 16 on List of 25 Greatest Female Screen Legends of the 20th Century from American Film Institute. **Records:** When Leigh picked up her second New York Film Critics award and Oscar for *A Streetcar Named Desire* in 1951, she and Laurence Olivier became the first married couple to both win acting Oscars and New York Critics awards. Leigh and Olivier married in 1940, a year after Leigh won her first Best Actress awards for *Gone with the Wind*. Olivier won Best Actor for *Hamlet* from both groups in 1948; Leigh won for *Streetcar* three years later. They divorced nine years after that.

Leighton, Margaret

Movie: 1954: *Carrington V.C.* (Best British Actress) British. 1971: *The Go-Between* (Best Supporting Actress) Academy, *British*. **Theater:** 1957: *Separate Tables* (Best Actress, Dramatic) *Tony*. 1960: *Much Ado About Nothing* (Best Actress, Dramatic) Tony. 1962: *The Night of the Iguana* (Best Actress, Dramatic) *Tony*. 1963: *Tchin-Tchin* (Best Actress, Dramatic) Tony. **Television:** 1966: *Dr. Kildare* (Best Single Performance by an Actress in a Leading Role in a Drama) Emmy. 1971: *"Hamlet," Hallmark Hall of Fame* (Best Supporting Actress in a Drama) *Emmy*.

Le Mat, Paul

Movie: 1973: *American Graffiti* (New Star of the Year — Actor) *Globe*. 1980: *Melvin and Howard* (Best Actor, Musical or Comedy) Globe. **Television:** 1984: *The Burning Bed* (Best Supporting Actor in a Series, Miniseries, or TV Movie) *Globe*.

Lemmon, Jack

Movie: 1955: *Mister Roberts* (Best Foreign Actor) British (Best Supporting Actor) *Academy*. 1959: *Some Like It Hot* (Best Actor) Academy (Best Actor, Musical or Comedy) *Globe* (Best Foreign Actor) British. 1960: *The Apartment* (Best Actor) Academy (Best Actor, Musical or Comedy) *Globe* (Best

Foreign Actor) *British.* 1962: ***Days of Wine and Roses*** (Best Actor) Academy (Best Actor, Drama) Globe (Best Foreign Actor) British. 1963: ***Irma La Douce*** (Best Actor, Musical or Comedy) Globe; ***Under the Yum Yum Tree*** (Best Actor, Musical or Comedy) Globe. 1964: ***Good Neighbor Sam*** (Best Foreign Actor) British (multiple nomination). 1965: ***How to Murder Your Wife*** (Best Foreign Actor) British (multiple nomination); ***The Great Race*** (Best Actor, Musical or Comedy) Globe. 1968: ***The Odd Couple*** (Best Actor, Musical or Comedy) Globe. 1970: ***The Out-of-Towners*** (Best Actor, Musical or Comedy) Globe. 1972: ***Avanti!*** (Best Actor, Musical or Comedy) *Globe.* 1973: ***Save the Tiger*** (Best Actor) Academy (Best Actor, Drama) Globe. 1974: ***The Front Page*** (Best Actor, Musical or Comedy) Globe. 1979: ***The China Syndrome*** (Best Actor) Academy, *Cannes, British* (Best Actor, Drama) Globe. 1980: ***Tribute*** (Best Actor) Academy, *Berlin* (Best Actor, Drama) Globe. 1982: ***Missing*** (Best Actor) Academy, *Cannes,* British (Best Actor, Drama) Globe. 1986: ***That's Life!*** (Best Actor, Musical or Comedy) Globe. 1989: ***Dad*** (Best Actor, Drama) Globe. 1992: ***Glengarry Glen Ross*** (Best Actor) *Venice, Board.* 1993: ***Short Cuts*** (Best Ensemble) *Venice* (special award). Theater: 1979: ***Tribute*** (Best Actor, Play) Tony. 1986: ***Long Day's Journey into Night*** (Best Actor, Play) Tony. Television: 1972: ***Jack Lemmon in 'S Wonderful, 'S Marvelous, 'S Gershwin*** (Best Single Program, Variety or Musical; Star) *Emmy.* 1976: ***The Entertainer*** (Best Actor in a Drama or Comedy Special) Emmy. 1987: ***Long Day's Journey into Night*** (Best Actor in a Miniseries or TV Movie) Globe. 1988: ***The Murder of Mary Phagan*** (Best Actor in a Miniseries or Special) Emmy (Best Actor in a Miniseries or TV Movie) Globe. 1993: ***A Life in the Theater*** (Best Actor in a Miniseries or TV Movie) Globe. 1997: ***12 Angry Men*** (Best Actor in a Miniseries or TV Movie) Emmy, Globe (Best Male Actor in a Television Movie or Miniseries) SAG. 1999: ***Inherit the Wind*** (Best Actor in a Miniseries or TV Movie) Emmy, *Globe*; ***"Tuesdays with Morrie," Oprah Winfrey Presents*** (Best Actor in a Miniseries or TV Movie) *Emmy,* Globe (Best Male Actor in a Television Movie or Miniseries) *SAG.* Tributes: 1986: Career Achievement Award from Board. 1988: Life Achievement Award from American Film Institute. 1989: Life Achievement Award from SAG. 1990: Cecil B. DeMille Award from Globe. 1993: Gala Tribute from Film Society of Lincoln Center. 1996: Honorary Golden Bear from Berlin; Honor from Kennedy Center for the Performing Arts. **Highlights:** Lemmon's professional impact on fellow performers is perhaps most recognizable in the effusive praise other award winning actors have given him in their acceptance speeches. Two of the most memorable: Kevin Spacey dedicated his second Oscar (for ***American Beauty***) to Lemmon for inspiring his performance, and for being his friend, mentor and even a father figure. Lemmon wasn't in attendance at the Shrine Auditorium that night, but was watching the live telecast with Gregory Peck at Peck's home and later told the press that he felt overwhelmed by Spacey's generous acknowledgment. Lemmon did attend the 1998 Golden Globe ceremony, where was nominated for Best Actor for the television production of ***12 Angry Men***. When fellow nominee Ving Rhames won for ***Don King: Only in America***, Rhames paid an even more personal tribute to Lemmon by calling him on stage. When a skeptical Lemmon reached the podium, Rhames hugged Lemmon and handed his award to Lemmon. At first refusing the award, Lemmon finally relented to Rhames' insistence. Later, the Hollywood Foreign Press made a duplicate of the award so that Rhames would have one in his possession as well.

Lemper, Ute

Movie: 1994: ***Prêt-à-Porter (Ready-to-Wear)*** (Best Ensemble) *Board.*

Lennix, Harry J.

Movie: 2004: ***Ray*** (Best Ensemble) SAG.

Lennon, Jerrett

Movie: 1993: ***Short Cuts*** (Best Ensemble) *Venice* (special award).

Lenya, Lotte

Movie: 1961: ***The Roman Spring of Mrs. Stone*** (Best Supporting Actress) Academy, Globe. Theater: 1956: ***The Threepenny Opera*** (Best Supporting or Featured Actress, Musical) *Tony.* 1967: ***Cabaret*** (Best Actress, Musical) Tony.

Lenz, Kay

Movie: 1973: ***Breezy*** (New Star of the Year — Actress) Globe. Television: 1975: ***"Heart in Hiding," ABC Afternoon Playbreak*** (Best Actress in a Daytime Drama Series) *Emmy.* 1976: ***Rich Man, Poor Man*** (Best Single Performance by a Supporting Actress in a Comedy or Drama Series) Emmy. 1988–1990 series ***Midnight Caller*** (Best Guest Actress in a Drama Series) 1989: *Emmy.* 1990: Emmy. 1991–1933 series ***Reasonable Doubts*** (Best Supporting Actress in a Drama Series) 1992: Emmy. 1993: Emmy.

Leon, Tara

Movie: 1994: ***Prêt-à-Porter (Ready-to-Wear)*** (Best Ensemble) *Board.*

Leonov, Yevgeni

Movie: 1979: *Osenniy marafon (Autumn Marathon)* (Best Actor) *Venice.*

Lerman, Logan

Movie: 2007: *3:10 to Yuma* (Best Ensemble) SAG.

Lerner, Michael

Movie: 1991: *Barton Fink* (Best Supporting Actor) Academy, *LA.*

Leroy, Phillipe

Movie: 1961: *Le Trou* (Best Foreign Actor) British. Television: 1973: *The Life of Leonardo da Vinci* (Best Continued Performance by an Actor in a Leading Role, Drama or Comedy — Limited Episodes) Emmy.

Leslie, Anthony

Movie: 2001: *Kaaterskill Falls* (Best Debut Performance) Spirit (nomination shared with costars).

Leung, Tony

Movie: 2007: *Lust, Caution* (Best Male Lead) Spirit.

Levin, Rachel

Movie: 1987: *Gaby—A True Story* (Best Actress, Drama) Globe.

Levine, Ted

Movie: 2007: *American Gangster* (Best Ensemble) SAG.

Levy, Eugene

Movie: 1997: *Waiting for Guffman* (Best Screenplay) Spirit. 2003: *A Mighty Wind* (Best Supporting Actor) *New York* (Best Screenplay) Spirit (Best Song, "A Mighty Wind") *Broadcast* (Best Ensemble) Broadcast. Television: 1981–1983 series *SCTV Network* (Best Writing in a Variety or Music Program) 1982: Emmy, Emmy, Emmy, *Emmy.* 1983: Emmy, Emmy, Emmy, Emmy, *Emmy.*

Lewis, Gary

Movie: 2000: *Billy Elliot* (Best Supporting Actor) British (Best Ensemble) SAG.

Lewis, Huey

Movie: 1985: *Back to the Future* (Best Song, "The Power of Love") Academy, Globe. 1993: *Short Cuts* (Best Ensemble) *Venice* (special award).

Lewis, Jerry

Movie: 1965: *Boeing, Boeing* (Best Actor, Musical or Comedy) Globe. 1983: *The King of Comedy* (Best Supporting Actor) British. Television: 1952: --- (Best Comedian or Comedienne) Emmy (nomination shared with costar, Dean Martin). Tributes: 1999: Career Golden Lion from Venice. 2004: Career Achievement Award from LA. Records: While Jerry Lewis proved a major success in the United States during his years as half of a comic duo with Dean Martin and afterwards when he starred in and often directed his own movies, it was the French who particularly embraced Lewis for his wit and creativity. From French moviegoers he earned the nickname "Le Roi du Crazy" (The King of Crazy) and in 1984 he received the French Legion of Honor, a first for an American comedic film actor.

Lewis, Juliette

Movie: 1991: *Cape Fear* (Best Supporting Actress) Academy, Globe. 1994: *Natural Born Killers* (Best Actress) *Venice.* 2002: *Hysterical Blindness* (Best Supporting Female) Spirit. Television: 2003: *Hysterical Blindness* (Best Supporting Actress in a Miniseries or TV Movie) Emmy.

Li, Gong

Movie: 1992: *Qui Ju da guan si* (Best Actress) *Venice.* 1993: *Farewell, My Concubine* (Best Supporting Actress) *New York.* 2005: *Memoirs of a Geisha* (Best Supporting Actress) *Board.* Tributes: 1993: Honorary Award from Berlin.

Lichtenstein, Mitchell

Movie: 1983: *Streamers* (Best Actor) *Venice* (win shared with costars). 1993: *The Wedding Banquet* (Best Male Lead) Spirit.

Lin, Cui

Movie: 2001: *Beijing Bicycle* (Best Young Actor) *Berlin* (win shared with costar).

Linares, Aida

Movie: 1996: *The First Wives Club* (Best Ensemble) *Board.*

Lincoln, Abbey

Movie: 1968: *For Love of Ivy* (Best Supporting Actress) Globe.

Lincoln, Andrew

Movie: 2003: *Love Actually* (Best Ensemble) Broadcast.

Linden, Jennie

Movie: 1970: *Women in Love* (Most Promising New-comer) British.

Lindfors, Viveca

Movie: 1962: *No Exit* (Best Actress) *Berlin* (win shared with costar). Television: 1978: *A Question of Guilt* (Best Supporting Actress in a Drama or Comedy Special) Emmy. 1990: *Life Goes On* (Best Guest Actress in a Drama Series) *Emmy*.

Lindo, Delroy

Movie: 1999: *The Cider House Rules* (Best Ensemble) SAG. Theater: 1988: *Joe Turner's Come and Gone* (Best Actor in a Featured Role, Play) Tony.

Ling, Bai

Movie: 1997: *Red Corner* (Best Breakthrough Performer — Female) *Board*.

Linney, Laura

Movie: 2000: *You Can Count on Me* (Best Actress) Academy, *New York*, *Society*, Broadcast (Best Actress, Drama) Globe (Best Female Actor in a Leading Role) SAG (Best Female Lead) Spirit. 2003: *Love Actually* (Best Ensemble) Broadcast; *Mystic River* (Best Supporting Actress) British (Best Ensemble) SAG, Broadcast. 2004: *Kinsey* (Best Female Actor in a Supporting Role) SAG (Best Supporting Actress) Academy, *Board*, Globe, Society, Broadcast. 2005: *The Squid and the Whale* (Best Actress, Musical or Comedy) Globe (Best Female Lead) Spirit. 2007: *The Savages* (Best Actress) Academy. Theater: 2002: *The Crucible* (Best Actress, Play) Tony. 2004: *Sight Unseen* (Best Actress, Play) Tony. Television: 2002: *Wild Iris* (Best Actress in a Miniseries or TV Movie) *Emmy*. 2004: *Frasier* (Best Guest Actress in a Comedy Series) *Emmy*.

Liotta, Ray

Movie: 1986: *Something Wild* (Best Supporting Actor) Globe. 2002: *Narc* (Best Supporting Male) Spirit. Television: 1998: *The Rat Pack* (Best Male Actor in a Television Movie or Miniseries) SAG. 2005: *ER* (Best Guest Actor in a Drama Series) *Emmy*.

Lipman, Maureen

Movie: 1983: *Educating Rita* (Best Supporting Actress) British.

Lipnicki, Jonathan

Movie: 1996: *Jerry Maguire* (Best Child Performance) *Broadcast*.

Lisi, Virna

Movie: 1994: *Queen Margot* (Best Actress) *Cannes*.

Lithgow, John

Movie: 1982: *The World According to Garp* (Best Supporting Actor) Academy, *New York, LA*. 1983: *Terms of Endearment* (Best Supporting Actor) Academy. Theater: 1973: *The Changing Room* (Best Supporting or Featured Actor, Dramatic) *Tony*. 1985: *Requiem for a Heavyweight* (Best Actor, Play) Tony. 1988: *M. Butterfly* (Best Actor, Play) Tony. 2002: *Sweet Smell of Success* (Best Actor, Musical) *Tony*. 2005: *Dirty Rotten Scoundrels* (Best Actor, Musical) Tony. Television: 1984: *"The Day After," An ABC Theatre Presentation* (Best Supporting Actor in a Limited Series or Special) Emmy. 1986: *"Resting Place," Hallmark Hall of Fame* (Best Actor in a Miniseries or Special) Emmy; *Amazing Stories* (Best Guest Performer in a Drama Series) *Emmy*. 1995: *My Brother's Keeper* (Best Actor in a Miniseries or Special) Emmy. 1996–2001 series *3rd Rock from the Sun* (Best Actor in a Comedy Series) 1996: *Emmy*. 1997: *Emmy*. 1998: Emmy. 1999: *Emmy*. 2000: Emmy. 2001: Emmy. (Best Actor in a Series, Musical or Comedy) 1996: *Globe*. 1997: Globe. 1998: Globe. (Best Male Actor in a Comedy Series) 1996: *SAG*. 1997: *SAG*. (Best Ensemble in a Comedy Series) 1996: SAG. 1997: SAG. 1998: SAG. 2000: *Don Quixote* (Best Actor in a Miniseries or TV Movie) SAG.

Little, Cleavon

Movie: 1974: *Blazing Saddles* (Most Promising Newcomer) British. Theater: 1970: *Purlie* (Best Actor, Musical) *Tony*. Television: 1989: *Dear John* (Best Guest Actor in a Comedy Series) *Emmy*.

Liu, Lucy

Movie: 2002: *Chicago* (Best Ensemble) *SAG, Broadcast*. Television: 1998–2002 series *Ally McBeal* (Best Female Actor in a Comedy Series) 1999: Emmy. (Best Ensemble in a Comedy Series) 1998: *SAG*. 1999: SAG. 2000: SAG.

Lloyd, Christopher

Movie: 1993: *Twenty Bucks* (Best Supporting Male) *Spirit*. Television: 1978–1983 series *Taxi* (Best Supporting Actor in a Comedy, Variety, or Music Series) 1982: *Emmy*. 1983: *Emmy*. 1992 series *Avonlea (Road to Avonlea* or *Tales of Avonlea)* (Best Actor in a Drama Series) 1992: *Emmy*.

Lloyd, Emily

Movie: 1987: *Wish You Were Here* (Best Actress) British, *Society*.

Lloyd, Harold

Movie: 1950: *Mad Wednesday* (Best Actor, Musical or Comedy) Globe. Tributes: 1952: Honorary Oscar statuette for being a master comedian and good citizen from Academy.

Lo Cascio, Luigi

Movie: 2001: *Luce dei miei occhi* (Best Actor) *Venice.*

Locke, Sondra

Movie: 1968: *The Heart Is a Lonely Hunter* (New Star of the Year—Actress) Globe (Best Supporting Actress) Academy, Globe.

Lockhart, Gene

Movie: 1938: *Algiers* (Best Supporting Actor) Academy.

Lockwood, Margaret

Movie: 1955: *Cast a Dark Shadow* (Best British Actress) British.

Logan, Phyllis

Movie: 1983: *Another Time, Another Place* (Most Oustanding Newcomer to Film) *British* (Best Actress) British.

Loggia, Robert

Movie: 1985: *Jagged Edge* (Best Supporting Actor) Academy. Television: 1989–1990 series *Mancuso F.B.I.* (Best Actor in a Drama Series) 1990: Emmy. 2001: *Malcolm in the Middle* (Best Guest Actor in a Comedy Series) Emmy.

Lohan, Lindsay

Movie: 2004: *Mean Girls* (Best Young Actress) Broadcast. 2006: *Bobby* (Best Ensemble) SAG, Broadcast; *A Prairie Home Companion* (Best Ensemble) Broadcast.

Lojodice, Giuliana

Movie: 1998: *La Vita è Bella (Life Is Beautiful)* (Best Ensemble) SAG.

Lollobrigida, Gina

Movie: 1954: *Bread, Love and Dreams* (Best Foreign Actress) British. 1968: *Buona Sera, Mrs. Campbell* (Best Actress, Musical or Comedy) Globe. Television: 1984–1985 series *Falcon Crest* (Best Supporting Actress in a Series, Miniseries, or TV Movie) 1984: Globe. Tributes: 1960: Henrietta Award for World Film Favorite from Globe. 1986: Honorary Award from Berlin.

Lombard, Carole

Movie: 1936: *My Man Godfrey* (Best Actress) Academy. Tributes: 1999: Ranked Number 23 on List of 25 Greatest Female Screen Legends of the 20th Century from American Film Institute.

Lone, John

Movie: 1985: *Year of the Dragon* (Best Supporting Actor) Globe. 1987: *The Last Emperor* (Best Actor, Drama) Globe. 1988: *The Moderns* (Best Supporting Male) Spirit.

Long, Shelley

Movie: 1984: *Irreconcilable Differences* (Best Actress, Musical or Comedy) Globe. Television: 1982–1987 series *Cheers* (Best Actress in a Comedy Series) 1983: *Emmy.* 1984: Emmy. 1985: Emmy. 1986: Emmy. (Best Actress in a Series, Musical or Comedy) 1984: Globe. 1985: *Globe.* (Best Supporting Actress in a Series, Miniseries, or TV Movie) 1983: *Globe.* 1993: *Cheers* (Best Guest Actress in a Comedy Series) Emmy. 1996: *Frasier* (Best Guest Actress in a Comedy Series) Emmy.

Lonsdale, Michael (Michel)

Movie: 1973: *The Day of the Jackal* (Best Supporting Actor) British.

Lopez, Jennifer

Movie: 1995: *My Family/Mi Familia* (Best Supporting Female) Spirit. 1997: *Selena* (Best Actress, Musical or Comedy) Globe.

López, Sergi

Movie: 1999: *Une liaison pornographique* (Best Actor) *Venice.*

Loren, Sophia

Movie: 1958: *The Black Orchid* (Best Actress) *Venice.* 1960: *It Started in Naples* (Best Actress, Musical or Comedy) Globe. 1961: *Two Women* (Best Actress) *Academy, New York, Cannes* (Best Foreign Actress) *British.* 1964: *Marriage, Italian Style* (Best Actress) Academy (Best Actress, Musical or Comedy) Globe. 1994: *Prêt-à-Porter (Ready-to-Wear)* (Best Supporting Actress) Globe (Best Ensemble) *Board.* Tributes: 1963, 1964, 1965, 1968, 1970, 1976: Henrietta Award for World Film Favorite. 1990: Honorary Oscar statuette for being one of the true treasures of world cinema who, in a career rich with memorable performances, has added permanent luster to our art form from Academy. 1994: Honorary Golden Bear from Berlin; Cecil B. DeMille Award from Globe. 1998: Career Golden Lion from Venice. 1999: Ranked Number 21 on List of 25 Greatest Female Screen Legends of the 20th Century from American Film Institute. **Records:** When Loren won the Best Actress Academy Award for the 1961 film, *Two Women*, she became the first person to win an acting Oscar for a foreign language performance. **Highlights:** Like Joan Crawford 16 years earlier, Loren stayed home the night she won her Oscar because she was too nervous to attend. In her memoir she later explained that sitting in plain view of millions of viewers while her fate was being judged seemed too unbearable. Anticipating fainting from disappointment if she lost or from joy if she won, Loren decided it would be better if she just fainted at home.

Lorring, Joan

Movie: 1945: *The Corn Is Green* (Best Supporting Actress) Academy.

Louise, Tina

Movie: 1959: *God's Little Acre* (New Star of the Year — Actress) *Globe.*

Love, Bessie

Movie: 1929: *The Broadway Melody* (Best Actress) Academy.

Love, Courtney

Movie: 1996: *The People vs. Larry Flynt* (Best Actress, Drama) Globe (Best Supporting Actress) *New York.*

Love, Victor

Movie: 1986: *Native Son* (Best Male Lead) Spirit.

Lovett, Lyle

Movie: 1993: *Short Cuts* (Best Ensemble) *Venice* (special award). 1994: *Prêt-à-Porter (Ready-to-Wear)* (Best Ensemble) *Board.*

Lovitz, Jon

Movie: 1998: *Happiness* (Best Ensemble) *Board.* Television: 1985–1990 series *Saturday Night Live* (Best Individual Performance in a Variety or Music Program) 1986: Emmy. 1987: Emmy.

Lowe, Arthur

Movie: 1973: *O Lucky Man!* (Best Supporting Actor) *British.*

Lowe, Rob

Movie: 1987: *Square Dance* (Best Supporting Actor) Globe. Television: 1983: *Thursday's Child* (Best Supporting Actor in a Series, Miniseries, or TV Movie) Globe. 1999–2003 series *The West Wing* (Best Actor in a Drama Series) 2000: Globe. 2001: Emmy, *Globe.* (Best Ensemble in a Drama Series) 2000: SAG. 2001: SAG. 2002: SAG.

Löwenadler, Holger

Movie: 1974: *Lacombe Lucien* (Best Supporting Actor) *Board, Society.*

Lowensohn, Elina

Movie: 1995: *Nadja (Nadia)* (Best Female Lead) Spirit.

Loy, Myrna

Tributes: 1983: Career Achievement Award from LA. 1988: Honor from Kennedy Center for the Performing Arts. 1990: Honorary Oscar statuette in recognition of her extraordinary qualities both on screen and off, with appreciation for a lifetime's worth of indelible performances from Academy.

Lucas, Josh

Movie: 2001: *A Beautiful Mind* (Best Ensemble) SAG.

Luchko, Klara

Movie: 1954: *Bolshaya semya (The Big Family)* Cannes (special ensemble award).

Lukas, Paul

Movie: 1939: *Confessions of a Nazi Spy* (Best Acting) *Board.* 1943: *Watch on the Rhine* (Best Acting) *Board* (Best Actor) *Academy, New York, Globe.* **Records:** With *Watch on the Rhine* Lukas became the first Best Actor Golden Globe winner. He also has the rare distinction of being one of the few stars selected Best Actor by the New York Film Critics on their first round of voting. He received 15 of the 17 votes tallied that year. By winning all four major awards given at the time, Lukas made one of the first award sweeps of any actor in film history.

Luke, Derek

Movie: 2002: *Antwone Fisher* (Breakthrough Performer — Male) *Board* (Best Male Lead) *Spirit.* **Highlights:** Luke's ascension to success at the Independent Spirit awards was swift and dramatic. Accepting his Best Actor prize for *Antwone Fisher*, Luke told the audience that just four years earlier he'd been waiting tables at the Spirit Awards, and now he was standing accepting their award.

Lukyanov, Sergei

Movie: 1954: *Bolshaya semya (The Big Family)* *Cannes* (special ensemble award).

Luna, Diego

Movie: 2001: *Y tu mamá también* (Best First Time Actor) *Venice* (win shared with costar).

Lung, Sihung

Movie: 1994: *Eat Drink Man Woman* (Best Male Lead) Spirit.

Lunt, Alfred

Movie: 1931: *The Guardsman* (Best Actor) Academy. Theater: 1954: *Ondine* (Best Director) *Tony*. 1955: *Quadrille* (Best Actor, Dramatic) *Tony*. 1959: *The Visit* (Best Actor, Dramatic) Tony. Television: 1965: *"The Magnificent Yankee," Hallmark Hall of Fame* (Best Individual Achievement in Entertainment, Actor or Performer) *Emmy*. Tributes: 1970: Special award from Tony. Records: Lunt is the only actor in Academy Award history to be the one star nominated in a category to go home empty handed. In 1931/32, the Academy nominated just three people in the acting categories. When Wallace Beery in *The Champ* and Fredric March in *Dr. Jekyll and Mr. Hyde* both won in Oscar's first tie, Lunt was the only one in that category without a win.

Lupino, Ida

Movie: 1941: *High Sierra* (Best Acting) *Board* (multiple win); *Ladies in Retirement* (Best Acting) *Board* (multiple win). 1942: *Moontide* (Best Acting) *Board*. 1943: *The Hard Way* (Best Actress) *New York*. Television: 1952–1956 series *Four Star Playhouse* (Best Continuing Performance by an Actress in a Leading Role in a Dramatic or Comedy Series) 1956: Emmy. 1957–1958 series *Mr. Adams and Eve* (Best Continuing Performance by an Actress in a Leading Role in a Dramatic or Comedy Series) 1957: Emmy. (Best Actress in a Leading Role — Continuing Character — in a Comedy Series) 1958: Emmy.

LuPone, Patti

Movie: 2000: *State and Main* (Best Ensemble) *Board*. Theater: 1976: *The Robber Bridegroom* (Best Featured Actress, Musical) Tony. 1980: *Evita* (Best Actress, Musical) *Tony*. 1988: *Anything Goes* (Best Actress, Musical) Tony. 2006: *Sweeney Todd* (Best Actress, Musical) Tony. Television: 1998: *Frasier* (Best Guest Actress in a Comedy Series) Emmy.

Lutter, Alfred

Movie: 1974: *Alice Doesn't Live Here Anymore* (Most Promising Newcomer) British.

Lynas, Jeffrey

Movie: 1975: *Lies My Father Told Me* (New Star of the Year — Actor) Globe.

Lynch, Jane

Movie: 2003: *A Mighty Wind* (Best Screenplay) Spirit (Best Ensemble) Broadcast.

Lynch, John

Movie: 1984: *Cal* (Best Newcomer to Film) British.

Lynch, Kelly

Movie: 1989: *Drugstore Cowboy* (Best Female Lead) Spirit. 1994: *The Beans of Egypt, Maine* (Best Supporting Female) Spirit.

Lynch, Susan

Movie: 1998: *Waking Ned Devine* (Best Ensemble) SAG.

Lynley, Carol

Movie: 1958: *The Light in the Forest* (New Star of the Year — Actress) Globe. 1959: *Blue Denim* (New Star of the Year — Actress) Globe. Records: Popular blonde ingénue Lynley has the rare distinction of being nominated twice as New Star of the Year for the Globe. While Lynley is the only actress to be considered for a New Star of the Year award twice, Michael Callan is the only actor. He lost his first bid for the award but won the second, leaving Lynley the only person up twice for New Star of the Year to never win.

Lynn, Diana

Movie: 1942: *The Major and the Minor* (Best Acting) *Board*.

Lyon, Sue

Movie: 1962: *Lolita* (New Star of the Year — Actress) *Globe*.

Mac, Bernie

Movie: 2001: *Ocean's 11* (Best Ensemble) Broadcast. 2004: *Ocean's Twelve* (Best Ensemble) Broadcast. Television: 2001–2006 series *The Bernie Mac Show* (Best Actor in a Comedy Series) 2002: Emmy. 2003: Emmy. (Best Actor in a Series, Musical or Comedy) 2002: Globe. 2003: Globe.

MacArthur, James

Movie: 1957: *The Young Stranger* (Most Promising Newcomer) British.

Maccario, Josette

Movie: 1993: *Short Cuts* (Best Ensemble) *Venice* (special award).

MacDonald, Kelly

Movie: 2000: *Two Family House* (Best Female Lead) Spirit. 2001: *Gosford Park* (Best Ensemble) *SAG, Broadcast.* 2007: *No Country for Old Men* (Best Supporting Actress) British (Best Ensemble) *Board, SAG,* Broadcast. **Television:** 2006: *The Girl in the Café* (Best Actress in a Miniseries or TV Movie) *Emmy,* Globe.

MacDowell, Andie

Movie: 1989: *sex, lies, and videotape* (Best Actress) *LA* (Best Actress, Drama) Globe (Best Female Lead) *Spirit.* 1990: *Green Card* (Best Actress, Musical or Comedy) Globe. 1993: *Short Cuts* (Best Ensemble) *Venice* (special award). 1994: *Four Weddings and a Funeral* (Best Actress, Musical or Comedy) Globe.

MacGraw, Ali

Movie: 1969: *Goodbye, Columbus* (New Star or the Year — Actress) *Globe* (Most Promising Newcomer) British. 1970: *Love Story* (Best Actress) Academy (Best Actress, Drama) *Globe.* **Tributes:** 1971: Henrietta Award for World Film Favorite from Globe.

Mackie, Anthony

Movie: 2004: *Brother to Brother* (Best Debut Performance) Spirit.

MacLaine, Shirley

Movie: 1955: *The Trouble with Harry* (New Star of the Year — Actress) *Globe* (Best Foreign Actress) British. 1958: *Some Came Running* (Best Actress) Academy (Best Actress, Drama) Globe. 1959: *Ask Any Girl* (Best Actress) *Berlin* (Best Actress, Musical or Comedy) Globe (Best Foreign Actress) *British.* 1960: *The Apartment* (Best Actress) Academy, *Venice* (Best Actress, Musical or Comedy) *Globe* (Best Foreign Actress) *British.* 1961: *The Children's Hour* (Best Actress, Drama) Globe. 1963: *Irma La Douce* (Best Actress) Academy (Best Actress, Musical or Comedy) *Globe* (Best Foreign Actress) British (multiple nomination). 1964: *What a Way to Go* (Best Foreign Actress) British (multiple nomination). 1966: *Gambit* (Best Actress, Musical or Comedy) Globe. 1967: *Woman Times Seven* (Best Actress, Musical or Comedy) Globe. 1969: *Sweet Charity* (Best Actress, Musical or Comedy) Globe. 1971: *Desperate Characters* (Best Actress) *Berlin.* 1975: *The Other Half of the Sky: A China Memoir* (Best Doc-

umentary Feature, Producer) Academy. 1977: *The Turning Point* (Best Actress) Academy. 1979: *Being There* (Best Actress) British (Best Actress, Musical or Comedy) Globe. 1983: *Terms of Endearment* (Best Actress) *Academy, New York, Board,* British, *LA* (Best Actress, Drama) *Globe.* 1988: *Madame Sousatzka* (Best Actress) *Venice* (Best Actress, Drama) *Globe.* 1989: *Steel Magnolias* (Best Supporting Actress) British. 1990: *Postcards from the Edge* (Best Actress) British (Best Supporting Actress) Globe. 1992: *Used People* (Best Actress, Musical or Comedy) Globe. 1994: *Guarding Tess* (Best Actress, Musical or Comedy) Globe. 2005: *In Her Shoes* (Best Supporting Actress) Globe. **Television:** 1975: *Shirley MacLaine: If They Could See Me Now* (Best Special, Comedy-Variety or Music; Star) Emmy. 1976: *Gypsy in My Soul* (Best Special, Comedy-Variety or Music; Star) *Emmy.* 1977: *The Shirley MacLaine Special: Where Do We Go from Here?* (Best Special, Comedy-Variety or Music; Star) Emmy. 1979: *Shirley MacLaine at the Lido* (Best Comedy-Variety or Music Program, Star) Emmy. 1980: *Shirley MacLaine ... "Every Little Movement"* (Best Variety or Music Program, Star) Emmy. 1987: *Out on a Limb* (Best Actress in a Miniseries or TV Movie) Globe. 2002: *Hell on Heels: The Battle of Mary Kay* (Best Actress in a Miniseries or TV Movie) Globe. **Tributes:** 1958: Special Achievement Award from Globe. 1995: Gala Tribute from Film Society of Lincoln Center. 1997: Cecil B. DeMille Award from Globe. 1999: Honorary Golden Bear from Berlin. **Records:** Of acting families, two-person sister and brother family Shirley MacLaine and Warren Beatty have the most total nominations for the major competitive awards included in this book. Three acting family dynasties, the Hustons, Fondas, and Redgraves, rank second, third, and fourth, respectively.

MacMahon, Aline

Movie: 1944: *Dragon Seed* (Best Supporting Actress) Academy.

MacMurray, Fred

Movie: 1961: *The Absent-Minded Professor* (Best Actor, Musical or Comedy) Globe.

MacRae, Duncan

Movie: 1953: *The Kidnappers* (Best British Actor) British.

Macy, William H.

Movie: 1991: *Homicide* (Best Supporting Male) Spirit. 1994: *Oleanna* (Best Male Lead) Spirit. 1996: *Fargo* (Best Male Lead) *Spirit* (Best Male Actor in a

Supporting Role) SAG (Best Supporting Actor) Academy. 1997: *Boogie Nights* (Best Ensemble) SAG. 1999: *Magnolia* (Best Ensemble) *Board*, SAG. 2000: *State and Main* (Best Ensemble) *Board*. 2003: *Seabiscuit* (Best Supporting Actor) Globe (Best Ensemble) SAG. 2006: *Bobby* (Best Ensemble) SAG, Broadcast. **Television:** 1997: *ER* (Best Guest Actor in a Drama Series) Emmy. 2000: *A Slight Case of Murder* (Best Actor in a Miniseries or TV Movie) Emmy; *Sports Night* (Best Guest Actor in a Comedy Series) Emmy. 2002: *Door to Door* (Best Actor in a Miniseries or TV Movie) *Emmy*, Globe (Best Male Actor in a Television Movie or Miniseries) *SAG* (Best Writing for a Miniseries, TV Movie, or Dramatic Special) *Emmy*. 2004: *Stealing Sinatra* (Best Supporting Actor in a Miniseries or TV Movie) Emmy. 2004: *The Wool Cap* (Best Actor in a Miniseries or TV Movie) Emmy, Globe (Best Male Actor in a Television Movie or Miniseries) SAG (Best TV Movie, Producer) Emmy. 2006: *Nightmares and Dreamscapes: From the Stories of Stephen King* (Best Actor in a Miniseries or TV Movie) Emmy (Best Male Actor in a Television Movie or Miniseries) SAG.

Madigan, Amy

Movie: 1982: *Love Child* (Best New Star of the Year — Actress) Globe. 1985: *Twice in a Lifetime* (Best Supporting Actress) Academy, Globe. 1988: *Prince of Pennsylvania* (Best Supporting Female) Spirit. 1997: *Loved* (Best Supporting Female) Spirit. 2007: *Gone Baby Gone* (Best Ensemble) Broadcast. **Television:** 1989: *Roe vs. Wade* (Best Actress in a Miniseries or Special) Emmy (Best Supporting Actress in a Series, Miniseries, or TV Movie) *Globe*.

Madison, Guy

Tributes: 1953: Special Achievement Award as Best Western Star from Globe.

Madonna

Movie: 1987: *Who's That Girl* (Best Song, "Who's That Girl") Globe. 1992: *A League of Their Own* (Best Song, "This Used to Be My Playground") Globe. 1994: *With Honors* (Best Song, "I'll Remember") Globe. 1996: *Evita* (Best Actress, Musical or Comedy) *Globe*. 1999: *Austin Powers: The Spy Who Shagged Me* (Best Song, "Beautiful Stranger") Globe. 2002: *Die Another Day* (Best Song, "Die Another Day") Globe.

Madsen, Michael

Movie: 2005: *Sin City* (Best Ensemble) Broadcast.

Madsen, Virginia

Movie: 2004: *Sideways* (Best Female Actor in a Supporting Role) SAG (Best Supporting Actress) Academy, *New York*, Globe, *Society, LA, Broadcast* (Best Supporting Female) *Spirit* (Best Ensemble) *SAG, Broadcast*. 2006: *A Prairie Home Companion* (Best Ensemble) Broadcast.

Magimel, Benoît

Movie: 2001: *La Pianiste (The Piano Teacher)* (Best Actor) *Cannes*.

Magnani, Anna

Movie: 1946: *Open City* (Best Actress) *Board*. 1947: *L'onorevole Angelina* (Best Actress) *Venice*. 1955: *The Rose Tattoo* (Best Actress) Academy, New York, Board (Best Actress, Drama) Globe (Best Foreign Actress) British. 1957: *Wild Is the Wind* (Best Actress) Academy, Berlin (Best Actress, Drama) Globe (Best Foreign Actress) British. 1969: *The Secret of Santa Vittoria* (Best Actress, Musical or Comedy) Globe. **Records:** Friend Tennessee Williams was so taken with Magnani that he wrote his stage play, *The Rose Tattoo* especially for her. Because her English was too poor to take the role, Maureen Stapleton performed it on stage, but four years later, when the film version was ready to roll, so was Magnani. The simmering part of Serafina Delle Rose, a widow romanced by a truck driver, earned Magnani five American and British Best Actress prizes and made her one of the only actresses to win awards for a character created expressly for her, by a multiple–Pulitzer Prize winning playwright, no less.

Maguire, Tobey

Movie: 1999: *The Cider House Rules* (Best Ensemble) SAG. 2003: *Seabiscuit* (Best Ensemble) SAG.

Mahmoodzada, Ahmad Khan

Movie: 2007: *The Kite Runner* (Best Young Actor) *Broadcast*.

Main, Marjorie

Movie: 1947: *The Egg and I* (Best Supporting Actress) Academy. 1956: *Friendly Persuasion* (Best Supporting Actress) Globe.

Makatsch, Heike

Movie: 2003: *Love Actually* (Best Ensemble) Broadcast.

Mako

Movie: 1965: *The Sand Pebbles* (Best Supporting Actor) Academy, Globe. **Theater:** 1976: *Pacific Overture* (Best Actor, Musical) Tony.

Malden, Karl

Movie: 1951: *A Streetcar Named Desire* (Best Supporting Actor) *Academy*. 1954: *On the Waterfront* (Best Supporting Actor) Academy. 1956: *Baby Doll* (Best Actor, Drama) Globe (Best Foreign Actor) British. 1962: *Gypsy* (Best Actor, Musical or Comedy) Globe. Television: 1972–1977 series *The Streets of San Francisco* (Best Actor in a Drama Series) 1974: Emmy. 1975: Emmy, Globe. 1976: Emmy. 1977: Emmy. 1985: *Fatal Vision* (Best Supporting Actor in a Limited Series or Special) *Emmy*. Tributes: 2003: Life Achievement Award from SAG.

Malkovich, John

Movie: 1984: *The Killing Fields* (Best Supporting Actor) *Society* (multiple win); *Places in the Heart* (Best Supporting Actor) Academy, *Board, Society* (multiple win). 1991: *Queen's Logic* (Best Supporting Male) Spirit. 1993: *In the Line of Fire* (Best Supporting Actor) Academy, Globe, British. 1999: *Being John Malkovich* (Best Supporting Actor) *New York* (Best Ensemble) SAG. 2007: *Juno* (Best Picture, Producer) Academy, *Spirit*, Broadcast (Best Picture, Musical or Comedy; Producer) Globe. Television: 1985: *Death of a Salesman* (Best Supporting Actor in a Miniseries or Special) *Emmy* (Best Supporting Actor in a Series, Miniseries, or TV Movie) Globe. 1994: *Heart of Darkness* (Best Male Actor in a Television Movie or Miniseries) SAG (Best Supporting Actor in a Series, Miniseries, or TV Movie) Globe. 2000: *RKO 281* (Best Supporting Actor in a Miniseries or TV Movie) Emmy. 2002: *Napoleon* (Best Supporting Actor in a Miniseries or TV Movie) Emmy.

Malone, Dorothy

Movie: 1956: *Written on the Wind* (Best Supporting Actress) *Academy*, Globe. Television: 1964–1968 series *Peyton Place* (Best Actress in a Series) 1965: Globe. 1966: Globe.

Malone, Jena

Movie: 1996: *Bastard Out of Carolina* (Best Debut Performance) Spirit. 2007: *Into the Wild* (Best Ensemble) SAG. Television: 1996: *Bastard Out of Carolina* (Best Female Actor in a Television Movie or Miniseries) SAG. 1997: *Hope* (Best Actress in a Miniseries or TV Movie) Globe.

Manheim, Camryn

Movie: 1998: *Happiness* (Best Ensemble) *Board*. Television: 1997–2004 series *The Practice* (Best Supporting Actress in a Drama Series) 1998: *Emmy*. 1999: Emmy. (Best Supporting Actress in a Series, Miniseries, or TV Movie) 1998: *Globe*. (Best Ensemble in a Drama Series) 1998: SAG. 1999: SAG. 2000: SAG. 2005: *Elvis* (Best Supporting Actress in a Miniseries or TV Movie) Emmy (Best Supporting Actress in a Series, Miniseries, or TV Movie) Globe.

Mann, Paul

Movie: 1963: *America, America* (Best Supporting Actor) Globe. 1971: *Fiddler on the Roof* (Best Supporting Actor) Globe.

Manning, Taryn

Movie: 2005: *Hustle & Flow* (Best Ensemble) SAG.

Mansfield, Jayne

Movie: 1956: *The Girl Can't Help It* (New Star of the Year — Actress) *Globe*.

Mantegna, Joe

Movie: 1988: *Things Change* (Best Actor) *Venice* (win shared with costar). Theater: 1984: *Glengarry Glen Ross* (Best Actor in a Featured Role, Play) *Tony*. Television: 1997: *The Last Don* (Best Supporting Actor in a Miniseries or Special) Emmy. 1998: *The Rat Pack* (Best Supporting Actor in a Miniseries or TV Movie) Emmy (Best Supporting Actor in a Series, Miniseries, or TV Movie) Globe. 2007: *The Starter Wife* (Best Supporting Actor in a Miniseries or TV Movie) Emmy.

Mantell, Joe

Movie: 1955: *Marty* (Best Supporting Actor) Academy.

Mapother, William

Movie: 2001: *In the Bedroom* (Best Ensemble) SAG.

March, Fredric

Movie: 1931: *The Royal Family of Broadway* (Best Actor) Academy. 1932: *Dr. Jekyll and Mr. Hyde* (Best Actor) *Academy, Venice*. 1937: *A Star Is Born* (Best Actor) Academy. 1946: *The Best Years of Our Lives* (Best Actor) *Academy*. 1951: *Death of a Salesman* (Best Actor) Academy, *Venice* (Best Actor, Drama) Globe (Best Foreign Actor) British. 1954: *Executive Suite* (Best Foreign Actor) British (Best Ensemble) *Venice* (special award). 1959: *Middle of the Night* (Best Actor, Drama) Globe. 1960: *Inherit the Wind* (Best Actor) *Berlin* (Best Foreign Actor) British. 1964: *Seven Days in May* (Best Actor, Drama) Globe. Theater: 1947: *Years Ago* (Best Actor, Dramatic) *Tony*. 1957: *Long Day's Journey into Night* (Best Actor, Dramatic) *Tony*. 1962: *Gideon* (Best Actor, Dramatic) Tony. Television: 1954: *"A*

Christmas Carol," *Shower of Stars* (Best Actor in a Single Performance) Emmy; *"The Royal Family," Best of Broadway* (Best Actor in a Single Performance) Emmy. 1956: *"Dodsworth," Producers' Showcase* (Best Single Performance by an Actor) Emmy. **Records:** March is the first (and so far only) male actor to win an Oscar and a Tony in the same year. In 1947, he won his second Best Actor Academy Award for *The Best Years of Our Lives*, and later that year took home a Best Actor Tony for *Years Ago*. The double accolade has since only been achieved by five others: Shirley Booth, Audrey Hepburn, Ellen Burstyn, Mercedes Ruehl, and Judi Dench.

Marchand, Colette

Movie: 1952: *Moulin Rouge* (New Star of the Year — Actress) *Globe* (Most Promising Newcomer) British (Best Supporting Actress) Academy.

Marconi, Saverio

Movie: 1977: *Padre Padrone* (Most Promising Newcomer) British.

Marcovicci, Andrea

Movie: 1976: *The Front* (New Star of the Year — Actress) Globe.

Margolin, Janet

Movie: 1962: *David and Lisa* (New Star of the Year — Actress) Globe. **Theater:** 1962: *Daughter of Silence* (Best Supporting or Featured Actress, Dramatic) Tony.

Margolis, Mark

Movie: 2007: *Gone Baby Gone* (Best Ensemble) Broadcast.

Margolyes, Miriam

Movie: 1993: *The Age of Innocence* (Best Supporting Actress) *British*.

Marley, John

Movie: 1968: *Faces* (Best Actor) *Venice*. 1970: *Love Story* (Best Supporting Actor) Academy, Globe.

Marsden, James

Movie: 2007: *Hairspray* (Best Ensemble) SAG, *Broadcast.*

Marsh, Linda

Movie: 1963: *America, America* (Best Supporting Actress) Globe.

Marshall, Kris

Movie: 2003: *Love Actually* (Best Ensemble) Broadcast.

Marte, Judy

Movie: 2003: *Raising Victor Vargas* (Best Debut Performance) Spirit. 2004: *On the Outs* (Best Female Lead) Spirit.

Martin, Andrea

Movie: 2002: *My Big Fat Greek Wedding* (Best Ensemble) SAG, Broadcast. **Theater:** 1993: *My Favorite Year* (Best Actress in a Featured Role, Musical) *Tony*. 1997: *Candide* (Best Actress in a Featured Role, Musical) Tony. 2002: *Oklahoma!* (Best Actress in a Featured Role, Musical) Tony. **Television:** 1976–1984 series *SCTV Network* (Best Supporting Actress in a Comedy or Variety Series) 1982: Emmy. (Best Writing of a Comedy or Variety Series) 1982: Emmy, Emmy, Emmy, *Emmy*. 1983: Emmy, Emmy, Emmy, Emmy, *Emmy*.

Martin, Dean

Movie: 1959: *Who Was That Lady?* (Best Actor, Musical or Comedy) Globe. **Television:** 1952: --- (Best Comedian or Comedienne) Emmy (nomination shared with costar, Jerry Lewis). 1965–1974 series *The Dean Martin Show* (Best Actor in a Series) 1966: *Globe.* 1967: Globe. 1968: Globe. (Best Actor in a Series, Musical or Comedy) 1969: Globe. (Best Variety or Musical Series, Star) 1969: Emmy. 1970: Emmy. 1972: Emmy.

Martin, Dean-Paul

Movie: 1979: *Players* (New Star of the Year — Actor) Globe.

Martin, Jesse L.

Movie: 2005: *Rent* (Best Ensemble) Broadcast. **Television:** 1999–2008 series *Law & Order* (Best Ensemble in a Drama Series) 1999: SAG. 2000: SAG. 2001: SAG. 2003: SAG.

Martin, Ross

Movie: 1962: *Experiment in Terror* (Best Supporting Actor) Globe. **Television:** 1965–1969 series *Wild, Wild West* (Best Continued Performance by an Actor in a Leading Role in a Dramatic Series) 1969: Emmy.

Martin, Steve

Movie: 1981: *Pennies from Heaven* (Best Actor, Musical or Comedy) Globe. 1984: *All of Me* (Best Actor)

New York, Society (Best Actor, Musical or Comedy) Globe. 1987: *Roxanne* (Best Actor) *Society, LA* (Best Actor, Musical or Comedy) Globe. 1989: *Parenthood* (Best Actor, Musical or Comedy) Globe. 1995: *Father of the Bride, Part II* (Best Actor, Musical or Comedy) Globe. **Television:** 1967–1969 series *The Smothers Brothers Comedy Hour* (Best Writing Achievement in Comedy, Variety, or Music) 1969: *Emmy.* 1971–1974 series *The Sonny and Cher Comedy Hour* (Best Writing Aachievement in Variety or Music) 1972: Emmy. 1976: *Van Dyke and Company* (Best Writing in a Comedy-Variety or Music Special) Emmy. 2001: *73rd Annual Academy Awards* (Best Individual Performance in a Variety or Music Program) Emmy. **Tributes:** 2007: Honor from Kennedy Center for the Performing Arts.

Martinelli, Elsa
Movie: 1956: *Donatella* (Best Actress) *Berlin.*

Martinez, Vanessa
Movie: 1999: *Limbo* (Best Supporting Female) Spirit.

Marvin, Lee
Movie: 1964: *The Killers* (Best Foreign Actor) *British* (multiple win). 1965: *Cat Ballou* (Best Actor) *Academy, Board* (multiple win), *Berlin* (Best Foreign Actor) *British* (multiple win), (Best Actor, Musical or Comedy) *Globe*; *Ship of Fools* (Best Actor) *Board* (multiple win). 1969: *Paint Your Wagon* (Best Actor, Musical or Comedy) Globe. **Television:** 1962: *"People Need People," Alcoa Premiere* (Best Actor in a Single Performance) Emmy. **Records:** Marvin is the first actor to win the Oscar (and several other awards) for playing more than one character in a single film. In the western comedy, *Cat Ballou*, Marvin played brothers: the intoxicated and usually worthless good guy, Kid Shelleen, and the steely villain in black, Tim Strawn. His broad caricatures hit the perfect note of parodying the genre and helped catapult the light fare into the award-winning sleeper hit of the year. Back in 1931/32, Fredric March won his first Oscar playing the title role of *Dr. Jekyll & Mr. Hyde*, but those divergent personalities were aspects of the same man, so technically March still portrayed one character.

Marx, Groucho
Television: 1951: --- (Best Personality) *Emmy.* **Tributes:** 1973: Honorary Oscar statuette in recognition of his brilliant creativity and for the unequalled achievements of the Marx Brothers in the art of motion picture comedy from Academy. 1999: Ranked Number 20 on List of 25 Greatest Male Screen Legends of the 20th Century from American Film Insti-

tute (honor shared with costars, The Marx Brothers). **Records:** When he received his honorary award from the Academy of Motion Picture Arts and Sciences in 1973, 83-year-old Marx became the oldest performer to receive an Oscar. Mary Pickford was less than two weeks from her 82nd birthday when she received a special Oscar from the Academy in 1975. Marx was healthy enough to attend the 1973 ceremony to accept his award; Pickford's appearance was pre-taped for the Oscar telecast. **Highlights:** Never one to bypass a comic moment or a beautiful woman, Marx sparked life into the staid 1950 Emmy Awards ceremony after winning the award for Best Television Personality. In his acceptance speech, Marx made a few quips while standing beside that year's Miss Emmy, former Miss America Rosemary LaPlanche. When he finished, Marx left his Emmy on the table, picked up LaPlanche and carried her offstage instead.

The Marx Brothers
Tributes: 1999: Ranked Number 20 on List of 25 Greatest Male Screen Legends of the 20th Century from American Film Institute.

Masina, Giulietta
Movie: 1955: *La Strada* (Best Foreign Actress) British. 1957: *Le Notti di Cabiria (Nights of Cabiria)* (Best Actress) *Cannes* (Best Foreign Actress) British.

Maskell, Virginia
Movie: 1962: *The Wild and the Willing* (Best British Actress) British. 1968: *Interlude* (Best Supporting Actress) *Board*, British.

Mason, James
Movie: 1953: *The Desert Rats* (Best Actor) *Board* (multiple win); *Face to Face* (Best Actor) *Board* (multiple win); *Julius Caesar* (Best Actor) *Board* (multiple win); *The Man Between* (Best Actor) *Board* (multiple win). 1954: *A Star Is Born* (Best Actor) Academy (Best Actor, Musical or Comedy) *Globe.* 1962: *Lolita* (Best Actor, Drama) Globe (Best British Actor) British. 1966: *Georgy Girl* (Best Supporting Actor) Academy. 1967: *The Deadly Affair* (Best British Actor) British. 1982: *The Verdict* (Best Supporting Actor) Academy, Globe.

Mason, Marsha
Movie: 1973: *Cinderella Liberty* (Best Actress) Academy (Best Actress, Drama) *Globe.* 1977: *The Goodbye Girl* (Best Actress) Academy, British (Best Actress, Musical or Comedy) *Globe.* 1979: *Chapter*

Two (Best Actress) Academy (Best Actress, Musical or Comedy) Globe; *Promises in the Dark* (Best Actress, Drama) Globe. 1981: *Only When I Laugh* (Best Actress) Academy. **Television:** 1997: *Frasier* (Best Guest Actress in a Comedy Series) Emmy. **Records:** In 1977, Mason (for *The Goodbye Girl*) and Diane Keaton (in *Annie Hall*) became the first actors to tie in a lead acting race at the Golden Globes.

Massey, Daniel

Movie: 1968: *Star!* (New Star of the Year — Actor) Globe (Best Supporting Actor) Academy, *Globe.* **Highlights:** Massey received his only award accolades portraying his real life godfather, Noel Coward, in the 1968 film *Star!*

Massey, Raymond

Movie: 1940: *Abe Lincoln in Illinois* (Best Actor) Academy.

Massie, Paul

Movie: 1958: *Orders to Kill* (Most Promising Newcomer) *British.*

Mastandrea, Valerio

Movie: 2002: *Velocità massima* (Best Actor) Venice (special award).

Masterson, Mary Stuart

Movie: 1989: *Immediate Family* (Best Supporting Actress) *Board.* **Theater:** 2003: *Nine, the Musical* (Best Actress in a Featured Role, Musical) Tony.

Mastrantonio, Mary Elizabeth

Movie: 1986: *The Color of Money* (Best Supporting Actress) Academy, Globe. **Theater:** 2003: *Man of La Mancha* (Best Actress, Musical) Tony.

Mastroianni, Chiara

Movie: 1994: *Prêt-à-Porter (Ready-to-Wear)* (Best Ensemble) *Board.*

Mastroianni, Marcello

Movie: 1962: *Divorce—Italian Style* (Best Actor) Academy (Best Actor, Musical or Comedy) *Globe* (Best Foreign Actor) *British.* 1963: *Yesterday, Today and Tomorrow* (Best Foreign Actor) *British.* 1964: *Marriage, Italian Style* (Best Actor, Musical or Comedy) Globe. 1970: *Dramma della gelosia ... tutti i particolari in cronaca (A Drama of Jealousy or Jealousy, Italian Style or The Pizza Triangle)* (Best Actor) *Cannes.* 1977: *A Special Day* (Best Actor) Academy (Best Actor, Drama) Globe. 1987: *Dark*

Eyes (Best Actor) Academy, *Cannes.* 1989: *Che ora è?* (Best Actor) *Venice* (win shared with costar). 1992: *Used People* (Best Actor, Musical or Comedy) Globe. 1993: *Un, deux, trios, soliel* (Best Supporting Actor) *Venice.* 1994: *Prêt-à-Porter (Ready-to-Wear)* (Best Ensemble) *Board.* **Tributes:** 1964, 1965: Henrietta Award for World Film Favorite from Globe. 1990: Career Golden Lion from Venice.

Matarazzo, Heather

Movie: 1996: *Welcome to the Dollhouse* (Best Debut Performance) *Spirit.*

Matlin, Marlee

Movie: 1986: *Children of a Lesser God* (Best Actress) *Academy* (Best Actress, Drama) *Globe.* **Television:** 1991–1993 series *Reasonable Doubts* (Best Actress in a Drama Series) 1991: Globe. 1992: Globe. 1994: *Picket Fences* (Best Guest Actress in a Drama Series) Emmy; *Seinfeld* (Best Guest Actress in a Comedy Series) Emmy. 2000: *The Practice* (Best Guest Actress in a Drama Series) Emmy. 2004: *Law & Order: Special Victims Unit* (Best Guest Actress in a Drama Series) Emmy. **Records:** Matlin's Academy Award win for *Children of a Lesser God* set three Oscar records. At 21, she became the youngest star to win a lead actor trophy. Hers was the first Oscar winning performance directed by a female (Randa Haines). After Harold Russell, who lost his hands in World War II and won Best Supporting Actor for *The Best Years of Our Lives* in 1946, Matlin became the second actor (and first female) with a physical handicap to win a competitive Oscar. (Matlin became deaf at 18 months of age as the result of a fever.)

Matthau, Walter

Movie: 1966: *The Fortune Cookie* (Best Actor, Musical or Comedy) Globe (Best Supporting Actor) *Academy.* 1968: *The Odd Couple* (Best Actor, Musical or Comedy) Globe; *The Secret Life of an American Wife* (Best Actor) British. 1971: *Kotch* (Best Actor) Academy (Best Actor, Musical or Comedy) Globe. 1972: *Pete 'n' Tillie* (Best Actor, Musical or Comedy) Globe (Best Actor) *British* (multiple win). 1973: *Charley Varrick* (Best Actor) *British* (multiple win). 1974: *The Front Page* (Best Actor, Musical or Comedy) Globe. 1975: *The Sunshine Boys* (Best Actor) Academy, British (multiple nomination), (Best Actor, Musical or Comedy) *Globe.* 1976: *The Bad News Bears* (Best Actor) British (multiple nomination). 1980: *Hopscotch* (Best Actor, Musical or Comedy) Globe. 1981: *First Monday in October* (Best Actor, Musical or Comedy) Globe. **Theater:** 1959: *Once More, with Feeling* (Best

Supporting or Featured Actor, Dramatic) Tony. 1962: *A Shot in the Dark* (Best Supporting or Featured Actor, Dramatic) *Tony*. 1965: *The Odd Couple* (Best Actor, Dramatic) *Tony*. Television: 1963: *"Big Deal in Laredo," DuPont Show of the Week* (Best Single Performance by an Actor in a Leading Role) Emmy. **Highlights:** Matthau was the only one of the four acting stars present to accept his Best Supporting Actor award for *The Fortune Cookie* on Oscar night. Best Actor Paul Scofield stayed home in London and let his *A Man for All Seasons* co-star, Wendy Hiller accept for him. Liz Taylor stayed away that year with husband and *Who's Afraid of Virginia Woolf?* co-star Richard Burton because it looked as though Burton would be snubbed once more by Oscar (he was), so Anne Bancroft picked up the prize for Taylor. Supporting Actress Sandy Dennis was in New York working on a film, explained *Woolf* director Mike Nichols when he accepted on her behalf. Yet of the four, Matthau was physically least able to attend, as he came to the podium with a bruised face and a cast on his arm after recently surviving a bicycle accident on the Pacific Coast Highway. On the arms of presenter Shelley Winters, Matthau looks beat up but beaming in Oscar photos.

Maura, Carmen

Movie: 2006: *Volver* (Best Actress) *Cannes* (win shared with costars).

Maxwell, Lois

Movie: 1947: *That Hagen Girl* (New Star of the Year — Actress) *Globe*. **Records:** In 1947, fifteen years before beginning her regular stint as Miss Moneypenny in the James Bond films, Canadian-born Maxwell won the first New Star of the Year — Actress award ever presented at the Golden Globes.

May, Elaine

Movie: 1971: *A New Leaf* (Best Actress, Musical or Comedy) Globe. 1978: *Heaven Can Wait* (Best Adapted Screenplay) Academy. 1998: *Primary Colors* (Best Adapted Screenplay) Academy (Best Screenplay) *British*. 2000: *Small Time Crooks* (Best Supporting Actress) *Society*.

May, Jodhi

Movie: 1988: *A World Apart* (Best Actress) *Cannes* (win shared with costars).

Mayniel, Juliette

Movie: 1960: *Kirmes* (Best Actress) *Berlin*.

Mayron, Melanie

Movie: 1978: *Girlfriends* (Most Promising Newcomer) British. **Television:** 1987–1991 series *thirtysomething* (Best Supporting Actress in a Drama Series) 1989: *Emmy*. 1990: Emmy. 1991: Emmy.

McAnally, Ray

Movie: 1986: *The Mission* (Best Supporting Actor) *British*. 1989: *My Left Foot* (Best Supporting Actor) *British*.

McAndrew, Marianne

Movie: 1969: *Hello, Dolly!* (New Star of the Year — Actress) Globe (Best Supporting Actress) Globe.

McAvoy, James

Movie: 2006: *The Last King of Scotland* (Best Supporting Actor) British. 2007: *Atonement* (Best Actor) British (Best Actor, Drama) Globe.

McCambridge, Mercedes

Movie: 1949: *All the King's Men* (New Star of the Year — Actress) *Globe* (Best Supporting Actress) *Academy, Globe*. 1956: *Giant* (Best Supporting Actress) Academy. **Theater:** 1972: *The Love Suicide at Schofield Barracks* (Best Supporting or Featured Actress, Dramatic) Tony. **Records:** McCambridge is the first actor to win two Golden Globes for the same performance. Her first film role, as mentally unstable Sadie Burke in *All the King's Men*, not only earned her the Best Supporting Actress prize, but also made her the Globe's New Star of the Year — Actress, a category given by the Hollywood Foreign Press only once before. That previous time, as well as in the case of the New Actor award in 1949, the New Star awards went to actors other than those who won in the familiar lead and supporting categories. During her Oscar acceptance speech, she encouraged aspiring actresses to never give up, and to hold on to their dreams.

McCamus, Tom

Movie: 1997: *The Sweet Hereafter* (Best Ensemble) *Board*.

McCarthy, Kevin

Movie: 1951: *Death of a Salesman* (New Star of the Year — Actor) *Globe* (Best Supporting Actor) Academy.

McCarthy, Nobu

Movie: 1988: *The Wash* (Best Female Lead) Spirit.

McCarthy, Sheila

Movie: 1991: *Bright Angel* (Best Supporting Female) Spirit.

McCarthy, Thomas

Movie: 2005: *Good Night, and Good Luck* (Best Ensemble) SAG, Broadcast.

McCartney, Paul

Movie: 1964: *A Hard Day's Night* (Most Promising Newcomer, with The Beatles) British. 1970: *Let It Be* (Best Song Score, with The Beatles) *Academy.* 1973: *Live and Let Die* (Best Song, "Live and Let Die") Academy. 1984: *Give My Regards to Broad Street* (Best Song, "No More Lonely Nights") Globe, British. 2001: *Vanilla Sky* (Best Song, "Vanilla Sky") Academy, Globe.

McCormack, Patty

Movie: 1956: *The Bad Seed* (Best Supporting Actress) Academy, Globe.

McCowen, Alec

Movie: 1972: *Travels with My Aunt* (Best Supporting Actor) Globe. Theater: 1969: *Hadrian VII* (Best Actor, Dramatic) Tony. 1971: *The Philanthropist* (Best Actor, Dramatic) Tony. 1979: *St. Mark's Gospel* (Best Actor, Play) Tony.

McCrea, Joel

Tributes: 1987: Career Achievement Award from LA.

McCutcheon, Martine

Movie: 2003: *Love Actually* (Best Ensemble) Broadcast.

McDaniel, Hattie

Movie: 1939: *Gone with the Wind* (Best Supporting Actress) *Academy.* 1942: *In This Our Life* (Best Acting) *Board.* Records: McDaniel's Best Supporting Actress Academy Award for *Gone with the Wind* in 1939 made her the first African-American to win an acting Oscar. She attended the Oscar ceremony that year, making her the first African-American to do that as well. When Fay Bainter announced Mc-Daniel's name as Best Supporting Actress, McDaniel shouted, "Hallelujah!" and bounded toward the stage. In her tearful acceptance speech, she said that winning the Oscar was the happiest moment of her life, and that she would always work to be a credit to her race and to the motion picture industry.

McDonnell, Mary

Movie: 1990: *Dances with Wolves* (Best Supporting Actress) Academy, Globe. 1992: *Passion Fish* (Best Actress) Academy (Best Actress, Drama) Globe. Television: 2002: *ER* (Best Guest Actress in a Drama Series) Emmy.

McDormand, Frances

Movie: 1988: *Mississippi Burning* (Best Supporting Actress) Academy, *Board.* 1993: *Short Cuts* (Best Ensemble) *Venice* (special award). 1996: *Fargo* (Best Actress) *Academy, Board,* British, *Broadcast* (Best Actress, Musical or Comedy) Globe (Best Female Actor in a Leading Role) *SAG* (Best Female Lead) *Spirit.* 2000: *Almost Famous* (Best Female Actor in a Supporting Role) SAG (Best Supporting Actress) Academy, Globe, British, *LA* (multiple win), *Broadcast* (multiple win), (Best Ensemble) SAG; *Wonder Boys* (Best Supporting Actress) *LA* (multiple win), *Broadcast* (multiple win). 2003: *Laurel Canyon* (Best Supporting Female) Spirit. 2005: *North Country* (Best Female Actor in a Supporting Role) SAG (Best Supporting Actress) Academy, Globe, British, Broadcast. 2006: *Friends with Money* (Best Supporting Female) *Spirit.* Theater: 1988: *A Streetcar Named Desire* (Best Actress, Play) Tony. Television: 1997: *Hidden in America* (Best Supporting Actress in a Miniseries or Special) Emmy.

McDowall, Roddy

Movie: 1941: *How Green Was My Valley* (Best Acting) *Board.* 1963: *Cleopatra* (Best Supporting Actor) Globe. Theater: 1960: *The Fighting Cock* (Best Supporting or Featured Actor, Dramatic) *Tony.* Television: 1961: *"Not Without Honor," Equitable's American Heritage* (Best Single Performance by a Supporting Actor or Actress) *Emmy.* 1964: *Arrest and Trial* (Best Single Performance by an Actor in a Leading Role) Emmy. Records: The Board of Governors of the Academy of Motion Picture Arts and Sciences unanimously decided to name the collection of still photographs in the Academy's official library, the Margaret Herrick Library, the Roddy McDowall Photograph Archive. No other actor has been so honored. McDowall, a respected actor since his youth and an Academy governor, was a revered still photographer. He had many famous clients such as his personal friends, Natalie Wood and Elizabeth Taylor, and some stars would only allow McDowall to photograph them.

McDowell, Malcolm

Movie: 1971: *A Clockwork Orange* (Best Actor, Drama) Globe.

McEnery, John

Movie: 1968: *Romeo and Juliet* (Best Supporting Actor) British.

McFadden, Davenia

Movie: 2001: *Stranger Inside* (Best Supporting Female) Spirit.

McGillis, Kelly

Movie: 1985: *Witness* (Best Actress) British (Best Supporting Actress) Globe.

McGiveney, Maura

Movie: 1965: *Do Not Disturb* (New Star of the Year — Actress) Globe.

McGovern, Elizabeth

Movie: 1981: *Ragtime* (New Star of the Year — Actor or Actress) Globe (Best Supporting Actress) Academy.

McGowan, Rose

Movie: 1995: *The Doom Generation* (Best Debut Performance) Spirit.

McGrath, Douglas

Movie: 1998: *Happiness* (Best Ensemble) *Board*.

McGregor, Ewan

Movie: 1998: *Little Voice* (Best Ensemble) SAG. 2001: *Moulin Rouge!* (Best Actor, Musical or Comedy) Globe (Best Ensemble) SAG. **Television:** 1997: *ER* (Best Guest Actor in a Drama Series) Emmy.

McGuire, Dorothy

Movie: 1947: *Gentleman's Agreement* (Best Actress) Academy. 1956: *Friendly Persuasion* (Best Actress) *Board*. **Television:** 1955: *"The Giaconda Smile," Climax* (Best Actress in a Single Performance) Emmy. 1976: *Rich Man, Poor Man* (Best Supporting Actress in a Drama Series) Emmy. 1986: *Amos* (Best Supporting Actress in a Miniseries or Special) Emmy.

McKean, Michael

Movie: 2003: *A Mighty Wind* (Best Screenplay) Spirit (Best Original Song, "A Kiss at the End of the Rainbow") Academy (Best Song, "A Mighty Wind") *Broadcast* (Best Ensemble) Broadcast.

McKellen, Ian

Movie: 1995: *Richard III* (Best Actor) British (Best Actor, Drama) Globe (Best Adapted Screenplay) British. 1998: *Apt Pupil* (Best Actor) *Broadcast* (multiple win); *Gods and Monsters* (Best Actor) Academy, *Board, LA, Broadcast* (multiple win), (Best Actor, Drama) Globe (Best Male Lead) *Spirit* (Best Male Actor in a Leading Role) SAG. 2001: *The Lord of the Rings: The Fellowship of the Ring* (Best Actor) British (Best Male Actor in a Supporting Role) *SAG* (Best Supporting Actor) Academy (Best Ensemble) SAG. 2002: *The Lord of the Rings: The Two Towers* (Best Ensemble) SAG. 2003: *The Lord of the Rings: The Return of the King* (Best Supporting Actor) British (Best Ensemble) *Board, SAG, Broadcast.* **Theater:** 1981: *Amadeus* (Best Actor, Play) *Tony*. 1984: *Ian McKellen Acting Shakespeare* (Best Actor, Play) Tony. **Television:** 1996: *Rasputin* (Best Supporting Actor in a Miniseries or Special) Emmy (Best Supporting Actor in a Series, Miniseries, or TV Movie) *Globe*. 2007: *Extras* (Best Guest Actor in a Comedy Series) Emmy. **Tributes:** 2006: Honorary Golden Bear from Berlin.

McKenna, Virginia

Movie: 1956: *A Town Like Alice* (Best British Actress) *British*. 1958: *Carve Her Name with Pride* (Best British Actress) British. 1966: *Born Free* (Best Actress, Drama) Globe.

McKeon, Doug

Movie: 1978: *Uncle Joe Shannon* (New Star of the Year — Actor) Globe.

McKern, Leo

Movie: 1968: *The Shoes of the Fisherman* (Best Supporting Actor) *Board*.

McLachlan, Rod

Movie: 1999: *Magnolia* (Best Ensemble) *Board, SAG*.

McLaglen, Victor

Movie: 1935: *The Informer* (Best Actor) *Academy*. 1952: *The Quiet Man* (Best Supporting Actor) Academy.

McNamara, Maggie

Movie: 1953: *The Moon Is Blue* (Most Promising Newcomer) British (Best Actress) Academy.

McNeil, Claudia

Movie: 1961: *A Raisin in the Sun* (Best Actress, Drama) Globe (Best Foreign Actress) British. **Theater:** 1960: *A Raisin in the Sun* (Best Actress, Dramatic) Tony. 1963: *Tiger Tiger Burning Bright* (Best

Actress, Dramatic) Tony. **Television:** 1962–1965 series *The Nurses* (Best Performance by an Actress in a Supporting Role) 1964: Emmy.

McNichol, Kristy

Movie: 1981: *Only When I Laugh* (Best Supporting Actress) Globe. **Television:** 1976–1980 series *Family* (Best Actress in a Drama Series) 1978: Globe. 1980: Emmy. (Best Continuing Performance by a Supporting Actress in a Drama Series) 1977: *Emmy*. 1978: Emmy. (Best Supporting Actress in a Drama Series) 1979: *Emmy*.

McQueen, Steve

Movie: 1963: *Love with the Proper Stranger* (Best Actor, Drama) Globe. 1966: *The Sand Pebbles* (Best Actor) Academy (Best Actor, Drama) Globe. 1969: *The Reivers* (Best Actor, Musical or Comedy) Globe. 1973: *Papillon* (Best Actor, Drama) Globe. **Tributes:** 1966, 1969: Henrietta Award for World Film Favorite from Globe.

McTeer, Janet

Movie: 1999: *Tumbleweeds* (Best Actress) Academy, *Board* (Best Actress, Musical or Comedy) *Globe* (Best Female Actor in a Leading Role) SAG (Best Female Lead) Spirit. **Theater:** 1997: *A Doll's House* (Best Actress, Play) *Tony*.

Meaney, Colm

Movie: 1993: *The Snapper* (Best Actor, Musical or Comedy) Globe.

Medford, Kay

Movie: 1968: *Funny Girl* (Best Supporting Actress) Academy. **Theater:** 1964: *Funny Girl* (Best Supporting or Featured Actress, Musical) Tony.

Medvedev, Vadim

Movie: 1954: *Bolshaya semya (The Big Family)* *Cannes* (special ensemble award).

Melvin, Murray

Movie: 1961: *A Taste of Honey* (Most Promising Newcomer) British (Best Acting) *Cannes* (special award shared with costar).

Menjou, Adolphe

Movie: 1931: *The Front Page* (Best Actor) Academy.

Menzel, Idina

Movie: 2005: *Rent* (Best Ensemble) Broadcast. **Theater:** 1996: *Rent* (Best Actress in a Featured Role,

Musical) Tony. 2004: *Wicked* (Best Actress, Musical) *Tony*.

Merchant, Vivien

Movie: 1966: *Alfie* (Most Promising Newcomer) *British* (Best Supporting Actress) Academy, *Board*, Globe. 1973: *The Homecoming* (Best Supporting Actress) British. **Theater:** 1967: *The Homecoming* (Best Actress, Dramatic) Tony.

Mercouri, Melina

Movie: 1960: *Never on Sunday* (Best Actress) Academy, *Cannes* (Best Foreign Actress) British. 1962: *Phaedra* (Best Foreign Actress) British (Best Actress, Drama) Globe. 1964: *Topkapi* (Best Actress, Musical or Comedy) Globe. 1970: *Promise at Dawn* (Best Actress, Drama) Globe. **Theater:** 1968: *Illya Darling* (Best Actress, Musical) Tony.

Mercure, Monique

Movie: 1977: *J. A. Martin, Photographer* (Best Actress) *Cannes*.

Meredith, Burgess

Movie: 1962: *Advise and Consent* (Best Supporting Actor) *Board*. 1975: *The Day of the Locust* (Best Supporting Actor) Academy, Globe, British. 1976: *Rocky* (Best Supporting Actor) Academy. **Theater:** 1974: *Ulysses in Nighttown* (Best Director, Dramatic) Tony. **Television:** 1977: *"Tail Gunner Joe," The Big Event* (Best Supporting Actor in a Comedy or Drama Special) *Emmy*. 1978: *"The Last Hurrah," Hallmark Hall of Fame* (Best Supporting Actor in a Comedy or Drama Special) Emmy. **Tributes:** 1960: Special award for *A Thurber Carnival* from Tony.

Merkel, Una

Movie: 1961: *Summer and Smoke* (Best Supporting Actress) Academy. **Theater:** 1956: *The Ponder Heart* (Best Featured Actress, Play) *Tony*.

Merkerson, S. Epatha

Movie: 2005: *Lackawanna Blues* (Best Female Lead) Spirit. **Theater:** 1990: *The Piano Lesson* (Best Actress in a Featured Role, Play) Tony. **Television:** 1990–present series *Law & Order* (Best Ensemble in a Drama Series) 1994: SAG. 1995: SAG. 1996: SAG. 1997: SAG. 1998: SAG. 1999: SAG. 2000: SAG. 2001: SAG. 2003: SAG. 2005: *Lackawanna Blues* (Best Actress in a Miniseries or TV Movie) *Emmy, Globe* (Best Female Actor in a Television Movie or Miniseries) *SAG*.

Merman, Ethel

Movie: 1953: *Call Me Madam* (Best Actress, Musical or Comedy) *Globe*. Theater: 1951: *Call Me Madam* (Best Actress, Musical) *Tony*. 1957: *Happy Hunting* (Best Actress, Musical) Tony. 1960: *Gypsy* (Best Actress, Musical) Tony. Tributes: 1972: Special award from Tony.

Metkina, Svetlana

Movie: 2006: *Bobby* (Best Ensemble) SAG, Broadcast.

Metzler, Jim

Movie: 1982: *Tex* (Best Supporting Actor) Globe.

Mezzogiorno, Giovanna

Movie: 1998: *L'Albero delle pere* (Best Actress) *Venice*. 2005: *La Bestia nel cuore (The Beast in the Heart)* (Best Actress) *Venice*.

Middleton, Noelle

Movie: 1954: *Carrington V.C.* (Best British Actress) British.

Midler, Bette

Movie: 1979: *The Rose* (New Star of the Year — Actress) *Globe* (Best Actress) Academy, British (Best Actress, Musical or Comedy) *Globe*. 1980: *Divine Madness* (Best Actress, Musical or Comedy) Globe. 1986: *Down and Out in Beverly Hills* (Best Actress, Musical or Comedy) Globe. 1987: *Outrageous Fortune* (Best Actress, Musical or Comedy) Globe. 1991: *For the Boys* (Best Actress) Academy (Best Actress, Musical or Comedy) *Globe*. 1996: *The First Wives Club* (Best Ensemble) *Board*. Television: 1978: *Bette Midler—Ol' Red Hair Is Back* (Best Comedy-Variety or Music Special, Star) *Emmy* (Best Writing of a Comedy-Variety or Music Special) Emmy. 1992: *The Tonight Show Starring Johnny Carson* (Best Individual Performance in a Variety or Music Program, Performer) *Emmy*. 1994: *Gypsy* (Best Actress in a Miniseries or Special) Emmy (Best Actress in a Miniseries or TV Movie) *Globe*. 1997: *Bette Midler: Diva Las Vegas* (Best Performance in a Variety or Music Program) *Emmy* (Best Variety, Music, or Comedy Special; Executive Producer) Emmy. 1998: *Murphy Brown* (Best Guest Actress in a Comedy Series) Emmy. 2000–2001 series *Bette* (Best Actress in a Series, Musical or Comedy) 2001: Globe. Tributes: 1974: Special award for adding luster to the Broadway season from Tony. Records: Midler has the rare distinction of winning both the Grammy for New Artist of the Year (where she beat Eumit Deodato,

Maureen McGovern, Marie Osmond, and Barry White) and the Golden Globe for New Female Star of the Year for her performance in *The Rose* (winning over Susan Anton, Bo Derek, Lisa Eichhorn, and Lynn-Holly Johnson).

Mifune, Toshirô

Movie: 1955: *The Seven Samurai* (Best Foreign Actor) British. 1961: *Yojimbo* (Best Actor) *Venice*. 1965: *Akahige* (Best Actor) *Venice*. Television: 1981: *Shogun* (Best Actor in a Limited Series or Special) Emmy.

Miles, Bernard

Movie: 1942: *In Which We Serve* (Best Acting) *Board*.

Miles, Sarah

Movie: 1962: *Term of Trial* (Most Promising Newcomer) British. 1963: *The Servant* (Best British Actress) British. 1970: *Ryan's Daughter* (Best Actress) Academy, British (Best Actress, Drama) Globe. 1976: *The Sailor Who Fell from Grace with the Sea* (Best Actress, Drama) Globe. 1987: *Hope and Glory* (Best Actress) British.

Miles, Sylvia

Movie: 1969: *Midnight Cowboy* (Best Supporting Actress) Academy. 1975: *Farewell, My Lovely* (Best Supporting Actress) Academy.

Milford, Penelope

Movie: 1978: *Coming Home* (Best Supporting Actress) Academy.

Milian, Tomas

Movie: 2000: *Traffic* (Best Ensemble) *SAG*.

Milicevic, Ivana

Movie: 2003: *Love Actually* (Best Ensemble) Broadcast.

Milland, Ray

Movie: 1945: *The Lost Weekend* (Best Actor) *Academy, New York, Board, Globe, Cannes*. 1952: *The Thief* (Best Actor, Drama) Globe. Television: 1976: *Rich Man, Poor Man* (Best Supporting Actor in a Drama Series) Emmy. Records: Few performances have gained as much award recognition as Milland's haunted alcoholic, Don Birnam, in Billy Wilder's *The Lost Weekend*, the film that tackled a social problem more unflinchingly than perhaps any before it. Besides sweeping every competitive and critical acting award given at the time, Milland also won the first Best Actor prize ever given at the Cannes Film Festival. Thanks to his Academy Award win for the movie, Milland holds the record for the shortest acceptance speech in Oscar history. When Ingrid Bergman announced him the winner, Milland's wife elbowed him in the ribs to prompt him to get his award. Once at the podium, the overwhelmed Milland said nothing. He simply grinned, bowed, and exited the stage.

Miller, Jason

Movie: 1973: *The Exorcist* (Best Supporting Actor) Academy. Theater: 1973: *That Championship Season* (Best Play, Writer) *Tony*.

Miller, Mandy

Movie: 1952: *Mandy* (Most Promising Newcomer) British.

Miller, Penelope Ann

Movie: 1993: *Carlito's Way* (Best Supporting Actress) Globe. Theater: 1989: *Our Town* (Best Actress in a Featured Role, Play) Tony.

Miller, Sienna

Movie: 2007: *Interview* (Best Female Lead) Spirit.

Mills, Hayley

Movie: 1959: *Tiger Bay* (Most Promising Newcomer) *British*. 1960: *Pollyanna* (New Star of the Year — Actress) *Globe* (Best Actress) British. 1961: *The Parent Trap* (Best Actress, Musical or Comedy) Globe; *Whistle Down the Wind* (Best Actress) British. 1963: *Summer Magic* (Best Actress, Musical or Comedy) Globe. Tributes: 1959: Silver Bear Extraordinary Prize of the Jury for *Tiger Bay* from Berlin. 1960: Special miniature Oscar statuette for the most outstanding juvenile performance during 1960 for *Pollyanna* from Academy. Records: Mills was the last young star to receive a special juvenile Academy Award. After she was honored for her appealing performance as the eternally optimistic *Pollyanna*, the Academy stopped giving children special awards (they gave 12 in all) and began including minors for consideration only in the competitive acting categories. Shirley Temple, the first person to receive the honor back in 1934, presented Mills with her miniature statuette.

Mills, John

Movie: 1942: *In Which We Serve* (Best Acting) *Board*. 1954: *Hobson's Choice* (Best British Actor) British. 1960: *Tunes of Glory* (Best Actor) *Venice* (Best British Actor) British. 1970: *Ryan's Daughter*

(Best Supporting Actor) *Academy, Globe*, British. Theater: 1962: *Ross* (Best Actor, Dramatic) Tony. Records: John Mills and daughter Hayley are the first to be father and daughter Oscar-winning actors. In 1960, Hayley received a special juvenile Academy Award for her performance in *Pollyanna*. Mills joined her in the winner's circle ten years later when he was named Best Supporting Actor for his much-lauded performance as a mute vagabond in David Lean's *Ryan's Daughter*.

Mills, Juliet

Movie: 1972: *Avanti!* (Best Actress, Musical or Comedy) Globe. Theater: 1960: *Five Finger Exercise* (Best Supporting or Featured Actress, Dramatic) Tony. Television: 1970–1971 series *Nanny and the Professor* (Best Actress in a Series, Musical or Comedy) 1971: Globe. 1975: *"QB VII,"* ABC Movie Special (Best Single Performance by a Supporting Actress in a Comedy or Drama Special) *Emmy*.

Mimieux, Yvette

Movie: 1959: *Platinum High School* (New Star of the Year — Actress) Globe. Television: 1964: *Dr. Kildare* (Best Actress in a Series) Globe. 1970–1971 series *The Most Deadly Game* (Best Actress in a Drama Series) 1970: Globe.

Mineo, Sal

Movie: 1955: *Rebel Without a Cause* (Best Supporting Actor) Academy. 1960: *Exodus* (Best Supporting Actor) Academy, *Globe*. Television: 1957: *"Dino,"* Studio One (Best Single Performance by an Actor) Emmy.

Minnelli, Liza

Movie: 1969: *The Sterile Cuckoo (Pookie)* (Most Promising Newcomer) British (Best Actress) Academy (Best Actress, Drama) Globe. 1972: *Cabaret* (Best Actress) *Academy, British* (Best Actress, Musical or Comedy) *Globe*. 1975: *Lucky Lady* (Best Actress, Musical or Comedy) Globe. 1977: *New York, New York* (Best Actress, Musical or Comedy) Globe. 1981: *Arthur* (Best Actress, Musical or Comedy) Globe. Theater: 1965: *Flora, the Red Menace* (Best Actress, Musical) *Tony*. 1978: *The Act* (Best Actress, Musical) *Tony*. 1984: *The Rink* (Best Actress, Musical) Tony. Television: 1973: *A Royal Gala Variety Performance in the Presence of Her Majesty the Queen* (Best Supporting Performer in Music or Variety) Emmy; *Singer Presents "Liza with a 'Z'"* (Best Single Program in Variety or Popular Music, Star) *Emmy*. 1980: *Goldie and Liza Together* (Best Variety or Music Program, Star) Emmy. 1985: *A Time to Live* (Best Actress in a Miniseries or TV Movie)

Globe. 1987: ***Minnelli on Minnelli: Liza Remembers Vincente*** (Best Informational Special, Host) *Emmy.* 1993: ***Liza Minnelli Live from Radio City Music Hall*** (Best Individual Performance in a Variety or Music Program) *Emmy.* **Tributes:** 1974: Special award for adding luster to the Broadway season from Tony. **Records:** Winning the Best Actress Oscar for 1972's ***Cabaret*** made Minnelli and her parents the first family of Oscar winners. Her mother, Judy Garland, received a special juvenile Oscar statuette in 1939, and her father, Vincente Minnelli, was named Best Director in 1958 for ***Gigi.***

Miracle, Irene

Movie: 1978: ***Midnight Express*** (New Star of the Year—Actress) *Globe.*

Miranda, Isa

Movie: 1949: ***The Walls of Malapaga*** (Best Actress) *Cannes.*

Mirren, Helen

Movie: 1984: ***Cal*** (Best Actress) *Cannes,* British. 1994: ***The Madness of King George*** (Best Actress) British, *Cannes* (Best Supporting Actress) Academy. 2001: ***Gosford Park*** (Best Female Actor in a Supporting Role) *SAG* (Best Supporting Actress) Academy, *New York,* Globe, British, *Society* (Best Ensemble) *SAG,* Broadcast; ***Last Orders*** (Best Ensemble) *Board.* 2003: ***Calendar Girls*** (Best Actress, Musical or Comedy) Globe. 2006: ***The Queen*** (Best Actress) *Academy, Venice, New York, Board, British, Society, LA, Broadcast* (Best Actress, Drama) *Globe* (Best Female Actor in a Leading Role) *SAG.* **Theater:** 1995: ***A Month in the Country*** (Best Actress, Play) Tony. 2002: ***Dance of Death*** (Best Actress, Play) Tony. **Television:** 1993: ***Prime Suspect 2 (Mystery!)*** (Best Actress in a Miniseries or Special) Emmy. 1994: ***Prime Suspect 3 (Mystery!)*** (Best Actress in a Miniseries or Special) Emmy. 1996: ***Prime Suspect: Scent of Darkness*** (Best Actress in a Miniseries or Special) *Emmy;* ***Losing Chase*** (Best Actress in a Miniseries or TV Movie) *Globe.* 1997: ***Prime Suspect 5: Errors of Judgment*** (Best Actress in a Miniseries or Special) Emmy. 1999: ***The Passion of Ayn Rand*** (Best Actress in a Miniseries or TV Movie) *Emmy,* Globe (Best Female Actor in a Television Movie or Miniseries) SAG. 2002: ***Door to Door*** (Best Actress in a Miniseries or TV Movie) Globe (Best Female Actor in a Television Movie or Miniseries) SAG (Best Supporting Actress in a Miniseries or TV Movie) Emmy. 2003: ***Tennessee Williams' The Roman Spring of Mrs. Stone*** (Best Actress in a Miniseries or TV Movie) Emmy, Globe (Best Female Actor in a Television Movie or Miniseries) SAG. 2004: ***"Prime Suspect 6: The Last Witness," Masterpiece Theatre*** (Best Actress in a Miniseries or TV Movie) Emmy. 2006: ***Elizabeth I*** (Best Actress in a Miniseries or TV Movie) *Emmy, Globe* (Best Female Actor in a Television Movie or Miniseries) SAG. 2007: ***"Prime Suspect: The Final Act," Masterpiece Theatre*** (Best Actress in a Miniseries or TV Movie) *Emmy,* Globe. **Records:** In 2006 Mirren set an acting record by playing both Queen Elizabeth I and II. When she won the title role for the ***Elizabeth I*** television production, Mirren considered it a role of a lifetime, gave it her all, and swept every major award. At some of those same awards shows, such as the Golden Globes and SAGs, she won two awards, as ***The Queen*** did as much on the big screen as ***Elizabeth I*** did on the small. Mirren had gained so much award momentum winning Best Actress prizes from the major film committees and critics' organizations that by the night of the SAGs none of her four competitors even bothered to attend. It was a uniquely noticeable moment and a telling sign when during the announcement of the nominees, the camera panned only to Mirren, who moments earlier had accepted her award for ***Elizabeth I.*** Despite Oscar's penchant for an occasional last minute surprise and a tendency to honor younger actresses, Mirren sustained the momentum and became the first Best Actress nominee over age 60 to win the award since Jessica Tandy had nearly twenty years earlier.

Misner, Susan

Movie: 2002: ***Chicago*** (Best Ensemble) *SAG,* Broadcast.

Mitchell, John Cameron

Movie: 2001: ***Hedwig and the Angry Inch*** (Best Male Lead) Spirit (Best Actor, Musical or Comedy) Globe (Best Director) Spirit.

Mitchell, Millard

Movie: 1952: ***My Six Convicts*** (Best Supporting Actor) *Globe.*

Mitchell, Radha

Movie: 2004: ***Finding Neverland*** (Best Ensemble) SAG.

Mitchell, Thomas

Movie: 1937: ***The Hurricane*** (Best Supporting Actor) Academy. 1939: ***Stagecoach*** (Best Acting) *Board* (Best Supporting Actor) *Academy.* 1940: ***The Long Voyage Home*** (Best Acting) *Board.* 1942: ***Moontide*** (Best Acting) *Board.* **Theater:** 1953: ***Hazel Flagg*** (Best Actor, Musical) *Tony.* **Television:** 1952:

--- (Best Actor) Emmy. 1953: --- (Best Actor) *Emmy*. 1955: *"Good of His Soul," Ford Theatre* (Best Actor in a Single Performance) Emmy. **Records:** Along with Helen Hayes, Thomas Mitchell became the first star to win both an Oscar and an Emmy. Hayes won her first Academy Award in 1931/1932 when she was named Best Actress for *The Sin of Madelon Claudet* and Thomas Mitchell picked up a Best Supporting Actor golden boy for 1939's *Stagecoach*. On February 5, 1953, the Emmys voted Hayes Best Actress and Mitchell Best Actor for their television work of 1952. **Highlights:** 1939 was a great year for Mitchell. Even though he confessed in his acceptance speech that he didn't think he was that good, he won the Best Supporting Actor Oscar for *Stagecoach*. That same year he also had supporting roles in two other Oscar-winning movies, *Mr. Smith Goes to Washington* and *Gone with the Wind*, which won a record-setting ten Academy Awards. Of the 17 regular competition awards presented that night to full-length motion pictures, 11 went to films in which he starred: eight to *Gone with the Wind* (its other two awards were in technical and special non-competitive categories), two to *Stagecoach*, and one to *Smith*.

Mitchell, Yvonne

Movie: 1954: *The Divided Heart* (Best British Actress) *British*. 1957: *Woman in a Dressing Gown* (Best Actress) *Berlin*. 1959: *Sapphire* (Best British Actress) British.

Mitchum, Robert

Movie: 1945: *G. I. Joe* (Best Supporting Actor) Academy. 1957: *Heaven Knows, Mr. Allison* (Best Foreign Actor) British. 1960: *Home from the Hill* (Best Actor) *Board* (multiple win); *The Sundowners* (Best Actor) *Board* (multiple win). **Tributes:** 1980: Career Achievement Award from LA. 1991: Cecil B. DeMille Award from Globe. 1999: Ranked Number 23 on List of 25 Greatest Male Screen Legends of the 20th Century from American Film Institute.

Mobley, Mary Ann

Movie: 1964: *Get Yourself a College Girl* (New Star of the Year — Actress) *Globe*.

Möck, Manfred

Movie: 1988: *Bear Ye One Another's Burdens...* (Best Actor) *Berlin* (win shared with costar).

Modine, Matthew

Movie: 1983: *Streamers* (Best Actor) *Venice* (win shared with costars). 1993: *Equinox* (Best Male Lead) *Spirit*; *Short Cuts* (Best Ensemble) *Venice*

(special award). **Television:** 1994: *And the Band Played On* (Best Actor in a Miniseries or Special) Emmy (Best Actor in a Miniseries or TV Movie) Globe. 1997: *What the Deaf Man Heard* (Best Actor in a Miniseries or TV Movie) Globe.

Moffett, D. W.

Movie: 2000: *Traffic* (Best Ensemble) *SAG*.

Mol, Gretchen

Movie: 2007: *3:10 to Yuma* (Best Ensemble) SAG.

Molina, Alfred

Movie: 1997: *Boogie Nights* (Best Ensemble) SAG. 1999: *Magnolia* (Best Ensemble) *Board*, SAG. 2000: *Chocolat* (Best Ensemble) SAG. 2002: *Frida* (Best Male Actor in a Supporting Role) SAG (Best Supporting Actor) British, Broadcast. **Theater:** 1998: *Art* (Best Actor, Play) Tony. 2004: *Fiddler on the Roof* (Best Actor, Musical) Tony.

Monaghan, Dominic

Movie: 2001: *The Lord of the Rings: The Fellowship of the Ring* (Best Ensemble) SAG. 2002: *The Lord of the Rings: The Two Towers* (Best Ensemble) SAG. 2003: *The Lord of the Rings: The Return of the King* (Best Ensemble) *Board, SAG, Broadcast*.

Monaghan, Michelle

Movie: 2007: *Gone Baby Gone* (Best Ensemble) Broadcast.

Moniz, Lúcia

Movie: 2003: *Love Actually* (Best Ensemble) Broadcast.

Monroe, Marilyn

Movie: 1955: *The Seven Year Itch* (Best Foreign Actress) British. 1956: *Bus Stop* (Best Actress, Musical or Comedy) Globe. 1957: *The Prince and the Showgirl* (Best Foreign Actress) British. 1959: *Some Like It Hot* (Best Actress, Musical or Comedy) *Globe*. **Tributes:** 1953, 1961: Henrietta Award for World Film Favorite from Globe. 1999: Ranked Number 6 on List of 25 Greatest Female Screen Legends of the 20th Century from American Film Institute.

Montalban, Ricardo

Theater: 1958: *Jamaica* (Best Actor, Musical) Tony. **Television:** 1978: *How the West Was Won* (Best Single Performance by a Supporting Actor in a Comedy or Drama Series) *Emmy*. **Tributes:** 1993: Life Achievement Award from SAG.

Montand, Yves

Movie: 1960: *Let's Make Love* (Best Foreign Actor) British. 1987: *Jean De Florette* (Best Actor) British. **Television:** 1962: *Yves Montand on Broadway* (Best Performance in a Variety or Musical Program) Emmy. **Tributes:** 1988: Gala Tribute from Film Society of Lincoln Center.

Montenegro, Fernanda

Movie: 1998: *Central do Brasil (Central Station)* (Best Actress) Academy, *Board, Berlin, LA* (Best Actress, Drama) Globe.

Montgomery, Robert

Movie: 1937: *Night Must Fall* (Best Acting) *Board* (Best Actor) Academy. 1941: *Here Comes Mr. Jordan* (Best Acting) *Board* (multiple win), (Best Actor) Academy; *Rage in Heaven* (Best Acting) *Board* (multiple win). **Theater:** 1955: *The Desperate Hours* (Best Director) *Tony*. **Television:** 1952: --- (Best Actor) Emmy.

Moody, Ron

Movie: 1968: *Oliver!* (Best Actor) Academy, British (Best Actor, Musical or Comedy) *Globe*. **Theater:** 1984: *Oliver!* (Best Actor, Musical) Tony.

Moon, So-ri

Movie: 2002: *Oasis* (Best First Time Actor or Actress) *Venice*.

Moore, Demi

Movie: 1990: *Ghost* (Best Actress, Musical or Comedy) Globe. 2006: *Bobby* (Best Ensemble) SAG, Broadcast. **Television:** 1996: *If These Walls Could Talk* (Best Actress in a Miniseries or TV Movie) Globe (Best TV Movie, Executive Producer) Emmy.

Moore, Dudley

Movie: 1978: *Foul Play* (Best Supporting Actor) Globe. 1979: *10* (Best Actor, Musical or Comedy) Globe. 1981: *Arthur* (Best Actor) Academy (Best Actor, Musical or Comedy) *Globe*. 1982: *Six Weeks* (Best Score, Composer) Globe. 1984: *Micki + Maude* (Best Actor, Musical or Comedy) *Globe*. **Tributes:** 1963: Special award with the ensemble of *Beyond the Fringe* for their brilliance which has shattered all the old concepts of comedy from Tony. 1974: Special award with Peter Cook, co-stars and authors of *Good Evening* from Tony.

Moore, Grace

Movie: 1934: *One Night of Love* (Best Actress) Academy.

Moore, Juanita

Movie: 1959: *Imitation of Life* (Best Supporting Actress) Academy, Globe.

Moore, Julianne

Movie: 1993: *Short Cuts* (Best Supporting Female) Spirit (Best Ensemble) *Venice* (special award). 1995: *Safe* (Best Female Lead) Spirit. 1997: *Boogie Nights* (Best Female Actor in a Supporting Role) SAG (Best Supporting Actress) Academy, Globe, *Society, LA* (Best Ensemble) SAG. 1999: *Cookie's Fortune* (Best Supporting Actress) *Board* (multiple win); *The End of the Affair* (Best Actress) Academy, British (Best Actress, Drama) Globe (Best Female Actor in a Leading Role) SAG; *An Ideal Husband* (Best Actress, Musical or Comedy) Globe (Best Supporting Actress) *Board* (multiple win); *Magnolia* (Best Female Actor in a Supporting Role) SAG (Best Supporting Actress) *Board* (multiple win), (Best Ensemble) *Board*, SAG; *A Map of the World* (Best Supporting Actress) *Board* (multiple win). 2002: *Far from Heaven* (Best Actress) Academy, *Venice, Board, LA* (multiple win), *Broadcast* (Best Actress, Drama) Globe (Best Female Lead) *Spirit* (Best Female Actor in a Leading Role) SAG; *The Hours* (Best Actress) *Berlin* (win shared with costars), *LA* (multiple win), (Best Female Actor in a Supporting Role) SAG (Best Supporting Actress) Academy, British (Best Ensemble) SAG, Broadcast. 2007: *I'm Not There* (Best Ensemble) *Spirit* (special award). **Television:** 1985–1988 series *As the World Turns* (Best Ingénue in a Daytime Drama Series) 1988: *Emmy*. **Tributes:** In addition to winning the Venice Film Festival's Volpi Cup for Best Actress for *Far from Heaven*, Moore won a second Best Actress audience award. **Records:** With six, Moore currently holds the record for most SAG nominations for individual performances. Factor in the three nominations she earned as part of an ensemble, and her nine nominations also make her the most nominated person overall. To date, she has never won a SAG award.

Moore, Mary Tyler

Movie: 1980: *Ordinary People* (Best Actress) Academy, British (Best Actress, Drama) *Globe*. **Television:** 1961–1966 series *The Dick Van Dyke Show* (Best Actress in a Series) 1964: *Globe*. (Best Continued Performance by an Actress in a Series) 1963: Emmy. 1964: *Emmy*. (Best Continued Performance by an Actress in a Comedy Series) 1966: *Emmy*. 1970–1977 series *The Mary Tyler Moore Show* (Actress of the Year) 1974: *Emmy*. (Best Actress in a Series, Musical or Comedy) 1971: *Globe*. 1973: Globe. 1974: Globe. 1975: Globe. 1976: Globe. 1977: Globe. (Best Actress in a Leading Role, Musical or Comedy

Series or TV Movie) 1972: Globe. (Best Continued Performance by an Actress in a Leading Role in a Comedy Series) 1971: Emmy. 1972: Emmy. 1973: *Emmy*. (Best Actress in a Comedy Series) 1974: *Emmy*. 1975: Emmy. 1976: *Emmy*. 1977: Emmy. 1979: *First You Cry* (Best Actress in a Limited Series or Special) Emmy. 1985: *"Heartsounds," An ABC Theatre Presentation* (Best Actress in a Limited Series or Special) Emmy. 1988: *Gore Vidal's Lincoln* (Best Actress in a Miniseries or Special) Emmy. 1993: *Stolen Babies* (Best Supporting Actress in a Miniseries or Special) *Emmy*. **Tributes:** 1980: Special award for *Whose Life Is It Anyway?* from Tony. 1986: Television Hall of Fame Inductee from Emmy. **Records:** When she won her seventh Emmy in 1993, Moore set the record for most Emmy Awards for acting. Her closest competitor has most often been her co-star and friend, Ed Asner, who won most of his Emmys for *The Mary Tyler Moore Show*. Moore held the record until 2006 when Cloris Leachman, who won her first two Emmys playing landlord Phyllis Linstrum on *The Mary Tyler Moore Show*, set a new record with a ninth Emmy win for her guest appearance on *Malcolm in the Middle*. **Highlights:** The television show starring and named after Moore set the record for most Emmy wins when it received its 29th in the show's final season. *The Mary Tyler Moore Show* also inspired the most spin-offs, as *Rhoda, Phyllis*, and *Lou Grant* all began as characters on that show. Incidentally, all those spin-off shows garnered either Emmy or Golden Globe wins for their stars. In 1980 Robert Redford convinced Moore to take the role of emotionally clenched Beth Garrett in his film adaptation of Judith Guest's young adult novel that became an adult best seller, *Ordinary People*. In the role of a mother who cannot forgive her less favored son for surviving a boating accident that killed her favorite, Moore dug deep and found a hardness in her character that most fans had never seen from her before. Sadly, the tragic circumstance that propelled the plot of the film paralleled Moore's own life, as around that time her only son died.

Moore, Roger

Tributes: 1979: Henrietta Award for World Film Favorite from Globe.

Moore, Terry

Movie: 1952: *Come Back, Little Sheba* (Best Supporting Actress) Academy.

Moorehead, Agnes

Movie: 1942: *The Magnificent Ambersons* (Best Acting) *Board* (Best Actress) *New York* (Best Supporting

Actress) Academy. 1944: *Mrs. Parkington* (Best Supporting Actress) Academy, *Globe*. 1948: *Johnny Belinda* (Best Supporting Actress) Academy. 1964: *Hush ... Hush, Sweet Charlotte* (Best Supporting Actress) Academy, *Globe*. **Television:** 1964–1972 series *Bewitched* (Best Supporting Actress in a Comedy) 1966: Emmy. 1967: Emmy. 1968: Emmy. 1969: Emmy. 1970: Emmy. 1971: Emmy. 1967: *Wild, Wild West* (Best Supporting Actress in a Drama) *Emmy*.

More, Kenneth

Movie: 1953: *Genevieve* (Best British Actor) British. 1954: *Doctor in the House* (Best British Actor) *British*. 1955: *The Deep Blue Sea* (Best Actor) *Venice* (Best British Actor) British. 1956: *Reach for the Sky* (Best British Actor) British.

Moreau, Jeanne

Movie: 1960: *Moderato Cantabile* (Best Actress) *Cannes*. 1961: *Jules et Jim* (Best Foreign Actress) British. 1965: *The Sleeping Car Murders* (Best Foreign Actress) *British*. **Tributes:** 1992: Career Golden Lion from Venice. 2000: Honorary Golden Bear from Berlin.

Moreno, Catalina Sandino

Movie: 2004: *Maria Full of Grace* (New Generation) *LA* (Best Actress) Academy, *Berlin*, Broadcast (Best Female Actor in a Leading Role) SAG (Best Female Lead) *Spirit*.

Moreno, Rita

Movie: 1961: *West Side Story* (Best Supporting Actress) *Academy, Globe*. 1976: *The Ritz* (Best Actress) British (Best Actress, Musical or Comedy) Globe. **Theater:** 1975: *The Ritz* (Best Supporting or Featured Actress, Dramatic) *Tony*. **Television:** 1975: *Out to Lunch* (Best Continuing or Single Performance by a Supporting Actress in Variety or Music) Emmy. 1977: *The Muppet Show* (Best Continuing or Single Performance by a Supporting Actress in Variety or Music) *Emmy*. 1978–1979 series *The Rockford Files* (Best Single Appearance by an Actress in a Drama or Comedy Series) 1978: *Emmy*. (Best Actress in a Drama Series) 1979: Emmy. 1982: *Portrait of a Showgirl* (Best Supporting Actress in a Limited Series or Special) Emmy. 1982–1983 series *9 to 5* (Best Actress in a Comedy Series) 1983: Emmy. (Best Actress in a Series, Musical or Comedy) 1983: Globe. **Records:** With her 1977 Emmy Award for her guest appearance on *The Muppet Show*, Moreno became the first actress to win an Oscar, Tony, Emmy, Golden Globe, and Grammy Award all in competitive categories. Barbra Streisand was the first to receive each of those awards, but her Tony was given to her not in competition, but as a special Star of the Decade tribute for her impact on Broadway during the 1960s. Moreno's Grammy came as one of the recording artists on 1972's *The Electric Company Album*, based on the children's television show.

Morgan, Debbi

Movie: 1997: *Eve's Bayou* (Best Supporting Female) *Spirit*. **Television:** 1982–1990, 2008–present series *All My Children* (Best Ingénue in a Daytime Drama Series) 1985: Emmy. (Best Supporting Actress in a Daytime Drama Series) 1988: *Emmy*.

Morgan, Frank

Movie: 1934: *The Affairs of Cellini* (Best Actor) Academy. 1942: *Tortilla Flat* (Best Supporting Actor) Academy. **Records:** Morgan is only one of three actors to receive a Best Actor Oscar nomination for a supporting role. Before the Academy instituted the supporting actor and actress categories in 1936, most supporting players were bypassed at award time. But Morgan's performance in *The Affairs at Cellini*, as well as Lewis Stone's in *The Patriot* (1928/1929) and Franchot Tone's in *Mutiny on the Bounty* (1935), made such an impression on Academy voters that their relatively small roles garnered them Oscar nods. None of the three actors won for those performances, nor did they end up winning Academy Awards for other films in either the Best Actor or Supporting Actor categories.

Morgan, Henry

Movie: 1943: *Happy Land* (Best Acting) *Board* (multiple win); *The Ox-Bow Incident* (Best Acting) *Board* (multiple win).

Morgan, Janet

Movie: 1963: *David and Lisa* (Most Promising Newcomer) British.

Morgan, Michèle

Movie: 1946: *La Symphonie Pastorale* (Best Actress) *Cannes*. **Tributes:** 1996: Career Golden Lion from Venice. **Records:** Morgan, the delicate beauty who became one of France's most popular stars in the middle of the twentieth century received the first Best Actress award ever given at the Cannes Film Festival. The festival began in 1939, but acting awards were not included as part of the festivities until 1946. In 1971, she became one of the first female jury presidents to preside over the festivities. Before her, Olivia de Havilland took the reigns in 1965 and Sophia Loren helmed the judging in 1966.

Morgenstern, Stephanie

Movie: 1997: *The Sweet Hereafter* (Best Ensemble) *Board*.

Moriarty, Cathy

Movie: 1980: *Raging Bull* (New Star of the Year — Actress) Globe (Most Promising Newcomer) British (Best Supporting Actress) Academy, Globe.

Morice, Tara

Movie: 1992: *Strictly Ballroom* (Best Actress) British.

Morita, Noriyuki "Pat"

Movie: 1984: *The Karate Kid* (Best Supporting Actor) Academy, Globe. **Television:** 1985: *Amos* (Best Supporting Actor in a Miniseries or Special) Emmy (Best Supporting Actor in a Series, Miniseries, or TV Movie) Globe.

Morley, Robert

Movie: 1938: *Marie Antoinette* (Best Acting) *Board* (Best Supporting Actor) Academy. 1978: *Who Is Killing the Great Chefs of Europe?* (Best Supporting Actor) Globe, *Society, LA*.

Morris, Chester

Movie: 1929: *Alibi* (Best Actor) Academy.

Morris, Garrett

Movie: 2001: *Jackpot* (Best Supporting Male) Spirit. **Television:** 1975–1980 series *Saturday Night Live (NBC's Saturday Night)* (Best Comedy-Variety or Music Program, Star) 1979: Emmy.

Morrow, Jane

Movie: 1968: *The Lion in Winter* (Best Supporting Actress) Globe.

Morse, David

Movie: 1995: *The Crossing Guard* (Best Supporting Male) Spirit. 1999: *The Green Mile* (Best Ensemble) SAG. **Television:** 2007: *House* (Best Guest Actor in a Drama Series) Emmy.

Mortensen, Viggo

Movie: 2001: *The Lord of the Rings: The Fellowship of the Ring* (Best Ensemble) SAG. 2002: *The Lord of the Rings: The Two Towers* (Best Ensemble) SAG. 2003: *The Lord of the Rings: The Return of the King* (Best Ensemble) *Board, SAG, Broadcast*. 2007: *Eastern Promises* (Best Actor) Academy, British,

Broadcast (Best Actor, Drama) Globe (Best Male Actor in a Leading Role) SAG.

Mortimer, Emily

Movie: 2002: *Lovely & Amazing* (Best Supporting Female) *Spirit.*

Morton, Joe

Movie: 2007: *American Gangster* (Best Ensemble) SAG. Theater: 1974: *Raisin* (Best Actor, Musical) Tony.

Morton, Samantha

Movie: 1999: *Sweet and Lowdown* (Best Supporting Actress) Academy, Globe. 2003: *In America* (Best Actress) Academy, Broadcast (Best Female Lead) Spirit (Best Ensemble) SAG. 2007: *Control* (Best Supporting Actress) British. Television: 2007: *Longford* (Best Supporting Actress in a Miniseries or TV Movie) Emmy (Best Supporting Actress in a Series, Miniseries, or TV Movie) *Globe.*

Moss, Carrie-Anne

Movie: 2000: *Chocolat* (Best Ensemble) SAG. 2001: *Memento* (Best Supporting Female) *Spirit.*

Moss, Elisabeth

Movie: 2003: *Virgin* (Best Female Lead) Spirit.

Mostel, Zero

Movie: 1968: *The Producers* (Best Actor, Musical or Comedy) Globe. 1976: *The Front* (Best Supporting Actor) British. Theater: 1961: *Rhinoceros* (Best Actor, Dramatic) *Tony.* 1963: *A Funny Thing Happened on the Way to the Forum* (Best Actor, Musical) *Tony.* 1965: *Fiddler on the Roof* (Best Actor, Musical) *Tony.* 1974: *Ulysses in Nighttown* (Best Actor, Dramatic) Tony.

Mouloudji, Marcel

Movie: 1953: *Nus sommes tous des assassins* (Best Foreign Actor) British.

Mueller-Stahl, Armin

Movie: 1992: *Utz* (Best Actor) *Berlin.* 1996: *Shine* (Best Supporting Actor) Academy (Best Ensemble) SAG. Tributes: 1997: Honorary Award from Berlin.

Mühe, Ulrich

Movie: 2006: *The Lives of Others* (Best Actor) British.

Mulkey, Chris

Movie: 1988: *Patti Rocks* (Best Male Lead) Spirit.

Mullan, Peter

Movie: 1998: *My Name Is Joe* (Best Actor) *Cannes.*

Münchmeyer, Gloria

Movie: 1990: *La Luna en el espejo* (Best Actress) *Venice.*

Muni, Paul

Movie: 1929: *The Valiant* (Best Actor) Academy. 1932: *I Am a Fugitive from a Chain Gang* (Best Actor) Academy. 1936: *The Story of Louis Pasteur* (Best Actor) *Academy, Venice.* 1937: *The Life of Emile Zola* (Best Actor) Academy, *New York.* 1959: *The Last Angry Man* (Best Actor) Academy. Theater: 1956: *Inherit the Wind* (Best Actor, Dramatic) *Tony.* Television: 1959: *"Last Clear Chance," Playhouse 90* (Best Single Performance by an Actor) Emmy. Records: Muni almost won a Best Actor Oscar for a race in which he wasn't even a nominee. In 1935, four men were up for Best Actor: Victor McLaglen for *The Informer* and Clark Gable, Charles Laughton, and Franchot Tone for *Mutiny on the Bounty.* After McLaglen won, the Academy released its vote tally, which it did for some years early in its history. At the time, the Academy also briefly allowed for write-in candidates on the winning ballot. In the final tally, all three *Mutiny* stars had fewer votes than Muni received as a write-in for *Black Fury.* Though never a nominee that year, Muni came in second in the race for Best Actor. No write-in candidate ever won an acting Oscar, but Muni came the closest. The next year, he was nominated and won for *The Story of Louis Pasteur,* often considered the first biography turned into a motion picture.

Munir, Mazhar

Movie: 2005: *Syriana* (Best Ensemble) Broadcast.

Muniz, Frankie

Movie: 1999: *My Dog Skip* (Best Child Performer) Broadcast. Television: 2000–2006 series *Malcolm in the Middle* (Best Actor in a Comedy Series) 2001: Emmy. (Best Actor in a Series, Musical or Comedy) 2001: Globe. 2002: Globe.

Munro, Janet

Movie: 1959: *Darby O'Gill and the Little People* (New Star of the Year — Actress) *Globe.* 1962: *Life of Ruth* (Best British Actress) British.

Murphy, Brittany

Movie: 2005: *Sin City* (Best Ensemble) Broadcast.

Murphy, Cillian

Movie: 2005: *Breakfast on Pluto* (Best Actor, Musical or Comedy) Globe.

Murphy, Eddie

Movie: 1982: *48 Hours* (New Star of the Year — Actor) Globe. 1983: *Trading Places* (Best Actor, Musical or Comedy) Globe. 1984: *Beverly Hills Cop* (Best Actor, Musical or Comedy) Globe. 1996: *The Nutty Professor* (Best Actor) *Society* (Best Actor, Musical or Comedy) Globe. 2001: *Shrek* (Best Supporting Actor) British. 2006: *Dreamgirls* (Best Male Actor in a Supporting Role) *SAG* (Best Supporting Actor) Academy, *Globe, Broadcast* (Best Ensemble) SAG, Broadcast. Television: 1980–1984 series *Saturday Night Live (NBC's Saturday Night)* (Best Supporting Actor in a Comedy, Variety, or Music Series) 1983: Emmy. (Best Individual Performance in a Variety or Music Program) 1984: Emmy. (Best Writing in a Variety or Music Program) 1984: Emmy. 1999–2001 series *The PJs* (Best Animated Program for Programming One Hour or Less, Executive Producer) 1999: Emmy.

Murray, Bill

Movie: 1984: *Ghostbusters* (Best Actor, Musical or Comedy) Globe. 1998: *Rushmore* (Best Supporting Actor) *New York*, Globe, *Society, LA* (Best Supporting Male) *Spirit*. 2001: *The Royal Tenenbaums* (Best Ensemble) Broadcast. 2003: *Lost in Translation* (Best Actor) Academy, *New York, British, Society, LA*, Broadcast (Best Actor, Musical or Comedy) *Globe* (Best Male Lead) *Spirit* (Best Male Actor in a Leading Role) SAG. 2004: *The Life Aquatic with Steve Zissou* (Best Ensemble) Broadcast. Television: 1976–1980 series *Saturday Night Live (NBC's Saturday Night)* (Best Comedy-Variety or Music Series, Star) 1979: Emmy. (Best Writing in a Comedy-Variety or Music Program) 1977: *Emmy*.

Murray, Don

Movie: 1956: *Bus Stop* (Most Promising Newcomer) British (Best Supporting Actor) Academy.

Mvusi, Linda

Movie: 1988: *A World Apart* (Best Actress) *Cannes* (win shared with costars).

Mýa (Harrison, Mýa)

Movie: 2002: *Chicago* (Best Ensemble) *SAG, Broadcast*.

Naceri, Samy

Movie: 2006: *Days of Glory* (Best Actor) *Cannes* (win shared with costars).

Nadal, Lymari

Movie: 2007: *American Gangster* (Best Ensemble) SAG.

Nader, George

Movie: 1954: *Four Guns to the Border* (New Star of the Year — Actor) *Globe*.

Naidu, Ajay

Movie: 1997: *SubUrbia (Suburbia)* (Best Supporting Male) Spirit.

Naish, J. Carrol

Movie: 1943: *Sahara* (Best Supporting Actor) Academy. 1945: *A Medal for Benny* (Best Supporting Actor) Academy, *Globe*.

Naji, Reza

Movie: 2007: *Avaze gonjeshk-ha (The Song of Sparrows)* (Best Actor) *Berlin*.

Namath, Joe

Movie: 1970: *Norwood* (New Star of the Year — Actor) Globe.

Nardini, Tom

Movie: 1965: *Cat Ballou* (New Star of the Year — Actor) Globe (Most Promising Newcomer) British.

Narita, Darling

Movie: 1997: *Bang* (Best Debut Performance) Spirit.

Nascarella, Arthur J.

Movie: 1998: *Happiness* (Best Ensemble) *Board*. Television: 2006–2007 series *The Sopranos* (Best Ensemble in a Drama Series) 2007: *SAG*.

Nat, Marie-José

Movie: 1974: *Les Violons du Bal* (Best Actress) *Cannes*.

Natwick, Mildred

Movie: 1967: *Barefoot in the Park* (Best Supporting Actress) Academy. Theater: 1957: *The Waltz of the Toreadors* (Best Supporting or Featured Actress, Dramatic) Tony. 1972: *70, Girls, 70* (Best Actress, Musical) Tony. Television: 1957: *"Blithe Spirit,"*

Ford Star Jubilee (Best Supporting Actress) Emmy. 1974: *"The Snoop Sisters," NBC Tuesday Mystery Movie* (Best Actress in a Limited Series) *Emmy.*

Naughton, James

Movie: 1996: *The First Wives Club* (Best Ensemble) *Board.* Theater: 1990: *City of Angels* (Best Actor, Musical) *Tony.* 1997: *Chicago* (Best Actor, Musical) *Tony.*

Neal, Elise

Movie: 2005: *Hustle & Flow* (Best Ensemble) SAG.

Neal, Patricia

Movie: 1963: *Hud* (Best Actress) *Academy, New York, Board* (Best Foreign Actress) *British* (Best Supporting Actress) Globe. 1965: *In Harm's Way* (Best Foreign Actress) *British.* 1968: *The Subject Was Roses* (Best Actress) Academy. Theater: 1947: *Another Part of the Forest* (Best Supporting or Featured Actress, Dramatic) *Tony.* Television: 1972: *The Homecoming—A Christmas Story* (Best Single Performance by an Actress in a Leading Role) Emmy (Best Actress in a Drama Series or TV Movie) *Globe.* 1977: *"Tail Gunner Joe," The Big Event* (Best Supporting Actress in a Comedy or Drama Special) Emmy. 1980: *"All Quiet on the Western Front," Hallmark Hall of Fame* (Best Supporting Actress in a Limited Series or Special) Emmy. **Records:** Although a few men have eked out lead actor Oscar nominations for supporting roles, Neal managed to become one of the only actresses to achieve the feat and then go one further and win the award. Her role as housekeeper Alma in *Hud* kept her in the background and gave her no major dramatic monologues to secure her Oscar chances, but Neal's stellar work as the only female in the cast raised her to the rank of Best Actress and made hers one of the shortest Best Actress winning performances in Oscar history.

Neely, Ted

Movie: 1973: *Jesus Christ Superstar* (New Star of the Year — Actor) Globe (Best Actor, Musical or Comedy) Globe.

Neeson, Liam

Movie: 1993: *Schindler's List* (Best Actor) Academy, British (Best Actor, Drama) Globe. 1996: *Michael Collins* (Best Actor) *Venice* (Best Actor, Drama) Globe. 2003: *Love Actually* (Best Ensemble) Broadcast. 2004: *Kinsey* (Best Actor) *LA* (Best Actor, Drama) Globe (Best Male Lead) Spirit. **Theater:** 1993: *Anna Christie* (Best Actor, Play) Tony. 2002: *The Crucible* (Best Actor, Play) Tony.

Nelligan, Kate

Movie: 1991: *Frankie and Johnny* (Best Supporting Actress) *Board, British*; *The Prince of Tides* (Best Supporting Actress) Academy. 1995: *How to Make an American Quilt* (Best Ensemble) SAG. 1999: *The Cider House Rules* (Best Ensemble) SAG. Theater: 1983: *Plenty* (Best Actress, Play) Tony. 1984: *A Moon for the Misbegotten* (Best Actress, Play) Tony. 1988: *Serious Money* (Best Actress in a Featured Role, Play) Tony. 1989: *Spoils of War* (Best Actress, Play) Tony. Television: 1992 series *Avonlea (Road to Avonlea* or *Tales of Avonlea)* (Best Actress in a Drama Series) 1992: Emmy.

Nelson, Gene

Movie: 1950: *Tea for Two* (New Star of the Year — Actor) *Globe.* Theater: 1972: *Follies* (Best Supporting or Featured Actor, Musical) Tony.

Nelson, Kenneth

Movie: 1970: *The Boys in the Band* (New Star of the Year — Actor) Globe.

Nelson, Rick(y)

Movie: 1959: *Rio Bravo* (New Star of the Year — Actor) Globe.

Nelson, Sean

Movie: 1994: *Fresh* (Best Debut Performance) *Spirit.*

Nero, Franco

Movie: 1967: *Camelot* (New Star of the Year — Actor) Globe.

Nesbitt, James

Movie: 1998: *Waking Ned Devine* (Best Ensemble) SAG. Television: 2007: *Jekyll* (Best Actor in a Miniseries or TV Movie) Globe.

Newman, Nanette

Movie: 1971: *The Raging Moon* (Best Actress) British.

Newman, Paul

Movie: 1956: *The Silver Chalice* (New Star of the Year — Actor) *Globe.* 1958: *Cat on a Hot Tin Roof* (Best Actor) Academy (Best Foreign Actor) British; *The Long, Hot Summer* (Best Actor) *Cannes.* 1961: *The Hustler* (Best Actor) Academy (Best Actor, Drama) Globe (Best Foreign Actor) *British.* 1962: *Adventures of a Young Man* (Best Supporting Actor) Globe; *Sweet Bird of Youth* (Best Actor, Drama) Globe. 1963: *Hud* (Best Actor) Academy (Best Actor, Drama) Globe (Best Foreign Actor) British. 1967:

Cool Hand Luke (Best Actor) Academy (Best Actor, Drama) Globe. 1968: ***Rachel, Rachel*** (Best Director) *New York, Globe* (Best Picture, Producer) Academy. 1969: ***Butch Cassidy and the Sundance Kid*** (Best Actor) British. 1981: ***Absence of Malice*** (Best Actor) Academy. 1982: ***The Verdict*** (Best Actor) Academy (Best Actor, Drama) Globe. 1986: ***The Color of Money*** (Best Actor) *Academy, Board* (Best Actor, Drama) Globe. 1994: ***Nobody's Fool*** (Best Actor) Academy, *New York, Berlin, Society* (Best Male Actor in a Leading Role) SAG (Best Actor, Drama) Globe. 2002: ***Road to Perdition*** (Best Supporting Actor) Academy, Globe, British, Broadcast. **Theater:** 2003: ***Our Town*** (Best Actor, Play) Tony. **Television:** 1981: ***The Shadow Box*** (Best Directing in a Limited Series or Special) Emmy. 2003: ***Our Town*** (Best Actor in a Miniseries or TV Movie) Emmy (Best Male Actor in a Television Movie or Miniseries) SAG. 2005: ***Empire Falls*** (Best Male Actor in a Television Movie or Miniseries) *SAG* (Best Supporting Actor in a Miniseries or TV Movie) *Emmy* (Best Supporting Actor in a Series, Miniseries, or TV Movie) *Globe* (Best Miniseries, Executive Producer) Emmy. **Tributes:** 1963, 1965: Henrietta Award for World Film Favorite from Globe. 1975: Gala Tribute from Film Society of Lincoln Center (honor shared with spouse, Joanne Woodward). 1983: Cecil B. De-Mille Award from Globe. 1985: Special Oscar statuette in recognition of his many and memorable compelling screen performances and for his personal integrity and dedication to his craft from Academy; Life Achievement Award from SAG. 1992: Honor from Kennedy Center for the Performing Arts (honor shared with spouse, Joanne Woodward). 1993: Jean Hersholt Humanitarian Award from Academy. **Records:** Newman's professional connection to wife Joanne Woodward resulted in some memorable award records. In 1968, he went behind the camera for the first time to direct Woodward in ***Rachel, Rachel***. His efforts made him the first actor to receive a Best Director award from the New York Film Critics, and, when Woodward was named Best Actress for the same film, they became the first husband and wife to both earn New York Film Critics Awards for a single project. When the Hollywood Foreign Press gave them the same awards, they set the record as Golden Globe winners as well. With his 2005 Emmy win as Max Roby in ***Empire Falls***, Newman and wife Joanne Woodward became the first married couple to both win acting Oscars and Emmys. **Highlights:** It took him 28 years and seven nominations to finally take home the Oscar, but Newman is in part responsible for not winning for so long. For most of his career, Newman not only refused to campaign for a win, but he also demanded that the studios releasing his films not lobby on his behalf. As a result, Newman's reprising a classic character, ***The Hustler***'s Fast Eddie Felson, in a comparatively light year for the Best Actor race (Brit Bob Hoskins in ***Mona Lisa*** was his strongest competition) enabled the Academy to finally reward Newman for his work in ***The Color of Money***. Newman won only one other award for that performance, from the National Board of Review. All other critics' awards went to Hoskins.

Newmar, Julie

Movie: 1960: ***The Marriage-Go-Round*** (New Star of the Year — Actress) Globe. **Theater:** 1959: ***The Marriage-Go-Round*** (Best Supporting or Featured Actress, Dramatic) *Tony*. **Television:** 1964–1965 series ***My Living Doll*** (Best Actress in a Series) 1965: Globe.

Newton, Thandie

Movie: 2005: ***Crash*** (Best Supporting Actress) *British* (Best Ensemble) *SAG, Broadcast*.

Newton-John, Olivia

Movie: 1978: ***Grease*** (Best Actress, Musical or Comedy) Globe.

Ngor, Haing S.

Movie: 1984: ***The Killing Fields*** (Best Newcomer to Film) *British* (Best Actor) *British* (Best Supporting Actor) *Academy, Globe*. **Records:** With four awards, Cambodian native Ngor won more acting honors for an English language film than any other actor of Asian descent. When he won the Oscar, the former doctor became only the second non-actor to give an Academy Award winning performance. In 1946, World War II soldier Harold Russell won the Best Supporting Actor prize, plus an Honorary Oscar, for his portrayal of a disabled veteran in ***The Best Years of Our Lives***.

Nicholson, Jack

Movie: 1969: ***Easy Rider*** (Best Supporting Actor) Academy, *New York*, Globe, British, *Society*. 1970: ***Five Easy Pieces*** (Best Actor) Academy (Best Actor, Drama) Globe. 1971: ***Carnal Knowledge*** (Best Actor, Drama) Globe. 1973: ***The Last Detail*** (Best Actor) Academy, *New York* (multiple win), *Cannes, British* (multiple win), *Society* (multiple win), (Best Actor, Drama) Globe. 1974: ***Chinatown*** (Best Actor) Academy, *New York* (multiple win), *British* (multiple win), *Society* (multiple win), (Best Actor, Drama) *Globe*. 1975: ***One Flew Over the Cuckoo's Nest*** (Best Actor) Academy, *New York, Board, British, Society* (Best Actor, Drama) *Globe*. 1981: ***Reds*** (Best

Supporting Actor) Academy, *Board*, Globe, *British*. 1983: ***Terms of Endearment*** (Best Supporting Actor) *Academy, New York, Board, Globe*, Society, *LA*. 1985: ***Prizzi's Honor*** (Best Actor) Academy, *New York, Society* (Best Actor, Musical or Comedy) *Globe*. 1987: ***Broadcast News*** (Best Actor) *New York* (multiple win); ***Ironweed*** (Best Actor) Academy, *New York* (multiple win), *LA* (multiple win), (Best Actor, Drama) Globe; ***The Witches of Eastwick*** (Best Actor) *New York* (multiple win), *LA* (multiple win). 1989: ***Batman*** (Best Actor, Musical or Comedy) Globe (Best Supporting Actor) British. 1992: ***A Few Good Men*** (Best Supporting Actor) Academy, *Board*, Globe; ***Hoffa*** (Best Actor, Drama) Globe. 1997: ***As Good as It Gets*** (Best Actor) *Academy, Board*, Broadcast (Best Actor, Musical or Comedy) *Globe* (Best Male Actor in a Leading Role) *SAG*. 2002: ***About Schmidt*** (Best Actor) Academy, British, *LA, Broadcast* (Best Actor, Drama) *Globe* (Best Male Actor in a Leading Role) SAG. 2003: ***Something's Gotta Give*** (Best Actor, Musical or Comedy) Globe. 2006: ***The Departed*** (Best Supporting Actor) Globe, British (Best Ensemble) *Board*, SAG, Broadcast. **Tributes:** 1994: Life Achievement Award from American Film Institute. 1998: Cecil B. DeMille Award from Globe. 2001: Honor from Kennedy Center for the Performing Arts. **Records:** Nicholson has received more awards from the major film groups than any other actor. He has set records by winning the most acting awards from four major film organizations with six awards from New York Film Critics, six Golden Globes, and five awards from both the National Board of Review and the National Society of Film Critics. With four L.A. Film Critics awards, he is only one award behind their champ, Meryl Streep. Along with Walter Brennan, who has all supporting actor Oscars, Nicholson is the only male actor with three acting Academy Awards (two for lead actor and one for supporting). With twelve, Nicholson also has more Oscar nominations than any other male actor. In 2002 Streep was one ahead of Nicholson, earning a thirteenth nomination for ***Adaptation*** as Nicholson got his twelfth for ***About Schmidt***. In 2006, Streep pulled ahead by two when she earned a Best Actress nomination for ***The Devil Wears Prada***, but Nicholson didn't garner his expected Best Supporting Actor nod for that year's Best Picture, ***The Departed***. As far as overall award nominations and wins, Streep holds the record for most movie acting nominations, followed closely by Nicholson and then Jack Lemmon. But for overall major award wins, Nicholson is the champion by a considerable margin over the second and third most awarded actors, Meryl Streep and Gene Hackman.

Nicholson, Julianne

Movie: 2002: ***Tully*** (Best Supporting Female) Spirit.

Nielsen, Connie

Movie: 2000: ***Gladiator*** (Best Ensemble) SAG.

Nighy, Bill

Movie: 2003: ***AKA*** (Best Supporting Actor) *LA* (multiple win); ***I Capture the Castle*** (Best Supporting Actor) *LA* (multiple win); ***Lawless Heart*** (Best Supporting Actor) *LA* (multiple win); ***Love Actually*** (Best Supporting Actor) *British, LA* (multiple win), (Best Ensemble) Broadcast. **Television:** 2005: ***The Girl in the Café*** (Best Actor in a Miniseries or TV Movie) Globe. 2006: ***Gideon's Daughter*** (Best Actor in a Miniseries or TV Movie) *Globe*.

Niven, David

Movie: 1953: ***The Moon Is Blue*** (Best Actor, Musical or Comedy) *Globe*. 1954: ***Carrington V.C.*** (Best British Actor) British. 1957: ***My Man Godfrey*** (Best Actor, Musical or Comedy) Globe. 1958: ***Separate Tables*** (Best Actor) *Academy, New York* (Best Actor, Drama) *Globe*. **Television:** 1955: ***"The Answer," Four Star Playhouse*** (Best Actor in a Single Performance) Emmy. 1957: ***Four Star Playhouse*** (Best Continuing Performance by an Actor in a Dramatic Series) Emmy.

Nivola, Alessandro

Movie: 2003: ***Laurel Canyon*** (Best Supporting Male) Spirit.

Noble, John

Movie: 2003: ***The Lord of the Rings: The Return of the King*** (Best Ensemble) *Board, SAG, Broadcast*.

Nogueira, Ana Beatriz

Movie: 1987: ***Vera*** (Best Actress) *Berlin*.

Noiret, Philippe

Movie: 1969: ***Topaz*** (Best Supporting Actor) *Board*. 1988: ***Cinema Paradiso*** (Best Actor) *British*.

Nolte, Nick

Movie: 1987: ***Weeds*** (Best Actor, Drama) Globe. 1991: ***The Prince of Tides*** (Best Actor) Academy, *LA* (Best Actor, Drama) *Globe*. 1998: ***Affliction*** (Best Actor) Academy, *New York, Society* (Best Actor, Drama) Globe (Best Male Lead) Spirit (Best Male Actor in a Leading Role) SAG. 2004: ***Hotel Rwanda*** (Best Ensemble) SAG. **Television:** 1976: ***Rich Man,***

Poor Man (Best Actor in a Limited Series) Emmy (Best Actor in a Drama) Globe.

Northam, Jeremy

Movie: 2001: *Gosford Park* (Best Ensemble) *SAG, Broadcast*.

Norton, Edward

Movie: 1996: *Everyone Says I Love You* (Best Supporting Actor) *Board* (multiple win), *LA* (multiple win); *The People vs. Larry Flynt* (Best Supporting Actor) *Board* (multiple win), *LA* (multiple win); *Primal Fear* (Best Supporting Actor) Academy, *Board* (multiple win), *Globe*, British, *LA* (multiple win). 1998: *American History X* (Best Actor) Academy. 2006: *The Painted Veil* (Best Male Lead) Spirit.

Novak, Kim

Movie: 1954: *Phffft!* (New Star of the Year — Actress) *Globe*. 1955: *Picnic* (Best Foreign Actress) British. Tributes: 1956: Henrietta Award for World Film Favorite from Globe. 1997: Honorary Golden Bear from Berlin.

Novarro, Ramon

Tributes: 1959: Special Achievement Award from Globe in honor of the performance of his career for playing Judah Ben-Hur in the 1925 silent version of *Ben-Hur*, given the year the new sound remake was released.

Novembre, Tom

Movie: 1994: *Prêt-à-Porter (Ready-to-Wear)* (Best Ensemble) *Board*.

Novents, Galya

Movie: 1985: *Mer mankutyan tangon* (Best Actress) *Venice*.

Nucci, Danny

Movie: 1997: *Titanic* (Best Ensemble) SAG.

Nuyen, France

Movie: 1958: *South Pacific* (New Star of the Year — Actress) Globe.

Oakie, Jack

Movie: 1940: *The Great Dictator* (Best Supporting Actor) Academy.

Oberon, Merle

Movie: 1935: *The Dark Angel* (Best Actress) Academy.

O'Boyle, Michael James

Movie: 2000: *State and Main* (Best Ensemble) *Board*.

O'Brian, Hugh

Movie: 1953: *Man from the Alamo* (New Star of the Year — Actor) *Globe*. Television: 1955–1961 series *The Life and Legend of Wyatt Earp* (Best Actor in a Dramatic Series) 1956: Emmy.

O'Brien, Edmond

Movie: 1954: *The Barefoot Contessa* (Best Supporting Actor) *Academy, Globe*. 1964: *Seven Days in May* (Best Supporting Actor) Academy, *Globe*.

O'Brien, Margaret

Movie: 1942: *Journey for Margaret* (Best Acting) *Board*. 1944: *Meet Me in St. Louis* (Best Acting) *Board*. Tributes: 1944: Honorary miniature Oscar statuette as outstanding child actress of 1944 from Academy. Records: O'Brien has perhaps the happiest ending to a lost Oscar story. A decade after she received an honorary Academy Award as outstanding child actress of 1944, her miniature statuette was stolen. A full forty years later, two baseball memorabilia collectors bought the long-missing Oscar at a swap meet and, after learning that the award had been stolen, returned it to O'Brien. Highlights: O'Brien appeared in five films the year she received an honorary miniature Oscar for her work in motion pictures. Besides strong performances in *The Canterville Ghost, Jane Eyre, Lost Angel*, and *Music for Millions*, she gave her most memorable performance as Judy Garland's comically morbid young sister, Tootie in director Vincente Minnelli's now-classic holiday staple, *Meet Me in St. Louis.*

O'Byrne, Brian F.

Movie: 2007: *Before the Devil Knows You're Dead* (Best Ensemble) Broadcast. Theater: 1998: *The Beauty Queen of Leenane* (Best Featured Actor, Play) Tony. 1999: *The Lonesome West* (Best Actor, Play) Tony. 2004: *Frozen* (Best Featured Actor, Play) *Tony*. 2005: *Doubt* (Best Actor, Play) Tony. 2007: *The Coast of Utopia* (Best Actor, Play) Tony.

O'Connell, Arthur

Movie: 1955: *Picnic* (Best Supporting Actor) Academy. 1959: *Anatomy of a Murder* (Best Supporting Actor) Academy.

O'Connell, Deirdre

Movie: 1991: *Pastime* (Best Supporting Female) Spirit.

O'Connor, Donald

Movie: 1952: *Singin' in the Rain* (Best Actor, Musical or Comedy) *Globe*. Television: 1954: --- (Best Personality) Emmy. 1950–1955 series *Colgate Comedy Hour* (Best Male Star, Regular Series) 1953: *Emmy*. 1956: --- (Best Specialty Act — Single or Group) Emmy. 1980: *52nd Annual Awards Presentation of the Academy of Motion Picture Arts and Sciences* (Best Individual Achievement — Special Events, Performer) Emmy.

O'Conor, Hugh

Movie: 2000: *Chocolat* (Best Ensemble) SAG.

Odom, George T.

Movie: 1991: *Straight Out of Brooklyn* (Best Supporting Male) Spirit.

O'Donnell, Chris

Movie: 1992: *Scent of a Woman* (Best Supporting Actor) Globe.

Ogier, Pascale

Movie: 1984: *Les Nuits de la pleine lune (Full Moon in Paris)* (Best Actress) *Venice*.

Oh, Sandra

Movie: 2004: *Sideways* (Best Ensemble) *SAG, Broadcast*. Television: 2005–present series *Grey's Anatomy* (Best Female Actor in a Drama Series) 2005: *SAG*. (Best Supporting Actress in a Drama Series) 2005: Emmy. 2006: Emmy. 2007: Emmy. (Best Supporting Actress in a Series, Miniseries, or TV Movie) 2005: *Globe*. (Best Ensemble in a Drama Series) 2005: SAG. 2006: *SAG*. 2007: SAG.

O'Hara Catherine

Movie: 2003: *A Mighty Wind* (Best Screenplay) Spirit (Best Ensemble) Broadcast. 2006: *For Your Consideration* (Best Female Lead) Spirit (Best Supporting Actress) *Board,* Broadcast. Television: 1976–1984 series *SCTV Network* (Best Writing in a Variety or Music Program) 1982: Emmy, Emmy, Emmy, *Emmy*. 1983: Emmy.

O'Herlihy, Dan

Movie: 1954: *Adventures of Robinson Crusoe* (Best Actor) Academy.

O'Keefe, Michael

Movie: 1980: *The Great Santini* (New Star of the Year — Actor) Globe (Best Supporting Actor) Academy.

Okonedo, Sophie

Movie: 2004: *Hotel Rwanda* (Best Female Actor in a Supporting Role) SAG (Best Supporting Actress) Academy (Best Ensemble) SAG. Television: 2006: *Tsunami, the Aftermath* (Best Actress in a Miniseries or TV Movie) Globe.

Oldman, Gary

Movie: 1987: *Prick Up Your Ears* (Best Actor) British. 1997: *Nil by Mouth* (Best Picture, Producer) *British* (Best Original Screenplay) *British*. 1991: *Rosencrantz & Guildenstern Are Dead* (Best Male Lead) Spirit. 2000: *The Contender* (Best Male Actor in a Supporting Role) SAG (Best Supporting Actor) Broadcast (Best Supporting Male) Spirit. Television: 2001: *Friends* (Best Guest Actor in a Comedy Series) Emmy.

Olin, Lena

Movie: 1987: *The Unbearable Lightness of Being* (Best Supporting Actress) Globe. 1989: *Enemies: A Love Story* (Best Supporting Actress) Academy, *New York*. 2000: *Chocolat* (Best Supporting Actress) British (Best Ensemble) SAG. Television: 2002–2003 series *Alias* (Best Supporting Actress in a Drama Series) 2003: Emmy. **Highlights:** Olin and *Enemies: A Love Story* co-star Anjelica Huston both achieved the difficult task of winning an award in a category that pits them against a co-star of the same film. In 1989 both Olin and Huston won rave reviews for their work as two of Ron Silver's three wives in *Enemies* and ended up taking turns winning a critical award, with Olin favored by the New York critics and Huston impressing the National Society of Film Critics. Both actresses were bypassed for Golden Globe consideration, but then made comebacks to nab Oscar nods. As is usually the case when actors compete against each other from the same film, the actresses' votes canceled each other out, and that year's Oscar laurels went to Brenda Fricker as a courageous mother who helps her son overcome the limitations of cerebral palsy in *My Left Foot*.

Oliver, Edna May

Movie: 1939: *Drums Along the Mohawk* (Best Supporting Actress) Academy.

Olivier, Laurence

Movie: 1939: *Wuthering Heights* (Best Acting) Board (Best Actor) Academy. 1940: *Rebecca* (Best Actor) Academy. 1946: *Henry V* (Best Actor) Academy, *New York, Board* (Best Picture, Producer) Academy, *Board*. 1948: *Hamlet* (Best Actor) *Academy, New York, Globe* (Best Director) Academy (Best

Picture, Producer) *Academy*, Board. 1952: **Carrie** (Best British Actor) British. 1956: **Richard III** (Best Actor) Academy (Best British Actor) *British*. 1957: **The Prince and the Showgirl** (Best British Actor) British. 1957: **The Devil's Disciple** (Best British Actor) British. 1960: **The Entertainer** (Best Actor) Academy (Best British Actor) British; **Spartacus** (Best Actor, Drama) Globe. 1962: **Term of Trial** (Best British Actor) British. 1965: **Othello** (Best Actor) Academy. 1969: **Oh! What a Lovely War** (Best Supporting Actor) *British*. 1972: **Sleuth** (Best Actor) Academy, *New York*, British (Best Actor, Drama) Globe. 1976: **Marathon Man** (Best Supporting Actor) Academy, *Globe*. 1978: **The Boys from Brazil** (Best Actor) Academy, *Board*. 1979: **A Little Romance** (Best Supporting Actor) Globe. **Theater:** 1958: **The Entertainer** (Best Actor, Dramatic) Tony. **Television:** 1960: **The Moon and Sixpence** (Best Single Performance by a Lead or Supporting Actor) *Emmy*. 1968: **"Uncle Vanya," NET Playhouse** (Best Dramatic Program, Producer) Emmy. 1970: **David Copperfield** (Best Single Performance by an Actor in a Leading Role) Emmy. 1973: **Long Day's Journey into Night** (Best Single Performance by an Actor in a Leading Role) *Emmy*. 1974: **"The Merchant of Venice," ABC Theatre** (Best Actor in a Drama) Emmy. 1975: **"Love Among the Ruins," ABC Theatre** (Best Actor in a Special Drama or Comedy Program) *Emmy*. 1982: **"Brideshead Revisited," Great Performances** (Best Supporting Actor in a Limited Series or Special) *Emmy*. 1984: **Laurence Olivier's King Lear** (Best Actor in a Limited Series or Special) *Emmy*. 1987: **"Lost Empires," Masterpiece Theatre** (Best Supporting Actor in a Miniseries or Special) Emmy. **Tributes:** 1946: Special Oscar statuette for his outstanding achievement as actor, producer, and director in bringing **Henry V** to the screen from Academy. 1978: Honorary Oscar statuette for the full body of his work and for the unique achievements of his entire career and his lifetime of contribution to the art of film from Academy. 1982: Cecil B. DeMille Award from Globe. 1983: Gala Tribute from Film Society of Lincoln Center. 1999: Ranked Number 14 on List of 25 Greatest Male Screen Legends of the 20th Century from American Film Institute. **Records:** Until Olivier, Shakespeare never met with such public and critical praise. Olivier's **Hamlet** became the first film from outside the United States to win the Best Picture Academy Award, and was the first (and still only) work by Shakespeare to win Best Picture. (Exactly fifty years after **Hamlet**, **Shakespeare in Love** won that prize, but the film was loosely about, not by Shakespeare.) By winning Best Actor for the film, Olivier also became the first actor to direct himself to an Oscar-winning performance. Of the three nominations he received for **Hamlet**,

Olivier only lost in the Best Director category, which John Huston won for **The Treasure of the Sierra Madre**. **Highlights:** Olivier won an Emmy for his American television debut playing emotionally tortured painter Paul Gaugin in **The Moon and Sixpence**. Three years earlier, Anthony Quinn played the same artist in **Lust for Life** on the big screen and won a supporting Oscar, making Gaugin the first historical figure to inspire portrayals that earned awards from motion pictures and television.

Olivos, Louie, Jr.

Movie: 2004: **Robbing Peter** (Best Debut Performance) Spirit.

Olmos, Edward James

Movie: 1988: **Stand and Deliver** (Best Actor) Academy (Best Actor, Drama) Globe (Best Male Lead) *Spirit*. **Theater:** 1979: **Zoot Suit** (Best Actor in a Featured Role, Play) Tony. **Television:** 1984–1989 series **Miami Vice** (Best Supporting Actor in a Drama Series) 1985: *Emmy*. 1986: Emmy. (Best Supporting Actor in a Series, Miniseries, or TV Movie) 1985: *Globe*. 1988: Globe. 1995: **The Burning Season** (Best Supporting Actor in a Miniseries or Special) Emmy (Best Supporting Actor in a Series, Miniseries, or TV Movie) *Globe*.

Olschewski, Gerhard

Movie: 1976: **Verlorenes Leben** (Best Actor) *Berlin*.

Olson, Nancy

Movie: 1950: **Sunset Boulevard** (Best Supporting Actress) Academy.

Olson, Olivia

Movie: 2003: **Love Actually** (Best Ensemble) Broadcast.

O'Neal, Ryan

Movie: 1970: **Love Story** (Best Actor) Academy (Best Actor, Drama) Globe. 1973: **Paper Moon** (Best Actor, Musical or Comedy) Globe.

O'Neal, Tatum

Movie: 1973: **Paper Moon** (New Star of the Year — Actress) *Globe* (Best Actress, Musical or Comedy) Globe (Best Supporting Actress) *Academy*. **Records:** 1973 turned out to have one of the tightest and most surprising Best Supporting Actress races in history, with the combined age of the two top contenders under 25. The box office punch of **The Exorcist** inspired the film's marketers to push heavily for nominations for 14-year-old Linda Blair in the role of a girl helplessly possessed by the devil. Momentum went her way when the Hollywood Foreign Press Association unexpectedly nominated O'Neal in the Best Actress category. Consequently, Blair won her Best Supporting Actress Golden Globe, but it was O'Neal who won the competition between the two young stars for New Star of the Year. (O'Neal lost Best Actress to Glenda Jackson in *A Touch of Class*.) At Oscar time, O'Neal and Blair were alternately odds-on favorites to win. When Charles Bronson and Jill Ireland announced O'Neal the winner, an approving roar swept across the Dorothy Chandler Pavilion, and an ebullient O'Neal sprinted to the podium to become the youngest star ever to win a competitive Academy Award, a record she holds to this day.

O'Neil, Barbara

Movie: 1940: *All This, and Heaven Too* (Best Supporting Actress) Academy.

Ontiveros, Lupe

Movie: 2000: *Chuck & Buck* (Best Supporting Actress) *Board* (Best Supporting Female) Spirit. Television: 2005: *Desperate Housewives* (Best Guest Actress in a Comedy Series) Emmy.

O'Quinn, Terry

Movie: 1987: *The Stepfather* (Best Male Lead) Spirit. Television: 2004–present series *Lost* (Best Supporting Actor in a Drama Series) 2005: Emmy. 2007: *Emmy*. (Best Ensemble in a Drama Series) 2005: SAG.

Ortiz, John

Movie: 2007: *American Gangster* (Best Ensemble) SAG.

Oscarsson, Per

Movie: 1966: *Sult (Hunger)* (Best Actor) *Cannes, Society*.

O'Shea, Milo

Movie: 1967: *Ulysses* (Most Promising Newcomer) British. Theater: 1968: *Staircase* (Best Actor, Dramatic) Tony. 1982: *Mass Appeal* (Best Actor, Play) Tony.

Osment, Haley Joel

Movie: 1999: *The Sixth Sense* (Best Child Performer) *Broadcast* (Best Male Actor in a Supporting Role) SAG (Best Supporting Actor) Academy, Globe.

2000: *Pay It Forward* (Best Child Performer) Broadcast. 2001: *A.I.: Artificial Intelligence* (Best Young Actor/Actress) Broadcast. **Records:** Osment's unforgettable performance in *The Sixth Sense* as the young boy who begs Bruce Willis for help from the paranormal phenomena that haunt him earned him praise as a child star as talented as Roddy McDowall or Natalie Wood at the height of their young stardom. His "I see dead people" ranks as one of the most familiar lines in film history, and the movie was so popular it became the top money making horror film of all time.

O'Toole, Peter

Movie: 1962: *Lawrence of Arabia* (New Star of the Year — Actor) *Globe* (Best Actor) Academy (Best Actor, Drama) Globe (Best British Actor) *British*. 1964: *Becket* (Best Actor) Academy (Best Actor, Drama) *Globe* (Best British Actor) British. 1968: *The Lion in Winter* (Best Actor) Academy (Best Actor, Drama) *Globe*. 1969: *Goodbye, Mr. Chips* (Best Actor) Academy, *Board* (Best Actor, Musical or Comedy) *Globe*. 1972: *Man of La Mancha* (Best Actor) *Board* (multiple win), (Best Actor, Musical or Comedy) Globe; *The Ruling Class* (Best Actor) Academy, *Board* (multiple win). 1980: *The Stunt Man* (Best Actor) Academy, *Society* (Best Actor, Drama) Globe. 1982: *My Favorite Year* (Best Actor) Academy (Best Actor, Musical or Comedy) Globe. 1987: *The Last Emperor* (Best Supporting Actor) British. 2006: *Venus* (Best Actor) Academy, British, Broadcast (Best Actor, Drama) Globe (Best Male Actor in a Leading Role) SAG. **Television:** 1981: *Masada* (Best Actor in a Limited Series or Special) Emmy (Best Actor in a Miniseries or TV Movie) Globe. 1999: *Joan of Arc* (Best Supporting Actor in a Miniseries or TV Movie) *Emmy* (Best Supporting Actor in a Series, Miniseries, or TV Movie) Globe. 2003: *Hitler: The Rise of Evil* (Best Supporting Actor in a Miniseries or TV Movie) Emmy. **Tributes:** 2002: Honorary Oscar statuette for an actor whose remarkable talents have provided cinema history with some of its most memorable characters from Academy. **Records:** Timing seemed to keep O'Toole from taking home Oscar, as he tended to lose to some of the giants of the silver screen. His first and arguably best chance to win came in 1962 for his lead in the epic *Lawrence of Arabia*. That year, however, Gregory Peck played Atticus Finch in *To Kill a Mockingbird*, a role that would eventually be cited by the American Film Institute as the most heroic character in American film history. On Oscar night, Peck won. In 1969, O'Toole was up for *Goodbye, Mr. Chips* against John Wayne, who'd never won after over 100 films, and The Duke came out the victor for **True Grit**. Three years later O'Toole won rave reviews for **The Ruling Class**, but ended up nominated against Marlon Brando in his classic role of Don Vito Corleone in the blockbuster, **The Godfather**. Brando won and refused the award. The 1980s were just as merciless for O'Toole. In 1980 he vied for the prize against Robert De Niro in **Raging Bull**, the film voted by a major critics' poll as the best of the decade, and in 1982 he lost to Ben Kingsley in the career-launching Best Picture, **Gandhi**. In 2006 O'Toole set the Academy Award record for most acting nominations without a single win when he lost to Forest Whitaker for **The Last King of Scotland**. A sentimental hopeful to win that year, O'Toole lost once again to someone who had everything going for him, as Whitaker had won virtually every major Best Actor award presented that year. But give O'Toole credit for fortitude and optimism. When the Academy honored him with a special Oscar in 2002, he at first hesitated to accept it because he didn't want that award to squelch his chances of winning a competitive Oscar, for which he still longed and still believed he would have an opportunity to win. Though he has yet to win, he still holds to the hope that he will. O'Toole does have one consolation for all his losses. In 1980 Robert De Niro won every major award for **Raging Bull** except one. The spoiler of his sweep was O'Toole, who took the Best Actor prize from the National Society of Film Critics for his work in **The Stunt Man**. He beat De Niro by one vote.

Otowa, Nobuko

Movie: 1979: **Kôsatsu** (Best Actress) *Venice*.

Otto, Miranda

Movie: 2002: **The Lord of the Rings: The Two Towers** (Best Ensemble) SAG. 2003: **The Lord of the Rings: The Return of the King** (Best Ensemble) *Board*, SAG, Broadcast.

Ouspenskaya, Maria

Movie: 1936: **Dodsworth** (Best Supporting Actress) Academy. 1937: **Conquest** (Best Acting) *Board*. 1939: **Love Affair** (Best Supporting Actress) Academy.

Outinen, Kati

Movie: 2002: **The Man Without a Past** (Best Actress) *Cannes*.

Owen, Clive

Movie: 2001: **Gosford Park** (Best Ensemble) *SAG*, Broadcast. 2004: **Closer** (Best Supporting Actor) Academy, *New York, Globe, British*, Broadcast (Best

Ensemble) *Board*, Broadcast. 2005: **Sin City** (Best Ensemble) Broadcast.

Özdemir, Muzaffer

Movie: 2003: **Uzak** (Best Actor) *Cannes* (win shared with costar).

Pace, Lee

Movie: 2003: **Soldier's Girl** (Best Male Lead) Spirit.

Pacino, Al

Movie: 1972: **The Godfather** (Most Promising Newcomer) British (Best Actor) *Society* (Best Actor, Drama) Globe (Best Supporting Actor) Academy, *Board*. 1973: **Serpico** (Best Actor) Academy, *Board*, British (Best Actor, Drama) *Globe*. 1974: **The Godfather Part II** (Best Actor) Academy, *British* (multiple win), (Best Actor, Drama) Globe. 1975: **Dog Day Afternoon** (Best Actor) Academy, *British* (multiple win), *LA* (Best Actor, Drama) Globe. 1977: **Bobby Deerfield** (Best Actor, Drama) Globe. 1979: **... And Justice for All** (Best Actor) Academy (Best Actor, Drama) Globe. 1982: **Author! Author!** (Best Actor, Musical or Comedy) Globe. 1983: **Scarface** (Best Actor, Drama) Globe. 1989: **Sea of Love** (Best Actor, Drama) Globe. 1990: **Dick Tracy** (Best Supporting Actor) Academy, Globe, British; **The Godfather, Part III** (Best Actor, Drama) Globe. 1992: **Glengarry Glen Ross** (Best Supporting Actor) Academy, Globe; **Scent of a Woman** (Best Actor) *Academy* (Best Actor, Drama) *Globe*. Theater Award: 1969: **Does a Tiger Wear a Necktie?** (Best Supporting or Featured Actor, Dramatic) *Tony*. 1977: **The Basic Training of Pavlo Hummel** (Best Actor, Play) *Tony*. Television: 2003: **Angels in America** (Best Actor in a Miniseries or TV Movie) *Emmy*, *Globe* (Best Male Actor in a Television Movie or Miniseries) *SAG*. Tributes: 1994: Career Golden Lion from Venice. 2000: Cecil B. DeMille Award from Globe; Gala Tribute from the Film Society of Lincoln Center. 2007: Life Achievement Award from American Film Institute. Records: Pacino shared the record for most acting race losses in Oscar history for less time than any actor — only 2 hours and 19 minutes. Nominated in his seventh and eighth Oscar competitions in 1992 for Best Supporting Actor in **Glengarry Glen Ross** and Best Actor in **Scent of a Woman**, Pacino risked becoming Oscar's biggest loser. When Gene Hackman from **Unforgiven** beat Pacino in the Best Supporting Actor race, Pacino joined Richard Burton and Peter O'Toole as actors who'd earned seven Oscar nominations without a win. When presenter Jodie Foster pronounced Pacino the Best Actor of 1992 less than two-and-a-half hours after he joined the ranks of Oscar's most overlooked nominees, the crowd at the Dorothy Chandler Pavilion rose to its feet. Pacino began his acceptance speech by telling the audience that they broke his streak of twenty years of Oscar losses. Besides pulling out of the ranks as one of Oscar's most defeated competitors, Pacino's win set another record by making him the first actor to win a Best Actor prize in a year he was up for lead and supporting awards.

Pacula, Joanna

Movie: 1983: *Gorky Park* (Best Supporting Actress) Globe.

Page, Ellen

Movie: 2007: *Juno* (Breakthrough Performance by an Actress) *Board* (Best Actress) Academy, British, Broadcast (Best Actress, Musical or Comedy) Globe (Best Female Actor in a Leading Role) SAG (Best Female Lead) *Spirit* (Best Ensemble) Broadcast.

Page, Geraldine

Movie: 1953: *Hondo* (Best Supporting Actress) Academy. 1961: *Summer and Smoke* (Best Actress) Academy, *Board* (Best Actress, Drama) *Globe*. 1962: *Sweet Bird of Youth* (Best Actress) Academy (Best Actress, Drama) *Globe* (Best Foreign Actress) British. 1963: *Toys in the Attic* (Best Actress, Drama) Globe. 1964: *Dear Heart* (Best Actress, Drama) Globe. 1966: *You're a Big Boy Now* (Best Supporting Actress) Academy, Globe. 1969: *Trilogy* (Best Actress) *Board*. 1972: *Pete 'n' Tillie* (Best Supporting Actress) Academy, Globe. 1978: *Interiors* (Best Actress) Academy, *British* (Best Actress, Drama) Globe. 1984: *The Pope of Greenwich Village* (Best Supporting Actress) Academy. 1985: *The Trip to Bountiful* (Best Actress) *Academy* (Best Actress, Drama) Globe (Best Female Lead) *Spirit*. Theater: 1960: *Sweet Bird of Youth* (Best Actress, Dramatic) Tony. 1975: *Absurd Person Singular* (Best Supporting or Featured Actress, Dramatic) Tony. 1982: *Agnes of God* (Best Actress, Play) Tony. 1987: *Blithe Spirit* (Best Actress, Play) Tony. Television: 1959: *"The Old Man," Playhouse 90* (Best Single Performance by an Actress) Emmy. 1967: *"A Christmas Memory," ABC Stage 67* (Best Single Performance by an Actress in a Leading Role in a Drama) *Emmy*. 1969: *The Thanksgiving Visitor* (Best Single Performance by an Actress in a Leading Role) *Emmy*. 1986: *Nazi Hunter: The Beate Klarsfeld Story* (Best Supporting Actress in a Series, Miniseries, or TV Movie) Globe. Records: Page finally won her Academy Award after eight nominations, a record for an actress. Had she lost, she would have overtaken Richard Burton and Peter O'Toole as the most nominated actor without a single win. When an interviewer later asked her how she would have felt if she lost the award and became the most losing actress in Oscar history, the roll-with-the-punches Page replied that she'd love to be the champion. Page won only one other award for the role but set another record in the process. Her victory at the newly launched Independent Spirit Awards made her the first person to win a Best Female Lead Spirit Award.

Page, Joanna

Movie: 2003: *Love Actually* (Best Ensemble) Broadcast.

Páger, Antal

Movie: 1964: *Pacsirta (The Lark)* (Best Actor) *Cannes*.

Palance, Jack

Movie: 1952: *Sudden Fear* (Best Supporting Actor) Academy. 1953: *Shane* (Best Supporting Actor) Academy. 1991: *City Slickers* (Best Supporting Actor) *Academy, Globe*. Television: 1956: *"Requiem for a Heavyweight," Playhouse 90* (Best Single Performance by an Actor) *Emmy*. Highlights: 73-year-old Palance made a graphic demonstration of the vitality of older actors when he came to the podium to accept his Best Supporting Actor Oscar for *City Slickers* and dropped to the floor to do a set of one-armed push-ups. The act drew a mix of amused and bemused responses from the audience, and quick-witted host Billy Crystal used the jarringly impromptu escapade as fodder for further quips throughout the rest of the award telecast. Good sport that he was, Palance helped Crystal continue the joke in his grand entrance as host the following year as well. Palance started the show by dragging huge ropes across the stage at the other end of which was Crystal riding a monstrous Oscar. Once he'd pulled Crystal on stage with him, Palance repeated his one-armed push-up routine, thereby getting the audience to laugh with rather than at him.

Palin, Michael

Movie: 1988: *A Fish Called Wanda* (Best Supporting Actor) *British*.

Palladino, Aleksa

Movie: 2007: *Before the Devil Knows You're Dead* (Best Ensemble) Broadcast.

Palmer, Keke

Movie: 2006: *Akeelah and the Bee* (Best Young Actress) Broadcast.

Palmer, Lilli

Movie: 1953: *The Four Posters* (Best Actress) *Venice*. 1957: *Anastasia—Die letzte Zarentochter (Is Anna Anderson Anastasia?* or *Anastasia—The Czar's Last Daughter)* (Best Foreign Actress) British. 1959: *But Not for Me* (Best Actress, Musical or Comedy) Globe. Television: 1986: *Peter the Great* (Best Supporting Actress in a Series, Miniseries, or TV Movie) Globe.

Palminteri, Chazz

Movie: 1994: *Bullets Over Broadway* (Best Male Actor in a Supporting Role) SAG (Best Supporting Actor) Academy (Best Supporting Male) *Spirit*. 1995: *The Usual Suspects* (Best Ensemble) *Board*.

Paltrow, Gwyneth

Movie: 1998: *Shakespeare in Love* (Best Actress) *Academy*, British (Best Actress, Musical or Comedy) *Globe* (Best Female Actor in a Leading Role) *SAG* (Best Ensemble) *SAG*. 2001: *The Royal Tenenbaums* (Best Ensemble) Broadcast. 2005: *Proof* (Best Actress, Drama) Globe.

PaMon, Bill

Movie: 1997: *Titanic* (Best Ensemble) SAG.

Pangborn, Franklin

Movie: 1944: *Hail the Conquering Hero* (Best Acting) *Board*.

Papas, Irene

Movie: 1971: *The Trojan Women* (Best Actress) *Board*. Highlights: 1971 seemed to be Jane Fonda's year, as her performance in *Klute* won every competitive Best Actress prize — except the one earned by Papas. The National Board of Review found Papas's performance as Helen of Troy so powerful that she stole the spotlight from her *Trojan Women* costars Katharine Hepburn, Vanessa Redgrave, and Genevieve Bujold — and proved the only actress who could interrupt Fonda's Best Actress sweep.

Paquin, Anna

Movie: 1993: *The Piano* (Best Supporting Actress) *Academy*, Globe, *LA*. 2000: *Almost Famous* (Best Ensemble) SAG. Television: 2007: *Bury My Heart at Wounded Knee* (Best Female Actor in a Television Movie or Miniseries) SAG (Best Supporting Actress in a Miniseries or TV Movie) Emmy (Best Supporting Actress in a Series, Miniseries, or TV Movie) Globe. Records: 11-year-old Paquin, a tremendously popular surprise Oscar winner for *The Piano*, was

not only the first New Zealander to win an acting Oscar, but she was also the first actress to beat a fellow nominee in the supporting category when that other actress was nominated for both Best Actress and Best Supporting Actress. Until that time, any actress nominated in both categories in a single year either won the supporting award or lost both races. Paquin's co-star in *The Piano*, Holly Hunter, won Best Actress for that film, but lost to Paquin in her supporting nomination for *The Firm*. Interestingly, Paquin's award was presented to her by Gene Hackman, the first actor to achieve the same feat in the men's acting categories. The year before, Hackman won Best Supporting Actor for *Unforgiven*, beating Al Pacino for *Glengarry Glen Ross*. Later that evening, Pacino won Best Actor for *Scent of a Woman*.

Paredes, Marisa

Movie: 1998: *La Vita è Bella (Life Is Beautiful)* (Best Ensemble) SAG.

Parfitt, Judy

Movie: 2003: *The Girl with the Pearl Earring* (Best Supporting Actress) British.

Parker, Eleanor

Movie: 1950: *Caged* (Best Actress) Academy, *Venice*. 1951: *Detective Story* (Best Actress) Academy. 1955: *Interrupted Melody* (Best Actress) Academy. Television: 1963: *The Eleventh Hour* (Best Single Performance by an Actress in a Leading Role) Emmy. 1969–1970 series *Bracken's World* (Best Actress in a Drama Series) 1969: Globe.

Parker, Molly

Movie: 2001: *The Center of the World* (Best Female Lead) Spirit. Television: 2004–2006 series *Deadwood* (Best Ensemble in a Drama Series) 2006: SAG.

Parker, Nicole Ari

Movie: 1997: *Boogie Nights* (Best Ensemble) SAG.

Parker, Paula Jai

Movie: 2005: *Hustle & Flow* (Best Ensemble) SAG.

Parker, Sarah Jessica

Movie: 1996: *The First Wives Club* (Best Ensemble) *Board*. 2000: *State and Main* (Best Ensemble) *Board*. 2005: *The Family Stone* (Best Actress, Musical or Comedy) Globe. Television: 1998–2004 series *Sex and the City* (Best Actress in a Comedy Series) 1999: Emmy. 2000: Emmy. 2001: Emmy. 2002: Emmy. 2003: Emmy. 2004: *Emmy*. (Best Actress in a Series,

Musical or Comedy) 1999: Globe. 2000: *Globe*. 2001: *Globe*. 2002: *Globe*. 2003: Globe. 2004: *Globe*. 2005: Globe. (Best Female Actor in a Comedy Series) 1999: SAG. 2000: *SAG*. 2001: SAG. 2004: SAG. (Best Ensemble in a Comedy Series) 2000: SAG. 2001: *SAG*. 2002: SAG. 2003: *SAG*. 2004: SAG. (Best Comedy Series, Producer) 2000: *Globe*. 2001: *Emmy, Globe*. 2002: Emmy, *Globe*. 2003: Emmy, Globe. 2004: Emmy, Globe. 2005: Globe.

Parks, Larry

Movie: 1946: *The Jolson Story* (Best Actor) Academy.

Parks, Taylor

Movie: 2007: *Hairspray* (Best Ensemble) SAG, *Broadcast*.

Parlo, Dita

Movie: 1938: *Grand Illusion* (Best Acting) *Board*.

Parrish, Leslie

Movie: 1963: *For Love or Money* (New Star of the Year — Actress) Globe.

Parsons, Estelle

Movie: 1967: *Bonnie and Clyde* (Best Supporting Actress) *Academy*. 1968: *Rachel, Rachel* (Best Supporting Actress) Academy. 1970: *Watermelon Man* (Best Supporting Actress) British. Theater: 1969: *Seven Descents of Myrtle* (Best Actress, Dramatic) Tony. 1971: *And Miss Reardon Drinks a Little* (Best Actress, Dramatic) Tony. 1978: *Miss Margarida's Way* (Best Actress, Play) Tony. 2002: *Morning's at Seven* (Best Actress in a Featured Role, Play) Tony.

Parton, Dolly

Movie: 1980: *9 to 5* (New Star of the Year — Female) Globe (Best Actress, Musical or Comedy) Globe (Best Song, "9 to 5") Academy, Globe. 1982: *The Best Little Whorehouse in Texas* (Best Actress, Musical or Comedy) Globe. 2005: *Transamerica* (Best Song, "Travelin' Thru") Academy, Globe. Television: 1978: *Cher ... Special* (Best Continuing or Single Performance by a Supporting Actress in Variety or Music) Emmy. Tributes: 2006: Honor from Kennedy Center for the Performing Arts.

Pascal, Adam

Movie: 2005: *Rent* (Best Ensemble) Broadcast. Theater: 1996: *Rent* (Best Actor, Musical) Tony.

Passgard, Lars

Movie: 1966: *Jakten* (Best Acting) *Berlin* (Silver Bear Extraordinary Jury Prize).

Patinkin, Mandy

Movie: 1983: *Yentl* (Best Actor, Musical or Comedy) Globe. Theater: 1980: *Evita* (Best Actor in a Featured Role, Musical) *Tony*. 1984: *Sunday in the Park with George* (Best Actor, Musical) Tony. 2000: *The Wild Party* (Best Actor, Musical) Tony. Television: 1994–1996, 1999–2000 series *Chicago Hope* (Best Actor in a Drama Series) 1995: *Emmy*, Globe. 2000: Emmy. (Best Guest Actor in a Drama Series) 1999: Emmy. (Best Male Actor in a Drama Series) 1994: SAG. 1996: *The Larry Sanders Show* (Best Guest Actor in a Comedy Series) Emmy.

Patrick, Nigel

Movie: 1952: *Breaking the Sound Barrier (The Sound Barrier)* (Best British Actor) British. 1957: *Raintree County* (Best Supporting Actor) Globe.

Patterson, Meredith

Movie: 2007: *Before the Devil Knows You're Dead* (Best Ensemble) Broadcast.

Pavan, Marisa

Movie: 1955: *The Rose Tattoo* (Best Foreign Actress) British (Best Supporting Actress) Academy, *Globe*.

Paxinou, Katina

Movie: 1943: *For Whom the Bell Tolls* (Best Acting) *Board* (Best Supporting Actress) Academy, Globe. Records: Greek actress Paxinou, the eighth to be named Best Supporting Actress by the Academy of Motion Picture Arts and Sciences, is the first to receive a full-sized Oscar statuette for the win. Until the ceremony honoring the films of 1943, supporting players received a plaque with a miniature statuette attached. In later years, the Academy replaced all those supporting plaques with a genuine Oscar statuette.

Paxton, Bill

Movie: 1995: *Apollo 13* (Best Ensemble) *SAG*. 1997: *Titanic* (Best Ensemble) SAG. Television: 1998: *A Bright, Shining Lie* (Best Actor in a Miniseries or TV Movie) Globe. 2006–present series *Big Love* (Best Actor in a Drama Series) 2006: Globe. 2007: Globe.

Paymer, David

Movie: 1992: *Mr. Saturday Night* (Best Supporting Actor) Academy, Globe. 2000: *State and Main* (Best Ensemble) *Board*. Television: 1996: *Crime of the Century* (Best Supporting Actor in a Series, Miniseries, or TV Movie) Globe.

Peach, Mary

Movie: 1959: *Room at the Top* (Most Promising Newcomer) British.

Pearce, Guy

Movie: 1997: *L.A. Confidential* (Best Ensemble) SAG.

Peck, Gregory

Movie: 1945: *The Keys of the Kingdom* (Best Actor) Academy. 1946: *The Yearling* (Best Actor) Academy, *Globe*. 1947: *Gentleman's Agreement* (Best Actor) Academy. 1949: *Twelve o'Clock High* (Best Actor) Academy, *New York*. 1953: *Roman Holiday* (Best Foreign Actor) British. 1962: *To Kill a Mockingbird* (Best Actor) *Academy* (Best Actor, Drama) *Globe* (Best Foreign Actor) British. 1963: *Captain Newman, M.D.* (Best Actor, Drama) Globe. 1977: *MacArthur* (Best Actor, Drama) Globe. 1978: *The Boys from Brazil* (Best Actor, Drama) Globe. Television: 1998: *Moby Dick* (Best Supporting Actor in a Miniseries or TV Movie) Emmy (Best Supporting Actor in a Series, Miniseries, or TV Movie) *Globe*. Tributes: 1950, 1954: Henrietta Award for World Film Favorite from Globe. 1967: Jean Hersholt Humanitarian Award from Academy. 1968: Cecil B. DeMille Award from Globe. 1970: Life Achievement Award from SAG. 1989: Life Achievement Award from American Film Institute. 1991: Honor from Kennedy Center for the Performing Arts. 1992: Gala Tribute from Film Society of Lincoln Center. 1993: Honorary Golden Bear from Berlin. 1999: Ranked Number 12 on List of 25 Greatest Male Screen Legends of the 20th Century from American Film Institute. **Records:** When he won the Best Actor Academy Award for playing compassionate lawyer Atticus Finch in the film adaptation of Harper Lee's *To Kill a Mockingbird*, La Jolla–born Peck became the first native Californian to win an acting Oscar. More than 40 years later, the American Film Institute selected Peck's interpretation of Finch as the most heroic character in film history.

Peet, Amanda

Movie: 2005: *Syriana* (Best Ensemble) Broadcast.

Pellegrino, Mark

Movie: 2005: *Capote* (Best Ensemble) SAG.

Peña, Elizabeth

Movie: 1996: *Lone Star* (Best Supporting Female) *Spirit*.

Pendleton, Austin

Movie: 2001: *A Beautiful Mind* (Best Ensemble) SAG. Theater: 1981: *The Little Foxes* (Best Director, Play) Tony.

Penn, Chris

Movie: 1993: *Short Cuts* (Best Ensemble) *Venice* (special award). 1996: *The Funeral* (Best Male Lead) Spirit (Best Supporting Actor) *Venice*.

Penn, Sean

Movie: 1983: *Bad Boys* (New Generation) *LA* (multiple win); *Fast Times at Ridgemont High* (New Generation) *LA* (multiple win). 1993: *Carlito's Way* (Best Supporting Actor) Globe. 1995: *Dead Man Walking* (Best Actor) Academy, *Berlin* (Best Actor, Drama) Globe (Best Male Lead) *Spirit* (Best Male Actor in a Leading Role) SAG. 1997: *She's So Lovely* (Best Actor) *Cannes*. 1998: *Hurlyburly* (Best Actor) *Venice* (Best Male Lead) Spirit. 1999: *Sweet and Lowdown* (Best Actor) Academy (Best Actor, Musical or Comedy) Globe. 2001: *I Am Sam* (Best Actor) Academy, Broadcast (Best Male Actor in a Leading Role) SAG. 2003: *21 Grams* (Best Actor) *Venice, Board* (multiple win), British, *Spirit* (special award shared with costars); *Mystic River* (Best Actor) *Academy, Board* (multiple win), British, *Broadcast* (Best Actor, Drama) *Globe* (Best Male Actor in a Leading Role) SAG (Best Ensemble) SAG, Broadcast. 2007: *Into the Wild* (Best Director) Broadcast (Best Picture, Producer) Board, Broadcast (Best Writer) Broadcast.

Peppard, George

Movie: 1960: *Home from the Hill* (Most Promising Newcomer) British (Best Supporting Actor) *Board*.

Pepper, Barry

Movie: 1998: *Saving Private Ryan* (Best Ensemble) SAG. 1999: *The Green Mile* (Best Ensemble) SAG. 2005: *The Three Burials of Melquiades Estrada* (Best Supporting Male) Spirit. Television: 2001: *61** (Best Actor in a Miniseries or TV Movie) Emmy, Globe. 2004: *3: The Dale Earnhardt Story* (Best Male Actor in a Television Movie or Miniseries) SAG.

Pera, Marilia

Movie: 1981: *Pixote* (Best Actress) *Society*.

Perez, Rosie

Movie: 1993: *Fearless* (Best Supporting Actress) Academy, Globe, *LA*. Television: 1990–1993 series *In Living Color* (Best Individual Achievement in

Choreography) 1990: Emmy. 1992: Emmy. 1993: Emmy.

Perier, François

Movie: 1956: *Gervaise* (Best Foreign Actor) *British*.

Perkins, Anthony

Movie: 1956: *Friendly Persuasion* (New Star of the Year — Actor) *Globe* (Best Supporting Actor) Academy. 1961: *Goodbye Again* (Best Actor) *Cannes*. Theater: 1958: *Look Homeward, Angel* (Best Actor, Dramatic) Tony.

Perlich, Max

Movie: 1989: *Drugstore Cowboy* (Best Supporting Male) *Spirit*. 1995: *Georgia* (Best Supporting Male) Spirit.

Perrin, Jacques

Movie: 1966: *Un Uomo a metà* (Best Actor) *Venice*. 1969: *Z* (Best Picture, Producer) Academy. 2002: *Winged Migration* (Best Documentary Feature) Academy.

Perrine, Valerie

Movie: 1974: *Lenny* (Most Promising Newcomer) *British* (Best Actress) Academy, *Cannes*, British (Best Actress, Drama) Globe (Best Supporting Actress) *New York, Board*.

Perrineau, Harold

Movie: 1995: *Smoke* (Best Supporting Male) Spirit.

Pesci, Joe

Movie: 1980: *Raging Bull* (Most Promising Newcomer) *British* (Best Supporting Actor) Academy, *New York, Board*, Globe, *Society*. 1990: *GoodFellas* (Best Supporting Actor) *Academy, Board*, Globe, *LA*.

Peters, Bernadette

Movie: 1976: *Silent Movie* (Best Supporting Actress) Globe. 1981: *Pennies from Heaven* (Best Actress, Musical or Comedy) *Globe*. Theater: 1972: *On the Town* (Best Supporting or Featured Actress, Musical) Tony. 1975: *Mack and Mabel* (Best Actress, Musical) Tony. 1984: *Sunday in the Park with George* (Best Actress, Musical) Tony. 1986: *Song and Dance* (Best Actress, Musical) *Tony*. 1993: *The Goodbye Girl* (Best Actress, Musical) Tony. 1999: *Annie Get Your Gun* (Best Actress, Musical) *Tony*. 2003: *Gypsy* (Best Actress, Musical) Tony. Television: 1976–1977 series *All's Fair* (Best Actress in a Series, Musical or Comedy) 1977: Globe. 1978: *The Muppet Show* (Best

Continuing or Single Performance by a Supporting Actress in Variety or Music) Emmy. 2001: *Ally McBeal* (Best Guest Actress in a Comedy Series) Emmy.

Peters, Brock

Theater: 1973: *Lost in the Stars* (Best Actor, Musical) Tony. Tributes: 1990: Life Achievement Award from SAG.

Peters, Susan

Movie: 1942: *Random Harvest* (Best Acting) *Board* (Best Supporting Actress) Academy.

Pfeiffer, Michelle

Movie: 1988: *Dangerous Liaisons* (Best Supporting Actress) Academy, *British*; *Married to the Mob* (Best Actress, Musical or Comedy) Globe. 1989: *The Fabulous Baker Boys* (Best Actress) Academy, *New York, Board*, British, *Society*, LA (Best Actress, Drama) *Globe*. 1990: *The Russia House* (Best Actress, Drama) Globe. 1991: *Frankie and Johnny* (Best Actress, Musical or Comedy) Globe. 1992: *Love Field* (Best Actress) Academy, *Berlin* (Best Actress, Drama) Globe. 1993: *The Age of Innocence* (Best Actress, Drama) Globe. 2002: *White Oleander* (Best Female Actor in a Supporting Role) SAG. 2007: *Hairspray* (Best Ensemble) SAG, *Broadcast*.

Phillippe, Ryan

Movie: 2001: *Gosford Park* (Best Ensemble) *SAG, Broadcast*. 2005: *Crash* (Best Ensemble) *SAG, Broadcast*.

Phillips, Leslie

Movie: 2006: *Venus* (Best Supporting Actor) British.

Phillips, Lou Diamond

Movie: 1988: *Stand and Deliver* (Best Supporting Actor) Globe (Best Supporting Male) *Spirit*. Theater: 1996: *The King and I* (Best Actor, Musical) Tony.

Phillips, Michelle

Movie: 1973: *Dillinger* (New Star of the Year — Female) Globe.

Phillips, Sian

Movie: 1969: *Goodbye, Mr. Chips* (Best Supporting Actress) Globe, *Society*. Theater: 1999: *Marlene* (Best Actress, Musical) Tony.

Phipps, William

Movie: 1954: *Executive Suite* (Best Ensemble) *Venice* (special award).

Phoenix, Joaquin

Movie: 2000: *Gladiator* (Best Male Actor in a Supporting Role) SAG (Best Supporting Actor) Academy, *Board* (multiple win), Globe, British, *Broadcast* (multiple win), (Best Ensemble) SAG; *Quills* (Best Supporting Actor) *Board* (multiple win), *Broadcast* (multiple win); *The Yards* (Best Supporting Actor) *Board* (multiple win), *Broadcast* (multiple win). 2004: *Hotel Rwanda* (Best Ensemble) SAG. 2005: *Walk the Line* (Best Actor) Academy, British, Broadcast (Best Actor, Musical or Comedy) *Globe* (Best Male Actor in a Leading Role) SAG.

Phoenix, River

Movie: 1988: *Running on Empty* (Best Supporting Actor) Academy, *Board*, Globe. 1991: *My Own Private Idaho* (Best Actor) *Venice, Society* (Best Male Lead) *Spirit.*

Phoenix, Summer

Movie: 2001: *The Believer* (Best Supporting Female) Spirit.

Piane, Carlo Delle

Movie: 1983: *Una Gita scolastica* (Best Actor) *Venice.* 1986: *Regalo di Natale* (Best Actor) *Venice.*

Piccoli, Michel

Movie: 1980: *A Leap into the Void* (Best Actor) *Cannes.* 1982: *A Strange Affair* (Best Actor) *Berlin.*

Piccolo, Ottavia

Movie: 1970: *Metello* (Best Actress) *Cannes.*

Pickford, Mary

Movie: 1929: *Coquette* (Best Actress) *Academy.* Tributes: 1975: Honorary Oscar statuette in recognition of her unique contributions to the film industry and the development of film as an artistic medium from Academy. 1999: Ranked Number 24 on List of 25 Greatest Female Screen Legends of the 20th Century from American Film Institute. Records: Pickford, one of the 36 founding members of the Academy of Motion Picture Arts and Sciences and "America's Sweetheart" of the silver screen, came out of retirement to star in *Coquette*, her first talking picture. When Pickford's name appeared among the nominees the day after Wall Street crashed, Pickford hungered for a win to prove she had survived the transition to talkies. Poor reviews for *Coquette* only made her more determined to find a way to increase her chances of winning. Because in those early days of Oscar the final winners were cho- sen by only a five-member panel of judges, Pickford invited them for tea at Pickfair, the famous estate she shared with husband Douglas Fairbanks. That gesture made her the first star to openly campaign to win an Oscar. When it worked and she received the award, she also became the first star to win a Best Actress Oscar for a single performance and for a film with sound. At the initial Oscar ceremony the previous year, Janet Gaynor won Best Actress for her work in three movies (***Seventh Heaven, Street Angel*** and ***Sunrise***), all silent pictures.

Picon, Molly

Movie: 1963: *Come Blow Your Horn* (Best Actress, Musical or Comedy) Globe. Theater: 1962: *Milk and Honey* (Best Actress, Musical) Tony.

Pidgeon, Rebecca

Movie: 2000: *State and Main* (Best Ensemble) *Board.*

Pidgeon, Walter

Movie: 1942: *Mrs. Miniver* (Best Actor) Academy. 1943: *Madame Curie* (Best Actor) Academy. 1954: *Executive Suite* (Best Ensemble) *Venice* (special award). Theater: 1960: *Take Me Along* (Best Actor, Musical) Tony. Tributes: 1974: Special Achievement Award from SAG.

Pierce, Justin

Movie: 1995: *Kids* (Best Debut Performance) *Spirit.*

Pigg, Alexandra

Movie: 1985: *A Letter to Brezhnev* (Best Actress) British.

Pilkes, Hannah

Movie: 2004: *The Woodsman* (Best Debut Performance) Spirit.

Pinchot, Bronson

Movie: 1996: *The First Wives Club* (Best Ensemble) *Board.* Television: 1986–1993 series *Perfect Strangers* (Best Actor in a Comedy Series) 1987: Emmy.

Pine, Larry

Movie: 1994: *Vanya on 42nd Street* (Best Supporting Male) Spirit.

Pischiutta, Bruno

Movie: 1972: *Uomini contro* (Best Supporting Actor) *Berlin.*

Pitt, Brad

Movie: 1994: *Legends of the Fall* (Best Actor, Drama) Globe. 1995: *12 Monkeys* (Best Supporting Actor) Academy, *Globe*. 2001: *Ocean's 11* (Best Ensemble) Broadcast. 2004: *Ocean's Twelve* (Best Ensemble) Broadcast. 2006: *Babel* (Best Supporting Actor) Globe (Best Ensemble) SAG, Broadcast. 2007: *The Assassination of Jesse James by the Coward Robert Ford* (Best Actor) *Venice* (Best Picture, Producer) Board; *A Mighty Heart* (Best Independent Film, Producer) Board (Best Picture, Producer) Spirit. Television: 2002: *Friends* (Best Guest Actor in a Comedy Series) Emmy.

Place, Mary Kay

Movie: 1996: *Manny & Lo* (Best Supporting Female) Spirit. 1999: *Being John Malkovich* (Best Ensemble) SAG. Television: 1974: *M*A*S*H* (Best Writing for a Comedy Series) Emmy. 1976–1977 series *Mary Hartman, Mary Hartman* (Best Continuing Performance by a Supporting Actress in a Comedy Series) 1977: *Emmy*. Highlights: Before she became an actress, Place had been Tim Conway's secretary. In 1977, both Place and her former boss won acting Emmys.

Placido, Michele

Movie: 1979: *Ernesto* (Best Actor) *Berlin*.

Pleshette, Suzanne

Movie: 1962: *Rome Adventure* (New Star of the Year — Actress) Globe. Television: 1962: *Dr. Kildare* (Best Single Performance by an Actress in a Leading Role) Emmy. 1972–1978 series *The Bob Newhart Show* (Best Actress in a Comedy Series) 1977: Emmy. 1978: Emmy. 1991: *Leona Helmsley: The Queen of Mean* (Best Actress in a Miniseries or Special) Emmy (Best Actress in a Miniseries or TV Movie) Globe.

Plimpton, Martha

Movie: 1987: *Shy People* (Best Supporting Female) Spirit. Theater: 2007: *The Coast of Utopia* (Best Actress in a Feature Role, Play) Tony. Television: 2002: *Law & Order: Special Victims Unit* (Best Guest Actress in a Drama Series) Emmy.

Plowright, Joan

Movie: 1960: *The Entertainer* (Most Promising Newcomer) British. 1977: *Equus* (Best Supporting Actress) British. 1992: *Enchanted April* (Best Supporting Actress) Academy, *Globe*. Theater: 1961: *A Taste of Honey* (Best Actress, Dramatic) *Tony*. Television: 1993: *Stalin* (Best Supporting Actress in a Miniseries or Special) Emmy (Best Supporting Actress in a Series, Miniseries, or TV Movie) *Globe*.

Plummer, Amanda

Movie: 1991: *The Fisher King* (Best Supporting Actress) British. Theater: 1982: *Agnes of God* (Best Actress in a Featured Role, Play) *Tony*; *A Taste of Honey* (Best Actress, Play) Tony. 1987: *Pygmalion* (Best Actress, Play) Tony. Television: 1988–1990 series *L.A. Law* (Best Supporting Actress in a Drama Series) 1989: Emmy. 1992: *"Miss Rose White," Hallmark Hall of Fame* (Best Supporting Actress in a Miniseries or Special) *Emmy* (Best Supporting Actress in a Series, Miniseries, or TV Movie) Globe. 1996: *The Outer Limits* (Best Guest Actress in a Drama Series) *Emmy*. 2005: *Law & Order: Special Victims Unit* (Best Guest Actress in a Drama Series) *Emmy*. Records: Along with Dana Ivey and Kate Burton, Plummer is one of only three actresses ever to be nominated for a Tony Award in two acting categories in the same year. In 1982, she was up for lead and featured actress. She won playing the part of delusional Sister Agnes in John Pielmeier's play, *Agnes of God*.

Plummer, Christopher

Movie: 1999: *The Insider* (Best Supporting Actor) *Society, LA*. 2001: *A Beautiful Mind* (Best Ensemble) SAG. 2002: *Nicholas Nickleby* (Best Ensemble) *Board*. 2005: *Syriana* (Best Ensemble) Broadcast. Theater: 1959: *J. B.* (Best Actor, Dramatic) Tony. 1974: *Cyrano* (Best Actor, Musical) *Tony*. 1982: *Othello* (Best Actor, Play) Tony. 1994: *No Man's Land* (Best Actor, Play) Tony. 1997: *Barrymore* (Best Actor, Play) *Tony*. 2004: *King Lear* (Best Actor, Play) Tony. 2007: *Inherit the Wind* (Best Actor, Play) Tony. Television: 1959: *"Little Moon of Alban," Hallmark Hall of Fame* (Best Single Performance by an Actor) Emmy. 1966: *Hamlet* (Best Single Performance by an Actor in a Leading Role in a Drama) Emmy. 1977: *"The Moneychangers," NBC World Premiere Movie, The Big Event* (Best Actor in a Limited Series) *Emmy*. 1983: *The Thorn Birds* (Best Supporting Actor in a Limited Series or Special) Emmy. 1994: *Madeline* (Best Voice-Over Performance) *Emmy*. 2000: *American Tragedy* (Best Supporting Actor in a Series, Miniseries, or TV Movie) Globe. 2005: *Our Fathers* (Best Male Actor in a Television Movie or Miniseries) SAG (Best Supporting Actor in a Miniseries or TV Movie) Emmy. Tributes: 2002: Career Achievement Award from Board.

Plummer, Glenn

Movie: 1991: *Pastime* (Best Supporting Male) Spirit.

Podemski, Tamara

Movie: 2007: *Four Sheets to the Wind* (Best Supporting Female) Spirit.

Poitier, Sidney

Movie: 1957: *A Man Is Ten Feet Tall* (Best Foreign Actor) British. 1958: *The Defiant Ones* (Best Actor) Academy, *Berlin* (Best Actor, Drama) Globe (Best Foreign Actor) *British.* 1959: *Porgy and Bess* (Best Actor, Musical or Comedy) Globe. 1961: *A Raisin in the Sun* (Best Actor, Drama) Globe (Best Foreign Actor) British. 1963: *Lilies of the Field* *Academy, Berlin* (Best Actor, Drama) *Globe* (Best Foreign Actor) British. 1965: *A Patch of Blue* (Best Actor, Drama) Globe (Best Foreign Actor) British. 1967: *In the Heat of the Night* (Best Actor, Drama) Globe (Best Foreign Actor) British. Theater: 1960: *A Raisin in the Sun* (Best Actor, Dramatic) Tony. Television: 1991: *Separate but Equal* (Best Actor in a Miniseries or Special) Emmy (Best Actor in a Miniseries or TV Movie) Globe. 1997: *Mandela and De Klerk* (Best Actor in a Miniseries or Special) Emmy (Best Male Actor in a Television Movie or Miniseries) SAG. Tributes: 1968, 1969, 1970: Henrietta Award for World Film Favorite from Globe. 1981: Cecil B. DeMille Award from Globe. 1992: Life Achievement Award from American Film Institute. 1994: Career Achievement Award from Board. 1995: Honor from Kennedy Center for the Performing Arts. 1999: Life Achievement Award from SAG; Ranked Number 22 on List of 25 Greatest Male Screen Legends of the 20th Century from American Film Insitute. 2001: Honorary Oscar statuette in recognition of his remarkable accomplishments as an artist and as a human being from Academy. Records: Poitier's 1963 Best Actor Academy Award for *Lilies of the Field* made him the first African-American to win an Oscar for a lead performance and the first Black male to win the award in a competitive acting category. (In 1947 James Baskett was honored with a special Oscar for his heartwarming interpretation of Uncle Remus in *Song of the South.*) After Poitier won, the city of New York gave Poitier a ticker-tape parade in recognition of his achievement, making him the first actor honored with a metropolitan parade for winning an Oscar.

Pollak, Kevin

Movie: 1995: *The Usual Suspects* (Best Ensemble) Board.

Pollard, Michael J.

Movie: 1967: *Bonnie and Clyde* (New Star of the Year — Actor) Globe (Most Promising Newcomer) British (Best Supporting Actor) Academy, Globe.

Polley, Sarah

Movie: 1997: *The Sweet Hereafter* (Best Ensemble) Board. 1999: *Go* (Best Supporting Female) Spirit. 2007: *Away from Her* (Best First Film, Director and Writer) New York (Best Adapted Screenplay) Academy (New Generation) *LA.*

Pollotta, Gabriella

Movie: 1962: *The Pigeon That Took Rome* (Best Supporting Actress) Globe.

Portillo, Blanca

Movie: 2006: *Volver* (Best Actress) *Cannes* (win shared with costars).

Portman, Natalie

Movie: 1999: *Anywhere but Here* (Best Supporting Actress) Globe. 2004: *Closer* (Best Supporting Actress) Academy, *Globe,* British, Broadcast (Best Ensemble) *Board,* Broadcast.

Pose, Jörg

Movie: 1988: *Bear Ye One Another's Burdens...* (Best Actor) *Berlin* (win shared with costar).

Posey, Parker

Movie: 2002: *Personal Velocity* (Best Female Lead) Spirit. 2003: *A Mighty Wind* (Best Screenplay) Spirit (Best Ensemble) Broadcast. 2007: *Broken English* (Best Female Lead) Spirit. Television: 2002: *Hell on Heels: The Battle of Mary Kay* (Best Supporting Actress in a Series, Miniseries, or TV Movie) Globe.

Postlethwaite, Pete

Movie: 1993: *In the Name of the Father* (Best Supporting Actor) Academy. 1995: *The Usual Suspects* (Best Ensemble) Board.

Potok, Charlotte

Movie: 2000: *State and Main* (Best Ensemble) Board.

Potts, Annie

Movie: 1978: *Corvette Summer* (New Star of the Year — Actress) Globe. Television: 1994–1995 series *Love & War* (Best Actress in a Comedy Series) 1994: Emmy. 1998–2002 series *Any Day Now* (Best Female Actor in a Drama Series) 1998: SAG. 1999: SAG.

Powell, Clifton

Movie: 2004: *Ray* (Best Ensemble) SAG.

Powell, William

Movie: 1934: *The Thin Man* (Best Actor) Academy. 1936: *My Man Godfrey* (Best Actor) Academy. 1947: *Life with Father* (Best Actor) Academy, *New York* (multiple win); *The Senator Was Indiscreet* (Best Actor) *New York* (multiple win).

Powers, Mala

Movie: 1950: *Cyrano de Bergerac* (New Star of the Year — Actress) Globe. 1953: *The Medium* (Best Foreign Actress) British.

Presnell, Harve

Movie: 1964: *The Unsinkable Molly Brown* (New Star of the Year — Actor) *Globe.*

Preston, Robert

Movie: 1962: *The Music Man (Meredith Willson's The Music Man)* (Best Actor, Musical or Comedy) Globe. 1981: *S. O. B.* (Best Supporting Actor) *Society.* 1982: *Victor/Victoria* (Best Actor, Musical or Comedy) Globe (Best Supporting Actor) Academy, *Board.* Theater: 1958: *The Music Man* (Best Actor, Musical) *Tony.* 1967: *I Do! I Do!* (Best Actor, Musical) *Tony.* 1975: *Mack and Mabel* (Best Actor, Musical) Tony. Tributes: 1982: Career Achievement Award from LA.

Price, Vincent

Movie: 1987: *The Whales of August* (Best Supporting Male) Spirit. Tributes: 1991: Career Achievement Award from LA.

Priest, Martin

Movie: 1990: *The Plot Against Harry* (Best Male Lead) Spirit.

Principal, Victoria

Movie: 1972: *The Life and Times of Judge Roy Bean* (New Star of the Year — Actress) Globe. Television: 1978–1987 series *Dallas* (Best Actress in a Drama Series) 1982: Globe.

Prochnow, Jürgen

Movie: 1996: *The English Patient* (Best Ensemble) SAG.

Prospero, Joe

Movie: 2004: *Finding Neverland* (Best Ensemble) SAG.

Pryce, Jonathan

Movie: 1995: *Carrington* (Best Actor) *Cannes,* British. Theater: 1977: *Comedians* (Best Actor in a Featured Role, Play) *Tony.* 1991: *Miss Saigon* (Best Actor, Musical) *Tony.* Television: 1993: *Barbarians at the Gate* (Best Supporting Actor in a Miniseries or Special) Emmy (Best Supporting Actor in a Series, Miniseries, or TV Movie) Globe.

Pucci, Lou Taylor

Movie: 2005: *Thumbsucker* (Best Actor) *Berlin.*

Pulver, Liselotte (Lilo)

Movie: 1963: *A Global Affair* (Best Supporting Actress) Globe.

Puri, Om

Movie: 1999: *East Is East* (Best Actor) British.

Qin, Shaobo

Movie: 2001: *Ocean's 11* (Best Ensemble) Broadcast. 2004: *Ocean's Twelve* (Best Ensemble) Broadcast.

Quaid, Dennis

Movie: 1987: *The Big Easy* (Best Male Lead) *Spirit.* 2000: *Traffic* (Best Ensemble) SAG. 2002: *Far from Heaven* (Best Male Actor in a Supporting Role) SAG (Best Supporting Actor) *New York*, Globe (Best Supporting Male) *Spirit.*

Quaid, Randy

Movie: 1973: *The Last Detail* (Best Supporting Actor) Academy, Globe, British. 1989: *Parents* (Best Male Lead) Spirit. 2005: *Brokeback Mountain* (Best Ensemble) SAG. Television: 1984: *"A Streetcar Named Desire," An ABC Theatre Presentation* (Best Supporting Actor in a Limited Series or Special) Emmy. 1987: *LBJ: The Early Years* (Best Actor in a Miniseries or Special) Emmy (Best Actor in a Miniseries or TV Movie) *Globe.* 2005: *Elvis* (Best Supporting Actor in a Miniseries or TV Movie) Emmy (Best Supporting Actor in a Series, Miniseries, or TV Movie) Globe.

Qualls, D. J.

Movie: 2005: *Hustle & Flow* (Best Ensemble) SAG.

Quayle, Anthony

Movie: 1958: *Ice-Cold in Alex* (Best British Actor) British. 1969: *Anne of the Thousand Days* (Best Supporting Actor) Academy, Globe. Theater: 1956: *Tamburlaine the Great* (Best Supporting or Featured Actor, Dramatic) Tony. Television: 1975: *"QB VII," ABC Theatre* (Best Single Performance by a Supporting Actor in a Comedy or Drama Special) *Emmy.* 1981: *Masada* (Best Supporting Actor in a Limited Series or Special) Emmy.

Quinlan, Kathleen

Movie: 1977: *I Never Promised You a Rose Garden* (Best Actress, Drama) Globe. 1995: *Apollo 13* (Best Supporting Actress) Academy, Globe (Best Ensemble) *SAG*.

Quinn, Aidan

Movie: 2004: *Cavedweller* (Best Supporting Male) Spirit. Television: 1985: *An Early Frost* (Best Actor in a Miniseries or Special) Emmy. 2007: *Bury My Heart at Wounded Knee* (Best Supporting Actor in a Miniseries or TV Movie) Emmy.

Quinn, Aileen

Movie: 1982: *Annie* (New Star of the Year — Actress) Globe (Best Actress, Musical or Comedy) Globe.

Quinn, Anthony

Movie: 1952: *Viva Zapata!* (Best Supporting Actor) *Academy*. 1956: *Lust for Life* (Best Supporting Actor) *Academy*, Globe. 1957: *Wild Is the Wind* (Best Actor) Academy. 1962: *Lawrence of Arabia* (Best Actor, Drama) Globe (Best Foreign Actor) British. 1964: *Zorba the Geek* (Best Actor) Academy, *Board* (Best Actor, Drama) Globe (Best Foreign Actor) British. 1969: *The Secret of Santa Vittoria* (Best Actor, Musical or Comedy) Globe. Theater: 1961: *Becket* (Best Actor, Dramatic) Tony. Television: 1988: *Onassis: The Richest Man in the World* (Best Supporting Actor in a Miniseries or Special) Emmy. 1996: *Gotti* (Best Supporting Actor in a Series, Miniseries, or TV Movie) Globe. Tributes: 1986: Cecil B. DeMille Award from Globe. Records: Quinn is the first two-time Oscar winner to receive both his awards playing biographical roles. In 1952 he was revolutionary Emilio Zapata's brother, Eufemio in *Viva Zapata!* In 1956, he portrayed fiery, egotistical painter Paul Gaugin in *Lust for Life*. Only on screen eight minutes for the latter film, that Oscar-winning performance is one of the shortest in Academy history.

Rabal, Francisco

Movie: 1984: *Los Santos Innocentes (The Holy Innocents)* (Best Actor) *Cannes* (win shared with costar).

Radcliffe, Daniel

Movie: 2001: *Harry Potter and the Sorcerer's Stone* (Best Young Actor/Actress) Broadcast. 2004: *Harry Potter and the Prisoner of Azkaban* (Best Young Actor) Broadcast. 2005: *Harry Potter and the Goblet of Fire* (Best Young Actor) Broadcast.

Raffin, Deborah

Movie: 1980: *Touched by Love* (Best Actress, Drama) Globe.

Railsback, Steve

Movie: 1980: *The Stunt Man* (New Star of the Year — Actor) Globe.

Raimu

Movie Awards: 1938: *Un Carnet de Bal* (Best Acting) Board. 1940: *The Baker's Wife* (Best Acting) *Board*.

Rainer, Luise

Movie: 1936: *The Great Ziegfeld* (Best Actress) *Academy, New York*. 1937: *The Good Earth* (Best Acting) *Board* (Best Actress) *Academy*. Records: Rainer set two Academy Award records in 1937 when she became the first person to win two acting Oscars and the first to win acting Oscars in consecutive years.

Rains, Claude

Movie: 1939: *Mr. Smith Goes to Washington* (Best Supporting Actor) Academy. 1943: *Casablanca* (Best Supporting Actor) Academy. 1944: *Mr. Skeffington* (Best Supporting Actor) Academy. 1946: *Notorious* (Best Supporting Actor) Academy. Theater: 1951: *Darkness at Noon* (Best Actor, Dramatic) *Tony*.

Rains, Luce

Movie: 2007: *3:10 to Yuma* (Best Ensemble) SAG.

Ralph, Sheryl Lee

Movie: 1990: *To Sleep with Anger* (Best Supporting Female) *Spirit*. Theater: 1982: *Dreamgirls* (Best Actress, Musical) Tony.

Rambeau, Marjorie

Movie: 1940: *The Primrose Path* (Best Supporting Actress) Academy. 1953: *Torch Song* (Best Supporting Actress) Academy. 1955: *A Man Called Peter* (Best Supporting Actress) *Board* (multiple win); *The View from Pompey's Head* (Best Supporting Actress) *Board* (multiple win).

Ramsey, Anne

Movie: 1987: *Throw Momma from the Train* (Best Supporting Actress) Academy, Globe.

Randall, Tony

Movie: 1957: *Will Success Spoil Rock Hunter?* (Best Actor, Musical or Comedy) Globe. 1959: *Pillow Talk*

(Best Supporting Actor) Globe. 1961: *Lover Come Back* (Best Supporting Actor) Globe. **Theater:** 1958: *Oh, Captain!* (Best Actor, Musical) Tony. 1993: *St. Joan* (Best Revival, Producer) Tony. 1994: *Timon of Athens* (Best Revival, Play; Producer) Tony. 1996: *Inherit the Wind* (Best Revival, Play; Producer) Tony. 1997: *The Gin Game* (Best Revival, Play; Producer) Tony. **Television:** 1952–1955 series *Mr. Peepers* (Best Series Supporting Actor) 1954: Emmy. 1970–1975 series *The Odd Couple* (Best Continued Performance by an Actor in a Leading Role in a Comedy Series) 1971: Emmy. 1972: Emmy. (Best Actor in a Comedy Series) 1973: Emmy. 1974: Emmy. 1975: *Emmy.* 1976–1978 series *The Tony Randall Show* (Best Actor in a Series, Musical or Comedy) 1976: Globe. 1981–1983 series *Love, Sidney* (Best Actor in a Series, Musical or Comedy) 1981: Globe. 1982: Globe.

Ransome, Prunella

Movie: 1967: *Far from the Madding Crowd* (Best Supporting Actress) Globe.

Rapp, Anthony

Movie: 2001: *A Beautiful Mind* (Best Ensemble) SAG. 2005: *Rent* (Best Ensemble) Broadcast.

Rappaport, Michael

Movie: 1992: *Zebrahead* (Best Male Lead) Spirit.

Rasuk, Victor

Movie: 2003: *Raising Victor Vargas* (Best Debut Performance) Spirit.

Rathbone, Basil

Movie: 1936: *Romeo and Juliet* (Best Supporting Actor) Academy. 1938: *If I Were King* (Best Supporting Actor) Academy. **Theater:** 1948: *The Heiress* (Best Actor, Dramatic) *Tony.*

Ray, Aldo

Movie: 1952: *Pat and Mike* (New Star of the Year — Actor) Globe.

Ray, Anthony

Movie: 1960: *Shadows* (Most Promising Newcomer) British.

Raye, Martha

Movie: 1962: *Jumbo* (Best Supporting Actress) Globe. **Television:** 1953: --- (Best Comedienne) Emmy. 1954: --- (Most Outstanding Personality) Emmy. 1976: *"McMillan and Wife,"* NBC Sunday *Mystery Movie* (Best Lead Actress for a Single Appearance in a Drama or Comedy Series) Emmy. **Tributes:** 1968: Jean Hersholt Humanitarian Award from Academy. 1973: Life Achievement Award from SAG. **Records:** The tenth time it was given, Raye became the first woman to be awarded the Jean Hersholt Humanitarian Award. Raye was cited for her diligent, high energy efforts to entertain Allied soldiers both on the home front and on the front lines overseas and for the equal dedication she showed performing for troops during her Vietnam USO tours. In all she ended up performing for literally millions of GIs. When her friend Bob Hope, with whom Raye had shared the spotlight during many of his tours entertaining the military, found out she was to be honored, he returned to the Oscars to present her award. When Hope referred to her as a great gal, great lady, and "Colonel Maggie of the Boondocks" a visibly moved Raye called that day the happiest of her life — stateside.

Razvi, Ahmad

Movie: 2006: *Man Push Cart* (Best Male Lead) Spirit.

Rea, Stephen

Movie: 1992: *The Crying Game* (Best Actor) Academy, British, *Society.* 1994: *Prêt-à-Porter (Ready-to-Wear)* (Best Ensemble) *Board.* **Theater:** 1993: *Someone Who'll Watch Over Me* (Best Actor, Play) Tony. **Television:** 1996: *Crime of the Century* (Best Actor in a Miniseries or TV Movie) Globe.

Read, Rufus

Movie: 1998: *Happiness* (Best Ensemble) *Board.*

Reagan, Ronald

Tributes: 1956: Hollywood Citizenship Award from Globe.

Reaser, Elizabeth

Movie: 2006: *Sweet Land* (Best Female Lead) Spirit. **Television:** 2007: *Grey's Anatomy* (Best Guest Actress in a Drama Series) Emmy (Best Ensemble in a Drama Series) SAG.

Reddy, Helen

Movie: 1974: *Airport 1975* (New Star of the Year — Female) Globe.

Redford, Robert

Movie: 1965: *Inside Daisy Clover* (New Star of the Year — Actor) *Globe.* 1969: *Butch Cassidy and the*

Sundance Kid (Best Actor) *British* (multiple win); *Downhill Racer* (Best Actor) *British* (multiple win); *Tell Them Willie Boy Is Here* (Best Actor) *British* (multiple win). 1973: *The Sting* (Best Actor) Academy. 1980: *Ordinary People* (Best Director) *Academy, Board, Globe.* 1992: *A River Runs Through It* (Best Director) Globe. 1994: *Quiz Show* (Best Director) Academy, Globe (Best Picture, Producer) Academy, British (Best Picture, Drama; Producer) Globe. 1998: *The Horse Whisperer* (Best Director) Globe. **Television:** 1963: *"The Voice of Charlie Pont," Alcoa Premiere Presented by Fred Astaire* (Best Supporting Actor) Emmy. **Tributes:** 1974, 1976, 1977: Henrietta Award as World Film Favorite from Globe. 1993: Cecil B. DeMille Award from Globe. 1995: Life Achievement Award from SAG. 2001: Honorary Oscar statuette as actor, director, producer, creator of Sundance, inspiration to independent and innovative filmmakers everywhere from Academy. 2005: Honor from Kennedy Center for the Performing Arts. **Records:** Picking up the Best Director Academy Award for *Ordinary People* in 1980 made Redford the first actor to win his Oscar in a non-acting category. While other Oscar-winning moviemakers, including Charlie Chaplin, Orson Welles, Woody Allen, and Richard Attenborough, act as well as direct, produce, and write, Redford is the first to make his niche in films as an actor but to win the Academy Award for non-acting work. **Highlights:** The year after Redford struck award gold for directing *Ordinary People*, he founded The Sundance Institute and took the reigns of the three-year-old Utah/United States Film Festival (renamed the Sundance Film Festival in 1991) which gave voice and strength to independent films and their creators.

Redgrave, Lynn

Movie: 1964: *Girl with Green Eyes* (Most Promising Newcomer) British. 1966: *Georgy Girl* (Best New Star of the Year — Actress) Globe (Best Actress) Academy, *New York* (Best Actress, Musical or Comedy) *Globe* (Best British Actress) British. 1996: *Shine* (Best Supporting Actress) British (Best Ensemble) SAG. 1998: *Gods and Monsters* (Best Female Actor in a Supporting Role) *SAG* (Best Supporting Actress) Academy, *Globe*, British (Best Supporting Female) *Spirit.* **Theater:** 1976: *Mrs. Warren's Profession* (Best Actress, Play) Tony. 1993: *Shakespeare for My Father* (Best Actress, Play) Tony. 2006: *The Constant Wife* (Best Actress, Play) Tony. **Television:** 1979–1981 series *House Calls* (Best Actress in a Comedy Series) 1981: Emmy. (Best Actress in a Series, Musical or Comedy) 1980: Globe. **Records:** Redgrave and Elizabeth Taylor both earned such favor from the New York Film Critics for their respective performances

in *Georgy Girl* and *Who's Afraid of Virginia Woolf?* that critics gave both the Best Actress prize in 1966. It was the first time the NYFC declared an acting tie in their 31-year history.

Redgrave, Michael

Movie: 1947: *Mourning Becomes Electra* (Best Actor) Academy, *Board.* 1951: *The Browning Version* (Best Actor) *Cannes.* 1955: *The Night My Number Came Up* (Best British Actor) British. 1957: *Time Without Pity* (Best British Actor) British. **Theater:** 1956: *Tiger at the Gates* (Best Actor, Dramatic) Tony.

Redgrave, Vanessa

Movie: 1966: *Morgan! (Morgan: A Suitable Case for Treatment)* (Best Actress) Academy, *Cannes* (Best Actress, Musical or Comedy) Globe (Best British Actress) British. 1967: *Camelot* (Best Actress, Musical or Comedy) Globe. 1968: *Isadora* (Best Actress) Academy, *Cannes* (Best Actress, Drama) Globe. 1969: *The Loves of Isadora* (re-cut version of *Isadora*) (Best Actress) *Society.* 1971: *Mary, Queen of Scots* (Best Actress) Academy (Best Actress, Drama) Globe. 1977: *Julia* (Best Supporting Actress) *Academy, Globe, LA.* 1984: *The Bostonians* (Best Actress) Academy, *Society* (Best Actress, Drama) Globe. 1985: *Wetherby* (Best Actress) *Society.* 1987: *Prick Up Your Ears* (Best Supporting Actress) *New York,* Globe, British. 1992: *Howards End* (Best Supporting Actress) Academy. 1995: *Little Odessa* (Best Supporting Actress) *Venice* (Best Supporting Female) Spirit; *A Month by the Lake* (Best Actress, Musical or Comedy) Globe. 2007: *Atonement* (Best Supporting Actress) Broadcast. **Theater:** 2003: *Long Day's Journey into Night* (Best Actress, Play) *Tony.* 2007: *The Year of Magical Thinking* (Best Actress, Play) Tony. **Television:** 1981: *Playing for Time* (Best Actress in a Limited Series or Special) *Emmy.* 1986: *Peter the Great* (Best Supporting Actress in a Miniseries or Special) Emmy; *Second Serve* (Best Actress in a Miniseries or Special) Emmy (Best Actress in a Miniseries or TV Movie) Globe. 1988: *A Man for All Seasons* (Best Actress in a Miniseries or TV Movie) Globe. 1991: *Young Catherine* (Best Supporting Actress in a Miniseries or Special) Emmy. 1997: *Bella Mafia* (Best Actress in a Miniseries or TV Movie) Globe. 2000: *If These Walls Could Talk 2* (Best Female Actor in a Television Movie or Miniseries) *SAG* (Best Supporting Actress in a Miniseries or TV Movie) *Emmy* (Best Supporting Actress in a Series, Miniseries, or TV Movie) *Globe.* 2002: *The Gathering Storm* (Best Actress in a Miniseries or TV Movie) Emmy, Globe (Best Female Actor in a Television Movie or Miniseries) SAG. 2007: *The Fever*

(Best Female Actor in a Television Movie or Miniseries) SAG. **Records:** Although their movie was entitled *Julia*, it was Jane Fonda as author Lillian Hellman who had the lead role. The Fred Zinnemann film, based on a section of Hellman's autobiographical story collection, *Pentimento*, shared Hellman's experiences with her childhood friend Julia, who as an adult and young mother became a World War II activist. Though the center of the film, Julia was truly a supporting character. When Redgrave took home the Oscar for her performance, she became the first person in Academy Award history to win a supporting Oscar playing a film's title character.

Redman, Joyce

Movie: 1963: *Tom Jones* (Best Supporting Actress) Academy. 1965: *Othello* (Best Supporting Actress) Academy, Globe.

Reed, Donna

Movie: 1953: *From Here to Eternity* (Best Supporting Actress) *Academy*. **Television:** 1958–1966 series *The Donna Reed Show* (Best Actress— Continuing Character — in a Comedy Series) 1959: Emmy. (Best Actress in a Series—Lead or Supporting) 1960: Emmy. (Best Actress in a Series) 1961: Emmy. (Best Continued Performance by an Actress in a Series) 1962: Emmy. (Best Actress in a Series) 1962: *Globe*.

Reed, Nikki

Movie: 2003: *Thirteen* (Best Debut Performance) *Spirit*.

Reed, Oliver

Movie: 2000: *Gladiator* (Best Supporting Actor) British (Best Ensemble) SAG.

Reeder, Ana

Movie: 2001: *Acts of Worship* (Best Debut Performance) Spirit.

Reeve, Christopher

Movie: 1978: *Superman* (Most Promising Newcomer) *British*. **Television:** 1997: *In the Gloaming* (Best Directing for a Miniseries or Special) Emmy; *Without Pity: A Film About Abilities* (Best Information Special, Narrator) *Emmy*. 1998: *Christopher Reeve: A Celebration of Hope* (Best Variety, Music, or Comedy Special; Executive Producer) Emmy; *Rear Window* (Best Actor in a Miniseries or TV Movie) Globe (Best Male Actor in a Television Movie or Miniseries) *SAG*. 2003: *Christopher Reeve: Courageous Steps* (Best Traditional Nonfiction Special, Narrator) Emmy.

Reeves, Dianne

Movie: 2005: *Good Night, and Good Luck* (Best Ensemble) SAG, Broadcast.

Régnier, Natacha

Movie: 1998: *The Dreamlife of Angels* (Best Actress) *Cannes* (win shared with costar).

Reid, Ann

Movie: 2003: *The Mother* (Best Actress) British.

Reid, Beryl

Movie: 1968: *The Killing of Sister George* (Best Actress, Drama) Globe. **Theater:** 1967: *The Killing of Sister George* (Best Actress, Dramatic) *Tony*.

Reid, Chris

Movie: 1990: *House Party* (Best Male Lead) Spirit.

Reid, Kate

Movie: 1973: *A Delicate Balance* (Best Supporting Actress) Globe. **Theater:** 1964: *Dylan* (Best Supporting or Featured Actress, Dramatic) Tony. 1966: *Slapstick Tragedy* (Best Actress, Dramatic) Tony. **Television:** 1963: *"The Invincible Mr. Disraeli,"* *Hallmark Hall of Fame* (Best Performance in a Supporting Role by an Actress) Emmy. 1985: *Death of a Salesman* (Best Supporting Actress in a Series, Miniseries, or TV Movie) Globe.

Reilly, John C.

Movie: 1997: *Boogie Nights* (Best Ensemble) SAG. 1999: *Magnolia* (Best Ensemble) *Board*, SAG. 2001: *The Anniversary Party* (Best Supporting Male) Spirit. 2002: *Chicago* (Best Supporting Actor) Academy, Globe (Best Ensemble) *SAG, Broadcast*; *The Good Girl* (Best Supporting Male) Spirit; *The Hours* (Best Ensemble) SAG, Broadcast. 2004: *The Aviator* (Best Ensemble) SAG. 2006: *A Prairie Home Companion* (Best Ensemble) Broadcast. 2007: *Walk Hard: The Dewey Cox Story* (Best Actor, Musical or Comedy) Globe (Best Original Song, "Walk Hard") Globe. **Theater:** 2000: *True West* (Best Actor, Play) Tony.

Reilly, Kelly

Movie: 2005: *Mrs. Henderson Presents* (Best Ensemble) *Board*.

Reiner, Carl

Movie: 2001: *Ocean's 11* (Best Ensemble) Broadcast. 2004: *Ocean's Twelve* (Best Ensemble) Broadcast.

Television: 1950–1954 series *Your Show of Shows* (Best Series Supporting Actor) 1954: Emmy. 1954–1957 series *Caesar's Hour* (Best Supporting Actor) 1955: Emmy. 1956: *Emmy.* (Best Continuing Supporting Performance by an Actor in a Dramatic or Comedy Series) 1957: *Emmy.* 1961–1966 series *The Dick Van Dyke Show* (Best Writing Achievement in Comedy) 1962: *Emmy.* 1963: *Emmy.* (Best Writing Achievement in Comedy or Variety) 1964: *Emmy.* (Best Individual Achievement in Entertainment, Writer) 1965: Emmy. (Best Program Achievement in Entertainment, Producer) 1965: *Emmy.* (Best Comedy Series, Producer) 1966: *Emmy.* 1966: *Linus the Lionhearted* (Best Special Classification of Individual Achievement, Voices) Emmy. 1967: *The Sid Caesar, Imogene Coca, Carl Reiner, Howard Morris Special* (Best Writing Achievement in Variety) *Emmy.* 1995: *Mad About You* (Best Guest Actor in a Comedy Series) *Emmy.* 2000: *Beggars and Choosers* (Best Guest Actor in a Comedy Series) Emmy. 2004: *The Dick Van Dyke Show Revisited* (Best Special Class Program, Executive Producer) Emmy. **Tributes:** 1999: Television Hall of Fame Inductee from Emmy. **Highlights:** Although he won Emmys for other professional responsibilities that came from being the creator, writer, and producer of *The Dick Van Dyke Show*, he was never honored for his memorable acting in the role of arrogant taskmaster Alan Brady on the show. But nearly thirty years after *The Dick Van Dyke Show* went off the air, Reiner resurrected the character for an appearance on *Mad About You* and earned an Emmy as Best Guest Actor in a Comedy Series.

Reiner, Rob

Movie: 1986: *Stand by Me* (Best Director) Globe, Spirit. 1989: *When Harry Met Sally...* (Best Director) Globe (Best Picture, Musical or Comedy; Producer) Globe. 1992: *A Few Good Men* (Best Director) Globe (Best Picture, Producer) Academy (Best Picture, Drama; Producer) Globe. 1995: *The American President* (Best Director) Globe (Best Picture, Musical or Comedy; Producer) Globe. 1996: *The First Wives Club* (Best Ensemble) *Board.* **Television:** 1971–1978 series *All in the Family* (Best Supporting Actor in a Comedy Series) 1972: Emmy. 1973: Emmy. 1974: *Emmy.* (Best Continuing Performance by a Supporting Actor in a Comedy Series) 1975: Emmy. 1978: *Emmy.* (Best Supporting Actor in a Series or TV Movie) 1971: Globe. (Best Supporting Actor in a Series, Miniseries, or TV Movie) 1972: Globe. 1973: Globe. 1975: Globe. 1976: Globe. **Records:** When Reiner and Sally Struthers earned acting Emmys for the second season of *All in the Family* just as their costars Carroll O'Connor and Jean Stapleton had done after the first, they became the first cast in television history to have every major member of the ensemble earn Emmys for the show. Since then, only the casts of *The Golden Girls* and *Will & Grace* have duplicated the feat.

Remick, Lee

Movie: 1959: *Anatomy of a Murder* (Best Actress, Drama) Globe. 1962: *Days of Wine and Roses* (Best Actress) Academy (Best Actress, Drama) Globe (Best Foreign Actress) British. **Theater:** 1966: *Wait Until Dark* (Best Actress, Dramatic) Tony. **Television:** 1973 series *The Blue Knight* (Best Actress in a Limited Series) 1973: Emmy. (Best Actress in a Drama Series) 1973: *Globe.* 1975: *"QB VII,"* ABC Movie Special (Best Single Performance by a Supporting Actress in a Comedy or Drama Special) Emmy. 1976: *"Jennie: Lady Randolph Churchill,"* Great Performances (Best Actress in a Limited Series) Emmy (Best Actress in a Drama Series) *Globe.* 1978: *Wheels* (Best Actress in a Limited Series) Emmy (Best Actress in a Drama Series) Globe. 1980: *Haywire* (Best Actress in a Limited Series or Special) Emmy. 1982: *The Letter* (Best Actress in a Miniseries or TV Movie) Globe. 1987: *Nutcracker: Money, Madness, & Murder* (Best Actress in a Miniseries or Special) Emmy. 1987: *"Eleanor: In Her Own Words,"* American Playhouse (Best Individual Achievement in Information Programming, Performer) Emmy.

Renner, Jeremy

Movie: 2002: *Dahmer* (Best Male Lead) Spirit.

Revere, Anne

Movie: 1943: *The Song of Bernadette* (Best Supporting Actress) Academy. 1945: *National Velvet* (Best Supporting Actress) *Academy.* 1947: *Gentleman's Agreement* (Best Supporting Actress) Academy. **Theater:** 1960: *Toys in the Attic* (Best Supporting or Featured Actress, Dramatic) *Tony.*

Revill, Clive

Movie: 1972: *Avanti!* (Best Supporting Actor) Globe. **Theater:** 1961: *Irma La Douce* (Best Supporting or Featured Actor, Musical) Tony. 1963: *Oliver!* (Best Actor, Musical) Tony.

Rey, Fernando

Movie: 1977: *Elise, Vida Mía (Elise, My Life)* (Best Actor) *Cannes.*

Reynolds, Burt

Movie: 1974: *The Longest Yard* (Best Actor, Musical or Comedy) Globe. 1979: *Starting Over* (Best Actor, Musical or Comedy) Globe. 1997: *Boogie*

Nights (Best Male Actor in a Supporting Role) SAG (Best Supporting Actor) Academy, *New York, Globe,* British, *Society, LA* (Best Ensemble) SAG. **Television:** 1970–1971 series *Dan August* (Best Actor in a Drama Series) 1970: Globe. 1990–1994 series *Evening Shade* (Best Actor in a Comedy Series) 1991: *Emmy.* 1992: Emmy. (Best Actor in a Series, Musical or Comedy) 1991: Globe. 1992: *Globe.* 1993: Globe.

Reynolds, Debbie

Movie: 1950: *Three Little Words* (New Star or the Year — Actress) Globe. 1956: *Bundle of Joy* (Best Actress, Musical or Comedy) Globe; *The Catered Affair* (Best Supporting Actress) *Board.* 1964: *The Unsinkable Molly Brown* (Best Actress) Academy (Best Actress, Musical or Comedy) Globe. 1996: *Mother* (Best Actress, Musical or Comedy) Globe. **Theater:** 1973: *Irene* (Best Actress, Musical) Tony. **Television:** 1969–1970 series *The Debbie Reynolds Show* (Best Actress in a Series, Musical or Comedy) 1969: Globe. 2000: *Will & Grace* (Best Guest Actress in a Comedy Series) Emmy.

Rhodes, Marjorie

Movie: 1967: *The Family Way* (Best Supporting Actress) *Board, Society.* **Theater:** 1965: *All in Good Time* (Best Actress, Dramatic) Tony. **Records:** Rhodes won the first Best Supporting Actress award from the National Society of Film Critics in 1967 when they began presenting awards. That year, Rhodes picked up her award for the British comedy, *The Family Way* while the other acting winners all won for dramas: Best Actor Rod Steiger played a bigoted Southern sheriff in *In the Heat of the Night*, Best Actress Bibi Andersson was a nurse in *Persona*, and Best Supporting Actor Gene Hackman was a Depression-era bank robber in *Bonnie and Clyde.* While Andersson and Hackman would each go on to win one more award from the society, this would be Steiger's only Society prize and Rhodes's only major acting award.

Rhys-Davies, John

Movie: 2001: *The Lord of the Rings: The Fellowship of the Ring* (Best Ensemble) SAG. 2002: *The Lord of the Rings: The Two Towers* (Best Ensemble) SAG. 2003: *The Lord of the Rings: The Return of the King* (Best Ensemble) *Board, SAG, Broadcast.* **Television:** 1981: *Shogun* (Best Supporting Actor in a Limited Series or Special) Emmy.

Ribisi, Giovanni

Movie: 1998: *Saving Private Ryan* (Best Ensemble) SAG. 2000: *The Gift* (Best Supporting Male) Spirit. **Television:** 2007: *My Name Is Earl* (Best Guest Actor in a Comedy Series) Emmy.

Ricci, Christina

Movie: 1998: *Buffalo 66* (Best Supporting Actress) *Board* (multiple win); *The Opposite of Sex* (Best Female Lead) Spirit (Best Supporting Actress, Musical or Comedy) Globe (Best Supporting Actress) *Board* (multiple win); *Pecker* (Best Supporting Actress) *Board* (multiple win). **Television:** 2006: *Grey's Anatomy* (Best Guest Actress in a Drama Series) Emmy.

Richard, Firmine

Tributes: 2002: Silver Bear for outstanding artistic contribution in *8 Femmes (8 Women)* from Berlin (special ensemble award shared with costars).

Richards, Beah

Movie: 1967: *Guess Who's Coming to Dinner* (Best Supporting Actress) Academy, Globe. **Theater:** 1965: *The Amen Corner* (Best Actress, Dramatic) Tony. **Television:** 1988: *Frank's Place* (Best Guest Performer in a Comedy Series) *Emmy.* 2000: *The Practice* (Best Guest Actress in a Drama Series) *Emmy.*

Richards, Dakota Blue

Movie: 2007: *The Golden Compass* (Best Young Actress) Broadcast.

Richards, Denise

Movie: 2003: *Love Actually* (Best Ensemble) Broadcast.

Richards, Jeff

Movie: 1954: *Seven Brides for Seven Brothers* (New Star of the Year — Actor) *Globe.*

Richardson, Janice

Movie: 2003: *Anne B. Real* (Best Debut Performance) Spirit.

Richardson, Joely

Movie: 1998: *Under Heaven* (Best Supporting Female) Spirit. **Television:** 2003–present series *Nip/Tuck* (Best Actress in a Series, Drama) 2004: Globe. 2005: Globe.

Richardson, Marie

Movie: 2003: *Om jag vänder mig om* (Best Ensemble) *Berlin* (special award).

Richardson, Miranda

Movie: 1992: *The Crying Game* (Best Supporting Actress) *New York* (multiple win), British; *Damage* (Best Supporting Actress) Academy, *New York* (multiple win), Globe, *British*; *Enchanted April* (Best Actress, Musical or Comedy) *Globe* (Best Supporting Actress) *New York* (multiple win). 1994: *Tom & Viv* (Best Actress) Academy, *Board*, British (Best Actress, Drama) Globe. 1997: *The Apostle* (Best Supporting Female) Spirit. 2002: *The Hours* (Best Ensemble) SAG, Broadcast. **Television:** 1994: *Fatherland* (Best Supporting Actress in a Series, Miniseries, or TV Movie) *Globe*. 1998: *Merlin* (Best Actress in a Miniseries or TV Movie) Globe. 1999: *The Big Brass Ring* (Best Supporting Actress in a Series, Miniseries, or TV Movie) Globe. 2004: *The Lost Prince* (Best Actress in a Miniseries or TV Movie) Globe.

Richardson, Patricia

Movie: 1997: *Ulee's Gold* (Best Supporting Female) Spirit. **Television:** 1991–1999 series *Home Improvement* (Best Actress in a Comedy Series) 1994: Emmy. 1996: Emmy. 1997: Emmy. 1998: Emmy. (Best Actress in a Series, Musical or Comedy) 1993: Globe. 1994: Globe.

Richardson, Ralph

Movie: 1938: *The Citadel* (Best Acting) *Board* (multiple win); *South Riding* (Best Acting) *Board* (multiple win). 1940: *The Fugitive* (Best Acting) *Board*. 1949: *The Fallen Idol* (Best Actor) *Board* (multiple win); *The Heiress* (Best Actor) *Board* (multiple win), (Best Supporting Actor) Academy. 1952: *Breaking the Sound Barrier (The Sound Barrier)* (Best Actor) *New York*, *Board* (Best British Actor) *British*. 1962: *Long Day's Journey into Night* (Best Acting) *Cannes* (win shared with costars). 1965: *Doctor Zhivago* (Best British Actor) British (multiple nomination). 1966: *Khartoum* (Best British Actor) British (multiple nomination); *The Wrong Box* (Best British Actor) British (multiple nomination). 1972: *Lady Caroline Lamb* (Best Supporting Actor) British. 1984: *Greystoke: The Legend of Tarzan, Lord of the Apes* (Best Supporting Actor) Academy, *New York*, British. **Theater:** 1957: *The Waltz of the Toreadors* (Best Actor, Dramatic) Tony. 1971: *Home* (Best Actor, Dramatic) Tony. 1977: *No Man's Land* (Best Actor, Play) Tony. **Records:** Throughout the early years of their giving awards, the National Board of Review and the New York Film Critics continuously disagreed on their acting favorites. But in 1952, Richardson impressed them so much with his portrayal of a fanatically determined and equally cold-hearted aircraft manufacturer in **Breaking the Sound Barrier** that he became the first to win Best Actor from both organizations for a single performance. Despite record-setting momentum, Richardson didn't make it into either the Golden Globe or Oscar race. But the British film, David Lean's first

independent project as director, fared better at the British Awards, earning Richardson his third Best Actor Prize. At the end of his career, Richardson set another record, this time with the Academy when he became the oldest male actor ever to be nominated for an Oscar. He was 82 when he portrayed the sixth Earl of Greystoke who succumbs to senility in *Greystoke: The Legend of Tarzan, Lord of the Apes*. Richardson died before the 1984 Oscar ceremony where *The Killing Field*'s Haing S. Ngor beat Richardson in the Best Supporting Actor category, making Richardson also one of the few actors to compete for an Oscar posthumously.

Rickman, Alan

Movie: 1991: *Robin Hood, Prince of Thieves* (Best Supporting Actor) *British*; *Truly, Madly, Deeply* (Best Actor) British. 1995: *Sense and Sensibility* (Best Supporting Actor) British (Best Ensemble) SAG. 1996: *Michael Collins* (Best Supporting Actor) British. 2003: *Love Actually* (Best Ensemble) Broadcast. 2007: *Sweeney Todd: The Demon Barber of Fleet Street* (Best Ensemble) Broadcast. **Theater:** 1987: *Les Liaisons Dangereuses* (Best Actor, Play) Tony. 2002: *Private Lives* (Best Actor, Play) Tony. **Television:** 1996: *Rasputin* (Best Actor in a Miniseries or TV Movie) *Emmy, Globe* (Best Male Actor in a Television Movie or Miniseries) *SAG*. 2004: *Something the Lord Made* (Best Actor in a Miniseries or TV Movie) Emmy. **Tributes:** 1997: CinemAvvernire Award for *The Winter Guest* from Venice; OCIC Award for *The Winter Guest* from Venice.

Ridgley, Robert

Movie: 1997: *Boogie Nights* (Best Ensemble) SAG.

Riegert, Peter

Movie: 2000: *By Courier* (Best Live Action Short Film, Producer) Academy; *Traffic* (Best Ensemble) *SAG*. **Television:** 1993: *Barbarians at the Gate* (Best Supporting Actor in a Miniseries or Special) Emmy.

Riemann, Katja

Movie: 2003: *Rosenstrasse* (Best Actress) *Venice*.

Rigg, Diana

Movie: 1971: *The Hospital* (Best Supporting Actress) Globe. **Theater:** 1971: *Abelard and Heloise* (Best Actress, Dramatic) Tony. 1975: *The Misanthrope* (Best Actress, Dramatic) Tony. 1994: *Medea* (Best Actress, Play) *Tony*. **Television:** 1966–1968 series *The Avengers* (Best Continued Performance by an Actress in a Leading Role in a Drama Series) 1967: Emmy. 1968: Emmy. 1975: *"In This House of Brede,"*

General Electric Theater (Best Actress in a Special Program — Drama or Comedy) Emmy. 1997: *Rebecca* (Best Supporting Actress in a Miniseries or Special) *Emmy*. 2002: *Victoria and Albert* (Best Supporting Actress in a Miniseries or TV Movie) Emmy.

Riggs, Mitchell

Movie: 2001: *Kaaterskill Falls* (Best Debut Performance) Spirit (nomination shared with costars).

Ringwald, Molly

Movie: 1982: *Tempest* (New Star of the Year — Actress) Globe.

Ritenberga, Dzidra

Movie: 1956: *Malva* (Best Actress) *Venice*.

Ritter, John

Movie: 1996: *Sling Blade* (Best Ensemble) SAG. Television: 1977–1984 series *Three's Company* (Best Actor in a Comedy Series) 1978: Emmy, Globe. 1979: Globe. 1981: Emmy. 1983: *Globe*. 1984: *Emmy*. 1987–1989 series *Hooperman* (Best Actor in a Comedy Series) 1988: Emmy, Globe. 1986: *Unnatural Causes* (Best Actor in a Miniseries or TV Movie) Globe. 1999: *Ally McBeal* (Best Guest Actor in a Comedy Series) Emmy. 2000–2003 series *Clifford the Big Red Dog* (Best Performer in an Animated Program) 2001: Emmy. 2002: Emmy. 2003: Emmy. 2002–2003 series *8 Simple Rules* (Best Actor in a Comedy Series) 2004: Emmy.

Ritter, Thelma

Movie: 1950: *All About Eve* (Best Supporting Actress) Academy, Globe. 1951: *The Mating Season* (Best Supporting Actress) Academy, Globe. 1952: *With a Song in My Heart* (Best Supporting Actress) Academy. 1953: *Pickup on South Street* (Best Supporting Actress) Academy. 1959: *Pillow Talk* (Best Supporting Actress) Academy. 1962: *Bird Man of Alcatraz* (Best Supporting Actress) Academy. 1965: *Boeing, Boeing* (Best Supporting Actress) Globe. Theater: 1958: *New Girl in Town* (Best Actress, Musical) *Tony*. Television: 1956: *"A Catered Affair," Alcoa Hour/Goodyear Playhouse* (Best Supporting Actress) Emmy. Records: With six, Ritter received more Best Supporting Actress Oscar nominations than any other actress. She also holds the record for being one of the most overlooked actresses in movie award history, as she never won a movie award despite her multiple nominations.

Riva, Emmanuelle

Movie: 1960: *Hiroshima Mon Amour* (Best Foreign Actress) British. 1962: *Thérèse Desqueyroux* (Best Actress) *Venice*.

Robards, Jason, Jr.

Movie: 1962: *Longs Day's Journey into Night* (Best Actor) *Board* (multiple win) *Cannes* (win shared with costars); *Tender Is the Night* (Best Actor) *Board* (multiple win). 1965: *A Thousand Clowns* (Best Actor, Musical or Comedy) Globe. 1976: *All the President's Men* (Best Supporting Actor) *Academy, New York, Board,* Globe, British, *Society*. 1977: *Julia* (Best Supporting Actor) *Academy*, Globe, British, LA. 1980: *Melvin and Howard* (Best Supporting Actor) Academy, Globe. 1999: *Magnolia* (Best Ensemble) *Board*, SAG. Theater: 1957: *Long Day's Journey into Night* (Best Supporting or Featured Actor, Dramatic) Tony. 1959: *The Disenchanted* (Best Actor, Dramatic) *Tony*. 1960: *Toys in the Attic* (Best Actor, Dramatic) Tony. 1964: *After the Fall* (Best Actor, Dramatic) Tony. 1965: *Hughie* (Best Actor, Dramatic) Tony. 1972: The *Country Girl* (Best Actor, Dramatic) Tony. 1974: *A Moon for the Misbegotten* (Best Actor, Dramatic) Tony. 1978: *A Touch of the Poet* (Best Actor, Play) Tony. Television: 1964: *"Abe Lincoln in Illinois," Hallmark Hall of Fame* (Best Single Performance by an Actor in a Leading Role) Emmy. 1976: *"A Moon for the Misbegotten," ABC Theatre* (Best Actor in a Drama or Comedy Special) Emmy. 1978: *Washington: Behind Closed Doors* (Best Actor in a Limited Series) Emmy. 1980: *F.D.R.: The Last Year* (Best Actor in a Limited Series or Special) Emmy. 1984: *Sakharov* (Best Actor in a Miniseries or TV Special) Globe. 1988: *Inherit the Wind* (Best Actor in a Miniseries or Special) *Emmy*. Tributes: 1999: Honor from Kennedy Center for the Performing Arts. Records: With two consecutive Oscar victories, Robards became only the fourth star to win back-to-back Academy Awards. Luise Rainer attained the landmark achievement first in 1937 followed immediately by Spencer Tracy in 1938 and then by Katharine Hepburn exactly thirty years after Tracy. All of those stars won in the lead actor category, so Robards holds the record for being the first to win the 1–2 accolades in supporting roles. Highlights: Like Anthony Quinn before him, Robards won two Best Supporting Actor Academy Awards in biographical roles. In 1976, he played *Washington Post* editor Ben Bradlee in *All the President's Men* and in 1977, he portrayed author Dashiell Hammett in *Julia*. For *All the President's Men*, Robards also received the Best Supporting Actor award from the New York Film Critics. At their ceremony, he was presented his award by none other than Ben Bradlee himself.

Robb, Anna Sophia

Movie: 2007: *Bridge to Terabithia* (Best Young Actress) Broadcast.

Robbins, Cindy

Movie: 1959: *This Earth Is Mine* (New Star of the Year — Actress) Globe.

Robbins, Tim

Movie: 1992: *Bob Roberts* (Best Actor, Musical or Comedy) Globe; *The Player* (Best Actor) *Cannes*, British (Best Actor, Musical or Comedy) *Globe*. 1993: *Short Cuts* (Best Ensemble) *Venice* (special award). 1994: *Prêt-à-Porter (Ready-to-Wear)* (Best Ensemble) *Board*; *The Shawshank Redemption* (Best Male Actor in a Leading Role) SAG. 1995: *Dead Man Walking* (Best Director) Academy (Best Screenplay) Globe. 2003: *Mystic River* (Best Male Actor in a Supporting Role) *SAG* (Best Supporting Actor) *Academy, Globe*, British, *Broadcast* (Best Ensemble) SAG, Broadcast. **Tributes:** 1999: Special Filmmaking Achievement Award for *Cradle Will Rock* from Board.

Roberts, Dallas

Movie: 2007: *3:10 to Yuma* (Best Ensemble) SAG.

Roberts, Eric

Movie: 1978: *King of the Gypsies* (New Star of the Year — Actor) Globe. 1983: *Star 80* (Best Actor, Drama) Globe. 1985: *Runaway Train* (Best Supporting Actor) Academy, Globe.

Roberts, Julia

Movie: 1988: *Mystic Pizza* (Best Female Lead) Spirit. 1989: *Steel Magnolias* (Best Supporting Actress) Academy, *Globe*. 1990: *Pretty Woman* (Best Actress) Academy, British (Best Actress, Musical or Comedy) *Globe*. 1994: *Prêt-à-Porter (Ready-to-Wear)* (Best Ensemble) *Board*. 1997: *My Best Friend's Wedding* (Best Actress, Musical or Comedy) Globe. 1999: *Notting Hill* (Best Actress, Musical or Comedy) Globe. 2000: *Erin Brockovich* (Best Actress) *Academy, Board, British, LA, Broadcast* (Best Actress, Drama) *Globe* (Best Female Actor in a Leading Role) *SAG*. 2001: *Ocean's 11* (Best Ensemble) Broadcast. 2004: *Closer* (Best Ensemble) *Board*, Broadcast; *Ocean's Twelve* (Best Ensemble) Broadcast. 2007: *Charlie Wilson's War* (Best Supporting Actress) Globe. **Television:** 1999: *Law & Order* (Best Guest Actress in a Drama Series) Emmy. **Records:** Throughout the early 2000s, Roberts was listed in the *Guinness World Record* books for continually evolving financial achievements. With $18.9 million, Roberts made the highest annual earning of an actress in 2000. Later that same year she topped that record by becoming the first actress to earn the most money for a single film, receiving $20,000,000 for starring in *Erin Brockovich*, which won her seven Best Actress trophies.

Roberts, Rachel

Movie: 1960: *Saturday Night and Sunday Morning* (Best British Actress) *British*. 1963: *This Sporting Life* (Best Actress) Academy (Best Actress, Drama) Globe (Best British Actress) *British*. 1979: *Yanks* (Best Supporting Actress) *British*. **Theater:** 1974: Performances with the New Phoenix Repertory Company (Best Actress, Dramatic) Tony. **Records:** When Roberts and Rex Harrison, who were married from 1962 to 1971, both received Oscar nominations in 1963, they became the first married couple to be up for acting Oscars from different films in the same year. In 1931/32, husband and wife Alfred Lunt and Lynn Fontanne received Oscar nods for their co-starring work in *The Guardsman*, making them the first couple to both be up in the same year.

Robertson, Cliff

Movie: 1968: *Charly* (Best Actor) *Academy, Board* (Best Actor, Drama) Globe. **Television:** 1961: *"The Two Worlds of Charlie Gordon," The U.S. Steel Hour* (Best Single Performance by an Actor in a Leading Role) Emmy. 1966: *"The Game," Bob Hope Presents the Chrysler Theatre* (Best Single Performance by an Actor in a Leading Role in a Drama) *Emmy*. **Highlights:** After giving an Emmy-nominated performance as Charlie Gordon, the mentally handicapped man who, thanks to a medical experiment, briefly becomes brilliant, Robertson did what few actors had done before him but many have done since in similar situations. He bought the film rights to Daniel Keyes' *Flowers for Algernon*, the novel upon which *The Two Worlds of Charlie Gordon* was based, to ensure that he would get the big screen role as well. The financial gamble paid off. Although he lost the Emmy in 1961 to actor Maurice Evans for Hallmark Hall of Fame's *Macbeth*, he took home Oscar and a Best Actor award from National Board of Review seven years later for *Charly*.

Robertson, Georgianna

Movie: 1994: *Prêt-à-Porter (Ready-to-Wear)* (Best Ensemble) *Board*.

Robinson, Edward G.

Movie: 1942: *Tales of Manhattan* (Best Acting) Board. 1949: *House of Strangers* (Best Actor) Cannes. **Theater:** 1956: *Middle of the Night* (Best Actor, Dramatic) Tony. **Tributes:** 1969: Life Achievement Award from SAG. 1972: Honorary Oscar statuette to Robinson who achieved greatness as a player, a patron of the arts, and a dedicated citizen ... in sum, a Renaissance man from Academy. 1999: Ranked Number 24 on List of 25 Greatest Male Screen Legends of the 20th Century from American Film Institute.

Robinson, Keith

Movie: 2006: *Dreamgirls* (Best Ensemble) SAG, Broadcast.

Robinson, Madeleine

Movie: 1959: *À Double Tour* (Best Actress) *Venice*.

Robinson, Roger

Movie: 2004: *Brother to Brother* (Best Supporting Male) Spirit. Theater: 1996: *Seven Guitars* (Best Actor in a Feature Role, Play) Tony.

Robson, Flora

Movie: 1939: *We Are Not Alone* (Best Acting) *Board*. 1946: *Saratoga Trunk* (Best Supporting Actress) Academy.

Robson, May

Movie: 1933: *Lady for a Day* (Best Actress) Academy.

Rocca, Daniela

Movie: 1961: *Divorce—Italian Style* (Best Foreign Actress) British.

Rochefort, Jean

Movie: 1994: *Prêt-à-Porter (Ready-to-Wear)* (Best Ensemble) *Board*. 2002: *L'homme du train* (Best Actor) *Venice*.

Rock, Crissy

Movie: 1994: *Ladybird, Ladybird* (Best Actress) *Berlin*.

Rocket, Charles

Movie: 1993: *Short Cuts* (Best Ensemble) *Venice* (special award).

Rockwell, Sam

Movie: 1999: *The Green Mile* (Best Ensemble) SAG. 2003: *Confessions of a Dangerous Mind* (Best Actor) *Berlin*.

Rodriguez, Freddy

Movie: 2006: *Bobby* (Best Ensemble) SAG, Broadcast. Television: 2001–2005 series *Six Feet Under*

(Best Supporting Actor in a Drama Series) 2002: Emmy. (Best Ensemble in a Drama Series) 2001: SAG. 2002: *SAG*. 2003: *SAG*. 2004: SAG. 2005: SAG.

Rodriguez, Michelle

Movie: 2000: *Girlfight* (Breakthrough Performance — Female) *Board*, Broadcast (Best Debut Performance) *Spirit*.

Roehm, David C., Sr.

Movie: 2001: *Ocean's 11* (Best Ensemble) Broadcast.

Rogers, Charles "Buddy"

Tributes: 1985: Jean Hersholt Humanitarian Award from Academy.

Rogers, Ginger

Movie: 1940: *The Primrose Path* (Best Acting) *Board*; *Kitty Foyle* (Best Acting) *Board* (multiple win), (Best Actress) *Academy*. 1941: *Tom, Dick and Harry* (Best Acting) *Board* (multiple win). 1942: *The Major and the Minor* (Best Acting) *Board* (multiple win); *Roxie Hart* (Best Acting) *Board* (multiple win). 1952: *Monkey Business* (Best Actress, Musical or Comedy) Globe. Tributes: 1992: Honor from Kennedy Center for the Performing Arts. 1999: Ranked Number 14 on List of 25 Greatest Female Screen Legends of the 20th Century from American Film Institute. Records: When she won the Best Actress Oscar for *Kitty Foyle*, Rogers did more than acknowledge a family member from a distance. Instead, she became the only star to bring her mother to the podium with her. A tearfully ebullient Rogers thanked her mother for being the one who stood by her faithfully throughout her career. The only other star to come to the podium with a family member after winning a competitive acting Oscar was Tatum O'Neal, but it was her grandfather who escorted her, as she was only ten years old when named Best Supporting Actress for *Paper Moon*.

Rogers, Mimi

Movie: 1991: *The Rapture* (Best Female Lead) Spirit.

Roland, Gilbert

Movie: 1952: *The Bad and the Beautiful* (Best Supporting Actor) Globe. 1964: *Cheyenne Autumn* (Best Supporting Actor) Globe.

Rollins, Howard E., Jr.

Movie: 1981: *Ragtime* (New Star of the Year — Actor or Actress) Globe (Best Supporting Actress) Academy, Globe. Television: 1982 series *Another World*

(Best Supporting Actor in a Daytime Drama Series) 1982: Emmy.

Roman, Ruth

Movie: 1949: *Champion* (New Star of the Year — Actress) Globe. **Records:** Roman's performance in *Champion* earned the first Best New Actress nomination ever given at the Golden Globes. Prior to 1949, the Globes named only winners but no nominees.

Romero, Cesar

Movie: 1962: *If a Man Answers* (Best Supporting Actor) Globe.

Ronan, Saoirse

Movie: 2007: *Atonement* (Best Supporting Actress) Academy, Globe, British (Best Young Actress) Broadcast.

Ronstadt, Linda

Movie: 1983: *The Pirates of Penzance* (Best Actress, Musical or Comedy) Globe. **Theater:** 1981: *The Pirates of Penzance* (Best Actress, Musical) Tony. **Television:** 1989: *"Canciones de mi padre," Great Performances* (Best Individual Performance in a Variety or Music Program) *Emmy*.

Rooker, Michael

Movie: 1990: *Henry, Portrait of a Serial Killer* (Best Male Lead) Spirit.

Rooney, Mickey

Movie: 1939: *Babes in Arms* (Best Actor) Academy. 1943: *The Human Comedy* (Best Actor) Academy. 1956: *The Bold and the Brave* (Best Supporting Actor) Academy. 1979: *The Black Stallion* (Best Supporting Actor) Academy. **Theater:** 1980: *Sugar Babies* (Best Actor, Musical) Tony. **Television:** 1958: *"The Comedian," Playhouse 90* (Best Single Performance by a Leading or Supporting Actor) Emmy. 1959: *"Eddie," Alcoa-Goodyear Theatre* (Best Single Performance by an Actor) Emmy. 1962: *Dick Powell Theatre* (Best Single Performance by an Actor) Emmy. 1964–1965 series *Mickey* (Best Actor in a Series) 1964: *Globe*. 1982: *Bill* (Best Actor in a Limited Series or Special) *Emmy* (Best Actor in a Miniseries or TV Movie) *Globe*. 1984: *Bill: On His Own* (Best Actor in a Limited Series or Special) Emmy. **Tributes:** 1938: Special miniature Oscar statuette for his significant contribution in bringing to the screen the spirit and personification of youth, and as a juvenile player setting a high standard of ability and achievement from Academy. 1982: Honorary Oscar in recognition of his 60 years of versatility in a variety of memorable film performances. **Records:** In 1938, Rooney won a miniature honorary Oscar as Best Juvenile performer. When he won his Special Academy Award in 1982, he became the first of the former child star winners to have both a miniature and a standard-sized Oscar. Three years later, at a special screening not on Oscar night, the Academy gave Shirley Temple a full-sized statuette. To date, they are the only stars to have both.

Rose, Anika Noni

Movie: 2006: *Dreamgirls* (Best Ensemble) SAG, Broadcast. **Theater:** 2004: *Caroline, or Change* (Best Featured Actress, Musical) *Tony*.

Rose, Gabrielle

Movie: 1997: *The Sweet Hereafter* (Best Ensemble) *Board*.

Ross, Annie

Movie: 1993: *Short Cuts* (Best Ensemble) *Venice* (special award).

Ross, Diana

Movie: 1972: *Lady Sings the Blues* (New Star of the Year — Female) *Globe* (Best Actress) Academy, British (Best Actress, Drama) Globe. **Television:** 1994: *Out of Darkness* (Best Actress in a Miniseries or TV Movie) Globe. **Tributes:** 1977: Special award from Tony. 2007: Honor from Kennedy Center for the Performing Arts.

Ross, Katharine

Movie: 1967: *Games* (New Star of the Year — Actress) *Globe; The Graduate* (New Star of the Year — Actress) Globe (Most Promising Newcomer) British (Best Supporting Actress) Academy. 1969: *Butch Cassidy and the Sundance Kid* (Best Actress) *British* (multiple win); *Tell Them Willie Boy Is Here* (Best Actress) *British* (multiple win). 1976: *Voyage of the Damned* (Best Supporting Actress) *Globe*.

Ross, Marion

Movie: 1996: *The Evening Star* (Best Supporting Actress) Globe. **Television:** 1974–1984 series *Happy Days* (Best Supporting Actress in a Comedy or Comedy-Variety or Music Series) 1979: Emmy. (Best Supporting Actress in a Comedy Series) 1984: Emmy. 1991–1993 series *Brooklyn Bridge* (Best Actress in a Comedy Series) 1992: Emmy. 1993: Emmy. 1999: *Touched by an Angel* (Best Guest Actress in a Drama Series) Emmy.

Ross, Matt

Movie: 2005: *Good Night, and Good Luck* (Best Ensemble) SAG, Broadcast.

Ross, Yolanda

Movie: 2001: *Stranger Inside* (Best Debut Performance) Spirit.

Rossellini, Isabella

Movie: 1986: *Blue Velvet* (Best Female Lead) *Spirit*. 1998: *Left Luggage* (Best Actress) *Berlin* (special award). Television: 1997: *Chicago Hope* (Best Guest Actress in a Drama Series) Emmy. 1998: *Crime of the Century* (Best Actress in a Miniseries or TV Movie) Globe.

Rossum, Emmy

Movie: 2000: *Songcatcher* (Best Debut Performance) Spirit. 2004: *The Phantom of the Opera* (Breakthrough Performance — Female) *Board* (Best Actress, Musical or Comedy) Globe (Best Young Actress) *Broadcast*.

Roth, Tim

Movie: 1984: *The Hit* (Best Newcomer to Film) British. 1995: *Little Odessa* (Best Male Lead) Spirit; *Rob Roy* (Best Supporting Actor) Academy, Globe, *British*. 1999: *The War Zone* (Best Director) *Berlin* (special award), (Best Foreign Film, and Director) Spirit.

Roud, Nick

Movie: 2004: *Finding Neverland* (Best Ensemble) SAG.

Roundtree, Richard

Movie: 1971: *Shaft* (New Star of the Year — Actor) Globe.

Rourke, Mickey

Movie: 1982: *Diner* (Best Supporting Actor) *Society*. 1987: *Barfly* (Best Male Lead) Spirit. 2005: *Sin City* (Best Ensemble) Broadcast.

Rowlands, Gena

Movie: 1974: *A Woman Under the Influence* (Best Actress) Academy, *Board* (Best Actress, Drama) *Globe*. 1977: *Opening Night* (Best Actress) *Berlin* (Best Actress, Drama) Globe. 1980: *Gloria* (Best Actress) Academy (Best Actress, Drama) Globe. 1996: *Unhook the Stars* (Best Female Actor in a Leading Role) SAG. Television: 1983: *Thursday's Child* (Best Actress in a Miniseries or TV Movie) Globe. 1986: *An Early Frost* (Best Actress in a Miniseries or Special) Emmy (Best Actress in a Miniseries or TV Movie) Globe. 1987: *The Betty Ford Story* (Best Actress in a Miniseries or Special) *Emmy* (Best Actress in a Miniseries or TV Movie) *Globe*. 1992: *Crazy in Love* (Best Supporting Actress in a Series, Miniseries, or TV Movie) Globe; *Face of a Stranger* (Best Actress in a Miniseries or Special) *Emmy*. 2000: *The Color of Love: Jacey's Story* (Best Actress in a Miniseries or TV Movie) Emmy. 2002: *Wild Iris* (Best Actress in a Miniseries or TV Movie) Emmy. 2003: *Hysterical Blindness* (Best Supporting Actress in a Miniseries or TV Movie) *Emmy* (Best Supporting Actress in a Series, Miniseries, or TV Movie) Globe. 2007: *What If God Were the Sun* (Best Actress in a Miniseries or TV Movie) Emmy (Best Female Actor in a Television Movie or Miniseries) SAG. Tributes: 1996: Career Achievement Award from Board.

Roxburgh, Richard

Movie: 2001: *Moulin Rouge!* (Best Ensemble) SAG.

Rozakis, Gregory

Movie: 1963: *America, America* (Best Supporting Actor) Globe.

Rudd, Paul

Movie: 1999: *The Cider House Rules* (Best Ensemble) SAG.

Rudolph, Maya

Movie: 2006: *A Prairie Home Companion* (Best Ensemble) Broadcast.

Ruehl, Mercedes

Movie: 1988: *Married to the Mob* (Best Supporting Actress) *Society*. 1991: *The Fisher King* (Best Actress) *LA* (Best Supporting Actress) *Academy, Globe*. Theater: 1991: *Lost in Yonkers* (Best Actress, Play) *Tony*. 1995: *The Shadow Box* (Best Actress in a Featured Role, Play) Tony. 2002: *Edward Albee's The Goat or Who Is Sylvia?* (Best Actress, Play) Tony.

Ruffalo, Mark

Movie: 2000: *You Can Count on Me* (Best Breakthrough Performer) Broadcast (Best Male Lead) Spirit. Theater: 2006: *Awake and Sing!* (Best Actor in a Featured Role, Play) Tony.

Rush, Barbara

Movie: 1953: *Hell and High Water* (New Star of the Year — Actress) Globe; *It Came from Outer Space* (New Star of the Year — Actress) *Globe*.

Rush, Geoffrey

Movie: 1996: **Shine** (Best Actor) *Academy, New York, British, LA, Broadcast* (Best Actor, Drama) *Globe* (Best Male Actor in a Leading Role) *SAG* (Best Ensemble) SAG. 1998: **Elizabeth** (Best Supporting Actor) British; **Shakespeare in Love** (Best Male Actor in a Supporting Role) SAG (Best Supporting Actor) Academy, Globe, *British* (Best Ensemble) *SAG*. 2000: **Quills** (Best Actor) Academy, British, Broadcast (Best Actor, Drama) Globe (Best Male Actor in a Leading Role) SAG. **Television:** 2004: **The Life and Death of Peter Sellers** (Best Actor in a Miniseries or TV Movie) *Emmy, Globe* (Best Male Actor in a Television Movie or Miniseries) *SAG*.

Russ, William

Movie: 1991: **Pastime** (Best Male Lead) Spirit.

Russell, Craig

Movie: 1978: **Outrageous!** (Best Actor) *Berlin*.

Russell, Harold

Movie: 1946: **The Best Years of Our Lives** (Best Supporting Actor) *Academy*. **Tributes:** 1946: Special Oscar statuette for bringing hope and courage to his fellow veterans through his appearance in **The Best Years of Our Lives** from Academy; Special Achievement Award for most natural performance in **The Best Years of Our Lives** from Globe. **Records:** Russell is the only actor to receive two Oscars for the same performance. In 1946, director William Wyler cast Russell, who had no acting background, in **The Best Years of Our Lives** in the role of a returning veteran who, like Russell himself, had both arms amputated. Russell won the Best Supporting Actor race and was also given a special Academy Award for bringing hope and courage to his fellow veterans. In 1992, Russell set another, more dubious Academy record by becoming the only actor to sell his Oscar. Despite the Academy's efforts to dissuade him, Russell put his Supporting Actor Oscar on the auction block to pay his ailing wife's medical bills. The award went for $60,000. Since then, several pre–1950s Oscars have been auctioned off posthumously, but in the 1950s the Academy began requiring winners to sign an agreement forbidding them to sell their Oscars.

Russell, Jane

Tributes: 1991: Honorary Award from Berlin.

Russell, Kurt

Movie: 1983: **Silkwood** (Best Supporting Actor) Globe. **Television:** 1979: **Elvis** (Best Actor in a Limited Series or Special) Emmy.

Russell, Rosalind

Movie: 1942: **My Sister Eileen** (Best Actress) Academy. 1946: **Sister Kenny** (Best Actress) Academy, Globe. 1947: **Mourning Becomes Electra** (Best Actress) Academy, *Globe*. 1958: **Auntie Mame** (Best Actress) Academy (Best Actress, Musical or Comedy) Globe (Best Foreign Actress) British. 1961: **A Majority of One** (Best Actress, Musical or Comedy) *Globe*. 1962: **Gypsy** (Best Actress, Musical or Comedy) Globe. **Theater:** 1953: **Wonderful Town** (Best Actress, Musical) *Tony*. 1957: **Auntie Mame** (Best Actress, Dramatic) Tony. **Tributes:** 1972: Jean Hersholt Humanitarian Award from Academy. 1975: Life Achievement Award from SAG. **Records:** Russell holds the record from the Golden Globes for having the longest winning record. From 1946 through 1962, she received five Globe nominations and won every time.

Russo, Rene

Movie: 1995: **Get Shorty** (Best Ensemble) SAG.

Rutherford, Margaret

Movie: 1963: **The V.I.P.s** (Best Supporting Actress) *Academy, Board, Globe*. **Records:** Earning an Academy Award at age 71 made Rutherford the first person in her 70s to win a supporting Oscar, proving that winning awards can revive enthusiasm for an acting career at any age. After learning that she'd won the Best Supporting Actress Academy Award for **The V.I.P.s**, Rutherford sent a written thank-you to the Academy from London that called her Oscar the climax of her 28 years in film. Even though she was about to turn 72, she hoped the award recognition might start a new phase of her career. It actually did. Rutherford lived another nine years and starred in 11 more films in the U.S., Spain, Switzerland, and her native England, including three more installments as Miss Marple in Agatha Christie mysteries.

Ryan, Amy

Movie: 2007: **Before the Devil Knows You're Dead** (Best Supporting Actress) *LA* (multiple win), (Best Ensemble) Broadcast; **Gone Baby Gone** (Best Female Actor in a Supporting Role) SAG (Best Supporting Actress) Academy, *New York, Board,* Globe, *LA* (multiple win), *Broadcast* (Best Ensemble) Broadcast.

Ryan, Meg

Movie: 1988: **Promised Land** (Best Female Lead) Spirit. 1989: **When Harry Met Sally...** (Best Actress, Musical or Comedy) Globe. 1993: **Sleepless in Seattle** (Best Actress, Musical or Comedy) Globe. 1994:

When a Man Loves a Woman (Best Female Actor in a Leading Role) SAG. 1998: *You've Got Mail* (Best Actress, Musical or Comedy) Globe.

Ryan, Robert

Movie: 1947: *Crossfire* (Best Supporting Actor) Academy. 1962: *Billy Budd* (Best Foreign Actor) British. 1973: *The Iceman Cometh* (Best Actor) *Board, Society* (special award).

Ryder, Winona

Movie: 1989: *Heathers* (Best Female Lead) Spirit. 1990: *Mermaids* (Best Supporting Actress) *Board,* Globe. 1993: *The Age of Innocence* (Best Supporting Actress) Academy, *Board, Globe,* British. 1994: *Little Women* (Best Actress) Academy. 1995: *How to Make an American Quilt* (Best Ensemble) SAG.

RZA

Movie: 2007: *American Gangster* (Best Ensemble) SAG.

Sábato, Antonio

Movie: 1966: *Grand Prix* (New Star of the Year — Actor) Globe.

Sacks, Michael

Movie: 1972: *Slaughterhouse-Five* (New Star of the Year — Actor) Globe.

Sagnier, Ludivine

Tributes: 2002: Silver Bear for outstanding artistic contribution in *8 Femmes (8 Women)* from Berlin (special ensemble award shared with costars).

Saint, Eva Marie

Movie: 1954: *On the Waterfront* (Most Promising Newcomer) British (Best Supporting Actress) *Academy.* 1957: *A Hatful of Rain* (Best Actress, Drama) Globe (Best Foreign Actress) British. Television: 1955: *"Middle of the Night," Philco TV Playhouse* (Best Actress in a Single Performance) Emmy. 1956: *"Our Town," Producers' Showcase* (Best Actress—Single Performance) Emmy. 1977: *How the West Was Won* (Best Actress in a Limited Series) Emmy. 1978: *"Taxi!!," Hallmark Hall of Fame* (Best Actress in a Drama or Comedy Special) Emmy. 1990: *People Like Us* (Best Supporting Actress in a Miniseries or Special) *Emmy.*

St. John, Jill

Movie: 1963: *Come Blow Your Horn* (Best Actress, Musical or Comedy) Globe.

Salmi, Albert

Movie: 1958: *The Bravados* (Best Supporting Actor) *Board* (multiple win); *The Brothers Karamazov* (Best Supporting Actor) *Board* (multiple win).

Samardzic, Ljubisa

Movie: 1967: *Jutro* (Best Actor) *Venice.*

Samoilova, Tatiana

Movie: 1958: *The Cranes Are Flying* (Best Foreign Actress) British.

Sanda, Dominique

Movie: 1976: *L'Eredita Ferramonti (The Inheritance)* (Best Actress) *Cannes.*

Sanders, Edward

Movie: 2007: *Sweeney Todd: The Demon Barber of Fleet Street* (Best Young Actor) Broadcast (Best Ensemble) Broadcast.

Sanders, George

Movie: 1940: *Rebecca* (Best Acting) *Board.* 1942: *The Moon and Sixpence* (Best Acting) *Board.* 1950: *All About Eve* (Best Supporting Actor) *Academy,* Globe.

Sandler, Adam

Movie: 2002: *Punch-Drunk Love* (Best Actor, Musical or Comedy) Globe. Television: 1991–1995 series *Saturday Night Live* (Best Writing for a Variety or Music Program) 1991: Emmy. 1992: Emmy. 1993: Emmy.

Sandlund, Debra

Movie: 1987: *Tough Guys Don't Dance* (Best Female Lead) Spirit.

Sandrelli, Stefania

Tributes: 2005: Career Golden Lion from Venice.

San Giacomo, Laura

Movie: 1989: *sex, lies, and videotape* (New Generation) LA (Best Supporting Actress) Globe, British (Best Supporting Female) *Spirit.* Television: 1997–2003 series *Just Shoot Me!* (Best Actress in a Series, Musical or Comedy) 1998: Globe.

Sangster, Thomas

Movie: 2003: *Love Actually* (Best Ensemble) Broadcast.

Santoro, Rodrigo

Movie: 2003: *Love Actually* (Best Ensemble) Broadcast.

Sarandon, Chris

Movie: 1975: *Dog Day Afternoon* (New Star of the Year — Actor) Globe (Best Supporting Actor) Academy.

Sarandon, Susan

Movie: 1981: *Atlantic City* (Best Actress) Academy. 1982: *Tempest* (Best Actress) *Venice*. 1988: *Bull Durham* (Best Actress, Musical and Comedy) Globe. 1990: *White Palace* (Best Actress, Drama) Globe. 1991: *Thelma & Louise* (Best Actress) Academy, *Board*, British (Best Actress, Drama) Globe. 1992: *Lorenzo's Oil* (Best Actress) Academy (Best Actress, Drama) Globe. 1994: *The Client* (Best Actress) Academy, *British* (Best Female Actor in a Leading Role) SAG. 1995: *Dead Man Walking* (Best Actress) *Academy* (Best Actress, Drama) Globe (Best Female Actor in a Leading Role) *SAG*. 1998: *Stepmom* (Best Actress, Drama) Globe. 2002: *Igby Goes Down* (Best Supporting Actress) Globe. Television: 2001: *Friends* (Best Guest Actress in a Comedy Series) Emmy. 2002: *Malcolm in the Middle* (Best Guest Actress in a Comedy Series) Emmy. Tributes: 2003: Gala Tribute from Film Society of Lincoln Center.

Sarno, John

Movie: 1971: *The Seven Minutes* (New Star of the Year — Actor) Globe.

Sarrazin, Michael

Movie: 1968: *The Sweet Ride* (New Star of the Year — Actor) Globe. 1969: *They Shoot Horses, Don't They?* (Most Promising Newcomer) British.

Sarsgaard, Peter

Movie: 2003: *Shattered Glass* (Best Supporting Actor) Globe, *Society* (Best Supporting Male) Spirit. 2004: *Kinsey* (Best Supporting Actor) Society, Broadcast (Best Supporting Male) Spirit.

Saß (Sass), Katrin

Movie: 1982: *Bürgschaft für ein Jahr (On Probation)* (Best Actress) *Berlin*. Tributes: 2005: Honorary Award from Berlin.

Savalas, Telly

Movie: 1962: *Bird Man of Alcatraz* (Best Supporting Actor) Academy, Globe. 1965: *Battle of the Bulge* (Best Supporting Actor) Globe. Television: 1973: *"The Marcus-Nelson Murders," CBS Thursday Night Movies* (Best Single Performance by an Actor in a Leading Role) Emmy. 1973–1978 series *Kojak* (Best Actor in a Drama Series) 1974: *Emmy, Globe*. 1975: Emmy, *Globe*. 1976: Globe. 1977: Globe. (Best Director of a Drama Series) 1975: Emmy.

Savic, Sonja

Movie: 1985: *Zivot je lep* (Best Actress) *Venice*.

Savinova, Yekaterina

Movie: 1954: *Bolshaya semya (The Big Family) Cannes* (special ensemble award).

Saxon, John

Movie: 1957: *This Happy Feeling* (New Star of the Year — Actor) *Globe*. 1966: *The Appaloosa* (Best Supporting Actor) Globe.

Scacchi, Greta

Movie: 1983: *Heat and Dust* (Best Newcomer to Film) British. Television: 1996: *Rasputin* (Best Supporting Actress in a Miniseries or Special) *Emmy* (Best Supporting Actress in a Series, Miniseries, or TV Movie) Globe. 2006: *Broken Trail* (Best Female Actor in a Television Movie or Miniseries) SAG (Best Supporting Actress in a Miniseries or TV Movie) Emmy.

Scardino, Hal

Movie: 1996: *Marvin's Room* (Best Ensemble) SAG.

Scarwid, Diane

Movie: 1980: *Inside Moves* (Best Supporting Actress) Academy. Television: 1996: *Truman* (Best Supporting Actress in a Miniseries or Special) Emmy.

Scheider, Roy

Movie: 1971: *The French Connection* (Best Supporting Actor) Academy. 1979: *All That Jazz* (Best Actor) Academy, British (Best Actor, Musical or Comedy) Globe. 1997: *The Myth of Fingerprints* (Best Supporting Male) Spirit.

Schell, Maria

Movie: 1953: *The Heart of the Matter* (Best Foreign Actress) British. 1956: *Gervaise* (Best Actress) *Venice* (Best Foreign Actress) British.

Schell, Maximilian

Movie: 1961: *Judgment at Nuremberg* (Best Actor) *Academy, New York* (Best Actor, Drama) *Globe*

(Best Foreign Actor) British. 1975: *The Man in the Glass Booth* (Best Actor) Academy (Best Actor, Drama) Globe. 1977: *Julia* (Best Supporting Actor) Academy, *New York,* Globe. 1986: *Marlene* (Best Documentary, Director) *Society.* **Television:** 1992: *"Miss Rose White," Hallmark Hall of Fame* (Best Actor in a Miniseries or Special) Emmy. 1993: *Stalin* (Best Supporting Actor in a Miniseries or Special) Emmy (Best Supporting Actor in a Series, Miniseries, or TV Movie) *Globe.* **Records:** With *Judgment at Nuremberg* Schell set two Academy Award records. Because he'd already portrayed Hans Rolfe in the 1959 production, Schell became the first actor to win Oscar gold for recreating a role he'd originated on the small screen. Not a headlining actor in 1961, Schell was billed below four other motion picture stars in the film: Spencer Tracy, Burt Lancaster, Richard Widmark, and Marlene Dietrich, making his the lowest credited performance to win a lead acting Oscar.

Schildkraut, Joseph

Movie: 1937: *The Life of Emile Zola* (Best Acting) Board (Best Supporting Actor) *Academy.* 1959: *The Diary of Anne Frank* (Best Actor, Drama) Globe. **Television:** 1963: *Sam Benedict* (Best Single Performance by an Actor in a Leading Role) Emmy.

Schneider, Romy

Movie: 1963: *The Cardinal* (Best Actress, Drama) Globe.

Schotte, Emmanuel

Movie: 1999: *L'Humanité (Humanity)* (Best Actor) *Cannes.*

Schrader, Maria

Movie: 1999: *Aimée & Jaguar* (Best Actress) *Berlin* (win shared with costar).

Schroder, Rick(y)

Movie: 1979: *The Champ* (New Star of the Year — Actor) *Globe.* **Television:** 1990: *The Stranger Within* (Best Actor in a Miniseries or TV Movie) Globe. 1998–2001 series *NYPD Blue* (Best Male Actor in a Drama Series) 1999: SAG. (Best Ensemble) 1999: SAG.

Schwarz, Helene

Tributes: 2005: Honorary Award from Berlin.

Schwarzenegger, Arnold

Movie: 1976: *Stay Hungry* (New Star of the Year — Actor) *Globe.* 1994: *Junior* (Best Actor, Musical or Comedy) Globe.

Schygulla, Hanna

Movie: 1979: *Die Ehe der Maria Braun* (Best Actress) *Berlin.* 1983: *Storia di Piera (Story of Piera)* (Best Actress) *Cannes.*

Sciorra, Annabella

Movie: 1989: *True Love* (Best Female Lead) Spirit. **Television:** 2001: *The Sopranos* (Best Guest Actress in a Drama Series) Emmy.

Scofield, Paul

Movie: 1955: *That Lady* (Most Promising Newcomer) *British.* 1966: *A Man for All Seasons* (Best Actor) *Academy, New York, Board* (Best Actor, Drama) *Globe* (Best British Actor) *British.* 1994: *Quiz Show* (Best Supporting Actor) Academy, British. 1996: *The Crucible* (Best Supporting Actor) Globe, *British.* **Theater:** 1962: *A Man for All Seasons* (Best Actor, Dramatic) *Tony.* **Television:** 1969: *"Male of the Species," Prudential's On Stage* (Best Single Performance by an Actor) *Emmy.*

Scott, Campbell

Movie: 1994: *Mrs. Parker and the Vicious Circle* (Best Male Lead) Spirit. 2002: *Roger Dodger* (Best Actor) *Board* (Best Male Lead) Spirit. **Records:** When Scott won the National Board of Review's Best Actor prize for *Roger Dodger* 32 years after his dad, George C. Scott won the same award for *Patton*, they became the first father and son to both win acting awards from the Board.

Scott, George C.

Movie: 1959: *Anatomy of a Murder* (Best Supporting Actor) Academy. 1961: *The Hustler* (New Star of the Year — Actor) Globe (Best Supporting Actor) Academy, Globe. 1970: *Patton (Patton: Lust for Glory)* (Best Actor) *Academy, New York, Board, British, Society* (Best Actor, Drama) *Globe.* 1971: *The Hospital* (Best Actor) Academy, British (multiple nomination), (Best Actor, Drama) Globe; *They Might Be Giants* (Best Actor) British (multiple nomination). 1978: *Movie, Movie* (Best Actor, Musical or Comedy) Globe. **Theater:** 1959: *Comes a Day* (Best Supporting or Featured Actor, Dramatic) Tony. 1960: *The Andersonville Trial* (Best Actor, Dramatic) Tony. 1974: *Uncle Vanya* (Best Actor, Dramatic) Tony. 1976: *Death of a Salesman* (Best Actor, Play) Tony. 1996: *Inherit the Wind* (Best Actor, Play) Tony. **Television:** 1962: *Ben Casey* (Best Supporting Actor) Emmy. 1963–1964 series *East Side, West Side* (Best Continued Performance by an Actor in a Series) 1964: Emmy. 1968: *The Crucible* (Best Single Performance by an Actor in a Drama)

Emmy. 1971: *"The Price," Hallmark Hall of Fame* (Best Single Performance by an Actor in a Leading Role) *Emmy*. 1972: *"Jane Eyre," Bell System Family Theatre* (Best Single Performance by an Actor in a Leading Role) Emmy. 1977: *"Beauty and the Beast," Hallmark Hall of Fame* (Best Actor in a Drama or Comedy Special) Emmy. 1985: *A Christmas Carol* (Best Actor in a Limited Series or Special) Emmy. 1997: *12 Angry Men* (Best Male Actor in a Television Movie or Miniseries) SAG (Best Supporting Actor in a Miniseries or TV Movie) *Emmy* (Best Supporting Actor in a Series, Miniseries, or TV Movie) *Globe*. 1999: *Inherit the Wind* (Best Actor in a Miniseries or TV Movie) SAG. **Records:** Nine years before he became the first actor to refuse an Academy Award (for *Patton*), Scott made clear to the Academy that he had no interest in their award. When nominated for Best Supporting Actor in 1961 for *The Hustler*, he became the first actor to decline a nomination, comparing the Oscars to a weird beauty or personality contest and insisting that actors should not be forced to out-advertise each other. Despite his wishes to be left off the ballot, the Academy left his name on it. He ended up losing to George Chakiras in *West Side Story*.

Scott, Martha

Movie: 1940: *Our Town* (Best Acting) *Board* (Best Actress) Academy.

Scott Thomas, Kristin

Movie: 1994: *Four Weddings and a Funeral* (Best Supporting Actress) *British*. 1996: *The English Patient* (Best Actress) Academy, British (Best Actress, Drama) Globe (Best Supporting Actress) *Board* (Best Female Actor in a Leading Role) SAG (Best Ensemble) SAG. 2001: *Gosford Park* (Best Ensemble) *SAG, Broadcast*.

Sears, Heather

Movie: 1957: *The Story of Esther Costello* (Best British Actress) *British* (Best Supporting Actress) Globe.

Seastrom (Sjöström), Victor

Movie: 1957: *Wild Strawberries* (Best Foreign Actor) British (Best Actor) *Board*.

Seberg, Jean

Movie: 1961: *Breathless* (Best Foreign Actress) British. 1963: *Lilith* (Best Actress, Drama) Globe.

Seda, Jon

Movie: 1994: *I Like It Like That* (Best Male Lead) Spirit.

Sedgwick, Kyra

Movie: 1995: *Something to Talk About* (Best Supporting Actress) Globe. 2004: *Cavedweller* (Best Female Lead) Spirit. **Television:** 1992: *"Miss Rose White," Hallmark Hall of Fame* (Best Actress in a Miniseries or TV Movie) Globe. 2005–present series *The Closer* (Best Actress in a Drama Series) 2005: Globe. 2006: Emmy, *Globe*. 2007: Emmy, Globe. (Best Female Actor in a Drama Series) 2005: SAG. 2006: SAG. 2007: SAG. (Best Ensemble in a Drama Series) 2005: SAG. 2007: SAG.

Segal, George

Movie: 1964: *The New Interns* (New Star of the Year — Actor) *Globe*. 1966: *Who's Afraid of Virginia Woolf?* (Best Supporting Actor) Academy, Globe. 1968: *No Way to Treat a Lady* (Best Supporting Actor) British. 1973: *A Touch of Class* (Best Actor, Musical or Comedy) *Globe*. **Television:** 1997–2003 series *Just Shoot Me!* (Best Actor in a Comedy Series) 1998: Globe. 1999: Globe.

Sellers, Peter

Movie: 1959: *I'm All Right Jack* (Best British Actor) *British*; *The Running, Jumping and Standing-Still Film* (Best Live Action Short Subject Film, Producer) Academy. 1962: *Only Two Can Play* (Best British Actor) British; *Lolita* (Best Supporting Actor) Globe. 1964: *Dr. Strangelove, or How I Learned to Stop Worrying and Love the Bomb* (Best Actor) Academy (Best British Actor) British (multiple nomination); *The Pink Panther* (Best British Actor) British (multiple nomination), (Best Actor, Musical or Comedy) Globe. 1975: *Return of the Pink Panther* (Best Actor, Musical or Comedy) Globe. 1976: *The Pink Panther Strikes Again* (Best Actor, Musical or Comedy) Globe. 1979: *Being There* (Best Actor) Academy, *Board*, British (Best Actor, Musical or Comedy) *Globe*. **Television:** 1978: *The Muppet Show* (Best Continuing or Single Performance by a Supporting Actor in Variety or Music) Emmy.

Serbedzija, Rade

Movie: 1994: *Before the Rain* (Best Actor) *Venice*.

Sergeyev, Nikolai

Movie: 1954: *Bolshaya semya (The Big Family)* *Cannes* (special ensemble award).

Serkis, Andy

Movie: 2001: *The Lord of the Rings: The Fellowship of the Ring* (Best Ensemble) SAG. 2002: *The Lord of the Rings: The Two Towers* (Best Ensemble) SAG. 2003: *The Lord of the Rings: The Return of the King*

(Best Ensemble) *Board, SAG, Broadcast.* **Television:** 2007: *Longford* (Best Supporting Actor in a Series, Miniseries, or TV Movie) Globe.

Seth, Roshan

Movie: 1982: *Gandhi* (Best Supporting Actor) British.

Severn, William

Movie: 1942: *Journey for Margaret* (Best Acting) *Board.*

Sevigny, Chloë

Movie: 1995: *Kids* (Best Supporting Female) Spirit. 1999: *Boys Don't Cry* (Best Female Actor in a Supporting Role) SAG (Best Supporting Actress) Academy, Globe, *Society, LA* (Best Supporting Female) *Spirit.*

Seweryn, Andrzej

Movie: 1980: *Dyrygent (Orchestra Conductor)* (Best Actor) *Berlin.*

Sexton, Brendan, III

Movie: 1996: *Welcome to the Dollhouse* (Best Debut Performance) Spirit.

Seymour, Cara

Movie: 2002: *Adaptation* (Best Ensemble) SAG.

Seyrig, Delphine

Movie: 1963: *Muriel* (Best Actress) *Venice.* 1969: *Stolen Kisses* (Best Supporting Actress) *Society.* 1973: *The Day of the Jackal* (Best Supporting Actress) British.

Shah, Naseeruddin

Movie: 1984: *Paar* (Best Actor) *Venice.*

Shalhoub, Tony

Movie: 1996: *Big Night* (Best Male Lead) Spirit (Best Supporting Actor) *Society.* **Theater:** 1992: *Conversations with My Father* (Best Actor in a Featured Role, Play) Tony. **Television:** 2002–present series *Monk* (Best Actor in a Comedy Series) 2003: *Emmy.* 2004: Emmy. 2005: *Emmy.* 2006: *Emmy.* 2007: Emmy. (Best Actor of a Series, Musical or Comedy) 2003: *Globe.* 2004: Globe. 2005: Globe. 2007: Globe. (Best Male Actor in a Comedy Series) 2002: SAG. 2003: *SAG.* 2004: *SAG.* 2006: SAG. 2007: SAG.

Shannon, Harry

Movie: 1954: *Executive Suite* (Best Ensemble) *Venice* (special award).

Shannon, Michael

Movie: 2007: *Before the Devil Knows You're Dead* (Best Ensemble) Broadcast.

Shannon, Molly

Movie: 1998: *Happiness* (Best Ensemble) *Board.* **Television:** 1995–2001 series *Saturday Night Live* (Best Individual Performance in a Variety or Music Program) 2000: Emmy.

Sharif, Omar

Movie: 1962: *Lawrence of Arabia* (New Star of the Year — Actor) *Globe* (Best Supporting Actor) Academy, *Globe.* 1965: *Doctor Zhivago* (Best Actor, Drama) *Globe.* 2003: *Monsieur Ibrahim et les fleurs du Coran* (Best Actor) *Venice.* **Tributes:** 2003: Career Golden Lion from Venice.

Sharkey, Ray

Movie: 1980: *The Idolmaker* (Best Actor, Musical or Comedy) *Globe.* **Television:** 1981: *The Ordeal of Bill Carney* (Best Actor in a Miniseries or TV Movie) Globe.

Sharp, Lesley

Movie: 1997: *The Full Monty* (Best Supporting Actress) British (Best Ensemble) *SAG.*

Sharpe, Karen

Movie: 1954: *The High and the Mighty* (New Star of the Year — Actress) *Globe.*

Shaw, Robert

Movie: 1966: *A Man for All Seasons* (Best Supporting Actor) Academy, *Board*, Globe. 1972: *Young Winston* (Best Actor) British.

Shaw, Victoria

Movie: 1955: *The Eddy Duchin Story* (New Star of the Year — Actress) *Globe.*

Shaw, Vinessa

Movie: 2007: *3:10 to Yuma* (Best Ensemble) SAG.

Shearer, Harry

Movie: 2003: *A Mighty Wind* (Best Screenplay) Spirit (Best Ensemble) Broadcast.

Shearer, Norma

Movie: 1929: *Their Own Desire** (Best Actress) Academy. 1930: *The Divorcée* (Best Actress) Academy. 1931: *A Free Soul* (Best Actress) Academy. 1934:

The Barretts of Wimpole Street (Best Actress) Academy. 1936: *Romeo and Juliet* (Best Actress) Academy. 1938: *Marie Antoinette* (Best Actress) Academy, *Venice*. **Records:** In the first two years of the Academy Awards, nominees were chosen by a group of twenty industry leaders and the winners by a panel of five judges. At the second awards ceremony when two founding members of the Academy, director Frank Lloyd and actress Mary Pickford, both won Oscars, critics balked, and the Academy decided to revamp its selection policies. As a result, the next year's winners were chosen by all 300 current Academy members, making Shearer and George Arliss, who won Best Actor for *Disraeli*, the first stars to win their Oscars by a vote from their peers. The year Shearer won (1929/1930), more Best Actress performances were nominated than any other time in Academy Award history. Although voters followed the standard five nominees per category rule, two actresses, Shearer and Greta Garbo, received separate nominations for two different performances, raising to seven the actual number of film performances in contention.

*For the 1929/1930 film season, Shearer's single nomination encompassed two films: *Their Own Desire* and *The Divorcée*, but her award was officially presented to her solely for *The Divorcée*. Academy researchers, experts, and even Shearer herself could never explain the mystery of the double nomination but single recognition. Many movie books no longer even mention her nod for *Their Own Desire*.

Sheedy, Ally

Movie: 1998: *High Art* (Best Actress) *Society, LA* (Best Female Lead) *Spirit*.

Sheen, Charlie

Movie: 1999: *Being John Malkovich* (Best Ensemble) SAG. **Television:** 2000–2002 series *Spin City* (Best Actor in a Comedy Series) 2001: *Globe*. 2003–present series *Two and a Half Men* (Best Actor in a Comedy Series) 2006: Emmy. 2007: Emmy. (Best Actor in a Series, Musical or Comedy) 2004: Globe. 2005: Globe. (Best Male Actor in a Comedy Series) 2004: SAG.

Sheen, Martin

Movie: 1968: *The Subject Was Roses* (Best Supporting Actor) Globe. 1979: *Apocalypse Now* (Best Actor) British. 2006: *Bobby* (Best Ensemble) SAG, Broadcast; *The Departed* (Best Ensemble) *Board*, SAG, Broadcast. **Theater:** 1965: *The Subject Was Roses* (Best Supporting or Featured Actor, Dramatic) Tony. **Television:** 1974: *"The Execution of Private Slovik,"* NBC Wednesday Night Movie (Best Actor in a Drama) Emmy. 1978: *"Taxi!!"* Hallmark Hall

of Fame (Best Actor in a Drama or Comedy Special) Emmy. 1979: *Blind Ambition* (Best Actor in a Drama Series) Globe. 1981: *Insight* (Best Individual Achievement in Religious Programming, Performer) *Emmy*. 1983: *Kennedy* (Best Actor in a Miniseries or TV Movie) Globe. 1994: *Murphy Brown* (Best Guest Actor in a Comedy Series) *Emmy*. 1999–2006 series *The West Wing* (Best Actor in a Drama Series) 1999: Globe. 2000: Emmy, *Globe*. 2001: Emmy, Globe. 2002: Emmy, Globe. 2003: Emmy, Globe. 2004: Emmy. 2006: Emmy. (Best Male Actor in a Drama Series) 1999: SAG. 2000: *SAG*. 2001: *SAG*. 2002: SAG. 2003: SAG. (Best Ensemble in a Drama Series) 2000: *SAG*. 2001: *SAG*. 2002: SAG. 2003: SAG. 2004: SAG. 2005: SAG. 2006: *Two and a Half Men* (Best Guest Actor in a Comedy Series) Emmy.

Sheen, Michael

Movie: 2006: *The Queen* (Best Supporting Actor) British, *LA*.

Shelton, Marley

Movie: 2005: *Sin City* (Best Ensemble) Broadcast.

Shepard, Sam

Movie: 1983: *The Right Stuff* (Best Supporting Actor) Academy. 1984: *Paris, Texas* (Best Screenplay) British. **Theater:** 1996: *Buried Child* (Best Play, Writer) Tony. 2000: *True West* (Best Play, Writer) Tony. **Television:** 1999: *Dash and Lilly* (Best Actor in a Miniseries or TV Movie) Emmy, Globe. 2007: *Ruffian* (Best Male Actor in a Television Movie or Miniseries) SAG.

Shepherd, Cybill

Movie: 1971: *The Last Picture Show* (New Star of the Year — Actress) Globe. **Television:** 1985–1989 series *Moonlighting* (Best Actress in a Drama Series) 1986: Emmy. (Best Actress in a Series, Musical or Comedy) 1985: *Globe*. 1986: *Globe*. 1987: Globe. 1995–1998 series *Cybill* (Best Actress in a Comedy Series) 1995: Emmy. 1996: Emmy. 1997: Emmy. (Best Actress in a Series, Musical or Comedy) 1995: *Globe*. 1996: Globe.

Sheppard, Stephen Lea

Movie: 2001: *The Royal Tenenbaums* (Best Ensemble) Broadcast.

Sher, Antony

Movie: 1998: *Shakespeare in Love* (Best Ensemble) *SAG*. **Theater:** 1997: *Stanley* (Best Actor, Play) Tony.

Sheridan, Ann

Movie: 1942: *Kings Row* (Best Acting) *Board*.

Shigeta, James

Movie: 1959: *The Crimson Kimono* (New Star of the Year — Actor) *Globe*.

Shimura, Takashi

Movie: 1955: *The Seven Samurai* (Best Foreign Actor) British. 1959: *Living* (Best Foreign Actor) British.

Shire, Talia

Movie: 1974: *The Godfather Part II* (Best Supporting Actress) Academy. 1976: *Rocky* (Best Actress) Academy (Best Actress, Drama) Globe (Best Supporting Actress) *New York, Board*. **Theater:** 1998: *Golden Child* (Best Play, Producer) Tony. **Records:** Shire's Best Supporting Actress nod for *The Godfather Part II* made her family the first with three members to receive Oscar nominations for a single film. Her brother, Francis Ford Coppola, directed the film and their father, Carmine Coppola, wrote the score. On Oscar night, both men won, but Shire lost her race to screen legend Ingrid Bergman, who picked up her third Oscar, and first in the supporting category, for *Murder on the Orient Express.*

Shirley, Anne

Movie: 1937: *Stella Dallas* (Best Supporting Actress) Academy.

Shue, Elisabeth

Movie: 1995: *Leaving Las Vegas* (Best Actress) Academy, British, *Society, LA* (Best Actress, Drama) Globe (Best Female Actor in a Leading Role) SAG (Best Female Lead) *Spirit*.

Siao, Josephine

Movie: 1995: *Nu ren sis hi (Summer Snow)* (Best Actress) *Berlin*.

Siddig, Alexander

Movie: 2005: *Syriana* (Best Ensemble) Broadcast.

Sidney, Sylvia

Movie: 1973: *Summer Wishes, Winter Dreams* (Best Supporting Actress) Academy, *Board*, Globe, British. Television: 1963: *The Defenders* (Best Single Performance by an Actress in a Leading Role) Emmy. 1986: *An Early Frost* (Best Supporting Actress in a Miniseries or TV Movie) Emmy (Best Supporting Actress in a Series, Miniseries, or TV Movie) *Globe*.

Sigel, Barbara

Movie: 1973: *Time to Run* (New Star of the Year — Actress) Globe.

Signoret, Simone

Movie: 1952: *Casque d'or* (Best Foreign Actress) British. 1957: *The Witches of Salem* (Best Foreign Actress) British. 1959: *Room at the Top* (Best Actress) Academy, Board, Cannes (Best Actress, Drama) Globe (Best Foreign Actress) *British*. 1965: *Ship of Fools* (Best Actress) Academy (Best Actress, Drama) Globe (Best Foreign Actress) British. 1967: *The Deadly Affair* (Best Foreign Actress) British; *Games* (Best Supporting Actress) British. 1971: *Le Chat* (Best Actress) *Berlin*. **Television:** 1966: *"A Small Rebellion," Bob Hope Presents the Chrysler Theatre* (Best Single Performance by an Actress in a Drama) *Emmy*. **Records:** French actress Signoret never made a Hollywood film before becoming the first female to win an Oscar for a movie made in a foreign country. Before her, only Charles Laughton had achieved the same feat among men. Both their movies (Signoret's *Room at the Top* and Laughton's *The Private Life of Henry VIII*) were British. **Highlights:** One of the most famous of all Academy archive photos is the shot of Signoret leaning forward in her seat at the RKO Pantages Theater unconsciously cupping the underside of her breasts as she awaits the announcement of the winner the year she was nominated for Best Actress for *Room at the Top*. Few other photos capture the blend of excitement and terror encompassed in that anticipatory moment. Seconds later, Signoret's anxiety made way for elation as her name was called as the winner.

Sillas, Karen

Movie: 1992: *Simple Men* (Best Supporting Female) Spirit. 1994: *What Happened Was...* (Best Female Lead) Spirit.

Silverstone, Alicia

Movie: 1995: *Clueless* (Breakthrough Performance — Female) *Board*. **Television:** 2001–2002, 2004–2005 series *Braceface* (Best Performer in an Animated Series) 2001: Emmy. 2003 series *Miss Match* (Best Actress in a Comedy Series) 2003: Globe. **Records:** For her starmaking turn as Cher Horowitz in *Clueless*, Silverstone became the first person to win a Breakthrough Performance award from the National Board of Review.

Sim, Alastair

Movie: 1952: *Folly to Be Wise* (Best British Actor) British.

Simmons, J. K.

Movie: 2007: *Juno* (Best Ensemble) Broadcast. **Television:** 2005–present series *The Closer* (Best Ensemble in a Drama Series) 2005: SAG. 2007: SAG.

Simmons, Jean

Movie: 1948: **Hamlet** (Best Actress) *Venice* (Best Supporting Actress) Academy. 1953: **The Actress** (Best Actress) *Board* (multiple win); **The Robe** (Best Actress) *Board* (multiple win); **Young Bess** (Best Actress) *Board* (multiple win). 1955: **Guys and Dolls** (Best Actress, Musical or Comedy) *Globe* (Best Foreign Actress) British. 1957: **This Could Be the Night** (Best Actress, Musical or Comedy) Globe. 1958: **Home Before Dark** (Best Actress, Drama) Globe. 1960: **Elmer Gantry** (Best Actress, Drama) Globe (Best Foreign Actress) British. 1969: **The Happy Ending** (Best Actress) Academy (Best Actress, Drama) Globe. Television: 1983: **The Thorn Birds** (Best Supporting Actress in a Limited Series or Special) *Emmy* (Best Supporting Actress in a Series, Miniseries, or TV Movie) Globe. 1989: **Murder, She Wrote** (Best Guest Actress in a Drama Series) Emmy. Tributes: 1957: Special Achievement Award as Most Versatile Actress from Globe.

Simmons, Robin

Movie: 2004: **Robbing Peter** (Best Supporting Female) Spirit.

Simon, Michel

Movie: 1939: **La Fin du jour** *(The End of a Day)* (Best Acting) *Board* (multiple win); **Le Quai des brumes** *(Port of Shadows)* (Best Acting) *Board* (multiple win). 1967: **Le Vieil homme et l'enfant** *(The Two of Us)* (Best Actor) *Berlin*.

Sinatra, Frank

Movie: 1953: **From Here to Eternity** (Best Supporting Actor) *Academy, Globe.* 1955: **The Man with the Golden Arm** (Best Actor) Academy (Best Foreign Actor) British; **Not as a Stranger** (Best Foreign Actor) British. 1957: **Pal Joey** (Best Actor, Musical or Comedy) *Globe.* 1963: **Come Blow Your Horn** (Best Actor, Musical or Comedy) Globe. Television: 1956: --- (Best Male Singer) Emmy. 1969: **Francis Albert Sinatra Does His Thing** (Best Variety or Music Program, Star) Emmy. 1970: **Sinatra** (Best Variety or Music Program, Executive Producer and Star) Emmy. 1974: **Magnavox Presents Frank Sinatra** (Best Comedy-Variety, Variety or Music Special; Star) Emmy. Tributes: 1970: Jean Hersholt Humanitarian Award from Academy; Cecil B. DeMille Award from Globe. 1972: Life Achievement Award from SAG. 1983: Honor from Kennedy Center for the Performing Arts.

Sinclair, John Gordon

Movie: 1981: **Gregory's Girl** (Most Promising Newcomer) British.

Singer, Lori

Movie: 1985: **Trouble in Mind** (Best Female Lead) Spirit. 1993: **Short Cuts** (Best Ensemble) *Venice* (special award).

Sinise, Gary

Movie: 1994: **Forrest Gump** (Best Male Actor in a Supporting Role) SAG (Best Supporting Actor) Academy, *Board*, Globe. 1995: **Apollo 13** (Best Ensemble) *SAG*. Theater: 1990: **The Grapes of Wrath** (Best Actor in a Featured Role, Play) Tony. 1996: **Buried Child** (Best Director, Play) Tony (Best Play, Producer) Tony. 2001: **One Flew Over the Cuckoo's Nest** (Best Actor, Play) Tony. Television: 1994: **Stephen King's The Stand** (Best Male Actor in a Television Movie or Miniseries) SAG. 1996: **Truman** (Best Actor in a Miniseries or Special) Emmy (Best Actor in a Miniseries or TV Movie) *Globe* (Best Male Actor in a Television Movie or Miniseries) *SAG*. 1997: **George Wallace** (Best Actor in a Miniseries or TV Movie) *Emmy,* Globe (Best Male Actor in a Television Movie or Miniseries) *SAG*.

Sinje, Angelica Lee

Movie: 2001: **Betelnut Beauty** (Best Young Actress) *Berlin*.

Sizemore, Tom

Movie: 1998: **Saving Private Ryan** (Best Ensemble) SAG. Television: 1999: **Witness Protection** (Best Actor in a Miniseries or TV Movie) Globe.

Skala, Lilia

Movie: 1963: **Lilies of the Field** (Best Supporting Actress) Academy, Globe. 1977: **Roseland** (Best Supporting Actress) Globe. Television: 1976: **"Eleanor and Franklin," ABC Theatre** (Best Single Performance by a Supporting Actress in a Comedy or Drama Special) Emmy.

Skarsgård, Stellan

Movie: 1982: **Den Enfaldige mördaren** *(The Simple-Minded Murderer)* (Best Actor) *Berlin*. 1997: **Good Will Hunting** (Best Ensemble) SAG.

Skelton, Red

Television: 1952: --- (Best Comedian or Comedienne) *Emmy*. 1957: **"The Big Slide," Playhouse 90** (Best Single Performance by an Actor) Emmy. 1951–1963 series **The Red Skelton Show** (Best Comedy Show, Star and Writer) 1952: Emmy. 1959: Emmy. (Best Program Achievement in the Field of Humor, Star and Writer) 1960: Emmy. 1962: Emmy.

(Best Writing Achievement in Comedy) 1961: *Emmy*. 1962: Emmy. 1963–1971 series *The Red Skelton Hour* (Best Individual Achievement in Entertainment, Performer) 1965: Emmy. (Best Program Achievement in the Field of Variety, Star and Writer) 1963: Emmy. (Best Variety Series, Star and Writer) 1966: Emmy. (Best Writing Achievement in Comedy) 1963: Emmy. **Tributes:** 1958: Special Television Achievement Award from Globe. 1977: Cecil B. DeMille Award from Globe. 1987: Life Achievement Award from SAG. 1989: Television Hall of Fame Inductee from Emmy.

Skerritt, Tom

Movie: 1977: *The Turning Point* (Best Supporting Actor) *Board*. Television: 1992–1996 series *Picket Fences* (Best Actor in a Drama Series) 1993: *Emmy*, Globe. 1994: Emmy, Globe. (Best Male Actor in a Drama Series) 1994: SAG.

Skinner, Anita

Movie: 1978: *Girlfriends* (New Star of the Year — Actress) Globe.

Slaine

Movie: 2007: *Gone Baby Gone* (Best Ensemble) Broadcast.

Slater, Christian

Movie: 1990: *Pump Up the Volume* (Best Male Lead) Spirit. 2006: *Bobby* (Best Ensemble) SAG, Broadcast.

Smart, Jean

Movie: 1999: *Guinevere* (Best Supporting Female) Spirit. Theater: 2001: *The Man Who Came to Dinner* (Best Actress, Play) Tony. Television: 2000–2001 series *Frasier* (Best Guest Actress in a Comedy Series) 2000: *Emmy*. 2001: *Emmy*. 2001: *The District* (Best Guest Actress in a Drama Series) Emmy. 2006–present series *24* (Best Supporting Actress in a Drama Series) 2006: Emmy. (Best Guest Actress in a Drama Series) 2007: Emmy. (Best Ensemble in a Drama Series) 2006: SAG.

Smith, Brooke

Movie: 1994: *Vanya on 42nd Street* (Best Supporting Female) Spirit. Television: 2007–present series *Grey's Anatomy* (Best Ensemble in a Drama Series) 2007: SAG.

Smith, Ian Michael

Movie: 1998: *Simon Birch* (Best Child Performer) *Broadcast*.

Smith, Jaden Christopher Syre

Movie: 2006: *The Pursuit of Happyness* (Best Young Actor) Broadcast.

Smith, Lionel Mark

Movie: 2000: *State and Main* (Best Ensemble) *Board*.

Smith, Liz

Movie: 1984: *A Private Function* (Best Supporting Actress) *British*.

Smith, Lois

Movie: 1970: *Five Easy Pieces* (Best Supporting Actress) *Society*. Theater: 1990: *The Grapes of Wrath* (Best Actress in a Featured Role, Play) Tony. 1996: *Buried Child* (Best Actress in a Featured Role, Play) Tony.

Smith, Louise

Movie: 1987: *Working Girls* (Best Female Lead) Spirit.

Smith, Maggie

Movie: 1958: *Nowhere to Go* (Most Promising Newcomer) British. 1963: *The V.I.P.s* (New Star of the Year — Actress) Globe. 1965: *Othello* (Best Actress, Drama) Globe (Best Supporting Actress) Academy; *Young Cassidy* (Best British Actress) British. 1969: *The Prime of Miss Jean Brodie* (Best Actress) *Academy*, *British* (Best Actress, Drama) Globe. 1972: *Travels with My Aunt* (Best Actress) Academy (Best Actress, Musical or Comedy) Globe. 1978: *California Suite* (Best Actress) British (Best Actress, Musical or Comedy) *Globe* (Best Supporting Actress) *Academy*; *Death on the Nile* (Best Supporting Actress) British. 1981: *Quartet* (Best Actress) British. 1984: *A Private Function* (Best Actress) *British*. 1986: *A Room with a View* (Best Actress) *British* (Best Supporting Actress) Academy, *Globe*. 1987: *The Lonely Passion of Judith Hearn* (Best Actress) *British*. 1993: *The Secret Garden* (Best Supporting Actress) British. 1996: *The First Wives Club* (Best Ensemble) *Board*. 1999: *Tea with Mussolini* (Best Supporting Actress) *British*. 2001: *Gosford Park* (Best Supporting Actress) Academy, Globe, British (Best Ensemble) *SAG*, *Broadcast*. Theater: 1975: *Private Lives* (Best Actress, Dramatic) Tony. 1980: *Night and Day* (Best Actress, Play) Tony. 1990: *Lettice and Lovage* (Best Actress, Play) *Tony*. Television: 1993: *"Suddenly, Last Summer," Great Performances* (Best Actress in a Miniseries or Special) Emmy. 2000: *"David Copperfield," Exxon Mobil Masterpiece Theatre* (Best Supporting Actress in a Miniseries or TV Movie) Emmy. 2003: *My House in Umbria* (Best Actress in a Miniseries or TV Movie) *Emmy*, Globe. **Records:** In *California Suite*, Smith played Diana Barry, a respected actress who'd done Ibsen and Shakespeare and Shaw, but then received her first Academy Award nomination for what she called a nauseating little comedy, *No Left Turns*. In Neil Simon's *Suite*, Smith gave a both hilareous and poignant performance as her character anticipates and loses her bid for the Oscar. When Smith won a Best Supporting Actress Academy Award for the role, she became the first star to win an Oscar playing someone who lost at the Oscars.

Smith, Toby

Movie: 1999: *Drylongso* (Best Debut Performance) Spirit.

Smith, Will

Movie: 2001: *Ali* (Best Actor) Academy, Broadcast (Best Actor, Drama) Globe. 2006: *The Pursuit of Happyness* (Best Actor) Academy, Broadcast (Best Actor, Drama) Globe (Best Male Actor in a Leading Role) SAG. **Television:** 1990–1996 series *The Fresh Prince of Bel-Air* (Best Actor in a Comedy Series) 1992: Globe. 1993: Globe.

Smits, Jimmy

Movie: 1995: *My Family/Mi Familia* (Best Male Lead) Spirit. **Television:** 1986–1992 series *L.A. Law* (Best Supporting Actor in a Drama Series) 1987: Emmy. 1988: Emmy. 1989: Emmy. 1990: *Emmy*, Globe. 1991: Emmy. 1992: Emmy. 1994–1998 series *NYPD Blue* (Best Actor in a Drama Series) 1995: Emmy, *Globe*. 1996: Emmy, Globe. 1997: Emmy. 1998: Emmy, Globe. 1999: Emmy. (Best Male Actor in a Drama Series) 1995: SAG. 1996: SAG. 1997: SAG. 1998: SAG. (Best Ensemble in a Drama Series) 1995: SAG. 1996: SAG. 1997: SAG. 1998: SAG. 2004–2005 series *The West Wing* (Best Ensemble in a Drama Series) 2005: SAG.

Smoktunovsky, Innokenti

Movie: 1965: *Hamlet* (Best Foreign Actor) British.

Smollett, Jurnee

Movie: 1997: *Eve's Bayou* (Best Child Performance) *Broadcast*.

Snape, William

Movie: 1997: *The Full Monty* (Best Ensemble) SAG.

Snipes, Wesley

Movie: 1992: *The Waterdance* (Best Supporting Male) Spirit. 1997: *One Night Stand* (Best Actor) Venice.

Snodgress, Carrie

Movie: 1970: *Diary of a Mad Housewife* (New Star of the Year — Actress) *Globe* (Most Promising Newcomer) British (Best Actress) Academy (Best Actress, Musical or Comedy) *Globe*.

Snow, Brittany

Movie: 2007: *Hairspray* (Best Ensemble) SAG, *Broadcast*.

Söderbaum, Kristina

Movie: 1942: *Die Goldene Stadt* (Best Actress) *Venice*.

Sohn, Sonja

Movie: 1998: *Slam* (Best Debut Performance) Spirit.

Solonizyn (Solonitsyn), Anotoli

Movie: 1981: *Dwadzat schest dnej is shisni Dostojewskogo* (Best Actor) Berlin.

Somerville, Geraldine

Movie: 2001: *Gosford Park* (Best Ensemble) *SAG*, *Broadcast*.

Sommer, Elke

Movie: 1963: *The Prize* (New Star of the Year — Actress) *Globe*.

Sondergaard, Gale

Movie: 1936: *Anthony Adverse* (Best Supporting Actress) *Academy*. 1946: *Anna and the King of Siam* (Best Supporting Actress) Academy. **Records:** Sondergaard set two Academy Award records in 1936. When she made history by receiving the first Best Supporting Actress Oscar ever given, she also became the first person to win an Academy Award for a debut film performance.

Soo-yeon, Kang

Movie: 1987: *Sibaji (Contract Mother)* (Best Actress) *Venice*.

Sordi, Alberto

Movie: 1961: *The Best of Enemies* (Best Foreign Actor) British (Best Actor, Musical or Comedy) Globe. 1963: *To Bed ... or Not to Bed* (Best Actor, Musical or Comedy) *Globe*. 1965: *Those Magnificent*

Men in Their Flying Machines (Best Actor, Musical or Comedy) Globe. 1971: *Detenuto in attesa di giudizio* (Best Actor) *Berlin*. **Tributes:** 1995: Career Golden Lion from Venice.

Sorvino, Mira

Movie: 1995: *Mighty Aphrodite* (Best Female Actor in a Supporting Role) SAG (Best Supporting Actress) *Academy, New York, Board, Globe*, British, *Broadcast*. **Television:** 1996: *Norma Jean and Marilyn* (Best Actress in a Miniseries or TV Movie) Emmy, Globe. 2005: *Human Trafficking* (Best Actress in a Series, Miniseries, or TV Movie) Globe.

Sothern, Ann

Movie: 1964: *The Best Man* (Best Supporting Actress) Globe. 1987: *The Whales of August* (Best Supporting Actress) Academy (Best Supporting Female) Spirit. **Television:** 1956: --- (Best Comedienne) Emmy. 1953–1957 series *Private Secretary* (Best Actress Starring in a Regular Series) 1955: Emmy. (Best Actress—Continuing Performance) 1956: Emmy. (Best Continuing Performance by a Comedienne in a Series) 1957: Emmy. 1958–1962 series *The Ann Sothern Show* (Best Actress in a Leading Role—Continuing Character—in a Comedy Series) 1959: Emmy. **Tributes:** 1958: Special Television Achievement Award from Globe. **Highlights:** Sothern was among the leading objectors when Nannette Fabray beat her (and Edie Adams, Gracie Allen, and Lucille Ball) for the 1956 Emmy. Fabray had left *Caesar's Hour* after the previous season and had not starred in one episode the next year, yet her name showed up on the ballot again and the TV Academy voted her the winner. To make matters worse, Sothern claimed never to have gotten an Emmy ballot to cast a vote, as it had been sent to her business manager's office instead of to her. The Academy Board explored the question concerning Fabray and ultimately concluded that she indeed earned her award. Although the awards ceremony was in March 1957, the awards were being considered for the 1956 calendar year, which included the second half of the 1955–1956 TV season, when Fabray was still filming *Caesar's Hour*. Sothern accepted the decision, but not too happily. Despite fine work in television and film, Sothern never ended up winning a competitive acting award.

Soule, Allen

Movie: 2000: *State and Main* (Best Ensemble) *Board*.

Spacek, Sissy

Movie: 1973: *Badlands* (Most Promising Newcomer) British. 1976: *Carrie* (Best Actress) Academy, *Society*. 1977: *Three Women* (Best Supporting Actress) *New York*. 1980: *Coal Miner's Daughter* (Best Actress) *Academy, New York, Board*, British, *Society, LA* (Best Actress, Musical or Comedy) *Globe*. 1981: *Raggedy Man* (Best Actress, Drama) Globe. 1982: *Missing* (Best Actress) Academy, British (Best Actress, Drama) Globe. 1984: *The River* (Best Actress) Academy (Best Actress, Drama) Globe. 1986: *Crimes of the Heart* (Best Actress) Academy, *New York* (Best Actress, Musical or Comedy) *Globe*. 2001: *In the Bedroom* (Best Actress) Academy, *New York*, British, *LA, Broadcast* (Best Actress, Drama) *Globe* (Best Female Actor in a Leading Role) SAG (Best Female Lead) *Spirit* (Best Ensemble) SAG. **Television:** 1994: *A Place for Annie* (Best Female Actor in a Television Movie or Miniseries) SAG. 1995: *The Good Old Boys* (Best Supporting Actress in a Miniseries or Special) Emmy. 2001: *Midwives* (Best Female Actor in a Television Movie or Miniseries) SAG. 2002: *Last Call* (Best Supporting Actress in a Miniseries or TV Movie) Emmy. 2007: *Pictures of Hollis Woods* (Best Actress in a Miniseries or TV Movie) Globe. **Highlights:** During the planning stages for her biopic, legendary country singer Loretta Lynn sorted through stacks of headshots of glamorous starlets in search of the actress she thought could best represent her on the big screen. Lynn recalled wading through volumes of *Charlie's Angels*–types until coming upon a freckle-faced strawberry blonde that convinced her she'd found the coal miner's daughter. 29-year-old Spacek so impressed critics and award voters by aging from 13 to her forties and doing her own singing that she swept every 1980 Best Actress award except the British (she was up for that award in 1981 and lost to Meryl Streep for *The French Lieutenant's Woman*). Spacek, who started her show business career singing at New York coffee houses under the name Rainbo, did all her own singing in *Coal Miner's Daughter*, so it is her voice, not Loretta Lynn's, on the movie soundtrack.

Spacey, Kevin

Movie: 1995: *Outbreak* (Best Supporting Actor) *New York* (multiple win), *Broadcast* (multiple win); *Seven* (Best Supporting Actor) *New York* (multiple win), *Board* (multiple win), *Broadcast* (multiple win); *Swimming with Sharks* (Best Supporting Actor) *New York* (multiple win), *Broadcast* (multiple win), (Best Male Lead) Spirit; *The Usual Suspects* (Best Male Actor in a Supporting Role) SAG (Best Supporting Actor) *Academy, New York* (multiple win), *Board* (multiple win), Globe, *Broadcast* (multiple win), (Best Ensemble) *Board*. 1997: *L.A. Confidential* (Best Actor) British (Best Ensemble) SAG. 1999: *American Beauty* (Best Actor) *Academy*, *British*

(Best Actor, Drama) Globe (Best Male Actor in a Leading Role) *SAG* (Best Ensemble) *SAG*. 2001: *The Shipping News* (Best Actor) British (Best Actor, Drama) Globe. 2004: *Beyond the Sea* (Best Actor, Musical or Comedy) Globe. **Theater:** 1991: *Lost in Yonkers* (Best Actor in a Featured Role, Play) *Tony*. 1999: *The Iceman Cometh* (Best Actor, Play) Tony. **Records:** Not since the early days of cinema, when films were shorter and the new studios could crank them out as if on an assembly line conveyor belt, did one actor succeed in doing so much so quickly. In 1995, Spacey was honored as Best Supporting Actor for an astonishing four performances from not one but two critics' organizations: the New York Film Critics and, in a tie with Ed Harris, from the Broadcast Film Critics Association in their first year of existence. In his winning roles he played a military medic in search of a deadly virus in **Outbreak**, a serial-killer obsessed with deadly sins in **Seven**, a kidnapped executive in **Swimming with Sharks**, and an eye-witness to a waterfront crime who might know the identity of the mysterious kingpin, Keiser Soze in *The Usual Suspects*. Except for **Outbreak**, each of those films earned him a nomination or win at other awards ceremonies that year, culminating in a surprise Oscar win for *The Usual Suspects* over frontrunner Ed Harris of *Apollo 13*.

Spader, James

Movie: 1989: *sex, lies, and videotape* (Best Actor) *Cannes* (Best Male Lead) Spirit. **Television:** 2003–2004 series *The Practice* (Best Actor in a Drama Series) 2004: *Emmy*. 2004–present series *Boston Legal* (Best Actor in a Drama Series) 2004: Globe. 2005: *Emmy*. 2007: *Emmy*. (Best Male Actor in a Comedy Series) 2005: SAG. (Best Male Actor in a Drama Series) 2006: SAG. 2007: SAG. (Best Ensemble in a Comedy Series) 2005: SAG. (Best Ensemble in a Drama Series) 2006: SAG. 2007: SAG.

Spain, Douglas

Movie: 1997: *Star Maps* (Best Debut Performance) Spirit.

Spall, Timothy

Movie: 1996: *Secrets and Lies* (Best Actor) British. 1999: *Topsy-Turvy* (Best Supporting Actor) British. 2002: *Nicholas Nickleby* (Best Ensemble) *Board*. 2007: *Sweeney Todd: The Demon Barber of Fleet Street* (Best Ensemble) Broadcast.

Sparv, Camilla

Movie: 1966: *Dead Heat on a Merry-Go-Round* (New Star of the Year — Actress) *Globe*.

Speer, Hugo

Movie: 1997: *The Full Monty* (Best Ensemble) *SAG*.

Spill, Luke

Movie: 2004: *Finding Neverland* (Best Ensemble) SAG.

Spriggs, Elizabeth

Movie: 1995: *Sense and Sensibility* (Best Supporting Actress) British (Best Ensemble) SAG. **Theater:** 1975: *London Assurance* (Best Supporting or Featured Actress, Dramatic) Tony.

Stack, Robert

Movie: 1956: *Written on the Wind* (Best Supporting Actor) Academy. **Television:** 1959–1963 series *The Untouchables* (Best Performance by an Actor in a Series — Lead or Supporting) 1960: *Emmy*. (Best Performance by an Actor in a Series — Lead) 1961: Emmy. 1987–1997 series *Unsolved Mysteries* (Outstanding Information Series, Host) 1995: Emmy.

Stafford, Chris

Movie: 1999: *Edge of Seventeen* (Best Debut Performance) Spirit.

Stahl, Nick

Movie: 2001: *In the Bedroom* (Best Ensemble) SAG. 2005: *Sin City* (Best Ensemble) Broadcast.

Stallone, Sylvester

Movie: 1976: *Rocky* (Best Actor) Academy, British (Best Actor, Drama) Globe (Best Original Screenplay) Academy, Globe, British.

Stamp, Terence

Movie: 1962: *Billy Budd* (New Star of the Year — Actor) *Globe* (Most Promising Newcomer) British (Best Supporting Actor) Academy. 1965: *The Collector* (Best Actor) *Cannes*. 1994: *The Adventures of Priscilla: Queen of the Desert* (Best Actor) British (Best Actor, Musical or Comedy) Globe. 1999: *The Limey* (Best Male Lead) Spirit.

Stanley, Kim

Movie: 1964: *Séance on a Wet Afternoon* (Best Actress) Academy, *New York, Board*. 1982: *Frances* (Best Supporting Actress) Academy, Globe. **Theater:** 1959: *A Touch of the Poet* (Best Actress, Dramatic) Tony. 1962: *A Far Country* (Best Actress, Dramatic) Tony. **Television:** 1963: *"A Cardinal Act of Mercy,"* Ben

Casey (Best Single Performance by an Actress in a Leading Role) *Emmy.* 1985: **"Cat on a Hot Tin Roof," American Playhouse** (Best Supporting Actress in a Limited Series or Special) *Emmy.*

Stanton, Harry Dean

Movie: 1999: **The Green Mile** (Best Ensemble) SAG.

Stanwyck, Barbara

Movie: 1937: **Stella Dallas** (Best Actress) Academy. 1941: **Ball of Fire** (Best Actress) Academy. 1944: **Double Indemnity** (Best Actress) Academy. 1948: **Sorry, Wrong Number** (Best Actress) Academy. 1954: **Executive Suite** (Best Ensemble) *Venice* (special award). Television: 1960–1961 series **The Barbara Stanwyck Show** (Best Performance by an Actress in a Series—Lead) 1961: *Emmy.* 1965–1969 series **The Big Valley** (Best Actress in a Dramatic Series) 1965: Globe. 1966: Globe. 1967: Globe. (Best Continued Performance by an Actress in a Leading Role in a Dramatic Series) 1966: *Emmy.* 1967: Emmy. 1968: Emmy. 1983: **The Thorn Birds** (Best Actress in a Limited Series or Special) *Emmy* (Best Supporting Actress in a Series, Miniseries, or TV Movie) *Globe.* Tributes: 1966: Life Achievement Award from SAG. 1981: Honorary Oscar statuette for superlative creativity and unique contribution to the art of screen acting from Academy; Career Achievement Award from LA; Gala Tribute from the Film Society of Lincoln Center. 1985: Cecil B. DeMille Award from Globe. 1987: Life Achievement Award from American Film Institute. 1999: Ranked Number 11 on List of 25 Greatest Female Screen Legends of the 20th Century from American Film Institute.

Stapleton, Maureen

Movie: 1958: **Lonelyhearts** (Best Supporting Actress) Academy, Globe. 1970: **Airport** (Best Supporting Actress) Academy, *Globe*, British. 1971: **Plaza Suite** (Best Supporting Actress) Globe. 1978: **Interiors** (Best Supporting Actress) Academy, *New York*, Globe, *LA*. 1981: **Reds** (Best Supporting Actress) *Academy*, Globe, *British, Society, LA*. Theater: 1951: **The Rose Tattoo** (Best Supporting or Featured Actress, Dramatic) *Tony.* 1959: **The Cold Wind and the Warm** (Best Actress, Dramatic) Tony. 1960: **Toys in the Attic** (Best Actress, Dramatic) Tony. 1968: **Plaza Suite** (Best Actress, Dramatic) Tony. 1971: **The Gingerbread Lady** (Best Actress, Dramatic) *Tony.* 1981: **The Little Foxes** (Best Actress in a Featured Role, Play) Tony. Television: 1959: **"All the King's Men," Kraft Television Theatre** (Best Single Performance by an Actress) Emmy. 1968: **"Among the Paths to Eden," Xerox Special** (Best Single Performance by an Actress in a Leading Role in a Drama) *Emmy.* 1975:

Queen of the Stardust Ballroom (Best Actress in a Drama or Comedy Special) Emmy. 1978: **The Gathering** (Best Actress in a Drama or Comedy Special) Emmy. 1989: **"B. L. Stryker," The ABC Monday Mystery Movie** (Best Guest Actress in a Drama Series) Emmy. 1992: **"Miss Rose White," Hallmark Hall of Fame** (Best Supporting Actress in a Miniseries or Special) Emmy. 1996: **Avonlea (Road to Avonlea** or **Tales of Avonlea)** (Best Guest Actress in a Drama Series) Emmy. **Records:** Stapleton (**Airport**) and Karen Black (**Five Easy Pieces**) tied for the Best Supporting Actress Golden Globe in 1970, marking the first dual win in an acting category in Globe history. **Highlights:** When Stapleton won her Oscar for the 1981 movie, **Reds**, she was the fourth Best Supporting Actress winner in a row with the initials M.S. Her predecessors were Maggie Smith (**California Suite**, 1978), Meryl Streep (**Kramer vs. Kramer**, 1979), and Mary Steenburgen (**Melvin and Howard**, 1980). At age 56, she was also the youngest Oscar winning actor that year, as Best Actor Henry Fonda, Best Actress Katharine Hepburn, and Best Supporting Actor John Gielgud were all in their 70s. In her acceptance speech, Stapleton made light of the personal problems she so candidly shared in her autobiography, **A Hell of a Life** by describing herself as thrilled, happy, delighted, and sober. She then concluded by thanking her inspiration, actor Joel McCrea, and, in what has become one of the most imitated lines in acceptance speech history, thanked everyone she ever met in her entire life.

Starr, Martin

Movie: 2001: **The Royal Tenenbaums** (Best Ensemble) Broadcast.

Staunton, Imelda

Movie: 1995: **Sense and Sensibility** (Best Ensemble) SAG. 1998: **Shakespeare in Love** (Best Ensemble) SAG. 2004: **Vera Drake** (Best Actress) Academy, *Venice, New York, British, Society, LA*, Broadcast (Best Actress, Drama) Globe (Best Female Actor in a Leading Role) SAG.

Steadman, Alison

Movie: 1991: **Life Is Sweet** (Best Actress) *Society.*

Steele, Tommy

Movie: 1967: **The Happiest Millionaire** (New Star of the Year—Actor) Globe. Theater: 1965: **Half a Sixpence** (Best Actor, Musical) Tony.

Steenburgen, Mary

Movie: 1978: **Goin' South** (New Star of the Year—Actress) Globe. 1980: **Melvin and Howard** (Best

Supporting Actress) *Academy, New York, Globe, Society, LA*. 1981: ***Ragtime*** (Best Supporting Actress) Globe. **Television:** 1988: ***"The Attic: The Hiding of Anne Frank," General Foods' Golden Showcase*** (Best Actress in a Miniseries or Special) Emmy. 1998: ***About Sarah*** (Best Female Actor in a Television Movie or Miniseries) SAG.

Stefani, Gwen

Movie: 2004: ***The Aviator*** (Best Ensemble) SAG.

Stehli, Edgar

Movie: 1954: ***Executive Suite*** (Best Ensemble) *Venice* (special award).

Steiger, Rod

Movie: 1954: ***On the Waterfront*** (Best Supporting Actor) Academy. 1965: ***The Pawnbroker*** (Best Actor) Academy, *Berlin* (Best Actor, Drama) Globe (Best Foreign Actor) *British*. 1967: ***In the Heat of the Night*** (Best Actor) *Academy, New York, Society* (Best Actor, Drama) *Globe* (Best Foreign Actor) *British*. **Television:** 1959: ***"A Town Has Turned to Dust," Playhouse 90*** (Best Single Performance by an Actor) Emmy. 1964: ***"A Slow Fade to Black," Bob Hope Presents The Chrysler Theater*** (Best Single Performance by an Actor) Emmy. **Highlights:** Steiger took home an impressive five awards for his role as bigoted Southern sheriff Bill Gillespie in the racially charged ***In the Heat of the Night*** including the first Best Actor prize ever bestowed by the newly formed National Society of Film Critics. His performance outranked stellar competitors including Dustin Hoffman for the career-launching ***The Graduate***, Warren Beatty for the groundbreaking ***Bonnie and Clyde***, and sentimental favorite posthumous nominee Spencer Tracy for ***Guess Who's Coming to Dinner***. He lost only one competition that year, from the National Board of Review, to Peter Finch whose performance in ***Far from the Madding Crowd*** didn't receive a single nomination from any other organization.

Stephane, Nicole

Movie: 1952: ***The Strange Ones*** (Best Foreign Actress) *British*.

Stephens, Harvey

Movie: 1976: ***The Omen*** (New Star of the Year — Actor) Globe.

Stephenson, James

Movie: 1940: ***The Letter*** (Best Acting) *Board* (multiple win), (Best Supporting Actor) Academy. 1941: ***Shining Victory*** (Best Acting) *Board* (multiple win).

Sterling, Jan

Movie: 1951: ***The Big Carnival (Ace in the Hole)*** (Best Actress) *Board*. 1954: ***The High and the Mighty*** (Best Supporting Actress) Academy, *Globe*.

Stevens, Andrew

Movie: 1978: ***The Boys in Company C*** (New Star of the Year — Actor) Globe.

Stevens, Gary

Movie: 2003: ***Seabiscuit*** (Best Ensemble) SAG.

Stevens, Kay

Movie: 1962: ***The Interns*** (Best Supporting Actress) Globe.

Stevens, Stella

Movie: 1959: ***Say One for Me*** (New Star of the Year — Actress) *Globe*.

Stevenson, Cynthia

Movie: 1998: ***Happiness*** (Best Ensemble) *Board*.

Stevenson, Juliet

Movie: 1991: ***Truly, Madly, Deeply*** (Best Actress) *British*. 2002: ***Nicholas Nickleby*** (Best Ensemble) *Board*.

Stewart, James

Movie: 1939: ***Mr. Smith Goes to Washington*** (Best Actor) Academy, *New York*. 1940: ***The Philadelphia Story*** (Best Actor) *Academy*; ***The Shop Around the Corner*** (Best Acting) *Board*. 1946: ***It's a Wonderful Life*** (Best Actor) Academy. 1950: ***Harvey*** (Best Actor) Academy (Best Actor, Drama) Globe. 1954: ***The Glenn Miller Story*** (Best Foreign Actor) *British*. 1959: ***Anatomy of a Murder*** (Best Actor) Academy, *Venice, New York* (Best Foreign Actor) *British*. 1962: ***Mr. Hobbs Takes a Vacation*** (Best Actor) *Berlin* (Best Actor, Musical or Comedy) Globe. **Television:** 1973–1974 series ***Hawkins*** (Best Actor in a Drama Series) 1973: Globe. **Tributes:** 1964: Cecil B. DeMille Award from Globe. 1968: Lifetime Achievement Award from SAG. 1980: Life Achievement Award from American Film Institute. 1983: Honor from Kennedy Center for the Performing Arts. 1984: Honorary Oscar statuette for fifty years of memorable performances and for his high ideals both on and off screen from Academy. 1990: Career Achievement Award from Board; Gala Tribute from Film Society of Lincoln Center. 1999: Ranked Number 3 on List of 25 Greatest Male Screen Legends of the 20th Century from American Film Institute. **Records:** Stewart won his Best Actor Oscar the first year that the Academy kept the winners a secret until awards night by securing the winners' names in sealed envelopes. Before then, winners were announced prior to the awards ceremony. The suspense of not knowing who won until presenters opened the envelope increased the popularity of the event, as well as future awards presentations, especially when they began being televised in the 1950s. Between his Oscar win and the award ceremonies broadcast over the TV airwaves, Stewart set another record. Before Pearl Harbor was bombed, Stewart enlisted in the Air Force, and served so valiantly during World War II that he eventually earned the Distinguished Flying Cross and the Croix de Guerre. Later he was promoted to Brigadier General in the Air Force, giving him the unprecedented status of highest ranking actor in U.S. military history. **Highlights:** Stewart's supporting role in **The Philadelphia Story** didn't keep him from winning the Best Actor Oscar in 1940. His biggest competition that year was his former roommate, Henry Fonda, who was up for **The Grapes of Wrath**. But **Grapes** had been released well over a year before the awards ceremony, so despite seven nominations for their film, star Fonda and director John Ford skipped the awards and went fishing. **The Philadelphia Story**, on the other hand, was a box office hit still going strong at theaters and still fresh in voters' minds. Stewart also benefited in 1940 by having lost the Best Actor award the year before to Robert Donat in **Goodbye, Mr. Chips** for his inspiring performance in **Mr. Smith Goes to Washington.** Those advantages gave Stewart his only competitive Oscar victory.

Stewart, Kristen

Movie: 2007: **Into the Wild** (Best Ensemble) SAG.

Stiles, Julia

Movie: 2000: **State and Main** (Best Ensemble) Board.

Stiller, Ben

Movie: 2001: **The Royal Tenenbaums** (Best Ensemble) Broadcast. Television: 1992–1993 series **The Ben Stiller Show** (Best Writing in a Variety of Music Program) 1993: Emmy. 2006: **Extras** (Best Guest Actor in a Comedy Series) Emmy.

Stiller, Jerry

Movie: 2007: **Hairspray** (Best Ensemble) SAG, Broadcast. Television: 1997: **Seinfeld** (Best Guest Actor in a Comedy Series) Emmy.

Stockwell, Dean

Movie: 1959: **Compulsion** (Best Actor) Cannes (win shared with costars). 1960: **Sons and Lovers** (Best Actor, Drama) Globe. 1962: **Long Day's Journey into Night** (Best Acting) Cannes (win shared with costars). 1988: **Married to the Mob** (Best Supporting Actor) Academy, New York (multiple win), Society (multiple win); **Tucker: The Man and His Dream** (Best Supporting Actor) New York (multiple win), Society (multiple win). Television: 1989–1993 series **Quantum Leap** (Best Supporting Actor in a Drama Series) 1989: Globe. 1990: Emmy, Globe. 1991: Emmy, Globe. 1992: Emmy, Globe. 1993: Emmy. Tributes: 1947: Special Achievement Award for Best Juvenile Performance in **Gentleman's Agreement** from Globe. **Records:** Several actors have portrayed legendary airman and eccentric millionaire Howard Hughes, but Stockwell was the first to play him to award-winning success. Jason Robards, Jr. received an Oscar and Golden Globe nomination playing Hughes in **Melvin and Howard** in 1980 but lost both his races to film newcomer Timothy Hutton in **Ordinary People.** When Stockwell put his own twist on interpreting Hughes for **Tucker: The Man and His Dream** eight years later, critics raved and those from the New York Circle and National Society voted him Best Supporting Actor for that performance and his comic mobster take in **Married to the Mob.** In 2004, Leonardo DiCaprio and director Martin Scorcese tackled the ambitious project of bringing a Howard Hughes epic biography to the screen to great success. **The Aviator** was a box office hit that racked up many nominations and awards. Of those, Best Actor DiCaprio was nominated for five and won one — a Best Actor, Drama Golden Globe from the Hollywood Foreign Press.

Stoltz, Eric

Movie: 1985: **Mask** (Best Supporting Actor) Globe. 1994: **Pulp Fiction** (Best Supporting Male) Spirit. Theater: 1989: **Our Town** (Best Actor in a Featured Role, Play) Tony.

Stone, Harold J.

Movie: 1962: **The Chapman Report** (Best Supporting Actor) Globe. Television: 1964: **The Nurses** (Best Single Performance by an Actor in a Leading Role) Emmy.

Stone, Lewis

Movie: 1928: **The Patriot** (Best Actor) Academy. **Records:** Stone is the first actor to receive a Best Actor Academy Award nomination for a supporting role. Because the Academy didn't begin giving supporting awards until 1936, actors in smaller roles before then usually failed to garner nominations no matter how fine their performance. But Stone earned a nod in only the second year of the Academy Awards (1928/1929). He lost to Warner Baxter for *In Old Arizona*.

Stone, Sharon

Movie: 1992: *Basic Instinct* (Best Actress, Drama) Globe. 1995: *Casino* (Best Actress) Academy (Best Actress, Drama) *Globe*. 1998: *The Mighty* (Best Supporting Actress) Globe. 1999: *The Muse* (Best Actress, Musical or Comedy) Globe. 2006: *Bobby* (Best Ensemble) SAG, Broadcast. **Television:** 2004: *The Practice* (Best Guest Actress in a Drama Series) *Emmy*.

Stormare, Peter

Movie: 2000: *Chocolat* (Best Ensemble) SAG.

Stowe, Madeleine

Movie: 1993: *Short Cuts* (Best Supporting Actress) *Society* (Best Ensemble) *Venice* (special award).

Straight, Beatrice

Movie: 1976: *Network* (Best Supporting Actress) *Academy*. **Theater:** 1953: *The Crucible* (Best Supporting or Featured Actress, Dramatic) *Tony*. **Television:** 1978: *The Dain Curse* (Best Single Performance by a Supporting Actress in a Comedy or Drama Series) Emmy. **Records:** At only 5 minutes, 56 seconds, Straight's two-scene appearance in *Network* makes hers the shortest Oscar-winning performance in film history. Her surprise win beat out Jane Alexander in *All the President's Men*, Jodie Foster in *Taxi Driver*, Lee Grant in *Voyage of the Damned*, and Piper Laurie in *Carrie*.

Strasberg, Lee

Movie: 1974: *The Godfather Part II* (New Star of the Year — Actor) Globe (Best Supporting Actor) Academy. 1980: *Going in Style* (Best Actor) *Venice* (win shared with costars). **Highlights:** Despite a lifetime of being known as the acting coach who helped catapult the careers of legendary stars such as Marlon Brando, James Dean, and Montgomery Clift, Strasberg did not act in a motion picture until he was 73 years old. His supporting role as mobster Hyman Roth earned him a Best Supporting Actor Oscar nomination for his first film, *The Godfather Part II*. He lost to co-star Robert De Niro who studied at the Actors Studio but did not always agree with Strasberg's approach to acting. In an even more astounding twist, after decades of being one of the world's preeminent acting coaches, Strasberg was nominated for a Golden Globe as Best New Star of the Year, but that prize went to Joseph Bottoms for *The Dove*.

Strasberg, Susan

Movie: 1955: *Picnic* (Most Promising Newcomer) British. 1962: *Adventures of a Young Man* (Best Actress, Drama) Globe. **Theater:** 1956: *The Diary of Anne Frank* (Best Actress, Dramatic) Tony.

Strathairn, David

Movie: 1987: *Matewan* (Best Supporting Male) Spirit. 1991: *City of Hope* (Best Supporting Male) *Spirit*. 1992: *Passion Fish* (Best Supporting Male) Spirit. 1997: *L.A. Confidential* (Best Ensemble) SAG. 1999: *Limbo* (Best Male Lead) Spirit. 2005: *Good Night, and Good Luck* (Best Actor) Academy, *Venice*, British, Broadcast (Best Actor, Drama) Globe (Best Male Lead) Spirit (Best Male Actor in a Leading Role) SAG (Best Ensemble) SAG, Broadcast.

Strauss, Robert

Movie: 1953: *Stalag 17* (Best Supporting Actor) Academy.

Streep, Meryl

Movie: 1978: *The Deer Hunter* (Best Actress) British (Best Supporting Actress) Academy, Globe, *Society*. 1979: *Kramer vs. Kramer* (Best Actress) British (Best Supporting Actress) *Academy, New York* (multiple win), *Board* (multiple win), *Globe, Society* (multiple win), *LA* (multiple win); *Manhattan* (Best Supporting Actress) *Board* (multiple win), British, *Society* (multiple win), *LA* (multiple win); *The Seduction of Joe Tynan* (Best Supporting Actress) *New York* (multiple win), *Board* (multiple win), *Society* (multiple win), *LA* (multiple win). 1981: *The French Lieutenant's Woman* (Best Actress) Academy, *British, LA* (Best Actress, Drama) *Globe*. 1982: *Sophie's Choice* (Best Actress) *Academy, New York, Board*, British, *Society, LA* (Best Actress, Drama) *Globe*. 1983: *Silkwood* (Best Actress) Academy, British (Best Actress, Drama) Globe. 1985: *Out of Africa* (Best Actress) Academy, British, *LA* (Best Actress, Drama) Globe. 1987: *Ironweed* (Best Actress) Academy. 1988: *A Cry in the Dark* (Best Actress) Academy, *New York, Cannes* (Best Actress, Drama) Globe. 1989: *She-Devil* (Best Actress, Musical or Comedy) Globe. 1990: *Postcards from the Edge* (Best Actress) Academy (Best Actress, Musical or Comedy) Globe. 1992: *Death Becomes Her* (Best Actress, Musical or Comedy) Globe. 1994: *The River Wild* (Best Female Actor in a Leading Role) SAG (Best

Actress, Drama) Globe. 1995: *The Bridges of Madison County* (Best Actress) Academy (Best Actress, Drama) Globe (Best Female Actor in a Leading Role) SAG. 1996: *Marvin's Room* (Best Actress, Drama) Globe (Best Ensemble) SAG. 1998: *One True Thing* (Best Actress) Academy (Best Actress, Drama) Globe (Best Female Actor in a Leading Role) SAG. 1999: *Music of the Heart* (Best Actress) Academy (Best Actress, Drama) Globe (Best Female Actor in a Leading Role) SAG. 2002: *Adaptation* (Best Supporting Actress) Academy, *Globe*, British, Broadcast (Best Ensemble) SAG; *The Hours* (Best Actress) *Berlin* (win shared with costars), British (Best Actress, Drama) Globe (Best Ensemble) SAG, Broadcast. 2004: *The Manchurian Candidate* (Best Supporting Actress) Globe, British. 2006: *The Devil Wears Prada* (Best Actress) Academy, British, Broadcast (Best Actress, Musical or Comedy) *Globe* (Best Female Actor in a Leading Role) SAG (Best Supporting Actress) *Society* (multiple win); *A Prairie Home Companion* (Best Supporting Actress) *Society* (multiple win), (Best Ensemble) Broadcast. **Theater:** 1976: *27 Wagons Full of Cotton* (Best Actress in a Featured Role, Play) Tony. **Television:** 1978: *"Holocaust," The Big Event* (Best Actress in a Limited Series) *Emmy*. 1997: *... First Do No Harm* (Best Actress in a Miniseries or Special) Emmy (Best Actress in a Miniseries or TV Movie) Globe. 2003: *Angels in America* (Best Actress in a Miniseries or TV Movie) *Emmy*, *Globe* (Best Female Actor in a Television Movie or Miniseries) *SAG*. **Tributes:** 1999: Honorary Award from Berlin Film Festival. 2004: Life Achievement Award from American Film Institute. 2008: Gala Tribute from Film Society of Lincoln Center. **Records:** With 14, Streep has the most Academy Award nominations for acting. In the earlier days of the awards, Bette Davis and Katharine Hepburn rivaled each other for top nominations, with Davis holding the lead at ten until Hepburn pulled ahead in the late '60s with back-to-back nominations and her second and third wins. Hepburn eventually topped out at 12 and earned a record-setting fourth Oscar in 1981 for *On Golden Pond*. In recent years, the nominations race has been between Streep and Jack Nicholson, with Streep always one step ahead. In 1999, she tied Hepburn's record with a twelfth nomination for *Music of the Heart*. Three years later, Nicholson joined the dozen-nomination group with a Best Actor bid for *About Schmidt*, but that same year Streep stayed ahead by pulling in another nomination, her first Supporting Actress nod since the 1970s, for her work in *Adaptation*. In 2006, both Streep and Nicholson were favored to be in contention for yet another Oscar, Streep for Best Actress in *The Devil Wears Prada* and Nicholson for Best Supporting Actor for *The Departed*. When that

year's nominees were announced, Streep made the cut, but Nicholson did not, making her now two nominations ahead of Nicholson, her nearest competitor for the record. Of these four performers, Hepburn won four Best Actress Oscars, Nicholson has three Oscars (two for Best Actor and one for Supporting Actor), Davis won two Best Actress awards, and Streep won two awards, first for Supporting Actress and then for Best Actress. For movie acting nominations from the major motion picture organizations and film festivals, Streep leads, followed by Jack Nicholson who is about eight nominations behind her. Her closest female competitor for movie awards is Shirley MacLaine, who has almost half as many nominations and about a third as many wins as Streep.

Streisand, Barbra

Movie: 1968: *Funny Girl* (Best Actress) *Academy*, British (multiple nomination), (Best Actress, Musical or Comedy) *Globe*. 1969: *Hello, Dolly!* (Best Actress) British (multiple nomination), (Best Actress, Musical or Comedy) Globe. 1970: *The Owl and the Pussycat* (Best Actress, Musical or Comedy) Globe. 1973: *The Way We Were* (Best Actress) Academy, British (Best Actress, Drama) Globe. 1975: *Funny Lady* (Best Actress, Musical or Comedy) Globe. 1976: *A Star Is Born* (Best Actress, Musical or Comedy) *Globe* (Best Song, "Evergreen, Love Theme from A Star Is Born") *Academy, Globe*, British. 1983: *Yentl* (Best Actress, Musical or Comedy) Globe (Best Director) *Globe*. 1987: *Nuts* (Best Actress, Drama) Globe (Best Picture, Drama; Producer) Globe. 1991: *The Prince of Tides* (Best Director) Globe (Best Picture, Producer) Academy (Best Picture, Drama; Producer) Globe. 1996: *The Mirror Has Two Faces* (Best Actress, Musical or Comedy) Globe (Best Song, "I've Finally Found Someone") Academy, Globe. **Theater:** 1962: *I Can Get It for You Wholesale* (Best Supporting or Featured Actress, Musical) Tony. 1964: *Funny Girl* (Best Actress, Musical) Tony. **Television:** 1964: *The Judy Garland Show* (Best Performance in a Variety or Musical Program or Series) Emmy. 1965: *My Name Is Barbra* (Best Individual Achievement in Entertainment by an Actor or Performer) *Emmy*. 1969: *Barbra Streisand: A Happening in Central Park* (Best Variety or Musical Program, Star) Emmy. 1974: *Barbra Streisand ... and Other Musical Instruments* (Best Comedy-Variety, Variety, or Music Special; Star) Emmy. 1995: *Barbra Streisand: The Concert* (Best Individual Performance in a Variety or Music Program) *Emmy* (Best Individual Achievement in Directing in a Variety or Music Program, Director of Stage) Emmy (Best Variety, Music, or Comedy Special; Producer) *Emmy*; *Serving in*

Silence: The Margarethe Cammermeyer Story (Best TV Movie, Executive Producer) Emmy. 2001: *Barbra Streisand: Timeless* (Best Individual Performance in a Variety or Music Program) *Emmy.* **Tributes:** 1969, 1970, 1974, 1977: Henrietta Award for World Film Favorite from Globe. 1970: Special award as Star of the Decade from Tony. 1999: Cecil B. DeMille Award from Globe. 2001: Life Achievement Award from American Film Institute. **Records:** When Ingrid Bergman announced a tie at the Oscars celebrating the films of 1968, her shock and the gasps that swept across the Dorothy Chandler Pavilion were genuine. It was the first and so far only legitimate tie in Academy Award history. Bergman named Katharine Hepburn and Streisand the winners. Perennial no-show Hepburn was not there, but Streisand accepted her prize and acknowledged her esteemed co-winner. Streisand had a unique reason to celebrate that win, as her vote alone may have resulted in her tie with Hepburn. For Streisand, the Academy relaxed its usually strict rules and let her become a member of the Academy before she finished filming *Funny Girl*, making her eligible to vote in that year's Oscar race. Assuming she voted for herself, her Best Actress bid created the exact tie that brought her to the podium in 1969. Eight years later, when Streisand won her Best Original Song Academy Award for co-writing "Evergreen" from *A Star Is Born* with Paul Williams, she became the first Oscar-winning actor to also win an Academy Award in another competitive category. In 1991, when her film, *The Prince of Tides* received a Best Picture nod, Streisand, who co-produced the film with Andrew Karsch, became the first actress to be nominated in three different categories: Best Actress, Best Song, and Best Picture.

Stricklyn, Ray

Movie: 1958: *10 North Frederick* (New Star of the Year — Actor) Globe. 1960: *The Plunderers* (Best Supporting Actor) Globe.

Strode, Woody

Movie: 1960: *Spartacus* (Best Supporting Actor) Globe.

Strong, Andrew

Movie: 1991: *The Commitments* (Best Supporting Actor) British.

Stuart, Gloria

Movie: 1997: *Titanic* (Best Female Actor in a Supporting Role) *SAG* (Best Supporting Actress) Academy, Globe (Best Ensemble) SAG. **Records:** 87-year-old Stuart, who helped found the Screen Actors Guild, became the oldest SAG and Academy Award nominee in history when she earned Best Supporting Actress nods for *Titanic*. She won the SAG in a tie with Kim Basinger of *L.A. Confidential*, making Stuart the oldest SAG winner and the first to win in a category with someone else. With the SAG win Stuart also set the record for winning an award for a comeback performance after the longest absence from films. Before *Titanic*, she hadn't made a film since *She Wrote the Book* 51 years earlier.

Stuart, Kim Rossi

Movie: 1998: *I Giardini dell'Eden* (Best Actor) *Venice.* 2004: *Le Chiavi di casa* (Best Actor) *Venice.*

Suchet, David

Movie: 1988: *A World Apart* (Best Supporting Actor) British. **Theater:** 2000: *Amadeus* (Best Actor, Play) Tony.

Sukowa, Barbara

Movie: 1981: *Die Bleierne Ziet* (Best Actress) *Venice* (win shared with costar). 1986: *Rosa Luxemburg* (Best Actress) *Cannes.*

Sullavan, Margaret

Movie: 1938: *Three Comrades* (Best Acting) *Board* (Best Actress) Academy, *New York.* **Television:** 1952: --- (Best Actress) Emmy.

Sullivan, David

Movie: 2004: *Primer* (Best Debut Performance) Spirit.

Sun, Jon Young

Movie: 1962: *To the Last Day* (Best Actor) *Berlin* (special award).

Sutherland, Donald

Movie: 1970: *M*A*S*H* (Best Actor, Musical or Comedy) Globe. 1973: *Don't Look Now* (Best Actor) British (multiple nomination); *Steelyard Blues* (Best Actor) British (multiple nomination). 1980: *Ordinary People* (Best Actor, Drama) Globe. 1998: *Without Limits* (Best Supporting Actor) Globe. **Television:** 1995: *Citizen X* (Best Supporting Actor in a Miniseries or TV Movie) *Emmy* (Best Supporting Actor in a Series, Miniseries, or TV Movie) *Globe.* 2002: *Path to War* (Best Supporting Actor in a Series, Miniseries, or TV Movie) *Globe.* 2005: *Human Trafficking* (Best Actor in a Miniseries or TV Movie) Emmy, Globe. 2005–2006 series *Commander in*

Chief (Best Supporting Actor in a Series, Miniseries, or TV Movie) 2006: Globe. 2007–present series *Dirty Sexy Money* (Best Supporting Actor in a Series, Miniseries, or TV Movie) 2007: Globe.

Suvari, Mena

Movie: 1999: *American Beauty* (Best Supporting Actress) British (Best Ensemble) *SAG*. Television: 2004 series *Six Feet Under* (Best Ensemble in a Drama Series) 2004: SAG.

Suzman, Janet

Movie: 1971: *Nicholas and Alexandra* (New Star of the Year — Actress) Globe (Most Promising Newcomer) British (Best Actress) Academy.

Swank, Hilary

Movie: 1999: *Boys Don't Cry* (Breakthrough Performance — Female) *Board* (Best Actress) *Academy, New York*, British, *LA*, *Broadcast* (Best Actress, Drama) *Globe* (Best Female Actor in a Leading Role) SAG (Best Female Lead) *Spirit*. 2004: *Million Dollar Baby* (Best Actress) *Academy, Society, Broadcast* (Best Actress, Drama) *Globe* (Best Female Actor in a Leading Role) *SAG* (Best Ensemble) SAG. Television: 2004: *Iron Jawed Angels* (Best Actress in a Miniseries or TV Movie) Globe (Best Female Actor in a Television Movie or Miniseries) SAG. Highlights: With *Boys Don't Cry*, Swank set a David and Goliath record by becoming the first breakout film star to win so many lead acting awards for an independent film. Swank's road to success began when the New York and L.A. critics saw *Boys Don't Cry* and rallied behind it so enthusiastically that they took the bold step of naming little-known Swank in the limited release film their Best Actress. Two weeks later, The National Society of Film Critics gave their Best Actress prize to Reese Witherspoon for *Election*, but thereafter Swank swept every competition except the SAG (Annette Bening won for *American Beauty*).

Swanson, Gloria

Movie: 1928: *Sadie Thompson* (Best Actress) Academy. 1929: *The Trespasser* (Best Actress) Academy. 1950: *Sunset Boulevard* (Best Actress) Academy, *Board* (Best Actress, Drama) *Globe*. Television: 1963–1964 series *Burke's Law* (Best Actress in a Drama Series) 1963: Globe.

Swayze, Patrick

Movie: 1987: *Dirty Dancing* (Best Actor, Musical or Comedy) Globe. 1990: *Ghost* (Best Actor, Musical or Comedy) Globe. 1995: *To Wong Foo, Thanks for*

Everything, Julie Newmar (Best Actor, Musical or Comedy) Globe.

Sweet, Blanche

Tributes: 1981: Special award from Board.

Swinton, Tilda

Movie: 1991: *Edward II* (Best Actress) *Venice*. 2001: *The Deep End* (Best Actress, Drama) Globe (Best Female Lead) Spirit. 2002: *Adaptation* (Best Ensemble) SAG. 2007: *Michael Clayton* (Best Female Actor in a Supporting Role) SAG (Best Supporting Actress) *Academy*, Globe, *British*, Broadcast.

Sylvie

Movie: 1966: *The Shameless Old Lady* (Best Actress) *Society*. Records: Sylvie won the first Best Actress award ever presented by the newly formed National Society of Film Critics, beating out such formidable competitors as Elizabeth Taylor in *Who's Afraid of Virginia Woolf?* and Lynn Redgrave in *Georgy Girl*, both of whom won the lion's share of Best Actress prizes that year.

Syms, Sylvia

Movie: 1957: *Woman in a Dressing Gown* (Best British Actress) British. 1959: *No Trees in the Street* (Best British Actress) British. 1974: *The Tamarind Seed* (Best Supporting Actress) British.

Tamblyn, Amber

Movie: 2006: *Stephanie Daley* (Best Supporting Female) Spirit. Television: 2003–2005 series *Joan of Arcadia* (Best Actress in a Drama Series) 2004: Emmy, Globe.

Tamblyn, Russ

Movie: 1955: *Hit the Deck* (New Star of the Year — Actor) *Globe*. 1957: *Peyton Place* (Best Supporting Actor) Academy.

Tamiroff, Akim

Movie: 1936: *The General Died at Dawn* (Best Supporting Actor) Academy. 1943: *For Whom the Bell Tolls* (Best Supporting Actor) Academy, *Globe*. Records: Tamiroff is the first actor whose Golden Globe win stood alone as his only award. He won the Best Supporting Actor trophy in 1943, the first year of the Golden Globes. The other three actors who won the Globes with him, Best Actor Paul Lukas in *Watch on the Rhine*, Best Actress Jennifer Jones in *The Song of Bernadette*, and Best Supporting Actress Katina Paxinou in *For Whom the Bell Tolls*, all repeated their wins at the Oscars. Though he was nominated, Tamiroff lost the Oscar race to Charles Coburn in the George Stevens comedy, *The More the Merrier*. While being the only one to lose the Oscar might seem disappointing, it marked an important milestone in film awards, as it established the Globes as a viable and unique award, not merely a mirror of the Academy.

Tanaka, Kinuyo

Movie: 1975: *Sandakan hachibanshokan, bohk yo (Sandaka 8)* (Best Actress) *Berlin*. Records: Tanaka made the *Guinness Book of World Records* as the actress with the most leading film roles in a career. Tanaka began acting in Japanese films at age 14. After a brief foray into light opera, she became a leading actress who went on to perform in a world record-setting 241 movies. Tanaka starred in nearly 240 films before she finally won her only major acting award outside of Japan: at the 1975 Berlin Film Festival she was voted Best Actress for one of her last screen performances.

Tandy, Jessica

Movie: 1962: *Adventures of a Young Man* (Best Supporting Actress) Globe. 1989: *Driving Miss Daisy* (Best Actress) *Academy, British* (Best Actress, Musical or Comedy) *Globe*. 1990: *Fried Green Tomatoes (Fried Green Tomatoes at the Whistle Stop Café)* (Best Actress) British (Best Supporting Actress) Academy, Globe. Theater: 1948: *A Streetcar Named Desire* (Best Actress, Dramatic) *Tony*. 1978: *The Gin Game* (Best Actress, Play) *Tony*. 1981: *Rose* (Best Actress in a Featured Role, Play) Tony. 1983: *Foxfire* (Best Actress, Play) *Tony*. 1986: *The Petition* (Best Actress, Play) Tony. Television: 1955: *"The Fourposter," Producers' Showcase* (Best Actress in a Single Performance) Emmy. 1988: *"Foxfire," Hallmark Hall of Fame* (Best Actress in a Miniseries or Special) *Emmy*. 1991: *The Story Lady* (Best Actress in a Miniseries or TV Movie) Globe. 1994: *"To Dance with the White Dog," Hallmark Hall of Fame* (Best Actress in a Miniseries or Special) Emmy. Tributes: 1986: Honor from Kennedy Center for the Performing Arts (honor shared with spouse, Hume Cronyn). 1989: Special Performance Award for *Driving Miss Daisy* from Berlin (win shared with costar, Morgan Freeman). 1994: Lifetime Achievement Award from Tony. Records: 80 years and 293 days old on the day she won the Best Actress Oscar for *Driving Miss Daisy*, Tandy became the oldest star in Academy Award history to win a competitive acting award.

Tarita

Movie: 1962: *Mutiny on the Bounty* (Best Supporting Actress) Globe.

Tate, Larenz

Movie: 2004: *Ray* (Best Ensemble) SAG. 2005: *Crash* (Best Ensemble) *SAG, Broadcast*.

Tate, Sharon

Movie: 1967: *Valley of the Dolls* (New Star of the Year — Actress) Globe.

Tatosov, Vladimir

Movie: 1954: *Bolshaya semya (The Big Family)* *Cannes* (special ensemble award).

Tatum, Channing

Movie: 2006: *A Guide to Recognizing Your Saints* (Best Supporting Male) Spirit.

Tautou, Andrey

Movie: 2001: *Amélie* (Best Actress) British. Records: After Tautou's award-winning film, *Amélie* (entire French titles: *Le Fabuleux destin d' Amélie* or *Amélie from Montmartre*) was first released in France on April 15, 2001, it caught like box office wildfire and quickly became the highest grossing French film in history with a world-wide box office take of $144,488,955 (£101,005,911). The endearing comedy has Tautou playing a young woman who ventures out into the world and then begins manipulating situations around the people she meets in order to make their lives happier.

Taylor, Dolores

Movie: 1971: *Billy Jack* (New Star of the Year — Actress) Globe.

Taylor, Elizabeth

Movie: 1957: *Raintree County* (Best Actress) Academy. 1958: *Cat on a Hot Tin Roof* (Best Actress) Academy (Best Foreign Actress) British. 1959: *Suddenly, Last Summer* (Best Actress) Academy (Best Actress, Drama) *Globe*. 1960: *Butterfield 8* (Best Actress) *Academy* (Best Actress, Drama) Globe. 1966: *Who's Afraid of Virginia Woolf?* (Best Actress) *Academy, New York, Board* (Best Actress, Drama) Globe (Best British Actress) *British*. 1967: *The Taming of the Shrew* (Best British Actress) British. 1972: *Hammersmith Is Out* (Best Actress) *Berlin*. 1973: *Ash Wednesday* (Best Actress, Drama) Globe. Theater: 1981: *The Little Foxes* (Best Actress, Play) Tony. Tributes: 1956: Special Achievement Award from Globe. 1965, 1968, 1973: Henrietta Award for World Film Favorite from Globe. 1984: Cecil B. DeMille Award from Globe. 1986: Gala Tribute from Film Society of Lincoln Center. 1992: Jean Hersholt

Humanitarian Award from Academy. 1993: Life Achievement Award from American Film Institute. 1997: Life Achievement Award from SAG. 1999: Ranked Number 7 on List of 25 Greatest Female Screen Legends of the 20th Century from American Film Institute. 2002: Honor from Kennedy Center for the Performing Arts. **Highlights:** Taylor may have withstood much negative publicity for marrying eight times, but husbands did tend to bring her award luck and generate extra attention on award night. In both her Academy Award–winning performances, she co-starred with her husband at the time. In 1960, Eddie Fisher co-starred with Taylor in *Butterfield 8*, then helped a frail Taylor, who was recovering from a near fatal bout of pneumonia, to the podium to accept her trophy. Five years later she co-starred with next husband, Richard Burton in *Who's Afraid of Virginia Woolf?* and both received Oscar nominations. Taylor was a no-show when she won on that Oscar night, and she had Anne Bancroft accept the award on her behalf. When Burton lost the Best Actor race, an irate Taylor considered giving back her award. Although she kept the prize, she incensed the Academy by refusing to issue a public statement of thanks the next morning. The disgruntled comments she made to the press instead kept the publicity fires flaring for several weeks.

Taylor, Lili

Movie: 1991: *Bright Angel* (Best Female Lead) Spirit. 1993: *Household Saints* (Best Supporting Female) *Spirit*; *Short Cuts* (Best Ensemble) *Venice* (special award). 1994: *Prêt-à-Porter (Ready-to-Wear)* (Best Ensemble) *Board*. 1995: *The Addiction* (Best Female Lead) Spirit. 1996: *Girls Town* (Best Supporting Female) Spirit. **Television:** 1998: *The X-Files* (Best Guest Actress in a Drama Series) Emmy. 2002–2005 series *Six Feet Under* (Best Guest Actress in a Drama Series) 2002: Emmy (Best Ensemble in a Drama Series) 2003: *SAG*. **Records:** With four, Taylor has more Independent Spirit award nominations than anyone.

Taylor, Noah

Movie: 1996: *Shine* (Best Male Actor in a Supporting Role) SAG (Best Ensemble) SAG. 2000: *Almost Famous* (Best Ensemble) SAG. 2004: *The Life Aquatic with Steve Zissou* (Best Ensemble) Broadcast.

Taylor, Robert

Tributes: 1953: Henrietta Award for World Film Favorite from Globe.

Taylor-Young, Leigh

Movie: 1968: *I Love You, Alice B. Toklas* (New Star of the Year — Actress) Globe. **Television:** 1993–1995 series *Picket Fences* (Best Supporting Actress in a Drama Series) 1994: *Emmy*. (Best Supporting Actress in a Series, Miniseries, or TV Movie) 1994: Globe.

Tedeschi, Valeria Bruni

Movie: 1999: *Rien à faire* (Best Actress) *Venice*. 2004: *5 × 2* (Best Actress) *Venice*.

Teller, Francis Kee

Tributes: 1952: Special Achievement Award for *Navajo* from Globe; Special Achievement nomination for Best Juvenile Performance in *Navajo* from Globe.

Temple (Black), Shirley

Tributes: 1934: Special miniature Oscar statuette in grateful recognition of her outstanding contribution to screen entertainment during the year 1934 from Academy. 1992: Career Achievement Award from Board. 1998: Honor from Kennedy Center for the Performing Arts. 1999: Ranked Number 18 on List of 25 Greatest Female Screen Legends of the 20th Century from American Film Institute. 2005: Life Achievement Award from SAG. **Records:** In 1934, 6-year-old Temple became the youngest Oscar winner ever (a record she still holds) and the first to receive the Academy's special miniature statuette presented to child performers. Initially, the special juvenile award was presented to minors for the entire body of work they did that given year. As a result, Temple also holds the record for winning a single Oscar for the most performances, as she starred in a staggering nine movies in 1934. Subsequent juvenile winners included Mickey Rooney, Judy Garland, and the last child to be so honored, Hayley Mills, who was presented her statuette for *Pollyanna* by Temple at the Oscars honoring the films of 1960. The year after Temple became the youngest Oscar winner, she earned the status of youngest number 1 box office star of 1935 and remained the number one box office draw until 1938. **Highlights:** Throughout the 1980s, the Academy of Motion Picture Arts and Sciences stepped up its efforts to find, preserve, and re-examine many of American film history's early classics. Part of that effort included special screenings and tribute nights, sometimes focusing on a film genre, a single motion picture, or an individual star. A 1985 tribute to Temple ended with the Academy presenting her a full-sized Oscar trophy to replace the miniature statuette that she earned in 1934.

Terry-Thomas

Movie: 1958: *Tom Thumb* (Best British Actor) British. 1963: *Mouse on the Moon* (Best Actor, Musical or Comedy) Globe.

Terselius, Lil

Movie: 1981: *Forfølgelsen (Witch Hunt)* (Best Actress) *Venice*.

Thaw, John

Movie: 1987: *Cry Freedom* (Best Supporting Actor) British.

Theaker, Deborah

Movie: 2003: *A Mighty Wind* (Best Screenplay) Spirit (Best Ensemble) Broadcast.

Theron, Charlize

Movie: 1999: *The Cider House Rules* (Best Ensemble) SAG. 2003: *Monster* (Breakthrough Performance — Female) *Board* (Best Actress) *Academy*, *Berlin*, British, *Society*, Broadcast (Best Actress, Drama) *Globe* (Best Female Actor in a Leading Role) *SAG* (Best Female Lead) *Spirit* (Best First Feature, Producer) *Spirit*. 2005: *North Country* (Best Actress) Academy, British, Broadcast (Best Actress, Drama) Globe (Best Female Actor in a Leading Role) SAG. Television: 2004: *The Life and Death of Peter Sellers* (Best Female Actor in a Television Movie or Miniseries) SAG (Best Supporting Actress in a Miniseries or TV Movie) Emmy (Best Supporting Actress in a Series, Miniseries, or TV Movie) Globe.

Thewlis, David

Movie: 1993: *Naked* (Best Actor) *New York, Cannes, Society*. 1995: *Hello, Hello, Hello* (Best Short Film, Director and Writer) British.

Thirlby, Olivia

Movie: 2007: *Juno* (Best Ensemble) Broadcast.

Thivisol, Victoire

Movie: 1996: *Ponette* (Best Actress) *Venice*. **Records:** Only five years old when she starred as a child coping with her mother's death in *Ponette*, Thivisol became the youngest star to win Best Actress from Venice.

Thomas, Henry

Movie: 1982: *E.T. The Extra-Terrestrial* (New Star of the Year — Actor) Globe (Most Promising Newcomer) British. **Television:** 1995: *Indictment: The McMartin Trial* (Best Supporting Actor in a Series, Miniseries, or TV Movie) Globe.

Thomas, Marlo

Movie: 1970: *Jenny* (New Star of the Year — Actress) Globe. **Television:** 1966–1971 series *That Girl* (Best Continued Performance by an Actress in a Leading Role in a Comedy Series) 1967: Emmy. 1968: Emmy. 1970: Emmy. 1971: Emmy. (Best Actress in a Series, Musical or Comedy) 1967: *Globe*. 1974: *Marlo Thomas and Friends in Free to Be ... You and Me* (Best Children's Special, Star and Producer) *Emmy*. 1981: *The Body Human: Facts for Girls* (Best Individual Achievement in Children's Programming, Performer) *Emmy*. 1985: *Consenting Adult* (Best Actress in a Miniseries or TV Movie) Globe. 1986: *Nobody's Child* (Best Actress in a Miniseries or Special) *Emmy* (Best Actress in a Miniseries or TV Movie) Globe. 1989: *Free to Be ... A Family* (Best Children's Program, Executive Producer) *Emmy*. 1996: *Friends* (Best Guest Actress in a Comedy Series) Emmy.

Thompson, Emma

Movie: 1991: *Impromptu* (Best Supporting Female) Spirit. 1992: *Howards End* (Best Actress) *Academy, New York, Board, British, Society, LA* (Best Actress, Drama) *Globe*. 1993: *In the Name of the Father* (Best Supporting Actress) Academy, Globe; *Much Ado About Nothing* (Best Female Lead) Spirit; *The Remains of the Day* (Best Actress) Academy, British (Best Actress, Drama) Globe. 1994: *Junior* (Best Actress, Musical or Comedy) Globe. 1995: *Carrington* (Best Actress) *Board* (multiple win); *Sense and Sensibility* (Best Actress) Academy, *Board* (multiple win), *British* (Best Actress, Drama) Globe (Best Female Actor in a Leading Role) SAG (Best Ensemble) SAG (Best Adapted Screenplay) *Academy*, British (Best Screeplay) *New York, Globe, Broadcast, LA*. 1997: *The Winter Guest* (Best Actress) *Venice*. 2003: *Love Actually* (Best Supporting Actress) British (Best Ensemble) Broadcast. 2006: *Stranger Than Fiction* (Best Supporting Actress) Broadcast. **Television:** 1998: *Ellen* (Best Guest Actress in a Comedy Series) *Emmy*. 2001: *Wit* (Best Actress in a Miniseries or TV Movie) Emmy, Globe (Best Female Actor in a Television Movie or Miniseries) SAG (Best Writing for a Miniseries or TV Movie) Emmy. 2003: *Angels in America* (Best Actress in a Miniseries or TV Movie) Emmy (Best Female Actor in a Television Movie or Miniseries) SAG. **Records:** Winning Academy Awards for Best Actress for *Howards End* and Best Screenplay for *Sense and Sensibility* made Thompson the first person to win Oscars in both the acting and writing categories.

Thompson, Sophie

Movie: 2001: *Gosford Park* (Best Ensemble) *SAG, Broadcast*.

Thorndike, Sybil

Movie: 1957: *The Prince and the Showgirl* (Best Supporting Actress) *Board*. Theater: 1957: *The Potting Shed* (Best Actress, Dramatic) Tony.

Thornton, Billy Bob

Movie: 1992: *One False Move* (Best Screenplay) Spirit. 1996: *Sling Blade* (Best Actor) Academy (Best Male Actor in a Leading Role) SAG (Best Adapted Screenplay) *Academy* (Best Ensemble) SAG. 1998: *Primary Colors* (Best Supporting Actor) *Broadcast* (multiple win); *A Simple Plan* (Best Male Actor in a Suppoarting Role) SAG (Best Supporting Actor) Academy, Globe, *LA, Broadcast* (multiple win). 2001: *Bandits* (Best Actor) *Board* (multiple win), (Best Actor, Musical or Comedy) Globe; *The Man Who Wasn't There* (Best Actor) *Board* (multiple win), (Best Actor, Drama) Globe; *Monster's Ball* (Best Actor) *Board* (multiple win). 2003: *Bad Santa* (Best Actor, Musical or Comedy) Globe; *Love Actually* (Best Ensemble) Broadcast. Tributes: 1996: Special Filmmaking Achievement Award for *Sling Blade* from Board.

Thulin, Ingrid

Movie: 1958: *Nara Livet (Brink of Life)* (Best Actress) *Cannes* (win shared with costars). 1973: *Cries and Whispers* (Best Supporting Actress) British.

Thurman, Uma

Movie: 1994: *Pulp Fiction* (Best Actress) British (Best Female Actor in a Supporting Role) SAG (Best Supporting Actress) Academy, Globe. 2001: *Tape* (Best Supporting Female) Spirit. 2003: *Kill Bill: Vol. 1* (Best Actress) British (Best Actress, Drama) Globe. 2004: *Kill Bill: Vol. 2* (Best Actress) Broadcast (Best Actress, Drama) Globe. Television: 2003: *Hysterical Blindness* (Best Actress in a Miniseries or TV Movie) *Globe* (Best Female Actor in a Television Movie or Miniseries) SAG.

Tibbett, Lawrence

Movie: 1930: *The Rogue Song* (Best Actor) Academy.

Tierney, Gene

Movie: 1945: *Leave Her to Heaven* (Best Actress) Academy.

Tiffin, Pamela

Movie: 1961: *Summer and Smoke* (New Star of the Year — Actress) Globe; *One, Two, Three* (Best Supporting Actress) Globe.

Tilly, Jennifer

Movie: 1994: *Bullets Over Broadway* (Best Supporting Actress) Academy.

Tilly, Meg

Movie: 1985: *Agnes of God* (Best Supporting Actress) Academy, *Globe*.

Todd, Ann

Movie: 1952: *Breaking the Sound Barrier (The Sound Barrier)* (Best British Actress) British.

Todd, Richard

Movie: 1949: *The Hasty Heart* (New Star of the Year — Actor) *Globe* (Best Actor) Academy, Globe. Records: Todd's Golden Globe nod for *The Hasty Heart* is the first nomination ever earned by anyone in the Best Actor race. Before 1949, the Hollywood Foreign Press chose a single winner like the film critics rather than a roster of nominees from which one came out victorious. In this first year, they named one winner and one nominee in each of the acting categories. Todd was runner up to Broderick Crawford, who won most every Best Actor award that year for *All the King's Men*.

Tognazzi, Ugo

Movie: 1967: *The Climax* (Best Actor, Musical or Comedy) Globe. 1981: *La Tragedia di un uomo ridicolo (Tragedy of a Ridiculous Man)* (Best Actor) *Cannes*.

Tomei, Marisa

Movie: 1992: *My Cousin Vinny* (Best Supporting Actress) *Academy*. 1996: *Unhook the Stars* (Best Female Actor in a Supporting Role) SAG. 2001: *In the Bedroom* (Best Supporting Actress) Academy, Globe, Broadcast (Best Ensemble) SAG. 2007: *Before the Devil Knows You're Dead* (Best Supporting Female) Spirit (Best Ensemble) Broadcast.

Tomlin, Lily

Movie: 1975: *Nashville* (New Star of the Year — Actress) Globe (Most Promising Newcomer) British (Best Supporting Actress) Academy, *New York*, Globe, *Society*. 1977: *The Late Show* (Best Actress) *Berlin*, British (Best Actress, Musical or Comedy) Globe. 1984: *All of Me* (Best Actress, Musical or

Comedy) Globe. 1991: *The Search for Signs of Intelligent Life in the Universe* (Best Female Lead) Spirit. 1993: *Short Cuts* (Best Ensemble) *Venice* (special award). 1996: *Flirting with Disaster* (Best Supporting Female) Spirit. 2006: *A Prairie Home Companion* (Best Ensemble) Broadcast. **Theater:** 1986: *The Search for Signs of Intelligent Life in the Universe* (Best Actress, Play) *Tony*. 2001: *The Search for Signs of Intelligent Life in the Universe* (Best Revival, Play; Producer) Tony. **Television:** 1969–1973 series *Rowan and Martin's Laugh-In* (Best Special Classification of Outstanding Program and Individual Achievement, Performer) 1971: Emmy. (Best Achievement by a Performer in Music or Variety) 1972: Emmy. (Best Achievement by a Supporting Performer in Music or Variety) 1973: Emmy. (Best Supporting Actress in a Series) 1971: Globe. 1973: *The Lily Tomlin Show* (Best Writing in a Variety or Music Special) Emmy. 1974: *Lily Tomlin* (Best Comedy-Variety, Variety, or Music Special; Star) *Emmy* (Best Writing for a Comedy-Variety or Music Special) *Emmy*. 1975: *Lily* (Best Comedy-Variety, Variety, or Music Special; Star) Emmy (Best Writing of a Comedy-Variety, Variety, or Music Special) Emmy. 1976: *Lily Tomlin* (Best Comedy-Variety, Variety, or Music Special; Star) Emmy (Best Writing of a Comedy-Variety, Variety, or Music Special) *Emmy*. 1978: *The Paul Simon Special* (Best Writing of a Comedy-Variety or Music Special) *Emmy*. 1981: *Lily: Sold Out* (Best Variety, Music, or Comedy Special; Star and Executive Producer) *Emmy*. 1984: *Live ... and in Person* (Best Individual Performance of a Variety or Music Program) Emmy. 1993: *The Search for Signs of Intelligent Life in the Universe* (Best Individual Performance in a Variety or Music Program) Emmy (Best Variety, Music, or Comedy Special; Star and Executive Producer) Emmy. 1994: *And the Band Played On* (Best Supporting Actress in a Miniseries or Special) Emmy; *Growing Up Funny* (Best Individual Performance in a Variety or Music Program) Emmy. 1996: *The Celluloid Closet* (Best Information Special, Co-Executive Producer and Narrator) Emmy; *Homicide: Life on the Street* (Best Guest Actress in a Drama Series) Emmy. 2002–2006 series *The West Wing* (Best Female Actor in a Drama Series) 2002: SAG. (Best Ensemble in a Drama Series) 2002: SAG. 2003: SAG. 2004: SAG. 2005: SAG. **Tributes:** 1977: Special award from Tony.

Tompkins, Angel

Movie: 1970: *I Love My Wife* (New Star of the Year — Actress) Globe.

Tomsett, Sally

Movie: 1970: *The Railway Children* (Most Promising Newcomer) British.

Tone, Franchot

Movie: 1935: *Mutiny on the Bounty* (Best Actor) Academy.

Topol

Movie: 1964: *Sallah* (New Star of the Year — Actor) *Globe*. 1971: *Fiddler on the Roof* (Best Actor) Academy (Best Actor, Musical or Comedy) *Globe*. **Theater:** 1991: *Fiddler on the Roof* (Best Actor, Musical) Tony.

Toprak, Mehmet Emin

Movie: 2003: *Uzak* (Best Actor) *Cannes* (win shared with costar).

Torn, Rip

Movie: 1983: *Cross Creek* (Best Supporting Actor) Academy. **Theater:** 1960: *Sweet Bird of Youth* (Best Supporting or Featured Actor, Dramatic) Tony. **Television:** 1985: *The Atlanta Child Murders* (Best Supporting Actor in a Limited Series or Special) Emmy. 1992–1998 series *The Larry Sanders Show* (Best Supporting Actor in a Comedy Series) 1993: Emmy. 1994: Emmy. 1995: Emmy. 1996: *Emmy*. 1997: Emmy. 1998: Emmy. 1996: *Chicago Hope* (Best Guest Actor in a Drama Series) Emmy.

Torocsic, Mari

Movie: 1976: *Deryne, Hol Van? (Where Are You, Mrs. Dery?)* (Best Actress) *Cannes*.

Torres, Fernanda

Movie: 1986: *Eu sei que vou te amar (Love Me Forever or Never* or *I Love You)* (Best Actress) *Cannes*.

Towles, Tom

Movie: 1990: *Henry, Portrait of a Serial Killer* (Best Supporting Male) Spirit.

Tracy, Lee

Movie: 1964: *The Best Man* (Best Supporting Actor) Academy, Globe. **Theater:** 1960: *The Best Man* (Best Actor, Dramatic) Tony.

Tracy, Spencer

Movie: 1936: *San Francisco* (Best Actor) Academy. 1937: *Captains Courageous* (Best Actor) *Academy*. 1938: *Boys Town* (Best Acting) *Board* (Best Actor) *Academy*. 1950: *Father of the Bride* (Best Actor) Academy. 1953: *The Actress* (Best Actor, Drama) *Globe* (Best Foreign Actor) British. 1955: *Bad Day at the Black Rock* (Best Actor) Academy, *Cannes*. 1956: *The Mountain* (Best Foreign Actor) British.

1958: *The Old Man and the Sea* (Best Actor) Academy, *Board* (multiple win), (Best Actor, Drama) Globe; *The Last Hurrah* (Best Actor) *Board* (multiple win), (Best Foreign Actor) British. 1960: *Inherit the Wind* (Best Actor) Academy (Best Actor, Drama) Globe (Best Foreign Actor) British. 1961: *Judgment at Nuremberg* (Best Actor) Academy. 1967: *Guess Who's Coming to Dinner* (Best Actor) Academy (Best Actor, Drama) Globe (Best Foreign Actor) *British*. Tributes: 1999: Ranked Number 9 on List of 25 Greatest Male Screen Legends of the 20th Century from American Film Institute. **Records:** With his Best Actor performances in 1937 for *Captains Courageous* and 1938 for *Boys Town*, Tracy became the first male star to win Oscars in consecutive years. He barely missed being the first performer to do so. Luise Rainer beat him by one year with her back-to-back Oscars in 1936 (*The Great Ziegfeld*) and 1937 (*The Good Earth*). Both of Tracy's Oscars have unique histories of their own. Tracy's first Academy Award was mistakenly inscribed to Dick Tracy. Because Spencer was in the hospital with appendicitis when he won his *Captains Courageous* Oscar, the Academy had a chance to fix their inscription error before sending it to their winning star. After Tracy won his Oscar for *Boys Town*, the Academy made a duplicate and gave it to the actual Boys Town compound in Nebraska. **Highlights:** Tracy was ill through most of the filming of *Guess Who's Coming to Dinner*, so director Stanley Kramer often adjusted daily schedules to accommodate the few hours Tracy had each day of feeling strong enough to work. In his climactic speech, Tracy's character finally supports the upcoming marriage between his daughter (played by Katharine Houghton) and her Black fiancé (Sidney Poitier) by relating how much he loves his wife (played by long time love Katharine Hepburn) as she looks on. The fact that Hepburn must have known Tracy didn't have long to live makes her tearful, affectionate gaze all the more stirring. Though Tracy remained married the entire time of his and Hepburn's long love affair, he was with Hepburn when he died of a heart attack just weeks after production on the film ended. During the next Oscar season, both Tracy and Hepburn were nominated for the film. Hepburn won her competition, but Tracy lost his posthumous bid for Best Actor to Rod Steiger in *In the Heat of the Night*.

Trantow, Cordula

Movie: 1961: *Hitler* (New Star of the Year — Actress) Globe.

Travers, Henry

Movie: 1942: *Mrs. Miniver* (Best Supporting Actor) Academy.

Travolta, John

Movie: 1977: *Saturday Night Fever* (Best Actor) Academy, *Board* (Best Actor, Musical or Comedy) Globe. 1978: *Grease* (Best Actor, Musical or Comedy) Globe. 1994: *Pulp Fiction* (Best Actor) Academy, British, *LA* (Best Actor, Drama) Globe (Best Male Actor in a Leading Role) SAG. 1995: *Get Shorty* (Best Actor, Musical or Comedy) *Globe* (Best Ensemble) SAG. 1998: *Primary Colors* (Best Actor, Musical or Comedy) Globe. 2007: *Hairspray* (Best Supporting Actor) Globe (Best Ensemble) SAG, *Broadcast*. Tributes: 1978: Henrietta Award for World Film Favorite from Globe. 1998: Alan J. Pakula Award from Broadcast. **Records:** For his work in 1999's *A Civil Action*, Travolta became the first, and so far only, actor to be honored with the Alan J. Pakula Award from the Broadcast Film Critics Association. The award, named after the director of such classics as *All the President's Men* and *Sophie's Choice*, honors artistic excellence by illuminating issues of great social and political importance.

Traylor, Susan

Movie: 1999: *Valerie Flake* (Best Female Lead) Spirit.

Trevor, Claire

Movie: 1937: *Dead End* (Best Supporting Actress) Academy. 1948: *Key Largo* (Best Supporting Actress) *Academy*. 1954: *The High and the Mighty* (Best Supporting Actress) Academy. Television: 1954: *"Ladies in Retirement," Lux Video Theatre* (Best Actress in a Single Performance) Emmy. 1956: *"Dodsworth," Producers' Showcase* (Best Single Performance by an Actress) *Emmy*.

Trintignant, Jean-Louis

Movie: 1968: *L'homme qui ment* (Best Actor) Berlin.1969: *Z* (Best Actor) *Cannes*.

Troisi, Massimo

Movie: 1989: *Che ora è?* (Best Actor) *Venice* (win shared with costar). 1995: *Il Postino (The Postman)* (Best Actor) Academy, British (Best Male Actor in a Leading Role) SAG (Best Adapted Screenplay) Academy, British. Tributes: 1989: A second Best Actor award for *Che ora è?* from Venice.

Truffaut, Francois

Movie: 1959: *Les Quatre cents coups (The 400 Blows)* (Best Story and Screenplay) Academy. 1970: *L'Enfant sauvage (The Wild Child)* (Best Director) *Board*. 1973: *Nuit américaine (Day for Night)* (Best Director) Academy, *New York, Society* (Best Original

Screenplay) Academy. 1975: *L'Histoire d'Adèle H. (The Story of Adele H.)* (Best Screenplay) *New York.* 1976: *L'Argent de poche (Small Change)* (Best Director) *Berlin* (special competitive award) *Berlin* (special jury award). 1977: **Close Encounters of the Third Kind** (Best Supporting Actor) British. **Tributes:** 1984: Special Award from LA.

Tryon, Tom

Movie: 1963: **The Cardinal** (Best Actor, Drama) Globe.

Tucci, Stanley

Movie: 1996: **Big Night** (Best Male Lead) Spirit (Best First Screenplay) *Spirit.* Theater: 2003: **Frankie and Johnny in the Clair de Lune** (Best Actor, Play) Tony. Television: 1995–1997 series **Murder One** (Best Supporting Actor in a Drama Series) 1996: Emmy. 1999: **Winchell** (Best Actor in a Miniseries or TV Movie) *Emmy, Globe* (Best Male Actor in a Television Movie or Miniseries) SAG. 2001: **Conspiracy** (Best Supporting Actor in a Miniseries or TV Movie) Emmy (Best Supporting Actor in a Series, Miniseries, or TV Movie) *Globe.* 2007: **Monk** (Best Guest Actor in a Comedy Series) *Emmy.*

Tucker, Larry

Movie: 1963: **Shock Corridor** (New Star of the Year — Actor) Globe. 1969: **Bob & Carol & Ted & Alice** (Best Story and Screenplay) Academy. Television: 1963–1967 series **The Danny Kaye Show** (Best Writing in Comedy or Variety) 1964: Emmy. (Best Writing in Variety) 1966: Emmy.

Tudyk, Alan

Movie: 2007: **3:10 to Yuma** (Best Ensemble) SAG.

Tully, Tom

Movie: 1954: **The Caine Mutiny** (Best Supporting Actor) Academy.

Tunie, Tamara

Movie: 2001: **The Caveman's Valentine** (Best Supporting Female) Spirit. Theater: 2007: **Radio Golf** (Best Play, Producer) Tony; **Spring Awakening** (Best Musical, Producer) *Tony.*

Tunney, Robin

Movie: 1998: **Niagara, Niagara** (Best Actress) *Venice* (Best Female Lead) Spirit.

Turkel, Ann

Movie: 1974: **99 and 44/100% Dead** (New Star of the Year — Actress) Globe.

Turner, Kathleen

Movie: 1981: **Body Heat** (New Star of the Year — Actor or Actress) Globe (Most Promising Newcomer) British. 1984: **Crimes of Passion** (Best Actress) *LA* (multiple win); **Romancing the Stone** (Best Actress) *LA* (multiple win), (Best Actress, Musical or Comedy) *Globe.* 1985: **Prizzi's Honor** (Best Actress, Musical or Comedy) *Globe.* 1986: **Peggy Sue Got Married** (Best Actress) Academy, *Board* (Best Actress, Musical or Comedy) Globe. 1989: **The War of the Roses** (Best Actress, Musical or Comedy) Globe. Theater: 1990: **Cat on a Hot Tin Roof** (Best Actress, Play) Tony. 2005: **Who's Afraid of Virginia Woolf?** (Best Actress, Play) Tony.

Turner, Lana

Movie: 1957: **Peyton Place** (Best Actress) Academy.

Turner, Tyrin

Movie: 1993: **Menace II Society** (Best Male Lead) Spirit.

Turturro, John

Movie: 1988: **Five Corners** (Best Supporting Male) Spirit. 1991: **Barton Fink** (Best Actor) *Cannes.* 1993: **Mac** (Best Director) *Cannes,* Spirit (Best First Feature, Producer) Spirit. 1994: **Quiz Show** (Best Male Actor in a Supporting Role) SAG (Best Supporting Actor) Globe. 1997: **Box of Moonlight** (Best Male Lead) Spirit. Television: 2002: **Monday Night Mayhem** (Best Male Actor in a Television Movie or Miniseries) SAG. 2004: **Monk** (Best Guest Actor in a Comedy Series) *Emmy.* 2007: **The Bronx Is Burning** (Best Male Actor in a Television Movie or Miniseries) SAG.

Turturro, Nicholas (Nick)

Movie: 1994: **Federal Hill** (Best Supporting Male) Spirit. Television: 1993–2001 series **NYPD Blue** (Best Supporting Actor in a Drama Series) 1994: Emmy. 1997: Emmy. (Best Ensemble in a Drama Series) 1994: *SAG.* 1995: SAG. 1996: SAG. 1997: SAG. 1998: SAG. 1999: SAG.

Tushingham, Rita

Movie: 1961: **A Taste of Honey** (New Star of the Year — Actress) *Globe* (Most Promising Newcomer) *British* (Best Acting) *Cannes* (special award shared with costar). 1964: **Girl with Green Eyes** (Best British Actress) British. 1965: **The Knack ... and How to Get It** (Best British Actress) British (Best Actress, Musical or Comedy) Globe.

Tutin, Dorothy

Movie: 1952: *The Importance of Being Earnest* (Most Promising Newcomer) British. 1972: *Savage Messiah* (Best Actress) British. Theater: 1968: *Portrait of a Queen* (Best Actress, Dramatic) Tony.

Twiggy

Movie: 1971: *The Boy Friend* (New Star of the Year — Actress) *Globe* (Best Actress, Musical or Comedy) *Globe*. Theater: 1983: *My One and Only* (Best Actress, Musical) Tony.

Tyler, Liv

Movie: 2001: *The Lord of the Rings: The Fellowship of the Ring* (Best Ensemble) SAG. 2002: *The Lord of the Rings: The Two Towers* (Best Ensemble) SAG. 2003: *The Lord of the Rings: The Return of the King* (Best Ensemble) *Board, SAG, Broadcast*.

Tyrrell, Susan

Movie: 1972: *Fat City* (Best Supporting Actress) Academy.

Tyson, Cathy

Movie: 1986: *Mona Lisa* (Best Actress) British (Best Supporting Actress) Globe, *LA*.

Tyson, Cicely

Movie: 1972: *Sounder* (Best Actress) Academy, *Board, Society* (Best Actress, Drama) Globe. 1974: *The Autobiography of Miss Jane Pittman* (Best Actress) British. Television: 1974: *The Autobiography of Miss Jane Pittman* (Best Actress in a Drama) *Emmy* (Best Actress of the Year in a Special) *Emmy*. 1977: *Roots* (Best Single Performance by a Supporting Actress in a Comedy or Drama Special) Emmy. 1978: *King* (Best Actress in a Limited Series) Emmy. 1982: *"The Marva Collins Story," Hallmark Hall of Fame* (Best Actress in a Limited Series or Special) Emmy. 1994: *Oldest Living Confederate Widow Tells All* (Best Female Actor in a Drama Series) SAG (Best Supporting Actress in a Miniseries or Special) *Emmy*. 1994–1995 series *Sweet Justice* (Best Actress in a Drama Series) 1995: Emmy. (Best Female Actor in a Drama Series) 1994: SAG. 1996: *The Road to Galveston* (Best Female Actor in a Television Movie or Miniseries) SAG. 1999: *A Lesson Before Dying* (Best Supporting Actress in a Miniseries or TV Movie) Emmy.

Uhl, Nadja

Movie: 2000: *Die Stille nach de Schuß (The Legends of Rita)* (Best Actress) *Berlin* (win shared with costar).

Ullman, Tracey

Movie: 1985: *Plenty* (Best Supporting Actress) British. 1994: *Prêt-à-Porter (Ready-to-Wear)* (Best Ensemble) *Board*. 2000: *Small Time Crooks* (Best Actress, Musical or Comedy) Globe. Television: 1987–1998 series *The Tracey Ullman Show* (Best Actress in a Series, Musical or Comedy) 1987: *Globe*. 1988: Globe. 1989: Globe. (Best Variety, Music, or Comedy Program; Host) 1987: Emmy. 1988: Emmy. 1989: *Emmy*. 1990: Emmy. (Best Writing for a Variety, Music, or Comedy Program) 1988: Emmy. 1989: Emmy. 1990: *Emmy*. 1990: *The Best of The Tracey Ullman Show* (Best Individual Performance in a Variety or Music Program) *Emmy*. 1993: *Love & War* (Best Guest Actress in a Comedy Series) *Emmy*. 1994: *Tracey Ullman: Tracey Takes on New York* (Best Individual Performance in a Variety or Music Program) *Emmy*. 1995: *Women of the Night* (Best Individual Performance in a Variety or Music Program) Emmy. 1996: *The Best of Tracey Takes on...* (Best Performance for a Variety or Music Program) Emmy (Best Variety, Music, or Comedy Special; Executive Producer) Emmy. 1996–1999 series *Tracey Takes on...* (Best Performance in a Variety or Music Program) 1997: Emmy. 1998: Emmy. 1999: Emmy. (Best Actress in a Musical or Comedy Series) 1996: Globe. (Best Female Actor in a Comedy Series) 1998: *SAG*. 1999: SAG. (Best Variety, Music or Comedy Series; Executive Producer) 1997: *Emmy*. 1998: Emmy. 1999: Emmy. (Best Writing for a Variety or Music Program) 1996: Emmy. 1997: Emmy. 1999: *Ally McBeal* (Best Guest Actress in a Comedy Series) *Emmy*. 2004: *Tracey Ullman in the Trailer Tales* (Best Individual Performance in a Variety or Music Program) Emmy. 2005: *Tracey Ullman Live and Exposed* (Best Individual Performance in a Variety or Music Program) Emmy.

Ullmann, Liv

Movie: 1968: *Hour of the Wolf* (Best Actress) *Board* (multiple win); *Shame* (Best Actress) *Board* (multiple win), *Society*. 1972: *Cries and Whispers* (Best Actress) *New York* (multiple win); *The Emigrants* (Best Actress) Academy, *New York* (multiple win), (Best Actress, Drama) *Globe*. 1973: *Forty Carats* (Best Actress, Musical or Comedy) Globe; *The New Land* (Best Actress) *Board, Society*. 1974: *Scenes from a Marriage* (Best Actress) *New York*, British, *Society* (Best Actress, Drama) Globe. 1976: *Face to Face* (Best Actress) Academy, *New York, Board*, British, *LA* (Best Actress, Drama) Globe. 1980: *Richard's Things* (Best Actress) *Venice*. 1989: *The Rose Garden* (Best Actress, Drama) Globe. Theater: 1975: *A Doll's House* (Best Actress, Dramatic) Tony. 1977: *Anna Christie* (Best Actress, Play) Tony. **Records:**

Ullmann became the first actress to win two National Society of Film Critics acting awards, earning her first in 1968 for *Shame* and her second for *The New Land* in 1973. The following year she broke her own record when her performance in *Scenes from a Marriage* made her the first to win three. Early in its existence, the Society consistently favored Swedish films, as Ullmann set her records for three Swedish productions, and Ullmann's *Scenes* co-star, Stockholm-born Bibi Andersson became the first actor to win two Society acting awards in different categories.

Ullrich, Luise

Movie: 1941: *Annelie* (Best Actress) *Venice*.

Ullrich, William

Movie: 2004: *Beyond the Sea* (Best Young Actor) Broadcast.

Umeki, Miyoshi

Movie: 1957: *Sayonara* (Best Supporting Actress) *Academy*, Globe. 1961: *Flower Drum Song* (Best Actress, Musical or Comedy) Globe. **Theater:** 1959: *Flower Drum Song* (Best Actress, Musical) Tony. **Television:** 1969–1972 series *The Courtship of Eddie's Father* (Best Supporting Actress in a Series) 1970: Globe. **Records:** Soft spoken, Japanese born Umeki was the first and still only female of pure Asian descent to win an acting Oscar. She won the year after Yul Brynner, who was born on Sakhalin, an island north of Japan, was named Best Actor for *The King and I*.

Urban, Karl

Movie: 2003: *The Lord of the Rings: The Return of the King* (Best Ensemble) *Board, SAG, Broadcast*.

Ure, Mary

Movie: 1960: *Sons and Lovers* (Best Supporting Actress) Academy, Globe. **Theater:** 1958: *Look Back in Anger* (Best Actress, Dramatic) Tony.

Urzì, Saro

Movie: 1964: *Sedotta e abbandonata (Seduced and Abandoned)* (Best Actor) *Cannes*.

Ustinov, Peter

Movie: 1951: *Quo Vadis?* (Best Supporting Actor) Academy, *Globe*. 1960: *Spartacus* (Best Supporting Actor) *Academy*, Globe. 1962: *Billy Budd* (Best British Screenplay) British. 1964: *Topkapi* (Best Actor, Musical or Comedy) Globe (Best Supporting Actor) *Academy*. 1968: *Hot Millions* (Best Story and Screenplay) Academy. 1978: *Death on the Nile* (Best Actor) British. **Theater:** 1958: *Romanoff and Juliet* (Best Actor, Dramatic) Tony (Best Play, Writer) Tony. **Television:** 1957: *"The Life of Samuel Johnson,"* *Omnibus* (Best Single Performance by a Lead or Supporting Actor) *Emmy*. 1967: *"Barefoot in Athens,"* *Hallmark Hall of Fame* (Best Single Performance by an Actor in a Drama) *Emmy*. 1970: *"A Storm in Summer,"* *Hallmark Hall of Fame* (Best Single Performance by an Actor in a Leading Role) *Emmy*. 1982: *Omni: The New Frontier* (Best Achievement in Informational Programming, Host) Emmy. 1985: *The Well-Tempered Bach with Peter Ustinov* (Best Classical Program in the Performing Arts, Host) Emmy. **Tributes:** 1972: Silver Bear for Outstanding Artistic Contribution to *Hammersmith Is Out* from Berlin. **Records:** Ustinov is the first Emmy Award winning star to later win an Oscar. In 1957, Ustinov won his first of three Emmys for *The Life of Samuel Johnson*. Three years later he took home one of the four Oscars won by Stanley Kubrick's lavishly produced Roman spectacle, *Spartacus*, making him the first star to win first an Emmy and then an Oscar. Before his wins, Helen Hayes and Thomas Mitchell had won both awards, but each had earned an Oscar first.

Vaccaro, Brenda

Movie: 1969: *Where It's At* (New Star of the Year — Actress) Globe; *Midnight Cowboy* (Best Supporting Actress) Globe. 1975: *Jacqueline Susann's Once Is Not Enough* (Best Supporting Actress) Academy, Globe. **Theater:** 1966: *Cactus Flower* (Best Supporting or Featured Actress, Dramatic) Tony. 1968: *How Now, Dow Jones* (Best Actress, Musical) Tony. 1969: *The Goodbye People* (Best Actress, Dramatic) Tony. **Television:** 1974: *The Shape of Things* (Best Supporting Actress in Comedy-Variety, Variety, or Music) *Emmy*. 1976 series *Sara* (Best Actress in a Drama Series) 1976: Emmy. 1991: *The Golden Girls* (Best Guest Actress in a Comedy Series) Emmy.

Valandrey, Charlotte

Movie: 1986: *Rouge baiser (Red Kiss)* (Best Actress) *Berlin*.

Vallee, Rudy

Movie: 1942: *The Palm Beach Story* (Best Acting) *Board*.

Valli, Alida

Movie: 1963: *The Paper Man* (Best Actress, Drama) Globe. **Tributes:** 1997: Career Golden Lion from Venice.

Vance, Courtney B.

Movie: 1998: *Blind Faith* (Best Male Lead) Spirit.
Theater: 1987: *Fences* (Best Actor in a Featured Role, Play) Tony. 1991: *Six Degrees of Separation* (Best Actor, Play) Tony.

Vance, Danitra

Movie: 1992: *Jumpin' at the Boneyard* (Best Supporting Female) Spirit.

Van Devere, Trish

Movie: 1972: *One Is a Lonely Number* (Best Actress, Drama) Globe.

Van Dyke, Dick

Movie: 1964: *Mary Poppins* (Best Actor, Musical or Comedy) Globe. **Theater:** 1961: *Bye Bye Birdie* (Best Supporting or Featured Actor, Musical) *Tony*. **Television:** 1961–1966 series *The Dick Van Dyke Show* (Best Continued Performance by an Actor in a Series) 1963: Emmy. 1964: *Emmy*. (Best Individual Achievement in Entertainment, Actor) 1965: *Emmy*. (Best Continued Performance by an Actor in a Leading Role in a Comedy Series) 1966: *Emmy*. 1971–1974 series *The New Dick Van Dyke Show* (Best Actor in a Series, Musical or Comedy) 1972: Globe. 1974: *"The Morning After," Wednesday Movie of the Week* (Best Actor in a Drama) Emmy. 1976 series *Van Dyke & Company (Van Dyke and Company)* (Best Comedy-Variety or Music Series, Star) 1977: *Emmy*. (Best Writing for a Comedy-Variety or Music Series) 1977: Emmy. (Best Writing for a Comedy-Variety or Music Special) 1977: Emmy. 1984: *"The Wrong Way Kid," CBS Library* (Best Performer in Children's Programming) *Emmy*. 1990: *The Golden Girls* (Best Guest Actor in a Comedy Series) Emmy. **Tributes:** 1995: Television Hall of Fame Inductee from Emmy.

Vanel, Charles

Movie: 1953: *Le Salaire de la peur (The Wages of Fear)* (Best Actor) *Cannes*.

Van Fleet, Jo

Movie: 1955: *East of Eden* (Most Promising Newcomer) British (Best Supporting Actress) *Academy*. **Theater:** 1954: *The Trip to Bountiful* (Best Supporting or Featured Actress, Dramatic) *Tony*. 1958: *Look Homeward, Angel* (Best Actress, Dramatic) Tony. **Highlights:** In 1955 Van Fleet had roles in three prominent, Oscar-winning pictures: *I'll Cry Tomorrow* (one award), *The Rose Tattoo* (three awards), and *East of Eden*, which earned her the Best Supporting Actress award for her film debut. Although reporters had warned her that she had no chance of winning if she didn't advertise, Van Fleet chose not to campaign to win, and ended up taking the prize anyway.

Vardalos, Nia

Movie: 2002: *My Big Fat Greek Wedding* (Best Debut Performance) *Spirit* (Best Actress, Musical or Comedy) Globe (Best Original Screenplay) Academy (Best Screenplay) Broadcast (Best Ensemble) SAG, Broadcast.

Vargas, Jacob

Movie: 2000: *Traffic* (Best Ensemble) *SAG*. 2006: *Bobby* (Best Ensemble) SAG, Broadcast.

Varsi, Diane

Movie: 1957: *Peyton Place* (New Star of the Year — Actress) *Globe* (Best Supporting Actress) Academy.

Vasquez, Yul

Movie: 2007: *American Gangster* (Best Ensemble) SAG.

Vaughn, Robert

Movie: 1959: *The Young Philadelphians* (Best Supporting Actor) Academy, Globe. 1960: *The Magnificent Seven* (New Star of the Year — Actor) Globe. 1968: *Bullitt* (Best Supporting Actor) British. **Television:** 1964–1968 series *The Man from U.N.C.L.E.* (Best Actor in a Series) 1965: Globe. 1966: Globe. 1978: *Washington: Behind Closed Doors* (Best Supporting Actor in a Drama Series) *Emmy*. 1979: *Backstairs at the White House* (Best Supporting Actor in a Limited Series or Special) Emmy.

Vaughn, Vince

Movie: 2007: *Into the Wild* (Best Ensemble) SAG.

Vega, Yenny Paola

Movie: 2004: *Maria Full of Grace* (Best Supporting Female) Spirit.

Veidt, Conrad

Movie: 1940: *Escape* (Best Acting) *Board*.

Veléz, Lauren

Movie: 1994: *I Like It Like That* (Best Female Lead) Spirit.

Venora, Diane

Movie: 1988: *Bird* (Best Supporting Actress) *New York*, Globe.

Verdon, Gwen

Movie: 1958: *Damn Yankees (What Lola Wants)* (Most Promising Newcomer) British. 1996: *Marvin's Room* (Best Female Actor in a Supporting Role) SAG (Best Ensemble) SAG. Theater: 1954: *Can-Can* (Best Supporting or Featured Actress, Musical) *Tony*. 1956: *Damn Yankees* (Best Actress, Musical) *Tony*. 1958: *New Girl in Town* (Best Actress, Musical) *Tony*. 1959: *Redhead* (Best Actress, Musical) *Tony*. 1966: *Sweet Charity* (Best Actress, Musical) Tony. 1976: *Chicago* (Best Actress, Musical) Tony. Television: 1988: *Magnum, P.I.* (Best Guest Actress in a Drama Series) Emmy. 1993: *Dream On* (Best Guest Actress in a Comedy Series) Emmy; *Homicide: Life on the Street* (Best Guest Actress in a Drama Series) Emmy.

Vereen, Ben

Movie: 1975: *Funny Lady* (New Star of the Year — Actor) Globe. Theater: 1972: *Jesus Christ Superstar* (Best Supporting or Featured Actor, Musical) Tony. 1973: *Pippin* (Best Actor, Musical) *Tony*. Television: 1977: *Roots* (Best Single Performance by an Actor in a Drama or Comedy Series) Emmy. 1977: *The Bell Telephone Jubilee* (Best Continuing or Single Performance by an Actor in Variety or Music) Emmy. 1984: *Ellis Island* (Best Supporting Actor in a Series, Miniseries, or TV Movie) Globe. 1992: *Intruders, They Are Among Us* (Best Supporting Actor in a Miniseries or Special) Emmy.

Verveen, Arie

Movie: 1996: *Caught* (Best Debut Performance) Spirit.

Vilbert, Henri

Movie: 1953: *Le Bon dieu sans confession* (Best Actor) *Venice*.

Vincent, Jan-Michael

Movie: 1971: *Going Home* (Best Supporting Actor) Globe. Television: 1983: *The Winds of War* (Best Supporting Actor in a Series, Miniseries, or TV Movie) Globe.

Vitti, Monica

Movie: 1960: *L'Avventura* (Best Foreign Actress) British. 1984: *Flirt* (Best Actress) *Berlin* (special award). Tributes: 1995: Career Golden Lion from Venice.

Vlady, Marina

Movie: 1963: *Una Storia Moderna: l'ape regina (The Conjugal Bed* or *Queen Bee)* (Best Actress) *Cannes* (Best Actress, Drama) Globe.

Vogel, Mitch

Movie: 1969: *The Reivers* (Best Supporting Actor) Globe.

Voight, Jon

Movie: 1969: *Midnight Cowboy* (New Star of the Year — Actor) *Globe* (Most Promising Newcomer) *British* (Best Actor) Academy, *New York, Society* (Best Actor, Drama) Globe. 1972: *Deliverance* (Best Actor, Drama) Globe. 1978: *Coming Home* (Best Actor) *Academy, New York, Board, Cannes, LA* (Best Actor, Drama) *Globe*. 1979: *The Champ* (Best Actor, Drama) Globe. 1985: *Runaway Train* (Best Actor) Academy (Best Actor, Drama) *Globe*. 1997: *John Grisham's The Rainmaker* (Best Supporting Actor) Globe. 2001: *Ali* (Best Supporting Actor) Academy, Globe, Broadcast. Television: 1992: *The Last of His Tribe* (Best Actor in a Miniseries or TV Movie) Globe. 2002: *Uprising* (Best Supporting Actor in a Miniseries or TV Movie) Emmy. 2004: *Mitch Albom's The Five People You Meet in Heaven* (Best Male Actor in a Television Movie or Miniseries) SAG. 2006: *Pope John Paul II* (Best Actor in a Miniseries or TV Movie) Emmy. Tributes: 2001: Career Achievement Award from Board.

Volonté, Gian Maria

Movie: 1983: *La Mort de Mario Ricci (The Death of Mario Ricci)* (Best Actor) *Cannes*. 1987: *Il Caso Moro (The Moro Affair)* (Best Actor) *Berlin*. Tributes: 1991: Career Golden Lion from Venice.

Von Stroheim, Erich

Movie: 1938: *Grand Illusion* (Best Acting) *Board*. 1950: *Sunset Boulevard* (Best Supporting Actor) Academy, Globe. Tributes: 1953: Certificate of Merit for his great services to film as director and actor on the occasion of the revival of *Greed* and other of his films at The National Film Theatre from British.

Von Sydow, Max

Movie: 1966: *Hawaii* (Best Actor, Drama) Globe. 1973: *The Exorcist* (Best Supporting Actor) Globe. 1982: *Ingenjör Andrées luftfärd (Flight of the Eagle)* (Best Actor) *Venice*. 1988: *Pelle the Conqueror* (Best Actor) Academy. Television: 1990: *Red King, White Knight* (Best Supporting Actor in a Miniseries or Special) Emmy.

Wadham, Julian

Movie: 1996: *The English Patient* (Best Ensemble) SAG.

Wagner, Robert

Movie: 1952: *Stars and Stripes Forever* (New Star of the Year — Actor) Globe. **Television:** 1968–1970 series *It Takes a Thief* (Best Actor in a Drama Series) 1969: Globe. (Best Continued Performance by an Actor in a Leading Role in a Drama Series) 1970: Emmy. 1979–1984 series *Hart to Hart* (Best Actor in a Drama Series) 1979: Globe. 1980: Globe. 1982: Globe. 1983: Globe.

Wahlberg, Mark

Movie: 1997: *Boogie Nights* (Best Ensemble) SAG. 2006: *The Departed* (Best Supporting Actor) Academy, Globe, *Society* (Best Ensemble) *Board*, SAG, Broadcast. **Television:** 2004–present series *Entourage* (Best Comedy Series, Executive Producer) 2007: Emmy.

Waits, Tom

Movie: 1982: *One from the Heart* (Best Song Score) Academy. 1993: *Short Cuts* (Best Ensemble) *Venice* (special award).

Walbrook, Anton

Movie: 1942: *The Invaders* (Best Acting) *Board*.

Walken, Christopher

Movie: 1978: *The Deer Hunter* (Best Supporting Actor) *Academy, New York*, Globe, British. 2002: *Catch Me If You Can* (Best Male Actor in a Supporting Role) *SAG* (Best Supporting Actor) Academy, *British, Society*. 2007: *Hairspray* (Best Ensemble) SAG, *Broadcast*. **Theater:** 2000: *James Joyce's The Dead* (Best Actor, Musical) Tony. **Television:** 1991: *"Sarah, Plain and Tall," Hallmark Hall of Fame* (Best Actor in a Miniseries or Special) Emmy.

Walker, Robert, Jr.

Movie: 1963: *The Ceremony* (New Star of the Year — Actor) *Globe*.

Wallace, Paul

Movie: 1962: *Gypsy* (New Star of the Year — Actor) Globe.

Wallach, Eli

Movie: 1956: *Baby Doll* (Most Promising Newcomer) *British* (Best Supporting Actor) Globe. **Theater:** 1951: *The Rose Tattoo* (Best Supporting or Featured Actor, Dramatic) *Tony*. **Television:** 1967: *"The Poppy Is Also a Flower," Xerox Special* (Best Performance by an Actor in a Supporting Role in a Drama) *Emmy*. 1968: *"Dear Friends," CBS Play-*

house (Best Single Performance by an Actor in a Drama) Emmy. 1987: *Something in Common* (Best Supporting Actor in a Miniseries or Special) Emmy. 2007: *Studio 60 on the Sunset Strip* (Best Guest Actor in a Drama Series) Emmy. **Tributes:** 2006: Career Achievement Award from Board.

Walsh, J. T.

Movie: 1996: *Sling Blade* (Best Ensemble) SAG. **Television:** 1997: *Hope* (Best Supporting Actor in a Miniseries or TV Movie) Emmy.

Walsh, Kay

Movie: 1958: *The Horse's Mouth* (Best British Actress) British (Best Supporting Actress) *Board*.

Walsh, M. Emmet

Movie: 1985: *Blood Simple* (Best Male Lead) *Spirit*. **Records:** Walsh received the first Best Male Lead at the Independent Spirit awards for playing double-crossing private detective Loren Visser in *Blood Simple*, earning the film's only Spirit Award for acting.

Walter, Jessica

Movie: 1966: *Grand Prix* (New Star of the Year — Actress) Globe. 1971: *Play Misty for Me* (Best Actress, Drama) Globe. **Television:** 1975: *"Amy Prentiss," NBC Sunday Mystery Movie* (Best Actress in a Limited Series) *Emmy*. 1977: *The Streets of San Francisco* (Best Single Performance by an Actress in a Drama or Comedy Series) Emmy. 1979–1986 series *Trapper John, M. D.* (Best Supporting Actress in a Drama Series) 1980: Emmy. 2003–2006 series *Arrested Development* (Best Supporting Actress in a Comedy Series) 2005: Emmy. (Best Ensemble in a Comedy Series) 2004: SAG. 2005: SAG.

Walters, Julie

Movie: 1983: *Educating Rita* (Most Outstanding Newcomer to Film) British (Best Actress) Academy, *British* (Best Actress, Musical or Comedy) *Globe*. 1987: *Personal Services* (Best Actress) British. 1991: *Stepping Out* (Best Supporting Actress) British. 2000: *Billy Elliot* (Best Female Actor in a Supporting Role) SAG (Best Supporting Actress) Academy, Globe, *British*, Broadcast (Best Ensemble) SAG.

Walters, Melora

Movie: 1997: *Boogie Nights* (Best Ensemble) SAG. 1999: *Magnolia* (Best Ensemble) *Board*, SAG.

Wanamaker, Zoë

Movie: 1998: *Wilde* (Best Supporting Actress) British. **Theater:** 1981: *Piaf* (Best Actress in a Featured Role,

Play) Tony. 1986: *Loot* (Best Actress in a Featured Role, Play) Tony. 1999: *Electra* (Best Actress, Play) Tony. 2006: *Awake and Sing!* (Best Actress in a Featured Role, Play) Tony.

Ward, Fred

Movie: 1993: *Short Cuts* (Best Ensemble) *Venice* (special award).

Ward, Mary B.

Movie: 1991: *Hangin' with the Homeboys* (Best Supporting Female) Spirit.

Ward, Rachel

Movie: 1981: *Sharky's Machine* (New Star of the Year—Actor or Actress) Globe. Television: 1983: *The Thorn Birds* (Best Actress in a Miniseries or TV Movie) Globe. 2000: *On the Beach* (Best Actress in a Miniseries or TV Movie) Globe.

Ward, Simon

Movie: 1972: *Young Winston* (New Star of the Year—Actor) Globe (Most Promising Newcomer) British.

Warden, Jack

Movie: 1975: *Shampoo* (Best Supporting Actor) Academy, British. 1978: *Heaven Can Wait* (Best Supporting Actor) Academy. Television: 1972: *"Brian's Song," ABC Movie of the Week* (Best Performance by an Actor in a Supporting Role in Drama) *Emmy*. 1984–1986 series *Crazy Like a Fox* (Best Actor in a Comedy Series) 1985: Emmy. 1986: Emmy.

Warner, David

Movie: 1966: *Morgan! (Morgan: A Suitable Case for Treatment)* (Best British Actor) British. 1997: *Titanic* (Best Ensemble) SAG. Television: 1978: *"Holocaust"* (Best Continuing Performance by a Supporting Actor in a Drama Series) Emmy. 1981: *Masada* (Best Supporting Actor in a Limited Series or Special) *Emmy*.

Warner, H. B.

Movie: 1937: *Lost Horizon* (Best Supporting Actor) Academy.

Warner, Steven

Movie: 1974: *The Little Prince* (New Star of the Year—Actor) Globe.

Warren, Lesley Ann

Movie: 1982: *Victor/Victoria* (Best Supporting Actress) Academy, Globe. 1984: *Songwriter* (Best Supporting Actress) Globe. Television: 1977 series *79 Park Avenue* (Best Actress in a Drama Series) 1977: *Globe*. 1990: *Family of Spies* (Best Actress in a Miniseries or Special) Emmy (Best Actress in a Miniseries or TV Movie) Globe.

Washbourne, Mona

Movie: 1978: *Stevie* (Best Supporting Actress) *New York, Board*, Globe, British, *LA*. Theater: 1971: *Home* (Best Supporting or Featured Actress, Dramatic) Tony. Highlights: Washbourne won her awards for *Stevie* three years apart. When the film was released in Los Angeles in 1978, Washbourne nabbed the Best Supporting Actress prize from the L.A. Film Critics and vied for the Golden Globe in a race ultimately won by Dyan Cannon for *Heaven Can Wait*. Distribution troubles for *Stevie* kept it in vaults for three years. When it finally opened throughout the U.S. in 1981, the New York Film Critics and the National Board of Review concurred with the L.A. critics, bestowing Best Supporting Actress accolades on Washbourne in one of the lengthiest winning streaks for a single performance in film history.

Washington, Denzel

Movie: 1987: *Cry Freedom* (Best Actor, Drama) Globe (Best Supporting Actor) Academy. 1989: *Glory* (Best Supporting Actor) *Academy*, *Globe*. 1992: *Malcolm X* (Best Actor) Academy, *New York*, *Berlin* (Best Actor, Drama) Globe. 1999: *The Hurricane* (Best Actor) Academy, *Berlin* (Best Actor, Drama) *Globe* (Best Male Actor in a Leading Role) SAG. 2001: *Training Day* (Best Actor) *Academy*, *LA* (Best Male Actor in a Leading Role) SAG (Best Actor, Drama) Globe. 2007: *American Gangster* (Best Actor, Drama) Globe (Best Ensemble) SAG; *The Great Debaters* (Best Picture, Drama; Producer) Globe. Television: 1995: *Hank Aaron: Chasing the Dream* (Best Information Special, Executive Producer) Emmy. 2001: *Half Past Autumn: The Life and Works of Gordon Parks* (Best Non-Fiction Informational Special, Producer) Emmy. Records: Winning the Best Actor Academy Award for *Training Day* in 2001 made Washington a record-setter twice over. He became the first African-American to win two acting Academy Awards and to win both a leading and supporting Oscar. Only nine other actors have achieved the dual category wins: five women (Helen Hayes, Ingrid Bergman, Maggie Smith, Meryl Streep and Jessica Lange) and four men (Jack Lemmon, Robert De Niro, Jack Nicholson and Gene Hackman). Highlights: Washington played a pivotal part in making Oscar history in 2001 when he and two other stars became the first three African-American actors to receive Academy Awards in a single night. Early in the evening, Sidney Poitier was heralded with a special award in recognition of his remarkable accomplishments as an artist and as a human being. Later that evening, Halle Berry of *Monster's Ball* made Oscar history by becoming the first African-American to win the Best Actress race. As the evening reached its climax, Washington was voted Best Actor for his memorable work as Alonzo Harris, a brutal police detective who overestimates his power in *Training Day*. At the podium, he smiled up at Poitier in the balcony and told him he'd always be proud to follow in Poitier's footsteps.

Washington, Kerry

Movie: 2001: *Lift* (Best Female Lead) Spirit. 2004: *Ray* (Best Ensemble) SAG.

Wasson, Craig

Movie: 1981: *Four Friends* (New Star of the Year — Actor or Actress) Globe.

Watanabe, Ken

Movie: 2003: *The Last Samurai* (Best Male Actor in a Supporting Role) SAG (Best Supporting Actor) Academy, Globe, Broadcast.

Waters, Ethel

Movie: 1949: *Pinky* (Best Supporting Actress) Academy. Television: 1962: *Route 66* (Best Single Performance by an Actress in a Leading Role) Emmy.

Waterston, Sam

Movie: 1974: *The Great Gatsby* (New Star of the Year — Actor) Globe (Best Supporting Actor) Globe. 1984: *The Killing Fields* (Best Actor) Academy, British (Best Actor, Drama) Globe. Theater: 1994: *Abe Lincoln in Illinois* (Best Actor, Play) Tony. Television: 1974: *The Glass Menagerie* (Best Supporting Actor in Drama) Emmy. 1982: *Oppenheimer* (Best Actor in a Miniseries or TV Movie) Globe. 1991–1993 series *I'll Fly Away* (Best Actor in a Drama Series) 1992: Emmy, Globe. 1993: Emmy, Globe. 1994: *I'll Fly Away: Then and Now* (Best Actor in a Miniseries or Special) Emmy. 1996: *Time Life's Lost Civilizations* (Best Informational Series, Host) *Emmy*. 1994–present series *Law & Order* (Best Actor in a Drama Series) 1995: Globe. 1997: Emmy. 1999: Emmy. 2000: Emmy. (Best Male Actor in a Drama Series) 1997: SAG. 1998: *SAG*. (Best Ensemble in a Drama Series) 1994: SAG. 1995: SAG. 1996: SAG. 1997: SAG. 1998: SAG. 1999: SAG. 2000: SAG. 2001: SAG. 2003: SAG.

Watson, Alberta

Movie: 1997: *The Sweet Hereafter* (Best Ensemble) Board.

Watson, Emily

Movie: 1996: *Breaking the Waves* (Best New Generation) *LA* (Best Actress) Academy, *New York*, British, *Society* (Best Actress, Drama) Globe. 1998: *Hilary and Jackie* (Best Actress) Academy, British (Best Actress, Drama) Globe (Best Female Actor in a Leading Role) SAG. 1999: *Angela's Ashes* (Best Actress) British. 2001: *Gosford Park* (Best Ensemble) *SAG, Broadcast*. Television: 2004: *The Life and Death of Peter Sellers* (Best Supporting Actress in a Series, Miniseries, or TV Movie) Globe.

Watson, Emma

Movie: 2004: *Harry Potter and the Prisoner of Azkaban* (Best Young Actress) Broadcast. 2005: *Harry Potter and the Goblet of Fire* (Best Young Actress) Broadcast.

Watson, Lucile

Movie: 1943: *Watch on the Rhine* (Best Supporting Actress) Academy.

Watts, Naomi

Movie: 2001: *Mulholland Drive* (Breakthrough Performance — Female) *Board* (Best Actress) *Society*. 2003: *21 Grams* (Best Actress) Academy, *Venice* (multiple win), British, *LA*, *Spirit* (special award shared with costars), Broadcast (Best Female Actor in a Leading Role) SAG; *Le Divorce* (Best Actress) *Venice* (multiple win).

Wayne, John

Movie: 1949: *Sands of Iwo Jima* (Best Actor) Academy. 1960: *The Alamo* (Best Picture, Producer) Academy. 1969: *True Grit* (Best Actor) *Academy* (Best Actor, Drama) *Globe*. Tributes: 1952: Henrietta Award for World Film Favorite from Globe. 1965: Cecil B. DeMille Award from Globe. 1999: Ranked Number 13 on List of 25 Greatest Male Screen Legends of the 20th Century from American Film Institute.

Wayne, Patrick

Movie: 1957: *The Searchers* (New Star of the Year — Actor) *Globe*.

Weaver, Sigourney

Movie: 1979: *Alien* (Most Promising Newcomer) British. 1986: *Aliens* (Best Actress) Academy (Best Actress, Drama) Globe. 1988: *Gorillas in the Mist* (Best Actress) Academy (Best Actress, Drama) *Globe*; *Working Girl* (Best Supporting Actress) Academy, *Globe*, British. 1997: *The Ice Storm* (Best Supporting

Actress) Globe, *British*. 1999: ***A Map of the World*** (Best Actress, Drama) Globe. **Theater:** 1985: ***Hurlyburly*** (Best Actress in a Featured Role, Play) Tony. **Television:** 1997: ***Snow White: A Tale of Terror*** (Best Actress in a Miniseries or TV Movie) Emmy (Best Female Actor in a Television Movie or Miniseries) SAG. **Records:** Weaver broke three award records in 1988: one an anomaly, one an achievement, and one a disappointment. At that year's Golden Globes, Weaver shared the first three-way tie in any category. Weaver's work as anthropologist Dian Fossey in ***Gorillas in the Mist*** took the Best Actress, Drama prize along with Jodie Foster in ***The Accused*** and Shirley MacLaine as ***Madame Sousatzka***. That night, Weaver also won Best Supporting Actress for her performance as Melanie Griffith's heartless boss in ***Working Girl***, making Weaver the first person in Globe history to win a lead and supporting award in a single year. The Oscar record she broke that year stands as one of most unfortunate records in Academy Award history. When she was nominated for Best Actress for ***Gorillas in the Mist*** and Best Supporting Actress for ***Working Girl***, she became only the fifth star to be nominated in both categories in one year. Before her, every star competing in both categories lost the lead actor race but took home the supporting prize. Pundits expected Weaver to follow the pattern and go home a winner. Instead, two dark horse nominees won both actress prizes. Geena Davis was named Best Supporting Actress for ***The Accidental Tourist*** and, in a Best Actress race dominated by Glenn Close (***Dangerous Liaisons***), Meryl Streep (***A Cry in the Dark***) and Weaver, Jodie Foster came from behind to win the award as a woman gang raped in ***The Accused***. Interviewed afterward, Weaver said she was especially disappointed to lose because she had brought with her to the award ceremony both her parents, former NBC President Sylvester "Pat" Weaver and actress Elizabeth Inglis.

Weaving, Hugo

Movie: 2001: ***The Lord of the Rings: The Fellowship of the Ring*** (Best Ensemble) SAG. 2002: ***The Lord of the Rings: The Two Towers*** (Best Ensemble) SAG. 2003: ***The Lord of the Rings: The Return of the King*** (Best Ensemble) *Board, SAG, Broadcast*.

Webb, Chloe

Movie: 1986: ***Sid and Nancy*** (Best Actress) *Society*. **Television:** 1989: ***China Beach*** (Best Guest Actress in a Drama Series) Emmy.

Webb, Clifton

Movie: 1944: ***Laura*** (Best Supporting Actor) Academy. 1946: ***The Razor's Edge*** (Best Supporting Actor) Academy, *Globe*. 1948: ***Sitting Pretty*** (Best Actor) Academy. 1952: ***Stars and Stripes Forever*** (Best Actor, Musical or Comedy) Globe.

Wedgeworth, Ann

Movie: 1977: ***Handle with Care*** (Best Supporting Actress) *Society*. **Theater:** 1978: ***Chapter Two*** (Best Actress in a Featured Role, Play) *Tony*.

Wei, Tang

Movie: 2007: ***Lust, Caution*** (Best Female Lead) Spirit.

Weisz, Rachel

Movie: 2005: ***The Constant Gardner*** (Best Actress) British (Best Female Actor in a Supporting Role) *SAG* (Best Supporting Actress) *Academy, Globe, Broadcast*.

Welch, Joseph N.

Movie: 1959: ***Anatomy of a Murder*** (Most Promising Newcomer) British (Best Supporting Actor) Globe.

Welch, Raquel

Movie: 1973: ***The Three Musketeers*** (Best Actress, Musical or Comedy) *Globe*. **Television:** 1987: ***Right to Die*** (Best Actress in a Miniseries or TV Movie) Globe. **Highlights:** Welch exploded into stardom as a tattered bikini clad cave woman in ***One Million Years B.C.*** (not the year, but the British film released in 1966). Her sex symbol status caused her to struggle for due credit as a serious actress, but her performance as the dimwitted, pratfalling Constance de Bonancieux in the comic spoof of Alexander Dumas' classic, ***The Three Musketeers*** earned her a Golden Globe. At the podium, tearfully delighted Welch poked good natured fun at her uphill climb to respectability by saying she'd been waiting for the award since ***One Million Years B.C.*** The crowd loved it.

Weld, Tuesday

Movie: 1959: ***The Five Pennies*** (New Star of the Year — Actress) *Globe*. 1972: ***Play It As It Lays*** (Best Actress, Drama) Globe. 1977: ***Looking for Mr. Goodbar*** (Best Supporting Actress) Academy. 1984: ***Once Upon a Time in America*** (Best Supporting Actress) British. **Television:** 1984: ***"John Steinbeck's The Winter of Our Discontent," Hallmark Hall of Fame*** (Best Supporting Actress in a Limited Series or Special) Emmy.

Welland, Colin

Movie: 1969: *Kes* (Best Supporting Actor) *British*.

Weller, Peter

Movie: 1993: *Partners* (Best Live Action Short Film) Academy. 2002: *ivans xtc.* (Best Supporting Male) Spirit.

Welles, Gwen

Movie: 1975: *Nashville* (Best Supporting Actress) British.

Welles, Orson

Movie: 1941: *Citizen Kane* (Best Acting) *Board* (Best Actor) Academy (Best Director) Academy (Best Picture, Producer) Academy, *New York, Board* (Best Original Screenplay) *Academy*. 1952: *Othello* (Best Picture, Director) *Cannes* (special Grand Prix award). 1959: *Compulsion* (Best Actor) *Cannes* (win shared with costars). 1966: *Chimes at Midnight* (Best Actor) British. 1981: *Butterfly* (Best Supporting Actor) Globe. Tributes: 1970: Career Golden Lion from Venice; Honorary Oscar statuette for superlative artistry and versatility in the creation of motion pictures from Academy. 1975: Life Achievement Award from American Film Institute. 1978: Career Achievement Award from LA. 1999: Ranked Number 16 on AFI's List of 25 Male Screen Legends from American Film Institute. **Records:** For his instant classic, **Citizen Kane**, Welles became the first person to receive four separate Oscar nominations for a single film. He won one, sharing the Best Screenplay honors with co-writer Herman J. Mankiewicz.

Welliver, Titus

Movie: 2007: *Gone Baby Gone* (Best Ensemble) Broadcast.

Wenham, David

Movie: 2002: *The Lord of the Rings: The Two Towers* (Best Ensemble) SAG. 2003: *The Lord of the Rings: The Return of the King* (Best Ensemble) *Board, SAG, Broadcast*.

Werner, Oskar

Movie: 1965: *Ship of Fools* (Best Actor) Academy, *New York* (Best Foreign Actor) British (Best Actor, Drama) Globe; *The Spy Who Came In from the Cold* (Best Foreign Actor) British (Best Supporting Actor) *Globe*. 1976: *Voyage of the Damned* (Best Supporting Actor) Globe.

Wessely, Paula

Movie: 1935: *Episode* (Best Actress) *Venice*.

West, Dominic

Movie: 2002: *Chicago* (Best Ensemble) *SAG, Broadcast*.

West, Mae

Tributes: 1999: Ranked Number 15 on List of 25 Greatest Female Screen Legends of the 20th Century from American Film Institute.

West, Samuel

Movie: 1992: *Howards End* (Best Supporting Actor) British.

Weston, Celia

Movie: 1995: *Dead Man Walking* (Best Supporting Female) Spirit. 2001: *In the Bedroom* (Best Ensemble) SAG. Theater: 1997: *The Last Night of Ballyhoo* (Best Actress in a Featured Role, Play) Tony.

Weston, Jack

Movie: 1976: *The Ritz* (Best Actor, Musical or Comedy) Globe. Theater: 1981: *The Floating Light Bulb* (Best Actor, Play) Tony.

Whishaw, Ben

Movie: 2007: *I'm Not There* (Best Ensemble) *Spirit* (special award).

Whitaker, Forest

Movie: 1988: *Bird* (Best Actor) *Cannes* (Best Actor, Drama) Globe. 1994: *Prêt-à-Porter (Ready-to-Wear)* (Best Ensemble) *Board*. 2006: *American Gun* (Best Male Lead) Spirit; *The Last King of Scotland* (Best Actor) *Academy, New York, Board, British, Society, LA, Broadcast* (Best Actor, Drama) *Globe* (Best Male Actor in a Leading Role) SAG. Television: 1994: *The Enemy Within* (Best Male Actor in a Television Movie or Miniseries) SAG. 2003: *Deacons for Defense* (Best Male Actor in a Television Movie or Miniseries) SAG; *Door to Door* (Best TV Movie, Co-Executive Producer) *Emmy*. 2007: *ER* (Best Guest Actor in a Drama Series) Emmy.

White, Mike

Movie: 2000: *Chuck & Buck* (Best Debut Performance) Spirit.

Whitelaw, Billie

Movie: 1960: *Hell Is a City* (Most Promising Newcomer) British. 1968: *Charlie Bubbles* (Best

Supporting Actress) *British* (multiple win), *Society*; ***Twisted Nerve*** (Best Supporting Actress) *British* (multiple win). 1976: ***The Omen*** (Best Supporting Actress) British. 1990: ***The Krays*** (Best Supporting Actress) British.

Whiteley, Jon

Tributes: 1954: Honorary miniature Oscar statuette for his outstanding juvenile performance in ***The Little Kidnappers*** from Academy.

Whiting, Leonard

Movie: 1968: ***Romeo and Juliet*** (New Star of the Year — Actor) *Globe.*

Whitman, Stuart

Movie: 1961: ***The Mark*** (Best Actor) Academy.

Whitmore, James

Movie: 1949: ***Battleground*** (Best Supporting Actor) Academy, *Globe.* 1975: ***Give 'Em Hell, Harry!*** (Best Actor) Academy (Best Actor, Drama) Globe. **Theater:** 1948: ***Command Decision*** (Best Performance by a Newcomer) *Tony.* **Television:** 2000: ***The Practice*** (Best Guest Actor in a Drama Series) *Emmy.* 2003: ***Mister Sterling*** (Best Guest Actor in a Drama Series) Emmy. **Records:** Receiving Golden Globe and Oscar nods for a taped version of his one-man stage show, ***Give 'Em Hell, Harry*** made Whitmore the first actor to be so honored for a film where he was the only actor to appear on screen.

Whitty, Dame May

Movie: 1937: ***Night Must Fall*** (Best Acting) *Board* (Best Supporting Actress) Academy. 1942: ***Mrs. Miniver*** (Best Supporting Actress) Academy.

Widmark, Richard

Movie: 1947: ***Kiss of Death*** (New Star of the Year — Actor) *Globe* (Best Supporting Actor) Academy. **Television:** 1971: ***"Vanished," World Premiere NBC Monday and Tuesday Night at the Movies*** (Best Single Performance by an Actor in a Leading Role) Emmy. **Tributes:** 2005: Career Achievement Award from LA. **Records:** In 1947, ***Kiss of Death***'s Widmark became the first actor to be named New Male Star of the Year by the Foreign Press Association, which added awards for male and female screen novices five years into their awarding Golden Globes. They didn't give New Star awards the following year, but resumed them in 1949 and continued giving them through 1982.

Wieman, Mathias

Movie: 1937: ***The Eternal Mask*** (Best Acting) *Board.*

Wiest, Dianne

Movie: 1986: ***Hannah and Her Sisters*** (Best Supporting Actress) *Academy, New York, Board,* Globe, *Society.* 1987: ***Radio Days*** (Best Supporting Actress) British. 1989: ***Parenthood*** (Best Supporting Actress) Academy, Globe. 1994: ***Bullets Over Broadway*** (Best Female Actor in a Supporting Role) *SAG* (Best Supporting Actress) *Academy, New York, Globe, Society, LA* (Best Supporting Female) *Spirit.* 1996: ***The Birdcage*** (Best Ensemble) *SAG.* **Television:** 1997: ***Avonlea (Road to Avonlea*** or ***Tales of Avonlea)*** (Best Guest Actress in a Drama Series) *Emmy.* 1999: ***The Simple Life of Noah Dearborn*** (Best Supporting Actress in a Miniseries or TV Movie) Emmy. 2000–2002 series ***Law & Order*** (Best Ensemble in a Drama Series) 2000: SAG. 2001: SAG. **Records:** Wiest is the first actor to win two SAG awards for different movie performances. In 1994 she won the Best Supporting Actress SAG as part of the sweep she made of nearly all awards in that category for ***Bullets Over Broadway.*** Two years later she played Louise Keeley in ***The Birdcage*** and shared a Best Ensemble SAG award with co-stars including Robin Williams, Nathan Lane, and Gene Hackman.

Wiig, Steven

Movie: 2007: ***Into the Wild*** (Best Ensemble) SAG.

Wilby, James

Movie: 1987: ***Maurice*** (Best Actor) *Venice* (win shared with costar). 2001: ***Gosford Park*** (Best Ensemble) *SAG, Broadcast.*

Wild, Jack

Movie: 1968: ***Oliver!*** (New Star of the Year — Actor) Globe (Most Promising Newcomer) British (Best Supporting Actor) Academy.

Wilde, Cornel

Movie: 1945: ***A Song to Remember*** (Best Actor) Academy.

Wilder, Gene

Movie: 1968: ***The Producers*** (Best Supporting Actor) Academy. 1971: ***Willy Wonka and the Chocolate Factory*** (Best Actor, Musical or Comedy) Globe. 1974: ***Young Frankenstein*** (Best Adapted Screenplay) Academy. 1976: ***Silver Streak*** (Best Actor, Musical or Comedy) Globe. **Television:** 2003: ***Will & Grace*** (Best Guest Actor in a Comedy Series) *Emmy.*

Wilkinson, Tom

Movie: 1995: *Sense and Sensibility* (Best Ensemble) SAG. 1997: *The Full Monty* (Best Supporting Actor) *British* (Best Ensemble) *SAG*. 1998: *Shakespeare in Love* (Best Supporting Actor) British (Best Ensemble) *SAG*. 2001: *In the Bedroom* (Best Actor) Academy, *New York*, British (Best Male Lead) *Spirit* (Best Male Actor in a Leading Role) SAG (Best Ensemble) SAG. 2007: *Michael Clayton* (Best Male Actor in a Supporting Role) SAG (Best Supporting Actor) Academy, Globe, British, Broadcast. **Television:** 2003: *Normal* (Best Actor in a Miniseries or TV Movie) Emmy, Globe.

Willard, Fred

Movie: 2003: *A Mighty Wind* (Best Screenplay) Spirit (Best Ensemble) Broadcast. **Television:** 2003–2005 series *Everybody Loves Raymond* (Best Guest Actor in a Comedy Series) 2003: Emmy. 2004: Emmy. 2005: Emmy.

Williams, Billy Dee

Movie: 2000: *The Visit* (Best Supporting Male) Spirit. **Television:** 1972: *"Brian's Song," ABC Movie of the Week* (Best Single Performance by an Actor in a Leading Role) Emmy.

Williams, Cara

Movie: 1958: *The Defiant Ones* (Best Supporting Actress) Academy, Globe. **Television:** 1960–1962 series *Pete and Gladys* (Best Continued Performance by an Actress in a Series—Lead) 1962: Emmy.

Williams, Cindy

Movie: 1973: *American Graffiti* (Best Supporting Actress) British. **Television:** 1976–1982 series *Laverne and Shirley* (Best Actress in a Comedy Series) 1977: Globe.

Williams, Clarence, III

Movie: 2007: *American Gangster* (Best Ensemble) SAG. **Theater:** 1965: *Slow Dance on the Killing Ground* (Best Supporting or Featured Actor, Dramatic) Tony.

Williams, Cynda

Movie: 1992: *One False Move* (Best Female Lead) Spirit.

Williams, Cyndi

Movie: 2005: *Room* (Best Female Lead) Spirit.

Williams, Darnell

Movie: 1993: *Short Cuts* (Best Ensemble) *Venice* (special award). **Television:** 1981–1988, 2008–present series *All My Children* (Best Supporting Actor in a Daytime Drama) 1982: Emmy. 1983: *Emmy*. (Best Actor in a Daytime Drama) 1985: *Emmy*.

Williams, Esther

Tributes: 1951: Henrietta Award for World Film Favorite from Globe. 1955: Hollywood Citizenship Award from Globe.

Williams, John

Movie: 1954: *Dial M for Murder* (Best Supporting Actor) *Board* (multiple win); *Sabrina* (Best Supporting Actor) *Board* (multiple win). **Theater:** 1953: *Dial M for Murder* (Best Supporting or Featured Actor, Dramatic) *Tony*.

Williams, Mark

Movie: 1998: *Shakespeare in Love* (Best Ensemble) *SAG*.

Williams, Michelle

Movie: 2003: *The Station Agent* (Best Ensemble) SAG. 2005: *Brokeback Mountain* (Best Female Actor in a Supporting Role) SAG (Best Supporting Actress) Academy, Globe, British, *Broadcast* (Best Supporting Female) Spirit (Best Ensemble) SAG. 2006: *Land of Plenty* (Best Female Lead) Spirit. 2007: *I'm Not There* (Best Ensemble) *Spirit* (special award).

Williams, Robin

Movie: 1984: *Moscow on the Hudson* (Best Actor, Musical or Comedy) Globe. 1987: *Good Morning, Vietnam* (Best Actor) Academy, British (Best Actor, Musical or Comedy) *Globe*. 1989: *Dead Poets Society* (Best Actor) Academy, British (Best Actor, Drama) Globe. 1990: *Awakenings* (Best Actor) *Board* (Best Actor, Drama) Globe. 1991: *The Fisher King* (Best Actor) Academy (Best Actor, Musical or Comedy) *Globe*. 1993: *Mrs. Doubtfire* (Best Actor, Musical or Comedy) *Globe*. 1996: *The Birdcage* (Best Ensemble) *SAG*. 1997: *Good Will Hunting* (Best Male Actor in a Supporting Role) *SAG* (Best Supporting Actor) *Academy*, Globe (Best Ensemble) SAG. 1998: *Patch Adams* (Best Actor, Musical or Comedy) Globe. 2002: *One Hour Photo* (Best Actor) Broadcast. **Television:** 1978–1982 series *Mork & Mindy* (Best Actor in a Comedy Series) 1979: Emmy. (Best Actor in a Series, Musical or Comedy) 1979: *Globe*. 1980: Globe. 1987: *A Carol Burnett Special: Carol, Carl, Whoopi & Robin* (Best Individual Performance in a Variety or Music Program) *Emmy*. 1988: *ABC Presents a Royal Gala* (Best Individual Performance in a Variety or Music Program) *Emmy*.

1994: *Homicide: Life on the Street* (Best Guest Actor in a Drama Series) Emmy. 1996: *Comic Relief VII* (Best Performance in a Variety or Music Program, Host) Emmy. 2003: *Robin Williams: Live on Broadway* (Best Individual Performance in a Variety or Music Program) Emmy (Best Writing of a Variety or Music or Comedy Program) Emmy. **Tributes:** 1992: Special award from Board; Special Achievement award for *Aladdin* from Globe. 2004: Cecil B. DeMille Award from Globe. **Records:** Williams is the first actor to win a SAG as part of an ensemble first and then win an individual SAG. In 1996, he and the cast of *The Birdcage* won Best Ensemble. The following year he took home the Best Supporting Actor SAG for his role of psychology professor Sean McGuire in *Good Will Hunting*.

Williams, Saul

Movie: 1998: *Slam* (Best Debut Performance) Spirit.

Williams, Treat

Movie: 1979: *Hair* (New Star of the Year — Actor) Globe. 1981: *Prince of the City* (Best Actor, Drama) Globe. 1985: *Smooth Talk* (Best Male Lead) Spirit. **Television:** 1984: *A Streetcar Named Desire* (Best Actor in a Miniseries or TV Movie) Globe. 1996: *The Late Shift* (Best Supporting Actor in a Miniseries or Special) Emmy. 2002–2006 series *Everwood* (Best Actor in a Drama Series) 2002: SAG. 2003: SAG.

Williamson, Nicol

Movie: 1968: *The Bofors Gun* (Best Actor) British. 1969: *Inadmissible Evidence* (Best Actor) British. **Theater:** 1966: *Inadmissible Evidence* (Best Actor, Dramatic) Tony. 1974: *Uncle Vanya* (Best Actor, Dramatic) Tony.

Willingham, Noble

Movie: 1999: *The Corndog Man* (Best Male Lead) Spirit.

Willis, Bruce

Movie: 1989: *In Country* (Best Supporting Actor) Globe. 2004: *Ocean's Twelve* (Best Ensemble) Broadcast. 2005: *Sin City* (Best Ensemble) Broadcast. **Television:** 1985–1989 series *Moonlighting* (Best Actor in a Drama Series) 1986: Emmy. 1987: *Emmy.* (Best Actor in a Series, Musical or Comedy) 1986: Globe. 1987: *Globe.* 1988: Globe. 2000: *Friends* (Best Guest Actor in a Comedy Series) *Emmy.*

Wills, Chill

Movie: 1960: *The Alamo* (Best Supporting Actor) Academy.

Wilson, Elizabeth

Movie: 1956: *Patterns of Power* (Most Promising Newcomer) British. **Theater:** 1972: *Sticks and Bones* (Best Supporting or Featured Actress, Dramatic) Tony. **Television:** 1987: *Nutcracker: Money, Madness, & Murder* (Best Supporting Actress in a Miniseries or Special) Emmy.

Wilson, George

Movie: 1962: *The Long Absence* (Best Foreign Actor) British.

Wilson, Luke

Movie: 2001: *The Royal Tenenbaums* (Best Ensemble) Broadcast. 2007: *3:10 to Yuma* (Best Ensemble) SAG.

Wilson, Owen

Movie: 2001: *The Royal Tenenbaums* (Best Ensemble) Broadcast (Best Original Screenplay) Academy. 2004: *The Life Aquatic with Steve Zissou* (Best Ensemble) Broadcast.

Wilson, Scott

Movie: 1980: *The Ninth Configuration* (*Twinkle, Twinkle, "Killer" Kane*) (Best Supporting Actor) Globe.

Wimbush, Mary

Movie: 1969: *Oh! What a Lovely War* (Best Supporting Actress) British.

Windsor, Barbara

Movie: 1963: *Sparrows Can't Sing* (Best British Actress) British. **Theater:** 1965: *Oh! What a Lovely War* (Best Supporting or Featured Actress, Musical) Tony.

Winfield, Paul

Movie: 1972: *Sounder* (Best Actor) Academy. **Television:** 1978: *King* (Best Actor in a Limited Series or Special) Emmy. 1979: *Roots: The Next Generation* (Best Supporting Actor in a Limited Series or Special) Emmy. 1995: *Picket Fences* (Best Guest Actor in a Drama Series) *Emmy.*

Winfrey, Oprah

Movie: 1985: *The Color Purple* (Best Supporting Actress) Academy, Globe. 2007: *The Great Debaters* (Best Picture, Drama; Producer) Globe. **Theater:** 2006: *The Color Purple* (Best Musical, Producer) Tony. **Television:** 1986–1999* *The Oprah Winfrey*

Show (Best Talk/Service Show Host) 1987: *Emmy.* 1988: Emmy. 1991: Emmy. 1992: *Emmy.* 1994: *Emmy.* 1995: *Emmy.* 1998: *Emmy.* (Best Talk/Service Show, Producer) 1987: *Emmy.* 1988: *Emmy.* 1989: *Emmy.* 1991: Emmy. 1992: *Emmy.* 1994: *Emmy.* 1995: *Emmy.* 1996: *Emmy.* 1997: *Emmy.* 1998: *Emmy.* 1989: *The Women of Brewster Place* (Best Miniseries, Executive Producer) Emmy. 1993: *ABC Afterschool Specials* (Best Individual Achievement in Children's Programming, Producer) *Emmy*; *Michael Jackson Talks ... to Oprah, 90 Primetime Minutes* (Best Information Special, Executive Producer) Emmy; *"Shades of a Single Protein," ABC Afterschool Special* (Best Children's Special, Producer) *Emmy.* 1999: *"Tuesdays with Morrie," Oprah Winfrey Presents* (Best Made-for-Television Movie, Executive Producer) *Emmy.* 2001: *A Prayer for America: Yankee Stadium Memorial* (Best Special Class Program, Producer) *Emmy.* **Tributes:** 1994: Television Hall of Fame Inductee from Emmy. 1998: Lifetime Achievement Award from Emmy. 2002: Bob Hope Humanitarian Award from Emmy.

*Although the span of *The Oprah Winfrey Show* is 1986–present, in 1999 Winfrey took herself out of Emmy competition for the show, and then withdrew the program from Emmy eligibility the following year. Consequently, the span of years above indicates those that Winfrey was eligible to be nominated for and win awards for this program.

Winger, Debra

Movie: 1980: *Urban Cowboy* (New Star of the Year — Actress) Globe (Most Promising Newcomer) British (Best Supporting Actress) Globe. 1982: *An Officer and a Gentleman* (Best Actress) Academy (Best Actress, Drama) Globe. 1983: *Terms of Endearment* (Best Actress) Academy, *Society* (Best Actress, Drama) Globe. 1993: *A Dangerous Woman* (Best Actress, Drama) Globe; *Shadowlands* (Best Actress) Academy, British. **Television:** 2005: *Dawn Anna* (Best Actress in a Miniseries or TV Movie) Emmy.

Winkler, Henry

Movie: 1977: *Heroes* (Best Actor, Drama) Globe. 1982: *Night Shift* (Best Actor, Musical or Comedy) Globe. **Television:** 1974–1984 series *Happy Days* (Best Actor in a Comedy Series) 1976: Emmy. 1977: Emmy. 1978: Emmy. (Best Actor in a Series, Musical or Comedy) 1976: *Globe.* 1977: *Globe.* 1979: *Who Are the Debolts—And Where Did They Get 19 Kids?* (Best Information Program, Executive Producer) Emmy. 1985: *"All the Kids Do It," CBS Schoolbreak Special* (Outstanding Children's Special, Producer) *Emmy.* 2000: *The Practice* (Best Guest Actor in a Drama Series) Emmy. 2003–present series *Clifford's*

Puppy Days (Best Performer in an Animated Program) 2003: Emmy. 2004: *Emmy.*

Winn, Kitty

Movie: 1971: *Panic in Needle Park* (Best Actress) *Cannes.*

Winningham, Mare

Movie: 1989: *Miracle Mile* (Best Supporting Female) Spirit. 1995: *Georgia* (Best Female Actor in a Supporting Role) SAG (Best Supporting Actress) Academy (Best Supporting Female) *Spirit.* **Television:** 1980: *Amber Waves* (Best Supporting Actress in a Limited Series or Special) *Emmy.* 1986: *"Love Is Never Silent," Hallmark Hall of Fame* (Best Actress in a Miniseries or Special) Emmy. 1996: *"The Boys Next Door," Hallmark Hall of Fame* (Best Supporting Actress in a Miniseries or Special) Emmy. 1997: *George Wallace* (Best Female Actor in a Television Movie or Miniseries) SAG (Best Supporting Actress in a Miniseries or TV Movie) *Emmy* (Best Supporting Actress in a Series, Miniseries, or TV Movie) Globe. 2004: *Law & Order: Special Victims Unit* (Best Guest Actress in a Drama Series) Emmy.

Winslet, Kate

Movie: 1995: *Sense and Sensibility* (Best Female Actor in a Supporting Role) *SAG* (Best Supporting Actress) Academy, Globe, *British* (Best Ensemble) SAG. 1997: *Titanic* (Best Actress) Academy (Best Actress, Drama) Globe (Best Female Actor in a Leading Role) SAG (Best Ensemble) SAG. 2000: *Quills* (Best Female Actor in a Supporting Role) SAG (Best Supporting Actress) Broadcast. 2001: *Iris* (Best Supporting Actress) Academy, Globe, British, *LA.* 2004: *Eternal Sunshine of the Spotless Mind* (Best Actress) Academy, British, Broadcast (Best Actress, Musical or Comedy) Globe (Best Female Actor in a Leading Role) SAG; *Finding Neverland* (Best Actress) British (Best Supporting Actress) Broadcast (Best Ensemble) SAG. 2006: *Little Children* (Best Actress) Academy, British, Broadcast (Best Actress, Drama) Globe (Best Female Actor in a Leading Role) SAG. **Television:** 2006: *Extras* (Best Guest Actress in a Comedy Series) Emmy. **Records:** When Winslet received her second Academy Award nomination for *Titanic* at the age of 21, she became the first person to earn two Oscar nods at so young an age. Since then, she has broken her own record with every subsequent nomination. With *Iris* she became the youngest person with three nominations, with *Eternal Sunshine of the Spotless Mind* the youngest person with four (reaching that milestone while still in her twenties), and with *Little Children*, the youngest person with five. She is also the only actor to be nominated twice for playing a character also portrayed by another Oscar nominee from the same film. In 1997, Winslet was up for Best Actress as young Rose in **Titanic** while co-star Gloria Stuart was up for Supporting Actress as Rose at age 101. Four years later, Winslet vied for Best Supporting Actress for **Iris** playing author Iris Murdock in her youth while co-star Judi Dench was up for Best Actress as the same character later in life as she succumbs to Alzheimer's disease.

Winslow, George

Tributes: 1952: Special award nomination for Best Juvenile Performance for **My Pal Gus** from Globe.

Winstead, Mary Elizabeth

Movie: 2006: **Bobby** (Best Ensemble) SAG, Broadcast.

Winstone, Ray

Movie: 1979: **That Summer** (Most Promising Newcomer) British. 1997: **Nil by Mouth** (Best Actor) British. 2001: **Last Orders** (Best Ensemble) **Board.** 2006: **The Departed** (Best Ensemble) **Board,** SAG, Broadcast.

Winter, Vincent

Tributes: 1954: Honorary miniature Oscar statuette for his outstanding juvenile performance in **The Little Kidnappers** from Academy.

Winters, Jonathan

Movie: 1963: **It's a Mad, Mad, Mad, Mad World** (Best Actor, Musical or Comedy) Globe. **Television:** 1991–1992 series **Davis Rules** (Best Supporting Actor in a Comedy Series) 1991: **Emmy.** 2002: **Life with Bonnie** (Best Guest Actor in a Comedy Series) Emmy.

Winters, Shelley

Movie: 1951: **A Place in the Sun** (Best Actress) Academy (Best Actress, Drama) Globe. 1954: **Executive Suite** (Best Ensemble) **Venice** (special award). 1959: **The Diary of Anne Frank** (Best Supporting Actress) **Academy,** Globe. 1962: **Lolita** (Best Actress, Drama) Globe. 1965: **A Patch of Blue** (Best Supporting Actress) **Academy.** 1966: **Alfie** (Best Supporting Actress) Globe. 1972: **The Poseidon Adventure** (Best Supporting Actress) Academy, **Globe,** British. 1976: **Next Stop, Greenwich Village** (Best Supporting Actress) Globe, British. **Television:** 1964: **"Two Is the Number," Bob Hope Presents The Chrysler Theatre** (Best Single Performance by an Actress in a Leading Role) **Emmy.** 1966: **"Back to Back," Bob Hope Presents The Chrysler Theatre** (Best Single Performance by

an Actress in a Leading Role in a Drama) Emmy. 1975: **"The Barefoot Girls of Bleecker Street," McCloud, NBC Sunday Mystery Movie** (Best Single Performance by a Supporting Actress in a Comedy or Drama Series) Emmy. **Records:** The category of Best Supporting Actress has had the fewest multiple winners at the Oscars. When Winters won for **A Patch of Blue** at the 38th annual ceremony, she became the only actress to win two Best Supporting Actress Academy Awards. She alone held the record for 29 years until Dianne Wiest tied her record. Winters' victory for 1965's **A Patch of Blue** also made her the first star to win an Emmy and Oscar in consecutive years. For the 1963–1964 television season, she took home an Emmy for the **"Two Is the Number"** episode of NBC's **Bob Hope Presents the Chrysler Theater. Highlights:** Winters met Anne Frank's father, Otto, on the set of the 1959 film, **The Diary of Anne Frank** and later promised him that she would donate her Oscar to the Anne Frank House if she won Best Supporting Actress for her performance as Mrs. Van Daan. She did win and in 1975 made good on her promise by going to Amsterdam and donating her award to the Anne Frank House at 263 Prinsengracht where it has been on display among the museum exhibits ever since.

Wisdom, Norman

Movie: 1953: **Trouble in Store** (Most Promising Newcomer) **British. Theater:** 1967: **Walking Happy** (Best Actor, Musical) Tony.

Wise, Ray

Movie: 2005: **Good Night, and Good Luck** (Best Ensemble) SAG, Broadcast.

Wise, William

Movie: 2001: **In the Bedroom** (Best Ensemble) SAG.

Wisener, Jayne

Movie: 2007: **Sweeney Todd: The Demon Barber of Fleet Street** (Best Ensemble) Broadcast.

Withers, Googie

Movie: 1942: **One of Our Aircraft Is Missing** (Best Acting) **Board.** 1996: **Shine** (Best Ensemble) SAG.

Witherspoon, Reese

Movie: 1999: **Election** (Best Actress) **Society** (Best Actress, Musical or Comedy) Globe (Best Female Lead) Spirit. 2001: **Legally Blonde** (Best Actress, Musical or Comedy) Globe. 2005: **Walk the Line** (Best Actress) **Academy, New York, British, Society,**

Broadcast (Best Actress, Musical or Comedy) *Globe* (Best Female Actor in a Leading Role) *SAG*.

Witt, Alicia

Movie: 1994: *Fun* (Best Debut Performance) Spirit.

Wolfington, Iggie

Theater: 1958: *The Music Man* (Best Supporting or Featured Actor, Musical) Tony. **Tributes:** 1984: Life Achievement Award from SAG.

Wolfit, Donald

Movie: 1954: *Svengali* (Best British Actor) British. 1959: *Room at the Top* (Best British Actor) British.

Wood, Elijah

Movie: 2001: *The Lord of the Rings: The Fellowship of the Ring* (Best Ensemble) SAG. 2002: *The Lord of the Rings: The Two Towers* (Best Ensemble) SAG. 2003: *The Lord of the Rings: The Return of the King* (Best Ensemble) *Board, SAG, Broadcast.* 2005: *Sin City* (Best Ensemble) Broadcast. 2006: *Bobby* (Best Ensemble) SAG, Broadcast.

Wood, Evan Rachel

Movie: 2003: *Thirteen* (Best Female Actor in a Leading Role) SAG (Best Actress, Drama) Globe (Best Young Actor/Actress) Broadcast.

Wood, John

Movie: 2000: *Chocolat* (Best Ensemble) SAG. Theater: 1968: *Rosencrantz & Guildenstern Are Dead* (Best Supporting or Featured Actor, Dramatic) Tony. 1975: *Sherlock Holmes* (Best Actor, Dramatic) Tony. 1976: *Travesties* (Best Actor, Play) *Tony*.

Wood, Natalie

Movie: 1955: *Rebel Without a Cause* (New Star of the Year — Actress) *Globe* (Best Supporting Actress) Academy. 1961: *Splendor in the Grass* (Best Actress) Academy (Best Actress, Drama) Globe (Best Foreign Actress) British. 1962: *Gypsy* (Best Actress, Musical or Comedy) Globe. 1963: *Love with the Proper Stranger* (Best Actress) Academy (Best Actress, Drama) Globe. 1965: *Inside Daisy Clover* (Best Actress, Musical or Comedy) Globe. 1966: *This Property Is Condemned* (Best Actress, Drama) Globe. Television: 1979: *From Here to Eternity* (Best Actress in a Series, Drama) *Globe*. **Tributes:** 1965: Henrietta Award for World Film Favorite from Globe. **Highlights:** Eager to make the transition from child star to adult actress, Wood strove to impress director Nicholas Ray and secure for herself the lead female

role as he was beginning work on his new film, *Rebel Without a Cause*. Spending time with Wood helped Ray rethink the character of Judy and, after initial hesitations, he decided that Wood could fit the part with a little aging. He required her to take speech and walking lessons and had the costume department create for her padded hips and a special push up brassiere that has since been known in the film business as the Natalie Wood bra. Wood's instincts that *Rebel* would secure her transition to adult film star were right: the film earned her a New Star of the Year Golden Globe as well as her first Oscar nomination.

Wood, Peggy

Movie: 1965: *The Sound of Music* (Best Supporting Actress) Academy, Globe. Television: 1953: --- (Best Actress) Emmy. 1949–1957 series *Mama* (Best Continuing Performance by an Actress in a Dramatic Series) 1957: Emmy.

Woodard, Alfre

Movie: 1983: *Cross Creek* (Best Supporting Actress) Academy. 1992: *Passion Fish* (Best Supporting Actress) Globe (Best Supporting Female) *Spirit*. 1998: *Down in the Delta* (Best Female Lead) Spirit. Television: 1984: *Hill Street Blues* (Best Supporting Actress in a Drama Series) *Emmy*. 1985: *"Words by Heart," Wonderworks* (Best Supporting Actress in a Limited Series or Special) Emmy. 1986: *St. Elsewhere* (Best Actress in a Drama Series) Emmy; *Unnatural Causes* (Best Actress in a Miniseries or Special) Emmy. 1987: *L.A. Law* (Best Guest Performer in a Drama Series) *Emmy*. 1988: *St. Elsewhere* (Best Guest Performer in a Drama Series) Emmy. 1990: *"A Mother's Courage: The Mary Thomas Story," The Magical World of Disney* (Best Actress in a Miniseries or Special) Emmy. 1995: *"The Piano Lesson," Hallmark Hall of Fame* (Best Actress in a Miniseries or Special) Emmy (Best Female Actor in a Television Movie or Miniseries) *SAG*. 1996: *Gulliver's Travels* (Best Supporting Actress in a Miniseries or Special) Emmy. 1997: *Miss Evers' Boys* (Best Actress in a Miniseries or Special) *Emmy* (Best Actress in a Miniseries or TV Movie) *Globe* (Best Female Actor in a Television Movie or Miniseries) *SAG*. 1998: *Homicide: Life on the Street* (Best Guest Actress in a Drama Series) Emmy. 2000: *Holiday Heart* (Best Actress in a Miniseries or TV Movie) Globe. 2003: *The Practice* (Best Guest Actress in a Drama Series) *Emmy*. 2005–2006 series *Desperate Housewives* (Best Supporting Actress in a Comedy Series) 2006: Emmy. (Best Ensemble in a Comedy Series) 2006: SAG. 2006: *"The Water Is Wide," Hallmark Hall of Fame* (Best Supporting Actress in a Miniseries or TV Movie) Emmy.

Woods, James

Movie: 1979: *The Onion Field* (Best Actor, Drama) Globe. 1986: *Salvador* (Best Actor) Academy (Best Male Lead) *Spirit.* 1987: *Best Seller* (Best Male Lead) Spirit. 1988: *The Boost* (Best Male Lead) Spirit. 1995: *Nixon* (Best Ensemble) SAG. 1996: *Ghosts of Mississippi* (Best Supporting Actor) Academy, Globe. **Television:** 1986: *"The Promise," Hallmark Hall of Fame* (Best Actor in a Miniseries or Special) *Emmy* (Best Actor in a Miniseries or TV Movie) *Globe.* 1987: *In Love and War* (Best Actor in a Miniseries or TV Movie) Globe. 1989: *Crimes of Passion* (Best Performance in Informational Programming) Emmy; *"My Name Is Bill W.," Hallmark Hall of Fame* (Best Actor in a Miniseries or Special) *Emmy* (Best Actor in a Miniseries or TV Movie) Globe. 1993: *Citizen Cohn* (Best Actor in a Miniseries or Special) Emmy (Best Actor in a Miniseries or TV Movie) Globe. 1995: *Indictment: The McMartin Trial* (Best Actor in a Miniseries or Special) Emmy (Best Actor in a Miniseries or TV Movie) Globe. 1996: *The Summer of Ben Tyler* (Best Actor in a Miniseries or TV Movie) Globe. 2000: *Dirty Pictures* (Best Actor in a Miniseries or TV Movie) Globe (Best Male Actor in a Television Movie or Miniseries) SAG. 2003: *Rudy: The Rudy Giuliani Story* (Best Actor in a Miniseries or TV Movie) Emmy. 2006: *ER* (Best Guest Actor in a Drama Series) Emmy.

Woodward, Joanne

Movie: 1957: *No Down Payment* (Best Actress) *Board* (multiple win), (Best Foreign Actress) British; *The Three Faces of Eve* (Best Actress) *Academy, Board* (multiple win), (Best Actress, Drama) *Globe* (Best Foreign Actress) British. 1963: *A New Kind of Love* (Best Actress, Musical or Comedy) Globe. 1968: *Rachel, Rachel* (Best Actress) Academy, *New York, British* (Best Actress, Drama) *Globe.* 1972: *The Effect of Gamma Rays on Man-in-the-Moon Marigolds* (Best Actress) *Cannes* (Best Actress, Drama) Globe. 1973: *Summer Wishes, Winter Dreams* (Best Actress) Academy, *New York, British* (Best Actress, Drama) Globe. 1987: *The Glass Menagerie* (Best Female Lead) Spirit. 1990: *Mr. & Mrs. Bridge* (Best Actress) Academy, *New York* (Best Actress, Drama) Globe (Best Female Lead) Spirit. **Television:** 1977: *"Sybil," The Big Event* (Best Actress in a Drama or Comedy Special) Emmy. 1978: *"See How She Runs," GE Theatre* (Best Actress in a Drama or Comedy Special) *Emmy.* 1981: *Crisis at Central High* (Best Actress in a Limited Series or Special) Emmy (Best Actress in a Miniseries or TV Movie) Globe. 1985: *Do You Remember Love* (Best Actress in a Limited Series or Special) *Emmy* (Best Actress in a Miniseries or TV Movie) Globe. 1990: *Broadway's Dreamers: The Legacy of the Group Theater* (Best Performance in Informational Programming) Emmy (Best Information Special, Producer) *Emmy.* 1993: *Blind Spot* (Best Actress in a Miniseries or Special) Emmy. 1994: *"Breathing Lessons," Hallmark Hall of Fame* (Best Actress in a Miniseries or Special) Emmy (Best Actress in a Miniseries or TV Movie) *Globe* (Best Female Actor in a Television Movie or Miniseries) *SAG.* 2005: *Empire Falls* (Best Female Actor in a Television Movie or Miniseries) SAG (Best Supporting Actress in a Miniseries or TV Movie) Emmy (Best Supporting Actress in a Series, Miniseries, or TV Movie) Globe. **Tributes:** 1975: Gala Tribute from Film Society of Lincoln Center (honor shared with spouse, Paul Newman). 1985: Life Achievement Award from SAG. 1992: Honor from Kennedy Center for the Performing Arts (honor shared with spouse, Paul Newman). **Records:** When the Hollywood Chamber of Commerce devised the concept for the Hollywood Walk of Fame, they chose six celebrities from a list of over 1,000 to honor with the first stars. They were Olive Borden, Louise Fazenda, Preston Foster, Burt Lancaster, Edward Sedgwick, and Joanne Woodward. On February 9, 1958, Woodward was the first to have her star set in place on the corner of Hollywood Boulevard and Highland Avenue. **Highlights:** Stories involving multiple personalities paved the way for Woodward's award success in both film and television. She received some of her first movie award nominations (and wins) for her starring role as Eve White (and "Eve Black" and "Jane"), a woman suffering from a split personality disorder in *The Three Faces of Eve.* Her first television award nomination came in the form of an Emmy nod for *Sybil* in which Woodward played the psychotherapist who helps a young woman played by Sally Field (who was nominated against Woodward that year and won) whose abuse as a child led her to developing 16 personalities.

Woof, Emily

Movie: 1997: *The Full Monty* (Best Ensemble) *SAG.*

Woolley, Monty

Movie: 1942: *The Pied Piper* (Best Acting) *Board* (Best Actor) Academy. 1944: *Since You Went Away* (Best Supporting Actor) Academy.

Woolridge, Susan

Movie: 1987: *Hope and Glory* (Best Supporting Actress) *British.*

Woronov, Mary

Movie: 1989: *Scenes from the Class Struggle in Beverly Hills* (Best Supporting Female) Spirit.

Worth, Irene

Movie: 1958: *Orders to Kill* (Best British Actress) *British*. Theater: 1960: *Toys in the Attic* (Best Actress, Dramatic) Tony. 1965: *Tiny Alice* (Best Actress, Dramatic) *Tony*. 1976: *Sweet Bird of Youth* (Best Actress, Play) *Tony*. 1977: *The Cherry Orchard* (Best Actress, Play) Tony. 1991: *Lost in Yonkers* (Best Actress in a Featured Role, Play) *Tony*. Television: 1990: *"The Shell Seekers," Hallmark Hall of Fame* (Best Supporting Actress in a Miniseries or Special) Emmy. 1996: *Remember WENN* (Best Guest Actress in a Comedy Series) Emmy.

Wright, Jeffrey

Movie: 1996: *Basquiat* (Best Debut Performance) Spirit. 2005: *Broken Flowers* (Best Supporting Male) Spirit; *Syriana* (Best Ensemble) Broadcast. Theater: 1994: *Angels in America: Perestroika* (Best Actor in a Featured Role, Play) *Tony*. 2002: *Topdog/Underdog* (Best Actor, Play) Tony. Television: 2003: *Angels in America* (Best Male Actor in a Television Movie or Miniseries) SAG (Best Supporting Actor in a Miniseries or TV Movie) *Emmy* (Best Supporting Actor in a Series, Miniseries, or TV Movie) *Globe*.

Wright, Michael

Movie: 1983: *Streamers* (Best Actor) *Venice* (win shared with costars).

Wright (Penn), Robin

Movie: 1994: *Forrest Gump* (Best Female Actor in a Supporting Role) SAG (Best Supporting Actress) Globe. 1997: *Loved* (Best Female Lead) Spirit; *She's So Lovely* (Best Female Actor in a Leading Role) SAG. 2005: *Nine Lives* (Best Supporting Female) Spirit. 2006: *Sorry, Haters* (Best Female Lead) Spirit. Television: 1984–1988 series *Santa Barbara* (Best Ingénue in a Daytime Drama Series) 1985: Emmy. 1986: Emmy. 1987: Emmy. 2005: *Empire Falls* (Best Female Actor in a Television Movie or Miniseries) SAG.

Wright, Teresa

Movie: 1941: *The Little Foxes* (Best Supporting Actress) Academy. 1942: *Mrs. Miniver* (Best Acting) *Board* (Best Supporting Actress) *Academy*; *The Pride of the Yankees* (Best Actress) Academy. 1943: *Shadow of a Doubt* (Best Acting) *Board*. Television: 1957: *"The Miracle Worker," Playhouse 90* (Best Single Performance by a Lead or Supporting Actress) Emmy. 1960: *"The Margaret Bourke-White Story," Breck Sunday Showcase* (Best Single Performance by an Actress in a Lead or Supporting Role) Emmy. 1989: *Dolphin Cove* (Best Guest Actress in a Drama Series) Emmy.

Wu, Chien-Lien

Movie: 1994: *Eat Drink Man Woman* (Best Female Lead) Spirit.

Wycherly, Margaret

Movie: 1941: *Sergeant York* (Best Supporting Actress) Academy.

Wyman, Jane

Movie: 1946: *The Yearling* (Best Actress) Academy. 1948: *Johnny Belinda* (Best Actress) *Academy, Globe*. 1951: *The Blue Veil* (Best Actress) Academy (Best Actress, Drama) *Globe*. 1954: *The Magnificent Obsession* (Best Actress) Academy. Television: 1956: *Jane Wyman Presents The Fireside Theatre* (Best Actress in a Leading Role — Continuing Character — in a Dramatic Series) Emmy. 1959: *Jane Wyman Theatre (Jane Wyman Show)* (Best Actress in a Continuing Character by an Actress in a Dramatic Series) Emmy. 1981–1990 series *Falcon Crest* (Best Actress in Dramatic Series) 1982: Globe. 1983: *Globe*. Tributes: 1950: Henrietta Award for World Film Favorite from Globe. Records: Because she played a deaf-mute in her Oscar-winning performance in *Johnny Belinda*, Wyman is the first actress to win an Oscar for a talkie without speaking a word. (Janet Gaynor, the first Oscar-winning Best Actress, received her award for three silent films.) For her Academy Award acceptance speech, Wyman quipped that because she'd won the award for keeping her mouth shut, she'd do it again, and exited the stage with her award.

Wynn, Ed

Movie: 1957: *The Great Man* (Best Foreign Actor) British (Best Supporting Actor) Globe. 1959: *The Diary of Anne Frank* (Best Supporting Actor) Academy. Television: 1949: *The Ed Wynn Show* (Best Live Personality) *Emmy*. 1956: *"Requiem for a Heavyweight," Playhouse 90* (Best Supporting Actor) Emmy. 1957: *"On Borrowed Time," Hallmark Hall of Fame* (Best Actor — Single Performance — Lead or Support) Emmy. 1961: *"The Man in the Funny Suit," Westinghouse-Desilu Playhouse* (Best Single Performance by an Actor in a Leading Role) Emmy. Highlights: Wynn's verbal slips at the 1949 Emmy's did little to help the reputation of the still-fledgling Emmy Awards. On January 27, 1950, Wynn came out as one of the presenters at the second Emmy ceremony joking about how he'd learned that he'd won the Best Live Personality award five weeks earlier. In truth, winners' names had been leaked, but only hours before the awards presentation. Later that evening, Wynn retracted his first flub by admitting he'd only learned about the win twenty minutes before the award was given. Since the winner's names were theoretically in top secret envelopes, Wynn's victory a few minutes later cast a bit of a pall over the event. Wynn's comments not only garnered plenty of unhappy press in *Daily Variety*, but they also remain one of the biggest gaffs in award show history.

Wynter, Dana

Movie: 1955: *The View from Pompey's Head* (New Star of the Year — Actress) *Globe*.

Wynyard, Diana

Movie: 1933: *Cavalcade* (Best Actress) Academy.

Yakusho, Kôji

Movie: 2006: *Babel* (Best Ensemble) SAG, Broadcast.

Yanne, Jean

Movie: 1972: *Nous ne vieillirons pas ensemble (We Will Not Grow Old Together)* (Best Actor) *Cannes*.

Yasutake, Patti

Movie: 1988: *The Wash* (Best Supporting Female) Spirit.

Yeoh, Michelle

Movie: 2000: *Crouching Tiger, Hidden Dragon* (Best Actress) British.

Yoakum, Dwight

Movie: 1996: *Sling Blade* (Best Ensemble) SAG.

York, Susannah

Movie: 1962: *Freud* (Best Actress, Drama) Globe. 1969: *They Shoot Horses, Don't They?* (Best Supporting Actress) Academy, Globe, *British*. 1972: *Images* (Best Actress) *Cannes*. Television: 1972: *"Jane Eyre," Bell System Family Theatre* (Best Single Performance by an Actress in a Leading Role) Emmy.

You, Ge

Movie: 1994: *To Live* (Best Actor) *Cannes*.

Young, Burt

Movie: 1976: *Rocky* (Best Supporting Actor) Academy.

Young, Gig

Movie: 1951: *Come Fill the Cup* (Best Supporting Actor) Academy. 1958: *Teacher's Pet* (Best Support-ing Actor) Academy, Globe. 1969: *They Shoot Horses, Don't They?* (Best Supporting Actor) *Academy, Globe*, British. Television: 1971: *"The Neon Ceiling," World Premiere NBC Monday Night at the Movies* (Best Single Performance by an Actor in a Leading Role) Emmy.

Young, Loretta

Movie: 1947: *The Farmer's Daughter* (Best Actress) *Academy*. 1949: *Come to the Stable* (Best Actress) Academy. Television: 1953: *Letter to Loretta* (Best Female Star, Regular Series) Emmy. 1953–1961 series *The Loretta Young Show* (Best Actress Starring in a Regular Series) 1954: *Emmy*. (Best Continuing Performance by an Actress in a Dramatic Series) 1956: *Emmy*. (Best Continuing Performance — Female — in a Series by a Comedienne, Singer, Hostess, Dancer, MC, Announcer, Narrator, Panelist or Any Person Who Essentially Plays Herself) 1957: Emmy. (Best Actress in a Leading Role — Continuing Character — in a Dramatic Series) 1959: *Emmy*. (Best Performance by an Actress in a Series — Lead or Supporting) 1960: Emmy. (Best Performance by an Actress in a Series — Lead) 1961: Emmy. 1955: *"Christmas Stopover," The Loretta Young Show* (Best Actress — Single Performance) Emmy. 1986: *Christmas Eve* (Best Actress in a Miniseries or TV Movie) *Globe*. 1989: *Lady in a Corner* (Best Actress in a Miniseries or TV Movie) Globe. Tributes: 1958: Special Television Achievement Award from Globe. Records: When Young won her second Emmy Award in 1956 for *The Loretta Young Show*, she became the first award-winning movie actress to become a multiple Emmy winner. Art Carney, the first actor to win multiple Emmy Awards (he earned his second in 1954 and ended up with a career total of seven) added film awards to his mantle late in his career for *Harry and Tonto, The Late Show,* and *Going in Style*. Highlights: Loretta Young pulled off what is still considered the biggest upset in Oscar history. In 1947, Rosiland Russell received rave reviews for the demanding role of Lavinia in the film adaptation of Eugene O'Neill's *Mourning Becomes Electra*. Seldom in Academy Award history did a win seem such a sure bet. *Daily Variety* even published a pre-ceremony poll of Academy members that ranked Russell first and Young a distant fourth among the nominees. According to *Variety*, the contenders ranked in this succession: Russell, Dorothy McGuire for *Gentleman's Agreement*, Susan Hayward for *Smash-Up*, Young, and Joan Crawford for *Possessed*. But when Best Actress was announced that night, Young became the unexpected winner. Just as surprising is the vehicle for which she won. *The Farmer's Daughter* was an implausible though enjoyable light comedy (which seldom win Oscars over heavy drama) about a Minnesota farm girl who gets a job as a congressman's maid and ends up winning a seat in congress herself.

Young, Robert

Movie: 1942: *H. M. Pulham, Esq.* (Best Acting) *Board* (multiple win); *Joe Smith, American* (Best Acting) *Board* (multiple win); *Journey for Margaret* (Best Acting) *Board* (multiple win). **Television:** 1954–1963 series *Father Knows Best* (Best Continuing Performance by an Actor in a Drama or Comedy Series) 1956: Emmy. 1957: *Emmy.* 1958: *Emmy.* 1959: Emmy. 1969–1976 series *Marcus Welby, M. D.* (Best Continued Performance by an Actor in a Leading Role in a Dramatic Series) 1970: *Emmy.* 1971: Emmy. 1972: Emmy. (Best Actor in a Drama Series) 1969: Globe. 1970: Globe. 1972: Globe. 1973: Globe. (Best Actor in a Drama Series or TV Movie) 1971: *Globe.* 1971: *"Vanished," World Premiere NBC Monday and Tuesday Night at the Movies* (Best Performance by an Actor in a Supporting Role in Drama) Emmy. **Records:** Having won two Best Actor Emmys for his comedic work as insurance salesman and understanding dad Jim Anderson in *Father Knows Best,* Young later took on the role of equally compassionate *Marcus Welby, M. D.* and snagged another Emmy in the show's first season. With that win, Young became the first actor in history to win Emmys for starring roles in a comedy and a drama series.

Young, Roland

Movie: 1937: *Topper* (Best Supporting Actor) Academy.

Young, Will

Movie: 2005: *Mrs. Henderson Presents* (Best Ensemble) *Board.*

Yu, Xia

Movie: 1994: *Yangguang Canlan de Rizi* (Best Actor) *Venice.*

Yuuya, Yagira

Movie: 2004: *Nobody Knows* (Best Actor) *Cannes.*

Zacconi, Ermete

Movie: 1941: *Don Buonaparte* (Best Actor) *Venice.*

Zadora, Pia

Movie: 1981: *Butterfly* (New Star of the Year — Actor or Actress) *Globe.* **Highlights:** Zadora is generally held accountable for the demise of the New Star of the Year award after her tycoon husband, Meshulam Riklis sought votes for Zadora by flying members to Vegas to catch Zadora's show and to preview *Butterfly* before it had even been released. Her Globe win sent shock waves across the Beverly Hilton Hotel the night of the Golden Globes and throughout Hollywood and beyond afterward. Foreign Press president Judy Solomon came to Zadora's defense, and the Foreign Press presented the award once more in 1982, but the credibility of the prize had lost its luster and the following year the categories for New Star of the Year had floated away on the wings of that unfortunate *Butterfly.*

Zahn, Steve

Movie: 1999: *Happy, Texas* (Best Supporting Male) *Spirit.* 2007: *Rescue Dawn* (Best Supporting Male) Spirit.

Zane, Billy

Movie: 1997: *Titanic* (Best Ensemble) SAG.

Zellweger, Renée

Movie: 1994: *Love and a .45* (Best Debut Performance) Spirit. 1996: *Jerry Maguire* (Breakout Artist of the Year) *Broadcast* (Breakthrough Performance — Female) *Board* (Best Female Actor in a Supporting Role) SAG; *The Whole Wide World* (Best Female Lead) Spirit. 2000: *Nurse Betty* (Best Actress, Musical or Comedy) *Globe.* 2001: *Bridget Jones's Diary* (Best Actress) Academy, British, Broadcast (Best Actress, Musical or Comedy) Globe (Best Female Actor in a Leading Role) SAG. 2002: *Chicago* (Best Actress) Academy, British (Best Actress, Musical or Comedy) *Globe* (Best Female Actor in a Leading Role) *SAG* (Best Ensemble) *SAG, Broadcast.* 2003: *Cold Mountain* (Best Female Actor in a Supporting Role) *SAG* (Best Supporting Actress) *Academy, Globe, British, Broadcast.* 2004: *Bridget Jones: The Edge of Reason* (Best Actress, Musical or Comedy) Globe. 2006: *Miss Potter* (Best Actress, Musical or Comedy) Globe. **Records:** When Renée Zellweger was named Breakout Artist of the Year by the Broadcast Film Critics for *Jerry Maguire* at the same event where Cuba Gooding, Jr. was voted Best Supporting Actor and six-year-old Jonathan Lipnicki was honored for Best Child Performance for the same film, they became the first trio to all win Broadcast awards for the same movie. Tom Cruise was considered for Best Actor for the title role, but he lost to Geoffrey Rush in *Shine.*

Zem, Roschdy

Movie: 2006: *Days of Glory* (Best Actor) *Cannes* (win shared with costars).

Zeta-Jones, Catherine

Movie: 2000: *Traffic* (Best Supporting Actress) Globe (Best Ensemble) *SAG.* 2002: *Chicago* (Best Actress, Musical or Comedy) Globe (Best Female Actor in a Supporting Role) *SAG* (Best Supporting Actress) *Academy, British, Broadcast* (Best Ensemble) *SAG, Broadcast.* 2004: *Ocean's Twelve* (Best Ensemble) Broadcast.

Zhang, Ziyi

Movie: 2000: *Crouching Tiger, Hidden Dragon* (Best Supporting Actress) British (Best Supporting Female) *Spirit.* 2004: *House of Flying Daggers* (Best Actress) British. 2005: *2046* (Best Supporting Actress) Society; *Memoirs of a Geisha* (Best Actress)

British (Best Actress, Drama) Globe (Best Female Actor in a Leading Role) SAG.

Zimbalist, Efrem, Jr.

Movie: 1958: *Too Much, Too Soon* (New Star of the Year — Actor) *Globe*; *Home Before Dark* (Best Supporting Actor) Globe. 1967: *Wait Until Dark* (Best Supporting Actor) Globe. **Television:** 1958–1964 series *77 Sunset Strip* (Best Actor in a Leading Role — Continuing Character) 1959: Emmy. 1965–1974 series *The F.B.I.* (Best Actor in a Series) 1968: Globe.

Zweig, Genevieve

Movie: 1999: *Magnolia* (Best Ensemble) *Board*, SAG.

Bibliography

Advanced Primetime Awards Search. *Academy of Television Arts & Sciences.* February 26, 2008. <http://www.emmys.tv/awards/awardsearch.php>

All Movie Guide. April 23, 2008. <www.allmovie.com>

Altman, Richard. *And the Envelope, Please.* Philadelphia: J. B. Lippincott, 1978.

American Film Institute. February 26, 2008.

Awards Database. *Academy of Motion Picture Arts and Sciences.* February 26, 2008. <http://awardsdatabase.oscars.org/ampas_awards/BasicSearchInput.jsp>

Berlinale. *Berlin International Film Festival.* February 26, 2008. <www.berlinale.de/en/HomePage.html>

La Biennale di Venezia. *International Venice Film Festival.* February 26, 2008. <www.labiennale.org/en/cinema/>

BFCA ... Broadcast Film Critics Association. February 26, 2008.

Bloom, Ken, and Frank Vlastnik. *Sitcoms: The 101 Greatest TV Comedies of All Time.* New York: Black Dog & Leventhal, 2007.

Brown, Gene. *Movie Time: A Chronology of Hollywood and the Movie Industry from Its Beginnings to the Present.* New York: Macmillan, 1995.

Cannes: Fifty Years of Sex & Celluloid. New York: Hyperion, 1997.

Carrier, Rhonda, ed. *Guinness World Records 1999.* New York: Guinness, 1998.

Corey, Melinda, and George Ochoa. *The American Film Institute Desk Reference.* New York: Dorling Kindersley, 2002.

Cunningham, Antonia, ed. *Guinness World Records 2002.* New York: Guinness, 2002.

"Ellen Burstyn Sounds Off on Controversial Emmy Nod." *FoxNews.Com,* January 16, 2007. <http://www.foxnews.com/story/0,2933,227440,00.html>.

Endres, Stacey, and Robert Cushman. *Hollywood at Your Feet: The Story of the World-Famous Chinese Theatre.* Los Angeles: Pomegranate, 1992.

Esso, Gabe. *The Book of Movie Lists.* Westport, CT: Arlington House, 1981.

Festival de Cannes. February 26, 2008. <www.festival-cannes.fr/en>

Film Independent. February 26, 2008.

Film Society of Lincoln Center. February 26, 2008.

Folkard, Claire, ed. *Guinness World Records 2003.* New York: Guinness, 2003.

_____. *Guinness World Records 2005.* New York: Guinness, 2004.

Franks, Don. *Entertainment Awards: A Music, Cinema, Theatre and Broadcasting Reference, 1928 through 1993.* Jefferson, NC: McFarland, 1996.

Fraser, Afton. *Hollywood Picks the Classics: A Guide for the Beginner & the Aficionado.* New York: Bulfinch, 2004.

Griffin, Nancy. "Mirren, Mirren on the wall..." *AARP: The Magazine.* March/April 2007, pp. 52–55, 112.

Gwinn, Alison. *The 100 Greatest Stars of All Time.* New York: Entertainment Weekly Books, 1997.

Hall of Fame Archives & Honorees. *Academy of Television Arts & Sciences.* February 26, 2008. <http://www.emmys.tv/awards/halloffame/hofarchive.php>

Hart, Samantha. *The Hollywood Walk of Fame: 2000 Sensational Stars, Star-Makers and Legends!* LCF, CA: Crybaby Books and Entertainment, 2000.

Hollywood Stars. San Francisco: Fog City Press, 2003.

Jones, Peter. *Stardust: The Bette Davis Story.* Atlanta: Turner Entertainment, 2006.

Karney, Robyn, ed. *Cinema Year by Year: 1994–2002.* London: Dorling Kindersley, 2002.

Katz, Ephraim. *The Film Encyclopedia, 3rd ed.* New York: HarperPerennial, 1998.

_____. *The Film Encyclopedia, 4th ed.* New York: HarperResource, 2001.

Kinn, Gail, and Jim Piazza. *Four-Star Movies: The 101 Greatest Films of All Time.* New York: Black Dog & Leventhal, 2003.

Krenz, Carol. *100 Years of Hollywood: A Century of Movie Magic.* New York: Metro, 1999.

Kuner, Mildred C. "Eva Le Gallienne." *Dictionary of World Biography, Volume VIII.* Pasadena: Salem Press, 1999.

Lackmann, Ron. *The Encyclopedia of American Television: Broadcast Programming Post–World War II to 2000.* New York: Facts on File, 2003.

LaCrosse, Babson, ed. "Get to the Bottom." *The Envelope: The Awards Insider from the Los Angeles Times,* January 16, 2007. <http://goldderbyforums.latimes.com/eve/forums/a/tpc/f/1106078764/m/5461097753>.

LAFCA. *The Los Angeles Film Critics Association.* February 26, 2008. <http://www.lafca.net/>

Levy, Emanuel. *All About Oscar: The History and Politics of the Academy Awards.* New York: Continuum, 2003.

Lloyd, Ann, and Graham Fuller, eds. *The Illustrated Who's Who of the Cinema.* New York: Portland House, 1987.

"Loretta Lynn with Sissy Spacek." *Entertainment Weekly* 901/902, October 13, 2006, p. 71.

Maltin, Leonard, ed. *1999 Movie & Video Guide.* New York: Plume, 1998.

_____. *2003 Movie & Video Guide.* New York: Plume, 2002.

Matthew, Peter, ed. *The Guinness Book of Records.* New York: Bantam, 1994.

Monush, Barry. *The Encyclopedia of Hollywood Film Actors from the Silent Era to 1965.* New York: Applause, 2003.

Morino, Marianne. *The Hollywood Walk of Fame.* Berkeley, CA: Ten Speed Press, 1987.

Morrow, Lee Alan. *The Tony Award Book: Four Decades of Great American Theater.* New York: Abbeville, 1987.

Murphy, Bruce, ed. *Benét's Reader's Encyclopedia, Fourth Edition.* New York: HarperCollins, 1996.

National Board of Review of Motion Pictures. February 26, 2008. <www.nbrmp.org/awards/>

Neame, Ronald, and Barbara Roisman Cooper. *Straight from the Horse's Mouth: Ronald Neame, an Autobiography.* London: Scarecrow, 2002.

New York Film Critics Circle. February 26, 2008. www.nyfcc.com/

The New York Times Online. April 19, 2006. movies2.nytimes.com/gst/movies/filmography.html>

O'Neil, Tom. *The Emmys: Star Wars, Showdowns, and the Supreme Test of TV's Best.* New York: Penguin, 1992.

_____. *Movie Awards: The Ultimate, Unofficial Guide to the Oscars, Golden Globes, Critics, Guild, & Indie Honors.* New York: Perigee, 2003.

_____. "What Emmy Records Can Be Broken This Evening?" *The Envelope: The Awards Insider from the Los Angeles Times.* January 16, 2007. <http://golddderby.latimes.com/awards_goldderby/2006/08/what_emmy_recor.Html>.

"Oprah Winfrey — The Story of an Entrepreneur." *ICMR Case Studies and Management Resources.* February 26, 2008. <http://www.icmrindia.org/free%20resources/casestudies/Oprah%20Winfrey13.htm>

Osborne, Robert. *75 Years of the Oscar: The Official History of the Academy Awards.* New York: Abbeville, 2003.

Past Honorees. *The John F. Kennedy Center for the Performing Arts.* February 26, 2008. <http://www.kennedy-center.org/programs/specialevents/honors/history/home.html>

Past Winners and Nominees. *British Academy of Film and Television Arts.* February 26, 2008. <http://www.bafta.org/awards/film/nominations/>

Past Winners Database. May 12, 2006. <http://theenvelope.latimes.com/extras/lostmind/year/1959/1959gg.htm>

Pickard, Roy. *The Award Movies: A Complete Guide from A to Z.* New York: Schocken, 1980.

Pirie, David, ed. *Anatomy of the Movies.* New York: Macmillan, 1981.

Pond, Steve. "The Hottest Races and Faces." *TV Guide,* February 19–25, 2007, pp. 28–30.

Scheuer, Steven H. *Movie Blockbusters: Hollywood's 50 Top-Grossing Films of All Time.* New York: Bantam, 1983.

Schwartz, Missy. "Being Catherine Keener." *Entertainment Weekly,* April 21, 2006, 42–44.

Schwarzbaum, Lisa. "'Murder' by Numbers." *Entertainment Weekly,* March 4, 2005, p. 53.

_____. "Playing a Different Tune." *Entertainment Weekly,* June 17, 2005, p. 60.

Screen Actors Guild. February 26, 2008.

Search. *Hollywood Foreign Press Association.* February 26, 2008. <http://www.goldenglobes.org/search/index.html>

Sheward, David. *The Big Book of Show Business Awards.* New York: Billboard Books, 1997.

Shipman, David. *The Great Movie Stars: The Golden Years.* New York: Bonanza Books, 1970.

_____. *The Great Movie Stars: The International Years.* New York: St. Martin's Press, 1972.

Slide, Anthony. *Silent Players: A Biographical and Autobiographical Study of 100 Silent Film Actors and Actresses.* Lexington: The University Press of Kentucky, 2002.

Stade, George, ed. "Agatha Christie," *British Writers, Supplement II.* New York: Charles Scribner's Sons, 1992.

Steinberg, Cobbett. *Film Facts.* New York: Facts on File, 1980.

Sullivan, Steve. *Va Va Voom! Bombshells, Pin-ups, Sexpots and Glamour Girls*. Los Angeles: General Publishing Group, 1995.

Terrace, Vincent. *Fifty Years of Television: A Guide to Series and Pilots, 1937–1988*. Cranbury, NJ: Cornwall, 1991.

Theodore, Terry. "Lillian Gish." *Dictionary of World Biography, Volume VII*. Pasadena: Salem Press, 1999.

Thomson, David. "The Goddess Brought Down to Earth," *Hollywood Life*, May/June 2006, pp. 94–97, 108–109.

Tony Awards. *The Official Website of the American Theatre Wing's Tony Awards*. February 26, 2008. <http://www.tonyawards.com/p/tonys_search>

Travers, Peter. *1,000 Best Movies on DVD*. New York: Wenner Books, 2006.

Vincendeau, Ginette, ed. *Encyclopedia of European Cinema*. New York: Facts on File, 1995.

Wikipedia, The Free Encyclopedia. February 26, 2008. <http://en.wikipedia.org>

Wiley, Mason, and Damien Bona. *Inside Oscar: The Official History of the Academy Awards*. New York: Ballantine, 1986.

Zacharek, Stephanie. "Olivier's Shakespeare (1944–1955)." *The New York Times*, May 7, 2006, p. 16.

Index